VALUES IN CULTURE AND CLASSROOM

HARPER'S SOCIAL SCIENCE SERIES

Under the Editorship of

F. STUART CHAPIN

VALUES IN CULTURE AND CLASSROOM

A STUDY IN THE SOCIOLOGY OF THE SCHOOL

H. Otto Dahlke
Associate Professor of Sociology
Concord College

HARPER & BROTHERS   PUBLISHERS   NEW YORK

To E. T. HILLER

Contents

Preface   xv

PART I. INTRODUCTION

1. Action and Values—A Cultural Approach to Education   3

The Meaning of Culture—Education and the Normative and
Functional Order—The School and Structural Elements of a
Society—Informal Social Relations in the School—The School
as a Group—The School a Group Among Groups—In Conclusion

**PART II. THE SOCIO-CULTURAL CONTEXT OF EDUCATION
AND THE SCHOOL**

2. The School as an Objective Fact   15

The Rise of Public Education in the United States—Types of
Schools—Trends in School Population—Education as an Aspect
of Public Economy—Groups Associated with Education—Sum
mary

3. Value Orientation, Social Models, and Education   41

Religion and Education—American Values and Education
Through Nativist Eyes—Individual Competitive Enterprise for
a Sound and Free America—A Sound and Free America
Through Collective Action—Labor—Educators and the Human-
istic Orientation—Summary—Suggested Typology of Value
Orientations

4. The Legal Order and Education   69

The Legal Order and Action—The School as Related to the
State—Life Chances, Legal Order, and School—School Person-
nel as Legally Prescribed—Functional Order of the School as
Defined by Law—Normative Order as Defined in Law—Corporal
Punishment and Discipline—Ceremonial Occasions and the
Law—Summary

5. The Community Context of the School   87

The Meaning of Community—Economic Order, Power, and Community Action—Economic Class and Status Group and the Principle of Inequality—Community Fragmentation—Nationality and Color Groups—Obstacles to the Realization of the Aesthetic Community—Community Ends Through Government—Community and School—Summary

PART III. THE STRUCTURE AND ORGANIZATION OF THE SCHOOL

6. Building and Equipment—Instruments for Action   125

Education Through Things—Cultural Values and the Material Order—Obsolete School Buildings—Architecture and Personality Growth—Architecture, Institutional Order, and Social Relations —Summary

7. The Functional Order   155

A Brief Glance Backwards—Entering the Functional Order— The Opening Minutes—Examinations as Recurrent Crises

8. The Functional Order (*Continued*)   183

The Functional Order as Constituted by Ceremonial Occasions— The School as a Vehicle of Mass Entertainment

9. The Functional Order as Group Process   206

A Few Experimental and Observational Considerations—A Few Sociological Principles—Paraphernalia of Techniques—The Practicality of Group Dynamics

10. The Normative Order in the School   227

The Normative Order as Explicitly Defined—Norms as Implicit —Normative Order as Teacher Defined—Summary

11. The Maintenance of the Functional and Normative Orders   255

Controls and Sanctions—Types of Control—Value Orientations and Control

12. The Meaning of the Institutional Order of the School   280

The Pupil's Interpretation of the School—The Teacher's Assessment of the Functional and Normative Orders—In Conclusion, the Significance of these Interpretations

PART IV. INFORMAL SOCIAL STRUCTURE AND RELATIONS WITHIN THE SCHOOL

13. Perspectives on the Nature of the Child   301

Unpopular, a Problem, Maladjusted—The Child in Terms of Sex and Age Status—Social Class and the Child—The Child in Nonwhite Groups—Problems that Bother Children—In Conclusion: Reconstructing Children by Reconstructing Worlds

14. Informal Order Versus Formal Order in the School   325

Informal Order in the Elementary School—The High School,

Ordered by the Structural Principles—Additional Factors Organizing the Informal Order—Generalized Structure of the Informal Order—The Informal Order as Irrationality

15. Reputational History and Evaluation in the School   353

The Process of Evaluation—Two Cases—Evaluation on the Basis of Social Class—Love and Obscenity as Points of Evaluation—Summary

PART V. THE TEACHER IN SCHOOL AND COMMUNITY

16. Teaching as a Vocation   383

The Social Recruitment of Teachers—The Recruiting Process—Teacher Training—On the Job—Teacher Organization—Summary

17. Teaching and Bureaucracy   422

The Nature of Bureaucratic Organization—School Systems as Bureaucratic Structures—Strains and Stresses in Bureaucratic Functioning—Value Orientations and Bureaucratic Structures

PART VI. THE SCHOOL IN THE CENTER OF CONTROVERSY

18. Special Interests and Education   463

Controversy and Consensus and the School—Control Through Coöperation—Direct Attack on the Schools

19. The Development of Mutuality   493

The NEA and Criticism of the Schools—Cases on Public Relations—The Quest for Objectivity

20. Educational Controversy and Law   523

Secularism, Religion, and the Courts—The Courts and Segregation in Education—The Status of Dissent—Value Orientations—the Basic Issue

Appendix: Sample of a Descriptive Report Card   557

Index of Names   561

Index of Subjects   566

Tables

1. Population, Pupils, Attendance, and Instructional Staff, 1869–70 Compared with 1951–52.   27

2. Percent of the Civilian Noninstitutional Population 5–29 Years by Age and Sex Enrolled in Public and Private Schools and Colleges, Continental United States, Urban and Rural, October, 1951.   29

3. Retention Rates, Fifth Grade Through High-School Graduation in

Public and Nonpublic Schools, Continental United States for Designated Years. 30

4. Median School Years Completed by Persons 25 Years and Over, by Sex, Color, and Residence, for the United States, 1950 and 1940. 31

5. Percentage Distribution of Revenue Receipts from Public Sources for Public Elementary and Secondary Day Schools for Forty-Eight States, 1951–52. 33

6. Total Revenue Receipts of Public-School Systems and Percentage Distribution by Source, United States, 1929–30 to 1951–52. 33

7. Percentage Distribution of Expenditures of Public-School Systems, by Purpose, United States, 1929–30 to 1951–52. 35

8. Annual Expenditures for Public Elementary and Secondary Education per Capita, per Child Aged 5–17, and per Pupil in Average Daily Attendance, by States, 1951–52. 36

9. Number of States and Territories Having Provisions for Revocation of Licenses. 78

10. Percent of Developed Urban Land Area in Use for Specified Purposes in Twenty-Two Cities by City Size. 93

11. Number of Manufacturing Establishments and Average Number of Wage Earners in Three Cities for Designated Years. 96

12. Percent Distribution of Population 14 Years Old and Over in Labor Force by Industry Group for Four Cities, 1940 and 1950. 97

13. Occupational Distribution in Four Cities, 1940 and 1950. 102

14. Percent Distribution of Population in Four Cities for 1900, 1940, and 1950 by Nativity and Color. 106

15. Age of Dwelling Units in Four Cities by Year Built. 110

16. Percent of Renter-Tenant-Occupied Dwelling Unit by Estimated Contract Monthly Rental for Four Cities, 1940 and 1950. 112

17. Total Scores and Scores of Five Areas on the McLeary Guide for Eight Elementary Schools, 1949. 131

18. Enrollment Housed in Various Buildings by Rating Categories, 1942. 132

19. Percent of City School Buildings of Specified Types That Are Overcrowded and Percent of Pupils Attending Schools in Overcrowded Buildings. 135

20. Occupation of Chief Breadwinner in Family and Enrollment in High-School Courses for 105 Freshmen. 164

21. Average Expenditures by Sex, Grade, and Occupation by High-School Students for the School Years 1942–43 and 1949–50. 167

22. Mean Expenditures by Items of Expenditure and Place of Residence. 168

23. School Practices in Providing Supplies, Equipment, and Services to Pupils as Reported by Principals of 78 Schools. 170

24. Truancy Reported by Truant Officer in Public and Nonpublic Elementary Schools of Mill City for Designated Years. 230

25. Relative Importance of 42 Specific Pupil Responsibilities as Judged by Faculty and Pupils, University of Chicago High School. 232

26. Total Number of Norms by Major Functional Areas as Specified by Pupils for Designated Grades. 239

27. Percent of Items of Undesirable Behavior as Listed by Teachers in the United States and Canada. 248

28. Seriousness and Frequency of Occurrence of Behavior as Listed and Rated by Teachers. 249

29. Subject Rating by a Class of Sixth Graders by Sex. 259

30. Positive and Negative Comments by Major Activity Area in Suggestion Box, Grade 6–7, March 17–April 15. 288

31. Percentage Relationship of Maladjustment at Each Grade Level in Three Schools, Columbus, Ohio. 304

32. Percentages of Children Showing Degrees of Adjustment in 1946 (N = 1500) and in 1947 (N = 340), Miami County. 305

33. Percentile Rank of 161 Pupils on the California Test of Personality for West School and by Grade, 1949. 306

34. Rorschach Test Interpretations of 24 Negro Subjects. 316

35. Percent Checking Selected Items in the SRA Junior Inventory by Sex, Grade, and Socio-Economic Class. 318

36. High-School Students' Problems as Determined by a Problem Check List. 319

37. Indexes of Self and Other Group Rejection by Economic Class, West School, Mill City. 332

38. Indexes of Self and Other Group Preference by Economic Class, West School, Mill City. 332

39. Groups Ranked from High to Low Self-Preference for Specified Sociometric Criteria of Choosing Leaders, Work Partners, Dates, and Friends in a High-School Population. 337

40. Degrees of Friendliness Among Specified Groups in Choosing Leaders, Work Partners, Dates, and Friends in a High-School Population. 330

41. School Enrollment and School Personnel for Elementary and High School, 1950–1960. 385

42. Social Origin of Teachers and Future Teachers According to Occupation of Father and by Sex, 1910 and 1948. 388

43. Percentage Distribution of Attitudes Toward Different Aspects of Teaching by Students Selecting and Not Selecting Teaching as a Profession. 392

44. Attitude Toward Different Aspects of Teaching by Students Selecting and Not Selecting Teaching as a Profession. 393

45. Percentage Distribution of Students Selecting and Not Selecting Teaching as a Vocation Based upon the Numbers Who Had Relatives with a Teaching Background. 395

46. Percentage Distribution of Teachers Prepared by Type of Institution, 1949–50. 399

47. Employability Quotients of Potential Applicants for Teaching Positions in the Public Schools.   401

48. Approval and Disapproval of Control by the School Board of Specific Behavior Patterns of Men and Women Teachers by Students Selecting and Not Selecting Teaching as a Profession.   410

49. Net Approval and Disapproval Reactions of Representative Groups to Teacher Behavior.   411

50. Work Stoppages Involving Teachers, 1940–52.   416

51. Size of High School by Enrollment, 1930, 1938, 1946.   428

52. Number and Percent of Groups Registered Under the Lobby Act by Value Orientation, 1946–49.   469

53. Distribution of Themes in Pamphlet Material of the National Council for American Education.   486

54. Practices and Usage in Aid to Sectarian Schools and Sectarianism in Public Schools as Reported by State Superintendents of Education.   527

Figures

1. The Development of the American Public-School System.   23

2. Enrollment in Full-Time Day Schools, by Level of Instruction and by Type of Control for Designated Years.   26

3. Population Growth of Chicago, Seattle, Mill City, and Elmtown, 1870–1950.   92

4. Size of School Sites.   145

5. Percent of Pupils per Acre of Site.   145

6. Age of School Buildings.   146

7. Percent of Pupils Housed in School Buildings of Various Ages.   146

8. Percent of Elementary School Plants *Not* Providing Certain Types of Rooms.   147

9. Percent of Secondary School Plants *Not* Providing Certain Types of Rooms.   148

10. Percent of Combined Elementary-Secondary Plants *Not* Providing Certain Types of Rooms.   149

11. Percent of Pupils Housed in Buildings Rated According to Fire Safety.   150

12. Number of New Classrooms Currently Needed.   150

13. Estimated Costs of Needed Site Acquisitions and Improvements.   151

14. Estimated Cost of New Construction Currently Needed.   152

15. Estimated Cost of New School Buses Currently Needed.   152

16. Current Per-Pupil Capital Outlay Needs and Deficits by Size of School District.   153

17. Current Capital Outlay Needs and Deficits by Size of School District.   153

18. Percent of Students of Three High Schools Rating Importance of Specified Factors as Influencing Their Choice of School.   162

19. Social Class, Controls and Learning.   275

20. Social Class Structure of Bronzeville, Chicago.   315

21. Social Atom of Two Siblings, West School, Mill City.   329

22. Legend for Sociogram.   342

23. Sociogram I, Grade 8.   343

24. Sociogram II, Grade 8.   344

25. Sociogram III, Grade 6–7.   344

26. Sociogram IV, Grade 6–7.   345

27. Sociogram V, Grade 4.   345

28. Sociogram VI, Grade 4.   346

29. Seating Arrangement, Grade 8, Showing Mutual Choosing and Rejecting Choices.   347

30. Organization with Independent Principal.   432

31. Large Organization with Specialized Staff.   433

ECOLOGICAL MAPS

Following page 110

1. Resident Population, Chicago, 1950.

2. Concentrations of Ethnic Groups, Chicago, 1950.

3. Per Cent Negro of Total Population, Chicago, 1950.

4. Median Income for Families in 1949, Chicago.

5. Per Cent of Occupied Dwelling Units with 1.51 or More Persons per Room, Chicago, 1950.

6. Generalized Redevelopment Areas, Chicago, 1953.

7. Mean Monthly Rental, Seattle, 1940.

8. Infant Mortality, Seattle: 1933–1937.

9. Seattle by Mean Monthly Rental, 1950.

10. Residential Areas of Mill City by Average Monthly Rental, 1940.

11. Dwelling Area of Jonesville-Elmtown.

Preface

"Whirl is king." With these words a Greek of the classic period characterized life in his times. The world had become disorganized. Civil strife and factionalism, spearheaded by ambitious men in the pursuit of their private goals, atomized society. Finally, a prolonged war gave the coup de grâce to this fluorescent culture, and it passed into history. Centuries later the breakup of the medieval society gave rise to the violent image of the four horsemen of the Apocalypse riding roughshod over land and bodies—famine, pestilence, war, and death. Today something of this whirl, this specter of catastrophe, haunts man's soul, and the new image is the whine of an intercontinental guided missile followed by a mushroom cloud.

A complacent belief in progress is no longer held. Nineteenth- and twentieth-century criticism objected to the mechanization of human relations, to the degradation of personality, to the ugliness and squalor in city and town, to the unchecked exploitation of natural resources, to recurrent economic breakdown and war. Would-be saviors rose in this social whirl, promising relief and security to followers, their efforts culminating in the totalitarian monstrosities of the planned mass society and genocide, a debacle of European society into planned terrorism and extermination. Democracies were on the defense. The assertion of democratic values was unsure, for times had changed, and the relation of these values to the modern society was not clear. What is the meaning of democracy in an urban, industrialized society? What is the meaning of political democracy in light of economic inequalities, discrimination, and the organization of economic life in large, private, collectivized units? Is dissenting opinion really welcomed? Is opportunity equal? How can the gap between democratic aspirations and level of achievement be overcome?

We find ourselves in a difficult challenge-response situation. The challenge is double. The first deals with the values of the American way of life. What are they and how do they fit together? The second is concerned with the relation between values and actions, between ideals and what is actually done. This book attempts to study this situation in a particular institution in our society—the school. No claim is made that this study is a special type of sociology, usually referred to as educational. Instead, an effort is made to examine the school in terms of a consistent general frame of reference: values and actions, their institutional expression, and the consequent social relations. This approach is stated in Chapter 1. The remainder of the book is an analytical, descriptive application of this conceptual schema.

In Part II we will study the general setting of the school. To use a big phrase, we say this setting is the sociocultural context of the school. First, we need to know something about the school as an objective fact in our society. While we will limit ourselves to the American public school, we will refer to nonpublic schools for comparison and contrast. To understand the school we must know something about the multiplicity of groups that make this sociocultural context. The focus is on the value orientations of these institutional groups. What specific set of values do these groups sponsor and support? How do the various value orientations fit together? What bearing does all this have on the school's organization and functioning? In this general view of the culture special attention must be directed to law as a basic factor in group action and organization. As the school is in the specific context of a community, we will focus on the structure of community life, considering only those phases which will aid us to understand and interpret the school.

Part III deals with the school as an institutional group, studying its structure and organization, its activities, its rules and regulations, its values, and the interplay of all these major factors. We are not concerned with learning theory or teaching skills. We will concern ourselves with coöperation, competition, and conflict, with questions of discipline, with power and authority, as these social factors are found in the school.

Parts IV and V center upon the children and the teacher. Our stress is upon the informal organization and system of evaluation that structures relations among the children. We will deal with the vocation and the bureaucratic setting of teaching.

In Part VI we come back to an aspect of the school in our complex sociocultural setting, the school as a center of controversy. This controversy is examined two ways: in terms of pressure groups and in terms of legal or court action. By studying the controversies we will know more about our society and about the destiny of our schools.

For those who are interested in social gimmicks and recipes on how to manipulate children or fellow teachers, this book will not offer pat formulas. Furthermore, it avoids many idealized anecdotes which dot traditional books in education. The professional educator supports a specific value orientation and uses his facts to promote and justify a particular form and content of schooling. In this volume the attempt is made to examine the different major types of value orientations on the assumption "if this type of value orientation, then this type of school." The effort has been made to be as objective as possible, though no social science is ultimately value neutral.

If genuflections are to be made, they are directed to the scholars whose works I have found useful, to the publishers for their permission to use materials, and to Ruth Stone Dahlke.

H. OTTO DAHLKE

February, 1958

PART I

INTRODUCTION

CHAPTER 1

Action and Values—
A Cultural Approach to Education

EVERYONE WHO enters a school building does not see the same thing. The same objects, the same people, and the same actions may be observed, but these are seen in the light and within the limitations of a person's experience and are related in the observer's mind to his interests and the reasons he has for being there. The social scientist comes in as a neutral observer with the sole purpose of describing and interpreting what he sees and hears, material that he collects in a systematic fashion.

Much as a botanist roaming the woods will see and understand a wealth of detail which will escape the hiker or hunter, a sociologist will see in the school what the child, the parent, or even the teacher does not see. As an observer he is equipped with preliminary knowledge of groups and of the processes of interaction between individuals and groups. An isolated incident falls into a theoretical framework. The following event will serve as an illustration.

As the nine o'clock bell rings, the children in the fifth grade stand at their desks, hands folded and heads bowed. Led by Jerry, who has been selected group leader for the week, they recite, "Our Father, who art in Heaven . . ." and so on to the final "Amen." At the conclusion of the prayer, the boys and girls snap into attention, direct their eyes to the American flag, and with proper arm motions pledge "allegiance to the flag of the United States and to the Republic for which it stands. . . ." With a scraping of chairs and a light buzzing conversation the children sit down at their desks. The teacher reminds them that the school day has begun and that some of them are behind in their work. After this brief warning the workday begins in earnest.

THE MEANING OF CULTURE

Here is a simple series of events that may take place almost every morning in many schools. At first glance these events seem quite obvious. Almost everybody has experienced such opening rituals. From the sociologist's perspective these events are a complex series of actions, fairly uniform and repetitive, which the boys, the girls, and the teacher carry out. The very way they move and handle their bodies, again in a fairly uniform and repetitive manner, indicates that they are acting out and living through different kinds of meanings— reverence on the one hand, patriotism on the other. The brief exercise in prayer has to do with ultimate meanings of life as defined in religion. The prayer also sets forth standards of conduct. It involves a comparative evaluation of the power and glory of the deity in contrast to the relative inferiority and impotence of the earthly creature. The whole pattern is a group activity in the sharing of meanings. The patriotic exercise is a highly concentrated lesson in nationalism and political belief. It defines the nature of American government and how it functions on the ideal level. The exercise symbolizes a claim by the state upon the loyalty of the children and the teacher, just as the prayer is also a claim made upon their loyalty by the churches. All these activities and meanings have been standardized for years. None of them represent the inventiveness of the participants. The pupils are organized, moreover, in the social relation of leader and follower with the teacher as an ultimate authority for the moment in the background. When the ceremonies are completed, the teacher becomes active in his role. With his opening statement, he makes an implicit distinction between good and bad pupils as far as work is concerned and sets up a standard of conduct, that work should be completed and handed in on time. These brief comments do not exhaust by any means the significance of this five-minute episode. We do learn something about culture, for all these actions are cultural.

Culture is a design for living. The prayer and the patriotic exercise in the above example are a small detail in this design. Culture is the accumulated action and thought ways of a people, and that is what these brief opening ceremonies represent. These action-thought ways are related to all aspects of human living, whether work, art, control of the body, coping with the physical environment, or dealing with other people. This very page is a complex of language, grammar, alphabet, reading and writing skills. It is also the result of our complex technology of the paper and printing industry.

As a design for living, a culture has three aspects. A culture is instrumental: from it people select the techniques of doing things, the means to reach an objective. A culture is regulative: the actions of persons and the use of the instruments are subject to rules and regulations, the dos and don'ts of living. They specify what should be done or must be done. A culture is directive: from it individuals derive their ultimate as well as immediate values, their interpretation of life, the goals for which they strive. Cultural behavior is action based upon a complex of evaluations, i.e., as to what is good or bad, proper or improper, efficient or inefficient, adequate or inadequate, beautiful or trivial, valuable or valueless, free or compulsory. Cultural reality is, thus, a value reality. The cultural approach to education is the approach which attempts to see it as part of this value reality and to analyze how the school reflects, conflicts with, or supports the culture.

EDUCATION AND THE NORMATIVE AND FUNCTIONAL ORDER

The parent may think of the school as the place where the child learns to read and write and acquire other skills. But in a very broad sense education may be interpreted as socialization, the growth process through which the child becomes an accepted adult in a society. "In every complex culture group the young are catechized and supplied with definitions of the situation which convey the accumulated wisdom of the past with respect to fortitude, frugality, industry, self-reliance, loyalty, unselfishness, cooperativeness, forbearance, or whatever the culture contains by way of the articulated regulation of social relations and personality standards." [1] As noted in the first example, the opening ceremonies in the class serve this end of instilling specific norms and values. The child is learning to act a religious or patriotic role. The approved social rules are taught to him through the family, the neighborhood, and the mass media of communication. School, church, court, and character-building organizations, such as Hi-Y or Gra-Y, are other agencies through which a boy or girl is taught and encouraged to act out the prescribed roles.

A specific rule or norm likely to be found in many schools is "no chewing of gum." Caught in the act, the youngster is requested or compelled by the teacher to throw the gum into the wastebasket. The pupil, none too happy, complies, and then sits down somewhat doggedly to continue his work. His friends in the class may indicate their sympathy and his enemies their pleasure at his being caught. Here is a rule that in its immediate effect means a denial of pleasure. Why should there be such a rule? This question is a question of value. The value may be a standard of conduct—self-restraint or discipline. The value from the point of view of the school may be purely utilitarian—keeping the schoolroom and desks clean. The "no gum chewing" rule is one of the hundreds of norms that compose the normative order of a school. The sociologist tries to get a comprehensive picture of this system of rules regulating conduct, imperatives pointing out the right or accepted ways of doing things. He tries to see how a normative order organizes and controls the actions of both teachers and pupils.

Values are made specific and effective through the norms. If one takes the value of cleanliness, a whole series of norms result—clean hands and face, teeth brushed, clothing neat, no sloppiness in the lavatory, no gum chewing, cleaning up after school, etc. All these rules stem from this one value. Furthermore, both norms and values define what is best for the individual and what is best for the group. Together they picture a model person, a social model of what the

[1] E. T. Hiller, *Principles of Sociology,* Harper & Brothers, 1933, p. 618.

child should be and of what he should eventually become. They also define ways of behaving that are important for the welfare of all and the achievement of common purposes. A norm of neatness involves largely a personal ideal. One requiring quiet and attentive behavior is directly related to the need for adequate communication between individuals in the classroom.

The picture the sociologist or the investigator is forming of the determining factors in the busy scheme he observes seems to fall into two main parts—the normative order, just described, and the functional order. The functional order refers to the variety of activities performed: teaching, learning, and administrative operations. The child must complete a specific lesson in arithmetic; the teacher must communicate certain specific information, take attendance, give grades; the principal must counsel children, allocate facilities. The tasks to be accomplished by the various members of the school constitute the functional order.

To itemize every activity and norm in a school would be an immense task. The most significant activities and crucial norms are the ones which need study. Their interrelations are important, for if they fit together, the chances are better that a school will operate efficiently and harmoniously. If they do not, there may be controversy and hostility. Since children are not mechanical puppets, they evaluate these activities and norms. They may even try to substitute some of their own. Their evaluations then become part of the dynamic process of an ongoing school, and so these must be included in observation and analysis. Let us rotate our perspective to another aspect of the school.

THE SCHOOL AND STRUCTURAL ELEMENTS OF A SOCIETY

The first-grader brings with him into the classroom certain expectations, antagonisms, or enthusiasms which he has absorbed from his short acquaintance with his society and the way it is organized. The youngster's position in his family and his family's prestige in the community are important in making him the sort of child he is. The sociologist looks for the influence of these factors on the school. The following observed example indicates some of these structural elements.

A small group in the class was studying something about agriculture. Tasks were being parceled out among the members of the group. An eager practice teacher placed some elaborate Diesel tractor diagrams in front of one of the girls. Looking at these diagrams in amazement, she turned to him and said in a somewhat embarrassed manner, "But Mr. Dexter, girls don't study such things. That's for boys!" The girl was stating what she thought was proper study inasmuch as she was a girl. She was relating school activities to her *sex status*. She was also informing him what she thought was proper for boys because they were boys. The use of the title "Mr." by the girl indicated a difference in *age status*. Sex and age status are positions into which people are placed. Such positions compose the structural elements of a society and together are termed the social structure of a society. Other statuses, in addition to age and sex, are occupation, race, nationality, and, from the point of view of large numbers of persons, social class.

Each status has its rights and obligations. The status of child means that the child has certain duties and claims with regard to the adult—a minimum of duties in terms of respect and obedience to the adult, a minimum of rights in terms of the essentials of life. Statuses may also involve the learning of specific character traits, as, for example, between the sexes in our country aggressiveness or meekness, harshness or gentleness. Similarly differences in rights and obligations and even in character traits would be found in the statuses of factory hand, professional man, and top executive.

The status structure carries or reflects values. The sociologist wants to know whether these values conflict with or support the ideal which the educator envisions. He will try to find out how these structural elements penetrate into the operation and structure of the school. How do they organize activities and social relations in the school? What is the significance to the educational process of the child-adult status, the male-female status, the class structure of a community? Are friendships and prestige among children the mere reflex of the family's position in the community structure? Is the curriculum organized according to sex status? Is school etiquette but an extension of child-adult relations of respect and submission? Is the relation of pupil-teacher the potential or actual conflict relation, as maintained, for example, by Waller? [2] What is the impact of this status order upon the school, as a whole, as a total ongoing process? These questions are not easy to answer, but the focus on the culture of the school is becoming sharper. Now you are beginning to note what must be looked for when using sociological lenses.

INFORMAL SOCIAL RELATIONS IN THE SCHOOL

John is considered a "good sport," George a "sissy," Susan a class "sweetheart," Dick a "tattle-tale," Mary a "tomboy." These terms indicate relations and evaluations among children that are outside the formal structure of teacher, pupil, and administrators. Children are interested in one another aside from their pupil role. Hatred, jealousy, love, fighting, and teasing are some of their informal social relations. The labels attached to the boy and girl are an indication of their rating, an informal prestige order. There are all sorts of pair relations, triads, cliques, gangs, even secret clubs, which create an informal social structure within the formal. A sociologist's analysis must take account of the creation and maintenance of this informal organization and structure—what its relation is to the formal, what problems it may pose for the teacher. The social world of the pupil in the school has many dimensions. Specialized techniques which are discussed in Chapters 9 and 14 are helpful in discovering something of these intricate, intense, personal relations.

THE SCHOOL AS A GROUP

Any school, whether public or private, is a distinctive group in its own right, with its own unique features. Yet certain generalizations about groups can be made. All schools, as institutional groups, have these common characteristics: *a degree of closure*, usually expressed in some test of admission (the child and family must meet certain conditions before they can participate; these are usually set by the state, except in the case of private schools); *a set of positions*, simple

[2] Willard Waller, *The Sociology of Teaching*, John Wiley and Sons, 1933.

or complex, to which the members are assigned, such as principal, supervisor, teacher, pupil, janitor; *a normative order*, which regulates the conduct of the members to each other and to outsiders; and *a functional order,* or the various activities and tasks that it is the business of the group to perform; *values* which the group serves or supports. A major problem is first to know what the test of admissions, norms, functions, and values are and secondly to analyze their interrelationship.

THE SCHOOL A GROUP AMONG GROUPS

Another important problem is to determine the degree to which schools are self-directive. To what extent are programs and goals set by educators? To what extent do other groups influence these programs and goals? The banning of certain textbooks is one obvious example of the impact of outside opinion.[3] It is necessary to investigate other and less obvious ways in which groups influence the schools. Any powerful special-interest group has a stake in the activities of the school. It will want the school to emphasize programs that agree with its ideas of education, with its interpretation of the American way of life. It may influence both the normative and functional orders of the school and will have some bearing on the values which the school elects to support. In Chapter 3 consideration will be given to diverse systems of value upheld by these groups, to the different images of the ideal person held by them. The extent to which these systems of value clash or fit together and how this affects the schools is an important fact to be determined.

IN CONCLUSION

In order to analyze an individual school or a particular teaching problem it is most helpful to have first the generalized picture of the principles and elements that make up a school. The picture con-

[3] *Hearings* before a subcommittee of the Committee on Education and Labor, House of Representatives, 81st Congress, 1st Session, on S. 246 and H.R. 4643, To Provide for Federal Financial Assistance to the States in Bearing Certain Costs of Public Elementary and Secondary School Education, Government Printing Office, 1949, p. 544.

structed thus far is admittedly an abstraction, but in order to think clearly theoretical conceptions are necessary. A weaver must know the materials which make up the finished cloth—the varicolored fibers and yarns, and the ways in which they are put together—the warp and the woof. In this type of study the materials are these principles of group structure and of cultural reality, and they are put together in a most complex crossing and interweaving of groups —the informal patterns of the school within the formal, the school against the background of the whole society, which is again a maze of competing groups. To understand the social fabric and the educational cloth is indeed an intricate business but one which must be attempted if catchwords and panaceas are to be eliminated as educational guides. The following list enumerates in detail questions which the sociologist asks about the school:

1. What values and norms organize social relations in the school and in the classroom?
   a. Are these values and norms unique to school and classroom or do they represent only general cultural values and norms?
   b. Do values and norms change as age and grade change? Why?
   c. Are these norms imposed by the teacher; pupil accepted or rejected; pupil originated?
   d. Do these norms and values fit together or are they inconsistent?
2. How are the norms enforced? What is the system of control, what are the rewards and punishments? How do pupils and teachers evaluate these controls?
3. What is significant about the activities in the school? How do pupils and teachers assess it? What interrelations are there between the values and norms of the school and the activities that are carried on?
4. What is the prestige order in the school? Which children and teachers rate high, which low? What are the consequences of this prestige order to the values intended and to the functional and normative orders?
5. What are the bases for rating conduct on the part of teachers and pupils?
6. To what extent do the community groups penetrate into the school, affecting its organization and operation? What impact does the community have upon the informal social relations within the school?
7. What is the significance of age and sex status, and class standing upon the school as a whole and the social relations within?
8. What makes for flexibility or rigidity in the organization and operation of the school?

9. What general values in American culture are supported by certain major groups? What bearing do these values have upon the operation of the school?

Important Terms

Culture, values, normative order, norm, functional order, status, age status, sex status, social structure, social class, status structure, informal social relations, informal structure, institutional group, special-interest group, test of admission.

Selected Readings

Biesanz, John, and Biesanz, Mavis, *Modern Society*, Prentice-Hall, Inc., 1954, chaps. 3, 4, 5, 7, 10.
Cuber, John, *Sociology*, Appleton-Century-Crofts, Inc., 1947.
Frank, Lawrence, *Society as the Patient*, Rutgers University Press, 1949.
Gerth, Hans, and Mills, C. Wright, *Character and Social Structure*, Harcourt, Brace and Company, 1953.
Hiller, E. T., *Principles of Sociology*, Harper & Brothers, 1933, chaps. 1–5.
Hiller, E. T., *Social Relations and Structures*, Harper & Brothers, 1947. The theoretical orientation in this book is adopted in this study. Definitions of terms are taken from this volume.
O'Brien, Robert, Schrag, Clarence, and Martin, Walter, *Readings in General Sociology*, Houghton Mifflin Company, 1951, Part III.
Williams, Robin M., *American Society*, Alfred A. Knopf, 1951, chap. 3.
Wilson, Logan, and Kolb, William L., *Sociological Analysis*, Harcourt, Brace and Company, 1949, Part I; Part II, chap. 7; Part III, chap. 11.

PART II

THE SOCIO-CULTURAL CONTEXT
OF EDUCATION
AND THE SCHOOL

CHAPTER 2

The School as an Objective Fact

FORMAL SCHOOLING is a cultural achievement. It is an outcome of differentiation of cultures in which institutional structures have become specialized. Such differentiation is not found in the folkways-mores type of society described by Sumner or in other anthropological accounts. The school as a socio-cultural fact cannot be taken for granted. While there are certain formal characteristics common to schools in any culture, there are qualitative distinctions, and this is true also of schools in the United States. A Lutheran parochial school is not the same as a secular public school. The significance of these qualitative variations will be discussed in the succeeding chapter on value orientations. This chapter will review (1) the rise of public education in the United States, (2) types of schools, (3) population trends and schooling, (4) schools as a phase of public economy, (5) groups associated with the school.

THE RISE OF PUBLIC EDUCATION
IN THE UNITED STATES

From the very outset of this country there was religious, private, philanthropic, and public concern about schooling. Frequently these different interests meshed. Thus, the 1606 charter of Virginia stressed the propagation of Christian religion to those who "as yet live in darkness and miserable ignorance of the true knowledge and worship of God" in the hope that it might "in time bring the infidels and savages . . . to human civility and quiet government. . . ." [1] This missionary interest in infidels and savages was shared by other groups, such as the Society for the Propagation of the Gospel in Foreign Parts. Colonial interest, however, was not merely in the Indian. It centered, too, in the apprenticeship or binding-out system, a way of taking care of poor or underprivileged, orphaned, or illegitimate children. This practice continued into the nineteenth century. The apprenticeship legislation of Virginia, 1642, indicates the point of view:

"Whereas sundry laws and statutes by act of parliament established, have with great wisdom ordained, for the better educateing of youth in honest and profitable trades and manufactures, as also to avoyd sloath and idlenesse wherewith such young children are easily corrupted, as also for reliefe of such parents whose poverty extends not to give them breeding. That the justices of the peace should at their discretion, bind out children to tradesmen or husbandmen to be brought up in some good and lawfull calling. . . ." [2]

The justices also had the power to compel such binding out "forasmuch as the most part the parents, either through fond indulgence or perverse obstinacy, are most averse and unwilling to parte with theire children." [3] The law shows a rather interesting legal phrasing of the Calvinistic work ethic. That the system was not too successful is indicated in the numerous reward bills for runaways.

Of greater importance in the furtherance of public education was the "Old Deluder Satan" Act passed by the Company of Massachusetts Bay in 1624. This act also shows the decisive significance of religion in the promotion of education. In this instance it is in the Protestant insistence that a man read and interpret the Scripture for himself; in order to achieve this objective, man must be taught to read.

It being one cheife proiect of ye ould deluder, Satan, to keepe men from the knowledge of ye Scriptures, as in formr times by keeping ym in an unknowne tongue, so in these latter times by perswading from ye use of tongues, yt so at least ye true sence & meaning of ye original might

[1] Edgar Knight and Clifton L. Hall, *Readings in American Educational History,* Appleton-Century-Crofts, Inc., 1951, p. 1.
[2] *Ibid.,* p. 9.
[3] *Ibid.*

be clouded by false glosses of saint seeming deceivers, yt learning may not be buried in ye grave of or fathrs in ye church and commonwealth, the Lord assisting or endeavors. . . .

It is therefore ordered, yt evry towneship in this iurisdiction, aftr ye Lord hath increased ym number to 50 householdrs, shall then forthwth appoint one with in their towne to teach all such children as shall resort to him to write & reade, whose wages shall be paid eithr by ye parents or mstrs of such children, or by ye inhabitants in genrall, by way of supply, as ye maior part of those yet ordr ye prudentials of ye towne shall appoint; provided, those yt send their children be not oppressed by paying much more yn they can have them taught for in othr towns; & it is further ordered, yt where any town shall increase to ye number of 100 families or householdrs, they shall set up a grammar schoole, ye mr thereof being able to instruct youth so farr as they shall be fited for ye university, provided yt if any towne neglect ye performance hereof above one yeare, yt every such towne shall pay 5 L to ye next schoole till they shall performe this order.[4]

This act served as a model for other New England colonies. Aside from the reason for educating the young, what is also important is the principle of public support of schooling. In addition the act provides for a simple educational structure. The idea of free, general, if not compulsory, education for all was the essence of the act. As New Englanders migrated into the interior of the country, they carried this educational ideal and educational practice with them, establishing schools as they duplicated their New England village life.

The colonial period thus already was complex in its educational pattern. The pattern was composed of the New England free public-supported school, the apprentice system, charity and pauper schools, and private tuition schools which were both secular and parochial. Cavalier America tended to develop a school system of which the last three types were the component parts, thus promoting a dual school system for the extremes in wealth and property. Many children from the plantation colonies were sent abroad for their education.

By the time the American Revolution came and passed, the basis for justifying education had also changed. Education was no longer advocated as protection against the old deluder Satan. In fact, the tendency was to loosen the tie between religion, education, and

[4] *Ibid.,* quoted on pp. 62–63.

state. The breaking up of this interconnection was a by-product of the move toward religious freedom, the effort to mitigate and to avoid sectarian strife. It represented the ultimate implication of Protestantism that religion is an individual, private affair and thus needs no public support. The point of view is summed up very succinctly in Jefferson's Bill for Establishing Religious Freedom in Virginia, 1779.[5] As religion was not to interfere in matters of state, so the state was to leave religion alone. Underlying the thinking of Jefferson and many of the other great men of this period was the theory of natural right, which involved religiously a deistic position. This theory includes among other points a profound respect for truth and the reasonableness of man. "Truth is great and will prevail if left to herself; that she is the proper and sufficient antagonist to error, and has nothing to fear from the conflict unless by human interposition, disarmed of her natural weapons, free argument and debate; errors ceasing to be dangerous when it is permitted freely to contradict them." [6] For truth to prevail, whatever the sphere of life, man had to be educated so that he could debate, and argue intelligently with information and insight.

After the Revolution the colonies adopted constitutional provisions for public-supported education. The Massachusetts Constitution of 1780 provided for "Wisdom and knowledge, as well as virtue, diffused generally among the body of the people, being necessary for the preservation of their rights and liberties . . . as these depend on spreading the opportunities and advantages of education in the various parts of the country, and among the different orders of people. . . ." [7] A similar idea is contained in the Northwest Ordinance of 1787, the first large-scale federal aid to education: "Religion, morality, and knowledge being necessary to good government and the happiness of mankind, schools and the means of education shall forever be encouraged." [8] Ignorance was equated with a servile, superstitious, docile population, with feudalism and arbitrary government. The new era the Revolution was ushering in would be the era of the enlightened citizen. In so far as man had been endowed

[5] Cf. Philip Foner (ed.), *Basic Writings of Jefferson*, Halcyon House, pp. 48–49.
[6] *Ibid.*, p. 49.
[7] Edgar Knight and Clifton Hall, *op. cit.*, p. 115.
[8] *Ibid.*, p. 116.

by his Creator with reason, he had a natural right to have his reason both respected and cultivated. Education was the means to implement this natural right.

That education was a form of public good was recognized. The attainment of this good was another matter. The specific policy was controversial from the very beginning. The differences in point of view have been described as the Jeffersonian and Jacksonian forces in American life.[9] The concept of an intellectual elite is associated with the former, as Jefferson put his case in his Bill for the More General Diffusion of Knowledge, 1779:

. . . Whence it becomes expedient for promoting the publick happiness that those persons, whome nature hath endowed with genius and virtue, should be rendered by liberal education worthy to receive, and able to guard the sacred deposit of the rights and liberties of their fellow citizens, and that they should be called to that charge without regard to wealth, birth, or other accidental condition or circumstance; but the indigence of the greater number disabling them from so educating, at their own expense, those of their children whom nature hath fitly formed and disposed to become useful instruments of the public, it is better that such should be sought for and educated at the common expense of all, than that the happiness of all should be confined to the weak or wicked.[10]

Jefferson's plan envisioned an overall system of public education but with a very rigid selection of the most qualified for higher education. The objective of university training was to prepare statesmen, judges, legislators, the guardians of the people's liberty. The objective of primary education was to prepare a good farmer- or artisan-citizen. The Jacksonian view is associated with equity and equality of opportunity. In Jackson's words, given in his first annual message, "The duties of all public offices are . . . so plain and simple that men of intelligence may readily qualify themselves for their performance. . . . No one man has any more intrinsic right to official station than another." [11] Equality of man, equality of opportunity, and equal

[9] *General Education in a Free Society,* Report of the Harvard Committee, Harvard University Press, 1948, pp. 27–35.

[10] Philip Foner, *op. cit.,* p. 40. Cf. also Jefferson's "Notes on Virginia," *op. cit.,* pp. 150–151, and excerpts from "The Report to the Legislature of Virginia Relative to the University of Virginia," August, 1818, *op. cit.,* pp. 400–401.

[11] Quoted in Samuel Morison and Henry Commager, *The Growth of the American Republic,* Oxford University Press, 1937, p. 368. Cf. Joseph Blau (ed.), *Social Theories of Jacksonian Democracy,* The Liberal Arts Press, 1947.

educational privileges for all were some of the cornerstones of Jacksonian democracy. Instead of selected students of "genius and virtue" who could profit by liberal education and a few select scholars, Jacksonianism wanted cheap, practical, vocational training for everybody, to produce better farmers, mechanics, merchants, etc.

As the development of education had made little progress up to the Jacksonian period, greater efforts were needed to make educational facilities available to all without the stigma of charity. The struggle for public support and control of education and compulsory attendance legislation sharpened and continued well into the twentieth century. The first compulsory attendance law was passed by Massachusetts in 1852 and the last by Mississippi in 1918. However, in 1925 the United States Supreme Court ruled in the Oregon School case (268 U.S. 510–513) that children of compulsory school age could not be compelled to attend public schools. The first permanent public-school fund was set up by Connecticut in 1795. The principle of public support for elementary education was firmly established by the middle of the nineteenth century. The legality of using taxes for secondary education was determined by the Supreme Court of Michigan in the Kalamazoo case, 1874. Thus, public support for secondary education was assured. Support for higher education was always forthcoming, as witnessed in the early establishment of universities and colleges, both private and public. A big impetus was given by the passage of the Morrill (Land-Grant) Act of 1862, the second large-scale federal aid to education.

THE CONTROVERSY ABOUT EDUCATION

The common, free, tax-supported, nonsectarian public school is rather recent in our history. The legal principles of public-supported and public-controlled schools were not settled until the 1860's and 1870's. For decades tremendous propaganda, public discussion, and memorializing of legislatures were waged for the institutionalizing of public education. There was disagreement about public education then, just as there is today.

In general the public school idea was promoted by middle class liberals, social and religious reformers, and humanitarians, by the labor movement and working classes of cities, and by the organized agrarian and Populist movements during the latter part of the [nineteenth] century. In general the public school idea was fought by social, political, and economic conservatives of all classes, by industrial and business interests that included large taxpayers, by the southern aristocrats, and by certain religious and non-English-speaking groups who saw a threat to their private control of religious and foreign-language schools.[12]

In addition operators of charity and private schools, some of whom received state support, also opposed the spread of free public-supported and public-controlled education. The public schools were regarded as a form of unfair competition.

The arguments for the establishment and expansion of public schools were: (1) the supremacy of the state and the state as *parens patriae*; (2) egalitarian values centering in the idea of equal worth and dignity of the individual; (3) the doctrine of the separation of state and church; (4) the necessity of having enlightened citizens; (5) the worth of the school as an instrument for social advance and progress; (6) equality of opportunity and self-advancement. Those opposed argued: (1) that the *status quo* should be preserved (the traditional is good, i.e., in terms of existing social classes, educational facilities, and property rights); (2) that there is a natural order as evidenced in a high association between intelligence and the distribution of property and wealth, and social class, and this order should not be violated; (3) that public education is irreligious, godless, and therefore contributes to social and moral decay; (4) that certain anti-equalitarian values are good; (5) that education is not the business of the state; (6) that public-controlled education is an interference with parental rights in the education of children; (7) that a public-school system is un-American; (8) that a public-school system would foster centralization of government power and bureaucratic control over people; (9) that education would cost too much.[13] Many of these arguments are still heard today. Public education remains controversial.

[12] R. Freeman Butts, *A Cultural History of Education,* McGraw-Hill Book Company, 1947, p. 472.
[13] Ellwood Cubberley, *Public Education in the United States,* Houghton Mifflin Company, 1919, pp. 120–123; Edgar Knight and Clifton Hall, *op. cit.,* pp. 143–150, 319–321, 340–343, 346–354, 368–372; Joseph Blau, *op. cit.,* pp. 46–47, 152, 271–272, 282–288, 337.

This brief survey of the rise of public education shows the following points: An educational system is based upon a set of values. These values may undergo change. As they do, the educational system likewise changes. The American school system is a cultural achievement, arising out of the competing differences of many groups. Public education had to be worked for. It was not something simply given. Lastly, the survey shows the relative recency of the educational system. The public-school system as it is known today in its major structural form is only eighty years old. Furthermore, what has been achieved may also be lost.

TYPES OF SCHOOLS

The increasing development and differentiation of the school system are shown in Figure 1. Lingering remnants of the older types of schools are still found in the New England region, but most of these will be gradually absorbed or converted into bona-fide public-supported and public-controlled schools. The different types of schools in an earlier period are suggested in the attempted definitions of the 1850 census:

Instead of the distribution of institutions into "universities and colleges," "academies and grammar schools," and "primary schools" adopted in 1840, in 1850 they were classified as first "colleges" or institutions empowered to grant degrees, as well as male or female, including law, medical, and theological institutions; secondly, "academies and other schools" or all such as are not embraced under third, "public schools," receiving their support in whole or in part from taxation or public funds. In framing the tables, however, it was found that female colleges, law institutions, etc., had been sometimes classed improperly with academies. In many of the states, particularly in the South, there is no general public school system, some counties, etc. supporting schools by taxation levied within their own limit, and in other cases the State contributing a proportion towards the support of public schools. Such schools are always considered as public in the census. Many academies also receive a limited support from public funds.[14]

The statement indicates this blending of private and public education, and the attempted classification represents an effort at a more

[14] *Statistical View of the United States*, U.S. Census, 1854, p. 141.

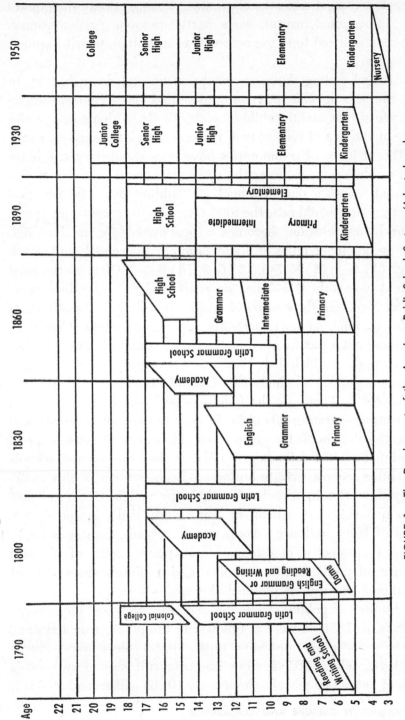

FIGURE 1. The Development of the American Public-School System. (Adapted and reprinted from Ellwood Cubberley, *Public Education in the United States,* Houghton Mifflin Company, 1919, p. 666.)

precise definition of educational practice. It suggests that the growth of our educational institutions is partly crescive, partly rational. The period referred to in the census is in transition, which Figure 1 also implies.

The school system shows an extension up and down in age. In some cities it is possible today to send a child to a prenursery school at the age of two, and the child may eventually graduate from a city college at the age of twenty-two. However, such instances are very few. The majority of communities have only elementary and high-school education. In so far as the child may spend from five to five and a half hours a day in school, not adding bus time for rural students, which would raise the total time in some cases to six, seven, or more hours, schooling becomes a focal experience for the child.

The predominant types of organization of the school are the following: (1) 8–4; (2) K–7–5; (3) 6–6; (4) 6–3–3. Of these the most prevalent type is the 6–3–3, i.e., six years of elementary, three years of junior high, and three years of senior high. Public education also includes evening, summer, part-time, and continuation schools.

To round out a picture of education in the United States, all other schools should be included. First there are the parochial schools. The more important are the Roman Catholic, Lutheran, and Seventh-Day Adventist. There are the federal schools for Indians. There is the private preparatory school for boys, for girls, or the type that is coeducational. Schools for exceptional children or the handicapped are maintained. The following would complete the picture: schools of art, Bible schools, private business schools, schools of chiropody, country day schools, schools of embalming and mortuary science, schools of fashion art, schools of home study and correspondence, schools of labor, military schools, music schools, nursing schools, schools of optometry, of osteopathy, of photography, of physical education, of public health, technical and trade schools, schools of occupational therapy, of physical therapy.

The number of public-school administrative units and the number of schools for 1951–52 were as follows: of the public-school system, ultimate or basic administrative units, 70,993, elementary schools 123,763 (of which 50,742 were one-teacher), secondary schools 23,746; of nonpublic schools, elementary 10,666 and secondary 3322;

residential schools for exceptional children (1945–46), public 307, private 137; institutions of higher learning, public 641, private 1191; schools of nursing not affiliated with colleges and universities, 984.[15]

TRENDS IN SCHOOL POPULATION

The trend of total population and school population for certain years is given in Figure 2. The figure shows the enormous growth of secondary education. It shows that the greater proportion of the child population age 5–17 years is in school. The decline in secondary education for 1949–50 may be the result of the birth rate of the thirties and war conditions. Inasmuch as the birth rate increased markedly during the forties, the elementary-school population in the fifties is very large, and this wave of population will eventually inundate the secondary schools. In 1951–52 enrollment in public elementary and secondary schools reached a new height, 26,562,663 pupils: 20,680,866 from kindergarten to grade 8 inclusive and 5,881,797, in grades 9–12 and postgraduate.

In Table 1 the changes in school population are contrasted for the years 1869–70 and 1951–52. It will be noted that the total population age 5–17 years of 1951–52 comes near the total United States population of 1869–70. Housing the school population today is almost equivalent to housing the entire nation of this early period. This point may suggest the magnitude of schooling as an objective fact. The data also indicate the effects of the compulsory school laws, so that 85 percent of the 5–17 year children are in the schools. The average daily attendance is considerably below the total enrollment, 60 percent in 1869–70 and 87 percent in 1951–52. This improvement may be due to the compulsory school laws, better health, and the urbanization of the country. The lengthening of the school term is also accompanied by better attendance of the children. The ADA of each pupil was 60 percent of the days of the school term in 1869–70 and 87 percent in 1951–52. In 1869–70, 37 percent of the year was used for schooling as compared to 50 percent of the year in 1951–52. This suggests an underuse of the school buildings in so far as the

[15] *Statistical Summary of Education,* 1951–52, Office of Education, U.S. Department of Health, Education, and Welfare, 1955, p. 4.

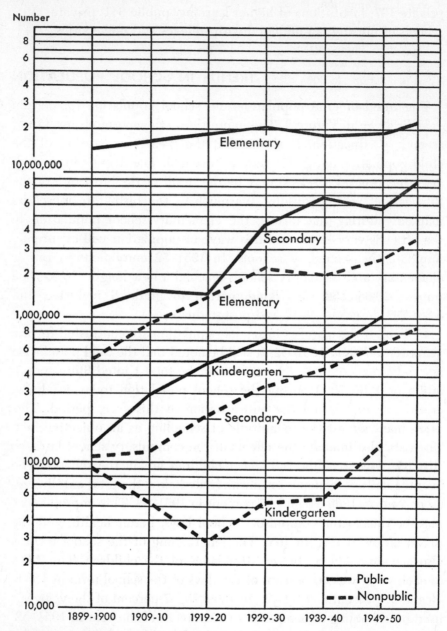

FIGURE 2. Enrollment in Full-Time Day Schools, by Level of Instruction and by Type of Control for Designated Years. (From *Biennial Survey of Education in the United States, 1950–52*, Office of Education, Government Printing Office, 1955, p. 7.)

TABLE 1. Population, Pupils, Attendance, and Instructional Staff, 1869–70
Compared with 1951–52

Population, Pupils, Attendance, and Instructional Staff	1869–70	1951–52
Total population (in 000)	38,588	153,383
Population age 5–17 years, inclusive (in 000)	12,055	31,379
Population age 5–17 years as percent of total population	31.3	20.5
Total number of pupils enrolled (in 000)	6,872	26,563
Elementary (kindergarten and grades 1–8) (in 000)	6,792	20,681
Secondary (grades 9–12, postgraduates) (in 000)	80	5,882
Percent of total population enrolled	17.8	17.3
Percent of population 5–17 years enrolled	57.0	84.7
Secondary enrollment (grades 9–12, postgraduates) as percent of total enrollment	1.2	22.1
Average daily attendance (in 000)	4,077	23,257
Percent of enrolled students in daily attendance	59.3	87.6
Average length of school term in days	132.2	178.2
Average number of days attended by each pupil enrolled during year	78.4	156.0
Total instructional staff, excluding supervisors and principals (in 000)	201	963
Men: Number (in 000)	78	235
Percent of total	38.7	24.4
Women (in 000)	123	728

SOURCE: *Statistical Summary of Education*, 1951 52, Office of Education, U.S. Department of Health, Education, and Welfare, 1955, p. 18.

equipment depreciates and becomes obsolescent whether in use or not. Unfortunately, most schools are not constructed for community use. The fact that most of the free time falls during the summer months has not been well explained. The usual explanation that this is a continuation of a rural pattern is not too acceptable. It was assumed that schools were not held in order to provide labor for the farms, but it is during these particular months that farm work is slack, a period between planting and harvesting. As a similar vacation pattern is found in Europe, the source of this pattern is perhaps not indigenous to America. Anyway, there is no rationale to the pattern. That teaching is a female occupation is a familiar stereotype, but this tendency began only at the turn of the century. There were 63 male teachers to every 100 female teachers in 1869–70, 42 males to 100 females in 1899–1900, 16 males to 100 females in 1919–20, and 32 males to 100 females in 1951–52. The explanation doubtless rests in the differential expansion of elementary and secondary education, and in World War I. With the enormous growth of secondary education after World War I more men went into teaching on that level, leaving the province of elementary education largely to females. Presumably the cultural definitions of the sex roles make it seem more appropriate for young children to be managed by adult females and older children by adult males.

Enrollment varies by age, sex, and place of residence, as is shown in Table 2. Almost all of the youth population that should be in the elementary school is attending it regardless of sex and residence. A marked difference occurs at the junior-high and senior-high levels. The proportion of each age group attending declines for both sexes and all areas. This decline is less for urban males and females than for rural farm males and females. In the latter group, the decline is greatest among males. The drop is linked with children's reaching the statutory age limit of the compulsory school laws. The problem of holding boys and girls in school seems to be more acute in rural nonfarm and rural farm areas. Attendance at college is associated with the urban population, primarily because more facilities are available to the urban older youth group.

The holding power of the school system is given in Table 3. The data show that the retention power on the elementary level on the whole is quite good, and it has improved. The high school has also increased its holding power but with less success than the elementary school. Thus, out of 1000 pupils in the fifth grade in 1944–45, 522 of them graduated from high school in 1952. Of this thousand 152 did not enter high school, and 326 students withdrew during high school. Secondary education is, hence, of no significance for almost half the youth population in the country.

Years of schooling completed is given in Table 4. The data, naturally, do not indicate the quality of the schooling. There has been an upward shift in the amount of schooling attained. The median is affected especially by the age structure. The younger the person is in this age group of 25 years or more, the larger the number of years of schooling completed. Thus, the median years of school completed in 1950 for those in the age group 25–29 for the United States was

TABLE 2. Percent of the Civilian Noninstitutional Population 5–29 Years by Age and Sex Enrolled in Public and Private Schools and Colleges, Continental United States, Urban and Rural, October, 1951

Age and Sex	Total	Urban	Rural Nonfarm	Rural Farm
Total, 5–29 years	52.8	50.4	54.4	59.1
5 years	18.9	18.7	17.9	20.5
6 years	93.1	94.0	93.8	89.6
7–9 years	99.0	99.7	99.1	96.9
10–13 years	99.2	99.6	99.6	96.9
14–15 years	94.8	99.7	96.3	86.3
16–17 years	74.9	79.2	74.1	63.8
18–19 years	26.2	29.3	24.7	17.7
20–24 years	8.6	10.3	5.1	5.3
25–29 years	2.5	3.3	0.8	0.8
Male, 5–29 years	56.8	55.9	57.5	58.9
5 years	19.6	20.0	20.4	17.2
6 years	93.5	95.5	93.9	87.1
7–9 years	99.1	99.8	99.3	96.9
10–13 years	99.1	99.6	99.3	97.9
14–15 years	95.1	97.8	95.3	88.7
16–17 years	74.3	82.0	71.6	58.2
18–19 years	32.4	39.3	31.9	15.8
20–24 years	14.3	17.8	9.1	7.2
25–29 years	4.2	5.6	1.5	1.6
Female, 5–29 years	49.1	45.5	51.5	59.2
5 years	18.1	17.3	15.4	24.4
6 years	92.7	92.5	93.8	92.2
7–9 years	98.9	99.7	98.8	96.8
10–13 years	99.3	99.7	99.8	97.8
14–15 years	94.5	97.6	97.2	83.6
16–17 years	75.4	76.6	76.4	70.5
18–19 years	21.3	22.3	19.0	20.1
20–24 years	4.3	5.1	2.1	3.4
25–29 years	1.0	1.4	0.3	—

Kindergarten enrollment is excluded.
SOURCE: *Statistical Summary of Education,* 1951–52, Office of Education, U.S. Department of Health, Education, and Welfare, 1955, p. 8. Slightly adapted.

12.1 as compared to a median of 8.2 for those in the age group 65 years and over. The data reflect thus the immigrants who come to this country with relatively little education and the educational facilities available to the native born. Since the high school first came into prominence in the decade 1910–20, most people over 40 in 1950 had primarily elementary education. This difference in access to educational facilities is also reflected in the years of schooling completed by those in urban, rural nonfarm, and rural farm areas, and by those in the white and nonwhite categories. Rural farm and the nonwhite are the educational have-nots.

TABLE 3. Retention Rates, Fifth Grade Through High-School Graduation in Public and Nonpublic Schools, Continental United States for Designated Years

Grade or Year	Retention [a] per 1,000 Pupils in the Fifth Grade in						
	1932–33	1934–35	1936–37	1938–39	1940–41	1942–43	1944–45
Elementary schools							
Fifth [b]	1,000	1,000	1,000	1,000	1,000	1,000	1,000
Sixth	935	953	954	955	968	954	952
Seventh	889	892	895	908	910	909	929
Eighth	831	842	849	853	836	847	858
High schools							
I	786	803	839	796	781	807	848
II	664	688	725	655	697	713	748
III	570	610	554	532	566	604	650
IV	510	512	425	444	507	533	549
Graduates	455	467	393	419	481	505	552
Year of graduation	1940	1942	1944	1946	1948	1950	1952

[a] Retention rates are approximate only.
[b] Fourth grade in eleven-grade systems; fifth grade in twelve-grade systems.
SOURCE: *Statistical Summary of Education*, 1951–52, Office of Education, U.S. Department of Health, Education, and Welfare, 1955, p. 9.

The trend of the birth rate and the death rate, immigration and internal migration, industrial expansion, and changing agricultural technology all interplay to affect the trends in school enrollment and educational achievement. The significance of regional variations remains to be explored. The present analysis can focus only on the broad picture.

EDUCATION AS AN ASPECT OF PUBLIC ECONOMY

Viewed in the aggregate, education is a big business. It is concerned with fixed and circulating capital. It is concerned with budgets and the estimates of future capital requirements. There is a

TABLE 4.   Median School Years Completed by Persons 25 Years and Over, by Sex, Color, and Residence, for the United States, 1950 and 1940

Item	Median School Years Completed	
	1950	1940
U.S.	9.3	8.6
Male	9.0	8.6
Female	9.6	8.7
Urban	10.0	8.7*
Male	9.9	8.6
Female	10.2	8.8
Rural nonfarm	8.9	8.4*
Male	8.7	8.2
Female	9.1	8.5
Rural farm	8.4	7.7*
Male	8.3	7.6
Female	8.6	7.9
White	9.7	8.7
Male	9.3	8.7
Female	10.0	8.8
Nonwhite	7.0	5.7
Male	6.5	5.4
Female	7.4	6.1

SOURCE: *Educational Attainment of the Population 25 Years Old and Over, for the United States,* 1950, Bureau of the Census, U.S. Department of Commerce, Series PC-7, No. 6, pp. 6–9; * U.S. Census 1940, *Population,* Vol. II, Pt. 1, Table 13, p. 40.

problem of depreciation, obsolescence, and replacement of equipment. There is the whole gamut of labor problems: recruiting, teachers' salaries, hours and conditions of work, pensions, teacher organization, and many more. In all of these phases, the school is like any other business establishment. The public-supported and public-controlled school, however, differs in three important ways from business. Its funds are not derived from the selling of its services and goods. It is not taxed. It is not operated for profit.

While schools receive funds from the sale of bonds, the ultimate source of revenue is the community itself. The funds represent an allotment by the community of its resources to the furtherance of a public objective. As the revenue is derived from taxes, education is a problem in public finance—what sort of taxes to be laid upon what types of sources. Traditionally, the tax has been a property tax, the amount of funds raised depending upon the assessed valuation of property, which may reflect the resource level of the community. Financing is thus a public policy and is either furthered or limited by legislative action and the specific procedures of implementing the legislative policy. This latter refers especially to the assessing of property values. At either point, i.e., on the legislative level or the local level, the impact of vested interests may make itself felt in such a way that the financing of the school is handicapped.[16] Bond proposals or increase in the tax levy may be rejected by the voters, especially if the issue is not clear. Voting depends on access to the polls. Unless workers are given time off, they cannot vote, and thus the issue may be carried by those middle- and upper-class property owners who have the free time. Unfortunately the financing of schools becomes roiled in the fracas of American politics, which is not especially noted for its straightforwardness and rationality. When this situation is coupled with ambivalent or one-sided reporting in the press, it is surprising that schools have fared as well as they have.

While the local community obtains its revenue from a tax on real estate, each individual state contributes funds for the support of schooling in each community. State funds are secured in different ways, varying from an income tax to a sales tax. The latter is not regarded as an equitable tax as it is not based on the principle of ability to pay. A regressive tax of this type is not good public policy. A graduated income tax on individuals and corporations would be preferable. The amount of money distributed to communities is usually based on the average daily attendance of pupils and other stipulations set by the state legislatures and/or boards of education. The revenue that a state obtains depends on the resources in that state. The ability to support education varies considerably among the forty-eight states.

How the source of revenue has changed during the past years is shown in Table 5. There is a fairly rapid shift from the local community as a source of revenue to the state. The relative insignificance of the county as a source of revenue is evident. This transfer of the

[16] For two cases: August Hollingshead, *Elmtown's Youth,* John Wiley and Sons, 1949, pp. 139–147; David Hulburd, *This Happened in Pasadena,* The Macmillan Company, 1951, pp. 62–98.

TABLE 5. Percentage Distribution of Revenue Receipts from Public Sources for Public Elementary and Secondary Day Schools for Forty-Eight States, 1951–52

Source	Percentage Distribution				
	None	Less than 25	25–49	50–74	75 and Over
Local	1	9	13	15	10
County	10	31	7	—	—
State	—	15	21	10	2
Federal	—	48	—	—	—

SOURCE: *Statistical Summary of Education*, 1951–52, U.S. Department of Health, Education, and Welfare, 1955, p. 28. Adapted.

financial responsibility to the state was doubtless ushered in by the depression decade. The extent to which the transfer has taken place varies tremendously. At one extreme is Louisiana, with 4.5 percent of revenue derived from local sources, and at the other extreme New Hampshire, with 91.0 percent of revenue locally derived. These variations are shown in Table 6.

TABLE 6. Total Revenue Receipts of Public-School Systems and Percentage Distribution by Source, United States, 1929–30 to 1951–52

Year	Total Amount [a] (000)	Revenue Receipts			
		Percentage From			
		Federal	State	County	Local
1929–30	$2,068,557	0.4	16.9	10.4	72.3
1931–32	2,068,029	0.4	19.8	8.8	71.0
1933–34	1,810,652	1.2	23.4	9.3	66.1
1935–36	1,971,402	0.5	29.3	7.1	63.1
1937–38	2,222,885	1.2	29.5	6.5	62.8
1939–40	2,260,527	1.7	30.3	6.7	61.2
1941–42	2,416,580	1.4	31.5	6.2	60.9
1943–44	2,604,322	1.4	33.0	5.6	60.0
1945–46	3,059,845	1.4	34.7	6.0	57.9
1947–48	4,311,534	2.8	38.9	5.3	53.0
1949–50	5,437,044	2.9	39.8	6.0	51.3
1951–52	6,423,816	3.5	38.6	6.0	51.8

[a] Includes income from subsidies from educational foundations, which amounts to less than 0.05 percent of the total.

SOURCE: *Statistical Summary of Education*, 1951–52, Office of Education, U.S. Department of Health, Education, and Welfare, 1955, p. 24.

Except for funds to support specialized vocational training, the federal government does not contribute directly to the public elementary and high schools. Its role is a matter of debate. In the 1955 White House Conference on Education the participants approved by a ratio of more than two to one the proposal that the federal government should increase its financial participation in public education. Of those approving, the majority favored federal funds primarily for the construction of school buildings. The participants divided almost evenly on the issue of federal funds to states for school operations. There was almost unanimous opposition to any federal control over educational use of funds in local school districts.[17] This opposition apparently has overlooked current federally supported and federally controlled programs in the public schools. In 1951–52 the federal government made the following contributions to the public schools: vocational training below college grade (agriculture, trade and industry, home economics, distributive occupations, teacher training), $26,273,383; assistance to federally affected areas for maintenance and operation and school construction, $79,-893,941; school facilities survey, $850,264; surplus property transferred to educational institutions (including higher education), $43,625,876; revenue from national forests, $14,081,321; school lunch program, $98,492,759.[18]

Expenditures of funds by public elementary and secondary school systems is given in Table 7. The proportion spent on administration appears constant. The percentage allotted to instruction has diminished to slightly over half of the expenditures while the proportions for auxiliary services and fixed charges have increased. The table implies that school construction almost ceased during the war years 1941–46. As a consequence an increasing proportion is now being spent on capital outlay.

As stated above, states and communities vary in their ability and perhaps also interest in supplying funds for the support of schools. A state or community with rich resources can acquire more funds with less effort than can poor communities and poor states. The latter

[17] *The Reports of the White House Conference on Education,* Washington, 1955, p. 15.
[18] *Statistical Summary of Education,* 1951–52, U.S. Department of Health, Education, and Welfare, 1955, pp. 14–15.

TABLE 7. Percentage Distribution of Expenditures of Public-School Systems, by Purpose, United States, 1929–30 to 1951–52

Purpose	1929–30	1939–40	1941–42	1943–44	1945–46	1949–50	1951–52
Total expenditures [a]	$2,313,791	$2,344,049	$2,322,697	$2,452,581	$2,906,887	$5,837,642	$7,344,237
Total	100.0	100.0	100.0	100.0	100.0	100.0	100.0
Current expenditures [a]	79.6	82.8	89.0	93.5	93.1	80.3	77.9
Administration	3.4	3.9	4.4	4.5	4.6	3.8	3.6
Instruction	56.9	59.9	62.8	64.9	63.8	53.3	51.5
Operation	9.3	8.3	9.0	9.7	9.3	7.3	6.9
Maintenance	3.4	3.1	3.4	3.2	3.5	3.7	3.4
Auxiliary services	4.4	5.5	6.0	6.9	7.3	7.7	7.8
Fixed charges	2.2	2.1	3.5	4.3	4.7	4.5	4.7
Capital outlay	16.0	11.0	5.9	2.2	3.8	17.4	20.1
Interest	4.0	5.6	4.7	3.9	2.6	1.7	1.6
Evening, summer, and adult schools	0.4	0.6	0.4	0.3	0.4	0.6	0.4

[a] Full-time day schools.
SOURCE: *Statistical Survey of Education*, 1951–52, U.S. Department of Health, Education, and Welfare, 1955, p. 24.
NOTE: Detail will not necessarily add to totals because of rounding.

must make a greater effort to secure their funds, i.e., to allocate a larger percentage of their resources to education. Even with such an effort they may not reach the level of those communities and states that are well off. The amount of funds spent by states for education per child and per pupil is given in Table 8. The bottom half is essentially the old South and the Great Plains states, and the top group is composed generally of the states constituting the manufacturing belt extending from New York to Illinois. It is to overcome this great differential that federal legislation to aid education is advocated as a measure to assure equality of opportunity to all of America's youth.

TABLE 8. Annual Expenditures for Public Elementary and Secondary Education per Capita, per Child Aged 5–17, and per Pupil in Average Daily Attendance, by State, 1951–52

State	Annual Expenditure per Child Aged 5–17, Full-Time Day Schools	Annual Expenditure per Pupil in Average Daily Attendance in Full-Time Day Schools
United States	$233.07	$312.68
Delaware	343.55	496.54
Oregon	327.33	417.70
New York	326.38	417.93
California	a	403.73
Washington	298.23	365.83
Wyoming	289.62	373.26
Kansas	288.07	354.02
Connecticut	282.09	388.53
Nevada	280.18	326.30
New Jersey	274.92	384.30
Montana	267.06	353.65
Michigan	264.65	351.95
Illinois	262.97	373.78
Maryland	258.63	374.41
Colorado	255.52	339.18
Iowa	250.73	315.17
Minnesota	245.99	338.93
Arizona	241.59	335.73
Ohio	239.20	317.71
Indiana	235.16	301.90
Florida	227.98	286.63
Utah	224.81	260.68

ᵃ No data.

SOURCE: *Biennial Survey of Education in the United States,* 1950–52, pp. 80–81.

TABLE 8. Annual Expenditures for Public Elementary and Secondary Education per Capita, per Child Aged 5–17, and per Pupil in Average Daily Attendance, by State, 1951–52 (*Continued*)

State	Annual Expenditure per Child Aged 5–17, Full-Time Day Schools	Annual Expenditure per Pupil in Average Daily Attendance in Full-Time Day Schools
New Mexico	221.88	315.33
South Dakota	216.85	289.58
Wisconsin	212.08	323.63
Massachusetts	210.24	313.89
Idaho	209.65	262.08
Nebraska	206.11	270.22
Texas	205.55	289.62
Oklahoma	205.22	261.10
Louisiana	202.80	294.15
Pennsylvania	201.91	291.90
North Dakota	200.77	279.24
Virginia	194.71	261.10
New Hampshire	194.38	303.81
North Carolina	190.38	235.97
Missouri	181.84	249.29
Rhode Island	181.23	296.14
Vermont	163.60	250.28
West Virginia	157.07	205.16
Maine	145.21	209.29
Georgia	143.66	192.93
Tennessee	128.69	187.76
South Carolina	128.68	173.46
Alabama	121.57	163.23
Arkansas	115.14	157.52
Kentucky	112.27	162.55
Mississippi	102.35	125.90

GROUPS ASSOCIATED WITH EDUCATION

The fact that schools have to be built and equipped of itself creates economic producers who specialize in furnishing educational materials. The relationship tends to be a reciprocal one. The livelihood of the producer depends upon the school system. What a school can do rests in part upon the type and quality of material that the producer furnishes. The initiative in specifying what the buildings and objects are to be like rests ultimately with the school and its theory of education. However, it is also to the interest of the producer to sell his product with an eye to the returns from the sales. The relationship, while reciprocal, is not necessarily good. A school may or may not receive quality products. The interests are not identical. The ramifications of the problem are quite complex and can only be suggested.

In *Patterson's American Education* a count of headings of educational equipment and materials which various firms are ready to furnish came to 994 areas. The following are a few samples: [19]

Addressing machines	Gymnasium Mats
Art materials	Janitors' supplies
Ash and refuse cans	Lifesaving equipment
Awnings	Minerals and rocks
Benches	Organs
Bird repellent	Paper towels
Blackboard erasers	Plastics
Bus bodies	Playground equipment
Communication systems	Prints and pictures
Cafeteria supplies	Ranges
Curtains	Recording equipment
Deodorants	Safes
Desks	Shop equipment
Dishwashing machines	Songbooks
Encyclopedias	Swimming pool equipment
Filmstrips	Tables
Flagpoles	Window shades
Flooring	Zoölogy charts
Grandstands	

The 994 areas do not exhaust the types of equipment and material which are furnished; 2258 manufacturers and publishers were listed in the directory,[20] though, again, this is an incomplete list. There is no area of the economy that remains untouched by the schools' demand for goods and services.

Since school contracts are frequently financial plums, all kinds of efforts are made to reap them. There is much advertising which indicates that a particular product is better than any other. A certain amount of wining and dining may take place, with a resultant alloca-

[19] *Patterson's American Education,* Educational Directories, Inc., 1954, pp. 7-61.
[20] *Ibid.*, pp. 62-67.

tion of contracts to "friends." Free offers of curriculum materials are made. Obviously, the greater part of contracting is bona fide, but fraud and collusion have not been absent in the zest to maximize returns. Politics has played its role in this too. Nevertheless, the school dollar should get its full value.

Economic groups are just one type among others that are linked with the school. There are the numerous educational associations and societies. A recent count showed 445 national, regional, state, and special-interest groups dealing with education in some form.[21] There are also the forty-eight state education associations which are affiliated with the National Education Association of America. In addition there are many other groups (church, patriotic, etc.) interested in education. The significance of these will be discussed in later chapters. If one adds the various local booster groups, the number of groups rotating around the school system is quite enormous.

SUMMARY

An educational system is a cultural achievement based on a system of values. Our free, public-controlled and public-supported school system is a creation of over 100 years' work; today schools exist for children of all ages from the pre-elementary age to post-high-school age. Education, however, is still a controversial issue, and the system may undergo additional changes. In order to exist, the schools are financed in many ways through support from local, state, and federal funds. The ability to support education varies, so that educational opportunity is distributed unequally throughout the nation. Various groups are bound up with the school through various ties. In the next chapter the educational implication and involvement of these groups is examined.

Selected Readings

Alexander, William M., and Saylor, Galen, *Secondary Education: Basic Principles and Practices*, Rinehart and Company, 1950.
Blau, Joseph (ed.), *Social Theories of Jacksonian Democracy*, The Liberal Arts Press, 1947.

[21] *Ibid.*, pp. 632–638.

Butts, R. Freeman, *A Cultural History of Education,* McGraw-Hill Book Company, 1947.

Harvard Committee, *General Education in a Free Society,* Harvard University Press, 1948.

Knight, Edgar, and Hall, Clifton, *Readings in American Educational History,* Appleton-Century-Crofts, Inc., 1951.

Morphet, Edgar L., and Lindman, Erick L., *Public School Finance Programs of the Forty-Eight States,* U.S. Government Printing Office, 1950.

Mulhern, James, *A History of Education,* The Ronald Press Company, 1946.

National Citizens Commission for the Public Schools, *How Have Our Schools Developed?*

CHAPTER 3

Value Orientation, Social Models, and Education

IT WAS pointed out in the first chapter that a culture is directive, but on closer examination it becomes apparent that a culture such as ours is signaling in various directions, and the result creates about the same confusion that would come from having several policemen on the same busy corner, each with a different idea of how the traffic should move! The policemen are the various major groups which have a distinctive value orientation and which try to train their members and to pass on their ideas from generation to generation. When a society has a consensus in most major areas of life and most of the values are core values, this process of cultural transmission is simple. But in a complex society there is nothing automatic about a son's believing as his father believed. Each major group has to work to gain acceptance of and continuing faith in its values. The youth are brought into many minor supporting groups. In the United States the American Legion supports baseball teams and youth camps organized to fit in with its conception of the American way of life. The church has its Sunday School and young people's organizations of all sorts. The universities have departmental clubs, honor societies, etc. In each case the attempt is to further the objectives of the parent organization or to socialize the young in accordance with a social model.

The social model crystallizes the value orientation of a group. The abstract idea is vividly symbolized in the life of a past or present hero of the group. Business groups will look to Henry Ford or Du Pont as epitomizing their ideals, labor to Samuel Gompers, Eugene Debs, or A. Philip Randolph, liberal educators to humanitarians and truth seekers such as Voltaire, Emerson, or Dewey. Patriotic groups will honor Washington, Lee, Eisenhower. Religious groups will seek to follow Jesus, St. Francis, Gandhi, Schweitzer, or other saintly characters who demonstrated by their dramatic life stories the values of this orientation.

Is there any way to distill from all these diversities something essentially American? Many efforts have been made to describe the typical American. Familiar expressions are "rugged individualism," "self-made man," and "go-getter." Americanism is also strongly connected with the traditional concepts of equality and tolerance. "The land of the free and the home of the brave" from the national anthem is commonly quoted to suggest national characteristics. Ritual and custom proclaim "freedom and justice for all." Religion is associated with many phases of public life. "In God We Trust," interestingly, appears on our money, "one nation under God" in the allegiance pledge. Prayers open the sessions of the legislatures. This is all very nearly second nature and familiar, but to get beyond platitudes and slogans it is necessary to do some digging. A little thought makes apparent the variety of meanings that can be ascribed to "freedom" by various groups. The agreement on such a concept may be purely formal, for a Catholic and a Protestant, or a worker and his boss, could never agree on the content of this handy word. "Equality" may mean anything from equality as children of God to equality before the law to equality as brothers in a lodge or fraternal order, and very different consequences flow from these various interpretations.

It is necessary to study the professed policies of outstanding public groups in the religious, economic, patriotic, and educational areas, and it is essential to examine in detail the statement of these groups in controversial situations. Controversy brings out more clearly the values the groups stand for and the values they condemn. The congressional hearings on federal aid to education are especially illuminating. These statements help delineate the social models of these groups, what they think the schools should do, what ideas they feel the schools should transmit, what they conceive to be the proper roles for teacher and pupil. Several value orientations and social models will now be examined. The objective is to understand them, not to criticize them.

RELIGION AND EDUCATION

Both Roman Catholic and Protestant groups are interested in education—Christian education, a type of training that results in the Christian man or Christian woman. The identity of goals between these groups is formal, since being a Christian comes to mean being a good Catholic or a good Protestant. Since these are the largest religious groups in our country, they need careful study, although non-Christian religious groups would be similarly interested in education as a means of passing on their values and beliefs.

THE RELIGIOUS SOCIAL MODEL

Here is the person whose life is focused on God and Christ. The aim is to be as Christlike as possible, to live a saintly or holy life. Rather than "life, liberty, and the pursuit of happiness" he seeks death of self, obedience to divine will and divine love, and the virtues of humility, patience, purity, fidelity, faith, and service. His is a life of prayer, penitence, repentance. "It is at the same time a spirit of revolutionary criticism when confronted with institutions which have become formal or oppressive." [1] These ideas are common to both Catholic and Protestant tradition. The Christian must be loyal to Christ without considering consequences, and for the Catholic this loyalty must be funneled through the church. Man is not the measure of all things. The holy and consecrated life presented by the religious social model is radically divergent from all others. The ends found in the other social models would be condemned as idolatry of things worldly and ephemeral.

[1] Gerald B. Smith, *Principles of Christian Living*, University of Chicago Press, rev. ed., 1942, p. 61.

THE ROMAN CATHOLIC POSITION

What education means officially to the Catholic church is stated in the encyclical letter of Pope Pius XI on *Christian Education of Youth*, issued December 31, 1927. Roman Catholic educational theory is an elaboration of this document. It is in fundamental disagreement with the view held by many today that education is primarily a secular function and not a religious one. The goal of education stems from end values. The goal is stated as follows:

. . . It is clear that there can be no true education which is not wholly directed to man's last end, and that in the present order of Providence, since God has revealed Himself to us in the Person of His Only Begotten Son, who alone is "the way, the truth, and the life," there can be no ideally perfect education which is not Christian education. . . . The proper and immediate end of Christian education is to cooperate with divine grace in forming the true and perfect Christian, that is, to form Christ himself in those regenerated by baptism. . . . For the true Christian must live a supernatural life in Christ: "Christ who is your life," and display it in all his actions "That the life also of Jesus may be manifest in our mortal flesh." For precisely this reason, Christian education takes in the whole aggregate of human life, physical and spiritual, intellectual and moral, individual, domestic and social, not with a view to reducing it in any way, but in order to elevate, regulate and perfect it, in accordance with the example and teaching of Christ. . . . Hence, the true Christian, product of Christian education, is the supernatural man who thinks, judges, and acts consistently and constantly in accordance with right reason illuminated by the supernatural light of the example and teaching of Christ; in other words, to use the current term, the true and finished man of character.[2]

This statement of a form of Christian education proceeds from a first value (God and Christ) to instrumental values (baptism and education). This passage also contains the social model, i.e., one who excels in religious functions, a special total character orientation.

Actually the model manifests itself in the monks and nuns of the various religious orders. For those who cannot devote themselves exclusively to the attainment of excellence in religious functions, the church has provided alternate channels in its lay orders. Such groups

[2] *Five Great Encyclicals,* The Paulist Press, 1939, pp. 39, 64–66.

are a means of fitting the model to the demands of the world, but the true ideal will always be located in the lives of the saints, in the priesthood, and in the monastic life. Here we find the church's heroes. Part of the function of the parochial or church-controlled school is to transmit the model and to recruit members for the orders and priesthood.

Since Catholic education involves a total life pattern, the Roman Catholic Church makes an absolute claim to the right to educate. This claim is based on its value orientation and is bolstered on historical grounds.

And first of all education belongs pre-eminently to the Church, by reason of a double title in the supernatural order, conferred exclusively upon her by God Himself; absolutely superior therefore to any other title in the natural order. The first title is founded upon the express mission and supreme authority to teach given her by her Divine Founder: "All power is given to Me in Heaven and earth. Going therefore, teach ye all nations. . . ." The second title is the supernatural motherhood, in virtue of which the Church, spotless spouse of Christ, generates, nurtures and educates souls in the divine life of grace with her Sacraments and her doctrines. . . . By necessary consequence the Church is independent of any sort of earthly power as well in the origin as in exercise of her mission as educator, not merely in regard to her proper end and object, but also in regard to the means necessary and suitable to attain this end.[3]

Upon the basis of these principles the church assumes the right to promote the letters, science, and arts "in so far as necessary or helpful to Christian education," and to found schools and institutions. The church will coöperate as far as possible with the state with regard to schooling. This coöperation will take the form of "civic education," by which is meant "information having an intellectual, imaginative, and emotional appeal, calculated to draw their wills to what is upright and honest . . . to include almost every activity of the state intended for the public good." [4] Although according to Catholic theory there should be a true harmony and mutual support between church and state, this relationship is not always maintained. Where harmony does not prevail and there is conflict, the church will always strive to have the last word, as it never moves from its absolute stand on these matters.

[3] *Ibid.*, p. 41.
[4] *Ibid.*, p. 50.

It also assumes as "inalienable right" and "indispensable duty" the supervision and checking of all education in public and private institutions which Roman Catholics attend. This check includes not only matters of religious instruction but also "every branch of learning and every regulation in so far as religion and morality are concerned." [5] In effect this means that every aspect of education should be under church control or supervision.

The Nature of Catholic Schools. To foster a Christian education which will put before young people the religious model, and more specifically the Catholic model, the church in conjunction with its orders, particularly the teaching orders, builds up schools on the basis of its value orientation. This building of a school is not just a question of instructional content; the ideas are built right into the architecture and equipment so that the physical structure of the school reinforces the values of the church which are to be transmitted. The religious garb of teachers also contributes to the symbolism. The following statement in the encyclical describes in some detail this educational environment:

This educational environment of the Church embraces the Sacraments, divinely efficacious means of grace, the sacred ritual, so wonderfully instructive, and the material fabric of her churches, whose liturgy and art have immense educational values; but it also includes the great number and varieties of schools, associations and institutions of all kinds, established for the training of youth in Christian piety, together with literature and the sciences, not omitting recreation and physical culture. . . . The mere fact that a school gives some religious instruction does not bring it into accord with lights of the Church and of the Christian family, or make it a fit place for Catholic students. To be this, it is necessary that all the teaching and the whole organization of the school, and its teachers, syllabus and textbooks in every branch, be regulated by the Christian spirit under the direction of the maternal supervision of the Church; so that religion may be in very truth the foundation and crown of the youth's entire training; and this in every grade of school, not only the elementary, but the intermediate and the higher institutions of learning as well.[6]

Catholics are instructed to agitate for Catholic schools as a "genuinely religious work and therefore an important task of 'Catholic Action.'" Also control is to be extended over "impious and immoral books . . . cinema and radio." These points again emphasize the

[5] *Ibid.*, p. 43.
[6] *Ibid.*, pp. 59–60.

conception of a total pattern of life based on religious principles.

Educational Malpractice from the Roman Catholic Point of View.
The church is very explicit not only in what it believes to be the
right way to educate but also in what is wrong. This comes down,
of course, to the matter of values. When the Catholic value system
is being transmitted, education is good; when different values are
basic to an educational system, it is bad. "Every form of pedagogic
naturalism which in any way excludes or weakens supernatural
Christian formation in the teaching of youth is false. Every method
of education founded, wholly or in part, on the denial or forgetful-
ness of original sin and of grace, and relying on the sole powers of
human nature, is unsound." [7]

It will be noted that these condemned principles are precisely
those found in most public schools and advocated by non-Catholic
professional educators. There are probably no nonreligious teacher-
training institution that base their educational philosophy on original sin and the doctrine of grace.

Another point of difference is with regard to the mingling of the
sexes in schools and the teaching of sex education. The church forbids sex education on the assumption that it is a family matter and
that parents should take care of it.[8] Coeducation is also proscribed.[9]
The church in this country has not consistently provided separate
schools for boys and girls, but the ideal still stands for the separation
of the sexes.

All so-called "neutral" or "lay" schools, from which religion is
excluded, are condemned as contrary to the fundamental principles
of education. The lay school, it is thought, is bound to become irreligious. It is from this point of view that public schools in the
United States have been evaluated as "godless" and "pagan." Thus,
Roman Catholics should not attend neutral or mixed schools.

THE PROTESTANT POSITION

Because of the great variety of Protestant groups in which doc-
trinal differences may become erected into end values, it may seem
somewhat difficult to define a common core to which all might give

[7] *Ibid.*, pp. 54–55.
[8] *Ibid.*, p. 56.
[9] *Ibid.*, pp. 56–57.

assent. If one reflects that Unitarians, Jehovah's Witnesses, Christian Scientists, Presbyterians, Holy Rollers, Baptists, Friends, and hundreds of other groups are part of this Protestant history, what could there be of a basic consensus?

End values have been defined by various Protestant groups and publicists. These popular accounts, written for the layman, are likely to be standard interpretations rather than sophisticated theological arguments about the nature and purposes of God. Certain generalizations can be made about these statements. The role of Christ and God tends to be similar in Protestant and Roman Catholic conceptions. Protestants, however, deny the exclusive relation between God and the Roman Catholic Church. They also deny the body of belief and practice centering in the saints. The sacramental system as propounded by the Roman Catholic Church is rejected. Yet there is

. . . a common belief in God as source of all existence. His ways are found in nature and within man through conscience. God's word has been proclaimed by prophets and in Jesus Christ God was made manifest in human life. Man is a child of God and he attains his full stature only as the Spirit of God dwells in him. The central teaching of Christianity is the principle of the love of God and the love of fellowmen. It seeks to bring in Fellowship all mankind, for all of whatever race or nation are children of God. . . . The purpose of the Church is to bring about the development of Christ-like persons and a more Christian society.[10]

The Committee on Religion and Education of the American Council on Education Studies took the following stand.

We who write this report are members of religious bodies to which we owe allegiance by conviction. For us, the democratic faith means the worth of persons and the increasing perfectibility of human institutions rests on a religious conception of human destiny. We believe that the Judaeo-Christian affirmation that man is a child of God expresses an authentic insight which underlies all particular theological formulas. . . . Underneath the cleavage is the stream of Judaeo-Christian tradition with its conception of the common source and spiritual equality of all men as the children of God; the obligation to respect the supreme worth of persons and the wickedness of exploiting them; the golden quality of mercy; the meaning of redemptive love, the inexorableness of the law that he that soweth to the wind shall reap the whirlwind. These are great cohesive

[10] Frank McKibben, *Christian Education Through the Church*, Abingdon-Cokesbury Press, 1937, pp. 13-14.

spiritual forces to which the secular order of society probably owes more than it suspects.[11]

These two statements are fairly typical of attempts to get at some core ideas to which most Protestants would assent. Other ideas which many Protestants would emphasize are: Christology, the Bible as an infallible source, the emphasis on individual conscience and private judgment, the stress upon individual effort to attain salvation, an emphasis on democratic church organization. It will be noticed that in the above statements there is the implication of a higher sphere of life (religion) and a lower sphere of life (the secular)—a kind of dualism found also in Roman Catholic doctrine with regard to the respective spheres of state and church.

False Values from the Protestant Point of View. There is frank questioning about the value of a nonreligious democracy, or humanistic ethics, and about the whole trend of thought associated with instrumentalism and pragmatism. A report adopted by the International Council of Religious Education in 1949 rejected "educational philosophies based on 'frankly materialistic and secularist views' and 'belief in spiritual values, conceived without reference to a transcendent religious faith.'" [12] This is similar to the Catholic attack on "false naturalism."

Educational Implications of the Protestant Position. Although there are some Protestant parochial schools, the parochial school as a means of fostering Protestant points of view is generally rejected. Such parochial schools as exist are regarded as a specific way of indoctrinating the Christian model. The Reverend Oswald C. J. Hoffman, director of the Lutheran Church Missouri Synod, states: "We erect our own schools in order that our children may build their lives wholly, not just partly, on Jesus Christ." [13]

In general the public school is accepted as the proper vehicle for the education of children. The principle of separation of church and state is accepted as basic. On the other hand there is an increasing desire on the part of Protestants to introduce religion or more religion in the public schools. The complete separation of religion and

[11] Committee on Religion and Education, *The Relation of Religion to Public Education,* American Council on Education Studies, Series I, No. 26, 1947, p. 47.
[12] *Information Service,* Federal Council of Churches, March 26, 1949, p. 1.
[13] *New York Times,* September 12, 1949, p. 5.

school is regarded as a mistake. While there is not the point of view of Roman Catholic officials that the education in public schools is godless and therefore undesirable, Protestants do point out that the public schools are irreligious, if not anti-religious. It is maintained that since religion is part of culture, and it is the function of schools to transmit the basic values in the culture, they should teach religion.

The controversy arises immediately as to the content and method of teaching religion, and while some educators seem to favor the teaching of religion, there is little agreement as to how it should be carried out. Some feel that a law should be enacted to compel the teaching of religion in the public schools. A model bill contains the following provisions:

. . . Whereas, the religion and moral standards of this state and the nation are those of the Bible.

THE BILL

Section 1. Immediately upon the passage of this act, the state department of public instruction shall prepare courses in nonsectarian religion and morals suitable for all grades of the common schools of this state, with special emphasis upon the Ten Commandments, the Shepherd Psalm, the Proverbs, the Sermon on the Mount, the Lord's Prayer, the Golden Rule, and the Judicial Oath used in all our courts. High schools shall also include courses in the historical and literary values of the Bible.[14]

This statement contains not only reference to ultimate values but also ways in which these are to be embodied in the school. The school would be compelled by law to carry out religious and Christian education.

Religious education on released time is another proposal. Children would be dismissed early from school, and the time so gained would be devoted to religious training. In practice each child would be instructed according to his church affiliation. This instruction would take place either on the premises of the school or in a nearby church. The whole issue is controversial, but it does illustrate how people want to put into effect religious values and train children accord-

[14] W. S. Fleming, *God in Our Public Schools,* National Reform Association, 1942, p. 235.

ingly. The program is regarded by some as a sound compromise on the principle of the separation of church and state.

There is some agreement between Roman Catholics and Protestants in this controversy between a religious education and a secular scientific education, but the opposition of the two groups remains as strong as ever, a matter of power and control, as evidenced by the continuous struggle and litigation on the question of federal or state aid to nonpublic schools. Such controversy is to be expected when there are contending groups proclaiming absolute values.

AMERICAN VALUES AND EDUCATION
THROUGH NATIVIST EYES

When different groups are competing with one another to have their ideas accepted, there are some groups which consider themselves the supporters of the traditional cultural heritage. They conceive the traditional values to be the true core of the culture. Other values are alien, destructive, bad, and false. The greater the struggle between groups the more rigidly will nativists assert these traditional goals. The nativist group in purest form is found in the patriotic societies, nationalistic organizations, and groups emphasizing national power. They support the nativist value orientation.

THE PATRIOT-WARRIOR SOCIAL MODEL

The nativist is the patriot *par excellence*, operating on the principle "my country right or wrong, my country, glory and power forever and ever." The measure of all things is the national culture. The nativist is a purveyor of legends and rituals that center on the past. From his point of view what was good for the Pilgrims at Plymouth Rock or George Washington and other founding fathers of the Republic is good today. He is a fervid supporter of patriotic occasions and ceremonials. Innovations, changes, controversy, questioning are disapproved. His mentality is immobile. Rigid conventionalism characterizes the life pattern. Personal honor is identified with national honor. He sincerely and devoutly believes that God has blessed America, its founding fathers, and the Constitution, and that in the fierce competitive struggles among nations the United States has triumphed by virtue of its institutions which are animated by a frontier spirit.

The nativist is not merely conventional but an aggressive fighter for conventionality, willing to slug it out with deviating groups if necessary. His heroes are the fighters, and he considers the important events in the culture its wars, for in war a nation proves its power and secures its glory, its triumphs.

TRADITIONS AS END VALUES

The preamble to the constitution of the American Legion contains the following statement:

For God and country we associate ourselves together for the following purposes: To uphold and defend the constitution of the United States of America; to maintain law and order; to foster and perpetuate a one hundred per cent Americanism; to preserve the memories and incidents of our association in the Great War; to inculcate a sense of individual obligation to the community, state and nation; to combat the autocracy of both the classes and the masses; to make right the master of might; to promote peace and good will on earth; to safeguard and transmit to posterity the principles of justice, freedom, and democracy; to consecrate and sanctify our comradeship by our devotion to mutual helpfulness.

Gellerman is of the opinion that, in the passage of time, chief emphasis has been placed upon upholding and defending the Constitution of the United States, maintaining law and order, and fostering and perpetuating a one hundred per cent Americanism.[15] If his interpretation is correct, Americanism is narrowed to a few traditional values. The nativist orientation would include the following main ideas:

1. The individual should be free to direct his own life.
2. Americanism rests upon the personal initiative of the individual, of the local community, and of the separate states.
3. The individual, community, and individual state should be self-supporting.
4. Private enterprise and a free economy are principles established by the founders of the country.

[15] William Gellerman, *The American Legion as Educator*, Teachers College, Columbia University, 1938.

5. The sovereignty of the United States is a supreme value.

6. Children and adults should have a "compelling sense of pride" in the country, and persons should willingly die for their country if need be.

7. Competition teaches rugged but inspiring lessons; the competitive life is the good life.

8. Teamwork makes a democracy.

9. Success is not dependent upon wealth, or social class of father, but is the triumph of talents in competition.

10. The Constitution is the most envied document in the world.

UN-AMERICAN "ISMS" AS NEGATIVE VALUES

Many of these groups struggle to preserve their conception of the American way of life by an unceasing fight against "isms," many of which are regarded as alien importations. The foremost "ism" during the past thirty years has been communism. Socialism falls in almost the same category. Pacifism is equally bad. Federal paternalism and centralization of control in Washingon are feared. Federal aid to education is considered by many, as a witness at the hearings said, "a crucial step toward the socialization of America." [16] Perhaps the latest ism which is feared is world federalism. "Patriotic women protest the use of their Federal tax dollars by left-wing educators to aid them in an educational endeavor to scrap America's hard-won Declaration of Independence for 'surrender to world organization.'" [17] There is fear of the indoctrination of school children, which is considered bad as long as the content does not fit in with traditional values and the nativist's viewpoint.

MALPRACTICE IN EDUCATION

Any deviation from the established traditional values is regarded with great animosity. This hostility, as expressed in the hearings, is directed particularly to the National Education Association and other educational organizations. Teachers and educators are pictured as betraying America. Controversial issues are considered dangerous unless the superiority of the American system are pointed out. Too

[16] *Public School Assistance Act of 1949, Hearings* before a special subcommittee of the Committee on Education and Labor, House of Representatives, 81st Congress, 1st Session, Government Printing Office, 1949, p. 557.

[17] *Ibid.*, p. 540.

many questions are raised. The "three R's" are neglected. Pupils know nothing about American history. There are too many frills. The following ideas are considered folderol: individualized teaching, extracurricular activities, progressive education in general, sex education, no homework. Schools are too easy. "This business of letting a child express himself is the reason we have so many unruly children now. They come home with the idea that they are a little law unto themselves. They bring it from schools, this principle of self-expression." [18] According to the House Un-American Activities Committee, Communists smash a school by destroying the teacher's authority, turning classrooms into madhouses of disorder "with 'student councils' deciding courses, discipline, and school policies." [19] Lastly, American public schools are controlled by power-hungry educational bureaucrats who can do with schools and children's minds anything they please, opposing parents and communities alike.

INDIVIDUAL COMPETITIVE ENTERPRISE FOR A SOUND AND FREE AMERICA

Via press, magazines, pamphlets, radio, and movies, industrial and business groups have set forth their conception of the "American System." This point of view will be referred to as the market orientation. The ideas are not a matter of slogans or catchwords, as some critics imply. The constant reiteration in writing, its affirmation in public discussion and in congressional hearings, suggests not only that these values have been internalized but that they also represent a base for policy formation.

According to the market value orientation, America is a system of unlimited opportunities for all. America has limitless possibilities. If physical frontiers are closed, production and management frontiers are open. America is a place to get ahead.

Coupled with the idea of freedom to do what you want is freedom of choice. These coalesce in the idea of competition. The result of unrestrained competition is believed to be abundance, happiness,

[18] *Ibid.*, p. 855.
[19] *Communism and Education*, Committee on Un-American Activities, House of Representatives, Government Printing Office, n.d., pp. 4–5.

and progress. For the individual it means success. Moreover, the attainment of success in this country, it is claimed, is unimpeded by social restrictions. Wealth, prestige of birth, and ability to "bluff" are irrelevant. Race, creed, political affiliation are unimportant. Education is a necessity but no guarantee, an ambivalent value. What does count? Initiative, courage, conviction, perseverance of the individual are the most important qualities.

The self-reliance of the individual will overcome all obstacles. Hard work will bring its rewards. However, while hard work is conceived of as a value, the highest success will depend on the willingness to take a risk. Wealth and high standards of living are regarded as a result of taking chances. Being venturesome correlates with self-initiative, freedom of choice, and opportunity.

Goods, wealth, profits, money, though sometimes depreciated, are also major values. This is seen in the instrumental evaluation of education as a means of providing more profitable markets and as an avenue to more lucrative careers. It is seen in the American admiration for bigness—in buildings, bridges, cities, conspicuous consumption, conspicuous leisure, and the fabulously high standard of living.

THE MARKET SOCIAL MODEL

The social model contained in this value orientation is that of the successful, hard-driving, self-made man, who may also be characterized as the market personality. Financial wizards and industrial giants are the heroes. Excellence lies in acquisition, self-reliance, inventiveness, planning. Skills lie in the manipulation of persons and things. Attitudes toward others are based on their utility or usefulness to the enterpriser. Traditional values are used to support the ends of power, authority, and wealth, and emphasis is on the need of unlimited freedom to make a triumphant struggle through the human jungle. Business is business; expediency and self-interest are primary.

A refined version of the self-made man is the successful manager. Contrasted with the entrepreneur who, starting with little, builds a business empire, the self-made manager is working within an organization which already existed before he came on the scene. He may start off as office boy or worker in the shop; by hard work, initiative, and other characteristic virtues he climbs the power and responsibility ladder. The two-fisted dynamic go-getter type is superseded by a suave public-relations, public-responsibility character. But the same traditional values are attached to both of these types.

"ISMS" AS NEGATIVE VALUES

Socialism, communism, collectivism, paternalism, statism—all these "isms" are much the same as those denounced by the patriotic and nativist groups. Wherever they are considered to be given any encouragement by schools, there is strong criticism and negative evaluation. The conception of malpractices in education closely resembles that of nativist groups.

THE SCHOOLS AS UPHOLDERS OF FREE, COMPETITIVE AMERICANISM

The schools are to transmit the true facts and values of the American way of life. This means, of course, those facts and values proposed by the industrial and business groups. Among other things the schools are to devote more attention to the importance of manufacturing as a force in American history. It is the function of schools to turn out trained workers so that the productive output in factories can be increased. Schools give rise to a more profitable market since there is some correlation between education and purchasing power. Schools can also produce a more contented citizenry. "I believe that the experts in this field are convinced that education produces not only a difference in the volume of opinon, but also a difference in the kind of opinion. People with information are inclined to more moderate opinions, whereas those without information are apt to be extremists. Business and industry have an ever increasing interest in an educated population—an enlightened electorate. I cannot think of a healthier climate for any private enterprise." [20] Schools must also inculcate self-discipline and respect for authority.

[20] Frank Abrams, *The Stake of Business in American Education*, Standard Oil Company of New Jersey, n.d., p. 7.

A SOUND AND FREE AMERICA THROUGH
COLLECTIVE ACTION—LABOR

The orientation of labor groups is in many respects similar to that of the industrial and business groups, but their interpretation amounts to a different way of life: the common man value orientation. The right of an individual to direct his own life is considered a sacred right. Labor groups, like others, are concerned with a democratic way of life. They resort to a traditional and historical appeal with a labor slant. They support, as do all groups, the ends implied in the Bill of Rights. Freedom of choice, equality of opportunity likewise represent end values. They are interested in material progress and the accumulation of goods. Participation of the worker in problems of organization, production, and distribution and in policy formation to them is an extension of the equality value to a collective and representative basis. This idea is rejected by most businessmen and business groups. Individual and collective responsibility for welfare is stressed as a desirable end. "Every free trade unionist holds that the essence of democracy is social discipline; a discipline based upon an ideal of mutual restraint for the common good." [21] Competence and independence are stressed. It is felt that ultimately what is good for labor is good for America.

Great emphasis is given to instrumental values. This has led to the opportunism of labor groups, to the practice of supporting only those who support labor. It also leads to the tremendous emphasis placed upon collective action.

Wage earners through their unions were the pioneers in working out the principles and technique of associated activity. We have passed from the age of individual self-sufficiency to a period of interdependence of interest. Practically the whole business world is now organized for carrying on associated practices and is developing for their functions the principles that Labor discovered. It, as Labor, has conformed to the necessities of the changed economic situation. Business, however, has made the basic mistake of attempting to carry over into the associated area the principles of personal gain regardless of the costs to others. . . . Mutuality stimu-

[21] *Labor and Education in 1947* (American Federation of Labor), Introduction.

lates cooperation—a much more fundamentally sound principle than profit at the expense of the co-workers.[22]

In this statement there is something of a messianic conception of labor, the vision of a new social order and greater progress, provided the methods of labor are accepted and some of the false values of business abandoned. The state is not regarded with the degree of repugnance expressed by business groups. The state is valued as the equalizer of opportunities and benefits.

NEGATIVE ASSESSMENTS—ANY IMPEDIMENTS TO LABOR'S PROGRESS

Labor protests against compulsion, coercion of workers, and governmental regimentation. The dominance and unequal allocation of property rights, as against human rights, is disapproved. Rugged individualism is assessed negatively. The incentive of profit and unrestrained competition are not considered unalloyed virtues though allegiance is accorded to the American free enterprise system. Big business as a system of power is condemned as totalitarianism from the right. Militarism and conscription have consistently been condemned because they deny the worker individuality and because these devices have been turned against him.

THE COMMON MAN SOCIAL MODEL

The common man, the toiler (the opposite of the self-made man or his modern version, the manager), is the little man (the salt-of-the-earth), who has to organize with others to make himself heard. The heroes of the labor movement are for the most part unsung and unknown. They are the men who suffered and struggled and had faith in the ideas that brought organized labor much of its current prominence and power. The labor leaders cannot supply a pattern for this social model because many of them have really left the ranks of the common man. The laborer, the unidentified individual who has to join with his fellows in the struggle to achieve a fair return for his work, is the best symbol of the model. He is not the competitive personality. He is the one who also counts. The value of the

[22] *Fifty Years of Service,* American Federation of Labor, 1941, pp. 9–10.

worth and dignity of the individual also applies to him. He is not merely a cost, or a salable abstraction called labor.

EDUCATION FOR THE WORKER-CITIZEN

Compulsory free public schools with equal opportunities for all children have regularly been supported by labor groups. Education is regarded as a tool to equip children "to think about, understand, and appreciate the blessings of the free way of life. . . . Good schools mean teachers who have the ability to impart learning to the young and who are ready to teach the truth—including the truth about the contributions which organized labor has made and is making to the attainment and maintenance by the United States of its position as a great and progressive nation." [23] Vocational and cultural education should be reunited. Control of schools should be local. Schools must meet the needs of the individual and his community. Schools should develop a sound social discipline. "Somewhere between the rigid, regimented discipline asked for by totalitarians, and the unbridled license which is misnamed as 'free discipline' by the pseudo-liberals, the school of tomorrow will develop a sound social discipline." [24]

Other items favored for education are: free discussion of all issues, federal aid to education, labor education extension services for workers, social security for teachers, more federal lunch programs, a federal scholarship program, better United States employment counseling, better guidance, smaller classes, trade unions for teachers, more pay for teachers, student councils, and student government.

Aspects of education looked upon unfavorably are: lack of labor representation on school boards, NAM-conducted industrial tours as part of social studies, unresponsive school bureaucracies, low status of vocational schools, verbalism and bookishness in the curriculum, antilabor materials in schools, or, as summarized by Philip Murray, "too much one-sided teaching, too much emphasis on militarism, palace-politics, business economics, nationalism, and not enough

[23] *Labor and Education in 1944,* Introduction.
[24] *Labor and Education in 1947,* p. 6.

emphasis on the story of the common people's role in American history." [25]

EDUCATORS AND THE HUMANISTIC ORIENTATION

The stress on education for democracy and citizenship is of comparatively recent origin. Although these terms were used in arguments for the establishment of a public-school system, they were imperfectly carried out according to popular consent by the established schools. At present the federal government, state boards of education, schools of education, and organizations of teachers emphasize the urgency of inspiring school children with democratic ideals and practicing democracy and citizenship. These groups constantly stress respect for personality and use such expressions as "a reverence for the essential sanctity of all that is human." In place of personal success, Americanism, patriotism, or godliness as most worth striving for, the humanist would count human welfare as the most important end. The Educational Policies Commission states that "The impact of education on a developing personality should lead that person to place human welfare at the very summit of his scale of values." [26] Here is admission that values are important and that the school has a role to play in their formulation. The Connecticut State Board of Education underlines this idea when it states in one of its bulletins that "The materialistic concept which circumscribes the purpose of education needs to be supplanted by a system of moral value and personal responsibility." [27]

This point of view and these values are elaborated in democratic theory, which has been formulated in many statements and definitions. The Educational Policies Commission sums its conception of democracy in five generalizations.

1. Democracy prizes a broad humanitarianism, an interest in the other fellow, a feeling of kinship to other people more or less fortunate than

[25] B. P. Brodinsky, "Labor Has Its Own Program for Public Education," *The Nation's Schools*, January, 1949, p. 21.

[26] Educational Policies Commission, *The Purposes of Education in American Democracy*, National Education Association, 1938, p. 73.

[27] *The Redirection, Reorganization, and Retooling of Secondary Education*, Bulletin 37, Connecticut State Department of Education, Bureau of Youth Service, 1945, pp. 4–5.

oneself. One who lives in accordance with democracy is interested not only in his own welfare but in the welfare of others—in general welfare.

2. Democratic behavior observes and accords to every individual "unalienable" rights and certain inescapable responsibilities.

3. Democratic processes also involve the assent of the people in matters of social control and the participation of all concerned in arriving at important decisions.

4. Peaceful and orderly methods of settling controversial questions are applied in a democracy. . . . The callous use of force and violence is rejected as unworthy of a civilized people.

5. Democracy sets high value upon the attainment of human happiness as a basis for judging the effectiveness of social life.[28]

THE HUMANIST SOCIAL MODEL

"The assent of the people," "inescapable responsibilities," and "participation" all suggest that this democratic theory stands or falls on the success of the various socializing and educating agencies, including the schools, in producing citizens who can fulfill these requirements. The social model, for groups with the humanistic orientation, is the good citizen—the man of freed intelligence, self-discipline, and a humanistic spirit. This person has scientific habits of thought, mental balance, and a willingness to accept and evaluate change. He is one who has a sense of responsibility for self and others, who has earned the regard of the group. He shows tolerance, sympathy, helpfulness, sharing. In short, he is "a self-directing social being, who has habits of analyzing, criticizing and evaluating his conduct in light of democratic ideals."[29]

THE SCHOOL AS A DEMOCRATIC LABORATORY

Democracy in the classroom means that education is a joint process between teacher and pupils in which all share in the planning and carrying out of plans. The instructional process, according to one educator, is "comprehension, insight, seeing both sides of a question, research, suspended judgment, criticizing, choosing, cooperating, lending a helpful hand."[30] The use of force, coercion, and

[28] Educational Policies Commission, op. cit., pp. 7–8.

[29] Weems Saucier, Theory and Practice in the Elementary School, The Macmillan Company, 1941, p. 92. Reprinted with the permission of the Macmillan Company.

[30] Ibid., p. 91.

compulsion is considered a lesser evil, to be avoided as much as possible, though in practice the occasional use is regarded by some as an unfortunate necessity. Of course, the crucial point is the general type of relationship that should prevail, so that the situation is democratic, rather than authoritarian or laissez faire. The following statement is a fairly typical description of how the schoolroom could be a democratic laboratory:

American education today is faced with the challenge of having children experience the democratic manner of living. This means opportunities to be provided for pupils to learn the principles of democratic living by playing and working together under conditions which foster respect for the rights and privileges of others, tolerance for the viewpoints of other persons, and a sharing of responsibility for decisions affecting the group. It means that children need to grow in an understanding of the balance between freedom and responsibilities and between right and duties. The school, if it is to educate for democratic living, will have to assist each pupil to find his place in the group and to become a contributing member of group enterprise. . . . The children learn to live with each other cooperatively and harmoniously. It must be a place in which arbitrary decisions are not made, but one in which control evolves from within the group and is exercised for the welfare of the majority. The general atmosphere of this laboratory is characterized by mutual understanding and mutual respect of pupil for pupil and pupil for teacher, and teacher for pupil. . . . Since the teacher is the one adult member in the group, his every act has to coincide with the democratic way of thinking and acting which he would have pupils acquire. The teacher cannot give lip service to democracy but must exemplify democratic ideals if he is to inspire children to democratic living.[31]

SUMMARY

Certain similarities are seen to exist between our five orientations, but more outstanding are their differences. These types of value orientations and social models have been worked out through methods of content analysis of documents, testimonies, hearings, etc.[32]

[31] Bernice Baxter, *Teacher-Pupil Relationships*, The Macmillan Company, 1941, pp. 1–3.

[32] For detailed documentation, see H. Otto Dahlke, "The Social Structure and Institutional Organization of an Elementary School," unpublished Ph.D. thesis, University of Wisconsin, 1950.

The differences become clearer as one examines the social images toward which the various groups wish to socialize the young. The humanist image is at variance with all the others except perhaps that of the "common man." The critical questioning mind is at odds with traditionalism. The stress upon group activity, coöperation, group responsibility is the reverse of individualism and competition. The concept of authority as mutual and shared is widely different from traditional domination-submission relationships. The absence of otherworldly reference is incompatible with a religious orientation.

The implications of the five positions for education have been explored, and it has been seen that in each case the group wants education to turn out a child according to its social image. What is right for one group is malpractice for another. When there seems to be unanimity on certain values these are seen to agree only when kept on an abstract level. Important qualitative differences become apparent when such a word as "freedom" or "equality" is spelled out by a group in terms of the kind of program it wants to see going into effect in a school.

On the basis of these data the schools are seen to be an area of contending value emphases. The schools are surrounded by a ring of special-interest groups which are watching, criticizing, and trying to exert their influence to see their own values realized. Later analysis will show in detail how these value orientations and social models are factors in shaping the structure and organization of the school.

Suggested Typology of Value Orientations

I. The Religious Value Orientation.
   A. *Ultimate ends:* God, Christ, salvation, immortality; otherworldly.
   B. *Character structure and life organization:*
      1. The saintly or holy character; the Christlike character.
      2. Virtues of humility, patience, purity, fidelity, faith, and service.
      3. A life of prayer, penitence, and repentance; obedience to divine will and to divine love.
   C. *Person:* each soul a unique and infinite value; worth of person and evaluation of person symbolized in the brotherhood and sisterhood ideal; redemption through love and grace.

D. *Competition:* devaluation of competition; man against man ultimately sacrilegious.

E. *Coöperation:* stress on mutual aid, sharing, communalism, service without ulterior motives.

F. *Wealth and property:* low valuation, a hindrance to the religious life; frugality and simplicity in living; stewardship concept.

G. *Social change, intellectual inquiry, and creativity:*
1. Criticism of social institutions if regarded as contrary to divine will or divine law; may even be revolutionary.
2. Change and inquiry of little significance, for the important values are not of this world.
3. Artistic creativity in service of the ultimate ends.

H. *War:* ambiguous, from pacificism to just-war principles, but ultimately the Kingdom of God is peace.

II. The Nativist Value Orientation.

A. *Ultimate ends:* the national culture and/or the state, power, glory, honor, greatness as national attributes; sovereignty.

B. *Character structure and life organization:*
1. The patriot-warrior.
2. Virtues: aggressiveness, discipline, toughness, hardness, ambition for fame, prestige in struggle.
3. Tradition-bound, mentally immobile, mentally conformist, ethnocentric.

C. *Person:* instrumental or tool conception of person.

D. *Competition:* life as a struggle for existence; survival of the fittest with the weak falling by the way, exterminated or subservient to the winner.

E. *Coöperation:* significant only as it contributes to the competitive struggle.

F. *Wealth and property:* as an expression of and in service of the nation-state, leads to public monumentalism and other display items of national power and glory.

G. *Social change, intellectual inquiry, and creativity:*
1. Conservative, *status quo* oriented; best ways are the old.
2. Fear of the new; inquiry suspect because questioning and skeptical; intellectualism debunked as mere talk, words.
3. Creativity to be channeled into the celebration of the grandeur and power of the nation and its heroes.

H. *War:* proves the mettle of man and nation, *the* or *a* main source of social progress.

III. The Market Value Orientation.

A. *Ultimate ends:* goods, wealth, profits, money, power, conspicuous consumption, prestige, fame.

B. *Character structure and life organization:*
   1. The self-made man image or the successful manager or executive.
   2. Virtues: exemplified in the hard-driving, shrewd, acquisitive, inventive, calculating, ambitious, aggressive individual, manipulative of persons and things.
C. *Person:* instrumental and tool conception of person; "everybody has his price."
D. *Competition:* competition as the mainspring in life.
E. *Coöperation:* same as nativist, and as coöperation contributes to the achievement of the main goals; *pseudo-Gemeinshaft.*
F. *Wealth and property:* accumulation for the individual the *summum bonum*; a symbol of respectability, prestige; all things valuated quantitatively in monetary units.
G. *Social change, intellectual inquiry, and creativity:*
   1. Inquiry into the manipulation of things (technology) and persons acceptable.
   2. Inquiry into social institutions suspect: hence, conservatism.
   3. Suspicion of intellectual and artist because they do not fit into the work categories.
H. *War:* as an opportunity to move or advance rapidly to the ultimate ends.
IV. The Common Man Value Orientation.
   A. *Ultimate ends:* collective action, mutualism, dignity of worker.
   B. *Character structure and life organization:*
      1. The little man image—salt of the earth; the toiler, the worker-citizen.
      2. Virtues: hard-work, self-sacrifice, coöperation, willingness to share; modest ambitions.
   C. *Person:* inherent worth and dignity of person; rejection of tool conception.
   D. *Competition:* collective action, working together, rather than individualistic competition.
   E. *Coöperation:* "Mutually stimulates coöperation—a much more fundamentally sound principle than profit at the expense of co-workers." (AFL)
   F. *Wealth and property:* a comfortable level of living regarded as desirable; unlimited accumulation as unsocial.
   G. *Social change, intellectual inquiry, and creativity:*
      1. Change as favoring the worker acceptable, but with the worker as the dominant factor in community living.
      2. Inquiry and creativity to be directed to the creation and support of a worker culture.

H. *War:* devaluation of war and peacetime conscription or military service.
V. The Humanist Value Orientation.
    A. *Ultimate ends:* knowledge, creativity, experimentation, man as the measure of things, the intelligent ordering of life as based upon knowledge.
    B. *Character structure and life organization:*
       1. The scientist-citizen, the man of freed intelligence.
       2. Virtues: scientific habits of thought, suspended judgment, analyzing, criticizing, investigating or exploring, seeing both sides of a question, impartiality and objectivity, tolerance and sympathy.
       3. Mental balance, willingness to accept and evaluate change, sense of responsibility to self and others, sensitivity to others.
    C. *Person:* persons as ends, not tools: creative personalities.
    D. *Competition:* destructive of human nature and social living.
    E. *Coöperation:* living as an essentially coöperative venture, sharing and exploring with others.
    F. *Wealth and property:* as a means for personal and community development; no inherent worth in wealth and property; things needed as instruments for action and the aesthetic life.
    G. *Social change, intellectual inquiry, and creativity:*
       1. Experimentalism as a fundamental way; no limits to inquiry; no blocks to creativity.
       2. Living as an exploration for and in support of intellectual, social, and aesthetic values.
       3. Ordering cultural living in terms of the findings of the sciences.
    H. *War:* a denial of man's human nature and of cultural living; war as cultural suicide.

Selected Readings

GENERAL

Brady, Robert, *Business as a System of Power,* Columbia University Press, 1943.
Commager, Henry Steele (ed.) *America in Perspective, the United States Through Foreign Eyes,* Mentor Books, 1948.
Davis, K., Bredemeier, H., and Levy, M., *Modern American Society,* Rinehart and Company, 1949, chaps, 2, 26.
Howe, Irving, and Widick, B. J., *The U.A.W. and Walter Reuther,* Random House, 1949.

Kallen, Horace, *Individualism, An American Way of Life,* Horace Liveright, Inc., 1933.

Kluckhohn, Clyde, and Kluckhohn, Florence, "American Culture: Generalized Orientation and Class Patterns," in Lyman Bryson, et al. (eds.), *Conflicts of Power in Modern Culture,* Harper & Brothers, 1947, pp. 106–128.

Lindeman, Eduard C., *Wealth and Culture,* Harcourt, Brace and Company, 1936.

Myrdal, Gunnar, et al., *An American Dilemma,* Harper & Brothers, 1944, vol. I, chap. 1.

Northrop, F. S. C., *The Meeting of East and West,* The Macmillan Company, 1946, chap. 3.

Stouffer, Samuel S., *Communism, Conformity, and Civil Liberties,* Doubleday and Company, 1955. See especially the data on tolerance of nonconformists.

Temporary National Economic Committee, *Economic Power and Political Pressures,* Monograph No. 26, 76th Congress, 3rd Session, Government Printing Office, 1941.

THE ROMAN CATHOLIC POSITION

Five Great Encyclicals, The Paulist Press, 1939. This volume contains the "Christian Education of Youth."

Immortale Dei, The Christian Constitution of States, The Paulist Press, 1941.

Woywood, Stanislaus, *A Practical Commentary on the Code of Canon Law,* J. F. Wagner, 1925, 2 vols.

    These volumes contain the church's canon law and the student should look up the canons regarding education, especially Canon 1372, Canon 1374, Canon 1375, Canon 1381.

Zollman, Carl, *American Church Law,* West Publishing Company, 1933.

    The student might also profitably examine any Catholic catechism as well as Catholic weeklies. These are important because they are addressed to the rank and file of Catholics rather than to the intellectuals.

Blanshard, Paul, *American Freedom and Catholic Power,* The Beacon Press, 1949.

    A very critical analysis of the role of the Roman Catholic Church in the United States written in a controversial manner.

Dunne, George H., *Religion and American Democracy,* The American Press, 1949.

    A critical reply to Blanshard's book by a Catholic priest.

Committee on Religion and Education, *The Relation of Religion to Public Education,* American Council on Education Studies, Series I, No. 26, 1947.

Fleming, W. S., *God in Our Public Schools,* National Reform Association, 1942.

McKibben, Frank, *Christian Education Through the Church,* Abingdon-Cokesbury Press, 1937.

Moehlman, Conrad, *The Church as Educator,* Hinds, Hayden, and Eldredge, Inc., 1947.

Moehlman, Conrad, *School and Church,* Harper & Brothers, 1944.

Smith, Gerald B., *Principles of Christian Living,* University of Chicago Press, rev. ed., 1942.
  The chapter on Christian virtues is significant for the Christian social model.

Thayer, V. T., *Religion in Public Education,* The Viking Press, 1947.
  This book might be categorized as representing the "secularist" value orientation.

Weigle, Luther, *Public Education and Religion,* International Council of Religious Education, 1940.
  Students might also consult the various catechisms of Protestant church groups and the denominational literature. The Federal Council of Churches of Christ in America, now the National Council of Churches, attempts to further the core values of Protestantism, and its literature is of importance in defining the common Protestant point of view and the values regarded as false.

  For a very enlightening expression of the value orientations of the church groups as well as of many other interest groups with specific reference to education, the student should sample: *Public School Assistance Act of 1949, Hearings* before a special subcommittee of the Committee on Education and Labor, House of Representatives, 81st Congress, 1st Session, Government Printing Office, 1949.

CHAPTER 4

The Legal Order and Education

THE LEGAL ORDER AND ACTION

LAW IS important in almost any situation in which individuals or groups wish to act. Relevant laws and court decisions must be taken into consideration so that the act may be successfully completed. Therefore in the study of education one must look at the legal order as a frame for the educational picture and as an element in the structuring of an educational system.

The creation of a legal order, through legislation, administrative rulings, and court decisions, is one major way in which human beings attempt to order a society. Events, persons, and groups are evaluated by the awarding of special privileges and responsibilities, by the observance of prescribed ceremonial occasions, and by penalties and other forms of punishment. Detailed duties and the establishment of schools are prescribed. The status of pupil and of teacher is defined. The legal order makes group action directed toward a particular social model possible or impossible, difficult or easy. As long as a group does not violate what legislatures and courts consider public morality, public safety, and welfare, it has the opportunity to pursue its objectives and to train youth accordingly. Where these authorities think that a group or a person is committing such violation, they will call on law-enforcing agents to prevent action. Legislative and court actions against communists illustrate this point. Such a group is then compelled to carry out its activities secretly, if at all. Criminal syndicalist laws, found in many states, serve the same purpose. The history of trade unions in the courts likewise illustrates the principle that whether action is open and accepted or furtive and unaccepted is determined by the legal order.

THE SCHOOL AS RELATED TO THE STATE

The definition of education and its function in society are indicated in the legal order, based on more fundamental assumptions about the individual, the state, and their relationship. What is prohibited, permitted, or prescribed in the legal order depends on the nature of the state. It makes a big difference in the life opportunities of the members and groups of a country whether assumptions about the state are democratic, aristocratic, totalitarian, theocratic, or oligarchic. The legal order is constructed in terms of these assumptions.

From the previous study of value orientations in the United States one would not expect to find the legal order presenting a completely consistent picture. Conceptions of the state are somewhat unclear. In colonial New England participation in town meeting was conditioned by church membership so that nonchurch people in the community were excluded. In addition privileges were awarded according to church standing.[1] To this degree theocratic assumptions mingled with democratic assumptions. At a later period property or wealth qualifications, of which the poll tax is still an example, determined the inclusion or exclusion of members in the political community, and the qualifications for holding office. These qualifications have been dropped by most states, but where they persist, they continue oligarchic assumptions of the state.

[1] "There were first the church members who allotted to themselves the best land, cattle, and meadows, monopolized the entire trade with the Indians, and all fishing rights. The second group, comprising the rest of the church members, were allotted good land and cattle. The third group, definitely inferior, were called 'inhabitants.' They were potential church members and were allotted land under such restrictions as the leaders deemed necessary. The fourth group were considered undesirable as church members or citizens. They received no land and their activities, including work, were directed and controlled by the leaders." Roland Usher, *Pilgrims and Their History,* The Macmillan Company, 1918, pp. 223–225, as quoted in Ernest Burgess and Harvey J. Locke, *The Family,* American Book Company, 1947, pp. 65–67.

Many state constitutions echo in their preamble the ideas of the Declaration of Independence and the Preamble of the Federal Constitution. They usually emphasize the natural rights of man to life, liberty, the pursuit of happiness, and safety in property. These ideas are also summed up in Bill of Rights sections and enacted into statutory law. Such assumptions are the democratic, liberal ideas that stemmed from the Enlightenment. The intent of these constitutions and laws apparently was to maximize action of the individual. Yet other conceptions minimize individual actions, conceptions expressed in the doctrine of absolute sovereignty that is implicit in much legal thought and government practice. The ideas about the divine right of kings have been transferred to the state. Without the religious support given the king by the belief that he was God's representative on earth, the modern "sovereign state" is an absolute authority, though allegedly democratized in the idea of "popular sovereignty." The effect of this concept is seen, for example, in the limitations placed upon suits against the state. No suit can be instituted without the consent of the state. There can be no strikes against the government. At this point the individual is reduced to a condition of helplessness.

While parents have the right to educate their children in any way they see fit, they have to comply with the state's requirements as to the content of that education. They must show that they are providing education equal to that offered in state institutions. Even private schools must comply. Education is a function of government. What the state does will vary according to the assumptions underlying it and its relation to other groups. Thus, in a state where there is a close relation with the church, as in Italy or Spain, the state may delegate to the church all major educational functions. It may, on the other hand, centralize educational functions into one system under its control, as in France.

In the United States, state constitutions contain provisions for a uniform system of public education. In the Ohio constitution, for example, on the premise that knowledge is essential to good government, the general assembly is to "encourage schools and the means of instruction." The legislature has plenary power with regard to education. This means, in general, the following: "The legislature may determine the type of schools to be established throughout the state, the means of their support, the organs of their administration, the content of their curricula, and the qualifications of their teachers. Moreover, all these matters may be determined with or without regard to the wishes of the localities, for in education the state is the unit, and there are no local rights except such as are safeguarded by the Constitution," [2] and, we might add, as safeguarded by the courts. For example, a law of Oregon compelling all children to go to public schools was declared unconstitutional, thus insuring the existence of parochial and other private schools. On occasion certain statutes dealing with curriculum have been declared invalid by the courts. The actions of individuals or local groups are strictly limited by the legal agencies of the state. The important point is the almost absolute position of the state in matters of education, and this strikes a rather undemocratic note.[3]

The American public school is one of possible types that might have developed. It so happens that state legislatures have decided that school districts would be formed, that these may establish schools, that there should be local boards of education in charge of the schools, that school officials may be elected, and so forth. Such a system of delegated power with local control and direction fits in with our notions of democracy and is thus supported by democratic values and hallowed by tradition. The parent group, however, is the state, and the public schools make up one of its delegated or subsidiary agencies.

LIFE CHANCES, LEGAL ORDER, AND SCHOOL

In countries, such as England, France, Italy, and Germany, where status groups have been an integral part of the society, the public-school system of the country became organized in terms of status considerations. These status considerations became embodied in law, as seen very explicitly in the following order issued in 1854 by the King of Prussia.

[2] Newton Edwards, *The Courts and the Public School,* University of Chicago Press, 1933, p. 5.
[3] A state is made up of constitutions, statutes, court decisions, administrative decisions, and some explicit or implicit value orientation. These are the decisive aspects.

The primary schools have only to work to the end that the common people may grasp and appreciate the Christian Faith . . . may be intelligent in regard to all matters within the narrow sphere to which God has called them . . . may learn to read and write, reckon, and sing, . . . may love their rulers and their fatherland, be contented with their social status and live peacefully and happy in their lot. . . . I do not think the principles enunciated will raise the common people out of the sphere designated for them by God and Society.[4]

The result was a dual school system, one part of it designed to keep people in the lower classes in their low status and the other to provide for an elite. The German school system evolved into a *Volkschule* for commoners, which was free and compulsory from the sixth to the thirteenth year, a *Mittelschule*, a tuition school from the sixth to the fourteenth year, and trade, vocational, and compulsory continuation schools for the ages 14–16. For the elite there was a *Vorschule* for those 6–8 years old, a *Gymnasium* (classical education), an *Oberrealschule* (scientific education), and a *Realgymnasium* (a compromise institution), all of which were tuition schools with few available scholarships, from the ninth to the seventeenth year. Graduation from this second type of school granted privilege to attend the university and higher technical schools, and this also was a step to careers in the army or navy as officers, or in the state as civil officials. Schools in the other countries mentioned developed in similar fashion. Since World War I and especially since World War II many efforts have been made in these countries to modify the system to a more open and freer one.

What this dual form of school system means can be seen in English experience.[5] A study of the personnel of the British Foreign Office and Diplomatic Service between 1851 and 1929 shows that 60 percent were drawn from the eleven most exclusive public schools, and of the remaining 40 percent over half attended lesser public schools, received a military or naval training, or were educated privately or abroad. A study of key positions in certain occupations for the year

[4] Quoted in Edgar Knight, *Twenty Centuries of Education*, Ginn and Co., p. 527.
[5] R. T. Nightingale, "The Personnel of the British Foreign Office and Diplomatic Service, 1851–1929," *The Realist*, 1929, pp. 333–334, 341, 343. M. Ginsberg, "Interchange between Social Classes," *Economic Journal*, December, 1929, p. 563.

1926 shows that a very large percentage of the men had attended the exclusive public schools: 71 out of 80 bishops and deans; 139 out of 181 members of the judiciary; 152 out of the 210 high officials in the public department; 63 out of 88 members of the India Service and Governers of Dominions; and 99 out of 132 directors of banks and railroads.

Since a tradition of entrenched aristocratic groups was lacking, and since the initial orientation came from the value order expressed in the Enlightenment, the public-school system of the United States has not been based on status group principles. The idea of public education was accepted only after a long struggle, but the system, as it exists in America today, expresses the democratic assumptions that are embodied in the state and the legal order. Even though practice differs widely from principle in some regions, there is still the assumption on the value level that educational opportunities and facilities should be equal for all citizens. This idea has been reaffirmed in the past ten years by some far-reaching Supreme Court decisions, notably Sweatt *v.* Painter, McLaurin *v.* Oklahoma State Regents, and especially Brown et al. *v.* Board of Education of Topeka et al.

SCHOOL PERSONNEL AS LEGALLY PRESCRIBED

A school, whatever its place in an educational system, is a relatively closed system. The degree of closure is indicated by tests of admission, which determine who may or may not be a member of the association, and in what way they may participate. Tests of admission and the assignment of the personnel are closely linked. Entrance to the positions of teacher and learner are prescribed by law.

THE TEACHER: A FREE CONTRACTING AGENT WITH PROFESSIONAL STATUS

A teacher is the occupant of a legal status and one whose life chances are set by his being in an educational system supported by public or private funds. The teacher position is determined by statute, as are other professions such as law, nursing, medicine, and architecture. A person has to meet certain tests of admission to the status of teacher. He qualifies when he is certified, receiving a license from the certifying agency, usually the state board of education. Certification means that the teacher has met the minimum requirements set by the statutes for a particular level of teaching. Certification is of itself taken as evidence of technical competence.

The requirements for the teaching certificate will vary from state to state. In general, two years of college or university training has been sufficient to qualify for elementary-school teaching and four years of college training to qualify for secondary-school teaching. In some states four years of training are required for elementary-school and five for high-school teaching. There may be other qualifications, such as citizenship, age, moral character, physical condition, or race, which will limit access to the teacher status. Local boards may add still other requirements. In general, tests of admission go far beyond requirements of technical efficiency.

Local boards of education have the power to employ and dismiss teachers. Employment is a contractual relation between school board and teacher, which must be concluded when the board is meeting as a legal body, if it is to be valid. In an abstract sense a teacher has complete freedom to arrange a contract with any school board, just as a worker was supposed to be free to contract and bargain with any employer. This freedom in both cases is fictitious, and for the teacher it is hedged in not only by the variety of legal rules but also by local expectations and school policies. Furthermore, haggling with a school board over salary is looked upon as unprofessional. As long as the teacher was unorganized, he was at a disadvantage in improving his fortune as compared with the organized workers. Nowadays teacher organizations act as pressure groups to improve the teacher's status by changing the statutes determining it. Thus the teacher must be politically active, though such activity is frequently viewed with disfavor in many communities.

Content of Teacher Status. The position of a teacher is that of public employee, not of a school official. The teacher does not represent the state in an official capacity. Consequently, the rights, duties, and immunities that apply to public officials do not apply to teachers. Teachers do not exercise any sovereign power or authority of a governmental nature. Their rights, privileges, and duties vary from state to state. Minimum rights and duties are set by law, though local boards may add other specifications. The legal definition of teacher status will include such items as tenure, salary, and retirement, leave of absence for illness, for professional study, or for other purposes, compensation for injury in line of duty, freedom from insult or abuse, exemption from jury service, etc. Other rights, duties, and powers are given in the following areas: instructional, administrative routine (e.g., keeping records), professional growth (e.g., attending institutes organized by a state board of education), maintenance of order, disciplining students, legal liability.

In regard to the control of the pupil, the teacher is *in loco parentis*, i.e., the teacher stands in place of the pupil's parents and may correct and discipline him accordingly. The teacher has the right to enforce obedience to any reasonable and lawful commands. In the performance of instructional duties and *in loco parentis*, a teacher is subject to legal liability.

Legal liability is a complex topic. It is an occasion for suit under liability for tort. The most relevant legal points for teachers are: assault and battery, negligence, and contributory negligence. The last two involve a failure on the part of the teacher in the performance of his duties which results in some injury to a child. The parent may sue for damages on the ground of negligence. Likewise, parents may institute suit for assault and battery when they feel that their child has been too severely punished. Legal liability affects the kind of norms that develop in a school. Many school norms are designed not only for the safety of children but for the legal safety of teachers, school bus drivers, and other personnel.

Loss of Status. Grounds for dismissal of teachers vary from state to state. In some states the legal causes are specified, though the phrases in the law are very broad. Where legal reasons are specified, no teacher may be dismissed except for the stated reasons.

In the absence of statutes providing for the dismissal of teachers, the school employing agency has the implied power to dismiss for good and sufficient cause. It is presumed in law, on the basis of court decisions, that a board will act in good faith and not from mere passion, prejudice, or caprice. It must be kept in mind that, while there are special legal causes for the dismissal of a teacher, the entire gamut of criminal law applies to him, such as offenses against humanity and morality, offenses against public property, offense against the person, and other sections of the code. Violations here could be interpreted under the general phrase "unprofessional conduct."

Loss of status can take place on two levels. The teacher may be dismissed by the local board or county superintendent, suffering only a temporary loss of status. Final expulsion from the legal status takes place only if the teaching certificate is revoked. Revocation of the certificate may be carried out by the state board of education or state superintendent of education, depending on state regulations. A summary of legal causes for revocation of a license is given in Table 9. The medical profession is the most closely regulated, the teaching profession apparently the least. Teachers are subject to the rules and regulations of the local board of education. Incompetence and immorality are the legal causes stressed by the majority of the states. The most frequently reported causes of trials for revocation of teaching certificates have been immorality, intemperance, and unprofessional conduct.

The right to a hearing in case of a revocation of a license is assured to the five professions mentioned in the table. Provisions for appeals are also included in the law. The teacher is not always so privileged. Fifteen states do not have provisions as to notice, hearing, and appeal. In twenty-one states the teacher has such a right. Only eleven states have the right to appeal the case to a higher school official or court. Only one state has provision for possible reinstatement.

THE CHILD AS A LEGAL ENTITY

What is a child? A child, according to the statute in one state, "shall mean any person under sixteen years of age and any person between the ages of 16 and 18 who has been transferred from the jurisdiction of a town, city, police, or borough court to the jurisdiction of the juvenile court." The legal definition may vary somewhat in other states, but the gist is in terms of age, the individual leaving

Legal Cause	Profession					
	CPA	Architect	Lawyer	MD	RN	Teacher
Good, Reasonable sufficient cause	30	2	1	0	9	10
Unprofessional conduct	22	12	25	28	12	7
Misdeameanor involving Moral turpitude	6	1	25	11	2	0
Conviction of felony	12	17	13	23	8	0
Fraud in obtaining license	8	26	4	32	17	0
Incompetency	9	33	1	6	24	26
Immorality	0	0	1	14	13	35
Fraud, deceit, dishonesty	14	27	16	15	23	3
Negligence	7	29	0	0	5	19
Violation of state regulations for prof.	3	6	4	11	7	2
Intemperance	0	6	2	36	22	13
Addiction to drugs	0	6	0	37	10	0
Insanity	3	0	1	6	0	0

CPA—certified public accountant; MD—physician; RN—registered nurse.

SOURCE: Summarized and reprinted from *Statutory Status of Six Professions*, Research Division, National Education Association, September, 1938, Table I, pp. 222–223.

the status usually between 16 and 18 years. As a rule the codes of the various states also make such other distinctions as: dependent child, uncared-for child, neglected child, defective child, and delinquent child. All these definitions apply to situations in which the state assumes the right to intervene for the sake of the child and for its own sake. In these definitions we find the theory of the state as the ultimate parent. This means that a parent's right to a child is limited, for in case of neglect the state may intervene and assume guardianship over the child.

We find in these statutes definitions of the child as he ought to be, and these rules of oughtness refer directly to the growth of the child. The laws will necessarily become part of the normative order of a school, and teachers are responsible for carrying them out. These ideas are most obvious in the definition of the "delinquent" child, who, according to one state, is

. . . one who violates any law of the state or local ordinance, is habitually truant, incorrigible, or knowingly or wilfully associates with vicious criminal or immoral persons or uses vile, indecent, or profane language or is guilty of indecent or immoral conduct or is growing up in idleness, ignorance, or vice, or absents himself from home without just cause or consent of his parents or wanders about at night-time without any lawful purpose or occupation, or knowingly at wilfully engages in any practice, employment or occupation prejudicial to his normal development physically, mentally, or morally.[6]

On reading this statute it appears that in some sections there is no difference between what is expected of child and of adult; in other sections, a child is forbidden conduct which is legal to an adult. The effort of this law, fumbling as it may be, is to define the conditions which make for a healthy growth of the child. It is the teacher's duty to see that in the school the child does not violate this law, and, if he does, that he is corrected.

In some states the statutes definitely instruct the teacher what he is to do with regard to the child. In Virginia, in both white and non-white schools, teachers "shall require of pupils cleanliness of person, punctuality, diligence, and good behavior during their attendance at school and on their way thither and back to their homes." In Idaho the law states that the teacher shall "keep himself or herself without reproach and endeavor to impress upon the minds of the pupils the principles of truth, justice, morality, patriotism, and refinement, and to avoid idleness, falsehood, profanity, vulgarity and intemperance; give attention during every school term to the cultivation of manners." In Florida the law states that the teacher is to

[6] *General Statutes of Connecticut*, Revision of 1949, Bond Press, Inc., 1949, vol. I, sec. 2802, pp. 1084–1085; cf. vol. III, sec. 85799, p. 3105, for obligations of parents.

"require the pupils to observe personal cleanliness, neatness, order, promptness, and gentility of manner, avoid vulgarity and profanity and cultivate in them habits of industry, and economy, a regard for the rights and feelings of others, and their own responsibilities and duties as citizens."

Tests of Admission to the School. To make sure that the child receives training the state compels attendance. Attendance laws, coupled with those prohibiting and limiting the employment of children, insure a supply of pupils as well as indicate the years of attendance required. Parents are obliged either to send their children to public schools or to show that the child is receiving equivalent instruction during school hours elsewhere. Such statutes, of course, are not absolute, and extenuating circumstances are recognized, as when it appears "that the child is destitute of clothing suitable for attending school, and the parent or person having control of such a child is unable to provide clothing, or its mental or physical condition is such as to render its instruction inexpedient or impracticable." [7]

Education is not a right of a child; it is a privilege conferred upon it by the state. Definite limitations are set up with regard to age and general mental and physical condition. The terms of the law are rather vague, though in some states definite procedure is provided to determine whether or not a child should be in school or receive special instruction elsewhere. If the child is incapable of fulfilling its obligations in terms of proper conduct or requisite abilities the privilege of education can be modified or taken away. Local boards have the power to do this by suspending or expelling a child for a definite period of time.

There is wide flexibility in the interpretation of the tests of admission. Teachers have had pupils who should have been institutionalized or should have received special care outside of the school. There may be a tendency to keep less fit children in school because of the funds received from state aid. The child, then, represents a lump sum of subsidy which a local board may be unwilling to forgo. This is an expression of the market orientation. Superintendents and teachers in such a case have no alternative, since they must accept all pupils that are of the proper school age.

[7] *Ibid.,* vol. I, sec. 1446, p. 539.

Race and color may be involved in tests of admission. In some states schools are open to all children over 6 without discrimination on this basis. In such cases equality, as a democratic value, is being supported. In other states there is distinction in terms of race and color, with the provision that facilities should be equal. This point of view represents an older conception of the state with emphasis on status groups. The phrase "equal facilities" is a bow to equalitarian theory, but the gap between ideal and practice is very great. Color as a test of admission, however, has been rejected by the United States Supreme Court.

FUNCTIONAL ORDER OF THE SCHOOL
AS DEFINED BY LAW

The legal order specifies or strongly suggests the content that is to be taught and other tasks that are to be performed in the school. It defines the length of the school year, the length of the school day, provisions for health and sanitation, dental hygiene, vaccination, use and construction of school buildings, safety regulations, cafeterias, pupil transportation. The following statute is fairly typical:

. . . reading, spelling, writing, English grammar; geography; arithmetic; United States, state and local history; the duties of citizenship which shall include a study of the town, state, and federal governments; hygiene, including the effects of alcohol and narcotics on health and character; physical and health education, to be employed in preventing and correcting bodily deficiency; instruction in the humane treatment and protection of animals and birds and their economic importance, such instruction when practicable to be correlated with work in reading, language and nature study, and such other subjects as may be prescribed by the board of education. Courses in health instruction and physical education shall be prepared by the secretary of the state board of education and when approved by the state board of education shall constitute the prescribed courses.[8]

How much of this program goes into effect depends upon local circumstances. Physical education, for example, is not available in many elementary schools, particularly in small rural schools, and poor facilities make a complete program difficult in many high schools.

[8] *Ibid.*, vol. I, sec. 1349, p. 512.

Most states provide for free textbooks, and some furnish supplies free.

Such laws as the above demonstrate the dependent position of the school as an agency of the state. In some states the curriculum is subject to the approval of the superintendent of public instruction, and if this principle were put into practice, it would mean an effective centralization of educational policy and program.

NORMATIVE ORDER AS DEFINED IN LAW

Norms (rules regulating conduct) are implied by the legal definition of a child, particularly that of a "delinquent child." They are suggested by a school board's power to suspend or expel a child for incorrigibly bad conduct. They are found in laws such as those prohibiting children from using tobacco. Laws set up rules of proper conduct, and this must be followed in the school. In the absence of specific statutes the school board has the authority to establish rules and regulations governing the conduct of teachers and pupils, and when school authorities do not state such rules, the teacher has the power to do so, for "the good order and discipline of the school," as the court puts it.[9] The rules and regulations may extend to the control of pupil conduct off school grounds and after school hours and they will tend to be upheld by the courts if it can be shown that such action is necessary to maintain the order, discipline, and welfare of the school.[10]

CORPORAL PUNISHMENT AND DISCIPLINE

While teachers are required to have good order in the school, the law is very vague as to means of attaining it. The two major devices of suspension and corporal punishment are restricted and limited in various ways. In one state corporal punishment is forbidden. It is permitted by law in a few states, and in others its use is implied. An example is the following court decision based on several previous court decisions in other jurisdictions:

[9] *Connecticut Records*, vol. 102, p. 130.
[10] *Ibid.*, p. 103.

The reasonableness of the punishment administered by a school teacher to a pupil is purely a matter of fact. A school teacher has the right to require obedience to reasonable rules and proper submission to this authority, and to inflict punishment for disobedience. . . . In inflicting corporal punishment the teacher must be governed, as to the mode and severity of it, by the nature of the offense, and by the age, size, and physical condition of the pupil. Where a boy has been habitually refractory and disobedient, the teacher, in punishing him for a particular offense, may take into consideration his habitual disobedience. And it is not necessary that he should inform the pupil at the time that he is punishing him for his past as well as his present misconduct.[11]

If injury has been inflicted in administering corporal punishment, a teacher or other administrator may be subject to a suit for damages by the parents, or to trial by the state on charges of assault and battery. He might also be dismissed for violating school laws or for unprofessional conduct.

The relation of teacher and pupil, in the decision cited, is conceived of as a power relation. Control can be imposed by the teacher by the inflicting of corporal punishment if necessary. Such legal statements supposedly insure the authority of the teacher and order within the school. This emphasis on the use of violence does not fit in with the child-centered, developmental point of view that is expressed in the value orientation of educators. Nevertheless, if pupils are fighting, a teacher must intervene directly, for the safety of the children is involved.

CEREMONIAL OCCASIONS AND THE LAW

Among the varied aspects of the normative order specified by statute are ceremonial occasions. We shall not consider at this time all the ceremonial occasions that are observed by schools, for some, and from the child's point of view the more important, are not specified in the statutes. Many of the statutes represent merely legislative approval of national occasions and traditions. Some of the more commonly observed ones are: New Year's Day, Lincoln's Birthday, Washington's Birthday, Memorial Day, Independence Day,

[11] *Ibid.,* vol. 53, p. 481.

Labor Day, Veterans' Day, Christmas. Thanksgiving and Good Friday are observed by proclamation.

States will vary again as to special occasions. Louisiana has Louisiana Purchase Day, Confederate Memorial Day, Lee Day. Connecticut has *Maine* Memorial Day, Indian Day, and Pan-American Day. Most states have a fire-prevention day or week and an arbor-bird day. In general, most of the occasions are patriotic, centering upon the state, which through these events recognizes and sustains its heritage. Two occasions, and there will be some variation here too, are religious events, and the significance of these is recognized in the legal order. To observe many of these occasions is mandatory upon the schools.

Associated with ceremonial occasions is the national symbol of the flag. There are all sorts of statutes regulating the use and misuse of the flag. Flag Day supposedly is devoted to instructions in displaying and respecting the flag. For some parents and groups, with a nativist orientation, this flag etiquette is almost an end in itself; for others, such as Jehovah's Witnesses, it is idolatry. However, for participants the result is often a daily routine. This routinization of the etiquette may make it less significant. Where there are divergent evaluations of it, the flag ceremony makes for disunity, so that the symbol does not fulfill its function. In most communities the ceremony is accepted and supported, and the symbol fulfills its integrating function.

SUMMARY

The legal order is composed of the constitutions, statutes, court decisions, and administrative rulings. It represents an effort at the intelligent ordering of the relations between persons, groups, and objects in a society. In order to act, both persons and groups must take into consideration the limitations or advantages set forth in the legal order. Their actions may be penalized or facilitated.

The laws formulated in the legal order are based upon certain assumptions about the nature of the state and society. In general, these conceptions involve the idea of a society based upon the principle of status groups or upon the principle of equality. In the former case, the state orders the society in terms of inequality and privilege; in the latter, it is ordered in terms of equal opportunity. The conception of the state in our country involves both principles, so that there is fundamental inconsistency. The problem is compounded by the ideas of absolute sovereignty and government by consent, mutually exclusive principles.

Since education is regarded as a function of sovereignty, the school is an agency of the state. While our educational system is locally controlled, this organization is brought about only through the consent of the state authorizing such "home rule" of schools. Practically, the state exerts a tremendous amount of influence by setting forth minimum conditions for schools and education and by assisting local units with financial aid. Teacher and pupil statuses may be looked upon as positions in the legal order. Thus, law spells out how persons occupying these statuses are to act, and what rights, privileges, and duties they have. The educational program designed by and for the state is to inculcate proper loyalties toward the state and the national culture, an orientation that does not fit completely with the religious and the humanistic. How a school carries out a program specifically is dependent upon local conditions and the value orientation of that school.

In the legal order the stress tends to be upon the welfare of the school and its order and discipline. For this reason there are definite suggestions concerning the normative order and methods of punishment.

How the schools are to function is a matter of law and the conceptions underlying the state. Until the inconsistencies that are found in our legal order are overcome, the schools will be subject to lack of integration, i.e., the educational structure will express these inconsistencies.

Students can examine the code of their state with special reference to the sections on education; the criminal code, particularly offenses against minors, assault and battery; child welfare, including ideas on delinquency, duties of parents to children, legal liability. Students might also examine in detail relevant court cases, many of which are cited in the code, to analyze judicial reasoning. If the law on education in foreign countries is available, it would be enlightening to compare it with ours. Students might also try to discover the assumptions of the state found in these laws. The student should make his analysis in terms of teacher status, pupil status, the functional and normative organization of the school.

Selected Readings

Butts, Robert Nelson, *A Cultural History of Education*, McGraw-Hill Book Company, 1947.

Cubberley, Ellwood P., *Public Education in the United States*, Houghton Mifflin Company, 1919.

Education Under Enemy Occupation in Belgium, China, Czechoslovakia, France, Greece, Luxembourg, Netherlands, Norway, Poland, U.S. Office of Education, Bulletin No. 3, Government Printing Office, 1945.

Edwards, Newton, *The Courts and the Public School*, University of Chicago Press, 1933.

Johnson, Alvin, *The Legal Status of Church-State Relationships in the United States*, University of Minnesota Press, 1934.

Legal Status of the Public School Pupil, Research Division of the National Education Association, February, 1948.

Legal Status of the Public School Teacher, Research Division of the National Education Association, April, 1947.

Raup, Bruce, *Education and Organized Interests in America*, G. P. Putnam's Sons, 1936.

Reisner, Edward, *Nationalism and Education Since 1789*, The Macmillan Company, 1923.

State and Sectarian Education, Research Division of the National Education Association, February, 1946.

Teacher Liability for Pupil Injuries, Research Division of the National Education Association, April, 1940.

CHAPTER 5

The Community Context
of the School

MAN IS a community dweller. The isolated man, the isolated family, if not a fiction, would be a social abnormality. Man and family, living their history, do so with others bounded in a locality they call their community. Neighborhood, hamlet, village, town, city, metropolis— these are the significant locality groups. Today 64 percent of the United States population live in towns and cities of 2500 and over. Another 4.3 percent live in communities of 1000–2500. The remainder of the population are in hamlets, villages, or open-country communities. The purpose of this chapter is to study the community not as the familiar and accepted background of our daily lives but critically and analytically. What effect do our ways of living together have upon us? What effect do they have on health, family life, educational possibilities? Our special interest in this matter of education will lead us to investigate all the important ways in which communities influence schools: the problems of population growth and crowded schools, the differences in children's backgrounds, the bearing that the needs of a community may have on the curriculum, the school plant. A teacher can fully understand her children only by knowing the community. He should have a good working knowledge of all the significant aspects of the community in order to understand the school-community relationship.

We will discuss communities in a general way, though we will illustrate our points with reference to four communities of very different size. At the end of the chapter there is a list of specific community studies. These will give further illustration of the ways in which social scientists have attempted overall analytical surveys of various towns and cities.

THE MEANING OF COMMUNITY

The community, like the school, is an objective order of functions, things, and persons; it is a social and cultural fact, a design for living. In some cases, the community order does not advance very far beyond the bare necessities of living and the rudiments of community institutions. On the other hand, some communities are such sprawling conglomerations of people and functions that despite wealth and facilities there seems to be no ordered community design. In either situation it is difficult for the school to operate effectively. When the order of life is rudimentary, the school itself is organized in terms of poverty and meagerness of means and experience. In the metropolitan community with its kaleidoscopic changes in groups and functions the schools feel the stress and strain of the inevitable tensions and disequilibria that exist.

Most of the people in the United States live in communities large enough to be called cities. The city is our dominant community form. The following is Lewis Mumford's lucid and comprehensive description of what the city means:

The city is a related collection of primary and purposive associations: the first, like family and neighborhoods, are common to all communities, while the second are especially characteristic of city life. These varied groups support themselves through economic organizations that are likewise of a more or less corporate, or at least publicly regulated, character; and they are all housed in permanent structures, within a relatively limited area. The essential physical means of a city's existence are the fixed site, the durable shelter, the permanent facilities for assembly, interchange, and storage; the essential social means are the social division of labor, which serves not merely the economic life, but the cultural processes. The city in its completest sense, then, is a geographical plexus, an economic organization, an institutional process, a theatre of social action, and an esthetic symbol of collective unity. . . . Without the social drama that comes into existence through the focusing intensification of group activity there is not a single function performed in the city that could not be performed—and has not in fact been performed—in the open country. . . . One may describe the city, in its social aspect, as a special framework directed toward the creation of differentiated opportunities for a common life and a significant collective drama.[1]

Since urban life is the distinctive feature of our living, the analysis focuses on this pattern. Even the open-country community that centers in a grange, a church, or a small school is pulled into the orbit of the small town which is its trade, service, and secondary-school center. The suburban community is also meshed in the life of its metropolitan center. This analysis will have to deal with the arrangement in space and time of these economic and cultural functions and groups, and with the sort of common life and collective drama that has developed. The community is built up through the activities of its members, a design that may express elements of good, aesthetic living, or one in which the manner of living is largely malignant and degrading. Since the school is a part of this total scheme, it will be affected by the achievement of order or the degree of disorder in a community.

VALUE ORIENTATION AND COMMUNITY DESIGN

The design of life which the community presents and the physical form it takes reflects the dominant value orientation of its citizens. Whereas most European cities have long histories, all American cities are relatively new. Original forms of settlement varied. In New England the church spire was the physical symbol of the theocratic community with privileges reserved for the higher-standing members and disadvantages falling upon the lesser members and non-believers. Life centered around the village green, an aspect of community life that became the Middle West's courthouse square when New Englanders migrated after mining out the virgin farm lands. In the South the attempt to reproduce Cavalier England developed the communities of plantation society. In the Southwest

---

[1] Lewis Mumford, *Culture of Cities*, Harcourt, Brace and Company, 1938, pp. 480–481.

and Far West Spaniards organized their original settlements around the mission, presidio, and alameda, a pattern typical of South American communities.

There are still traces of these earlier forms in American communities, but the dominant mood of settlement in the nineteenth century, when our big cities developed rapidly, was one of individualism, with the emphasis on the market value orientation. The community design expressed the drive toward power, success, and wealth, tempered with whatever effect the religious and humanistic orientations asserted.

Magic Middletown, Thread City, Reno, "greatest little city in the world"—every community became a prospective metropolis, had aspirations to be bigger, better, boosting its name, wares, and greatness throughout the country. Each struggled to attract transportation facilities and industry, and all sorts of concessions and subsidies were offered. In this primarily unplanned growth our communities developed a pattern based on the assumption that self-interest was identical with the interest of the community as a whole. Municipal governments made weak attempts to organize this rapid growth intelligently, but comprehensive city design plans have appeared only during recent years. The basic trend that developed as a result of the vigorous strivings of many individuals to attain wealth and power will be found to be similar in communities of various sizes: Chicago, with a population of over 3,000,000; Seattle, with around 400,000; Mill City with 12,000; and Elmtown with 6000.

PEOPLE AND LIVING SPACE

In the depths of many a city the only view of nature involves sky, clouds, and sun. All the rest is man-made, cultural. Even the air has become a cultural object, filled with dirt, soot, and obnoxious gases coming from homes, factories, office buildings, and motor vehicles. Sound, except for an occasional overpowering thunderstorm, is mostly man-made. Through this cultural atmosphere, this cultural landscape, myriads of persons jostle, scurrying along the streets, in and out of buildings, bent on their own ends. Even the small town takes on this metropolitan character on week ends. People are everywhere, and the struggle for space to park, space to move, to act, to live, becomes paramount.

A community has boundaries, and therefore limited space. The growth of population creates a demand for the use of this space. To what end shall it be put? What facilities shall be constructed, and for whom? These are the crucial questions, and they become more urgent as cities grow.

The rise of many American communities can be characterized as meteoric, tremendous spurts of growth followed by a leveling off. As Figure 3 shows, this picture is true of three of the cities. Elmtown varies from this pattern of rapid growth. It had a fairly stable period between 1900 and 1920 with a slow increase during the following decades. Mill City became stabilized around 1910 and remained on that level. The other two cities slowed up around 1920. All of them show a slight spurt during 1940–50. The child population has followed somewhat the general growth pattern, except for the thirties, when there was a marked drop in the birth rate.

The rapid growth of cities has been due to two main factors—immigration, most of which came from Europe and the Near East and today comes from Canada and Mexico, and internal migration, primarily from the South since 1910. Migration of Negroes and whites was tremendously stimulated by World War II and the demands of industry and port cities in North, East, and West. The birth rate in most cities is too low to maintain a constant population; consequently, their growth involves precisely this immigration and internal migration.

The mere flood of population in these periods of rapid growth would have made planning for the community as a whole difficult. In the absence of overall plans, use was organized primarily by the possibilties of sale and rental of ground, as one would expect with the dominance of the market orientation. The layout of most American cities is in a gridiron street plan, and this holds true even where there are some radial arterial streets. The gridiron plan maximizes street frontage and the number of building lots that can be carved out of the land. The original plot for Manhattan Island, for example, was completely subdivided without any special regard as to the functional areas into which a city can be organized. Even the Cen-

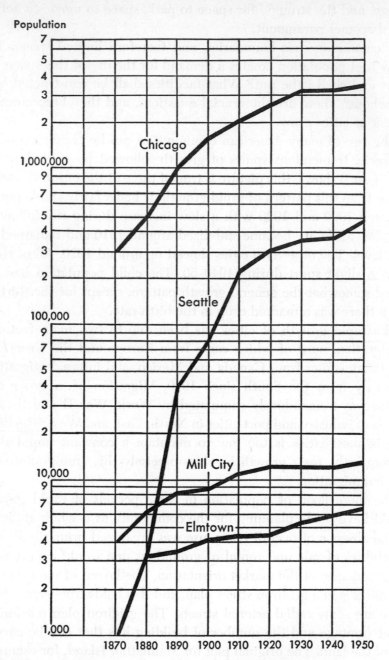

FIGURE 3. Population Growth of Chicago, Seattle, Mill City, and Elmtown, 1870–1950. (From U.S. Censuses, *Population Characteristics*, 1870–1950.)

tral Park area was subdivided, but because the land was too rocky and uneven it could not be sold as real estate. If the area had been usable, there is little doubt that there would be no Central Park today.

The gridiron plan was applied to land to maximize returns and sales. It was the plan which lent itself best to the exploitation of the housing and living needs of a growing population. Whoever had the price would get his bit of living space. In general, it meant that the most accessible and desirable locations were converted to business and industrial usages. Many areas along water fronts which could have been reserved for community use, for park and play space, were lost. In fact, cities have had to buy back land which was sold to private interests in order to make the community design more intelligent and to improve community living. Communal ends in city growth apparently were secondary to the commercial, so that the evolving pattern was a hodgepodge of industry, business, residences, schools, and churches. The significance of the gridiron plan is shown in Table 10.

TABLE 10.   Percent of Developed Urban Land Area in Use for Specified Purposes in Twenty-Two Cities by City Size

City Size	Use					
	Resi- dential	Indus- trial	Com- mercial	Streets, Alleys	Parks, Etc.	Public Insti- tutions
Over 500,000	34.5	14.2	5.1	31.1	7.9	7.2
250,000–500,000	39.2	10.3	3.4	27.2	8.2	11.7
100,000–250,000	39.1	10.8	2.7	30.3	8.8	8.3
50,000–100,000	42.7	9.8	2.8	30.6	5.4	8.7

SOURCE: National Housing Agency, November, 1944.

One-third of the developed area need not be used on streets and alleys. This has meant a wastage of municipal funds and of land that could have gone into communal purposes. It has meant increased costs in the construction of water mains and of sewage lines, in the collection of refuse, and in the mere upkeep of these miles of streets and alleys. It has also meant higher costs in the installation of private utilities—gas, electricity, and telephones. It is not surprising that the streets and alleys became playgrounds, for they were the main open space for children in the overbuilt cities.

Population growth, gridiron subdivision, and market orientation combine to create the lack of intelligent order, in terms of human needs, in our community design. Since city governments are dependent upon the state legislatures for their powers, they frequently were unable to act in terms of the whole. The belated zoning power granted to city government is an example. In addition, the municipal authorities were so besieged by private interest groups that even much of zoning was of little consequence. A government of weak power is in line with the market orientation. Communal provision of services and facilities was to be kept at a minimum: first, in the interest of some private groups that wanted to exploit the opportunity themselves; second, to keep down the tax rate. As a result, community facilities, including schools, were likely to deteriorate. In Elmtown the main schools were so obsolete that the state university and the North Central Association finally refused to accredit the school. In Mill City the annual reports for twenty years made constant reference to equipment that was wearing out, to facilities that were obsolete, to the need for new equipment. The 1941 Annual Report of the Board of Education expressed the hope that a continuing decline of the birth rate would solve the problem of overcrowding in the schools.

Since schools are a phase of the community's history, they are subjected to the population factor and the unintegrated order characteristic of our cities. The growth of population not only created a demand for new facilities but placed a strain through overuse on existing services and equipment. A growing youth population raises problems of adding, locating, remodeling, or tearing down school buildings, problems that have been persistent and that have become more acute since 1940. The larger the community, the more complex these problems have become, for the school is one detail in the overall pattern. To plan adequately for the school implies adequacy of plan for the community as a whole—including the location of factory districts, wholesale and retail areas, transportation lines and areas, parks, playgrounds, the street plan, etc. To what extent are the schools to be designed for a youth population, for all age groups, for a stabilizing population? What can be done about schools submerged on inadequate sites in the industrial-commercial areas of a city? What is adequate living space for a school? There seems to be increasing realization that if education is an expression of communal ends it cannot, perhaps should not, be limited by market orientation considerations of land use. The school is for people, and to realize its purpose, it demands an adequate land area with a functional localization of other activities, as suggested, for example, in the neighborhood unit plan and the garden city idea.

ECONOMIC ORDER, POWER, AND COMMUNITY ACTION

The community is not only an arrangement in space of physical structures, services, individuals, families, and other groups. It is also an area of opportunity. The career possibilities of persons are tied up with the vocational structure of the community. While the living space of the community is the result of the conflux of value orientations expressed in the actions of a variety of groups and of the community organized politically as public order, the vocational opportunities set forth in the economic order are relatively independent of community and school action. This economic order is not the expression of communal or public ends, as community and education are. It is true, however, that the school and the community as politically organized provide career possibilities, and both are in the market for goods and services. Furthermore, however they be instituted, municipal policies may have a directive influence on the economic order, for example through zoning and taxes. The problem is to examine the nature and the significance of the economic order to the community and to the school. To analyze this interrelationship certain points are important: a community's function and services are linked up with those of other communities, regions, and countries; and the economic order continuously changes, either through depletion of resources, through the vagaries of the business cycle, or through inventions that make some functions obsolete while creating new ones.

In Table 11 the industrial history of three of the cities is shown as a very general cycle. There is an expansion in establishments during World War I, a slight contraction in the twenties, a major decline during the thirties, a resurgence, perhaps temporary, during World War II. Opportunities will vary with the rise and decline of these establishments. If there is a persistent decline or a leveling off, youth in the community will be stranded or will have to look for opportunities elsewhere.

Career possibilities must be thought of in terms of major economic activities. Major foci of services and functions are shown in Table 12. The table suggests the world of opportunity within these communities. Drastic changes in these percentages are unlikely. Mill City will remain a small manufacturing city and a retail trade center. Seattle's more evenly distributed working population is indicative of its function as a port city. Chicago will continue to be hog butcher of the nation, steel center, and trade center. Elmtown will remain a rural trade center. These data do not mean that there is no growth in urban life, but most of the growth is in the metropolitan regions rather than in the central cities. Immediate profound shifts in the

TABLE 11. Number of Manufacturing Establishments and Average Number of Wage Earners in Three Cities for Designated Years

City	Year					
	1909	1914	1919	1929	1939	1947
Manufacturing establishments						
Mill City	47	51	43	24	22	16
Seattle	753	1,014	1,229	1,219	1,023	1,060
Chicago	9,656	10,115	10,537	10,201	8,476	10,240
Average wage earners for Year						
Mill City	3,020	3,507	3,625	2,230	2,167	2,947
Seattle	11,523	12,429	40,843	23,003	20,352	50,214
Chicago	293,977	313,710	403,942	405,399	347,839	667,407

(In Elmtown there were three major plants, employing from 65 to 700 persons. There were also several processing establishments for agricultural products.)
SOURCE: U.S. Census, 1940, 1930, 1920; Census of Manufactures, 1947.

TABLE 12. Percent Distribution of Population 14 Years Old and Over in Labor Force by Industry Group for Four Cities, 1940 and 1950

Industry Group	Mill City		Seattle		Chicago		Elmtown	
	1940	1950	1940	1950	1940	1950	1940	1950
Agriculture and forestry	1.7	0.9	1.6	2.1	0.1	0.1		1.9
Mining	—	—	0.3	0.1	0.1	—		1.8
Construction	3.8	5.7	5.4	5.8	3.9	4.3		7.2
Manufacturing	47.4	50.4	19.4	18.5	34.1	36.8		35.9
Transportation, communication, and other public utilities	5.7	5.0	11.0	11.0	10.0	10.6		7.6
Wholesale and retail trade	17.5	15.4	26.1	25.4	22.9	21.5		22.8
Finance, insurance, real estate	2.2	1.9	6.7	6.4	5.4	4.9		2.3
Business and repair service	1.5	1.7	2.7	3.0	2.6	2.4		2.8
Personal services	7.7	4.4	9.4	7.0	8.5	5.6		5.2
Amusement and related services	0.5	0.5	1.2	1.2	1.1	1.1		1.1
Professional and related services	8.6	0.1	9.5	11.2	6.8	7.3		7.6
Government	2.4	2.4	5.3	7.2	3.5	4.3		3.6
Not reported	1.0	0.9	1.3	1.1	1.0	1.2		0.6
Total number	4,954	6,505	147,952	190,246	1,352,218	1,614,867		2,694

SOURCE: U.S. Census, 1940, 1950, *Population*, "General Characteristics."
NOTE: There is no data for Elmtown in 1940.

occupational groupings, excluding obliteration through atomic or bacteria warfare, are not likely to take place. Long-time trends, however, suggest the following: a very large decrease in the farming occupations and in unskilled labor, an increase in professional workers and managers, a marked increase in semiskilled, sales and clerical workers, relative stability in proprietors. Coupled with these trends is on-the-job training through which a worker acquires his skills within a few weeks or months.[2]

Since the economic activities within a community are given, the school has to formulate a policy in relation to them. Schools have been characterized as activity-centered, child-centered, or community-centered. What does it mean to say that a school should center on a community, and in what ways should this focus work itself out? If the range of activities is small, as in a coal-mining town, textile town, or agriculture-centered town, the breadth of the educational process will be restricted because of the limited nature of the community. Field trips and community exploration may vivify social studies but at the same time may contribute to a provincial point of view. Furthermore, the *prime facie* sense experience cannot convey the institutional structure implicit in these activities within the community, for this structure can be "seen" only conceptually. From a guidance point of view the problem is a matter of selecting and fitting students, among other things, into the vocational order. To what extent should the local community set this guidance program? Perhaps, as the life adjustment program suggests, the focus should be on the nation, on living in the United States, an institution-centered approach, living in the factory, the office, the store, the trade union, the family, the church, in a private and corporate property system, etc. The question can be raised to what extent schools in rural communities should prepare their students for urban living, and whether urban schools should provide education so that students can migrate anywhere and make a satisfactory vocational adjustment.

[2] Alfred C. Kahler and Ernest Hamburger, *Education for an Industrial Age,* Cornell University Press, 1948, chaps. 2–11; C. W. Mills, *White Collar: The American Middle Classes,* Oxford University Press, 1951; Alba Edwards, *Sixteenth Census of the United States: 1940, Population,* "Comparative Occupation Statistics for the United States, 1870–1940," Government Printing Office, 1943.

POWER IN THE COMMUNITY

The world of opportunity in the community is not developed automatically. Controls are asserted, and they are a matter of power. Functions and services are organized through business groups. The larger the group, the greater is its economic power and the greater the probabilities of its using that power for political influence. Pressure is exerted not only on the municipality directly but also through local boards of trade, chambers of commerce, or trade associations. Mill City is dominated by the great Connecticut Yarn Company, part of a wide flung English textile empire. It is essentially a one-company town, of which there are many in the United States. In the pure type, the company owns and controls almost all aspects of the community. In Mill City the company exercised its influence through the local chamber of commerce. It was believed that the company was responsible for keeping out new industries in order to control the local labor market, and many also contended that the company always had a spokesman for its viewpoint on the city's board of finance. The company broke a strike by dispossessing striking workers from company homes and by importing French Canadians as strikebreakers. This is one way in which the world of opportunity can be organized by power.

In the other cities similar struggles have taken place. Elmtown might also be regarded as a company town. The mill and the foundry dominate. Absentee ownership prevails, but about four local families have important interests in these businesses. A strike in the earlier days of the community was broken by importing Poles. These business interests control both political parties on both town and county levels. In this way municipal policies are directed from their point of view. In cities such as Chicago and Seattle the situation is more complex. The "company" is superseded by several big companies and corporations. These are not unrelated. Corporate managements develop a common climate of opinion, outlook, and values, a common ground in shaping of general corporation politics. Some ways of doing this are through holding companies or the owning of stock in other companies, interlocking directorates, use of common firms for financial, legal, accounting, and similar services, interrelationships stemming from the control of investment funds, corporate interest groups, and special business and trade organizations. In Chicago corporate interest groups, i.e., groupings of related companies, include three banks, four industrial corporations, and three utilities. In Cleveland they include one bank and four industrial corporations; in Boston, two banks, two utilities, and four industrial corporations. What has happened in Mill City and Elmtown with regard to strikes, strikebreaking (by either foreign born or Negroes), municipal policy, and schools is duplicated in the history of these cities.[3]

Community action is, then, hedged in by the wielding of economic power. In some cases communities deliver themselves to the business groups by providing free buildings, tax exemptions, and other subsidies for the establishing of factories. Threats of removal, a standard technique, are likely to immobilize communal planning. Under such circumstances the municipality cannot operate as an instrument for public ends.

School planning may become hampered or made easier in the presence or absence of such opposition and power manipulation by interest groups. Frequently this power play attempts to force a rather exclusive vocational policy upon the school whereas the latter has to maintain its orientation to the humanities, the arts, and the social studies. In addition to such a curriculum problem, the question of finances comes into play inasmuch as the property tax is a major source of revenue for the schools.

ECONOMIC CLASS AND STATUS GROUP AND THE PRINCIPLE OF INEQUALITY

A man's work is not merely a source of income. The work places a tag on him, as professional, manager, laborer, etc. The job or the vocation is man's key position in the community and in a society.

[3] Cf. National Resources Committee, *The Structure of the American Economy*, Government Printing Office, 1940; *Small Business and Civic Welfare*, Document No. 135, 79th Congress, 2nd Session, Senate, Report of the Smaller War Plants Corporation to the Special Committee to Study Problems of American Small Business, Government Printing Office, 1946; Delbert Miller and William Form, *Industrial Sociology*, Harper & Brothers, 1951, chap. 21; Wilbert E. Moore, *Industrial Relations and the Social Order*, The Macmillan Company, 1946, chap. 21; H. R. Cayton, and G. S. Mitchell, *Black Workers and the New Unions*, University of North Carolina Press, 1939, pp. 5, 46–47, 256.

Occupational differences may also be thought of as differences in economic class and status. Economic class and status group are here to be understood in Weber's sense:

. . . as the typical chance for a supply of goods, external living conditions, and personal life experiences, in so far as this chance is determined by the amount and kind of power, or lack of such, to dispose of goods or skills for the sake of income in a given economic order. . . . With some oversimplification, one might thus say that "classes" are stratified according to their relations to the production and acquisition of goods; whereas "status groups" are stratified according to the principles of their consumption of goods as represented by special "styles of life." An "occupational group" is also a status group. For normally, it successfully claims social honor only by virtue of the special styles of life which may be determined by it. The differences between classes and status groups frequently overlap. [The status group is characterized by] distance and exclusiveness . . . with a monopolization of ideal and material goods or opportunities.[4]

Economic classes in the four cities are suggested by Table 13. The occupational distribution is based upon three criteria: skills and training required for performance, amount of supervision, and amount of authority. In general, one finds that semiskilled and unskilled workers and laborers tend to make up the lowest status groups; professionals, managers, and proprietors the highest; clerks, salesmen, and craftsmen in between. Mill City and Elmtown would have a very large proportion of the population in low economic class and status groups. Chicago and Seattle are more diffuse. Only the extremes are clearly demarcated.

These divisions of the population within the community stand for differences in living opportunities. The upper group is upper precisely because of the things the lower has not. The more this group can monopolize ideal and material goods or opportunities, including such intangibles as prestige, the more it consolidates its position and strengthens the social distance and social exclusiveness between itself and the less advantaged. Sumptuary laws would be the ultimate outcome of such an arrangement. The greater the prestige an upper group arrogates to itself, the greater the inferiority and deference the lower groups must or should display; the more upper it can be,

[4] From Max Weber: Essays in Sociology, edited by H. H. Gerth and C. Wright Mills, Oxford University Press, 1947, pp. 181, 193, 191.

TABLE 13. Occupational Distribution in Four Cities, 1940 and 1950

Occupational Group	City							
	Chicago		Seattle		Mill City		Elmtown	
	1940	1950	1940	1950	1940	1950	1940	1950
Professional and technical	7.7	8.8	10.0	12.5	6.8	7.7	8.3	7.9
Farmer, Farm manager	—	—	0.1	0.1	0.2	0.3	0.6	0.8
Proprietor, manager	8.2	8.7	13.3	12.7	8.0	6.2	11.8	10.6
Clerical and sales	27.5	26.8	26.0	28.8	16.0	17.5	15.0	19.5
Craftsman, foreman	14.2	15.1	14.0	14.3	10.0	15.4	14.0	18.0
Operative, etc.	22.0	23.0	14.2	12.6	38.4	36.0	18.2	25.5
Domestic service	2.6	1.3	3.3	1.8	3.6	1.5	4.4	1.8
Service	10.9	9.7	11.4	10.7	8.0	7.8	8.5	8.4
Farm laborer, foreman	—	—	0.2	0.1	0.6	0.4	1.0	0.7
Farm laborer, unpaid	—	—	—	—	—	—	—	—
Laborer	6.5	5.6	8.6	5.5	7.4	6.1	17.0	6.3
Not reported	0.5	1.0	0.6	0.9	1.0	1.1	1.1	0.5
Numbers in labor market	1,352,218	1,614,867	147,952	190,246	4,954	6,505	2,164	2,694

SOURCE: U.S. Census, 1940 and 1950, *Population Characteristics*.

even in such intangibles as prestige. The more prestige the upper person has, the more deference must the lower person show.

The relationship may also be characterized as a system of contempt and resentment. Such attitudes can be seen most clearly in the extremes. In Elmtown the lowest group is "looked upon as the scum of the city by the higher classes." It is the opinion of the upper classes that:

1. They have no respect for the law, or themselves.
2. They enjoy their shacks and huts along the river or across the tracks and love their dirty, smoky, low-class dives and taverns.
3. Whole families—children, in-laws, mistresses, and all—live in one shack.
4. This is the crime class that produces the delinquency and sexual promiscuity that fills the paper.
5. Their interests lie in sex and its perversions. The girls are always pregnant; the families huge; incestual relations occur frequently.
6. They are not inspired by education, and only a few are able to make any attainments along this line.
7. They are loud in their speech, vulgar in their actions, sloppy in their dress, and indifferent toward their plight. Their vocabulary develops as profanity is learned.
8. If they work, they work at menial jobs.
9. Their life experiences are purely physical, and even these are on a low plane.
10. They have no interest in health and medical care.
11. The men are too lazy to work or do odd jobs around town.
12. This group lives for a Saturday of drinking or fighting. They are of low character and breed and have a criminal record for a pedigree.[5]

The lower group has been characterized as "being resigned to live a life of frustration and defeat," [6] passive and fatalistic. The upper status group justifies its superiority in assuming that its members are of a superior biological stock as compared with the lower groups.

This relationship of unwilling submission to others can be duplicated in almost any community. Yankee City, Plainville, Middletown, Mill City—all have the same principle of inequality "organizing" the community. In a small South Dakota community the people in the top group agreed that those in the lower lacked ambition,

[5] Reprinted with permission from August Hollingshead, *Elmtown's Youth*, 1949, John Wiley & Sons, Inc., pp. 110–111.
[6] *Ibid.*, p. 111.

spent money unwisely, and failed to make full use of opportunities. They also agreed that the bottom group was mentally dull, had low moral standards, drank too much, was irreligious, behaved in an ill-mannered fashion, and failed to appreciate those who were trying to help them. The low status persons failed to treat the upper group with proper respect and did not seem to know their place. Viewing the upper status group, the lower group agreed that the top group tried to show off, acted as if they were inherently better than others, drank to excess, failed to live up to the religious teachings of their churches, used too much profanity, and had easy jobs. They thought that these people were not well behaved, were unkind and unsympathetic to the less fortunate, tried to run everybody's business, and discriminated against the bottom people. The community and educational implication of this system of inequality and mutual resentment was striking. Separate playgrounds and separate grade schools were built to insure isolation of the children of the top and lower status groups.[7]

Such separate school facilities are an extreme case but demonstrate the logical outcome of a community organized on the status group principle. While studies of high schools show that relations among students are strongly influenced by their social class background, this factor may be of little significance in the elementary school. In the Mill City study it was found to be negligible. There is no inherent reason to assume that the variety of functions which call forth economic classes must result in a divisive status group system.

Great extremes of economic class and the accompanying emphasis on status tend to split a community rather than hold it together. If the lower group has a life that is relatively disorganized, the upper group fails to develop an integrated and balanced view because it cannot recognize the essential common humanity of man. To this extent the life patterns of the upper group are distorted with contempt and possibly also with fear of the lower groups, who it feels really cannot be trusted. It can realize its style of life primarily through control and use of the lower groups to its ends. A community organized on a status group principle is a feudal structure, an

[7] John Useem, Pierre Tangent, and Ruth Useem, "Stratification in a Prairie Town," *American Sociological Review,* June, 1942, pp. 331–342.

organization of privilege and opportunity concentrated in the upper groups and lacking in the lower. Such a community is less of a community because common ends are not shared, because the collective life is particularized into antagonistic bewildered segments, because the significant social drama that could develop remains unrealized.

COMMUNITY FRAGMENTATION— NATIONALITY AND COLOR GROUPS

"Wops, bohunks, dagos, kikes, pachucos, niggers"—these are a few of the stereotyped epithets directed against members in a community. While not all American communities are a cosmopolitan mixture, most of them are. In the South, Southwest, and West, Negroes and Mexicans primarily compose the group that is hated and feared. In the North, the many different European nationality groups, the French Canadians, and in recent years the Negroes, are the groups viewed with contempt and hostility by native whites. These groups themselves view each other with similar suspicion. Perhaps their distrust came about because the groups were first related to each other economically. A relation that is based upon the utility of a person is likely to be an exploitable one.

A very large proportion of the population in our four communities is composed of these nationality and color groups (Table 14). What is also important is the large group of persons having foreign or mixed parentage. Taken together with the foreign-born white the proportion comes to over 50 percent in 1900 in the four cities. It is possible that the proportion in 1940 may have been 20 to 30 percent. This information suggests, first, that these groups manage to maintain their identity and, second, that there is also a certain amount of assimilation.

The specific groups vary in these cities. In Chicago the more important have been the Germans, Poles, Russians, Italians, Swedes, Czechs, and Irish; in Seattle, the Japanese, Canadians (other than French), Italians, Germans, Swedes, Norwegians, and English; in Mill City, English, Irish, Poles, Italians, Russians, French Canadians; in Elmtown, Irish, Germans, Norwegians, and Poles. The result is community cleavage, except in those communities where the nation-

TABLE 14. Percent Distribution of Population in Four Cities for 1900, 1940, and 1950 by Nativity and Color

Nativity and Color	Chicago			Seattle			Mill City			Elmtown		
	1900	1940	1950	1900	1940	1950	1900	1940	1950	1900	1940	1950
Native white	63.7	80.0	69.0	74.9	—	82.3	81.4	81.4	84.3	77.4	92.6	94.5
Native parentage	20.9	—	—	50.0	—	—	39.3	—	—	39.5	—	—
Foreign or mixed parentage	42.8	—	—	24.9	—	—	32.9	—	—	37.9	—	—
Foreign-born white	34.5	19.7	17.6	20.2	—	11.7	27.2	18.1	15.3	22.1	7.2	5.3
Negro	1.8	8.2	13.0	0.5	1.0	3.3	0.8	0.6	0.4	0.5	—	0.1
Other [a]	—	0.1	0.4	4.4	2.8	2.4	—	—	—	—	—	—

[a] Includes Japanese, Chinese, Indian, etc. Mexicans are classed as white.
SOURCE: U.S. Census, 1900, 1940, and 1950.

ality or colored group is the dominant or almost exclusive factor or where the community is almost exclusively native white and native born. In the latter community economic class and status group is the more important principle. In the others the community cleavage is compounded with the nationality and color factor.

What is important is not only the mere presence or absence of these groups but how they are evaluated, what their position in the community life is, how they are manipulated, or how they try to manipulate others. Since most of these migrants came from farm or peasant background as unskilled or semiskilled labor and with little money, it is not surprising that many of them stepped onto the bottom rungs of the economic ladder and lived in the disadvantaged sections of the community. These groups maintained their identity through clubs and other associations, particularly the church, the church school, and the parochial school. Clubs functioned as recreational, social, and benefit associations and as a means of political expression, e.g., Pulaski clubs, Knights of Columbus, St. Jean de Baptiste, Sons and Daughters of Italy, Steuben Club, the *Turnverein*, and myriads of others.

Relations with other groups may be antagonistic or distrustful. In Mill City an informant stated: "The Polish people, more so the first generation, appear to rank only the Irish and the Jews on a scale higher than themselves. The Italians follow them and last come the French. Polish people hate the French. One of the chief reasons is because the French were imported from Canada, Maine, and New Hampshire to replace the strikers at the local mill. They became a threat to the security of the Polish people who formed a large part of the strikers." In Elmtown the stereotyped interpretations and epithets were as follows:

Irish: Catholics, Democrats, hell raisers, fighters, boozers, cheap politicians, troublemakers, and philanderers.

Germans: good, thrifty people, hard workers, money makers, a good element, some of finest people.

Norwegians: clannish, cold sexually, disinterested in education, religious, a good, thrifty sort, hard workers, good citizens.

Poles: scabs, filthy, ignorant, law breakers, dumb, unable to learn American ways, pretty good citizens, a problem in school.[8]

[8] Hollingshead, *op. cit.*, p. 62.

An Italian settlement in New York City was bordered by Irish and Bohemians. The Italians viewed them as follows: "The Irishwomen are considered wives of drunkards, and as all of the husband's salary goes to the bartender, the wives are believed to earn a living in prostituting themselves. The Bohemians are libertarians; the girls are free; and, moreover, Bohemians and Hungarians are looked upon as bastard peoples." [9]

Life among these groups is in transition. Jack Dureille, writing about his life in Mill City, said:

I was born and spent my early childhood in the company houses of the Connecticut Thread Company. These homes were rented to the employees of the thread company. There were so many Canadian families living in them that they should have called it "Little Canada." French was the only language spoken and became the first language I spoke. Being able to speak the French language fluently later became a handicap when I went to grammar school. . . . Life in the little colony was pretty rough. People didn't have everything they wanted. There weren't many car and radio owners. . . . There was close tie in kin relationships. The women would go shopping with each other. Some would meet during the week or on holidays to form some kind of pastime by playing cards, singing, dancing. . . . The group loves to have a good time, gets along well with other nationality groups, and some give them the honor of being heavy drinkers.

And Eddie Ostrowski wrote about his group:

Polish families as a rule are very large, especially the first generation. They average about six children per family. The Polish people believe children to be assets when they are full-grown. Parents expected their children to work for them a long time. . . . The first generation Poles feel that they are not true Americans, but they are just as good as the next person. They feel especially handicapped by their inability to speak English fluently and their lack of formal education. Only the late second generation and the third generation children as a group went through high school and some on to college.

Both of these documents suggest adjustment problems that the children of these nationality groups undergo. In general they may go through three phases, though some are fixated in the first or

---

[9] Robert E. Park and Herbert Miller, *Old World Traits Transplanted*, Harper & Brothers, 1921, pp. 149, 150.

second: "1. engaging in behavior that violates the standards of both the nationality and American groups, adventurous, spectacular and dangerous activities, gang activities, truancy, stealing; intellectually —escape into esoteric religious and political movements; 2. renouncing the traditions of the nationality group and embracing 100 per cent Americanism; 3. reconciling the nationality and American culture by, a. with others of his age, joining nationality associations with symbols predominantly American, b. taking the place of the dying generation in the nationality community and at the same time assuming many American elements." [10]

The community falls apart into a variety of nationality and color groups. The nationality groups are bound by common ties of kin, language, religion, occupation, and area of residence. The color groups, such as the Negro, Japanese, and Mexican, are pushed together by their high social visibility, i.e., their color and other physical features. Intermarriage and inter-dining take place primarily within these groups. Special schools, clubs, and other associations support the nationality cultures. Members in these groups are linked to others outside their group primarily through economic and political relations. There is mutual suspicion, and in extreme cases violence breaks out, as in race riots. The degree of community integration is low, and community action is impeded by the presence or dominance of these nationality and color groups.

The educational implications are interesting. In so far as these nationality groups maintain their own schools, the differences are maintained, and integration into the surrounding culture is resisted and slowed. Competitive relations, whether in music, debate, or athletics, may further solidify these differences, resulting in we-they group attitudes. Public schools at one time simply tried to Americanize, though the earlier attitude of disparagement has now given way to an appreciation of differences of cultural groups. The stress on intergroup education in recent years represents an effort to clear away ignorance and prejudice and make way for understanding, for coöperation, for appreciating the worth of cultural differences.

[10] William Lloyd Warner and Leo Srole, *The Social Systems of American Ethnic Groups,* Yale University Press, 1945, p. 147.

OBSTACLES TO THE REALIZATION
OF THE AESTHETIC COMMUNITY

The city as "esthetic symbol of collective unity," to return to the Mumford quotation, is in general very inadequately realized today. The inequalities in residential areas seem to symbolize disunity and self-seeking rather than unity. In some cases there are rather grandiose monuments to the civic ideal in the form of parks or "civic centers," but while there is blight and slum, a community cannot be an aesthetic object, nor can there be a good life.

TABLE 15. Age of Dwelling Units in Four Cities by Year Built

Year Built [a]	Percent of Units			
	Chicago	Seattle	Mill City	Elmtown
1935–40	1.0	3.7	1.7	11.4
1930–34	2.0	6.4	2.4	5.7
1925–29	18.3	18.8	5.0	9.0
1920–24	12.0	12.4	6.2	4.5
1910–19	19.8	27.2	15.5	13.7
1900–09	19.9	25.0	14.9	18.0
1890–99	16.6	5.2	15.2	14.0
1880–89	7.7	1.2	14.7	12.7
1860–79	2.4	0.1	11.6	7.0
1859 and earlier	0.3	—[b]	12.8	4.0
Based on units	955,310	129,254	2,914	1,217

[a] Of the dwelling units reported in the 1950 census, 11 percent were built since 1940 in Mill City, 12 percent in Elmtown, 4.8 percent in Chicago, and 20 percent in Seattle.
[b] 0.002 percent.
SOURCE: U.S. Census, 1940, *Housing Characteristics.*

A slum is defined as "an area in which housing is so unfit as to constitute a menace to the health and morals of the community." [11] The United States Housing Act of 1937 defines a slum: "Any area where dwellings predominate which by reason of dilapidation, overcrowding, faulty arrangement or design, lack of ventilation, light or sanitation facilities, or any combination of these factors, are detrimental to safety, health, or morals." [12] While slum areas may be

[11] Mabel Walker, *Urban Blight and Slums*, Harvard University Press, 1938, p. 3.
[12] *Ibid.*, p. 4.

ECOLOGICAL MAPS

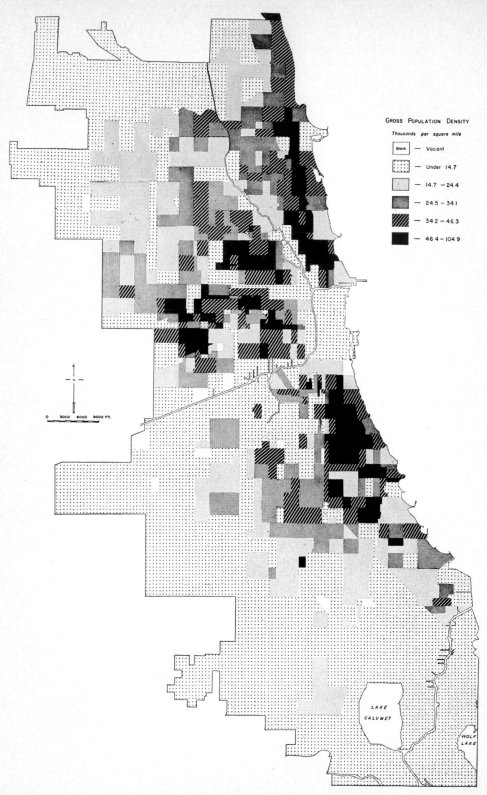

LAKE
CALUMET

WOLF
LAKE

0   3000   6000   9000 FT.

MAP 1. Resident Population, Chicago, 1950. (Reprinted by permission of Chicago Plan Commission.)

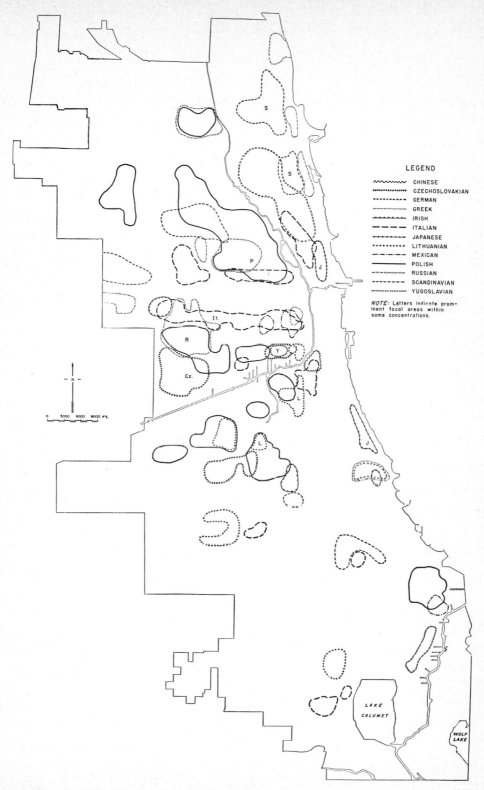

LEGEND

∿∿∿∿	CHINESE
●●●●●●	CZECHOSLOVAKIAN
- - - -	GERMAN
··········	GREEK
▬▬▬▬	IRISH
— — —	ITALIAN
+++++	JAPANESE
✦✦✦✦✦	LITHUANIAN
—·—·—	MEXICAN
——————	POLISH
—··—··—	RUSSIAN
- - - - -	SCANDINAVIAN
·-·-·-·	YUGOSLAVIAN

NOTE: Letters indicate prominent focal areas within some concentrations.

N

0   3000   6000   9000 FT.

LAKE CALUMET

WOLF LAKE

MAP 2. Concentrations of Ethnic Groups Based on Dot Map of Each Group, Chicago, 1950. (Reprinted by permission of Chicago Plan Commission.)

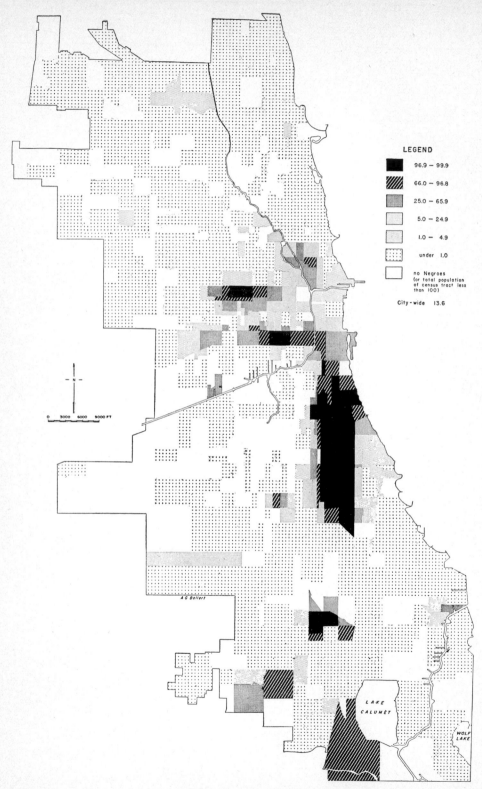

N

0 3000 6000 9000 FT

A G Bollert

LAKE
CALUMET

WOLF
LAKE

MAP 3.   Percent Negro of Total Population, Chicago, 1950. (Reprinted by permission of
Chicago Plan Commission.)

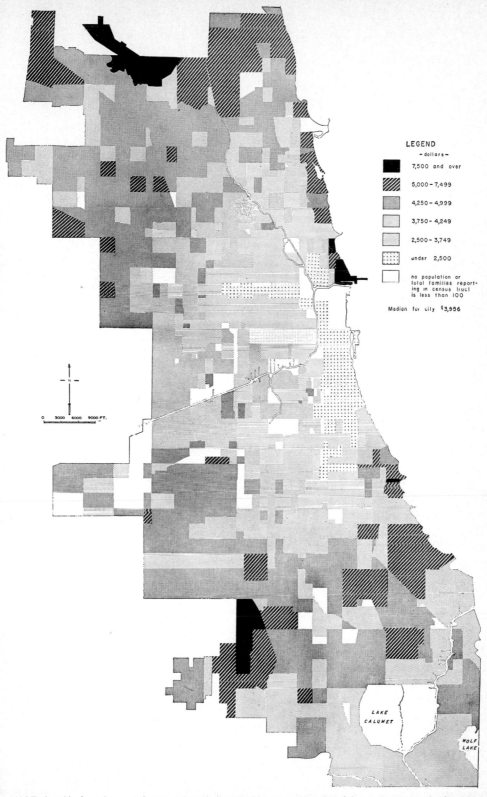

LEGEND

— dollars —

■	7,500 and over
▨	5,000 – 7,499
▦	4,250 – 4,999
▨	3,750 – 4,249
▨	2,500 – 3,749
▦	under 2,500
☐	no population or total families report- ing in census tract is less than 100

Median for city $3,956

LAKE CALUMET

WOLF LAKE

N

0   3000   6000   9000 FT.

MAP 4.   Median Income for Families in 1949, Chicago. (Reprinted by permission of Chicago Plan Commission.)

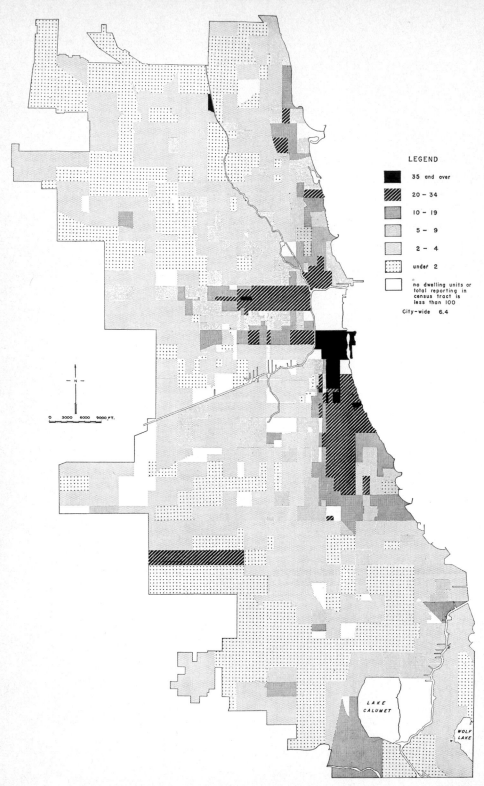

LEGEND

■	35 and over
▨	20 – 34
▦	10 – 19
▨	5 – 9
░	2 – 4
⣿	under 2
□	no dwelling units or total reporting in census tract is less than 100

City-wide 6.4

N

0   3000   6000   9000 FT.

LAKE
CALUMET

WOLF
LAKE

MAP 5.   Percent of Occupied Dwelling Units with 1.51 or More Persons per Room, Chicago, 1950. (Reprinted by permission of Chicago Plan Commission.)

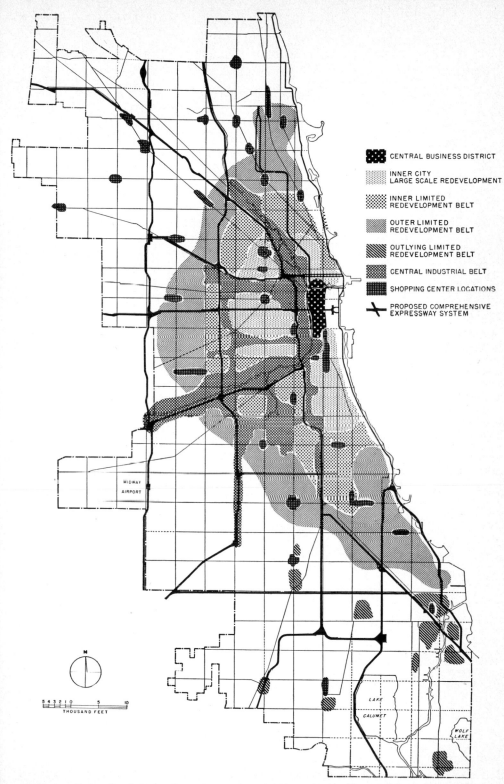

	CENTRAL BUSINESS DISTRICT
	INNER CITY LARGE SCALE REDEVELOPMENT
	INNER LIMITED REDEVELOPMENT BELT
	OUTER LIMITED REDEVELOPMENT BELT
	OUTLYING LIMITED REDEVELOPMENT BELT
	CENTRAL INDUSTRIAL BELT
	SHOPPING CENTER LOCATIONS
	PROPOSED COMPREHENSIVE EXPRESSWAY SYSTEM

MIDWAY AIRPORT

N

5 4 3 2 1 0   5   10
THOUSAND FEET

LAKE CALUMET

WOLF LAKE

MAP 6. Generalized Redevelopment Areas, Chicago, 1953. (Reprinted by permission of Chicago Plan Commission.)

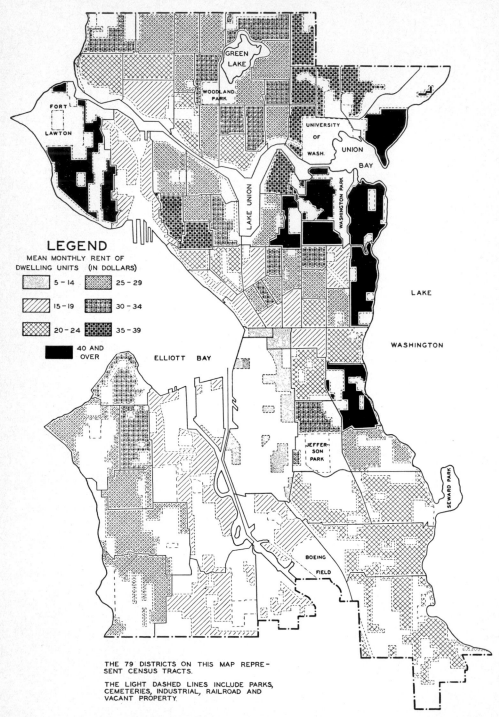

THE 79 DISTRICTS ON THIS MAP REPRE-
SENT CENSUS TRACTS.

THE LIGHT DASHED LINES INCLUDE PARKS,
CEMETERIES, INDUSTRIAL, RAILROAD AND
VACANT PROPERTY.

MAP 7.   Mean Monthly Rental, Seattle, 1940. (Reprinted from *Social Trends in Seattle* by Calvin Schmid, by permission of University of Washington Press. Copyright 1944 by Calvin Schmid.)

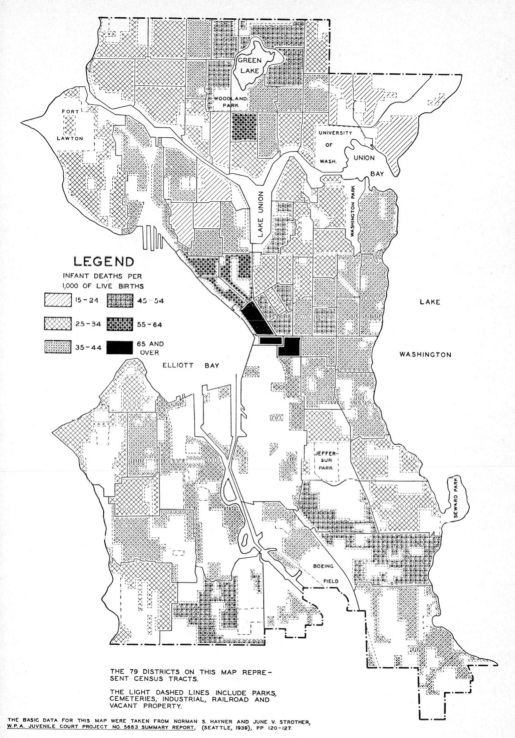

LEGEND

INFANT DEATHS PER 1,000 OF LIVE BIRTHS

15 - 24		45 - 54	
25 - 34		55 - 64	
35 - 44		65 AND OVER	

THE 79 DISTRICTS ON THIS MAP REPRE-SENT CENSUS TRACTS.

THE LIGHT DASHED LINES INCLUDE PARKS, CEMETERIES, INDUSTRIAL, RAILROAD AND VACANT PROPERTY.

THE BASIC DATA FOR THIS MAP WERE TAKEN FROM NORMAN S. HAYNER AND JUNE V. STROTHER, W.P.A. JUVENILE COURT PROJECT NO. 5683 SUMMARY REPORT, (SEATTLE, 1939), PP 120-127.

MAP 8. Infant Mortality, Seattle, 1933–1937. (Reprinted from *Social Trends in Seattle* by Calvin Schmid, by permission of University of Washington Press. Copyright 1944 by Calvin Schmid.)

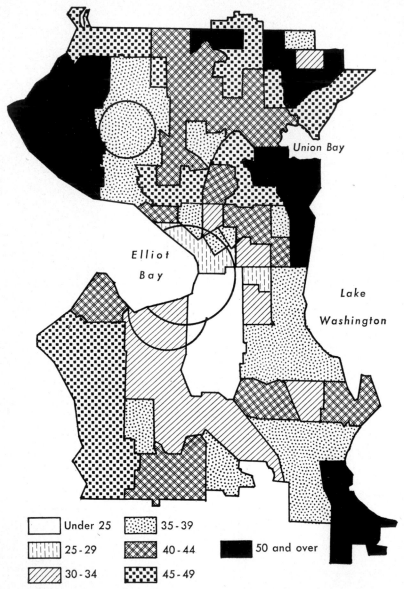

Union Bay

Elliot
Bay

Lake

Washington

	Under 25		35 - 39
	25 - 29		40 - 44
	30 - 34		45 - 49		50 and over

MAP 9.   Seattle by Mean Monthly Rental, 1950. Circled sections cover major problem areas.

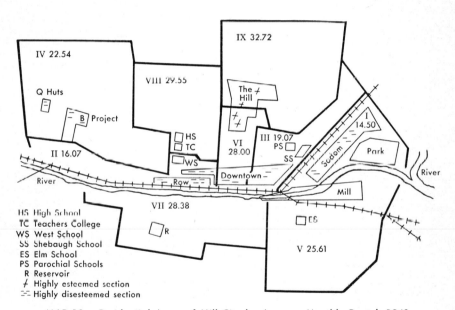

IV 22.54

Q Huts

B Project

II 16.07

VIII 29.55

IX 32.72

The Hill

HS
TC
WS
Row

VI 28.00

Downtown

III 19.07
PS
SS

I 14.50

Sodom

Park

River

River

Mill

VII 28.38

R

ES

V 25.61

HS High School
TC Teachers College
WS West School
SS Shebaugh School
ES Elm School
PS Parochial Schools
R Reservoir
✗ Highly esteemed section
═ Highly disesteemed section

MAP 10.   Residential Areas of Mill City by Average Monthly Rental, 1940.

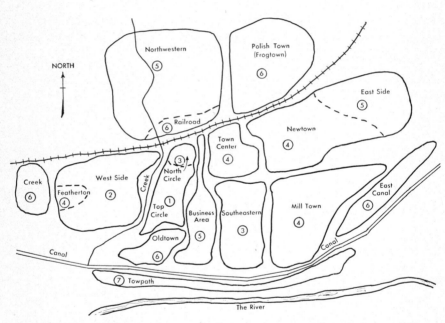

MAP 11. Dwelling Area of Jonesville-Elmtown. Areas rate from 1 (very good) to 7 (very poor). (Slightly adapted and reprinted from *Democracy in Jonesville* by W. Lloyd Warner et al., by permission of Harper & Brothers. Copyright 1949 by Harper & Brothers.)

dangerous, they may also be profitable because of rentals derived from congestion and improper use, as for vice, gambling, risqué entertainment. A blighted area is one in which it is not profitable to make or maintain improvements. It is an area that is deteriorating.

Much city living takes place in old structures, old houses. The age of these units varies with the history of the community. Thus, Seattle has the smallest proportion of old residential structures and Mill City the largest. These old and dilapidated houses are generally located in areas of first settlement which are now the central district and near other industrial areas, but there may be blight and shacktowns at the edges of the communities. The central areas of Chicago, Seattle, and Mill City are characterized by blight and slum. In Elmtown these areas are "below the canal" (shacks), "down by the canal," and "north of the tracks" at the west boundary.

Rentals paid in the community are indicative of the quality of housing. Though higher rentals were paid in 1950, this does not necessarily mean that quality improved in like fashion. It may mean that it cost more to live in the same old housing. We may assume that the lower the rental, the poorer will be the facilities and the structure of the dwelling unit. Cheap rental is concentrated in tenant-occupied units, ranging from 24.5 percent in Chicago to 60 percent in Mill City. Cheap rents usually coincide with the older areas and structures, but for some families, especially of nationality and colored groups, the rent in terms of space secured and quality of accommodations may be quite expensive.

The ecological maps of Chicago, Seattle, Mill City, and Elmtown show the spatial distribution of certain social facts. The Chicago maps indicate that the foreign-born and Negro populations are concentrated in areas of greatest population density, lowest income, and greatest overcrowding. These are the major blight and slum areas that need redevelopment. They are located around the central business districts, along the North and South Branches of Chicago River, near the Stockyards, along the railroad lines funneling into the city, and in the steel mill area to the east of Lake Calumet and Calumet River. These areas are also characterized by the lowest educational achievement, the highest juvenile delinquency rates, the highest insanity rates, the highest illegitimate birth rates, the highest tuberculosis death rate, and the highest infant mortality rate (a good sensitive indicator of living conditions). As the redevelopment map shows, the amount of physical, not to say social, reconstruction is enormous. The two Seattle maps also suggest a confluence of social pathologies. The central area of Seattle, roughly at the middle of the map, contained in 1940 in addition to the foreign-born white, the Negroes, and the Japanese, the greatest number of unemployed, the greatest proportion of houses built in 1899 or earlier, the largest proportion of dwelling units needing major repairs, low rentals, overcrowding, lack of private flush toilets and private bath, the highest suicide rates, and the highest infant mortality rates. It is an area predominantly of laborers and semiskilled workers. Two other prob-

TABLE 16. Percent of Renter-Tenant-Occupied Dwelling Units by Estimated Contract Monthly Rental for Four Cities, 1940 and 1950

Rent in Dollars	Chicago 1940	1950	Seattle 1940	1950	Mill City 1940	1950	Elmtown 1940	1950
Less than 10	1.0	0.4	3.4	0.4	5.4	1.4	5.4	0.3
10–19	11.6	8.4	15.6	5.5	54.2	27.7	31.5	4.5
20–29	23.8	15.4	26.4	15.7	29.1	29.4	35.4	16.3
30–39	23.9	15.8	24.4	26.1	7.9	18.1	22.2	20.5
40–49	20.5	20.0	13.3	20.1	2.5	12.9	4.7	23.1
50–59	9.7	15.7	6.6	11.4	0.3	3.8	0.6	18.6
60–74	5.3	11.5	5.0	7.0	0.1	2.1	0.1	8.6
75–99	2.4	6.0	2.7	5.7	0.1	0.4	0.1	1.4
100 and up	1.8	3.7	2.6	2.3	0.1	—	—	0.1
Free or not reported	—	4.3	—	5.6	—	3.9	—	6.5

SOURCE: U.S. Census, 1940 and 1950, *Housing Characteristics*.

lem areas are in the city: one, south and southeast of Elliott Bay; the other, along the river coming from Lake Union to the ocean. These areas show the same characteristics as the central area, though in lesser degree. There are, for example, more skilled workers in these areas. That the pattern has maintained itself is suggested by the generalized mean monthly rental map for 1950. The exception, perhaps, is the absence of the Japanese, who were relocated during the war. Their place was no doubt taken by the wartime influx of Negroes.

In Mill City, Area I and the indicated sections in Areas II, III, and IV are the major slum, blighted, and disesteemed areas. The major nationality groups are concentrated here. Sodom, for example, is French-Canadian and Polish. Forty-eight percent of the workers in the area are either semiskilled or unskilled. It is an area of tenants rather than owners. Of the structures within the area 61 percent needed major repairs or had no private bath. Many of the ethnic club houses are located here. Saturday night conviviality results in a large number of arrests for drunkenness or disorderly conduct, but this takes place at the periphery of the area toward the business center.

Area II contains some of the most disesteemed sections, known as Yellow Row, Brick Row, and Stone Row. These border the railroad tracks. Italians have concentrated in these two areas, though they are not the predominant occupants of the row sections. Semiskilled and unskilled workers account for almost 36 percent of the workers. Persons in service occupations are next with 21 percent. It is a dominant tenant area with over half of the dwelling units needing major repairs or lacking private bath. The Radiotron Company operates here. West Street School is located at the northern boundary touching Area VIII.

Area III is largely Polish and French. It contains the two Roman Catholic churches, the two parochial schools, and the Shebaug Elementary School. Several smaller factories center their activities here. The section toward the business center and along the tracks contains some of the most decrepit housing, even less attractive than Sodom because of the intermingling of smaller businesses, taverns, and industry. Semiskilled and unskilled workers compose 32 percent of the working population. Small proprietors and skilled workers appear in almost equal proportion, 18 percent. Most of the people rent. One-third of the dwelling units have deficiencies.

Area IV was open space until the addition of Baker Project, which gives the area its reputation. The project consists of two-story, tar-paper-covered, barrack-type buildings. The project does not have high prestige. At the end of World War II it is claimed that the skilled workers and people with initiative left, leaving the social dregs behind. Because of a housing shortage at one time, quite a few students from a nearby university lived there. There was a sharp division between students and non-students, their differences reflected in the terms "diaper alley" and "snob hill." The students account for 24 percent of the working population and semiskilled and unskilled workers for 21 percent. This latter proportion would change to 42 percent if the students were omitted. The section that is built up near the main street contains the older tenements and manufacturing concerns. Better housing does not appear until the community hospital is passed.

The three problem areas in Elmtown have already been described. It might be noted that the factors involving the location of these areas are the same as in the other communities.

What we now see is that large areas of our big cities are incubators of sickness, insanity, and death. The same thing occurs on a more modest scale in smaller communities. It is not merely an American phenomenon but characteristic of cities in other countries, e.g., Glasgow, Manchester, London, or Rouen.[13] While slum clearance has some effect, the major pattern remains unaltered.

COMMUNITY ENDS THROUGH GOVERNMENT

The community through political organization takes on a form by which reflection on the whole of community life can issue in wide plans and actions toward their accomplishment. In its form as a municipality communal ends can be thought out and objectified. Government has no content of its own. Its content is the life of the community, its health, its safety, its protection, its housing, its recreation, its morality, and its beauty of design. The powers of government are related to the ordering of this social and cultural content, achieved through law and administrative decision or by services instituted by the municipality. For example, the municipality of Detroit carried out twenty-eight functions in the period 1824–33, and these involved functions of general government and protection.[14] By 1924–33, 306 functions were carried on in such areas as safety

[13] Robert Sinclair, *The Big City*, Reynal and Hitchcock, 1938; R. H. Tawney, *Equality*, Harcourt, Brace and Company, 1931, pp. 144–145; Michel Quoist, *La Ville et l'Homme*, Éditions Ouvrières, 1952.
[14] L. D. Upson, *The Growth of City Government*, pp. 13–17, quoted in *Contemporary Society*, ed. Staff, Social Science, University of Chicago Press, 1939.

engineering, conservation of health, sanitation, promotion of cleanliness, highways, charities, hospitals and correction, education, recreation, public-service enterprises. The expansion of these activities correlates with growth and concentration of population. Any municipality must develop in similar fashion, for this is the only way the design of the whole city can be envisioned and made real.

The intentions of a community as organized in municipal form may not be realized. Some limits are set by the state from which a city receives its charter. A legislature can effectively block municipal action by the conditions and powers granted at incorporation. Since many legislatures are dominated by representatives of rural areas, town-country suspicion may influence legislative acts. Malfunction of government, however, is not merely a matter of a city's charter. The perversion of municipal government was examined in detail by Lincoln Steffens around 1900 in his book *The Shame of the Cities*. Forty-seven years later the shame was still there as documented in *Our Fair City* and in the hearings of the congressional crime investigation committee.

Large-scale corruption, "honest" or dishonest graft, bribery, protection, and favors have been common to most of the large cities. A scandal of some sort characterizes our large cities about once in every ten years. This distortion of municipality is a process involving a complicated pattern of underworld organization, business interests, political parties, and the legal framework of government. Despite advances in merit systems and civil service, the market orientation is basic, i.e., to use office for power, money, and success, for patronage and spoils. The result is wastage of funds, reluctance to plan, and subservience to private interests. Even small communities such as Mill City are affected. Not that there were any public scandals, but the government did not act. For twenty years it watched the deterioration of its equipment and facilities, hamstrung apparently by interests that wanted to keep the tax rate down.

The fact that there is planning and that efforts are made at reconstructing communities means that the municipality has not succumbed 100 percent to the market orientation; the possibilities of creating an ordered community design are always present. The vision of the good life, however obscure and ill defined, is ever at hand. It is inherent in the very nature of the corporate community to see its life as a whole and to organize it as a whole through its agency the government. The idea of the ordered society and of the aesthetic community also animates many private volunteer groups. While they may not have the synoptic vision, yet their action is civic, for their contribution is shared by the community as a whole— instance the contribution of playgrounds. Furthermore, such groups have acted as checks and gadflies on the governmental activities of the corporate community; that is to say, they function to keep the focus of the government on its job. While private groups in this way play an important role, they still lack the authority, the means, and perhaps the total view of the community. Nor should a community's services and facilities be dependent upon the inclinations of these groups. The organization of living as a civic or public function, and the efforts of larger cities to redesign themselves evidence this inner propulsion to the whole life and the subordination of the market orientation.

COMMUNITY AND SCHOOL—SUMMARY

Our cities have grown tremendously during the past 100 years. Much of this growth was brought about by immigration. Today cities are sustained by internal migration, since their birth rates are too low to maintain a stable population. In many of the larger cities the schools built around and before 1900 are now in the slum and blighted areas. Children of these areas, usually immigrant children, have the structure and equipment of an educational plant from fifty to eighty years old. Many teachers have the prospect of working in these old structures with a "difficult" child population. It is not surprising that they are reluctant to teach in the back-of-the-yards or black belt areas. Schools become typed as "slum schools" or "nice schools in better neighborhoods."

A community is divided into economic classes and status groups. The latter represent a principle of privilege and inequality that is destructive of unity and causes fragmentation of a community. Since those on top want to maintain their prestige and power, a variety of mechanisms must be used, including the school. These people either send their children to private schools or make sure that local schools handle their children according to their wishes, expecially in high school. They can monopolize privileges and awards. Through discriminatory practices and other pressures the lower groups tend to drop out of the schools. Here is a fundamental problem, for the school is caught between two principles: equal opportunity for all and special opportunity for the favored. The school has only three possibilities: (1) to accept and maintain the distinctions, (2) to try to ignore or minimize them, (3) to change them. The last means that the community must be reformed.

Community cleavage also arises through the existence of nationality and color groups. The Negro has been assimilated but through segregation and discrimination continues to live in a world quite separate from that of the rest of the community. The members of the various nationality groups are being assimilated into American culture, but the life experiences of their children will differ markedly from those of native white children. They live in many worlds, shifting daily several times from one culture to another. Family, church, and other special groups try to hold them to the nationality culture. The American school attempts to pull them into American values and practices. Since many of these groups are Catholic, one of the great cleavages in the school system is brought about by the split into parochial and public school. If there are competitive activities between the schools the cleavages will be accentuated. The problem of the financing of these schools automatically arises, with resultant hostility and recrimination. The whole schooling process, the personality development of the children, and the stability of their family life are upset by these clashing cultures.

The community is organized into areas, some of which are stable, some undergoing transition, others disorganized. Sickness, delinquency, poor housing, high mortality are built into many community structures. The nationality and color groups, the lower economic classes and status groups are especially concentrated in these areas, predestined to a life of disorder and frustration. They live in areas which are a mixture of industry, commerce, residence, smog, noise, and dirt, areas which show a lack of community plan. A school can function only with difficulty in such a social disorder.

Some schools have capitulated to this disorder; others have refused to accept it and attempt to change the deteriorated areas. For the schools are concerned with training for living, preparing for the variety of roles that society has developed. But preparing for these roles means a selection of appropriate ones and in a setting that is enriching. Thus, what sort of life is it for which children are to be prepared? How does the slum, the black ghetto, the unskilled job, the business executive, or the union fit into an educational program? A basic policy problem is involved. Should the school teach experimentalism, adventure, reconstruction of our social world or do nothing, simply standing by amidst the substandard housing, the lack of play space, the taverns, the vice and crime that infiltrates around it, or perhaps snugly tucked into the sheltered life of the well-kept suburb? This involves a decision as to what is good in the present for the foundation of the future. Democracy in the abstract is not enough and democracy within the school only is not enough. The principle must be manifest in the total physical and social order of the community.

Designing and planning, or replanning a city as a whole can be carried out only through the community organized as municipality. Special corporations, such as the Port Authority of New York, can be organized to carry out specific tasks that integrate a region. The knowledge necessary for redesigning communities has been developed. The principles of the "garden city" and of the neighborhood unit plan have been formulated and tested. The school and the municipality can put this knowledge to work in light of the synoptic principle with a view to ordering an enriching life in all its manifold patterns. The school can prepare the knowledge and the enlightened citizen who can translate this knowledge into the structure of the community through the instrument of government.

Selected Readings

GENERAL WORKS

Bergler, Egon, *Urban Sociology*, McGraw-Hill Book Company, 1955.
Bernard, Jessie, *American Community Behavior*, The Dryden Press, 1949.
  An analysis of problems confronting American communities today.

Brunner, Edmund de S., and Hallenbeck, Wilbur C., *American Society: Urban and Rural Patterns*, Harper & Brothers, 1955.

Gist, Noel, and Halbert, L. A., *Urban Society*, Thomas Y. Crowell Company, 3rd rev. ed., 1948.

Hatt, Paul K., and Reiss, Albert, *Reader in Urban Sociology*, The Free Press, 1951.

Kolb, J. H., and Brunner, Edmund de S., *A Study of Rural Society*, Houghton Mifflin Company, 1946, chaps. 12–14.

Mumford, Lewis, *The Culture of Cities*, Harcourt, Brace and Company, 1938, chap. 3, "The Insensate Industrial Town," chap. 4, "Rise and Fall of Megalopolis," and chap. 6, "Social Basis of the New Urban Order."

Stein, Clarence, *Toward New Towns for America*, Public Administration Service, 1950. Shows, among other things, how later private building continued all the defects of urban design which Greenbelt demonstrated were unnecessary.

ON COMMUNITY PLANNING AND THE SCHOOL

"Building the Future City," *Annals of the American Academy of Political and Social Science*, November, 1945.

Caplow, Theodore (ed.), *City Planning*, University of Minnesota Press, 1950.

Dahir, James, *The Neighborhood Unit Plan, Its Spread and Acceptance*, Russell Sage Foundation, 1947.

Dewey, Richard, "The Neighborhood, Urban Ecology, and City Planning," *American Sociological Review*, August, 1950, pp. 502–507.

Gallion, Austin, *The Urban Pattern*, D. Van Nostrand Company, 1950.

Hillman, Arthur, *Community Organization and Planning*, The Macmillan Company, 1950.

Howard, Ebenezer, *Garden Cities of To-Morrow*, Faber and Faber, Ltd., 1949. The classic pioneering proposal for city reconstruction.

COMMUNITY STUDIES

Anderson, E. L., *We Americans*, Harvard University Press, 1937. Study of Burlington, Vt., with emphasis on the ethnic groups.

Bell, Earl, *Culture of a Contemporary Rural Community, Sublette, Kansas*, Bureau of Agricultural Economics, Government Printing Office, 1942.

Carr, Lowell, and Stermer, James, *Willow Run*, Harper & Brothers, 1951. A study of the unplanned war boom town under dominance of the market orientation.

Davis, Allison, Gardner, Burleigh B., and Gardner, Mary R., *Deep South*, University of Chicago Press, 1940. A study of Natchez, Miss., with emphasis on class relations and Negro-white relations.

Dollard, John, *Caste and Class in a Southern Town,* Yale University Press, 1937.

Drake, St. Clair, and Cayton, Horace, R. *Black Metropolis,* Harcourt, Brace and Company, 1945. A study of the Negro sub-community in Chicago.

Kollmorgen, Walter, *Culture of a Contemporary Rural Community, The Old Order Amish of Lancaster County, Pennsylvania,* Bureau of Agricultural Economics, Government Printing Office, 1942.

Leonard, Olson, and Loomis, Charles P., *Culture of a Contemporary Rural Community: El Cerrito, New Mexico,* Bureau of Agricultural Economics, Government Printing Office, 1942.

Lynd, Robert S., and Lynd, Helen M., *Middletown,* Harcourt, Brace and Company, 1929. Some interesting observations on the social and intellectual interests and activities in 1890 as compared with the life of the community in the middle twenties; chaps. XIII–XVI on the education of the young, with high-school emphasis, position of teachers in a middlewestern community.

Lynd, Robert S., and Lynd, Helen M., *Middletown in Transition,* Harcourt, Brace and Company, 1937.

MacDonald, Lois, *Labor Problems and the American Scene,* Harper & Brothers, 1938, chap. V, "Company Towns: Coal Camps," and chap. VI "Company Towns: Textile Mill Villages."

MacDonald, Lois, *Southern Mill Hills,* Alex L. Hillman, 1928.

McKay, Claude, *Harlem: Negro Metropolis,* E. P. Dutton and Company, 1940.

McLeish, Kenneth, and Young, Kimball, *Culture of a Contemporary Rural Community, Landaff, New Hampshire,* Bureau of Agricultural Economics, Government Printing Office, 1942.

Moe, Edward, and Taylor Carl, *Culture of a Contemporary Rural Community, Irwin, Iowa,* Bureau of Agricultural Economics, Government Printing Office, 1942.

Morgan, Arthur E., *The Small Community,* Harper & Brothers, 1942. An attempt to state the place of small communities in our contemporary society.

Pope, Liston, *Millhands and Preachers,* Yale University Press, 1942. A study of Gastonia.

Tuck, Ruth, *Not with the Fist,* Harcourt, Brace and Company, 1946. A community study with special emphasis on the life problems of Mexican-Americans in a southwest town.

Walker, Charles R., *Steeltown,* Harper & Brothers, 1950.

Warner, William Lloyd, *The Social Life of a Modern Community,* Yale University Press, 1941. Study of a New England City; chapter on the educational system.

Warner, W. Lloyd, et al., *Democracy in Jonesville*, Harper & Brothers, 1949. Summarizes research over a series of years in a small (6000 population) town in Illinois; emphasis on social class.

Warner, William Lloyd, and Srole, L., *The Social Systems of American Ethnic Groups*, Yale University Press, 1945. Discusses the significance of the school to the perpetuation and breakdown of ethnic groups.

West, James, *Plainville*, Columbia University Press, 1945. A detailed study of a small rural community in Missouri.

Whyte, William, *Street-Corner Society*, University of Chicago Press, 1943. Study of an Italian slum area.

Winslow, Jones, *Life, Liberty, and Property*, J. B. Lippincott Company, 1941. Study of Akron, Ohio, community conflict in a one-industry town.

Wynne, Waller, *Culture of a Contemporary Rural Community, Harmony, Georgia*, Bureau of Agricultural Economics, Government Printing Office, 1943.

Zimmerman, Carle Z., *The Changing Community*, Harper & Brothers, 1938. Contains a series of descriptions of New England communities.

Zimmerman, Carle Z., and Frampton, Merle, *Family and Society*, D. Van Nostrand Company, 1935. A series of case studies on communities.

PART III

THE STRUCTURE
AND ORGANIZATION
OF THE SCHOOL

Building and Equipment—
Instruments for Action

In Part II the analysis centered upon the socio-cultural context of the school. Three phases of this context were emphasized: (1) the value orientations, (2) the legal order, and (3) the community. These constitute the matrix in which the school exists. The school, as was emphasized in the beginning chapter, is a relatively independent, self-directing organization. Attention now will focus on the school as such, though, as the analysis proceeds, the interplay of the context with the structure and organization of the school will be worked out. The first point of analysis is the housing of education.

Most people have been in several school buildings during their educational life. Here is a physical stage on which the educational drama is taking place. The scene shifts from elementary school to high school to college, each distinctive in building and equipment. Have you ever considered what this equipment, the books, the rooms, the playgrounds, really meant to you? You may look back on it all with a feeling of satisfaction and pleasure or remember it as a drab, meager, depressing experience. To understand the school it is necessary to reflect on this material, objective aspect. What one does and even how one feels in the school is related to the physical structure. Why must this be so?

To act effectively man creates a physical world of structures, tools, and instruments. Without this material culture man is relatively impotent. In addition, the aesthetic qualities of life are revealed through the material cultural environment. The following autobiographical account illuminates this point and suggests the importance of the principle of education through things.

A teacher began her work in a school located in a small coal-mining town at a time when coal mining was a declining industry. In 1933, three years after she started to teach, the mines closed down completely. The village was located in a so-called backward area, rather isolated and without the refinements of town living. On her first day she hiked the regular two and one-half miles to the school.

The schoolhouse itself was the worst of the picture. Every pane of glass was broken, a form of vandalism I did not then understand. Its interior beggars description. The benches and desks were battered, carved, and broken. The floor was covered with glass, stones, sticks, and leaves. Everything was blanketed with dust. I wished I had brought my new broom—this, with a box of chalk, being the regular issue for a country school at that time. . . . I did manage to clean up the worst of the litter and heave it outside. . . . I gave the pupils book lists but soon found what I should have known, namely, their parents were too poor to buy books. Many families could not buy even paper and pencil. Last winter I taught geography out of a mail-order catalogue, history out of the community's own past, and health out of my own knowledge concerning human needs. Many a lesson has been brought in from our homes, mines, fields, stores and surroundings.

With a first enrollment of thirty-eight, she went after others who should be in school. With hard work and persuasion she ran up the total to seventy pupils at the end of the first month. This increase automatically added another teacher to the school by state law. At the end of three months the school had 110 pupils.

That first year we expanded into the Hardshell Baptist Church, only a few steps away. By the end of the next year, our log school had been transformed into a neat three-room frame building, a structure that was the pride and joy of the community. Between two of its rooms were folding doors, so that we could make an auditorium for school plays and other programs. Last year the enrollment was 158. As time went on, my thoughts flowed out more and more into community affairs. When I came to Cove, leisure pursuits were few and far between—prayer meetings, baptisms, a dance now and then, and neighborly visiting. By desperate efforts, I secured play equipment for the boys; a bat and ball, marbles, and other things. I got permission to use a level meadow across the creek, and soon adults were playing with us. More recently we bought a basketball and nets, and the game has swept over the Cove like wildfire. How I worked to get a rattlebox piano! It has proved to be the most educative piece of apparatus we possess, for it gives pinched little souls a taste of melody and rhythm.[1]

Here a sensitive, perceptive young woman tackled a problem with determination. Out of the meager resources and the great need she worked with others to build up this school as a vital community center. While she used the school to achieve certain narrow or immediate ends, such as teaching skills and techniques, her concern was with the whole of life, with leisure, with health, with aesthetics, with the school as part of the community. For the time being Shakespeare and Plato may remain unknown in Cove, but the community has become electrified with the opportunities in new experience. In helping the teacher build the school, the community also began to rebuild itself.

One of the more significant aspects of this world-building is the fact that people need things through which they can act, by which they can achieve their objectives. Education requires objects, things, so that schooling can really take place. A broken-down building, a broom, a box of chalk, and a mail-order catalogue are not the things that make for adequate education. To be sure, some kind of education can take place within the poverty of this scene. Note how the teacher determinedly acquired better buildings and more equipment so that she could reach her educational objectives. Richness and variety of experience is provided through these culture objects that she had organized into the school. She became even more of a teacher because she had these things. Education takes place through the use of things: the books, instruments, laboratories, kitchens, toys,

[1] Alvin Harlow, *Schoolhouse in the Foothills,* Simon and Schuster, 1936, quoted in Lloyd Cook, *Community Backgrounds of Education,* McGraw-Hill Book Company, 1938, pp. 8–12.

maps, chemicals, and the hundreds of items that constitute an order of buildings and equipment. The teacher aids the pupils to acquire skill in the manipulation of these things.

For most students and for the teacher as well this order of material things is already created, a preëxisting fact that is frequently difficult to change. The organization of equipment, facilities, classrooms, school building, and site involves some principle that sets it in motion, that brings the various items into a meaningful relationship. The nature of this organization will vary with the principle in it, which variation in the physical order is now to be examined.

CULTURAL VALUES AND THE MATERIAL ORDER

The material order of the school will express the value orientations described in Chapter 3. Parochial schools take on a religious coloration. St. Patrick's Elementary School in Mill City, for example, is a unit among other religious buildings. There is the convent for the teaching nuns, the parish house for the priests, and, across the street, St. Patrick's Church. As religion is the most important feature, the location of the buildings facilitates the inclusion of special religious activities in the school program. The boys and girls can readily be taken to the church. Every building proclaims its close religious connection—the name inscribed in the cornerstone, the crosses against the blue sky, the white statues of saints in the green grass. The dark fluttering garb of the nuns is also part of this physical world that symbolizes religion. The school in general expresses the architecture of the turn of the century: long high-ceilinged halls, large archways, long wooden stairways and wood floors, rooms about twenty-two by thirty foot long capable of holding twenty-five to forty chairs or screwed-down desks. All seems permeated with religion, for in each class the pictures, the decorations, even the books themselves portray this dominant value orientation. What differences will be found in the other value orientations?

The humanist view implies, to William Caudill, architect, a trend in educational practice toward an activity program, the project and unit method. "The architect," he says, "should interpret the curriculum in terms of architecture." What does this idea mean? If education and the curriculum stand for certain things, then architecture must meet these educational demands. Here are some aspects of this relationship, according to Mr. Caudill.[2]

Education	*Architecture*
1. Courses of study never regarded as finished products . . . always revised to meet arising needs.	1. Classrooms designed for flexibility . . . structure designed for future expansion . . . use of movable partitions.
2. Children aided in developing their interests and abilities.	2. Nook or corner in classrooms for individual instruction.
3. Children taught to work together . . . to develop a spirit of coöperation.	3. Classroom unit permits children to work in groups . . . movable furniture used.
4. Home, church, and community integrated by school . . . education of the adults as well as children.	4. Conference rooms provided for parents . . . meeting rooms for PTA neighborhood culture programs . . . night school.
5. Mathematical problems taken from the experiences and environment of the children.	5. Flower gardens, vegetable gardens and school ground landscape laid by students to teach arithmetic.
6. Health and physical development of the child given importance as well as the mental development.	6. Small health clinics essential for most schools, storage for records, medical supplies, sight-saving classrooms.
7. Flexible schedules provide activity programs as the need arises . . . no fixed schedule of classes.	7. Classrooms insulated from outside disturbances . . . while one class is having rhythm drills, an adjacent class may be having a quiet study period.

While this could be further elaborated, the principle is clear. The building, the equipment, the space are considered in terms of educational objectives and functions.

Our two examples have covered the religious and humanist orientations. If the point of view is that of the patriot-warrior than the equipment and the organization of space express his principles, the more extreme forms coming ever closer to approximating army camp life. If the business or common man orientation prevails, there may

[2] William Caudill, *Space for Teaching*, Bulletin of the Agricultural and Mechanical College of Texas, Vol. 12, No. 9, 1941, pp. 42–46.

be more vocational emphasis, more shops and labs and equipment for learning vocational skills. Perhaps proximity to hospitals, farms, factories, or businesses where part-time apprentice work can be experienced would be important.

OBSOLETE SCHOOL BUILDINGS

Modern educational practices are extremely difficult to carry out in obsolete buildings. The building not only sets the stage but determines in large part, or limits in any case, what activities, procedures, and schedules can be attempted. What is meant by an obsolete building?

An obsolete building may be structurally sound. It may last many more years.

These buildings usually have good walls, and good roofs, but lack many of the requirements for accommodating a modern educational program. They are generally of nonfireproof construction, with poor lighting; have no special rooms for art, music, shops, cafeteria, library, offices, clinics, gymnasium, and the like; and have inadequate heating plants, toilets in dark basement rooms, and poor plumbing. Moreover, these buildings are generally rectangular in shape, with windows on all four sides so that additions cannot be made generally without cutting off the light from some of the classrooms. These buildings generally have small sites and are set in the center of the site so that such playground as exists is badly cut up by the placement of the building.[3]

The classroom, moreover, is likely to be painted in dark brownish colors; desks are in fixed rows with very little free space; windows are to the left of the children when they are seated.

There are several guides for scoring the adequacy of school buildings. They represent an effort to make the evaluation of school buildings precise. Many communities have been scored. The following examples indicate the building and equipment problem in specific communities. These studies mean that communities have become concerned about the problem, and one of the first steps is to define its nature and extent. Since scoring guides are readily available, other communities can inaugurate such inventories.

[3] *American School Buildings,* American Association of School Administrators, 1949, p. 267.

Table 17 is taken from a survey of elementary schools in a small city of around 15,000 located near the Muskingum and Ohio rivers. It is a slowly growing city. Diversified business and industry and the surrounding rich agricultural area make for a stable community. There is a small college. Recreational, religious, and social opportunities are above average. It seems to be a pleasant community, except for the school housing. Three of the schools were so unfit that they were not scored in detail. Of the other five none is really satisfactory with the possible exception of Washington.

TABLE 17.   Total Scores and Scores of Five Areas on the McLeary Guide, for Eight Elementary Schools, 1949

| Name of Building | Total Score | Site (120) | Score on Major Areas | | | |
			Building Design and Structure (170)	Service Systems (225)	Class-rooms (315)	Special Rooms (170)
Washington	492	77	102	113	138	62
Norwood	383	28	64	133	117	41
Marion	341	36	58	94	111	42
Harmar	281	65	17	74	106	19
Willard	247	33	36	67	85	26
Fairview	150					
Pike	150					
Terberg	100					

Possible total score for each area is in parentheses. Scores of more than 900, excellent buildings; of 700–800, generally satisfactory; of 600–700, subsatisfactory but can be rehabilitated; of 500–600, borderline; of 400–500, generally unfit building; lower than 400, definitely unfit, inadequate, obsolete, or even dangerous.

SOURCE: F. H. McKelvey, *A Survey of Elementary School Building Needs in Marietta, Ohio*, College of Education, Ohio University, 1949, p. 30.

In Mill City three elementary schools scored 276, 559, 588 out of 1000 points on the Holy Arnold score card. The Shebaug school with a score of 559 is constructed along the traditional lines given above. West School with a score of 588 is a mixture of traditional and "modern" with movable furniture, gym, library, and other special facilities which Shebaug does not have. Oak School building was completely obsolete.

The two cities cited are rather small, but schools in larger cities may not be much better. A study of schools in a city of 430,000 was completed in 1942. There were sixty-eight school buildings: forty-nine were elementary schools, seven of which included ninth grade and above. Included also were one junior high school, eight high schools, and ten special schools. Two of the schools dated to 1840–49, and only four were built after 1930. On the basis of the Strayer-Engelhardt 1000-point score cards, twenty-eight were rated as poor or inferior, nineteen as fair, and twelve as good or superior. Forty-six percent of the buildings were obsolete. Most of these were elementary schools. Children will then have very different experiences because of these differences in structure. Inequality of opportunity is evident in the very physical structure; it is not a planned discrimination but one resulting from negligence in keeping both city and schools up to date. Obsolete school buildings are but a phase in the general blight of cities—the cited case is not unusual. The survey states, "A similar problem exists in Manhattan of New York City, in Philadelphia, Pittsburgh, Cleveland, St. Louis, and in the other giant cities of America." [4] Nor is the problem merely urban, for many rural schools are equally out of date.

TABLE 18.   Enrollments Housed in Various Buildings
by Rating Categories, 1942

Rating of School Building	Number of Pupils	Percent of Enrollment
Inferior	7,637	10.9
Inferior or poor	28,040	40.0
Superior	10,092	14.4
Superior or good	15,652	22.3

SOURCE: *Report of a Survey of Public Schools of Newark, New Jersey,* Teachers College, Columbia University, 1942, p. 110.

A 1937 school survey in Texas showed the following inadequacies. One out of ten schools had *no* toilet facilities. Seven out of ten had pit toilets. Two out of ten had flush toilets. In 3634 schools there was no artificial illumination. About an equal number used oil; about 600 used gas. Only 3193 out of the 11,068 schools surveyed had electricity, but having electricity is no guarantee that the lighting is ade-

[4] *Ibid.*, p. 110.

quate. Six out of every seven Texas schools had inadequate sites. It was estimated that about 40 percent of the schools were run-down and obsolete.[5]

The Office of Education stated in 1937: "During the pre-World War [I] period there was little or no scientific schoolhouse planning. The majority of buildings constructed at that time are now obsolescent from the standpoint of both educational needs and of modern school building construction." [6] It estimated that 39.3 percent of all buildings in 506 cities of 10,000 and over were obsolete.[7]

In 1943 the National Resources Planning Board, in a report to the House of Representatives, stated: "From information available it appears probable that half of the school children below college grade are now housed in school buildings that are either obsolete or poorly located. These pupils should be rehoused as rapidly as possible in structures adapted to modern educational techniques and community needs. . . . Structures likely to outlast the educational theories they exemplify are to be avoided." [8]

SOME CURRENT ASPECTS OF THE BUILDING PROBLEM

One cannot ignore the fact that there are many fine school buildings.[9] Mrs. Hobart, an Ohio elementary-school teacher, comments about her new school building, which is a separate unit in addition to an old one built in 1889:

This year, 1951, a modern twelve room building was completed. It is all one floor except for the boiler room and shower rooms. The building contains twelve class rooms, a clinic, library, kindergarten room, office, supply rooms, adequate toilets, and a multiple purpose room which serves as a dining hall, gymnasium, and an auditorium. In planning the building it was thought that this plan and this amount of space would be ample. Now that we are in the building we find we need an extra room to house the large first grade. There are now two first grades. We need room for

[5] William Caudill, op. cit., p. 2–3.
[6] Alice Barrows, The School Building Situation and Needs, U.S. Department of the Interior, Office of Education, Bulletins 1937, No. 35, p. 1.
[7] Ibid., pp. 59–60.
[8] National Resources Planning Board, Development Report for 1943, Post-war Planning and Progress, Government Printing Office, 1943, p. 1.
[9] Cf. William Caudill, op. cit.; Alfred Roth, The New School, Grisberger (Zurich), 1950; Good and Bad School Plants in the United States, U.S. Department of Health, Education, and Welfare, Special Publication No. 2, Government Printing Office, 1954.

a third one. We also need storage space for extra desks and other large items. We also find that the gymnasium, which we needed so badly for indoor games during the noon hours, will be in use as a lunch room for both elementary and high school during practically all of the noon hour.

Otherwise the building is quite adequate. The blonde moveable furniture permits varied seating arrangements, as do also the non-glare windows and desk tops. In each class room there is more than ample storage space in the form of cupboards and drawers. There is a sink in each room which solves the problem of cleaning up after the use of paste, paints, etc. Green glass boards placed at the correct height for the use of the child are pleasant both to look at and to use. Asphalt-tile flooring is easy on the feet and also tends to minimize noise. The building has sound-proof walls which is a boon to teacher's nerves. This new building has so many, many improvements over the old one that the few inadequacies can be overlooked. [Document prepared for the author.]

This new school is not a perfect one, but note how pleased and satisfied the teacher is. At the same time we should note the trends that account for the housing problem in education.

The growth of the child population is one of the major factors in today's school housing program, but the spurt of the birth rate during the first part of the 1940's is not the whole explanation. For about twenty years little was done about the housing of pupils. During the depression that began in 1929 school building except for WPA construction was at a standstill. In those days there was not even enough money to pay teachers regularly. Many schools could not afford adequate maintenance. During World War II and the Korean conflict supplies and raw materials had to be used for war purposes, and thus little was available for school construction. The tremendous internal migration that took place during the war years, especially to the centers where war plants and camps were located, hastened the overuse of schools and their obsolescence.

One of the important factors perpetuating obsolete building practices is the school building codes. These legislative prescriptions for school buildings are dated. Many of them are so restrictive that they prevent the adoption of newer methods, materials, and design. The law is in this instance a drag upon the progressive possibilities in school architecture. Where the codes have been revised or where they are flexible enough, there has been a trend away from schools as civic monuments, from dominating, columned fronts, from multi-storied structures to informal, single-storied buildings with inviting entrances in park-like settings, the scale of the buildings adapted to the children's needs. Scaled fountains, blackboards, etc., are created to fit the primary and intermediate ages.

Despite modern trends in school building the plight of school housing remains. The situation in the immediate past is as follows.

A survey in 1947 based upon 1600 reports of communities having 2500 population and up highlights some of the school housing needs of city school systems. Fifty-one percent of the cities had one or more overcrowded schools. Overcrowding increased consistently with city size, from 46 percent in the very small cities to 75 percent in those with a population of 100,000 and over. The problem is predominantly an elementary-school problem at present. It will become more and more a senior-high-school problem as the war-born children reach high-school age.

The overload in the overcrowded school buildings is estimated as 31 percent more than their rated capacity. This overcrowding is emphasized in Table 19.

Many boards of education have resorted to makeshift housing arrangements to avoid either overcrowding or half-day sessions. Arrangements for temporary use include (1) portable or other temporary building; (2) rented space in churches, halls, residences, etc.; (3) continued use, on a temporary and special-permit basis, of

TABLE 10. Percent of City School Buildings of Specified Types That Are Overcrowded and Percent of Pupils Attending Schools in Overcrowded Buildings

Type of Building	Percent Buildings Overcrowded	Pupils in Overcrowded Buildings
Elementary school	18	22
Junior high	15	15
Senior high	21	25
Other types	17	24
All schools	18	22

SOURCE: School Housing Needs in City School Systems 1947–48, NEA *Research Bulletin,* December, 1948, p. 151, adapted from Figure IV.

obsolete buildings that have been officially condemned as unsafe, unsanitary, or otherwise unfit for use. Of the cities reporting, 15 percent used a portable or other temporary building, 9 percent rented buildings, and 24 percent used buildings condemned as obsolete. About 400,000 pupils in these cities are housed for at least part of the day in these temporary, rented, or obsolete buildings. For the nation as a whole this figure might come to 675,000 to 700,000, around 5 percent of the pupils. This percentage must be viewed in relation to the overcrowded buildings and double-session days that many schools have. Smaller communities tend to use condemned buildings for school use whereas the larger cities use temporary structures.

Half-day sessions were used in 5 percent of the cities involving 2 percent of the total enrollments. This would come to around 123,000 pupils. For the nation as a whole this figure might come to 200,000 pupils. Many school superintendents, moreover, thought that they would have to add half-day sessions. The half-day sessions fall heaviest on the first, second, and third grades.

The following data summarize the results of the most recent nation-wide survey, 1952. On the basis of forty-three states, 37 percent of the elementary schools were unsatisfactory, 38 percent were fair, and 25 percent were satisfactory. Many of the unsatisfactory elementary buildings were outmoded one- and two-room frame structures. Of secondary-school plants for the forty-three states 14 percent were unsatisfactory, 38 percent were fair, and 48 percent were satisfactory. Of combined elementary- and secondary-school plants 21 percent were unsatisfactory, 51 percent were fair, and 28 percent were satisfactory. For all types combined, 33 percent were unsatisfactory, 40 percent were fair, and 27 percent were satisfactory.[10]

The school plants surveyed housed 20,156,045 pupils. The data did not include pupils housed in churches, warehouses, garages, and other types of rented or donated structures. Of this number 18 percent were housed in unsatisfactory school plants, 42 percent in

[10] *Report of the Status Phase of the School Facilities Survey*, Office of Education, U.S. Department of Health, Education, and Welfare, Government Printing Office, December, 1943, pp. 56–57.

those rated fair, and 40 percent in those rated satisfactory. Again the elementary population was poorly housed, 22 percent in unsatisfactory school plants, 39 percent in plants rated fair, and 39 percent in structures rated satisfactory. High-school students were better housed, with 10 percent in plants rated unsatisfactory, 36 percent in structures rated fair, and 54 percent in satisfactory school plants. Of the population in combined elementary and secondary school plants 15 percent were in unsatisfactory structures, 53 percent in fair, and 32 percent in satisfactory.[11]

A total of 124,437 acres of land is needed for school sites, 82,362 acres for new sites and 42,075 acres for enlarging existing areas. Costs would be as follows: $360,022,064, with $169,541,893 for new sites and their improvements, $137,340,268 for the enlargement of existing sites, and $53,139,903 for the improvement of existing sites.[12]

Increase in pupil capacity through remodeling and rehabilitation was estimated at 122,114 pupils for elementary schools and 55,668 for secondary schools. With a thirty-pupil maximum per classroom, the net increase in pupil capacity possible would be 251,463—equivalent to the construction of 8382 classrooms.[13]

Pupils needing new housing in 1952 came to 6,984,596, including 3,575,699 in obsolete or otherwise unsatisfactory plants; 2,111,916 to relieve overcrowded conditions in satisfactory and fair classrooms; and 1,296,981, the anticipated increase in enrollment March, 1951–September, 1952. The estimated total cost for new housing was $7,408,267,989 to relieve overcrowded classrooms, to house enrollment increases, to replace obsolete buildings, and for noninstructional additions to existing buildings.[14]

The total number of school buses needed for all purposes, minus duplication, came to 28,583: 10,737 of these to replace obsolete publicly owned equipment; 6080 to improve and extend service; 3688 to accommodate pupils involved as a result of school consolidation; 7175 to convert from private contracts and common carriers to school-owned buses; and 2265 to accommodate increased

[11] *Ibid.*, pp. 58–59.
[12] *Ibid.*, pp. 70–72.
[13] *Ibid.*, pp. 66–68.
[14] *Ibid.*, pp. 74–127.

school enrollments. The total cost was estimated at $122,666,584.[15]

For 1950–51 the total capital outlay need for forty-three states was $8,309,621,034. The applicable resources were $4,578,301,970, and the total remaining deficit was $3,731,319,064. The total cost needs of the nation's school plants as of September, 1952, were estimated at $10,566,213,639 with a total estimated deficit or lack of resource of $4,744,610,401.[16] Capital outlay adjusted to 1951 cost levels came to $1,725,000—24 percent of total expenditures in 1952.[17]

These statistics must be viewed in human terms; i.e., schooling for a large proportion of children is carried out under very unfavorable circumstances. What should be an enriching, creative experience, considering the amount of time a child spends in school, under these conditions is likely to be drab, barren, and meager. Fortunate are those in well-designed school plants.

ARCHITECTURE AND PERSONALITY GROWTH

Buildings and equipment either contribute to good personality growth or inhibit it. "Personality" and "growth" are broad terms, involving many aspects of our being. Physical, intellectual, aesthetic, and social factors all enter the picture and are affected by the day-to-day experiences in school. Compare those two pictures, and their probable effect on personality development:

It was a rather dark basement room. The children were sitting with their backs to the windows. The walls were bare of decoration. There was no evidence of paintings or other creative work by the children. The teacher was dressed in sober black, speaking in a loud, strained voice. The children showed little animation and interest in what she said. They squirmed in their seats. They were noisy.

The classroom was a sunny room, overlooking a great expanse of rolling hills. The teacher's bright smock made a colorful spot wherever she happened to be. For the most part the children's own drawings, clay models and woodwork adorned the display places in the room.[18]

Without staying to watch the activities of either of these groups,

[15] *Ibid.*, pp. 82–83.
[16] *Ibid.*, p. 86.
[17] *Ibid.*, p. 19.
[18] Bernice Baxter, *Teacher-Pupil Relations,* The Macmillan Company, 1941, pp. 77–78.

we could surmise certain things merely from this brief impression of the physical scene. The value placed on creativity is apparent in the second example, as is the emphasis on color, action, and closeness to the world of nature. The contrast with the static, barren, shut-between-walls atmosphere of the first example is sharp indeed.

The various aspects of growth are interlinked, as are the various aspects of the school as a physical fact. To analyze a fact or a process it is necessary to split up the whole into parts and examine them separately. Some features of the surrounding physical world of the school which are of direct importance and should be examined carefully are: air, heat, sound, color and light, safety.

A home economics teacher in an Indiana high school, reflecting on "my ideal school facilities," emphasizes consideration for beauty:

> Schools should be the most beautiful, most colorful of all gathering places, but in reality they are the most desolate of places. All rooms should be made colorful, and we should avoid institutionalization of color. We now have four choices of color: cream, gray, green and yellow. I am sick of buff and dado brown. Perhaps the art teacher can appreciate gray. The classroom should be restful and comfortable and should provide an emotional environment conducive to study. "Color is not a neutral factor in education. . . . Good combinations of color are an outward sign of cultural activities. Children should acquire a feeling for color and skill in the use of it." [19]

She is discussing what has been called "chromo-therapy," the use of color in inducing moods or emotional feelings. A drab world of buff and dado-brown floors, furniture, walls, and moldings, flanked by blackboards, is not an aesthetically exciting world and may produce equally drab feelings in the person who must live in these surroundings.

Color is also a question of adequate lighting. How many classrooms are there where students seated near the windows have a problem of glare and those seated farthest away do not have enough light? In either case, there is strain, possible headache, poor work. If a child has deficiencies in vision, they may become worse. Sight-saving ought to be built into the structure.

[19] Indiana and Midwest School Building Planning Conference, *Proceedings,* vol. XXIV, No. 5, Division of Research and Field Services, Indiana University, 1948, p. 13.

Let us consider briefly the question of sound. The author has been an observer in a classroom where the teacher speaking at one end of the room could be heard only as an indistinct mumble at the other. By shifting around one could find dead and live spots in the rear of this room. Meanwhile street noises would frequently rush in with such power that all communication would momentarily fail. Halls and stairways often function as resonating chambers, compounding any noise or disturbance. Sound activities from the first floor work their way up to the second floor. Noise may screech in from neighboring rooms. In many schools with makeshift arrangements the problem becomes almost unbearable. Mrs. Keen, commenting on the physical structure of her school, says,

Lincoln was and still is a modern building, highly rated by state inspectors, but due to the increased population many makeshift adjustments have had to be made in order to convert more space into classrooms. For example, my room was at one time a very large room used for music, art and meetings of the Girl Scouts and of the Mothers' Club. Now it is divided by a thin, definitely *not* [her italics] soundproof wall. Between the clamor of would-be musicians on the other side of the wall, and the noise of screeching saws in the Industrial Arts Department across the hall, I endeavor to teach in a constant cacophony of noise. [Document written for the author.]

The obvious answer lies in the constitution of soundproof buildings, or possibly in soundproofing existing structures if funds for such improvement could be secured.

Direct dangers to physical well-being may be inherent in the equipment of a school—furniture that makes for poor posture, ventilating systems that distribute disease germs, heating systems that produce unequal temperatures, drafty rooms, shops and workrooms that have safety hazards. In the effort to bring about the fullest development of the child's body, mind, and whole personality the teacher should have every possible support from the physical arrangements of the school. Inadequacies in these physical factors do not declare themselves openly to anyone. To find them takes careful study.

ARCHITECTURE, INSTITUTIONAL ORDER, AND SOCIAL RELATIONS

Building, layout, and equipment are points of reference for action. They become elements in action. They organize the normative and functional orders, the institutional order of the school.

It may seem obvious that architecture is a determinant of the functional order. No gym, no auditorium, no stage, no manual training room, no school kitchen facilities, little playground equipment, no audio-visual aids equipment—as soon as such a list is made, one can almost feel the area of experience contracting, the possibilities of a curriculum becoming limited. On the other hand, if these facilities are available, then the potentialities for enriched experience are great. It is perhaps equally obvious that size of classroom and type of furniture put strict limits on the functional order. A teacher at the Banholm School comments, "All seats are stationary and cover most of the floor space. There is practically no opportunity for arranging the children for discussion groups or project work. There is little space for recreational activity." (Document written for the author.) Fixed desks don't allow flexibility in program. Where there is unattached furniture, the organization of the physical order expresses a principle of freedom and spontaneity, and both children's and teacher's opportunities are potentially greater.

It is not surprising that there are a host of norms regulating conduct around the drinking fountains. In West School in Mill City, for example, there were four drinking fountains in the halls. Three were on the second floor and two of these were condemned as unhygienic and were not used. The other fountain was on the first floor. Since the means of securing water were scarce, the situation was an obvious setup for the dissociative effects of competition. Crowd behavior was likely to result if the restraining influence of the teacher was absent. During hot weather the thirsty children, particularly after a playground session, rushed pell-mell for the fountain. A huge line of pushing, struggling, arguing children wound around the hall, while the teacher, spurred by possibilities of legal liability, endeavored to maintain order, manners, and safety.

Scarcity of equipment such as balls and bats, easels and paints, etc., may also create situations of limited opportunities so that there is a regular grab or scramble for what equipment there is. Competition, recrimination, dislikes, arguments, if not violence, result. Again the teacher has to intervene, via a system of rules, to try to organize the situation equitably. However, if a girl is enthusiastic about an idea she has for painting a picture today, the fact that her "turn" for painting comes next week may not console her for the loss of this activity at a time when she was interested in it.

If the architecture of the school ignores the informal social relations and social needs of children, they will reinterpret the facilities in ways not originally intended. In one school, at least in some of the lower grades observed, the lavatory became a place of social privacy, a place where the child could loaf by himself or with close friends, where he could get away from the numerous children and interstimulation in the classrooms. It was a place where plans were hatched, also a place where a child could have an emotional release without many eyes staring at him. In a crisis which a child could not control, the lavatory, unless the teacher took him elsewhere, was the place of refuge.

The distance between school and home is itself a fact of great consequence, especially in rural areas where the distance is too great to walk. For the young child it means riding away part of his life on a school bus. The longer the ride, the earlier the child must get up and the later he returns home. On the high-school level this means that participation in extracurricular activities is either negligible or entirely impossible. The bus cannot wait. Unless such activities are merged with the day's schedule, all these supposedly rich opportunities are denied, and this denial may be viewed as a result of the relation between home and school site. It also means that the home activities of these children are geared to the time schedule of the school bus.

Perhaps another aspect should be mentioned, in view of the large number of proponents for consolidated schools. On field trips in rural areas the author was always impressed by an argument offered in opposition of this movement. "Every time," said a 72-year-old chicken farmer, "one of our little neighborhood schools close and they start taking the children to the consolidated school, the neighborhood falls apart." Now it is maintained by researchers that special-interest groups are taking the place of the rural neighborhood, and that they are dying out anyway. If so, the consolidated school has assisted in giving the neighborhood its coup de grâce. This is an instance of the wider context of social relations which can be influenced by the school.

A last point about the school building is its influence on scheduling. The inclusion of special rooms, such as gym, auditorium, art and music rooms, was introduced in an effort to bring more variety and richness into the program. However, at the same time that the content of the program was expanding, the idea of flexibility and spontaneity in school experience was being advocated. The idea was to get away from the humdrum routine drabness of school drill and to move toward something more like the normal patterns of growth resulting from participation in meaningful experiences and spontaneous interests. However, the very fact that there are these facilities to be shared by various classes almost automatically produces a routinized time schedule, with special activities set for certain times and other regular activities worked in around them.

SUMMARY

Education goes on in a physical world which limits and defines in very important ways the possibilities for learning and growth. The stage is set, and the play is thereby already partially determined. The means are rich with possibilities and offer many alternatives, or they are meager and inadequate. They may unleash creative potentialities or may be a stunting and depressing element in a child's life. The building and equipment may be a factor in making for coöperative or antagonistic social relations. They become an element in organizing the normative and functional order of the school. In so far as they tend to be a routinizing factor, they may limit spontaneity.

Our values are built into our schools. The design and layout of the building and grounds express assumptions about how a school should function. Freedom and spontaneity in school experience will be achieved by arranging the building and its objects so that they can serve these principles. Larger amounts of space, unattached furniture, and more special facilities for varied activities are likely to be features. If rigidity, strict order, and performance of standardized tasks are desired, the building too will tend to express these ideas. If aesthetic values are important, they should be embodied in the school building, rather than being simply relegated to a course an art teacher gives. Safety and health, likewise, are influenced by the engineer and architect as well as by the curriculum builders. The choice of a school site is itself an expression of certain values. The physical fact of great distance between home and school will lessen the possibility of the school's being an important element in the total life of the community.

Since many of our school buildings were built in accordance with older educational ideas, there is a distinct clash between educational theory and this material order, which acts as a cultural drag. Much of school housing is not adequate, but since most of it will not be replaced in the near future, there is a real challenge to teachers and parents to rehabilitate this physical world as much as possible if they want to make the child's school experience emotionally, intellectually, and aesthetically satisfying.

Figures 4–17, which follow, constitute a graphic summary of the school housing problem (from *Report of the Status Phase of the School Facilities Survey*, Office of Education, U.S. Department of Health, Education, and Welfare, December, 1953).

Selected Readings

American School Building, Twenty-Seventh Yearbook, American Association of School Administrators, 1949.

Caudill, William, *Space for Teaching*, Bulletin of the Agricultural and Mechanical College of Texas, Fourth Series, Vol. 12, No. 9, 1941.

Cocking, Walter, and Perkins, Laurence B., *Schools*, Reinhold Publishing Corporation, 1949.

Designing Elementary Classrooms, U.S. Department of Health, Education, and Welfare, Special Publication No. 1, Government Printing Office, 1953.

Engelhardt, N. L., Engelhardt, N. L. Jr., and Leggett, *Spaces and Their Sizes*, published by authors, 1950.

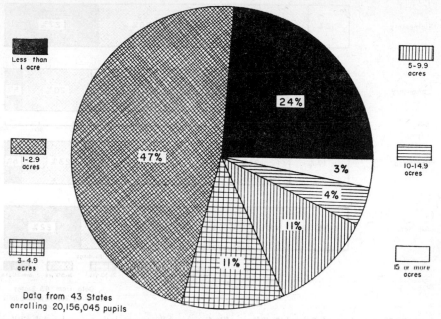

Less than 1 acre

5-9.9 acres

1-2.9 acres

10-14.9 acres

3-4.9 acres

15 or more acres

24%

3%

4%

11%

11%

47%

Data from 43 States
enrolling 20,156,045 pupils

FIGURE 4. Size of School Sites. Suggested standards by the National Council on Schoolhouse Construction (*Guide for Planning School Plants,* George Peabody College for Teachers, 1953 ed., pp. 26–28): elementary school, minimum site of five acres plus an additional acre for each 100 pupils of predicted ultimate maximum enrollment; junior and senior high school, minimum site of ten acres plus an additional acre for each 100 pupils of predicted ultimate enrollment.

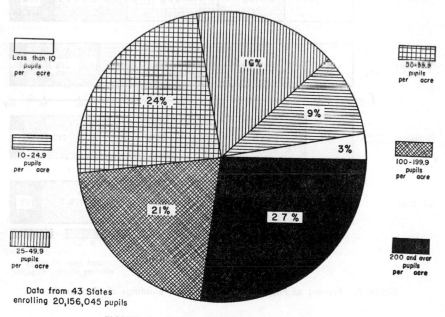

Less than 10 pupils per acre

30-99.9 pupils per acre

10-24.9 pupils per acre

100-199.9 pupils per acre

25-49.9 pupils per acre

200 and over pupils per acre

16%

9%

3%

24%

21%

27%

Data from 43 States
enrolling 20,156,045 pupils

FIGURE 5. Percent of Pupils per Acre of Site.

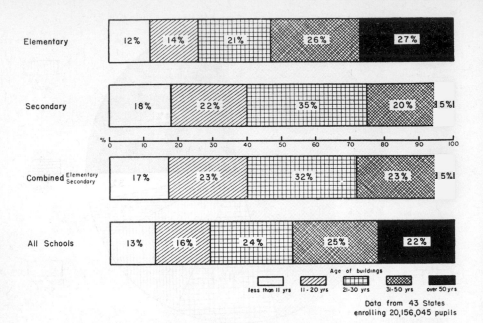

FIGURE 6. Age of School Buildings. "It is generally agreed that a school building more than 30 years old is beginning to reach a stage of educational obsolescence unless it has been extensively remodeled and modernized."

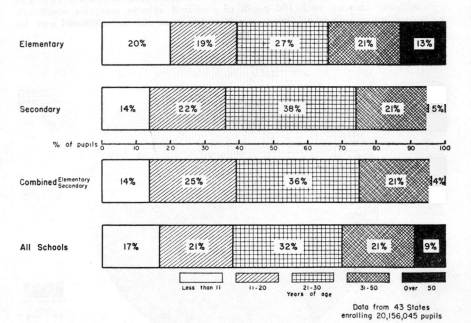

FIGURE 7. Percent of Pupils Housed in School Buildings of Various Ages.

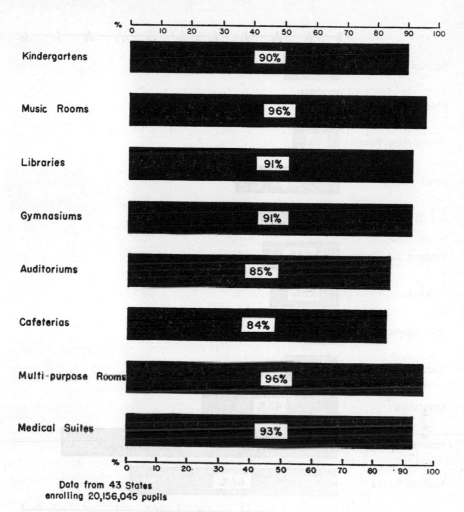

%

| | 0 | 10 | 20 | 30 | 40 | 50 | 60 | 70 | 80 | 90 | 100 |

Kindergartens   90%

Music Rooms   96%

Libraries   91%

Gymnasiums   91%

Auditoriums   85%

Cafeterias   84%

Multi-purpose Rooms   96%

Medical Suites   93%

%

| | 0 | 10 | 20 | 30 | 40 | 50 | 60 | 70 | 80 | 90 | 100 |

Data from 43 States
enrolling 20,156,045 pupils

FIGURE 8. Percent of Elementary-School Plants *Not* Providing Certain Types of Rooms. Figure does not give an evaluation of the adequacy of special room facilities in school plants having them. It shows only the degree of absence of such special rooms. School plants having combination facilities such as auditorium-gymnasium are considered as having both.

147

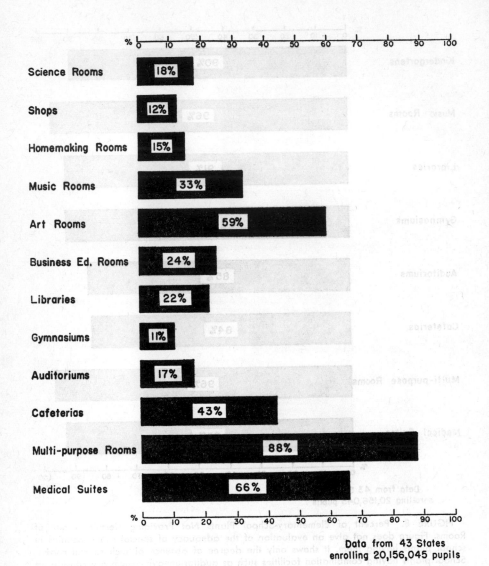

FIGURE 9. Percent of Secondary-School Plants *Not* Providing Certain Types of Rooms.

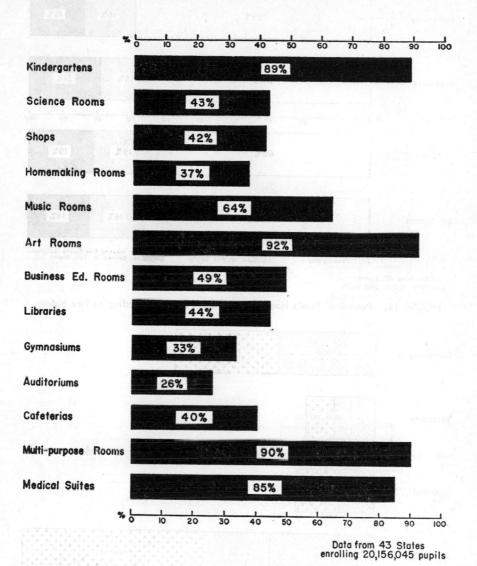

%

| | 0 | 10 | 20 | 30 | 40 | 50 | 60 | 70 | 80 | 90 | 100 |

Kindergartens — 89%

Science Rooms — 43%

Shops — 42%

Homemaking Rooms — 37%

Music Rooms — 64%

Art Rooms — 92%

Business Ed. Rooms — 49%

Libraries — 44%

Gymnasiums — 33%

Auditoriums — 26%

Cafeterias — 40%

Multi-purpose Rooms — 90%

Medical Suites — 85%

%

Data from 43 States
enrolling 20,156,045 pupils

FIGURE 10. Percent of combined Elementary-Secondary Plants *Not* Providing Certain Types of Rooms.

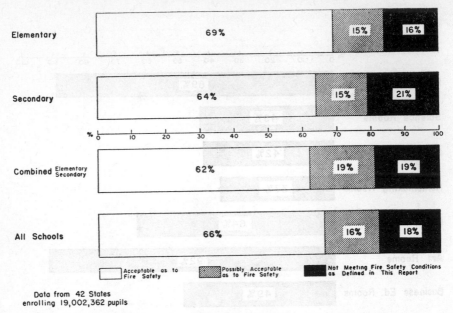

Elementary   69%   15%   16%

Secondary   64%   15%   21%

% 0   10   20   30   40   50   60   70   80   90   100

Combined Elementary Secondary   62%   19%   19%

All Schools   66%   16%   18%

☐ Acceptable as to Fire Safety   ▨ Possibly Acceptable as to Fire Safety   ■ Not Meeting Fire Safety Conditions as Defined in This Report

Data from 42 States
enrolling 19,002,362 pupils

FIGURE 11. Percent of Pupils Housed in Buildings Rated According to Fire Safety.

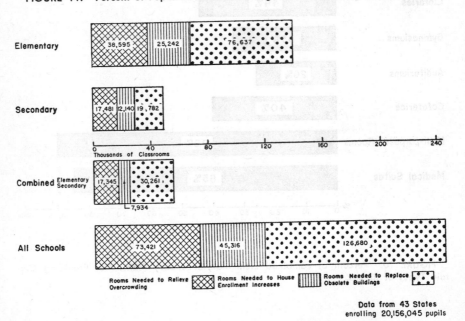

Elementary   38,595   25,242   76,637

Secondary   17,481   12,140   19,782

0   40   80   120   160   200   240
Thousands of Classrooms

Combined Elementary Secondary   17,345   30,261
└ 7,934

All Schools   73,421   45,316   126,680

▨ Rooms Needed to Relieve Overcrowding   ▧ Rooms Needed to House Enrollment Increases   ▥ Rooms Needed to Replace Obsolete Buildings

Data from 43 States
enrolling 20,156,045 pupils

FIGURE 12. Number of New Classrooms Currently Needed.

150

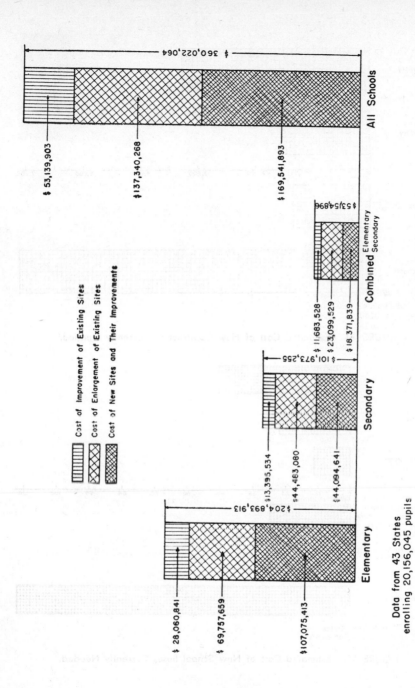

FIGURE 13. Estimated Costs of Needed Site Acquisitions and Improvements.

Data from 43 States
enrolling 20,156,045 pupils

Cost of Improvement of Existing Sites

Cost of Enlargement of Existing Sites

Cost of New Sites and Their Improvements

All Schools

$ 360,022,064

$ 53,139,903

$137,340,268

$169,541,893

Combined Elementary
Secondary

$ 53,154,896

$ 11,683,528

$ 23,099,529

$ 18 371,839

Secondary

$ 101,973,255

$13,395,534

$44,483,080

$44,094,641

Elementary

$ 204,893,913

$ 28,060,841

$ 69,757,659

$107,075,413

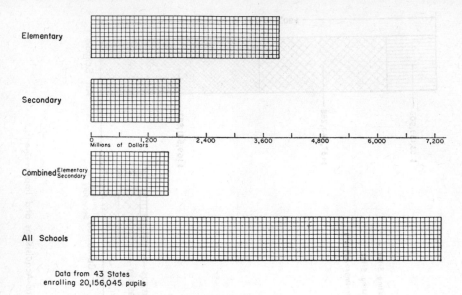

FIGURE 14. Estimated Cost of New Construction Currently Needed.

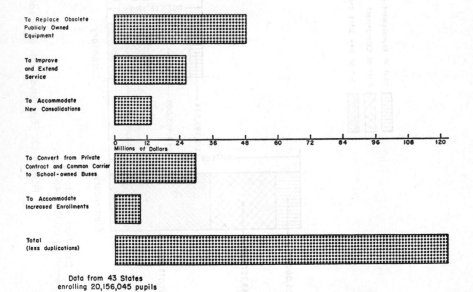

FIGURE 15. Estimated Cost of New School Buses Currently Needed.

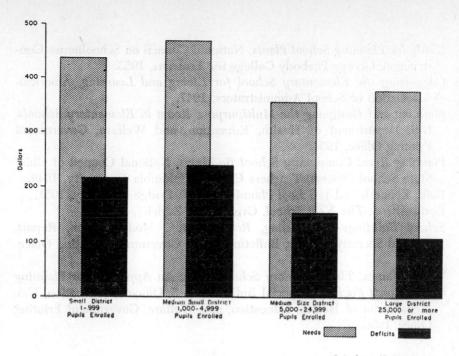

Data from 43 States
enrolling 20,156,045 pupils

FIGURE 16. Current Per-Pupil Capital Outlay Needs and Deficits by Size of School District.

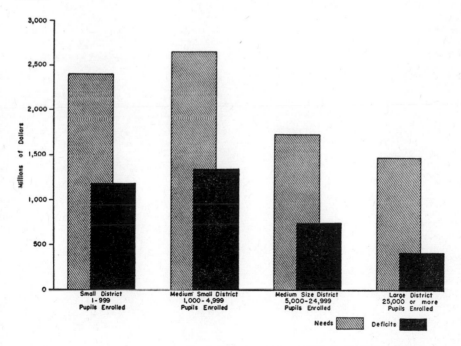

Data from 43 States
enrolling 20,156,045 pupils

FIGURE 17. Current Capital Outlay Needs and Deficits by Size of School District.

Guide for Planning School Plants, National Council on Schoolhouse Construction, George Peabody College for Teachers, 1953.

Organizing the Elementary School for Living and Learning, American Association of School Administrators, 1947.

Planning and Designing the Multipurpose Room in Elementary Schools, U.S. Department of Health, Education, and Welfare, Government Printing Office, 1954.

Planning Rural Community School Buildings, National Council of Chief State School Officers, Teachers College, Columbia University, 1949.

Reid, Kenneth (ed.), *School Planning*, F. W. Dodge Company, 1951.

Roth, Alfred, *The New School*, Grisberger (Zurich), 1950.

School Buildings—Remodeling, Rehabilitation, Modernization, Repair, Federal Security Agency, Bulletin No. 17, Government Printing Office, 1950.

Taylor, James, *The Secondary School Plant: An Approach for Planning Functional Facilities*, Special Bulletin No. 5, Office of Education, U.S. Department of Health, Education, and Welfare, Government Printing Office, 1956.

CHAPTER 7

The Functional Order

A BRIEF GLANCE BACKWARDS

THE FUNCTIONAL order of the school today is a changing one. Putting current battle cries and controversies aside, we can look at the mildest and most conservative of our schools and see that momentous changes have taken place. Our present "traditional" schools are quite different from the earlier forms of education, and the label "modern" doubtless was hurled at these schools at one time. What was the earlier form like and what changes have taken place?

THE SCHOOL AS FACTORY

The idea that a school should be organized like a factory is an old view that was correlated with the rise of the factory system. The factory was the model. How many pupils could be educated at the lowest possible cost; how was the school to be organized to educate them? The answer to these questions was the Lancasterian and Madras systems. Originating in England, they became quite widespread in the United States during the 1830's and 1840's. What were these educational factories like?

In the Manchester Lancasterian School [the observer] would have found over a thousand close-packed children, sitting on benches, all being taught in one room, with only two masters and one mistress in charge.

At first the noise would have been deafening, the crowd bewildering but soon he would have noticed that there was order and system in the apparent chaos, that the multitude obeyed certain words and commands such as "sling hats," "clean slates," and acted as one child, that each nine or ten boys were in charge of another boy called a monitor, who taught them the lesson that he had lately learned himself, either summoning them to stand round him in one of the semicircles marked in the passage at the end of the forms and teaching them to read from a board with the lesson printed large upon it, or else standing at the end of the form on which they were sitting and dictating to them words of the number of syllables suitable to their particular class. Dictation for the whole school was a triumph of organization. On the platform at one end sat the master, and at a signal from him, or from the "monitor-general," a sort of sergeant-major among children, the monitor of the highest class would lead off with his four-syllabled word, followed in turn by each monitor in the hierarchy down to the bottom. When the process had been repeated for six words, each monitor examined the slates of his charges and signalled to the master by means of a "telegraph" or signboard fixed at the end of the form; as soon as corrections were made, and all the telegraphs turned the right way, the master gave the signal again and another six words were dictated.[1]

It is not surprising that Lancaster claimed he had "invented, under the blessing of Divine Providence, a new and mechanical system of Education," and that Bell, inventor of the rival Madras system, wrote in eulogy, "While it bears a manifest analogy to the mechanical powers, it infinitely surpasses them in simplicity, economy, force, and effect. With great propriety it has been called the *steam engine* of the moral world." [2] The monitorial system was acclaimed for two reasons: the mass handling of pupils, and low cost. It worked by creating a strictly uniform and rigid functional order, emphasizing drill, rote memory, and question-answer recitation.

Just as these rival systems had their supporters in England, so too a certain amount of factionalism developed in the United States when they were imported.

Yet for all the huffing and puffing of these steam engines of the moral world and the blessing of Divine Providence, the wheels wobbled to a lurching stop as the educational steam vanished in a

[1] J. L. Hammond and Barbara Hammond, *The Bleak Age*, Penguin Books, rev. ed., 1947, p. 143. Reprinted with the permission of Longmans Green & Co., Ltd.
[2] *Ibid.*, p. 150.

faint sigh from the empty monitorial cylinders. The pistons of progress clattered to the floor. The systems simply did not work. They were, no doubt, a triumph in formalism and routine, a "mechanization" of human relations, but the results were reading, writing, and answering questions without comprehension. One English school inspector who deviated from the routine pattern of questioning secured chaotic results:

Q. Who were the Gentiles?   A. People of God.
Q. Who was Moses?   A. Apostle of Christ.
Q. Who was Peter?   A. An angel.
Q. Where was Christ crucified?   A. In England.
Q. Who was Jesus Christ the Son   A. Son of David.
    of?
Q. Who then was David?   A. Son of Jesus.[3]

While mass education, the teaching of 500 or more children in one room, is past, some of the practices—the emphasis on drill, rote memory, questions and answers based on a textbook—are still current method. It is this sole reliance on book-centered, question-answer routine in which all children, regardless of intelligence, emotion, and home background, had to participate that modern education has tried to modify. The school as modeled on the factory is past history.

NEW CONTENT IN THE CURRICULUM

In efforts to find optimum learning conditions, educational theory and research have pointed directly away from the older methods of mass education. To individualize instruction and yet also to provide for group participation represented innovations in method. New content in the curriculum recognizes the changing content of culture. Modifications are always going on.

Past and present content of both elementary and high school is an indicator of the different social worlds that have developed, of shifts in value orientations. In 1800 the elementary-school curriculum typically consisted of reading, spelling, writing, catechism and Bible, and arithmetic. By 1900 catechism and Bible was dropped and thirteen new subjects were added. A list for 1945 includes:

[3] *Ibid.*, pp. 159–160.

reading
literature
spelling
printing and script writing
citizenship
arithmetic
oral presentation
correct usage
geography
history (local, national, backgrounds)

Constitution
general science
art
music
hygiene
physical education
vocational education
home making
foreign languages
trips and excursions
extracurricular activities

Obviously few elementary schools would include the complete range of these subjects. The significant point is the expansion of experience that these subjects indicate.

Similar expansion is found in high schools. In 1849 an Ohio high school taught seventeen subjects: English grammar, composition, rhetoric, Greek, Latin, vocal music, United States history, mental philosophy, logic, higher arithmetic, algebra, geometry, trigonometry, botany, chemistry, geology, and bookkeeping. In 1949, a hundred years later, the total subjects were fifty.

American literature
English literature
grammar and compo-
sition
Latin
French
German
Spanish
art
vocal music
band
journalism
United States history
world history
civics
economics
sociology

psychology
economic geography
commercial law
practical mathematics
plane geometry
solid geometry
trigonometry
advanced algebra
college algebra
biology
chemistry
physics
practical science
bookkeeping
salesmanship
retail selling
stenography

typing
office machines
automotives
woodwork
drawing
aircraft mechanics
metalcraft
metal casting
Smith-Hughes
vocational machine shop
drafting
printing
sheet metal
home economics
driver education
physical education
business mathematics

Here large blocks of time are devoted to the humanities and the arts, the social sciences, the natural sciences and mathematics, and vocational courses. We need not assume that all high schools have programs of this type. Some may have more, others less. The 1939–40 high-school program in the hamlet of Plainville [4] included English, speech, American history, citizenship, music, theory and harmony, glee club, orchestra, algebra, arithmetic, geography, typewriting, bookkeeping, agriculture, sewing, and physical education—only sixteen subjects.

ENTERING THE FUNCTIONAL ORDER

The changing attitudes toward the question "What are the functions of the school?" are reflected in the expanded curriculum and the changing methods of instruction. As education has become nearly universal, it has become more concerned with vocational studies. It is not within the scope of this discussion to pass judgment on the hot controversy which rages over this trend. But a sociological inquiry will keep probing into questions arising out of this situation, such as: (1) How do the variations in the functional order of schools influence the life opportunities of their graduates? (2) What factors influence individuals in the choice of a type of school or type of course? (3) What value implications are found in the various aspects of the functional order?

SELECTING THE SCHOOL

On the elementary level there is little choice. A child goes to the school in his particular district. The exception is in those areas where segregation is or has been practiced. The child enters the school when it meets the minimum legal requirements or the additional tests of admission as set forth by the parochial and private school. In many communities there is no choice because there is only one school. It is only in larger communities that transfer to a school in another district is possible, depending of course on the policies of the board of education and of the principals. Reasons for transfer are various: opportunity and reputation, for example. The reputation of the school also becomes part of the reputation of the

[4] James West, *Plainville*, Columbia University Press, 1945, p. 179.

child. An unsavory reputation and situation may prompt many a parent to request a transfer. This happened in the following situation, in which a large number of transfer requests were made: "In the case of both Public School 121 Manhattan and Junior High School 40 Bronx, the school community was characterized by gross disorder, widespread racial antagonisms, wholesale street fighting by both boy and girl students, pernicious 'shake-down' rackets, countless intruders, flagrant rowdyism, assaults on teachers, and community apathy." [5] It is not implied that this situation still exists in these schools, but, given the situation, some parents tried every device to get their children transferred. In some cities, however, children are compelled to attend certain schools by a gerrymandering of school districts so that children from the lower economic class, "race," or nationality will be segregated from the middle and upper classes. This can become a controversial issue. An attempt to change such gerrymandered districts in Pasadena to a more democratic and equitable arrangement was a factor, according to some observers, leading to an opposition which forced the dismissal of the superintendent of schools.[6] It has been noted that the more obsolescent school structures are found near the center of cities and the more modern toward the areas of later development. The elementary school, then, that a child attends is a consequence of his family's position in the social structure and ecological order of the community, the policies of the board of education, and the parents' intentions about the education of their children.

On the high-school level wider choice is possible, though this is dependent on size of community. As with the elementary school, many communities have a single high school, and selection of a school is precluded. In communities with a variety of high schools, choice is possible. Let us examine this situation in a Connecticut city of around 30,000 population.[7] This city had three private high schools at the time of the study, which charged the town a tuition for each child enrolled. Billings Memorial Institute, with an enroll-

[5] Michael Levine, "The Changing School Community," *Social Education*, December, 1946, p. 384.
[6] David Hulburd, *This Happened in Pasadena*, The Macmillan Company, 1951, pp. 79–81.
[7] Based on a study supervised by the author.

ment of 600, is open only to girls; Greeley, with about 400 enrolled, is for boys. Burchard Technical, with about 1000 enrolled, is co-educational with a ratio of six boys to four girls. Billings and Greeley offer three courses of study—commercial, general, and college. Burchard Technical (hereafter "Tech"), with no specific courses, requires four years of English, one year of math, one year of United States history, and four years of technical work, all other choices being electives. Nearby towns, too small to support a high school, send their students to these schools.

How do the principals interpret the situation? The headmaster of Greeley thought that the principals of the schools in Bradford (an adjoining town) very definitely influenced the eighth-grade graduates to come to Tech, feeling that Greeley was prepared only to handle the college-bound students. The headmaster of Tech stated that many of the eighth-grade teachers and principals of the city schools pushed the better athletes and students toward Billings and Greeley and sorted out the "dummies" for Tech. He also felt that eighth-grade students were given the impression that if college was the objective they should go to Greeley or Billings; if it was work after graduation, they should go to Tech.

Among townspeople there was a definite feeling that attendance at Greeley and Billings Memorial was a step up, or at least a step toward maintaining status on the social ladder. The better athletes of the grade schools generally picked Greeley because of the greater success the Greeley teams had in sports. This tendency was mutually reinforcing.

Class and nationality groups are unequally distributed among the schools. Native-born Americans, English, and Irish attend Billings and Greeley in greater proportion than Tech. Italians attend Tech in greater proportion. This is true of students from lower economic classes and status groups in general. Figure 18 shows another aspect. Parental influence was most important in affecting choice of school, especially for Billings and Greeley. While the parental factor is important for Tech, the older sister or brother influence was of equal significance. This is explained by the ethnic factor. A rather high percentage of Italian parents do not have a high-school education, and they feel that the older brother or sister who has graduated from

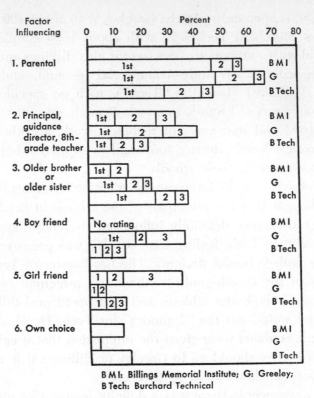

Factor Influencing

| | Percent |
| | 0 10 20 30 40 50 60 70 80 |

1. Parental — 1st ... 2 3 B M I; 1st ... 2 3 G; 1st ... 2 3 B Tech

2. Principal, guidance director, 8th-grade teacher — 1st 2 3 B M I; 1st 2 3 G; 1st 2 3 B Tech

3. Older brother or older sister — 1st 2 B M I; 1st 2 3 G; 1st 2 3 B Tech

4. Boy friend — No rating B M I; 1st 2 3 G; 1 2 3 B Tech

5. Girl friend — 1 2 3 B M I; 1 2 G; 1 2 3 B Tech

6. Own choice — B M I; G; B Tech

B M I: Billings Memorial Institute; G: Greeley;
B Tech: Burchard Technical

FIGURE 18. Percent of Students of Three High Schools Rating Importance of Specified Factors as Influencing Their Choice of School.

high school is in a better position to help form a decision as to choice of school. The influence of boys (especially athletes) is important among Greeley students. The girl-friend factor in Billings is high as a third factor among girls. The proportion of students who claim that they made up their own minds is not large, 25 percent. The people important in affecting high-school choice are those with whom one has a primary group relationship. The effect of principals and other school personnel seems to be of secondary importance.

TAKING COURSES AND SUBJECTS

Course sequences vary with high schools. In the twenties, for example, Middletown Central had twelve different course sequences, of which eight were practical and vocational.[8] Many high schools, especially the smaller ones, are organized around three courses: general, commercial, and college preparatory. What a student takes will vary with the overall school organization and policy.

The principal of a junior high school in a city of about 40,000 indicated the official policy for assignment of students as follows: If a child has a B average or better, choice of courses is left to child and parents. No child is permitted to take Latin with a B— average unless the parents insist. If they insist, the child is given a six-weeks trial. As a rule he drops out. Children are informed early in the second semester of the eighth grade that unless they have a B average they will not be permitted to take Latin or the college course. An exception to this is made for children with a high IQ (110 and over) and straight C average all the way through the lower grades. They are encouraged to take the college course in the hope that with a little more effort on their part they can make the grade. The principal encourages children to take the home economics course.[9]

Such a policy of selecting in terms of ability may be colored in two ways—by the principles according to which students are graded and by social background. The latter may also influence how teachers grade students. In Yankee City all of the lower-upper class, 88 percent of the upper-middle, 45 percent of the middle-lower, 28 percent of the upper-lower, and 26 percent of the lower-lower class took the scientific or Latin courses, which are college preparatory. Children from the lower-middle and lower class took the general and commercial courses.[10] In Elmtown a similar relationship between social class and course was found.[11] Table 20, based on the total freshman class in the junior high school mentioned above, also shows a relationship between occupation of the chief breadwinner in the family and the course the child takes. The practical and vocational courses are taken primarily by those in the lower economic class and status group.

[8] Robert Lynd and Helen M. Lynd, *Middletown*, Harcourt, Brace and Company, 1929, p. 192.
[9] Based on a document secured by the author.
[10] W. Lloyd Warner et al., *Who Shall Be Educated?* Harper & Brothers, 1944, p. 61.
[11] August Hollingshead, *Elmtown's Youth*, John Wiley and Sons, 1949, p. 462.

TABLE 20. Occupation of Chief Breadwinner in Family and Enrollment in High-School Courses for 105 Freshmen

Occupation of Chief Breadwinner	Course in High School										Total	
	College		General		Commercial		Industrial		Home Economics			
	Number	Percent	Number	Percent	Number	Percent	Number	Percent	Number	Percent	Number	Percent
Professional, proprietor, managerial	11	52	2	29	2	6	6	23	5	33	24	23
Clerical and sales	2	10			4	11	4	15	1	7	11	11
Craftsmen, foremen	3	14	5	71	13	36	8	31	3	20	32	30
Service workers					4	11			2	13	6	6
Semiskilled workers	5	24			13	36	8	31	4	27	32	30
Total	21	100	7	100	36	100	26	100	15	100	105	100

Includes all freshmen except seven who could not be classified.

The fact that this relationship between courses and social class is found in some communities does not mean that it holds in all communities. It is not an invariable, repetitive, uniform relation or what some social scientists are prone to dub a causal relation. It is bedded in human decisions and policies as these express one or the other value orientation. Thus, in some communities the relationship is not found.[12] By requiring traditional courses for all students, by use of the core curriculum (or general education or multiple-period classes), with many individual electives and no sharp divisions into course sequences, there is no longer the handy hook on which invidious social distinctions can be hung. The bolstering of social class differences is not a necessary and inherent phase of the functional order.

The bearing of the two structural elements of age status and sex status upon the functional order is much more decisive. Unless the school is monosexual in composition, these elements as organizing factors of the functional order are found in all schools. Of the two, the sex status factor is the more important. The relation is reciprocal. Sex status structures the functional order, and the fact that this order is so organized also helps to support the sex status. Not every aspect of the functional order is so organized. The most obvious instance is in use of the showers and lavatories, and the use of the gym. Other instructional content is also divided along sex lines. These divisions emphasize and maintain the distinction between male and female sex roles. It would be possible to work out gym activities in which both girls and boys participate, and some schools do this. The emphasis, however, is on separate physical education activities for the sexes. Cooking, sewing, and manual training in elementary schools, when facilities are available, are usually allocated by sex status. On the high-school level the home economics course is designed for the girl. This means that girls are given special training to fit them into their future domestic role. Many practical and vocational courses are primarily for boys, for they are the future breadwinners, and they must have some skill to offer in the labor market. Those vocational courses that girls take are for such occupations as fit our cultural definition of the female sex role and

[12] W. Lloyd Warner, *op. cit.*, pp. 66–70.

feminine character. The girl is most likely to enter the domestic and personal service occupations, the clerical and sales occupations, or teaching, nursing, and social work professions. In some schools, very few, these "traditional" distinctions are disregarded so that girls can take the so-called boys' courses and vice versa. Division of labor in classes is carried out along sex lines. Jobs that require manual dexterity and strength, such as sawing and using hammers, are usually assigned to boys. Children are thus fitted into their appropriate sex roles. The degree to which sex status is an organizing principle depends upon the policy of the school.

HOW COST IS INVOLVED IN FUNCTION

One assumption underlying public education is that school should be free to those enrolled in it, that the costs should be shared by the community as a whole. While the overall expense is carried by the community, many minor fees tend to slip in. Complete participation in the school depends upon the family's ability to pay for these extra costs. They have been described as hidden tuition costs and involve not only special fees in connection with courses but also expenses involved in the athletic and social events of the school, extracurricular activities, school publications, and so on.

While such hidden tuition costs have been studied primarily on the high-school level, they also occur on the elementary. What parents have to pay varies with school policy. For example, in West Virginia in some counties textbooks are provided by the school, but in other counties they must be purchased by the parent. Depending on the grade level, such expenditures may range from ten to thirteen or more dollars. Some schools rent textbooks at a nominal cost. In addition the child has to furnish other supplies—paper, pencil, ink, rulers, etc. Special activities, such as band, may require the purchase of an instrument unless the school rents them to the pupils or furnishes them free. Graduation from elementary school may also involve additional expenditures. The problem of hidden tuition costs on the elementary level needs further study.

On the high-school level investigation has brought results that have surprised investigators inasmuch as the findings conflict with the ideal of the free public school. Expenditures according to one study averaged around $125 per year. Costs increased sharply from year to year as follows: freshman, $95; sophomore, $117; junior, $134; senior, $155. The total was $501.[13] Almost identical results were obtained in a study made in Wisconsin.[14] Tables 21 and 22 compare the results of the two studies. Table 21 shows the variations of expenditures according to several factors, as by sex status, economic class, and grade. The higher expenditure for the later study is in part accounted for by inflation. The table suggests the differ-

TABLE 21. Average Expenditures by Sex, Grade, and Occupation by High-School Students for the School Years 1942–43 and 1949–50

| | 1942–43 | | 1949–50 |
Item of Comparison	Wisconsin Schools	All Schools	Wisconsin Only
Boys	$ 64.67	$ 73.75	$109.16
Girls	85.94	87.67	136.75
9th grade	63.65	62.96	91.63
10th grade	65.96	69.32	105.43
11th grade	77.69	88.16	131.40
12th grade	101.17	109.14	166.36
Proprietors	93.84	83.21	152.42
Professional	78.43	96.53	149.98
Sales and clerical	76.27	76.20	143.67
Protective	73.87	83.09	125.90
Craftsmen	73.41	89.96	121.22
Service	74.44	74.94	117.78
Operatives	82.39	71.43	116.17
Domestic	80.76	76.98	114.24
Farmers	78.73	94.52	110.49
All Pupils	77.03	81.96	124.02

SOURCES: For 1942–43, Paul B. Jacobson, "The Cost of Attending High School," *Bulletin of the National Association of Secondary-School Principals*, January, 1944, p. 23. For 1949–50, Russel T. Gregg and Raymond E. Schultz, *Personal Expenditures for High-School Education*, School of Education, University of Wisconsin, 1951, p. 22; this study dealt only with Wisconsin students.

[13] Harold C. Hand, *How the Illinois Secondary School Curriculum Basic Studies Can Help You Improve Your High School*, Circular Series A, No. 51, Illinois Secondary Curriculum Program Bulletin, No. 13, Office of Public Instruction, pp. 12–13.
[14] Russel T. Gregg and Raymond E. Schultz, *Personal Expenditures for High-School Education*, School of Education, University of Wisconsin, 1951, p. 33.

TABLE 22. Mean Expenditures by Items of Expenditure and Place of Residence

Item of Expenditure	Year		Residence		
	1942–43	1949–50	Rural	Village	City
Activity card	$ .53	$ 1.51	$ .98	$ .58	$ 2.47
Admission to athletic contests	.58	1.70	1.42	2.08	1.77
Admission to other school activities	.96	1.79	1.38	1.77	2.14
Transportation	7.72	4.66	3.61	2.54	6.28
Uniforms and equipment	2.05	3.70	3.93	4.76	3.10
School dues	1.56	3.83	4.22	3.91	3.15
Lunches	16.18	16.48	23.67	17.52	10.55
School excursions, trips	.88	1.40	1.46	1.69	1.31
School fees and fines	1.54	2.18	1.84	1.93	2.55
School supplies	4.30	7.58	6.69	7.01	8.45
School publications	.69	1.25	1.10	1.24	1.36
Candy sales, drives, etc.	1.17	1.48	1.65	1.61	1.34
Clothing	41.46	62.23	48.03	59.64	80.68
Miscellaneous	9.98	11.23	10.13	12.10	11.71
Total	$89.60	$124.02	$110.11	$118.38	$136.86

SOURCES: For 1942–43, Paul B. Jacobson, "The Cost of Attending High School," *Bulletin of the National Association of Secondary-School Principals,* January, 1944, p. 18, based on a sample of 464 pupils out of the total study. For 1949–50 and for the residence data, Russel T. Gregg and Raymond E. Schultz, *Personal Expenditures for High-School Education,* School of Education, University of Wisconsin, 1951, pp. 22–23.

ential monetary requirements called for by the two sex roles, the increasing monetary requirements of the school as the pupil advances in grade, and the differential ability of families to meet these requirements. Table 22 shows the amounts spent on specific items. The study concludes, "The out-of-pocket expense to the pupil in attending high school today is apparently of the same relative magnitude as it was some years ago." [15] It also shows that the cost increases from rural to urban areas. The average rural family, however, spends more of its income (5.2 percent) to support a child in high school as compared with the average urban family (4.1 percent).[16] That the financial burden on families supporting more than one child in high school becomes great is obvious. "The median family

[15] *Ibid.,* p. 22.
[16] *Ibid.,* p. 23.

income for families with one child in high school was $2,881 and the mean total expenditure for one child was $128.66 or 4.5 per cent of the family income. The median family income for families with three children enrolled was only $2,433 and the combined expenditures for the three children was $306.45, or 12.6 per cent of the family income. . . . Such expenditures are, of course, in addition to taxes paid by the families for school purposes." [17] Expenditures also vary considerably among schools. The mean expenditure in the schools in the lowest quartile of the seventy-eight schools studied was $69.79, in those in the median quartile $122.35, and in those in the highest quartile $197.60.[18] Much of the difference lies in the expenditures for school events, transportation, uniforms and equipment, and lunches.

The inclusion of clothing in the items of expenditure may seem somewhat strange as parents would have to purchase clothing for the children whether they went to school or not. The fact that the child does go to school makes a difference. This point was recognized in the Middletown study. Appearance values are associated with clothing for class and for social or formal occasions. Clothing is also subject to fads and fashions and thus may involve a kind of peer conspicuous consumption. As some of the mothers in Middletown expressed the problem: "We couldn't dress him like we'd ought to and he felt out of place," or "The two boys and the oldest girl all quit because they hated Central High School. They all loved the Junior High School down here, but up there they're so snobbish. If you don't dress right you haven't any friends." [19] Twenty-five years later, in the Wisconsin study cited, the same difficulty was found. In technical language, "pupil drop-out rates were negatively related to family income." [20]

High schools vary considerably in providing supplies, equipment, and services to pupils, as shown in Table 23. Only three items of the thirteen were given free of charge in a majority of the schools where the items were required. Free textbooks, free supplies, free admission to school events, free transportation would lighten the burden

[17] *Ibid.*, p. 24.
[18] *Ibid.*, p. 25.
[19] Robert Lynd and Helen Lynd, *op. cit.*, p. 186.
[20] Russel T. Gregg and Raymond E. Schultz, *op. cit.*, p. 34.

TABLE 23. School Practices in Providing Supplies, Equipment, and Services to Pupils as Reported by Principals of 78 Schools

Item Supplied	Number of Schools Where Item Is Needed	Furnished by School		Purchased by Pupil		Rented or Partly Paid for by Pupil	
		Number	Percent	Number	Percent	Number	Percent
Textbooks	78	45	58	14	18	19	24
Workbooks	78	16	21	47	60	15	19
Newspapers and magazines	78	23	31	40	50	15	19
Fine art supplies	32	17	51	6	19	9	30
Home economics supplies	74	25	34	4	4	46	62
Industrial arts supplies	62	11	18	7	11	44	71
Hall, gym locks, lockers	70	44	62	11	16	15	22
Gym suit and shoes	74	—	—	68	92	6	8
School publications	71	14	20	53	74	4	6
Musical instruments	77	7	9	5	7	65	84
Admission to athletic contests	78	3	4	72	92	3	4
Caps and gowns	78	6	8	64	82	8	10
Pupil insurance	68	27	40	32	47	9	13

SOURCE: Russel T. Gregg and Raymond E. Schultz, *Personal Expenditures for High-School Education*, School of Education, University of Wisconsin, 1951, p. 31.

considerably and make education "more free." The children from low-income families, however, are handicapped. Unless the family's financial power increases or the child has the opportunity to earn money (which may also affect his schooling adversely), he will drop out of school early. There is no inherent reason why families have to shoulder completely these hidden tuition costs. In Bloomington, Illinois, the school board, after analyzing the problem, put most of the high-school extracurricular activities on the free list.[21] Some schools—and this has been the policy of many parochial schools—solve the clothing problem by requiring a standard dress.

VALUE IMPLICATIONS

It becomes apparent that many of the same principles that organize society in general also influence the smaller world of the school. If a person's place in society is defined by his age, sex, color, nationality, and economic status, his opportunities in education are likewise influenced by these factors. The fact that these social classifications are arbitrary and unrelated to the individual child's talents and potentialities make their desirability as principles of organization in school districts, courses, or other school activities doubtful, from a humanistic, common man, and perhaps religious value orientation. If equality of opportunity is to be more than a catchword, schools must reassess some of their policies and practices. Some schools have done that to minimize the influence of these social irrationalities.

The discussion of the functional order cannot be limited to subject matter. Opening exercises, activities outside the curriculum, the system of examinations and grading, the ceremonial occasions, and sports spectacles are all extremely important parts of what pupils do in school. It is important to our understanding of the meaning of the value reality of the school to study these aspects.

THE OPENING MINUTES

The following account indicates one of the many variations of the beginning of a school day:

[21] Harold C. Hand, *op. cit.*, p. 17.

As visitors we do not follow the prescribed route into the class. As we enter, we note that the class library, reading table, and easels are located in the rear of the room. The movable desks are arranged in rows so that the light from the windows falls upon the desk from the left. This arrangement, according to the teacher, was to insure proper lighting. She did not follow a common practice in the school of arranging the desks so that children would face one another. "I don't think a child could stand looking at the same face for a whole day throughout a year." Too many children and the arrangement of the desks gave the room an over-crowded appearance. The dominant color was a very vivid exciting yellow. Paintings by pupils were hung at various points along the wall. These pictures would be changed. On a bulletin board inside the class were announcements and inter-class correspondence. The functional order so far is teacher planned.

As the children gradually settle down, Jane, who is class leader, rings a bell several times as she sits in a chair in front of the class and says, "Good morning, boys and girls." The class responds, "Good morning, Jane." Jane and the group bow heads and recite the Lord's Prayer. During this recitation the children are still settling down in their seats, mumbling in a half-hearted monotone, staring at the desk with folded hands or peering around at late comers. The class then rises and, led by Jane, recites the pledge of allegiance, followed by the song "My Country 'Tis of Thee." Since Jane pitches the key too high, the class barely gets through the song. The class sits down. Jane climbs a chair, erases yesterday's date and asks the class for the current date. Class recites, "Friday was the 13th, Saturday was the 14th, Sunday was the 15th, today is Monday the 16th, 1956." Jane writes the date on the board, including the new total of days spent in school. She asks, "How many of you have not brushed your teeth this morning?" Three have not, and a three is placed on the board. Jane climbs off the chair and goes from desk to desk to inspect hands.

In this room the remainder of the opening exercise might be devoted to the reading of a story by one of the pupils, announcements, or a special project. Interest in the proceedings was extremely diverse, with much whispering, shifting in seats, and restlessness. Some children might decide to complete their "household" duties. Collection of lunch money was taken care of by a practice teacher during the opening period. In the main, the opening exercise was completely routine, rather uninteresting and boring to the children. The child leadership showed that the class was attempting to operate along democratic lines.

Opening exercises may set the temper of the day, inspiring or routine. They may give expression to a variety of cultural values. In Mill City, in those classes where opening rituals took place, they tended to follow patriotic and religious patterns. In other rooms, class discussion would precede the standard tasks. In some classes there were no opening rituals. The children went immediately to work on their activities, checking numbers and spelling, tending to household duties, etc. The amount of variation within the school was great. Teachers' attitudes differed—some thought that such exercises were routine and meaningless, some objected to an over-emphasis on patriotism, some thought opening rituals were an invaluable experience.

A group of twenty-three elementary teachers were asked about their opening rituals. Their response produced the following list of activities:

Bible stories	16	Flag salute and pledge of	
Lord's Prayer or other prayer	16	allegiance	11
Hymns	3	Patriotic songs	2
Group sing	15	Collecting money	10
Stories	10	Attendance report	7
Sharing period	8		
Poems	3	Planning	8
Songs	2		
Dramatizing stories and stunts	3		

Other activities included: announcements, playing records, talks, folk dance, election of officers, household duties, preparing for assembly program, working on art, none. (In the last case the school had a chapel meeting on an afternoon once a week.) In one school the first portion of the opening ritual came through a PA system. These periods varied from ten minutes to forty-five minutes. In the lower grades (1–3) the teacher played a more important role. The most interesting aspect of this list is the mingling of traditional and new, but the traditional outweighs the new. Teachers try to vary the program, though the tendency is to fall into a pattern.

The pure mechanics of attendance reports and collecting money are an aspect of the list deserving of thought. As a second-grade teacher in a rural school commented to the author, "The first thing I do is to check on lunches and take lunch money and attendance. This is required so that others may make their reports and necessary arrangements. This is the period I dislike in the morning as nothing seems to interest or amuse the pupils while the money is being taken care of. They seem to feel it is a time that they call their own. In addition to that, I often have picture show money, work book money, pictures [individuals in class], PTA dues, or something to collect. This takes from fifteen minutes to half an hour in the morning." These duties the teachers regarded as harassing and a waste of their time as well as of the children's time. It might be added that the home-room period in high school frequently becomes a matter of fulfilling administrative tasks and bookkeeping.

EXAMINATIONS AS RECURRENT CRISES

The opening rituals may set the mood for a day, but an event that has deeper repercussions is the examination. The opening ceremonies may not be closely related to the formal activities of the day's work. As a rule the flow of work moves along without engendering much emotion, but as soon as the word "examination" is cast into the social scene, the mood typically changes. Tension and anxiety develop and increase. Worry sets in. An exaggerated bustle takes place as pencils are sharpened, chairs pushed around. Smiles of encouragement are flashed. The examination begins.

Examinations need not be recurrent crises, but they tend to be interpreted and acted upon in such a way that they finally become a crisis situation. They become a disturbing experience not only to the pupils but also to the teacher, who is affected by the nervous crisis actions of the pupils. At whatever level, the examination is a task that must or should be not only conquered but very thoroughly conquered. Students must be successes.

TIMING OF EXAMINATIONS

The scheduling of examinations depends on the level of the school. In the elementary school the schedule will vary with the units and material covered. If report cards come at stated intervals, say four times a year, then examinations will be planned so that a grade can be assigned to the pupil. The formalization of examinations increases until the college level is reached. At this level, the schedule culminates in the final examination week, during which the test periods may range from two to three hours. The student as a rule will be subjected to three hour examinations during the semester. These tests are grouped because grades must be turned in at seven weeks, mid-semester, twelve weeks, or some such schedule, depending on the school. The tendency is for examination periods in various courses to fall together. Roughly speaking, students and teachers may be subjected to four examination periods a semester or eight for the year. Eight times a student faces a critical period involving success or failure—thirty-two times for the four-year college course. If the total number of examination periods for an entire school career could be estimated, the total pressure, the nervous tension, the worry, would be seen to be immense. The situation is more severe on the college level, for career possibilities are involved.

EXAMINATIONS AS A FORM OF COMPETITION

Examinations have a variety of objectives. The ostensible and accepted objective is to find out how a pupil's skills are developing —be they communicative, appreciative, computative, physical, etc. The examination may serve as a measure of progress. In some schools such an objective may be realized. Other schools may have no examinations whatsoever, but a series of completed projects involving the development of skills and insight. The formal examination has a tendency not to be used as a diagnostic tool and a means of measuring progress. To the children it becomes a matter of self-other competition and a means of mutual as well as of self-evaluation. In a school oriented to a humanist viewpoint, where grades were given only in the seventh and eighth grade, the administration of a personality test to a group of sixth-graders brought forth the response "Will it count against us?" In spite of the efforts of teachers to encourage a different point of view, the success-failure-competition pattern had become a reality at this level. Why does this concept of the examination come to the fore?

Teachers, as has been said, may try to minimize the competitive element in examinations by emphasizing their function as a check on self-improvement. They try to impress on the child that the test has no bearing upon his ranking with others but refers only to his individual progress. Self-improvement charts are often made and filed in a pupil's notebook. Sometimes the teacher slips, and the charts are publicly displayed. The process is still an evaluative one. The child is evaluating himself and his progress by some standard. This may be a scientifically derived norm or it may involve, and usually does, a self-other reference. The standard may thus be the brightest student in the class. In any case, however much the self-competition is stressed, the process takes place in a social situation. While the teacher may think only in terms of the degree of progress made by the individual, the child, who may not even understand what the teacher is intending, will make the self-other rating. In this way the teacher's intention is subverted. The net result of all rating will tend to be the same—the typing of children (especially in very large classes) as good and poor pupils by the teacher, the labeling as "brain" or "dumbbell" and so on by the children. The typing establishes a reputation, and the child has to compete under a good or poor reputation. Students may eventually be graded on reputation rather than on achievement.

Competing to be a success may spur a person to greater effort and output in simple situations, such as running a race, working a punch press, crossing out every third letter in a series, or adding up small columns of numbers. In many "experiments in competition" such effort was found to take place. Whether such competitive testing produces the same result in the case of more complicated intellectual problem solving is debatable, and when the test puts a premium upon speed, the results may be even more suspect. As a matter of fact, students develop all sorts of emotional blockages so that they do not function at their best. When two or three examinations follow in succession, as happens on the college level during a final examination week, a student is exhausted. To immediately shift from one field of knowledge and pour out another within minutes requires a flexibility and a power of concentration that many students do not possess. The very way the system of examination is organized may guarantee their defeat.

It is not surprising that efforts are made to "beat the game." Since success is the goal to be achieved through competition, all sorts of devices are developed to get ahead. In the wake of competition flows a series of unethical actions, and as long as the system of examinations, as described above, is maintained, such actions will continue. The variety of means to facilitate cheating are well known, and it is an unfortunate commentary upon the educational system that students spend their time trying to figure out ways and means to be a success rather than centering their attention upon the content of their education. Cheating in many forms, stealing examinations, the extensive development of files which contain book reports and term papers in addition to copies of examinations, attempts to bribe secretaries to get tests—all these actions are part of the success-failure-competition complex, a norm deviation that is duplicated in any area of life where competition is regarded as the central fact. This mixture of ethical and unethical action imparts to examinations an added crisis quality, the fear of getting caught. It also builds a certain corruption of character.

The evil effects of competitive examinations are recognized, but instead of radically changing the system, teachers and administrators tinker with techniques of control. These techniques of control also support the crisis nature of testing. That taking an examination is a critical event is shown by the elaborate precautions used to prevent any cheating. In Mill City desks were moved in such a way that no child could look at another's paper. This procedure had been routinized in all classes from the third up. The use of alternate seats, squads of circulating proctors, if the class is large enough, examinations in which pages are scrambled, special instructions, exhortation to do one's own work, not to cheat, and threats of penalties are a few of these ineffective devices. No matter what has been tried, the problem has not changed, even in schools where the honor system is in vogue. No threats or appeals to such subjective traits as honor and fair play work. The change must be in the system.

THE WIDER CONTEXT OF EXAMINATIONS

Outside pressures or cross pressures are elements that help to create the crisis character of examinations. Some of these pressures arise from within the educational system and some from the outside. Problems are more noticeable on the high-school and college level.

A typical cross pressure within the school arises from extracurricular activities, such as dramatics, band, or athletics, which are especially effort- and time-consuming. The significance of such cross pressure attracted national attention to one of the military academies noted for successful football teams and an honor system in examinations. Eighty out of ninety investigated cadets were dismissed. The school, the alumni, booster groups, and public wanted a very successful team. Educationally the school had high requirements. The players could not meet both demands. They were caught in a dilemma which they could resolve only by an immoral act. This case is the type resulting from cross pressures from within, which can occur on any educational level. Others follow the same pattern.

Pressures from without include home problems, personal problems, such as love affairs, time and effort spent on a job or some sort of outside work, the demands of other groups, such as fraternities and sororities, and competing for prestige. A student who is a member of organizations must contribute his time to their special activities or pay fines. Since he cannot attack his own in-group, criticism is directed against the faculty (as out-group), its assignments and examinations. It is in these groups that the more devious ways of coping with examinations and reports are taught. At one university, students requested that the faculty not schedule examinations during a week of heavy social activities such as Junior Prom week. In this case there was the frank solution of cross pressures by minimizing educational concerns for the period. Students active in church foundations encounter similar demands for time and effort. In these cases there is no integration between the educational institution and the groups outside. It is doubtful, because of varying objectives, whether any integration could take place.

THE GRADE—SUCCESS AS A FORMAL ACHIEVEMENT

In many schools, to be a success means to have a high score. The end is the grade, not the skill, content, or problem mastered. These aspects are incidental to the grade and the accumulation of credits. In the lower grades, success is also shown through promotion. Units of credit, promotion, and grade become the crucial points. What are the implications of this peculiar focus of attention?

Grades become a source of invidious comparisons, involving complicated processes of assessment. There is first the assessment by the teacher. Although the teacher may be grading in term of the child's own progress rather than in comparison with others and may try to indicate this fact, an assessment is made, and a figure appears on the card. Secondly, the child is led to a self-assessment, and this contributes to the development of his self-image, whether negative or positive. Thirdly, there is the assessment by other pupils, whether they are in his class or in another class, a mutual evaluation on the part of peers. Fourthly, there may be the assessment made by his parents, his siblings, and by neighbors or neighboring children that might be involved. A report card becomes a community affair.

Since the mark becomes an important item in this evaluating process and is, in fact, the main way through which the process can take place, attention must become centered on the high score. The standing on the report card becomes a major end, and how a teacher grades of major significance. This emphasis represents a displacement of ends from education to technique.

Since grades take on such a crucial significance, it is of interest to know on what basis they are assigned. A current sociological interpretation emphasizes grading according to social class, the higher grades being given to children of the upper economic class and status group and vice versa. Grading in this manner takes place especially in high school, as shown in the Elmtown study [22] and implied in the book *Who Shall Be Educated?* However, the theory needs further study. For example, a study of marks in West School

[22] Hollingshead, *op. cit.*, p. 172.

seventh and eighth grades did not show this relationship. If the principle were generally true, children in so-called slum schools should all rate low, but since teachers usually operate on a "normal distribution" policy, they do not. Even in schools where various classes are represented and preferential grading is possible, it will not take place if the school practices a policy of nullifying the social class distinctions as an intrusive factor. Such a basis for grades is not necessary or unavoidable.

Pupils may try to nullify the significance of grades by withholding their best efforts and approximating what is thought to be an average norm. Thus, the better student may conceal his grade from others or give a false statement to his peers as to his achievement. During a study the author witnessed a sixth-grader pleading with the teacher to lower her grades so that she would not be too different from her companions. The drift to mediocrity may vary in schools, depending on to what degree achievement is an approved overall objective.

There are schools where teachers do not assign grades. The report card is regarded as an outmoded device, arbitrary and meaningless. In Mill City, West School pupils up to the seventh grade receive a written statement commenting on their general development—not only on ability to read, write, and do arithmetic but also on social skills, artistic appreciation, and so on. Such analytical and descriptive statements, some of which become quite lengthy documents, may tell a parent and another person more than a 5, 4, 3, 2, 1 or A, B, C, D, F. Over a period of eight years in elementary school quite a development can be seen if the documents are taken as a unit and an overall brief is prepared.[23] The approach is very time-consuming, since it involves a different mode of keeping records, conferences with parents, etc. Size of class would have a considerable impact on this approach. It may tend to become as stereotyped as the awarding of grades on a report card. Parents may not understand or may misinterpret. Any mode of reporting thus has its drawbacks, but the advantage of the written statements over the traditional report card with its rows of marks is the fact that invidious

[23] See Appendix for sample statement.

comparisons are difficult to make and the competitive-success-failure pattern is minimized.

Unfortunately the tests within the class may take the place of the report card in causing a displacement of educational goals. The getting of a grade may center around these tests, even though the final statement is a written report, as described above. If the examination as a crisis is to be avoided, and if the displacement of educational goals is to be inhibited, then some of the reforms now taking place should become more widespread. These are (1) the non-graded school; (2) replacement of the report card by the descriptive statement of progress plus a good cumulative file; (3) the abolition of examinations and the substitution of a series of projects, units, or problems that must be worked through or solved. Skills and insight developed by working through such material will be evaluated in the descriptive statements, involving greater counseling on the part of the teacher. The chances that such a shift will take place may seem slim, but steps have been made in this direction. Ungraded elementary schools are beyond the experimental stage.[24] Other schools have done away with grades, using instead broader divisions or units; still others have ungraded classes.[25] Plans for individualized instruction, such as the Winnetka plan, the Dalton plan, and others, are increasingly used.[26] For those who prefer the nativist and market orientation, the competitive examination complex is an acceptable if not preferable pattern; but those who try to put a humanistic philosophy into effect will want this pattern to be replaced by the suggested innovations.

Selected Readings

Baxter, Bernice, Lewis, Gertrude, and Cross, Gertrude, *The Role of Elementary Education*, D. C. Heath and Company, 1952, Part IV.

[24] "Doing Away with Grade Levels," *NEA Journal*, April, 1948, pp. 222–223; Florence Kelley, "Ungraded Primary Schools Make the Grade," *NEA Journal*, December, 1951, pp. 645–646; John Goodlad, "Ungrading the Elementary Schools," *NEA Journal*, March, 1955, pp. 170–171; John Goodlad, "More About the Ungraded Unit," *NEA Journal*, May, 1955, pp. 295–296.

[25] NEA Research Bulletin, *Trends in City-School Organization, 1938–1948*, February, 1949, pp. 18–19.

[26] *Ibid.*, pp. 20–21.

Lafferty, H. M., *Sense and Nonsense in Education,* The Macmillan Company, 1947.

Rugg, Harold, and Brooks, Marian, *The Teacher in School and Society,* World Book Company, 1950, chaps. 13, 14.

Stiles, Dan, *High Schools for Tomorrow,* Harper & Brothers, 1946.

Strang, Ruth, *Reporting to Parents,* Teachers College, Columbia University, rev. ed., 1952.

Waller, Willard, *The Sociology of Teaching,* John Wiley and Sons, 1932, chap. 9.

Wrinkle, William, *Improving Marking and Reporting Practices in Elementary and Secondary Schools,* Rinehart and Company, 1947.

Yeager, William, *Administration and the Pupil,* Harper & Brothers, 1949, Part VI.

CHAPTER 8

The Functional Order (Continued)

THE FUNCTIONAL ORDER AS CONSTITUTED
BY CEREMONIAL OCCASIONS

IN OUR DISCUSSION of the relationship of the legal order to the school we noted that several legal holidays and additional ceremonial observances initiated by proclamation were to be observed in the schools with appropriate exercises. Many of these occasions have no intrinsic connection with education. Schools can function without these ceremonial events. Yet the time and event of the ceremony is considered of importance for the society as a whole so that the school is either required or pressured into observing it. The occasion, then, may be viewed as a structural element that penetrates into the school and so organizes its activities. Not all ceremonial events are outside the school. Schools develop their own. The functional order is constructed or organized in part by this twofold aspect of ceremonial occasions.

The total number of ceremonial events is quite large. There are twelve chief legal or public holidays, sixty other legal or public holidays, twenty-five other special days, and twenty other weeks or months that are generally observed. There are also observances that are not society-wide but particular to some group, such as a church, a nationality group, and so on. These are observed only in certain schools. Northern schools obviously will not observe the Southerner's Robert E. Lee Day or Confederate Memorial Day. Public schools in general will not observe Epiphany, Ascension, Corpus Christi, and other major church occasions which are important in parochial schools. The fact that schools observe different kinds of ceremonies gives them their unique or special cultural quality. On the elementary-school level certain occasions are regarded as very important, especially by pupils. These tend to drop out on higher levels, where other ceremonial events take precedence. Sometimes special occasions lose their meaning and are not carried out. This was true of *Maine* Memorial Day and Indian Day in Mill City. In fact, some teachers were not even aware that these occasions were to be observed, nor did they know the significance of the days.

SANTA CLAUS AND GIFTS IN THE ELEMENTARY SCHOOL

While most of the legal holidays refer overwhelmingly to patriotic figures and events, due recognition is given to certain religious events, such as Christmas and Good Friday. Their relative importance as viewed by the pupils differs from that intended by law, so that Christmas outweighs all the patriotic holidays and Easter outweighs Good Friday. If ceremonial events are ranged in order of importance as far as the elementary school as a whole is concerned, Christmas is the most important. Valentine's Day is next, then, Halloween, and lastly, Thanksgiving and Easter. For the eighth-grade student graduation ceremonies are obviously important, but these do not affect the school as a whole.

We started our Christmas planning immediately after Thanksgiving. It is a joyous, busy, noisy time. Out of our work and play we expect to enrich our experience in thinking of others, sharing, music, public appearance, writing of invitations, spelling, reading, English, art, and a better understanding of the real meaning of Christmas. We're making gifts for our friends and family, getting ready for a Christmas operetta, planning for a Christmas party, and trying to keep up to date on all lessons. We're having a wonderful time and everyone is getting tired. Before we're through, we'll all be worn out, and nerves edgy, but Christmas is a wonderful time and is worth it all.

This very apt description summarizes also the interpretation of Christmas of thirty-one elementary teachers who were asked to write up a log of activities during this part of the year. Every grade in every elementary school in the country does not follow the described pattern completely, but where there is any emphasis on Christmas, this description of activities is valid. Furthermore, teachers cannot avoid putting this pattern into effect. It will demanded by the children, by parents, by the community, and despite all the turmoil teachers also welcome the season.

Both Christians and non-Christians are drawn into the vortex of activities that the Christmas pattern demands. For about three weeks attention is focused on a set of activities that finally crescendos in the climax of the Christmas play and party. Christmas is the only event that dominates the school for such a long period. The teaching content becomes saturated with Christmas ideas, secular and sacred. With decorations, songs, stories, Bible stories, compositions, art work, serenading in the halls, and interclass visits, the whole school becomes tuned to the season. The school is transformed into a Christmas world. Not only are the activities Christmas saturated, but the rooms themselves become holiday rooms with decorations of snowmen, ornaments, trees, and nativity scenes. To do all this properly entails an expanded workday for child and teacher. After-school work to make for a bright and proper Christmas is considered all right. As a teacher commented, "It seems the only time of the year when children learn with interest and enthusiasm."

"Our school board states that we must have a Christmas program. The teachers with the music teachers decided to give an operetta. We chose one the week of Thanksgiving. We had pupils try out for parts and the characters were chosen. Costumes had to be made, scenery gathered in, etc. This was the beginning."

The amount of time devoted to such a program will vary. In one school two hours a day, in another the three forty-five-minute music periods each week were devoted to practice. Chorus, band, and orchestra also concentrate for the final performance. Class attendance becomes somewhat irregular as children leave to practice their parts. Those who cannot perform may feel unhappy. There is a tendency for the activities to lose their educational orientation if they become too imbued with a drive for a smash performance, which will demonstrate to parents and others in the community that the school is doing a bang-up job. The meaning of the production angle of the Christmas activities, then, arises out of this interplay between school and community. Many are the parents making a costume at their own expense for the event.

Another major aspect of the pattern is the giving of gifts, and this culminates as a rule in the class party. The pattern is not a simple one. It involves gifts from child to child, child (more accurately the parent) to teacher, teacher to child, class to other school personnel. "The week of December 3–7, the Primary room decided to choose names for gift exchange. They also decided to bring money for gifts for two bus drivers, the janitor, cook, and music teacher." The name of a child is drawn secretly, and everybody must be included, even the children of different color, or social class, who may be rejected. Even cross-sex giving will take place. The gift-giving must be controlled on grounds of equity and the spirit of the season. Costs for such gifts vary. They may range from ten to thirty cents. If money for others is included, the total amount may not be inconsiderable, especially if the family is large. Gifts may be wrapped in class or at home. Sometimes the name of the donor is included.

Whether the teacher should accept a gift is a debatable question, but the practice is established. There are some who may not want to receive gifts and so inform the children, but inevitably the gifts turn up. If the room is operating according to the self-government principle, the teacher may be overruled. If gifts are accepted, then the problem of opening them in class occurs, for there may be no limits placed on the price of the gift, and the poorer child is disadvantaged. Consequently, many teachers take the presents home unopened.

The Christmas season has a tremendous impact on the school, an impact strengthened by the commercialization of the event with the constant exhortation to buy gifts, blaring of carols from loud-speakers, and an assortment of Santa Clauses on the streets. Religious groups counteract by emphasizing the original nature of the event. The school's observation of Christmas is the extreme example of its support of a recurrent cultural event which in this case largely determines and organizes the functional order for weeks.

WITCHES AND HEARTS

Two other events are regarded as important by the children. They are not prescribed in the legal order, nor are they viewed as very important by adults, except perhaps by police and storekeepers. Still Halloween and Valentine's Day are high points for the children, the former because of the fun element, the latter because of the rating element and whatever there may be of romanticism. Schools will vary in their observance of Halloween. In some the afternoon will be devoted to a dress-up party; in others the occasion may be ignored. It will be difficult to avoid the events because the children will demand them, and this is especially true of Valentine's Day. As a result both events penetrate into the instructional content. In each instance, as at Christmas time, there is an anticipatory period, the making of objects, drawing, decorations, plans for a party. Because of the tremendous personal significance of Valentine's Day for each child, teachers feel especially obligated to make sure that no child is slighted. Here again is an event that cuts through all color, class, intelligence, and personal differences. Everybody is to count, everyone is the object of a present. Some may give with evident good feelings, others as a matter of form if they do not especially care for the child. Procedures vary. The policy of some teachers is to have each child give valentines to everybody in class. In this way preferential giving is avoided, and every child has a nice stack as they are distributed. Or there is a drawing of names, and a child has to send one but may in addition add others. Here preferential choices may loom. Teachers also invest in valentines so that everyone will receive at least two valentines.

Valentine's Day supposedly focuses attention on heterosexuality, a preferential appreciation of the opposite sex. Its origin may rest in some fertility rite which became christianized, the kissing on February 14 of the "first-met," who was then the special love for the year. The event today supports the differences in sex status and the traditional approval of romantic love. In practice it is a generalized sociality or friendliness as evidenced in the indiscriminate awarding of valentines in the earlier grades when no controls are asserted. Preferential giving may occur in later grades, where the hetero-sexual component may be more important. Control of giving on grounds of equity tends to be resisted. If there is a sex-avoidance pattern during certain periods of growth, as some claim, it is not reflected in but contravened in the institutional arrangement of Valentine's Day. The occasion is a very rarified form of sex educa-tion.

"TIME MUST COME WHEN SOME MUST LEAVE US"

Commencement is an intertwined pattern of commercial, patriotic, religious, and educational interests. The graduation period is some-what like a *rite de passage*, a community ceremony suggesting arrival at adult status, a time when childish things are put away and one becomes a man. On the elementary level the exercise repre-sents a stage toward the adult status, but on the high-school level for many the conclusion of the rite signifies entry into the world of work and family. For the few who attend college this final movement into career and domesticity is postponed for four years with a consequent retention of the late adolescent play and courtship interests.

Commencement as a serious occasion is but one aspect of the total pattern. There is the school annual, class flowers, class song, class colors, class motto, and class pin, honors day sometimes combined with an athletic awards day, a junior-senior banquet, a senior day, a senior play, a dance, a senior reception, baccalaureate services, and commencement. At many schools there will also be an alumni re-union, replete with reception, banquet, and dance. It takes about a week or more to cover all the activities. The preparations take a much longer time, especially when band or orchestra and choral groups have to perform. In addition, arrangements have to be made and funds collected for the banquets, the dances, the various class emblems, the awards days, and a host of activities involving stu-dents, faculty, and outside groups. School and outside world inter-penetrate. In this interrelationship one effort is to maximize the glamour of the situation, for it pays off. Another phase is the opportunity for special-interest groups to state their case through baccalaureate and commencement speakers.

The content of an awards day illustrates the varying value emphases in our culture. It also shows the impact of special-interest groups which furnish various certificates and awards. Here are a few samples (names are fictitious):

Main High School

University scholarship
DAR award for girls
American Legion essay awards
State department of education certificates in scholarship
County educational scholarship
County educational scholarship pins
Danforth award
Magazine sales award
Babe Ruth sportsmanship award
State FHA award
Merit award pins
Band letter awards for juniors and seniors
Senior band keys
Athletic letter awards in basketball, football, baseball; cheerleader letters (girls)
Typing pins
School bank certificates
FHA awards of merit
Vocal music awards
Perfect attendance certificates
County spelling awards
Service certificates for student librarians

Middleport High School

Reader's Digest award
Highest scholastic achievement certificate
DAR award
American Legion delegate to boys' state convention (and to girls' state convention)
Scholarship by University High
Placement in state General Scholarship Test for seniors
Outstanding senior boy and girl with the Danforth Foundation leadership certificate
Service certificates to student librarians
Typewriting awards
Medals to Girls' Glee Club
Medals to Boys' Glee Club
Student Activities Association pins; special awards to college aspirants; commerce and technical career people; commerce and industry awards

Palos High School

Basketball medal and letters
Cheerleading awards
Orchestra awards
Glee club awards
Girls' intramurals
Senior medals and letters
Scholarship recognition in English, algebra, geometry, stenography, chemistry, office practice
Baseball awards
DAR award
Reader's Digest award
Honor keys
Perfect attendance certificates

Sports and cheerleading, music, scholarship, leadership, and service are the main emphases. Patriotic and commerical groups are the recurring award-giving societies.

The culmination of the graduation exercises is in the baccalaureate services and commencement. In the first, benedictions flow upon the robed attendants, and in the second, the final award is the diploma. Both occasions serve to reaffirm traditional values. The baccalaureate is primarily a religious service. A minister keynotes the situation, emphasizing that Christ and Christianity are the way of life. Hymns and other weighty processional tunes sanctify the solemnity of the event. The commencement speakers may include ministers, educators, judges, business people, columnists, radio commentators, and so on. Invocations and blessings at the recessional emphasize the religious values of the culture. The speakers generally reaffirm a mixture of the nativist, market, and religious orientations. The common man and the humanist orientations are usually by-passed. Content analysis of commencement speeches shows that graduating students are given a "Let's carry on the traditions in this land of unlimited freedom and opportunity, hard work, the Constitution, God, and Christ" type of message. Class mottoes echo these ideas: "Today we follow, tomorrow we lead"; "Life is a game; we will play it"; "We finish to begin"; "The greater the trials, the more glorious the triumph."

IMPLICATION OF THESE CEREMONIAL EVENTS

These occasions are an important phase of the functional order. Some of them are prescribed by law so that the school is the carrier of the traditions and sentiments which support the state and the nation. Many events are not prescribed by law and serve other values. Christmas, Halloween, Valentine's Day, pep rallies, baccalaureate services, and commencement exercises involve a multiplicity of values and groups. Each of these occasions involves the organization of the instructional content to express the nature of the event, demanding up to a couple of weeks of concentrated attention on the part of teacher and pupils. The ceremonial event is one major way in which the school integrates with other phases of the culture.

The incorporation of this diverse culture content makes for diverse objectives in the school program and, especially when public productions are stressed, may divert teachers from realizing their primary educational goals.

THE SCHOOL AS A VEHICLE OF MASS ENTERTAINMENT

> Newark Hi, Newark Hi,
> We're the finest in the land.
> We *debate* to beat the band.
> Newark Hi, Newark Hi,
> Wahoo! Wahoo! Rip, Zip, Bazoo!
> Newark Hi!
>   [Italics ours]

A pep rally for a debating team, the high school auditorium filled at 25¢ a head, proceeds used to support athletics—today such action would seem rather fantastic. Fifty years ago, even thirty-five years ago, the literary and debating societies were the elite groups in schools. Newspapers featured the exploits and victories of the debating teams. Today only a few brief lines are included to the effect that a debate took place. "Although not as avidly supported since the Booster's Club began to push athletics, debate still plays an important part in the school community." [1] So runs a comment in the Newark High School *Centennial History*. A former and old member of the debating team looking at the past stated: "In this town the present popularity of football and basketball leaves little room for the enthusiasm necessary to make a high school student feel the labor involved in debating is worth while. Something is lost there." According to the *Centennial History*: "Of all the extracurricular services performed by the Newark public schools, athletic contests are probably the best known and most avidly followed." [2] One culture pattern prevails, new ones come into being, and a new order of activity results. Viewing many activities of the school, not only sports, we find that they are a form of mass entertainment, and the school functions to provide such mass entertainment.

[1] Gordon R. Kingery, *A Brief Centennial History of the Newark Public Schools*, n.d., p. 33.
[2] *Ibid.*, p. 25.

GROWTH OF THE MASS ENTERTAINMENT SPECTATOR PATTERN

No culture pattern springs into life without some antecedents. The mass entertainment spectator pattern roots in earlier types of large gatherings of highly emotionalized people, although the content of such gatherings has changed considerably and has been greatly amplified by modern technoloy and the strategies of the hoopla public relations experts. In the county fair, the Chautauquas, minstrel shows, cabarets, religious revivals, and especially political rallies of older vintage we find the essential ingredients that make for the mass gathering with its highly charged emotions and theatrical trimmings. The form of an audience with crowd characteristics remains generally the same, sometimes passive, sometimes aggressive, but always with an intensive interaction that results in irrational and often nonsocial behavior. The older forms of mass gathering and public entertainment have declined in significance, partly because of the invention of new forms and the according of respectability to others. Chautauquas were given the coup de grâce with the invention of the film and the development of the movie industry. Showboats and minstrel shows, quaint anachronisms in the twentieth century, likewise became peripheral as a form of public entertainment. The local political rally has been superseded by the planned manipulation of the political convention. These semiorgiastic occasions are complemented by many other annual conventions, often featuring horseplay and drinking in the twentieth-century megalopolis, as participants seek release from local community restraints.

Sports, originally amateur, became commercialized. Professionalized athletics, the mild gladiatorism of modern times, became acceptable. Baseball, boxing, and wrestling are good examples. The great sports became something to watch, not to participate in. The invention and acceptance of football and basketball added more possibility for the spectacle, for commercialization. The mass entertainment spectator pattern is not peculiar to schools. It is a major aspect of modern culture and society, of Western civilization. The school, unintentionally perhaps, supports this pattern.

Mass spectatoritis, as an almost daily or weekly occurrence, depending on the event, is something new. The older forms were characterized by relatively long in-between periods of calm, at least for the years before 1890. It was after the nineties that the mass entertainment spectator pattern grew, as part of the general shift from the agricultural, small-town society to the urban, industrialized society. This is the period characterized by the newer methods of transportation, communication, and entertainment, the invention of new sports, and so on. It is a period marked by the development of the high school. It is a time of increasing leisure. Communality disappears and special-interest groups take over. Social distinctions become stronger. Competition for distinctive styles of living develops. Community integration weakens. This pattern of change accelerates until the new alignments appear between 1915 and 1920. By 1920 the change has been completed. The twenties add their hedonistic touch to the elaboration of the mass entertainment spectator pattern. A total change has taken place, illustrated as follows:

College Mirror, vol. I, No. 8 (May, 1875): "Croquet, baseball, and football come in for about an equal amount of patronage now."

Athens Messenger, December 4, 1890: We were lately gratified in witnessing a game of football on the college campus, particularly as it awakened hope of the permanent introduction here of that healthy, harmless, and interesting diversion."

Alston Ellis, *Annual Report of the President for 1907,* p. 35: "Athletics in college life means little more than preparation for and participation in intercollegiate games. Systematic drill in the gymnasium is not popular with the students. I am not a football enthusiast. The whole athletic effort in college, as I see it, is a necessary evil. . . ."

Athens Messenger, November 1, 1915: "To denature football and put it on par with tag and leap frog would be a national misfortune. For it represents the last stand of natural vigorous American youth against encroaching softness and enervation. Football is not for the weak, of course. . . . But for the sturdy youngster there's nothing better. It turns mollycoddles into men. It has the virtues of war without war's evil."

Athens Messenger, November 11, 1915: "Dr. Ellis made quite a strenuous speech in eulogy of the team. . . . He rubbed something into the tightwads among the faculty who, he said, draw big incomes from the state but are too stingy to go away from home to encourage the boys who risk life and limb to bring glory, honor, and more students to the university."

Athens Messenger, October 13, 1915: "The secret of success is support.
. . . If an educational institution or a town falls down at football and
baseball, the trouble is not always with the players. It is more often the
community they represent. There are many people who will sour on a
team and stay away if it loses a game or two. But where a team has an
enthusiastic bunch of rooters behind it who are loyal through both victory
and defeat, sooner or later it is apt to make a record."

On a par with croquet in 1875, football by 1915 becomes a national symbol of collective effort, honor, and heroics—a major
change. This overall transformation is also suggested by a study of
the biography of heroes in popular magazines from 1900 to 1941.[3]
The major shift in the nature of these heroes occurs in 1910–20,
corresponding to the change mentioned above. The heroes in the
earlier publications were primarily "idols of production," people in
industry, business, and scientific research. Heroes in the twenties
and thereafter are primarily "idols of consumption," people in the
world of sports and entertainment.

High school and college were growing rapidly in this expanding,
secularizing world. The expansion of the school system itself was
marked with internal conflicts over the curriculum. In this reorganization the sciences and practical courses won out. The emphasis on
athletics fits in with the secularizing tendency. It is also a rational-
izing tendency, for early competition between schools was somewhat
haphazardly organized and carried out. The new trend definitely
organized this competition, institutionalized it through special associations and rules. Such hyper-development is an extension of the
physical education program into areas that were not commercialized,
such as football and basketball. The sports early commercialized
played a minor role. The newer sports, relatively untainted, became
the hubs around which the school rotated. With community support
and demand, demand of students, demand of alumni, mass sports
entertainment was on its march to the giant spectacles of the twenties and ensuing decades. This development also centered in the
school in the smaller towns, for the school, especially the high
school, is the only group that can furnish common ground and focus

[3] Leo Lowenthal, "Biographies in Popular Magazines," in Paul Lazarsfeld and
Frank Stanton (eds.), *Radio Research, 1942–1943*, Duell, Sloan and Pearce, 1943,
pp. 507–520.

to a community. The rest of the community is particularized in the variety of its associations. The school also became the focus for the 14-year to 18-year population, which had no significant function to perform in the community and society at large. To integrate the focus of attention, to create in-group solidarity in the absence of unifying intellectual interests, the mass entertainment spectator pattern as centered in the team provided the necessary social mechanism. Other functions of the school, such as the band, the yearbook, awards day, assemblies, were geared into promoting this loyalty-creating pattern. Eventually the pattern became an end in itself.

STRUCTURE OF MASS ENTERTAINMENT

For the thousands that come together to be entertained there may be no realization of the complex structure that organizes the whole pattern. In the three fields of football, basketball, and band there is a highly integrated structure, a structure that becomes relatively independent of the schools which created it. High schools are organized in the High School Athletic Association, which is the state-wide organization divided into a variety of districts, sections, and counties. Within the district, schools will be graded as to the class in which they compete. The Athletic Association formulates the code according to which the contests run. Both football and basketball are organized in this way. On the college level there are the various conferences, Big Ten, Ivy League, Southwest Conference, etc., which organize the various universities and colleges. These again are united in a national organization, the National Collegiate Athletic Association, which attempts to deal with general rules concerning the games and the athletics.

Bands, which predominate with the decline of the school orchestra, are similarly organized. A state association organizes the annual band competition in section, district, and state band contests. This organization, as a rule, hands out the composition that all bands must play in addition to two other selections, typically a march and two overtures.

In all three there is a drive to be champion or at least a medalist. Football, on the high-school level, as a rule is not fought to a finish as is basketball, where a state champion is proclaimed. It is for this reason that intense interest and hope follows the high-school basketball team.

There will be a chance for the individual to be selected on an all-conference, all-tournament, all-state, or all-American team. Events may be capped by participating in various national tournaments. The operation of the pattern entails a vast expenditure of intelligence, effort, funds, and facilities. It is on the basis of this structure that the hundreds and thousands of spectators gather.

Emphasis so far has been upon the structure that developed within the schools. Support is given by many outside groups and especially by the mass media of communication. Special booster clubs for the various teams and band are found in almost every community. For example, in Newark the Booster Club erected a scoreboard and installed a public-address system on the football field. The Newark High School Band Parents Club, which includes others interested in the band, coöperates with and assists the band director in securing needed instruments, uniforms, and other equipment, and in furnishing transportation for the band members to football games and other places where they are to play.

To give an adequate performance in the mass entertainment pattern involves an intense specialization and concentration of effort. Football practice starts in late August, a couple of weeks before school proper begins. During these weeks there may be two practices a day ranging from two to two and one-half hours. When school is in session, practice is daily for about two hours, usually in the afternoon. Four to five games are played at home and an equal number away. The playing nowadays is often on a Friday evening with an afternoon pep assembly and, on the previous evening, a pep rally. Basketball training starts toward the end of the football season, with the first game early in November and the final state championship game sometime in March or April. The marching band also starts its practice early, sometimes a week or more before school starts. Several hours a week are devoted to preparation for the performance at half-time, which is a competition of showmanship between local and visiting bands. Drum major, drum majorettes, and cheerleaders also swing into practice. The bands, drum major and majorettes play a more important role during the football season, with cheerleaders minor, but during basketball season the situation is reversed.

MEANING OF THE PATTERN—APPRECIATION, HEROICS, COMMUNALISM [4]

A devotee in the mass entertainment pattern is not a mere puppet letting a flood of stimulation agitate his sensibilities. The play is the thing, and he has to know what it is all about if he wants to get the most out of his experience. This appreciative meaning of the pattern, from the viewpoint of the spectator, emphasizes that the play is an important, rich event intrinsically, an end in itself. Good, high-quality play must be striven for by the participant and is appreciated by the spectator. Hence the jeers, boos, or roars of approval that accompany games. This appreciative aspect of the pattern extends also to the intricate marching movements of the band, the contortions and gyrations of the drum major and drum majorettes, and the cheerleaders.

The heroics in the pattern are demonstrations of strength, courage, skill, and endurance. Here is the chance to prove oneself in the masculine sex role. These virtues are called out through the game. The participants channel their conduct to the achievement of courage and skill and to the demonstration of endurance and the ability to take punishment. When such conduct is exhibited, the approval of the spectators roars out and so reinforces the pattern to achieve heroics.

While the appreciative and heroic aspects of the pattern center upon a glorification of the virile young man, they also involve the glorification of the physical female. Selection of females to fill majorette and cheerleader roles takes place with an eye to physical form. Dress and uniform are designed to bring out and emphasize physical attributes. The glorification of the physical female in this situation is but a phase of the diffusion of techniques and erotic values from the demimonde, burlesque, cabaret, and night club into the culture at large. The majorettes posture, strut, kick their legs.

[4] Much of this analysis is derived from Philip Frohlich, "Sports and the Community," unpublished doctoral dissertation, University of Wisconsin, 1952.

The scanty, abbreviated skirts are designed to focus on exposed leg and thigh. Hence, erotic and sexual overtones are imparted, and this is just another instance of the voyeurism characteristic of our culture. The acceptance and diffusion of this cute playing around with sex and physical form is so pervasive that it infiltrates into the elementary school. The author has observed fourth-grade girls playing by themselves go through a cancan routine including the appropriate lifting of skirts. Varsity shows may be a bit more sophisticated, but the emphasis is still the suggestive same. Sex receives its due homage.

The communal aspect of the mass entertainment pattern, especially in the one-high-school community, involves the creation of an in-group solidarity. Community members and participants are united in a common cause of upholding honor and fame in the community or bringing them to it. The participants contribute by playing well and winning, and the spectators by their mutual support, praise and blame, and general recognition of the community importance of the team:

I'm overwhelmed, as are all the rest of you. The final minutes of that game tonight and this reception for the team is just about as wonderful a moment as I've ever had. It's wonderful for Nelsonville and wonderful for the school. [Superintendent L. C. Gray]

I've been looking for this for 23 years. [Principal J. K. Kinneer]

A proud moment for the citizens of Nelsonville, a great honor for the team, the school, and the community. We're truly proud of the boys and the school officials. Thursday will be Greyhound day in Nelsonville. I hereby proclaim it officially. [Mayor Paul Galvin] [5]

So began the homage to the fighting, clean, sportsmanlike performance of this basketball team which had won the district basketball championship. A full-page ad sponsored by seventy-three firms showered congratulations upon the team. "We and all of Southeastern Ohio are proud of you. On to Columbus to final victory!" The year of all this ebullience is 1952. Twenty-seven years ago the same pattern was found in *Middletown*.[6] It is more entrenched now.

[5] *Athens Messenger*, March 16, 1952, p. 4.
[6] Robert S. Lynd and Helen M. Lynd, *Middletown*, Harcourt, Brace and Company, 1929, pp. 217, 284, 484–486.

FURTHER IMPLICATIONS OF THE PATTERN—
ANTI-INTELLECTUALISM AND COMMERCIALIZATION

The mass entertainment spectator pattern expresses the nativist and market orientations. The humanistic orientation becomes secondary. As long as there is this focus on mass entertainment, the school exploits the bodies and minds of its students. The growth of the student is less important than the achievement of success and community recognition. The school heroes are the "idols of consumption." To be called "a brain" is to be given a derogatory epithet. Serious students are awarded "greasy grind" and other uncomplimentary labels. Recognition of scholarship pales beside the adulation heaped upon those who excel in public performance. Students must specialize to be successes, for themselves and for the school.[7] The variety of pep rallies, special assemblies, dances, games, and other performances produce a culture that makes study not only difficult but undesirable. Intellectual values are by-passed, and this is also facilitated by the whole competitive arrangement. For example, musical education is minimized because time is spent learning marching patterns, marches, and school songs and preparing the few pieces for state competition; result: incessant practice within a narrow range of musical experience. The whole structure of the mass entertainment pattern results in a narrowing of experience and a subversion of intellectual values.

That this emphasis is regarded as undesirable has been recognized by educators.[8] The extension downward to the elementary and junior-high level is deplored. The persistence of the mass entertainment means recruitment of personnel. The college secures its material from the high school, the high school from the junior-high or elementary school. The competitive pattern, minus the big crowd, organizes activities in the lower grades.

Yet, "Inasmuch as pupils below the tenth grade are in the midst of the period of most rapid growth, with the consequent bodily weaknesses and maladjustments, partial ossification of the bones,

---

[7] "We Have to Win," *NEA Journal*, October, 1953, pp. 418–420.
[8] Educational Policies Commission, *School Athletics: Problems and Policies*, National Education Association, 1954, pp. 5–13.

mental and emotional stresses, physiological readjustments, and the like: Be it, therefore, RESOLVED, that the leaders in the field of physical education should do all in their power to *discourage* interscholastic competition at this age level because of its strenuous nature." [9] This resolution was passed in 1938 by the American Association for Health, Physical Education, and Recreation after consulting the National Education Association and the American Medical Association. In 1946 the resolution was reaffirmed. Similar resolutions have been passed by the Society of State Directors of Physical Education, the Western Conference of Physical Education Directors, and many state associations of physical education.[10] However, the trend seems to be to organize such competition even on fifth- and sixth-grade level. Here is a peculiar situation. Complete opposition is voiced to such athletic competition on the basis of certain physical and social growth factors, opposition that is against the mass entertainment pattern. Yet the very people who state this opposition on humanistic principles seem compelled to support the pattern on all school levels. In spite of their concern, children are still used for ends which make for an unbalanced, if not unhealthy, growth. Furthermore, children may approve and enjoy this competition even though according to the facts they are also injuring themselves. The practical implications of knowledge are rejected.

It is no doubt true that in competition there will be demonstration of "dirty" tactics and poor sportsmanship. Where competition is exceedingly strong, there will be a greater tendency to "dirty playing" which can be carried out in a very skillful, unobtrusive fashion. The great number of rules forbidding certain tricks of the game are ample evidence. They place obstacles to a tendency in the pattern "to win at any cost." The following are samples from the football rules: [11]

The mandatory suspension for striking an opponent with a fist or for kicking or kneeing him has been expanded to apply also to striking an opponent with the forearm, elbow, or locked hands.

[9] Elmer Mitchell, "The Case Against Interscholastic Athletics in the Junior High School," University of Michigan School of Education *Bulletin*, November, 1951, pp. 23–24.

[10] *Ibid.*, p. 23.

[11] Norm Nevard, "Stiffer Penalties in 1952," *Football Digest*, p. 67.

Clipping (old rule): throwing the body across or running into the back of an opponent, other than the runner, below the waist. (new rule) blocking an opponent, other than the runner, from behind, i.e., the rule has been redefined to include blocking from behind above the waist as well as below it.

In Elmtown, during the basketball game with the arch rival, supporters of the team offered a dollar per point which a player made. Three boys were barred from playing because of unnecessary roughness; one of them knocked down a member of the opposing team.[12] Even without the formal competition situation mutual recrimination, expressions of hostility, and aggressiveness tend to occur. Interclass baseball, for example, at West School in Mill City was played with a deadly seriousness, particularly by children in the younger grades when they challenged an upper grade. The mutual disgust and hostility that frequently occurred after a bad play or a lost game was very violent. The children would scream and bellow at the offending child with venomous ferocity. Arguments would be carried from the field into the classroom, where the teacher finally stopped the bickering.

If one considers also the problems centered on the selection of a team and on winning, the unsocial implications are wide. Girls are automatically excluded and relegated to a subordinate position. The arguments as to who is a good or bad player become vicious in the rather blunt approach children take (as, "He's no good!"). If there is a clique, the other, unorganized boys are at its mercy. The interschool competition of the elementary schools in Mill City duplicated the pattern of the high school, including the crowd-spectator behavior, on a rather small scale.

The recruitment, the subsidization, and the disregard of scholarship requirements reinforce the tendency to anti-intellectualism and commercialization. These three aspects vary on the different school levels. They are least significant on the elementary level. On the distortion in the educational program the Educational Policies Commission makes this comment:

Teachers are sometimes under pressure to excuse athletes from regular assignments or to lower academic standards to keep athletes on the eligi-

[12] August Hollingshead, *Elmtown's Youth,* John Wiley and Sons, 1949, p. 194.

bility list. Scheduled classes in physical education are sometimes used to give extra practice time for the varsity. Athletes' opportunities to profit from the total school program are reduced when they are absent from academic classes for practice or play—and when their minds are preoccupied with last night's exciting contest or tomorrow's crucial game. Athletes' absences also hamper the orderly progress of instruction in regularly scheduled classes to the disadvantage of others as well as of themselves.[13]

On the financial aspects, the Commission states:

When the support of a school's athletic program depends largely on gate receipts, bad practices almost certainly follow. To make as much money as possible, games are played at night during the week, and too many games are scheduled. Moreover, to prevent having to forego income, games are played in bad weather. To attract spectators, games are scheduled with unequal opponents. To accommodate large crowds, fire and safety codes may be violated. . . . The feeling that spectators are necessary to get money to pay the bills is often a prime cause for exaggerated emphasis on winning games. Schools sometimes accept financial help from "downtown" merchants and "interested" citizens in the form of direct contributions, buying advertising space in programs, or favors of various kinds. Often such benefactors feel they have a greater right than other citizens to influence school athletic policy.[14]

These problems likewise continue on the college level, especially when the capital investment in competitive contests is huge. Malpractices of various types were found during the 1920's in a survey of college athletics carried out by the Carnegie Foundation for the Advancement of Teachers.[15] In 1950, an effort to oust seven colleges and universities for violating the National Collegiate Athletic Association's "sanity code" failed by twenty-five votes.[16] The demoralization that takes place when success in football becomes a major objective was shown in the irregularities in the athletic program and resultant administrative changes at a large university.[17] The pattern

[13] Educational Policies Commission, *op. cit.*, p. 8.
[14] *Ibid.*, p. 9.
[15] Cf. Savage, *American College Athletics*, Bulletin No. 23, Carnegie Foundation for the Advancement of Education, 1929.
[16] Watson Fenimore, "The Football Frankenstein," *The Progressive*, January, 1951, p. 17.
[17] "The Faculty of William and Mary Responds to Responsibilities," *American Association of University Professors Bulletin*, Autumn, 1951, pp. 476–496.

of anti-intellectualism and commercialization is one with different nuances on the various school levels.

The culmination of the commercialization principle has been noted in the rash of post-season football bowl games, reaching a high of thirty-two bowl games in 1948–49, including a Cigar, Cattle, Flower, Fish, Freedom, etc., Bowl. In basketball the national games played at Madison Square Garden are big business. Since mass entertainment is big money, it attracts "shady" customers. The result has been the flare-up in 1951 of bribery and corruption charges in basketball. About forty players, several of whom were All-American champions, six colleges, and one referee were involved. An immediate reform movement was instituted, raising again the problems of recruitment, subsidization, scholarship requirements, and the effort of the athlete to turn his achievement into cash value while professing amateur status. As long as the mass entertainment spectator pattern prevails and as long as it provides big money, the difficulties are likely to remain.

While the mass entertainment pattern has a community unifying function, as discussed above, it also has the opposite tendency, i.e., the fostering and perpetuation of community cleavages and disorder. The community solidarity feeling created by the mass spectacle lasts as long as the spectacle, as long as there is the audience-crowd behavior. A community is not based on uniformity of emotional feeling, but if such feeling is to be a major factor, it can be maintained only by greater spectacles, more spectacles, constant propaganda, and crisis situations. But the outcome is theoretically a crowd, so that the community vanishes into mass emotion. The community mass spectacle may produce a spurious solidarity. When the event is over, the existing cleavages and differences continue.

Frequently rowdyism and vandalism have been associated with pep rallies that culminate in mob attacks on the rival high-school students, the high-school building, and the police with youthful zest, enthusiasm, and ingenuity. More serious implications arise when the cleavage involves ethnic and religious groups. The type case is the competition between parochial school and public school. In Mill City when West School defeated a parochial school team for the championship, a fight which was developing in the locker room was stopped with some difficulty. In Burlington, Vermont, at one time, the hostilities that developed during the playing of basketball games on the high-school and elementary level between public and parochial school teams became so serious that the series of games had to be played off without an audience.[18] A by-product of the pattern is intensification of community cleavages or intercity hostility.

CHANGES IN THE PATTERN—A QUESTION OF ENDS

There is no inherent reason for schools to promote the mass entertainment pattern. The very elaborate associational structure, the investment in stadium and other equipment, and the tradition of the pattern insure its continuance, however. Defense has been made in economic terms: the proceeds help to finance other school activities, though, of course, the greater proportion may be used to underwrite the mass spectacle. There is an effort today to deëmphasize and yet continue the mass pattern. The effort as carried out by the variety of athletic associations on college and high-school level is to put into effect more rules to control the problems that continue to erupt, as in the case of the basketball briberies of 1951.

Another possible way of dealing with the problem is to make a radical evaluation, putting into effect the humanistic orientation, i.e., to abandon the mass entertainment pattern. The outstanding instance here is the abandonment of football by the University of Chicago. A less drastic approach was used by Johns Hopkins University. This approach first emphasized a physical education program for the students' benefit and enjoyment, teaching skills that might be of use in later life. Second-year students may participate in either intramural or intercollegiate sports, but with a major difference. The university abolished paid admission to all of its home games and abolished financial guarantees to visiting athletic teams. It supports athletics from regular college funds just as any other department is supported. Johns Hopkins athletic authorities "are convinced that the elimination of gate receipts and of guarantees is the only answer to the problem of keeping college athletics on a rea-

[18] Elin Anderson, *We Americans,* Harvard University Press, 1937, p. 217.

sonable and amateur basis." [19] The assertion of intellectual values over commercial and hedonistic ones underlies the action and policy of these two universities. Sports are no longer the major foci but take their place among other pursuits.

High-school athletics can be similarly reëvaluated, as the Educational Policies Commission shows. The thinking expressed in the summary of its report on athletics has much in common with the views of the policy makers at the universities mentioned.[20] The Commission realizes that the problem involves faculty, superintendent, board of education, state departments of education, the state associations, parents, booster clubs, etc. The high school, junior high, and elementary school are not in a cultural vacuum, so the intended change will be extremely difficult to realize. For the present, therefore, the mass entertainment pattern with all its implications will remain.

> Oskie Wow Wow—Skinnie Wow Wow
> Rah, rah, rah
> Yeaaaaaaaaaaaaaaa, Team.

Selected Readings

Danford, H. C., "Why Interscholastic Athletics?" *Wisconsin Journal of Education,* January, 1947, pp. 221–222.

Educational Policies Commission, *School Athletics: Problems and Policies,* National Education Association, 1954.

Folger, O. Herschel, "Are Commencements Bunk?" *School Activities,* February, 1952, pp. 194–195.

Group, Don, "I'm Through with High School Football," *Saturday Evening Post,* October 11, 1952, pp. 42–43, 83, 86–87, 90.

Gruber, Frederick, and Beatty, Thomas, *Secondary School Activities,* McGraw-Hill Book Company, 1954, chaps. 10, 15.

Hess, Walter, "The Commencement Program," *Bulletin of the National Association of Secondary-School Principals,* February, 1952, pp. 195–203.

Stuber, G. M., "Championship Athletics Without Gate Receipts," *High School Journal,* November, 1950, pp. 180–182.

Waller, Willard, *The Sociology of Teaching,* John Wiley and Sons, 1932, chap. 10.

[19] Watson Fenimore, *op. cit.,* p. 19; corroborated in a letter by Dean G. Wilson Shaffer of Johns Hopkins University.

[20] Educational Policies Commission, *op. cit.,* pp. 81–84.

CHAPTER 9

The Functional Order
as Group Process

CHILDREN AND teachers carry out the various tasks, skills, projects, and events which compose the functional order. In the coördination of efforts required, coöperative or opposing relations arise among children or between children and teacher. Such relations constitute a social aspect of the functional order. For present purposes this phase is abstracted from the functional order. The title of this chapter means that the functional order can be viewed as a system of coöperation and opposition. In recent years [1] there has been much emphasis on group relations, group dynamics, or human relations in the school and in the curriculum, a stress which recognizes the significance of this social dimension. At present the analysis, while isolating this phase, still relates to the functional order. In a later chapter the same dimension will be examined apart from the formal structure and organization of the school.

A FEW EXPERIMENTAL AND
OBSERVATIONAL CONSIDERATIONS

To introduce the topic, several reports will be discussed. In this way the student may see how the findings were secured and interpreted. Approaches differ, though conclusions tend to be similar.

[1] See Selected Readings at the end of this chapter.

This corroboration or convergence of findings is significant, though such agreement of itself is no criterion for the validity of the studies.

DEMOCRATIC AND AUTOCRATIC GROUPS

If there has ever been a study much quoted, popularized, and anthologized, it has been the research in democratic and authoritarian group atmosphere.[2] This bit of work has had an extraordinary diffusion and acceptance. The findings came at an appropriate time, for the Nazis were on the march. Democracy was being debunked and disparaged by the totalitarians. The country was reeling out of the depths of the depression and recoiling from the recession of 1938. The study provided a reassuring function: that all was well with democracy and that autocracy was bad. The superiority of democracy was, thus, "proved" by science. An appeal to science was more reassuring than a mere assertion of traditional values. All is well, for science says so! Acceptance was largely uncritical, and the limitations of the study as indicated by the researchers, especially by Kurt Lewin, have been overlooked. Nevertheless, the conclusions from the study may be considered as "basic" to much of current thinking about groups, especially by educators. The report must be carefully examined.

What did this study attempt to investigate? There were three major objectives. The first was to find out what happened to a group under specific kinds of leadership. The types of leaders were labeled democratic, autocratic, and laissez-faire. The democratic leader was to play a coöperative role, the autocratic a dominating role, and the laissez-faire a passive role. The second aim was to find out what occurred to the group when the leadership changed from one type to another, a study in social change. The third objective was to develop and improve observational and recording techniques in group study.

The groups were composed of boys from the Iowa University Laboratory School. They were similar as to age, IQ, popularity as

[2] Kurt Lewin, Ronald Lippitt, and Ralph K. White, "Patterns of Aggressive Behavior in Experimentally Created 'Social Climates,'" *Journal of Social Psychology*, May, 1939; Ronald Lippitt, "An Experimental Study of Authoritarian and Democratic Group Atmospheres," *Studies in Topological and Vector Psychology* I, University of Iowa Studies in Child Welfare, No. 16, 1940.

measured by sociometric tests, teacher rating, personality adjustment, and socio-economic background (essentially upper middle class). These boys, scientifically viewed, were homogeneous units, each like the other, upon whom the leadership stimuli were to play. The question as to whether the homogeneity of the group had any effect on the stimulus was not considered. Each group contained five boys, either 10 or 11 years old, depending on the account one reads, working on handicraft activities, such as soap carving and the making of masks from plaster casts. The groups starting with the democratic leadership had a discussion on what to do and were skillfully led by the leader to accept the handicraft work he had in mind. The autocratic groups were simply informed what the projects were.

The first experiment had one group under democratic leadership and one under autocratic. The second experiment had four clubs, each experiencing five democratic sessions, five autocratic, and two laissez-faire. Each group in the second investigation met for fifty minutes once a week for five months. A change of leadership took place every sixth meeting.

The autocratic leader, despite his dominating influence, was a "nice" autocrat. Radical autocratic methods, such as corporal punishment, use of threats, or instilling fear, could not be used. In addition, the men who played the leader roles maintained a friendly and congenial relationship with each member outside of the regular club situation. If the experimenters had been consistent, the autocratic leader should have been autocratic both inside and outside the club meetings. This dual role of the leaders may have affected the results of the experiment. In addition, there was no check as to the extent to which the children discussed their experiences among themselves outside the club meetings. It must also be kept in mind that the children did not live in an autocratic or laissez-faire society and that they were selected from a presumably "progressive" school. The problem, then, is one of noting how children, socialized democratically, respond to certain kinds of adults.

As the experiments were carried out, two clubs met together in the same room, though in different areas. The researchers attempted to discount this fact as unimportant. The presence of the two groups did affect responses, as indicated by statements in the reports that the children in one group observed those in the other with friendly or unfriendly comments. In addition they had the chance to observe the differences of leadership in action. These observations in turn may have affected their interaction. The presence of observers, of which there were several, apparently was of no significance. This can easily be explained by the fact that in most "laboratory" schools children are accustomed to frequent visitors.

The study, in simple terms, leads to certain conclusions. Children (at least these children) will work hard in an unpleasant situation if they have to. These 10- or 11-year-olds usually responded without relish, but work they did. Playful conduct was conspicuously absent. Four out of the five groups subjected to autocratic leadership responded in this way. Only one, and this group is usually emphasized in most accounts, responded aggressively to the leader and among themselves. In the absence of leadership, these groups almost completely stopped working. In the groups under democratic leadership the amount of work was mediocre but more continuous than in the others in the absence of leadership. Relations to leaders and among members were more friendly. Play behavior was organized rather than disorderly. The laissez-faire situation, never a really organized group, showed essentially that young children need direction and guidance if they are to accomplish any work. They are apparently not competent to plan and organize a set of integrated activities for a long period of time. The children in this situation worked with difficulty. Play behavior tended to be more disorderly. The most marked changes took place during changes of leadership, so that the study might more aptly be described as an investigation of reactions to breaks in leadership. The disruption caused by the change in leadership may have been more important than type of leadership.

An aspect of the study underplayed or just omitted were the "wars" that developed between the groups in the room. (These wars, of course, show that the two groups in the same room had no effect on each other.) The conflicts took place after critical comments about the projects had been made by a stranger (a graduate student in the role of a janitor) during a planned absence of the leader. Apparently these groups could not take the criticism and expressed their hostility by throwing things at the other group. The groups were in one instance a laissez-faire (the aggressor) and a democratic club, and in the second instance two democratic clubs. Although an enormous amount of generalization has been based on this experiment, no one has ever drawn the conclusion that democratic and laissez-faire groups are prone to war or conflict. That would be an unpalatable finding. Yet none of the autocratically controlled groups were so involved! The corollary that autocratic groups are peacefully inclined was also not drawn, for such a finding would be not very acceptable. Thus, it seems that people draw out of this research only those conclusions and findings that they want. Nevertheless, it did appear that the children under a system of sharing and co-planning had a more enjoyable time.

The problem as to the general implication of the study is the most important aspect. Lewin, who directed the study and also furnished the theoretical framework, suggests great caution: "Generalization from an experimental situation should, therefore, always go to those life situations which show the same or sufficiently similar general patterns."[3] In other words, what life situations are similar to that faced by a group of five 10-year-old boys, carving soap or making masks from plaster casts, meeting once a week for fifty minutes with a drastic change in leadership every six weeks? The obvious answer is that there are no identical or even similar situations. The designed experiment is a unique historical event, and furthermore, there is much to suggest that the actions within the groups cannot be accounted for by the leadership. One variable recognized as extremely important was the handicraft club activity. The experimenter realized that the activities selected were individualizing, i.e., did not make for group integration or much mutual assistance. The children became bored with the activity. How much of the observed conduct arose out of the handicraft tasks was not worked out. There was little recognition on the part of the investigators of the normative order that organizes a group. In addition, there was the assumption, a fallacious one, that as soon as three people meet there is an institutional group. None of these groups were bona-fide groups. Perhaps they were groups in the making, but they were not established, were

[3] Kurt Lewin et al., *op. cit.*, p. 297.

without a history, without tradition; in short, they were lacking a developed social system and without clarity as to the values supported, unless it was the experiment itself.

Some of the findings do not arise out of the interrelation but from the nature of the experiment. Thus, the person playing the autocrat was instructed in the delineation of the role to issue orders, the laissez-faire leader to issue none, and the democratic leader few. The findings are that the autocrat issues lots of orders, the laissez-faire leader almost none, and the democratic leader few. This is a kind of experimental or verbal juggling similar to that of the magician who puts the rabbit in the hat and then pulls it out. The intellectual superstructure of program and policy erected on this flimsy foundation is enormous, and the words "autocratic," "democratic," "laissez-faire" group atmospheres, climates, and leadership have become intellectual clichés. Much of the material found in this study can be interpreted through some sociological principles which will be mentioned below. The limitations, however, must be firmly grasped. The nature of society is not revealed in temporary aggregations of five 10-year-olds meeting fifty minutes once a week.

DOMINATIVE AND INTEGRATIVE BEHAVIOR

A series of observational studies made in nursery, kindergarten, and higher grades in the elementary school tend to substantiate the findings of the experiment just described.[4] Instead of contriving a social situation, the investigators worked out a set of categories to classify behavior and then observed life situations.

What is the difference between integrative and dominative behavior? The former is characterized as a harmony of differences, the

[4] Harold Anderson, "Educational Implications of Research in Dominative and Socially Integrative Behavior," *Journal of Educational Sociology*, April, 1940; Harold Anderson, "Dominative and Socially Integrative Behavior," in Roger G. Barker et al., *Child Behavior and Development*, McGraw-Hill Book Company, 1943; Harold Anderson and Helen Brewer, *Studies of Teachers' Classroom Personalities*, American Psychological Association, Stanford University Press, 1945; Harold Anderson and Joseph Brewer, *Studies of Teachers' Classroom Personalities*, II, *Effects of Teachers' Dominative and Integrative Contacts on Children's Classroom Behavior*, American Psychological Association, Stanford University Press, 1946; Harold Anderson, Joseph Brewer, and Mary Reed, *Studies of Teachers' Classroom Personalities*, III, *Follow-up Studies of the Effect of Dominative and Integrative Contacts on Children's Behavior*, American Psychological Association, Stanford University Press, 1946.

finding of common purposes among differences. It implies flexibility of response, spontaneity, and insight into others. Dominative behavior is characterized as a conflict of differences leading to a stifling of differences in others. It involves a rigidity of response and a minimum of understanding of others, an "inability or unwillingness to admit the contribution of another's experience, desires, purposes or judgment in the determining of goals which concern others." [5]

The findings are as follows. Dominative behavior brought forth a similar response in the other. Integrative behavior induced similar behavior in the other. These relations held true for interchild relations and teacher-child relations. Teachers who used an integrative approach brought forth more spontaneity and initiative in children, and the converse held true for teachers with dominative contacts. Teachers tended to be consistent over time in their use of integrative or dominative behavior, though they tended to express dominative behavior more than the integrative.

A third study, included for matters of convenience in this section, reaches the conclusion that history teachers who are more autocratic teach significantly more historical information as measured by mean scores on a test than teachers who are more congenial and democratic.[6] This conclusion is explained on the assumption, which is not proved, that students expect teachers to force them to learn; hence the better showing of the autocratic teachers. This report tends to support the experimental findings that children work harder under "autocratic" leadership. In this study, however, the conception of the autocratic leader is not well worked out since the term is equivalent to an unpopular person—a sissy, somebody peculiar, not admired, not helpful. On this assumption, so-called autocratic behavior is a response to a student expectation and not something that originates solely within the teacher.

These studies tend to corroborate each other. To be more meaningful, they should be viewed in a systematic way. The following

[5] Harold Anderson and Helen Brewer, *op. cit.*, p. 9.
[6] Wilbur Brookover, "The Social Role of Teachers and Pupil Achievement," *American Sociological Review*, August, 1943, pp. 389–393; cf. Arthur Katoona, "Comment on Brookover," *American Sociological Review*, February, 1945, pp. 108–109, for a critical note.

general principles are offered to give this unity, and they will be applied to the above studies. The student may wail that here is more of the intellectual jargon that social scientists perpetrate. Every science, however, has a jargon, as do the humanities. In each area a student must learn the specialized vocabulary, not as an end in itself but for the order and insights engendered. The following points constitute part of the systematic framework utilized in this book.

A FEW SOCIOLOGICAL PRINCIPLES

The word "social" will be used to refer to mutuality, to interdependent living, coördinated effort. Anything that promotes this will be termed "sociative." Anything that interferes with the social will be termed "dissociative." Human relations may be viewed as fostering and maintaining or as obstructing and even destroying the social.

The findings and observations of the reviewed studies may be understood as expressing the following principles: augmentation of dissociative relations, complementary dissociative relations, augmentation of sociative relations, and complementary sociative relations.[7]

The autocratic leader of the experimental study and the dominative behavior of the observational express the two dissociative relations. The complementary dissociative relation is a paired relation, involving necessarily at least two parties, the dominator and the dominated, the coercer and the submitter. Such a relation may involve two or more persons, two or more groups. It may be formally or informally organized. The crux of the complementary dissociative relation is one of coerced or forced domination or submission. It is a relation of actual or implied power over others. The submitting or subordinated person or group will remain in that position as long as the force remains. Since the submission is unwilling, the person or group will reassert itself when the power is weakened or absent. The gas chamber, the concentration camp, corporal punishment, social and economic deprivations or discriminations, threats, harsh

[7] E. T. Hiller, *Social Relations and Structures,* Harper & Brothers, 1947, pp. 178–190.

disapproval, ridicule, or criticism are ways involving complementary dissociative relations. In the studies, the repressive behavior of the leader forced the children to stick to their tasks. Upon his absence the work remained undone. If the power is regarded as weak or weakening, behavior on the part of the submitters may become aggressive and nonconforming to the directives of the dominator. The augmentation of dissociative relations involves increasing mutual hostility. An unfriendly response when met by an unfriendly response tends to confirm the negative relationship. The longer such a relation obtains, the more each participant is convinced as to the antagonism of the other, and the more set he will be to respond hostilely. Thus, the autocratic leader creates a hostile response. The children respond negatively. This antagonism tends to reinforce the negative actions of the dominator. If the submitters cannot voice hostility to the dominator, they may express it among themselves.

The democratic leader and integrative behavior involve the two sociative relations. The complementary sociative relation is one of willing and admiring subordination. The star-follower relation is an example, e.g., a movie star and his fan clubs, Father Divine and his disciples, the democratic leader and his five boys. In the last case the leader and boys are as nearly on an equal plane as possible within the age status relation of adult-child. The invidious comparisons between the various leader types made by the boys indicate their preferential appreciation for the democratic type, who was regarded as a "good sport" and "nice." The democratic leader is the friendly, coöperative adult in contrast to the authoritarian adult. The age statuses in themselves put the boys in a subordinate position, but admiration and enjoyment of the leader make it willing subordination. The second principle, that of the augmentation of sociative relations, states that in so far as a friendly inclination is met by a friendly response it is thereby reinforced. Mutual aid and mutual love are examples of this relationship. The assistance given or the love demonstrated is shared, confirmed, and deepened. This principle can be seen structuring the behavior of the democratic groups in the first study and characterizing the integrative behavior observed in the second study.

Deliberately maintained dissociative relations demonstrate another principle that is pertinent to the experimental study, i.e., to the relations between the autocratic and laissez-faire leaders and the boys. By the design of the experiment they had to resist any sociative effort to change their negative actions to sociative ones. The necessary failure of these leaders to respond to such friendly overtures by the boys may also have contributed to the observed results. This principle stresses the continuance of dissociative actions by design or policy and resistance to sociative acts of others by design and policy. The tendency here is to maintain a *status quo* situation. Diplomatic negotiations frequently are of this type. Relations between business groups and unions have often been organized by this principle.

The converse of this principle is a purposive change of a negative relation into a positive social direction. This also represents a planned or deliberately maintained policy. An example is an adult's deliberately refraining from making negative responses to an angry child and so intending to change the angry responses to neutral or friendly ones. The principle is especially pertinent in psychotherapeutic situations where the worker attempts to maintain positive responses despite negativism on the part of the client. The sociative act of the agent encounters a negative response. The agent deliberately continues to act in a sociative manner in order to convert the dissociative response to a positive one.

The last two principles involve spontaneous or unplanned responses. In the one case an unplanned negative act is changed to a positive relation when met by a friendly response. An angry relation can be modified or overcome when a calm, conciliating response is introduced. Conversely, an unplanned, spontaneous positive relation is transformed into a negative relation when met by an unfriendly response. A curt rejection or a brusque refusal to a friendly gesture may bring about hostility.

These principles are not automatic in effect. They are linked up in a context of norms and values. They are linked up with the various statuses. A situation is ordered by these principles as conditioned by functions, rules, and major goals. They apply to interpersonal as well as to intergroup relations. This total setting must be kept in intellectual focus.

A SITUATION ANALYZED

The following is from a study conducted by the author. By working through this example, we can make our point clearer. Comments on the actions are made in parentheses.

The seating in this particular grade was according to sex status. The boys were sitting nearest the windows and the girls on the other side of the room. A light test had shown that the lighting on the girls' side was relatively poor as compared to that on the boys' side. On the basis of this finding, a long-standing controversy had arisen over a new seating arrangement such that the light would be shared more equitably or at least so that the boys could not monopolize it. The class was organized for a discussion. The president of the class was in the chair. Observation began as the teacher was saying:

TEACHER: It is up to the boys if you move. (General negative reaction on part of boys shown by vigorous shaking of heads, frowns, and agitated whispering. From past discussions the boys know she wants them to change, so the relation is one of domination and submission because she is both teacher and adult. They counter with a negative tendency. The teacher responds with an appeal to norms and values to which the boys should assent. She tries to change this negative response to a sociative one. This effort is weakened because of the tonal quality in the voice, which suggests annoyance and anger.)

TEACHER: Now, there is a question of generosity. (value and norm) Consider that I'm not deciding for you. (democratic value implying that the teacher does not intend to solve the situation in terms of complementary dissociative relations) It's a question of being fair. (appeal to norm) It's like asking a favor of you. (implied sociative relation) Ask yourself that. You have to learn to give in. (appeal to norm of compromise) It's the most difficult thing to do. The girls have been here all year. It's not fair. (appeal to norm) Argue with common sense, not with emotion: I will, I won't. (defines procedure of carrying out discussion in terms of norms) Make your mind rule your body.

MARTIN: (at far end of room and one of the social isolates seated together) I don't care where I sit. (This remark is directed dissociatively to the dominant clique of boys at the window and associatively to the teacher and to the girls. The teacher snaps up this comment.)

TEACHER: His argument is very good common sense. (Her statement is dissociatively directed to the clique so that the relationship between teacher and clique is of the augmenting negative type just as the implied relation to the girls is the augmenting sociative type. The girls realize this.)

HELEN: Gee, we've been sitting here a long time. It's only fair if we can see the room from another point. (Appeal to norm, and this reinforces what the teacher and Martin have been saying. The girls nod their heads to indicate approval of the statement so that their ranks are being closed as against the dominant boy clique. Relations are becoming increasingly structured in terms of the augmenting dissociative principle, as Peter says . . .)

PETER: We've been here a long time too, and we like it here.

TEACHER: (bluntly) Are you selfish? (Negative evaluation of Peter in terms of values of goodness, sharing, and so on. Relation dissociative augmenting with a touch of dissociative complementary for she is still the teacher and adult.)

PETER: (emphatically) No! (Dissociative augmenting relation. Peter reassures himself that he is not selfish nor are the members of his clique. Some fast pro and con between boys and girls—augmentation of dissociative relations.)

TEACHER: You boys have had the best light. The light was measured and your side has the best light. (statement of facts, but communicated in a hostile tone so that the impartial facts are socially negative as far as the boys are concerned) Why not share it with the girls? (appeal to norm) Are you selfish? (emphatically to the boys, negative assessment of boys) You have had the best light from September to March. It's hard to give it up. (introduces a sociative response to change the dissociative of the boys through an appeal to norm of sacrifice) Why don't you make yourself do the hard thing? I'd go over there (i.e., to the girls' side) and sit in pitch dark. (slight tittering and laughter among the girls realizing their solidarity with the teacher; scowls from the clique) DON'T SIT THERE CLOSE MINDED! (dissociative climax)

JOHN: You're the teacher of this room. You're the boss of this room. You make . . . (Defines the significance of the status relation of teacher-pupil, realizing that the situation can be either complementary sociative or dissociative. John implies the latter, suggests nondemocratic setup.)

TEACHER: I don't feel that way at all. I'm just one of the group. (reaffirms democratic value orientation) Sometimes your ideas are better than mine. I know a little more than you as in arithmetic, but on this subject you handle the question. (John's statement has thrown the teacher morally off-balance, and hence, she tries to right the situation by an appeal to equalitarian values. These are sociative tendencies but again weakened by the tonal quality of the voice.) We've had this over and over again. Where you sit has been argued all year. I'll give you one more minute and then table it. (complementary dissociative) Why do you keep your minds closed? (The teacher suggests a committee to work out a new seating arrangement. She ignores Peter's request that the committee be composed of two boys and one girl.) There will be no more discussion till tomorrow. It's closed. (The discussion concluded both sociatively, through the selection of a committee to solve the problem, and dissociatively, through the final remarks.) You're not president. (to the boy who is presiding, spontaneous dissociative act) Now that makes me cross. Adjourn the meeting. (dissociative complementary) (The meeting is closed and so voted, an associative action.)

TEACHER: The motion is carried; I can see that. (dissociative complementary)

PRESIDENT: (weakly) Motion is carried.

(A new seating arrangement was finally worked out by the committee. Note that the procedure for solving the problem was teacher originated. The new arrangement was put into effect. A few boys, however, continued to voice their objections in these discussion meetings.)

This meeting as a whole was organized sociatively between teacher and girls and the boys outside the clique, dissociatively between the clique and the rest of the room, sociatively among the clique members. The discussion included appeals to facts, norms, and values, which also structured the interaction pattern that took place. In fact, the functional order becomes meaningful and the social relations that took place become understandable only in relation to these facts, norms, and values. While the class is organized as a committee as a whole to consider common problems, the formal structure of the school (teacher status, pupil status) and the informal structure of the class (clique versus the others) affected the trend of relations. Possibly adult-child status was an additional element which could make for complementary relations, and lastly, there was sex status, boy versus girl, in the sense of "we don't want to sit by girls." There is also the general orientation of the school which the teacher is trying to put into effect, i.e., children should solve their problems through group discussion, and that is the humanistic orientation.

The situation also illustrates the difficulty of carrying on the functional order on humanistic principles. The teacher oscillates between dominative and integrative behavior. The children shift from one type to the other. Since the issue is controversial, the tendency to dominative behavior is increased unless there is a planned policy to change dissociative actions to sociative. The incident described was unplanned, and in view of this fact and the absence of deliberately maintained sociative relations, the actions in the group discussion (i.e., the functional order) took on a dominantly dissociative character. While a count of the relations could be made, what is more important is the quality of the relation. If a situation is organized in terms of the complementary dissociative principle, a continuous stream of negative actions will flow on. This is identical with the autocratic group atmosphere. The aggressiveness in the above situation is abetted by the democratic values of the culture, possibly also by social class and minority conflict patterns. Instead of suppression and apathy, the release of aggressiveness is stimulated. The teacher is not the sole source of the kind of relations that organize a situation. Relations arise out of the total culture patterns as they find expression in the classroom, and in the special culture of the school.

PARAPHERNALIA OF TECHNIQUES

The functional order as group process is not only an analytical problem but also a practical one. Activities have to be carried out in some manner. In recent years much attention has been devoted to group discussion and group problem solving. New techniques have been developed, many of them in therapeutic situations and with adults so that the carry-over into school may be uncertain.

In group discussion a variety of functions must be carried out. These have been described as:

(1) group task roles—functions that coordinate and facilitate the problem solving; (2) group building and maintenance functions, those activities that keep the group working as a group. Under the task functions would appear the following: information seeking and giving; value or objective seeking and giving; initiating proposals or ideas in relation to means and/or ends; coordinating ideas; suggestions, or activities of members and subgroups; evaluating progress, logic, facts, procedures; recording suggestions, decision. Under the building and maintenance functions are the following: mediating differences between members, praising and

accepting ideas and contributions of others, encouraging participation, observing and commenting on group progress and group difficulties.[8]

There is nothing new in this particular listing, but it does make explicit some of the functions in group discussion that the members and leaders must keep in mind. For better discussion and problem solving, the participants must maximize the task, building, and maintenance functions. All of these, as can be seen, are sociative in nature. The converse of these functions will lead to a disorganized discussion and frustrated problem solving.

Of the various devices to expedite the working of groups on problems the group recorder, group observer, resource person, and sociodrama are newer developments. What was done originally in an unsystematic way is now to be done in a more formal fashion. The function of the group recorder is to keep a record of the development of the discussion or the working on the problem. At any time he can be asked to report on what has been done, where there are cleavages of ideas, points of agreement, uncertainties, and so on. The main function of the observer is to help the group work better. He "takes responsibility for watching how the group works as it works, and interpreting what he sees; what the leader does and what happens as a result; what different members do, why they do it, and its effects on the group; how well the group stays on the problem, etc. . . . He doesn't talk down to the group or tell the group what it should have done. His job is to raise questions about what happened so the group can discuss why and decide what should be done about this kind of happening next time."[9] As the term "resource person" indicates, the individual is a specialist or one who has considerable practical experience. He may perform both task and maintenance functions, though his major contribution lies in the former. If the person is not much of a verbalist, he may act out or portray in some situation his methods of dealing with it. This way of working out a problem leads us to a consideration of the sociodrama technique.

[8] Kenneth D. Benne and Paul Sheats, "Functional Roles of Group Members," *Journal of Social Issues*, Spring, 1948, pp. 42–47.
[9] Kenneth D. Benne and Bozidar Muntyan, *Human Relations in the Curriculum*, The Dryden Press, 1951, pp. 158–159.

The sociodrama, first systematized as a technique by Moreno,[10] is a method of analyzing a problem by playing it out; that is, it is problem understanding through role playing. Members in a group or class take on the roles of characters in the problem situation and act out spontaneously what they would do in dealing with it. The technique has a variety of aspects. There is a warming-up period. The group leader by encouraging audience or class participation tries to bring out problems which are shared. The members of the group, by posing the problems, are brought into the situation, have a stake in the discussion. Once a general problem is finally decided upon, it is narrowed down to a size that will lend itself to the sociodrama technique. The group then decides what characters are included in the problem—how many and what they are like. The setting of the problem may be defined in general terms. Members of the group will be selected or will volunteer to take on specific roles. They may be briefed a little more in detail before they spontaneously act out the situation. A few other techniques might be mentioned. The use of the soliloquy is a method in the form of an aside or comment showing what one of the participants really thinks about the matter as the problem is being acted out. The group leader may cut in to emphasize a point. At the conclusion of the sociodrama members of the group may be interviewed. Roles may be exchanged, e.g., a superintendent plays the role of teacher, and vice versa. The role playing may be evaluated as to its accuracy. The problem may be played again by the same members or by different members. The problem playing will involve the sociative and dissociative principles discussed, norms of conduct, cultural values, and the various statuses. The solution of the problem, moreover, may be purely theoretical rather than actual, in any discussion or class group. The sociodrama is not the actual world, but there seems to be a carry-over from the discussion group to the actual situation.[11]

With emphasis on the group as well as problem solving in educa-

[10] J. L. Moreno, *Who Shall Survive?* Nervous and Mental Disease Monographs, Series No. 58, Nervous and Mental Disease Publishing Company, 1934, rev. ed., 1953. Cf. *Group Psychotherapy*, vol. 1, Beacon House, n.d.; Robert Haas, *Psychodrama and Sociodrama in American Education*, Beacon House, n.d.
[11] Kurt Lewin, "Group Decision and Social Change," in Theodore Newcomb et al., *Readings in Social Psychology*, Henry Holt and Company, 1947, pp. 330–344.

tional practice, it is not surprising that a class should be subdivided into work groups. Some of these groups represent merely a difference in ability, say in reading and arithmetic. There is no organization in these groupings, so it is doubtful whether such a gathering of children should even be designated as a group. In others a division of labor may be worked out. Different aspects of a topic are parceled out to interested members, or several committees may be formed, each to prepare a section on the topic. Such a system of committees, according to some educators, is the crux of the core curriculum in operation.[12] The class, to describe it politically, sits as a committee of the whole to listen to and to discuss the reports. Committees may be created or disbanded as the occasion demands. Committee work is the democracy in action that educators deem desirable. How this system is to work out in such fields as chemistry, biology, physics, shop, etc., has never been clearly stated. Most of the examples of committee systems are taken from the social studies. The use of this device puts on a tremendous pressure for coöperation, though frequently one or two dominant children do all the work for the subgroup, and the rest are followers. The use of the committee system poses the whole problem of the relation between the formal structure of the school and the informal structure among children.

THE PRACTICALITY OF GROUP DYNAMICS

Quite often the opinion seems to be that if the teachers would only stop being autocratic and carry on school activities through committees, the school as an experiment in democratic living would be assured. Group dynamic techniques, such as use of the group observer and group recorder, are theoretically designed to facilitate the democratic process. But to what extent are these techniques really useful?

Size of class and the way the physical order is arranged will affect the answer to this question. Let us consider the first, a perennial problem, i.e., what is optimum size. The greater the number of children in a class, the less likely it becomes that democratic pro-

[12] Roland Faunce and Nelson Bossing, *Developing the Core Curriculum*, Prentice-Hall, Inc., 1951, pp. 108–130; Edward A. Krug, *Curriculum Planning*, Harper & Brothers, 1950, pp. 201–208.

cedures will prevail. The strain of handling a large number of children, especially on the elementary level where contact is persistent for several hours, may so affect the teacher that her conduct will bring forth tensions. In an evening class the author had a teacher who dealt with about fifty-three 6- and 7-year-old children in a combined first and second grade. The teacher was fundamentally friendly but was also tense, high strung, and aggressive. She was quite frank to admit that she did not see how she could put into effect democratic procedures with these fifty-three young children. About four months later the class was divided as an additional teacher was hired. The change in our teacher was remarkable, almost overnight. She was relaxed and at ease. The tenseness and the aggressiveness were no longer noticeable.

A study on teacher loads, based on 3707 teachers, brought out the marked physical and nervous strain that teachers experienced when classes were large. The study also showed that teachers were less able to put into effect individualized instruction and less likely to use desirable methods and procedures. The large classes increased problems of classroom management. Pupil achievement was less satisfactory. Undesirable work habits developed.[13] The large class on elementary and high-school levels tended to be structured in terms of the augmenting and complementary dissociative principles. Perhaps this is unavoidable.

Size of class must be considered in relation to age. Many of the described techniques have been developed with and used by adults. Obviously in a prenursery school situation there cannot be, among the 2- and 3-year-old members, a group observer and group recorder, for they do not have the skills that make the playing of such roles possible, nor do they have the requisite social insight to know what it means for a group to function effectively. Would third-grade pupils—8 years old—do better? If the class is not too large, there is a good chance for some of these techniques to work, with adroit supervision. The committee method, to be efficient, requires a good deal of guidance. That such help from an adult is necessary is implied in the results of the laissez-faire experimental study. To com-

[13] NEA Research Bulletin, *The Teacher Looks at Teacher Load,* November, 1939, pp. 251–252.

plete their projects even the 10-year-olds needed an adult who worked with them in a friendly way.

Size of group and age of its members must also be related to the nature and meaning of the activity or the problem. Activities may be individualizing or integrative. They are individualizing in the sense that a person can perform the activity without reliance upon the help of another person. Many art and handicraft activities are of this nature. Reading and writing also fall into this category. A reading group is composed of persons performing the same activity. They usually are of the same reading ability. The effort to read does not depend upon the others, though their presence may serve as a stimulus. The child stumbling laboriously through a reader, however, may bore the other children with the resultant restlessness which accompanies boredom. Individualizing activities pose problems in classroom control or management different from those produced by the integrative activities. In the latter, the successful completion of the project rests directly upon the coördination of functions and coöperation of the participating members. The need for coöperation inheres in the activity, not in the persons. A puppet play, a dramatic performance, a basketball game, folk dancing are examples of integrative activities. Such functions furnish their own group dynamics, and there is no need to resort to special manipulative techniques. The problem, then, becomes one of discovering within the range of the school's program such integrative activities and problems. The trouble with a committee system is that it frequently becomes a mechanical way of subdividing the topic to be investigated. Educators have rightly been concerned with problems that are really meaningful and significant to the children, but this whole idea has been explored only in general terms. Much of the evidence and discussion is anecdotal. The dilemma may be seen in reading, for a child already has a rich and varied life before he enters school, an adequate speaking vocabulary, and then, he is reduced to reading "Run, Bobby, run." This comment is not intended to disparage readers but to indicate a problem in significance and meaning.

The sociodrama may be too explosive a technique to be handled in an uncritical fashion. A similar technique, the psychodrama, is used in mental hospitals to work out emotional and interpersonal living problems. The sociodrama can do a lot of damage if it is unintentionally converted to a psychodrama. The teacher is not a psychiatrist or a mental hygienist. While the teacher must be aware of personality problems, he should realize his limitations in helping the child solve them. On issues in which personal involvement may not be overly great, issues that are widespread, or historical, sociodrama may become an effective teaching device.

The reorganization of a school's functional order cannot be a piecemeal process. It has to be tackled as a whole and on all fronts simultaneously. Group dynamic techniques, for example, must be used in the school as a whole. If they are not, the children go through a bewildering set of experiences—group dynamics in the third grade, traditionalism in the fourth, a combination of the two in the fifth, and so on. Furthermore, the process must be carried out through the whole educational system. One or two instructors cannot effect a total change. The change must be on the elementary, high, and college level. If elementary-school graduates trained in a traditional school enter a high school with a core curriculum approach, a fundamental reëducation must take place. This reorientation may take a couple of years. Or let us assume that a student graduates from a traditional elementary school and high school and enters a college where one department tries a "group dynamics" approach—the chances of failure will be high. To be thoroughly effective the change must be total.

Selected Readings

Benne, Kenneth D., and Muntyan, Bozidar, *Human Relations in Curriculum Change,* The Dryden Press, 1951.

Cartwright, Davis, and Zander, Alvin (eds), *Group Dynamics, Research and Theory,* Row, Peterson, and Company, 1953.

Cunningham, Ruth, et al., *Understanding Group Behavior of Boys and Girls,* Columbia University Press, 1951.

"Curriculum in Intergroup Education," *Bulletin of the National Association of Secondary-School Principals,* February, 1949.

Group Dynamics and Education, reprint of articles appearing in *NEA Journal,* 1948–49.

Group Process in Supervision, Association for Supervision and Curriculum Development, National Education Association, 1948.

Haas, Robert, *Psychodrama and Sociodrama in American Education,* Beacon House, n.d.

Hiller, E. T., *Social Relations and Structures,* Harper & Brothers, 1947, Part 3.

Improving Human Relations, National Council for the Social Studies, 1949.

Life Adjustment in the Secondary School Curriculum, National Association of Secondary-School Principals, May, 1950.

Miels, Alice, *Cooperative Procedure in Learning,* Columbia University Press, 1952.

Olson, Willard, "Human Relations in the Classroom," *NEA Journal,* December, 1947, pp. 640–641.

Report of the Second Summer Session in the National Laboratory in Group Development, Committee on Adult Education, National Education Association, 1948.

CHAPTER 10

The Normative Order in the School

IN ALMOST any classroom, especially in the lower grades of an elementary school, an observer will note a recurrent phrase, sometimes put in terms of a plea, a request, or a command. "No talking now." "Let's be more quiet." "SILENCE!" The teacher is putting into effect a norm about conduct. Pupils are to act in certain approved ways. The rules which describe the approved way are called norms. They also apply to the teacher. In fact, both teacher and pupil have always lived in norm-regulated conduct. Some of the rules that controlled the New Haven Grammar School and the church meeting in the early days included the following:

That the Schollars being called together the Mr shall every morning begin his work with a short Prayer for a blessing on his labours and theire laboring. That ye Schollars behave themselves at all tymes, especially in Schoole tyme with due Reverence to theire Master, & with Sobriety & quietness among themselves, without fighting, Quarreling or calling one another or any othrs, bad names, or useing bad words in Cursing, taking the name of God in vaine, or other prophane, obscene, or Corrupt speeches which if any doe, that ye Mr Forthwith give them due Correccion. . . . That if any of ye Schoole Boyes be observed to play, sleep, or behave themselves rudely, or irreverently, or be any way disorderly att meeting on ye Sabbath Dayes or any other tymes of ye Publiqu worships of God that upon information or Complaint thereof to ye due Conviction of the offender or offenders the Master shall give them the Correccion to ye degree of ye Offense. And yt all Correccions be with Moderacion.[1]

These rules of conduct were about the same in the school and in the church. Most of them are still effective norms today. Three hundred years later almost identical rules! How can that fact be explained? Why these norms exist, what they are supposed to accomplish, and how they operate are the questions to be explored in this chapter.

The spirit of any rule of conduct will flow from the values of those who frame it. Norms are instituted for some reason, and reasons always lead us back to values. However, sometimes norms seem to become almost ends in themselves. The original value is lost sight of and the rule continues on its traditional momentum.

Norms are proscriptive (forbidding certain conduct) or prescriptive (specifying desired conduct). In the New Haven example, most of the norms are stated in proscriptive terms. Within the extremes of proscribed or prescribed conduct there may be a range of permissive conduct. Actually, even in the case of a rigid norm like "no fighting" there is a certain permissive latitude. On the playground scuffling usually must become violent and antagonistic before sanctions or controls are exerted to bring about an acceptable level of conformity.

Roles of pupil and of teacher are defined by the norms. A pupil must act in certain ways toward his teacher and the teacher likewise is bound by the norms to certain behavior toward his students. Other interpersonal relations are controlled by norms. Often the expected behavior is generally known in the culture and is remarked upon only when it is not forthcoming. Punishment and how it should be carried out is part of the normative order. This is usually not formally stated, except in the extreme cases of violation where suspension is the ultimate and specified result.

Despite the mountains of research devoted to the school and education, the analysis of the normative order has generally been by-passed or ignored. As a result, little information is available, and much of the material will deal with the West School in Mill City.

[1] Alvin Johnson, *The Legal Status of Church-State Relationships in the United States,* University of Minnesota Press, 1934, p. 9, quoting Brown, *The Making of Our Middle Schools.*

THE NORMATIVE ORDER AS EXPLICITLY DEFINED

We have already noted that within the legal order there is ample reference to the normative order of the school. Statutes, court rulings, and administrative decisions are to be followed by the school. Principal and teachers are responsible for the enforcement of these norms. They may have the aid of the police and the courts, if necessary. It might be well to recall the legal definition of juvenile delinquent (p. 79).

In the statutes, truancy is proscribed. In addition to trying to find out why a child is truant, a teacher must take some action which indicates that nonattendance cannot be tolerated. In extreme cases the truant officer will step in. If he is not successful, the juvenile court, if there is one, is called into action.

Table 24 shows the amount of violation with regard to school attendance in Mill City. There is a real difference between the schools. The difference between West and Shebaug is one of procedure and values. West School, with its more humanistic orientation, investigates a child very thoroughly and attempts an adjustment before action is taken. In Shebaug cases are turned over more readily to the truant officer. Here the enforcement of the legal norm is relative to the value assumptions of the school. The enforcement may also involve social class, so that action will be more lenient to higher-status children and more severe to lower-status children. There is some evidence that upper class children are so favored in high school. However, the topic needs more investigation, particularly in large school systems.

The all-around well-being of the child is one of the ultimate ends in the humanistic orientation. The legal order supports this in its emphasis on child safety and welfare, provision for healthy physical growth and intellectual and social development. Even though these ends may occasionally be subverted, principals and teachers are constrained by the legal order to fulfill them. They are legally responsible for the child from the time he leaves home until he returns. Relevant parts of the legal order which prescribe good conditions for growth are incorporated into the normative order of the school.

EXPLICIT NORMS WITHIN THE SCHOOL

School level and size of school system will influence the extent to which norms are stated in written form. The elementary school may have very few explicit norms. There may be an occasional note on

TABLE 24. Truancy Reported by Truant Officer in Public and Nonpublic Elementary Schools of Mill City for Designated Years

Year	Total	Nonpublic	Total	Public	
				West	Shebaug
1932–33	88	20	68	32	36
1934	100	45	55	25	30
1935	43	9	34	15	19
1936	50	7	43	26	17
1937	64	14	50	29	21
1938	47	13	34	16	18
1939	53	17	36	11	25
1940	63	16	47	10	37
1941	73	27	46	8	38
1942	84	18	66	26	40
1943	70	8	62	35	27
1944	51	4	47	21	26
1945	50	12	38	8	30
1946	33	n.r.	33	11	22
1947–48	18	n.r.	18	3	15

SOURCE: Truant Officer's Report, in Annual Report of the Board of Education for the designated years. N.r.: not reported. Average number of cases: West School, 17.5; Shebaug, 26.3.

the bulletin board, "No snow-balling on playground" for example, but otherwise pupils receive no formal set of norms. Teachers may receive written instructions concerning norms, but there is nothing of a codified nature. On the high-school and college level there may be handbooks for both students and faculty, defining norms and listing sanctions to be applied for violations. When there are no handbooks for students, the first issue of the student paper is frequently replete with normative suggestions. If there are only instructions for faculty, these formal norms may be transmitted to the students in the homeroom, during orientation week, and by other means. Where there is student government, many norms will be formulated in constitutions and bylaws.[2] In general, most of the norms are implicit and are learned in specific situations, but the groundwork for learning these norms is in the elementary school.

Two Cases of Explicit Norms on the High-School Level. Students of Holland High School formulated the following ordinances, backed up by a set of penalties and enforced through a student court. "It shall be unlawful for students of Holland High School: (1) to conduct themselves in a disorderly manner in the assembly room of said school, (2) to conduct themselves in a disorderly manner in any hall, cloak, room, or room not being used as recitation room of said school." [3] These are the first two ordinances. The remaining nine deal with unexcused absence during school hours, loitering around the school building during school, stealing or damaging property, use of tobacco in any form, disorderly conduct when the regular teacher is absent, gambling in any form, eating in the school building during school hours, resisting or insulting an officer of the school while performing his duties, and a series of rules dealing with the parking of cars. Most of these norms deal with the order and welfare of the school, and a few touch on general norms of honesty and probity. These norms also emphasize status relations between teachers and pupils.

In the following case the faculty was concerned with developing more student responsibility.[4] The faculty made out a list of specific situations in which they expected pupils to accept responsibility. The students were asked to describe specific things for which they were willing to accept responsibility without the need for continued supervision. The material was tabulated and circularized. In this manner norms of the school were made explicit. Table 15 contains the major areas and specific situations which faculty and pupils rated. There is a great similarity in the two ratings, but there are also some significant differences, differences that did not fit in with the faculty's value orientation. In addition the faculty expected the pupils to be prompt, to meet deadlines, and to be friendly to new

[2] Theral Herrick, *School Patterns for Citizenship Training*, Bureau of Educational Reference and Research, University of Michigan, 1947, especially pp. 119–125.

[3] *Ibid.*, pp. 120–121.

[4] Stephen Corey and Gustav Froehlich, "A High-School Staff Studies Pupil Responsibility," *School Review*, October, 1942, pp. 568–576.

TABLE 25. Relative Importance of 42 Specific Pupil Responsibilities as Judged by Faculty and Pupils,
University of Chicago High School

Responsibility	Percent of Faculty			Percent of Pupils		
	Very Important	Rather Important	Slightly Important	Very Important	Rather Important	Slightly Important
Pupil as individual						
Plays fair, does not cheat	100	—	—	87	2	13
Plans ahead, does something about own progress	96	4	—	72	26	2
Uses knowledge in new situations	77	23	6	60	36	4
Admits mistakes, takes consequences	77	23	—	70	25	7
Gets to class on time	64	36	—	69	27	4
Relates exercise to group goals	55	36	9	47	17	19
Gets going under own steam	55	45	—	61	34	5
Hands in neat, legible papers	36	64	—	61	34	5
Relation of pupil and his peers						
Considerate of others in gym and on playground	86	14	—	50	44	6
No ridiculing or unkind laughter at mistakes of others	86	14	—	65	30	5
Quiet when others want to listen, work, or write	73	23	—	80	18	2

Listens courteously at assemblies, coöperates on programs	77	23	—	58	40	2
Avoids interrupting others in class or meetings	73	27	—	65	32	3
Does not tease during class	59	36	5	30	45	24
Helps all members feel at home	32	64	4	36	42	22
Supports pupil activities, teams	27	68	5	48	40	12
Helps absent classmate get assignments, materials	—	68	32	21	59	20
Relations of pupils and staff						
Keeps appointments and promises	96	4	—	81	11	2
Does assignments and accepted tasks as well as possible	86	14	—	87	17	2
Takes care of school property and equipment	77	23	—	75	23	2
Takes care of own make-up work and extra-help needs	73	27	—	73	24	3
Completes assignment promptly, hands in on time	68	32	—	83	17	—
Gets to work, does not disturb others	68	32	—	79	18	—
Behaves appropriately in library	68	32	—	61	34	4
Reasonable conduct in corridor	55	45	—	33	54	13
Behaves appropriately in lunchroom	50	50	—	37	59	4
Takes part in group work and discussion	45	55	—	53	42	5
Takes lead when necessary to get things done	41	59	—	36	50	14

TABLE 25. Relative Importance of 42 Specific Pupil Responsibilities as Judged by Faculty and Pupils, University of Chicago High School (*Continued*)

Responsibility	Percent of Faculty			Percent of Pupils		
	Very Important	Rather Important	Slightly Important	Very Important	Rather Important	Slightly Important
Reports breakage and loss of school equipment immediately	41	50	9	49	36	15
Plans ahead for class group project	36	59	5	29	56	15
Plans ahead for club programs	32	54	14	14	26	49
Gets assignments straight first time	27	68	5	60	37	3
Uses bookstore for "business only"	5	50	45	14	40	46
Presents absence slips, excuses, etc., without reminder	—	59	41	20	52	28
General relations						
Shows courtesy to visitors	64	32	5	27	61	12
Takes care of own and other people's property	55	45	—	43	47	10
Helps keep class and building neat without too much urging	27	68	5	45	42	12
Takes part in drives, etc.	27	68	5	45	42	13
Leaves building by 5:00 P.M.	18	18	5	45	42	13
Informs parents of important happenings at school	9	64	64	12	36	52
Informs parents of progress in school work	4	73	23	47	40	13

SOURCE: Stephen Corey and Gustav Froehlich, "A High-School Staff Studies Pupil Responsibility," *School Review*, University of Chicago Press, October, 1942, pp. 570–571.

pupils in the halls, while they themselves did not live up to these standards.

Study of the table will bring out the following points:

1. The norms in the table are not exhaustive. The general norm of "appropriate behavior" in library, lunchroom, and corridor becomes particularized in a host of subsidiary norms.

2. Teachers evaluate activities more rigidly than do the pupils. The range of permissiveness in conduct is greater among the pupils. Here is a possible source of mutual misunderstanding and resultant dissociative tendencies.

3. The emphasis of the norms is upon work, property, and etiquette. They are general, applying to both sexes alike. There are norms, of course, which foster sex distinction.

4. Those areas which 70 percent of faculty and pupils rate very important deal mostly with work.

5. Teachers rated more than 25 percent higher than pupils the following: shows courtesy to visitors, does something about own progress, is considerate of others in gym and playground, does not tease others during class period. This shows faculty emphasis upon work, etiquette, and classroom order.

6. Pupils rated more than 25 percent higher than teachers the following points: hands in neat, legible papers, gets assignments straight first time, informs parents of progress in school. The emphasis is upon work. How well he can live up to the second norm depends upon the efficiency of the teacher.

7. Norms which a considerable percentage of pupils regard as of slight importance as compared to faculty rating are: does not tease during class, helps all members feel at home, plans ahead for club programs.

Explicit Norms on the Elementary Level—West School. Aside from an occasional prohibition that appeared on the bulletin boards, there were only three instances of explicitly formulated norms, and these were directed to the teachers who in turn had to impart them to the pupils.

The first set of norms dealt with fire drill. The mechanics of the drill are the functional pattern, but how the pupil should act constitutes the normative aspect. In this instance the norms carry out the statutes, framed to insure safety of the child. Almost all schools have fire drill, and norms may be similar to the West School pattern, which is as follows:

1. Select group leader.
2. Plan for wraps before leaving, November through April.
3. Close all doors and windows.
4. Room teacher leaves last, end of line.
5. *Single line always.*
6. Walk rapidly.
7. *Absolute silence.*
8. Teacher count children outside.
9. Special teachers responsible for children with them.
10. Children out of class and not with teacher, leave building by nearest exit and join their class group outside.
11. Any teacher in auditorium with class alone above grade 4 may use fire escapes.
12. Groups on playground at time fire alarm sounds must line up immediately with teacher.

Action is organized for both children and adults. The instructions can be viewed functionally—walking rapidly, silence, etc.—but they also can be viewed normatively. To run, to loiter would be bad. To talk would be bad. Not closing windows or doors constitutes a failure to adhere to a norm of technical efficiency. The prescribed path out of the building must be followed. Any failure in carrying out the functional pattern is subject to criticism. The whole occasion is a serious matter, and a breach cannot be treated lightly. "Absolute silence" is an indication of the seriousness and significance of the pattern. From the teacher's point of view there may be a possibility of legal liability.

A second set of instructions relates to the playground. Again this pattern is concerned with function as well as norm. The end value of the pattern involves the safety and welfare of the child. Possible legal liability is a likely element in framing these rules.

1. Positively no bicycle riding on playground.
2. Positively no stone throwing on playground.
3. Children must be kept off fire escapes.
4. All apparatus must be closely supervised at all times.
5. No child shall leave playground without written *permission* (request from parent signed by teacher and principal). Names of children who

have such permit should be reported to principal's office by room teacher.

6. Lawns on West Street and Vale Street sides are not to be used as playgrounds.
7. South playground (West Street) is reserved for primary children.
8. No basketball played on south playground or in courts.

Here are found rights and obligations that define the content of pupil status, but some also apply to the teacher status. Several rules safeguard the younger children. Breach of rule 5 is considered especially serious, again because of possible legal action in case of an accident to a child. Rules 7 and 8 are designed for the sake of the lower grades and make for the internal differentiation of the school. Rule 7 confers a right and a duty. Rule 8 is a proscription directed especially to older children. The rules take into consideration the various age statuses of the children. Rules 1, 2, and 3, 5 and 6 would apply to all pupils. These formal rules do not, however, exhaust permissible and prohibited conduct on the playground.

The third instance relates to conduct in the halls. The teachers decided: "It is generally agreed among members of our staff that: Children should learn to enter, to conduct themselves, and to leave a school building, in a manner in which they will enter, conduct themselves and leave all public buildings in later life." The statement means that the child should act like an adult. Putting the idea into practice, teachers have been converted into hall guards, checking, praising, and punishing the pupils as they behave or misbehave coming into the school. Conduct as enforced involves taking off hat on entering, saying "good morning" to adults, walking rather than running or pushing, and waiting one's turn at the fountain quietly, though these latter norms are conventional and unwritten. Both children and adults must express courtesy and etiquette. However, safety of the child is also important.

NORMS AS IMPLICIT

Most of the norms in a school are not explicitly formulated. Our analysis will deal with conduct norms that are directly linked with the school, for there are other norms that deal with sex status, age status, social class, and other positions in a society. A wide variety of situations can be studied. In West School the following areas were observed: playground, halls, library, cafeteria, classroom. Children were interviewed about the rules they had to live by. To complete the normative picture of the school would involve analysis of norms as applied to the gym, the lavatories, the showers, coming to school and going home. Many norms overlap in various situations, as will be seen, but nevertheless, they may take on a specific qualitative experience because of the differences in these situations. For example, the norm "be quiet" has a different feeling tone and significance in the classroom, in the hall, in the auditorium, and on the playground.

In the observed situations 158 norms were found. There may be more, but this was the number collected from observation and interview. Information from the various grades was unequal, as Table 26 shows. The total number represents unduplicated norms. Over half apply to activities in the classroom. The actual number of norms in a school must be enormous, and they are transmitted informally from teachers to pupils or from pupil to pupil. In order to make clear the variations and pervasiveness of the norms we shall examine two grades in detail, the second and the sixth.

WEST SCHOOL—IMPLICIT NORMS IN GRADE 2

Children should be in class on time. In the morning children are expected to start work of their own accord. At the start of the afternoon session at one o'clock the child should have secured his blanket from an adjoining room, placed it on the floor, and started to rest. This bit of functional routine is bolstered with norms of efficiency. The rest period involves a set of specific norms: to be quiet, not to wiggle, not to play "footsies," not to whisper. "Let's have a room full of rag dolls, right away," says the teacher, but the "rag dolls" need more than command and exhortation. The proscriptions indicate how the rest period actually works out. A child is evaluated as a good or bad rester. In some classes the poor resters are isolated in another room. Children, as the "no footsies" rule indicates, should not be too close together when choosing a resting space. Those who are too close will be separated. Such separation has been routinized and possibly converted into a bit of play, and this last point means that the children have redefined the situation on their own terms. If the children are too close, they put up their arms and are pulled to another place. Pupils must rest till 1:30, and this demand makes for difficulty as time goes on. There is gradually more noise, throat clearing, twisting, and shifting on the mats. Toward the end of the rest period more control is needed to enforce the required conduct. At 1:30 the children are asked to get up. They pick up their blankets and pile them neatly in the adjoining room.

TABLE 26. Total Number of Norms by Major Functional Areas as Specified by Pupils for Designated Grades

Area	Total	Grade					
		2	4	5	6	6–7	8
Playground	25	4	7	9	10	4	13
Halls	19	3	5	4	14	5	10
Cafeteria	23	–	–	–	18	–	14
Library	11	–	4	5	6	4	8
Classroom	57	7	22	23	19	10	15
School work	23	7	8	10	12	9	7
Total	158	21	46	51	79	32	67

Children who fall asleep are not awakened. They usually are allowed to sleep up to fifteen minutes after the other children. They apparently do not feel embarrassed at waking up late. This means that individual differences are recognized to a certain extent, but on the other hand, there may be some children who do not need the rest and yet are compelled to go through the pattern. In this instance individual differences are ignored. The norms apply, nevertheless, with the resulting valuations of the child by teacher and other children. Resting is a complicated physical-social situation for the young child and imposes a great demand for self-control, adherence to norms, and an effort to fulfill the requirements of this function. It seemed to this observer that in view of the total situation the rest period had become formalized routine, a sort of end in itself, and this routinization made for the problems indicated.

Decorum and work are two main areas around which norms center. There is a general emphasis upon quietness. That means specifically: not to talk when someone else is talking, not all to talk at once, to move quietly, to move chairs quietly. For example, the teacher suddenly says during a class meeting: "Do you know what I think? Tell me what I think!" The children chorus: "Too much noise!" The teacher responds: "Too much chatter, too much chatter"; then a little later: "There you go again!" Admonitions to be quiet, to be patient, not to talk loudly are frequent, up to twelve times during half an hour. There is some laxity on this general norm of etiquette. It is more rigidly enforced during recitations and class meetings and less stringently during free periods of work. When to talk and how loudly to talk falls within a permissive range. The ultimate limits are reached when the teacher judges that communication is becoming difficult, or that work is being interfered with.

Work norms include: to do the work well, to do work alone, to hand it in on time, not to ask help from others unless permitted, to pay attention, to follow instructions, not to prompt, not to wave hands too much after a question has been asked. Children who did the last were dubbed "teasers" by a trainee student, but the waving of the hands may indicate interest and enthusiasm on the part of the children which is repressed or restrained. There is also the possibility that the waving becomes an end in itself from the point of view of the children and tends to make for a kind of crowd behavior. The work rules support certain values, such as efficiency, individualism and self-reliance, self-control, niceness of manners. Here there are suggestions of the market model. Coöperation is limited. In arithmetic it is usually proscribed. If a child completes work ahead of time, he is rewarded. He may choose an activity of his own, such as reading in the class library. The reward supports both the norm and the function. The following observation deals with this phase:

Teacher tells Danny that he has to play hide and seek with two wrong answers on page 85 on his workbook and that he must find them before the day is over. She shows art work done by children at the beginning of the year. She gives each his, commenting on how improved they are, as, "Isn't this a nice one? Here is a pretty one of Mary's; you've got a beautiful one over there." The teacher announces to the class they have a long and hard assignment, referring to the book work for the afternoon, and ends by saying, "I expect better work." . . . During a reading period the class is in two groups, one in the classroom and one in the adjoining room. The trainee student criticized Carl for talking too loudly while helping Patricia. Later she tells him that he's done enough and for him to do his own work and she hers. The children try to help each other by whispered prompting. Children also "sh . . . sh" one another. Annette and Helen have finished their work and thus have free time which they decide to spend at the little library table. The trainee student breaks this up saying that they should go back and read more as they were not so good yesterday.

The situation is a teacher-dominated one, though her actions comprise both positive and negative relations by extending praise and by criticizing. Work goals are set for the children by the adult and the amount of effort expected is similarly set. Rewards are not automatic. Children may have a sense of inconsistency when the job is completed and the reward denied. This last point indicates the formalized relations of domination and submission that obtain between teacher and pupil status. The submission may be willing or unwilling. If it is willing and even admiring, then the relations will be positive; if coerced, the relations will be negative, i.e., hostility, resentment.

Mutual aid among children is apparently very strong despite the norms which, at certain points, suppress it. As we have noted, in other situations mutual help is supported and approved. The problem, then, is one of defining distinctly those areas in which the conduct is or is not permitted.

The following observed situation is a complex interrelation of unction, norm, interpupil relations, teacher-pupil relations, and teacher-trainee-student relations.

The children go through the routine of forming a circle for a general discussion. They come in waves, quietly, arranging their chairs. The discussion deals with birds, apparently a testing of the children's ability to report orally for a future parents' visit. Teacher begins with some instructions to fill out forms for summer school if they wish to come. Children ask questions spontaneously. Teacher answers each briefly. She finishes and attempts to walk in back of the group. One chair blocks her, and she says, "I'm not going to walk around!" The child moves the chair into the circle, and the teacher continues around to the other side of the room. Then the bird discussion begins.

Children are chosen to report on a bird. Mary tries. Teacher asks specific questions, "What is its name?" (colors, etc.). Mary is slow. Teacher says loudly, "Come on dearie, don't waste our time." Trainee prompts girl, and the teacher calls her down. Jean replaces Mary and she is replaced. Others follow in rapid succession. Teacher interrupts throughout somewhat impatiently, as, "If you can't do better than that I'm not going to bother with you." Children try to help by prompting. Carl whispers to Alice. Teacher says, "Who is going to talk about the catbird?" Dorothy says, "Oh, let Helen." Teacher responds, "I'm not talking to you! Annette, do you think you could?" Johnny and Danny also try. Teacher leaves room. Trainee says she won't choose teasers. Children meow like catbird. The children laugh at Johnny because he says "boid." Trainee responds by saying, "People, let's not be silly. Let's see if we can hear the clock." All sit still until clock ticks the next minute. Johnny and Mary squirm in their chairs to make them squeak and smile with hands over mouth. Danny starts on the catbird but says he won't if they are silly. Carl whispers. Rachel pretends she is playing piano. Kathleen sniffles. Bob blows nose noisily. Feet shuffle. Teacher enters and without even hearing Danny says, "You can't do it. Sit down." He seems to accept this calmly, saying, "I don't care. I'm going to dance in the program." Teacher taps his head and remarks that everyone will have something to do. Gail does a good job reporting on the catbird. Children meow again. Teacher chooses Danny to speak on robin. Jean whispers. Rachel pulls skirt above thighs. Children yawn and wave arms. Danny sits after reporting. Next Carol speaks. Danny says, "Don't be afraid like I was when I started." Helen reports next, apparently badly, for the teacher says aloud, "That girl has the best head in the class and that's how she uses it." Mike talks next and does well. Tom and Danny appear well versed in bird lore and volunteer numerous bits of information. At 2:30 everyone stands up and stretches, then sits down again to prepare for music.

This situation, lasting about half an hour, is a complex of routine and spontaneity, interest and boredom, approval and disapproval, domination and submission, mutual assistance, adherence to norms, violation of norms, and control techniques. The organizing factor is the discussion of birds, the content of the functional pattern at the moment. This particular situation is also oriented to the parents. The expectations of the parents, as the teacher, trainee, and children imagine them, become integrated into the situation. The teacher can instruct about birds without reference to parents, but since a demonstration is to be given, the teacher becomes involved with success as a goal. A good performance, parental applause and approval take the place of educational goals. The introduction of the parents tends to subvert the humanistic orientation of the school. Parents may wish to see their children do well. The teacher wants the same because her self-esteem is involved and she wants the parents to rate her work favorably. Since her work is representative of the school, the school's prestige is also involved. All these distort the educational process, by the emphasis on the goal of a smooth performance.

WEST SCHOOL—IMPLICIT NORMS IN GRADE 6

The continuity of norms in this class with the previous schools and class discussed is clear. We shall merely enumerate them without comment. The statements are taken verbatim from interviews.

With regard to the playground:
  No throwing of stones, rocks, snowballs
  No squirt guns allowed
  No hard baseball permitted
  Not to go off playground during recess or lunch hour if eating in
    school (formal)
  No fighting or hitting others
  Not to ride bike on playground (formal)
  Not to go into school before bell rings
  To play on assigned playground (formal)
  Not to snatch hats
  Not to play rough
With regard to halls and stairs:
  To be quiet, not to yell or to make noise
  Not to run, but walk
  Not to write on walls
  Not to bounce balls
  Not to play in halls
  Not to push around
  To take off your hat
  Not to slide down bannister
  Not to fool (hitting, punching, i.e., in a friendly manner)
  To use own stairs and door
  Not to argue or push in line at fountain

To move in two lines
To be clean (i.e., not throwing candy wrappers on floor)
Not to slam doors
With regard to the classroom:
To do things quietly
Not to talk loudly
Not to make noise
Not to yell
No fighting
No teasing
No pushing
Not to speak out of turn
Not to "butt in" when teacher or someone else is talking
Not to fool around
Not to sass teacher back
Not to teeter on chairs
To do one's household duties
With regard to work:
To be neat
No talking when whole class or group is working
Not to help others unless teacher approves
To do work alone
To get work done on time
To pay attention to the teacher
To ask teacher or trainee for information
To raise hand during discussions
Not to prompt
Not to copy
With regard to the library:
Not to talk loudly or much
To talk softly or whisper
Not to throw books around
To act right (not laughing, fooling)
Not to visit or gossip
Supposed to read

It will be noted that many of the rules prohibit aggressive and conflict behavior, or, to state the case positively, that friendly and coöperative relations are expected. On the other hand, some rules interdict sociability. Many of the norms recur in a variety of situations, and these tend to be the more important ones.

The following description of this class in action shows the dominant role of the teacher, how the norms which pupils are expected to live up to come into action, how the teacher defines these norms and by their application determines a pupil's rating as relatively good or bad. It shows the norm of fairness to which both teachers and pupils assent.

At 9:42 the class meeting has come to an end. The room is reorganized for math. The teacher is handling Group II. The other groups are seated at the desks. Group II (an ability grouping), which includes almost everybody in the room, stands in a single line by the door, equipped with pencils. There is a general shuffling around as the pupils take other seats. Group II boys seat themselves together. (functional order implicitly organized by differences in sex status) Jeanette is stuck between the boys and seems embarrassed, smiling self-consciously to the other girls. Terry forces Mary to move by pushing her violently so that he will not be flanked by girls. (dissociative relations related to sex status) In the meanwhile the teacher, Miss Lewis, is telling Group III so that everyone can hear that they have done well on some problems and made foolish mistakes on others. (norm of work, teacher-dominant relation, praise and blame control technique) She instructs them to take separate desks so that they can work alone. (work norm organizing functional order) She emphasizes by saying, "I want you to work alone." (work norm with individualistic value orientation)

Two long lines have been arranged in front of the blackboard, some separation of pupils along sex lines. During the whole period Maisie seems stuck on a problem and sits drooping, doing nothing. (violation of work norm) At 9:45 the teacher begins the blackboard session, which is interspersed with comments to the other groups, as "Gregory, don't get help. (coöperation forbidden) You miss too many. I'll teach you." (control of alleged violation of work norm, individualistic emphasis, teacher dominant, pupil subordinate) Examples have been written on the board. There is a sort of competitive hand-waving situation. "Who can give me an example of so and so?" Hands fly up in the air, arms are waved vigorously until the teacher, looking up and down the two long rows, makes a choice. The hubbub temporarily subsides. (teacher dominant, pupils subordinate, individualist emphasis, moderate crowd behavior) In this manner the groups work through four rows of five examples each. Harold leaves his desk and comes to the teacher's and asks a question. (freedom of movements as norm) Teacher says loudly, "No, you don't have to go till ten!" (relation of domination and submission) "Go back to your seat!" Terry, Group II, speaks up: "Will we go out today?" Teacher: "We'll go out for half an hour. Let's keep our minds on arithmetic." (relation of domination and submission with teacher emphasizing functional order)

The other groups are working at the desks. Miss Lewis suddenly says (and thereby focuses attention on the event): "Gregory, are you getting help?" (alleged violation of work norm and second calling down of Gregory) Lucille rises to his defense (pupil-versus-teacher relation, Lucille introducing a sociative response to counteract the teacher's negative act) by explaining that he was not looking but getting an eraser from her. Teacher: "I didn't mean that you were really cheating, Gregory." (alleged norm violaton stated, third calling down of Gregory) "I want you to understand and work out problems for yourself." (affirming work norms with individualistic emphasis) The teacher has a couple of problems worked out on the board, selecting a couple of reluctant pupils. Miss Lewis: "Time is going so fast, we will not be able to cover what we want to do." (work emphasis with negative evaluation of progress) At this point Harold leaves the room with Andy. Miss Lewis checks other group: "Are you finished, Maisie, Gerald? Gerald, collect papers of your group!" (teacher dominant, pupils subordinate, emphasis on work progress) Bruce collects papers of the other group, which has been working away steadily except for the interruptions by the teacher. At 10:00 the arithmetic session stops. Teacher: "Everybody, without talking (norm), go back to your seats." (function) "Don't waste time." (norm) Pupils go back to their seats. "Very well done." (praise technique) There is a quick scramble by the boys for basketballs and baseballs. (competition for scarce goods coupled with mutual recrimination, dissociative relations among boys) The teacher finally distributes the materials. (relations of domination and submission) Someone raises the question of taking off coats and the teacher says, "All right for basketball, but otherwise, no!" (domination and submission)

NORMS IN THE CAFETERIA—WEST SCHOOL

Many schools have hot lunch programs and cafeterias. In the large high school the cafeteria is on a par with any large commercial restaurant. Though there may be vast differences in the size of these enterprises and a large variation in the quality of the food, the normative order may be pretty much the same. West School's pattern may indicate the general outline.

The cafeteria is located in the basement. The room is not attractive and rather small. Pupils have no choice in foods. Meals are planned a week in advance, and the menu is posted. Originally the lower grades ate between 11:30 and 12:00. This arrangement did not prove workable because of limited facilities and the short eating time through which the children had to rush. This last point seems to be a perennial problem in many schools. The actual eating time may be very short if the time spent in securing the food and finding a seat is deducted from the lunch period. To solve the problem the teachers at West School originally decided to cut down the number eating and to limit the hot lunch program, a decision in direct opposition to the humanistic orientation of the school. Eventually it was decided to serve the lower grades in their "B" rooms. Some thought this was successful, resulting in less rush and better manners, though one teacher using a B room objected because of the food that was spilled on desks and chairs. Inspection of chairs and desks did show quite a bit of food deposit.

The upper grades ate between 12 and 12:30. The children line up by grades in front of the door, walk in, secure their food, sit at the same table, and are dismissed as a group, usually at 12:30, provided all the children have finished and have behaved properly. They then go out to the playground or, in case of rain, to an assigned room.

Norms that apply are the following:

To walk in with your room
No cutting in
No shoving
No playing games
No loud talking in line
To keep voices down, not to yell
Not to talk too much
Not to laugh
Not to sass
Not to talk with mouth full
To eat at least half the food on the plate
To keep leftover food on plate
Not to throw food (as peels)
Not to grab for dessert (e.g., apples)
Not to eat until all are at table
To have good manners
Not to take food out
Not to fuss about food
Not to leave until all are finished
Not to race in eating
Friday waiters to put chairs on table

In grade 6 conduct in the lunchroom was discussed during a class meeting. A motion was made to stop playing flinching while in line, to stop tripping, and to stop making remarks about the food. The motion was defeated despite the support of the teacher, but a new motion forbidding tripping and fussing about the food passed.

NORMATIVE ORDER AS TEACHER DEFINED

The information about West School has been derived mainly from observation and the questioning of children. Let us examine some teachers' ideas about conduct. While the following two studies dealt with so-called undesirable personality traits or maladjustment of school children, they actually deal with the evaluation of conduct, i.e., the normative order.[5] Teachers will abide by and enforce the normative order as verbalized by the children, but the teacher may have an additional emphasis of his own.

Table 27 summarized the major areas in which violations of norms took place. Differences between the American and the Canadian studies may be due in part to difference in classification. Both studies stress violations of general standards of morality and conduct in the classroom, including work.

In Table 28 the ten most serious and the ten least serious points

TABLE 27. Percent of Items of Undesirable Behavior as Listed by Teachers in the United States and Canada

Behavior	U.S.	Canada
Violations of general standards and morality, etc.	18.1	21.64
Transgressions against authority	6.4	7.41
Violations of classroom rules	16.7	6.55
Violations of general school regulations	7.1	5.42
Violations of school work and requirements	9.8	18.6
Difficulties with other children	9.1	10.8
Undesirable personality traits	32.5	29.1

SOURCE: S. R. Laycock, "Teacher's Reactions to Maladjustments of School Children," *British Journal of Educational Psychology*, February, 1934, p. 15.

[5] S. R. Laycock, "Teachers' Reactions to Maladjustments of School Children," *British Journal of Educational Psychology*, February, 1934, pp. 11–29; E. K. Wickman, *Children's Behavior and Teachers' Attitudes*, Commonwealth Fund, 1928.

U.S.	Canada	U.S.	Canada
Most Serious		*Most Frequent*	
Heterosexual activity	Masturbation	Whispering	Whispering
Stealing	Heterosexual activity	Inattentiveness	Bad posture
Masturbation	Stealing	Carelessness in work	Carelessness in work
Obscene notes, pictures	Homosexual activity	Tattling	Forgetting
Untruthfulness, lying	Forgery	Disorderliness in class	Inquisitiveness
Truancy	Lack of honor	Interrupting	Restlessness
Impertinence, defiance	Lying	Failure to study	Inattentiveness
Cruelty, bullying	Obscene notes, stories	Shyness, with-drawn attitude	Lack of concentration
Cheating	Deceitfulness	Daydreaming	Untidiness
Destroying school materials	Lack of ambition	Lack of interest	Teasing
Disobedience	Untrustworthiness	Overactivity	
Unreliableness, irresponsibility	Lack of effort	Cheating	

U.S.	Canada	U.S.	Canada
Least Serious		*Least Frequent*	
Unsocial attitude, withdrawing	Boisterousness	Masturbation	Cradle courtship
Dreaminess	Tattling	Enuresis	Grouchiness
Imaginative lying	Inquisitiveness	Being a sissy (tomboy)	Truancy
Interrupting, talkativeness	Desire to show off	Suspiciousness	Unsocial attitude
Inquisitiveness	Chewing gum	Cruelty, bullying	Forgery
Being overcrit-ical of others	Overimagina-tiveness	Profanity	Unhappiness, depression
Tattling	Cradle courtship	Truancy	Smoking
Whispering	Shyness	Temper outburst	Temper tantrum
Sensitiveness	Over conscien-tiousness	Stealing money	Stammering
Restlessness		Obscene notes, talk	Heterosexual activity
Shyness		Smoking	Masturbation
			Homosexual activity

Source: E. K. Wickman, *Children's Behavior and Teachers' Attitudes*, Commonwealth Fund, 1928, pp. 244–245, 31; S. R. Laycock, "Teachers' Reactions to Maladjustments of School Children," *British Journal of Educational Psychology*, February, 1934, pp. 17–19, 22, 24.

are listed in addition to those occurring most and least frequently. The seriousness of a norm is not measured by the frequency of its occurrence.

Many of these norms go beyond the school. The serious ones deal with sexual conduct, and the order of the school. It is also of note that violations of sex norms occur least frequently. The violation of norms that occurs most frequently deals with the order of the school and the accomplishment of work. By this indirect way we can see the normative order as viewed by the teacher. It deals not only with conduct related to the pupil status but also with the relation of pupil to teacher, pupil to pupil, and the sex statuses. These implied norms read like a statute defining juvenile delinquency. A modified replication of the 1927 Wickman study by Mitchell in 1940 showed slight change in rating of behavior items. Nearly 400 teachers checked again forty-nine of the behavior items which had been rated earlier. Lack of sociability and fearfulness rated among the first twelve behavior problems in the 1940 study. In 1927 they rated thirty-ninth and thirty-sixth respectively. Truancy and defiance, which rated among the first twelve behavior problems in the 1927 study, rated sixteenth and twenty-first in the later study.[6]

These studies show the continuity of the school's normative order with that of the society at large. In addition, they demonstrate a variety of norms that seem characteristic of the school. The studies also pointed out the contrast between the teachers' emphasis in rating traits and the evaluation of mental hygienists, who emphasized the importance of studying the child who is shy, sensitive, and withdrawing.

SUMMARY

THE CONCLUSIONS IN GENERAL

There is a solid code of norms that permeates the entire educational system. These norms are found from kindergarten through high school.

[6] J. C. Mitchell, "A Study of Teachers' and Mental Hygienists' Rating of Certain Behavior Problems of Children," *Journal of Educational Research*, vol. 36, 1943, pp. 292–307. Cf. also Margaret L. Hayes, *A Study of Classroom Disturbances of Eighth-Grade Boys and Girls*, Teachers College, Contributions to Educataion, No. 871, 1943, p. 20.

The norms refer to these points: work and punctuality; care of building and grounds; self-control, self-direction, and individual responsibility; safety and welfare of the children; respect, deference, and obedience to the teacher; ordering relations among pupils, limiting of conflict and aggressiveness, facilitating sharing, coöperation, considerateness, and politeness; general standards of morality, such as prohibitions of swearing, smoking, and stealing.

The effort of enforcing norms which are not readily acceptable may create conflict.

Teachers especially proscribe conduct that deviates from conventional sexual behavior and moral rectitude. Though the most frequent norm violations involve school work and classroom conduct, they regard such violations as less serious.

The greatest permissive range within the norms is in the lower grades and decreases as the child progresses into the upper grades.

Many of the norms are compatible with norms stated or implied in the legal order and in the community. None of the persistent norms are pupil or even teacher originated. Most of the norms are traditional. They are pupil and teacher accepted.

Persons are judged by their adherence to or violation of norms. Through such conformance or nonconformance they develop a reputational history. Both teachers and pupils judge each other in terms of the school's normative order.

The permissive range with regard to norms is a result of the value orientation of the school—narrow if the orientation falls into the nativist-market models, wider if it involves the humanistic and common man models.

INTERPRETATION

The normative order represents the rules regulating conduct, sometimes clearly defined, sometimes less sharply defined. Before the child enters school, he has been responding to a network of norms. In the family and among his peers these may be diffuse, but in the school, beginning with the earliest grades, they become more precise.

The legal order sets the minima of the rights and duties that define the pupil role. It likewise establishes, as we have seen, the rights and duties of teachers. This is very important. The normative order of the school, inasmuch as it incorporates the prescriptions and proscriptions of the legal order, accepts and maintains the valuations that are expressed in the statutes and court decisions. The legal order, moreover, stands for what is considered to be the public welfare, public order, and public morality. From this point of view a normative system is likely to be traditional and conventional rather than divergent. Any divergencies in "progressive" or modern education have always been justified with reference to the furtherance of democracy.

The amount of visiting and gossiping which may be observed in classes indicates very wide and flexible limits between the prescribed and the proscribed conduct. The enforcement of norms, however, becomes increasingly strict in the upper grades. The strictness or freedom of norms varies with the social situation and the school's value system. This means that a child may be consistently socialized along the lines of the humanist model or the nativist-market models. It may also mean that because teachers recognize differences in children's capacity for responsibility or accountability children will be socialized according to one social model in the lower grades and another in the upper grades. In the upper grades there may, then, appear the competitive, patriotic, individualistic characteristics supported by nativist and business groups.

If a question is raised about the general personality pattern which the norms of West School seemed to support, the best description is that of the well-behaved girl, specifically the characteristics imputed to the female sex status in our society. If "men are expected to be oriented toward assertiveness, strength, authority, responsibility, and impersonal dealing," and if females are expected to be oriented toward "gentleness, weakness, compassion, service, and affection," [7] then the norms favor the latter. A free play of the former would disrupt the order of the school as well as entail the consequences of legal liability. There is no lack of assertiveness and display of strength among boys and girls in the school, though there will be less of it in the older girls. Actual conduct deviates from the dominant model.

[7] E. T. Hiller, *Social Relations and Structures*, Harper & Brothers, 1947, pp. 428–429.

Variations in the functional order will also make for deviation from the model. In the instructional process proper, within the school building, the model of the female sex status prevails. Outside the school building, and particularly in play and athletic competition, the model based on male sex status prevails. To the extent that girls participate in such activities, this would apply to them.

In addition, as a reading of the norms shows, the various social models are found on different grade levels and in the various functional areas of the school. There is a mixture of the humanist, nativist, market, and common man models with a slight gesture toward the religious. These models diverge even more when sex status comes into the picture. Children are, hence, socialized inconsistently. The norms support a variety of inconsistent goals, and as a result they sometimes facilitate coöperative relations and inhibit conflict relations, and they sometimes do the reverse.

Despite all this, a school as an institutionalized group is an ongoing system which must have some order if it is to function. This refers not only to the tasks that must be performed but also to the kinds of relations that should take place among pupils and between pupils and teacher. Only through a stable order can the purposes of the school be realized, and among these is the socialization of the children according to certain social models. Norms are, hence, not fully understood only with reference to end goals, but in terms of the total order and operation of the school. In short, many norms are not explained by or made most meaningful in terms of the legal order, the social models, or specific tasks, but in terms of the school as an ongoing group.

A current interpretation of the public school is that it merely reflects and upholds middle-class values. The norms apparently support this idea, but continuity of school and middle-class norms is incidental. Many of the norms and even value emphases occur not because of middle-class influence but because the school is a group. Emphasis on work, punctuality, getting the job done, control of aggression, avoidance of conflict, and being relatively quiet are necessary conditions if any group is to persist. In this way we also account for the continuity of norms found in the New Haven Grammar School and the modern school today.

There is no question for educators whether or not there will be norms or no norms, many or few. They will always be found. The problem is to recognize them and to trace out their meaning so that inconsistencies may be overcome. Another aspect deals with the enforcement of norms: leniency or strictness, harshness or friendliness, understanding or literalness. This problem will now be examined.

Selected Readings

The study of norms is relatively undeveloped. For a general discussion, see:

Hiller, E. T., *Social Relations and Structures,* Harper & Brothers, 1947, chaps. 3, 4.

Piaget, Jean, *The Moral Judgment of the Child,* Harcourt, Brace and Company, 1932.

Sorokin, Pitirim, *Society, Culture and Personality,* Harper & Brothers, 1947, pp. 71–91, 122–127, 620–627.

The Maintenance of the Functional and Normative Orders

WHAT DO I do about control? Well, that's not so complicated. The group of children under my supervision this year are easily controlled. If a child is committing a misdemeanor, usually a stern glance in his direction will suffice. However, if he continues to misbehave, a quiet talk with him will straighten things out. I have found it necessary only once this year to send a child out of the room for bad conduct.

Work must be finished in the allotted time or it means remaining after school to finish. Certain rules concerning library books, art paper, and other supplies must be obeyed or the children will be denied some of their privileges. If a child is inattentive in reading class, he is segregated from the group for a short time. Misbehavior in the halls or on the playground means being reprimanded by the principal.

Very often we hold group discussions concerning the meaning of right and wrong. In this connection it is remarkable what sane and sensible statements can be made by seven-year-old children.

A soft low voice in my opinion is a great asset to a teacher. I have found it to be true that the more a teacher shouts and blusters, the more noise the children are apt to make. I have a paddle in my desk, but I never use it. I feel that corporal punishment is a very poor means by which to establish discipline.[1]

Let us summarize the main methods of control suggested by this second-grade teacher: a stern look, segregating the child from the

[1] From a document secured by the author.

others (two ways), staying after school, reprimands, group discussion on ethics, a low voice, a paddle. All these techniques are involved in the problem labeled by that elusive word "discipline."

CONTROLS AND SANCTIONS

THE NATURE OF THE PROBLEM

The maintenance of order is a necessary prerequisite for a group to achieve its objectives. No social system functions automatically or mechanically. It must be maintained by the efforts of its members. These efforts, moreover, must be so directed that coöperation is maximized and opposition minimized. In so far as the actions of the members incorporate the functional and normative orders, and the objectives, there will be a fairly smooth, continuous operation of the group. The sharing of objectives may be less in a school than in other groups. The ends of the teachers may not be the ends of the children. Belonging to the school is not a matter of choice. Children may accept the school in varying degree. A child may refuse to participate in the program, put forth a reluctant or feeble effort, or vigorously support the program. Children may "hate school," or "love school."

In so far as the school is not accepted, controls become necessary. Most children have internalized the norms to a great extent, and so the operation of the normative and functional order is relatively assured. To some degree the activities will make sense to the child. The rationality inherent in the activity has its binding power and hence, brings acceptance and participation. Discipline arises from the nature of the activity. The artist, in order to function, has to accept the discipline of his materials, his colors, his canvasses, his brushes, his painting medium. The mechanic is disciplined by the motors that he repairs. Virtues (knowledge, patience, honesty) are brought into action as the individual completes the task that is set, as the painting takes shape, as the motor is restored to efficiency. From this point of view control is a matter of planning meaningful projects and activities and facilitating student participation.

Control is not mere fiat, though ordering and forbidding techniques are generally used. Through them a social order can be established which is essentially punitive in nature, an order of force. The extreme case is the prison. An educational counterpart is the type of school which serves a primarily custodial function. It might be questioned whether there is a social order at all when organized on such a control principle. The most desirable control is based on rationality embodied in the school as a total structure. Rationality is the knowledge of man and of the world receiving a special type of objectification in the school. To the degree that rationality is lacking, the so-called discipline problems arise as an attribute of the school's deficient organization. Conversely, the problems will tend to disappear to the extent that rationality is embedded in the functional and normative order.

SOURCES OF PROBLEMS

The most general source of problems is found in the irrationalities in the society and culture in which the school functions. A lack of cultural integration and institutions operating at cross-purposes will create problems in the operation of the school. For the moment the more immediate sources of "discipline" problems will be examined. These sources are: (1) the functional order, (2) interpersonal relations, and (3) class organization. All of these are internal to the school.

The Function Order as a Source of Discipline Problems. Dissatisfaction with school work may take various forms. The subject may be too difficult or too easy. The work load may be too heavy or too light. Standards of work may be too high or too low. Activities may be too verbal, not allowing enough motor expression. The lesson may be poorly explained, and thus, not understood by the children, so that they cannot act. The work may be poorly scheduled, lack variation. The work may be meaningless to the child. Many of these faults may occur in combination, so that the cumulative effect may be disastrous to both children and teacher. This situation would be increasingly characterized by dissociative relations, a class full of boredom, resentment, feelings of guilt, aggressiveness, restlessness, and criticism.

On the elementary level, given the confines of a set of activities, the teacher can find out directly how the children feel about their activities by asking them. Though such a procedure may seem obvious, it is doubtful whether many teachers have ever done this. The teacher need only list the major activities and ask the children to rank them in order of preference. Table 29 shows such a breakdown as carried out by a teacher at the suggestion of the author. Clusters of interests can be seen for the group as a whole and also by sex status. Taking the individual ranking, the teacher can recognize individual differences. In this way planning can take place for the class as a whole as well as for the individual. Boys tend to prefer motor activities, but even girls are incapable of meeting the demands of the eternal immobile sitting. The paltry minutes of recess may not be enough release. The problem, of course, is the total structure of activity. To discover the ranking of activities as the children view them is but a step in probing the significance of the functional order, and in this way the problem of discipline is also being resolved.

The same principles apply to the high school. Where the activity appears unrelated to the life of the student and when the activity, furthermore, is not understood because of deficient tool skills, intelligence, etc., boredom, restlessness set in. Substitute activities are resorted to by the student. Note passing, blank staring at book or out of the window, whispering, and pranks are ways of relieving ennui. The culmination of this creates the dropout problem. Many pupils stay in school only as long as the law compels them. They drop out at the age level at which the law no longer requires attendance. "The result is that while 78 percent enter high school, only 48 percent graduate,"[2] i.e., nationally. To cope with the "educationally neglected student as learner" the Implementation Committee of the National Association of Secondary-School Principals offered the following suggestions:

1. The need for emphasis upon the concrete and specific in terms of both problem and materials.
2. The need for instruction directed toward the satisfaction of more immediate and clearly recognized needs.
3. The desirability of increasing the opportunity for more continuous

[2] *Life Adjustment Education in the American Culture*, Office of Education, Federal Security Agency, Circular No. 335, 1951, p. 6.

TABLE 29. Subject Rating by a Class of Sixth Graders by Sex

Rating	Recess B	Recess G	Gym B	Gym G	Arith. B	Arith. G	Spell. B	Spell. G	Art B	Art G	Read. B	Read. G	Library B	Library G	Sing. B	Sing. G	Hist. B	Hist. G	Eng. B	Eng. G
1st	1		6	4	1	2	1		3	1		1				1				
2	2	1	3		2		1		2	2					1	1	1			1
3	2		1		3	1	1		3	1										
4			2		1		1	1			2	1	1	1			1	1	1	1
5	2			1			1		2		1	1	1		1		1			1
6	1							2			4			1	2	1	3			1
7			1			2	1		1		1		1	1	1		1			
8		2									2									
9	1								1		1	1	1	1	1	2		1		
10								2			1	1	2		2		1	1		1
11					1		1					1			1	1				
12							1													
13	1	1			1		1				1		5	1	1	1	1	1	2	1
14	1				1		1			1			1		1		2	1	3	
15	1														1			2	4	
16th		2																		

SOURCE: Study directed by author.

and longer contact with teachers in order to provide more adequate teacher guidance.

4. The need for less exclusive dependence upon conventional printed materials.
5. The need for greater use of out-of-school resources through the medium of field trips.
6. The need for greater utilization of visual and auditory aids.
7. The need for organization of learning units around life problems rather than around subjects.[3]

These suggestions amount to a reconstruction of the functional order. The assumption seems to be that the objectification of these principles in the school's program will not only hold students but also minimize the so-called discipline problem.

Interpersonal Relations and Class Organization as a Source of Discipline Problems. Difficulties in interpersonal relations will likewise upset a class. Teachers are usually aware of the extreme cases or may become suddenly aware of them when confronted with a crisis. Trouble in this area will be among children and also between children and teacher. Friendship relations, love relations, bullying relations, clowning behavior can produce interpersonal tensions and unrest in a class. More important and also more difficult to cope with are clique and other subgroup formations. The dominant clique, closed to the other children in the class, becomes a major disruptive factor. It attempts to control opportunities, the distribution of equipment, choice class positions, and so on. It may produce counteraction on the part of those who are discriminated against.

"Say, do you think it's fair for a teacher to have favorites?" This topic, which was bothering a fifth-grader, is indicative of one of the ways in which the teacher's relations with students may be a source of problems. Discrimination, either in the direction of "favorites" or against "bad" boys and girls, produces resentment. Breaches of etiquette with resultant dignity violations and over-reaction may develop into augmented negative relations. Lack of tact, wrong use of punishment and reward, inconsistency in carrying out threats or promises—these are other aspects of the problems that center in the way a teacher carries out his role.

[3] *Life Adjustment Education for Every Youth,* Office of Education, Federal Security Agency, Bulletin No. 22, 1951, p. 49.

Class organization may be a source of problems in a variety of ways. The class may be too large and hence difficult to handle. The class may be too heterogeneous, or unbalanced as to age, sex, emotional and social development, race, or social class. There may be too few or too many rules in the class. Democratic organization may be attempted for children who are not ready, or it may be subtly manipulated by a controlling clique. The tendency to dump so-called problem boys and girls into certain courses, especially the vocational, compounds the problem of the teacher. What are these children likely to be? They often, if not usually

1. Come from families the members of which are engaged in unskilled and semi-skilled occupations.
2. Come from families with low incomes.
3. Come from families with low cultural environments.
4. Are retarded in school.
5. Begin school later than other children.
6. Make considerably poorer scores on intelligence tests (not only verbal traits but all mental traits).
7. Make considerably lower achievement test scores for age than average.
8. Make somewhat lower achievement test scores for grade than the average. (Since they are usually retarded, their achievement is nearer their grade group than their age group.)
9. Make lower marks than other students.
10. Are less emotionally mature—nervous, feel less secure.
11. Lack interest in school work.[4]

A roomful of such children will make extraordinary demands upon the skills of a teacher. If program and equipment are wanting, the teacher may be confronted with an insoluble problem, and that fact must be recognized. The idea that a teacher can cope with any situation is a mirage, if coping means more than exercising a custodial function.

THE COMMUNITY AS A SOURCE OF DISCIPLINE PROBLEMS

That community tensions and disorganization should reverberate into the school and affect discipline problems may seem obvious. The disorder in the school may correlate with the disorder in the

[4] *Ibid.*, pp. 45–46.

community. A case to demonstrate the point is the following document:

In a sixth-grade room the teacher is telling the students about an idea she has in mind. The idea is to form a club of all the girls in the grade, that is, all the white girls. The colored girls glance at one another and then back to the teacher. She continues to talk about a party they are going to have and entertain the fellows of the class, all the white fellows. Some of the Negro and white students live in the same community and play together. Some ask why their friends aren't invited. The teacher replies that she doesn't believe in Negroes and whites mixing together and where she came from they didn't. . . . Notes are going back and forth among the students as the teacher talks, especially among the Negro students. One is going to tell her mother, another is going to throw something at her, another is going to poison her, one wishes she would drop dead. On the way home that noon the main topic of discussion is the teacher's sermon. A white girl accidentally or intentionally, no one really knows, pushes a Negro girl. The Negro girl turns on her and beats her pretty badly.[5]

The upshot of the event is a call from the white mother to the principal, who calls the Negro girl in and starts to paddle her. The girl warns him. He calls in her mother, and the actions of the teacher come out. The club is disbanded. The teacher is warned that she will be discharged if any repetition of racial prejudice occurs. Such a dramatic event in all its ramification is not likely to be forgotten by these children. In similar fashion, ethnic group and social class may become sources of "discipline" problems, accompanied by student strikes and protests, police escort for the children of the minorities, and patrolling of the streets by riot details.[6]

In order to root out such a disturbing influence there has been a great emphasis on intergroup or intercultural education in recent years. The underlying theme seems to be "Americans all" despite differences in race, religion, color, and national origin. Problems of intergroup or intercultural relations may be worked over in group discussions or through sociodrama. Frequently problems arising

[5] From a document secured by the author.
[6] For recent development, cf. *Improving Intergroup Relations in School and Community*, North Central Association of Secondary Schools and Colleges, 1946; C. I. Chatto and Alice Hallegan, *Story of the Springfield Plan*, Barnes and Noble, 1945; Howard H. Cummings (ed.), *Improving Human Relations*, Bulletin No. 25, National Council for Social Studies, 1949.

within the school because of the very mixed population are used as a source to work out the "We Americans" theme, how to get along with others, and the significance of diverse nationality groups. Children will gather facts or read novels, biographies, autobiographies, or plays dealing with various ethnic and colored groups. There may be projects to show that the United States is a melting pot, a nation of immigrants. The observance of Brotherhood Week, Tolerance Week, I Am an American Day focuses on the problem, and there will be appropriate displays (books, posters), speeches, assembly or class programs on the theme of such occasions. Folk festivals may be sponsored. Other community-wide events organized by the schools, PTA, and other interested groups reëmphasize the unity-in-diversity principle. Prize contests on how to combat discrimination and prejudice may be sponsored by school or outside groups. The facts of race, prejudices, and superstitions about other groups will be subjected to analysis. Interschool visits are organized. Greater emphasis is placed upon the practice of democracy within the school.

The school may be relatively successful in curbing intolerance within its own closed orbit. The school is, however, only one factor in the total situation. The community life may contradict the theme taught in school. To be effective, intercultural education within the school must be correlated with real occupational, financial, and social opportunities outside the school. Democratic appeals in school may appear to the children as just so much blarney when the community life seems structured on the law of the jungle. The indoctrination effort of the school may boomerang and fail in its objective, as propaganda oftimes does. On the other hand, the reiteration of the basic themes may provide a point of reference for action so that the gap between ideal and practice may be narrowed. The coalescence of value and action must be in the community as a whole and not merely in the school.

Community events pose problems in other ways. Industrial conflict between labor and management, families on relief, broken homes, culture conflicts are all sources of problems in the school. Life is not compartmentalized, except in scientific analysis. Any major community event ramifies into the school, through the school board, the administrators, the teachers, and the children. Community and family tensions are relived in the school. In such situations the teacher is relatively impotent.

TYPES OF CONTROL

How a teacher controls a child and how children assert controls among themselves or in relation to a teacher or teachers will vary with the situation. The class, the auditorium, the halls, the cafeteria, the gym or playground, the library, and other locales may call for different methods or different use of similar methods. Methods used will vary with the value orientation structuring the total school organization. The techniques discussed below all work for the immediate situation, and that is why they are used. Teachers who use them primarily evaluated them on their immediate technical efficiency. "Sh! Sh!" (to bring about quiet) may serve as an example; it arouses a temporary sense of guilt at violating a norm and annoying the teacher. The technique may be effective, for the class may and usually does simmer down.

Techniques fall into two types of approaches to the question of control. The first is subjective. The control is directed toward the agent; it tends to be external and rather mechanical. The second is objective. The control is indirect, through the nature of the activity. When children are absorbed in their work, there is no need for any control of the first type. The fact that such controls are used is an indication of the unsatisfactoriness of the school "work." A school involves both types of control, but the most ostensible one is the subjective.

CONTROL AS SUBJECTIVE—DOMINATION AND SUBMISSION

It is not possible to catalogue all specific methods of control, but control involves social relations, so that it may promote either sociative or dissociative relations and tendencies. The following list includes the techniques given most frequently by a group of elementary-school teachers: denial of or shortening of recess; segregation of child in some area in the room or sending child outside of the room; use of corporal punishment or some other form of physical manipulation (as a shaking); talking with the child or group; standing child in corner; denial of privilege; having child return to seat or children stay in seats; humiliating the child; keeping after school; refusing requests; no gym or cutting gym time short; doing work over; some sort of pupil court. Many other techniques were listed, but these were the more important ones. The idea of "arranging for a good work program" was frequently mentioned. This approach to "control" indicates a flexibility in the search for ways to keep a schoolroom running smoothly and with an atmosphere of willing participation.

Many of the techniques listed above will also apply to the high school. Ordering and forbidding techniques are found in almost all groups. On the high-school level one need not necessarily expect unique techniques of control. In some high schools where there is a real guidance program, counseling may be of some effect. The routine type of control, however, will be similar to that of the elementary school.

In Mill City's West School, enforcement of the normative order varied from appeals to the moral self, to the withdrawal of privilege, to the isolation or segregation of the child, to the expectation of physical coercion. In some classes group discussions were attempted as a means of controlling conduct. Some of the techniques used there, such as the denial of recess, keeping children after school, the expectation of coercion, were not in agreement with the professed value orientation of the school, for they introduced an incompatible authoritarian element. While most of the methods were negative in effect, some positive techniques used were praise, humor, statements of approval and satisfaction, display of good work on bulletin boards and shelves, awarding of special honors or benefits. Yet most of the techniques were of the forbidding type. Some are a perversion of the activity, e.g., the denial of recess as a control technique. Something that is designed for the child is used against him.

What is the significance of these domination-submission control techniques? They curtail the movement of the child, limiting freedom as well as opportunity. Since the techniques are public, they will always brand a child as a malefactor, thus involving a certain amount of humiliation. The following devices of a second-grade teacher may serve to illustrate deliberately humiliating techniques: putting gum on the end of his nose when he is caught chewing; putting a sign on his back to be worn all day for everyone to see, if caught swearing, which says "THIS LITTLE BOY SWEARS" (a most effective technique, according to the teacher); if child is doing something that annoys the classroom (like making faces), making that child stand up in front of the class and continue whatever he was doing so everyone can see. The technique of humiliation works. It is effective, just as a third degree or torture chamber is effective. The analogy is appropriate because all of these methods express the principle of complementary dissociative relations, with all the consequent latent hate, hostility, and aggression that may break loose at some later time, provided the person has not been so cowed that he feels incapable or fearful of responding. What is of deeper significance is the implied evaluation of the person, i.e., contempt, denying respect to him as a person, violating his integrity. The person is relegated to a thing-status and is, therefore, humiliated and manipulated to the ends of the person in authority. The teacher may do this, even though not desirous of being brutal or cruel. The technique is justified on the grounds that the well-being of the school demands that good order be maintained.

Segregation has the same effect, especially if an area in the room becomes a symbol, as a "naughty chair" or detention corner. The child sitting or standing there is effectively labeled bad. This technique works only in the lower grades, probably being less effective by the fifth grade.

Corporal punishment is the ultimate reduction of human relations to the irrational, a failure in human relations: no persuasion, no reasoning, no consideration except strength and the big stick, massive retaliation on the part of the powerful adult, who is a certain winner in relation to the child. Yet this pure power relation is limited by definitions of law and court decision, by community and parental attitude, and by what the punisher thinks he can get away with. Threats of punishment, the brandishing of a strap or paddle, is but a step to their use. Corporal punishment is a last resort, excluding suspension, which is not a control technique but, as most teachers will admit, a failure to cope with a situation. Paradoxically, children most likely to receive corporal punishment will usually be the ones the least likely to be intimidated by it.[7] On the principle of augmenting dissociative relations the mutual hostility will be affirmed. That teachers may have to physically manipulate a child is obvious. To stop a fight, to prevent injury in the immediate situation the teacher may have to participate physically, but this intervention should be of the same type found in hospitals when some form of temporary restraint may be placed upon a patient. Such a use of "force" must be followed up later by other methods in working with the child or children involved.[8]

CONTROL AS SUBJECTIVE—EXHORTATION AND DISCUSSION

Appeals to the "better self" of the child, moral exhortation, seem to evince a more positive approach, though perhaps instead of a physical crackdown the impact is psychological and social—psychological in the sense that the child feels guilty or inadequate for deviating; social in the sense that the exhortation is in the open, for this sort of appeal may also be coupled with group discussion. This type of approach is more likely to work with the middle-class child, but even here the results may be temporary. In Chapter 9, a class discussion was presented on a problem of inadequate lighting and dissatisfaction with the seating arrangement. As a review of the discussion shows, moralistic and emotional appeals brought no results. The technique, as has been stated, is subjective in principle, that is, it deals with the individual and his emotional states and self-feelings. By creating sufficient anxiety and feelings of remorse, the emotions are to push the contrite individual into the correct pattern as he receives the approval of his peers. As the case shows, the children are not as other-directed as is now somewhat fashionably maintained.[9] Their social antennae are not sweeping radar-like through the social at-

[7] Cf. Fritz Redl and David Wineman, *Children Who Hate*, The Free Press, 1951.

[8] George V. Sheviakov and Fritz Redl, *Discipline for Today's Children and Youth*, Department of Supervision and Curriculum Development, National Education Association, 1944, pp. 25–34.

[9] David Riesman, *The Lonely Crowd*, Yale University Press, 1950.

mosphere of their peers to see whether they all approve or disapprove. As the case shows, the group discussion became sterile and was converted into a propaganda effort. After a couple of months there is nothing to discuss; the social antennae have ossified. Since the boys cannot be propagandized or talked into the "right attitude," the whole effort comes to naught. The problem is not solved and on a subjective principle cannot be solved. A social order does not rest upon the right feelings or correct attitudes. Any effort to build a social order on such "facts" relies on continuous propaganda, exhortation, emotional appeals, and crises. These are the techniques associated with the formation and maintenance of a crowd, which cannot, in fact, be considered a social order.

To continue the discussion of this case: A possible alternate approach would involve the creation of some general class project. With a division of labor of the project, the class could be reseated without any moral appeals. This solution, however, by-passes the light problem. Some children will still be sitting in inadequate light. A completely objective approach and discussion would raise the question of how the light could be improved in this room. The problem, then, is not a question of selfishness or reseating but one of reconstructing the physical structure of the room. If progressive principles were followed, this would lead presumably to the development of a unit on light—what it is, how it is related to the person, how we get it, how much it costs, etc., so that the child learns something about physics, physiology, architecture, and public utilities. In the process the children might also learn that the solution of the problem involves tearing out light fixtures, getting new ones, getting money to pay for all this electrical material, installation, and so on. Since they cannot do anything or much on their own as children, the objective solution is given up, and resort will be made to the subjective principle: "Don't be selfish! Share! Be fair!"

A Case of Control. The following discussion lasting twenty minutes in a sixth-seventh grade illustrates this seesawing back and forth from subjective to objective approach.

The class is seated in a circle for a meeting. The teacher, Miss Hendry, asks Bill about some arrangements about some folk dance instructions and a demonstration the class is to put on. There was a slight mixup in dates, Bill seems rather flustered, and Miss Hendry asks him to check the dates. (Note, no exhortation, accusation, but a request to check on an objective fact. Bill may feel derelict in duty, but he won't feel like a heel.) Sue raises her hand and introduces a problem in regard to play equipment: there is only one bat. What is to be done? There is great interest, and a forest of arms is waving in the air. The teacher takes up the discussion of what to do. Bobby suggests other rooms. (Apparently some bats have been misplaced or lost.) Lew suggests a monitor to check on play equipment. As Mack leaves, he indicates that he was to have done that. (Note that the discussion is fairly objective. It now changes and becomes subjective.) Gerald says girls do not take care of bats and leave them out on the playground. Doris objects to blaming the girls. Gerald continues that girls are more forgetful. Miss Hendry breaks in by reminding that everybody forgets, both boys and girls, and that Gerald had left his coat on the playground, which he somewhat shamefacedly admits. The discussion then shifts to another topic. (Note that the teacher tries to handle the situation by referring to a general principle or idea which takes out some of the sting in her rebuke to Gerald.)

Ruth states that the boys have been catching the girls' flies during recess and interfering with their baseball game. When the teacher comes on the scene, the boys melt away. (Control by anticipation of consequences.) Miss Hendry says that something must be wrong. Vigorous denials indicated through gesture by the boys, especially by Mack and Larry. Larry says he wanted to umpire. Teacher asks: "How many girls want boys around?" All girls raise hands rejecting the idea. (At this stage of the discussion, this response was the most probable.) Lew makes a comment about someone having caught a ball and that then the boys played catch among themselves. Mack adds that the ball was a foul ball. Bobby suggests that some of the boys play ball with the girls and the others play basketball. (A compromise solution in terms of limited equipment.) Betsy states that the boys watch us and tease us, see how badly we play. Sue, Patsy, and Mary smirk at this observation. Gladys states it would be all right for the boys to play with them if they wouldn't tease. (Appeal to norms of etiquette.) Doris seconds the idea. Larry observes that girls do not play so badly. (Sociative response.) Loud snorts emanate from Gerald and Tom. Betsy objects on the grounds that the boys pitch too fast. Miss Hendry comments that one should be considerate. Betsy then says it would be all right for the boys to play with the girls if they are considerate and play fair. Dave states that some girls can play as well as the boys. There is then a general discussion on this point. Miss Hendry finally asks how many girls will play with boys if the boys will coöperate. The girls raise their hands, Betsy after all the others. Miss Hendry concludes: "Let's see how this works out." (No final, ultimate decision; freedom of action is not completely constrained; possibilities of remodification and change.)

It would seem that provision for more play equipment, an objective solution, might solve the problem in the long run, but there are these cross-sexual attractions, primarily a teasing behavior, for which there is no permanent and final solution. Nor may this teasing be so very serious, especially if it is distributed among several persons. The girls together can take it quite well; a solitary girl could not. As this group discussion shows, a consensus is reached on how a game should be played and at the same time distinctions in sex status are recognized and taken into consideration. Moral exhortation is at a minimum.

Group discussion, as a technique, will be valuable only if it meets the following requirements: promotes sociative relations, seeks objective solutions to problems, seeks to deal with problems whose solutions are within the ability of the class to find.

The group discussion technique has been used in the effort to transfer authority from one individual, the teacher, to the whole group. The discipline or control was to be self-imposed, not teacher imposed. That group discussion could be very valuable for learning about democratic process does not, however, make it effective for solving all situations where students are failing to participate or are violating norms.

CONTROL AS SUBJECTIVE—STUDENT COURTS

The student court as a device of social control has been tried on both elementary and high-school level. In the former it frequently is found in a particular class whereas in the latter a court is one phase of the administrative machinery of student government or student councils. An advantage in this device over the teacher-imposed decision is the supposedly wider base of authority when children sit in judgment on one another. The analysis will confine itself to the student court without examining the question of student government. It will also center on the high school. In one case the author encountered on the elementary level the children composing the court were so severe, so excessive in their punishment that the teacher was compelled to abandon the practice. Tyranny of children over one another, given an opportunity, is difficult to match, a social exercise in sadism.

The pros and cons for the student court are as follows:

For: 1. Students in later life will be judged by their peers. Why not start doing this while they are in high school and thus accustom them to what they may eventually expect when they leave school?

2. Students, while actually participating in all of the activities of a student court, are learning much about how a real court of law functions.

3. If a student council is to set standards for the school, it must have the right and the facilities to see that such standards are maintained.

Against: 1. The school administrator cannot delegate the actual management of the school to the students. Therefore, if the student court is to handle any cases at all, they must necessarily be minor, inconsequential ones. Serious cases must go to the principal or someone designated by him. The student court is then, really, only "play-acting."

2. The student council will minimize its own citizenship activities, if it, at the same time, is called upon to "punish" student offenders.

3. Unless the court is exceptionally well-handled, students will either resent its functioning or will laugh at the puerile attempts of other students to discipline them. The effect then is worse than if nothing had been attempted.

4. There is no real punishment which the student court can give that will do much good.[10]

A court may be a small committee that will deal with a student informally concerning school rules and regulations. On the opposite extreme is the effort to duplicate as completely as possible the operations of a criminal court, with judge, bailiffs, sergeant at arms, attorneys for the defense and for the prosecution, recorders, and other personnel. The powers delegated to the court by the principal or superintendent vary with the particular situation. The point to stress is that the student court is analogous to a criminal court and thus subject to all the traditional deficiencies that penologists have

[10] *The Student Council in the Secondary School, a Handbook for Student Councils and Their Sponsors*, National Association of Secondary-School Principals, National Education Association, 1950, p. 275. Cf. Earl C. Kelley, *Student Cooperation*, National Self-Government Committee, n.d., p. 19; Gerald Van Pool, "Student Court vs. Student Council Policy," *Clearing House*, March, 1949, pp. 397–400.

leveled at the courts.[11] To presume that children can do successfully what in general has failed is simply astonishing.

The operation of such courts has not been objectively examined, though in the *Student Council Handbook* thirty schools report a satisfactory and successful court.[12] However, repeating and serious offenders are finally sent to the principal or a student personnel committee for disposal except in those cases where the student court has been granted the power to expel a student. The data from the schools suggest that the conceptions of punishment do not vary from the traditional concepts of deterrence (that inflicting pain on the convicted offender will deter others from crime), of retribution (the "an eye for an eye, and a tooth for a tooth" view), and of reformation (that punishment will reform the offender by creating a fear of the repetition of the punishment or by creating the belief that crime does not pay). Thus, one finds schools fostering as desirable educational experience such penologically obsolete ideas as "The sentence fits the offense," or "The court has a definite list of punishments for certain crimes."[13] What is the nature of some of these offenses and punishments? The following samples are not unrepresentative of the schools:

The following is a list of offenses and the penalty inflicted for each of the offenses. As the need arises, more penalties for new offenses are added. Penalties are tripled for second offenders. (1) Offense: Sneaking in line or making a disturbance in the cafeteria; running in the halls or downstairs. Penalty: Stand in back of the lunch line for a week. (2) Offense: Talking loudly in halls. Penalty: Give a speech to the home room or do not speak to friends for a week. (3) Offense: Putting tacks on seats; snapping others with rubber bands, pea shooters, water squirters, and guns. Penalty: Forfeit ninth-period privileges for a week. (4) Offense: Misbehavior when the teacher is out of room. Penalty: Erase blackboards in every room he attends for a day or week. (5) Offense: Walking in the halls without a pass during classes, fifth and ninth periods. Penalty: Detention. (6) Offense: Sliding down banisters. Penalty: Detention. (7) Offense: Throwing snow balls in front of school; walking across lawns or on the dike. Penalty: Walk around the track backwards.

[11] Cf. Edwin Sutherland and Paul Cressey, *Principles of Criminology*, J. B. Lippincott Company, 5th ed., 1955, chap. XV.
[12] *Op. cit.*, pp. 279–289.
[13] *Ibid.*, p. 288.

Punishments range from keeping an offender from assembly programs to having an offender make a public apology in assembly.

The punishments for the offenses are: first offense—severe reprimand; second offense—all school activities and privileges are taken away; third offense—suspension.

Students found guilty are given penalties of assigned work after school with the janitor.

Sentences may consist of themes, memorization of rules, periods made up in library, apologies made to persons concerned with the offense, helping with assemblies, or some serious cases may be taken to the deans for suspension or to the student's parents for discussion.

Student police, student informers ("any student who sees another student violating a rule of the student council may write the name, date, and offense on a piece of paper and hand it to the court clerk") become part of the Neanderthal mentality operating in these ordering and forbidding techniques. Acquitted in such a court, how does a student stand in the school? Does he become marked? How the penalties are enforced is not quite clear, though the reports suggest that the social pressure is so great that students conform, apologies (public shaming) being an extreme example. The penalties, moreover, in some cases work against the educational efforts of the school. Penalties such as writing themes, reporting on books, library work, etc., equate school work with a distasteful task and thus help to promote anti-intellectualism. In addition, there is the problem of selecting the officials. Some are appointed by the school administration; some are appointed by the student council; some are elected. In the latter case, the various problems of school politics enter into the picture, though one school found that "frequent elections make the judges *less unpopular* with the students and the courts more democratic." [15] The value orientation appears to be a variant of the nativist, in school terms: a student's poor conduct "neither improved his standing nor the school's reputation"; "The council brings up the name of the student who is injuring the standing and honor of the school"; ". . . offenses against the school." [16] In so far as the student

[14] *Ibid.*, pp. 285, 286, 287, 284. Cf. Theral Herrick, *School Patterns for Citizenship Training*, Bureau of Educational Reference and Research, School of Education, University of Michigan, 1947, p. 121.
[15] *Ibid.*, p. 280. Italics supplied.
[16] *Ibid.*, p. 280, 281.

court exemplifies the subjective principle, it is to that extent an unsound idea.

Furthermore, the concept of student self-government, of which the court idea is a part, needs more analysis. A self-governing class could not, for instance, legislate itself out of existence. The authority which the legal order confers upon the school administration and upon the teachers cannot be delegated away or denied. The teacher is held accountable while the children are not. Any self-government program will be limited by the question of accountability and liability as defined in the legal order, but this point is not to deny that students should make decisions in those areas for which they are qualified and furnish suggestions in areas outside of their jurisdiction.

WHO IS PUNISHED?

The obvious answer is anyone who performs ineffectively in the functional order or anyone who deviates from the norms. Any boy or girl is thus subject to controls, but do these controls fall upon boys and girls unequally? Are controls administered impartially? As our schools are now constituted, controls fall more heavily upon boys than girls. The hand and voice of authority is light and conciliatory upon the upper- and middle-class children, harsh and rebuking upon the lower class. The tendency is also for punishment to be more severe and rewards to be less for children categorized as members of racial and ethnic groups. The same holds true for a child with a "bad" reputational history. These are tendencies, not inevitabilities, for enlightened, discerning school policy and personnel can work with the child on his own merits as a person so that these other factors lose their influence.

The social class interpretation is shown in Figure 19. This interpretation may apply to some situations; however, not all lower-class children are subjected to this pattern of privation, nor do all middle- and upper-class children inevitably garner all rewards and avoid all punishment. This pattern, which seems to depend on the teacher, but which may be reinforced by clique formations in the school, is probably more operative on the high-school than on the elementary-school level. It is to be found in smaller communities more fre-

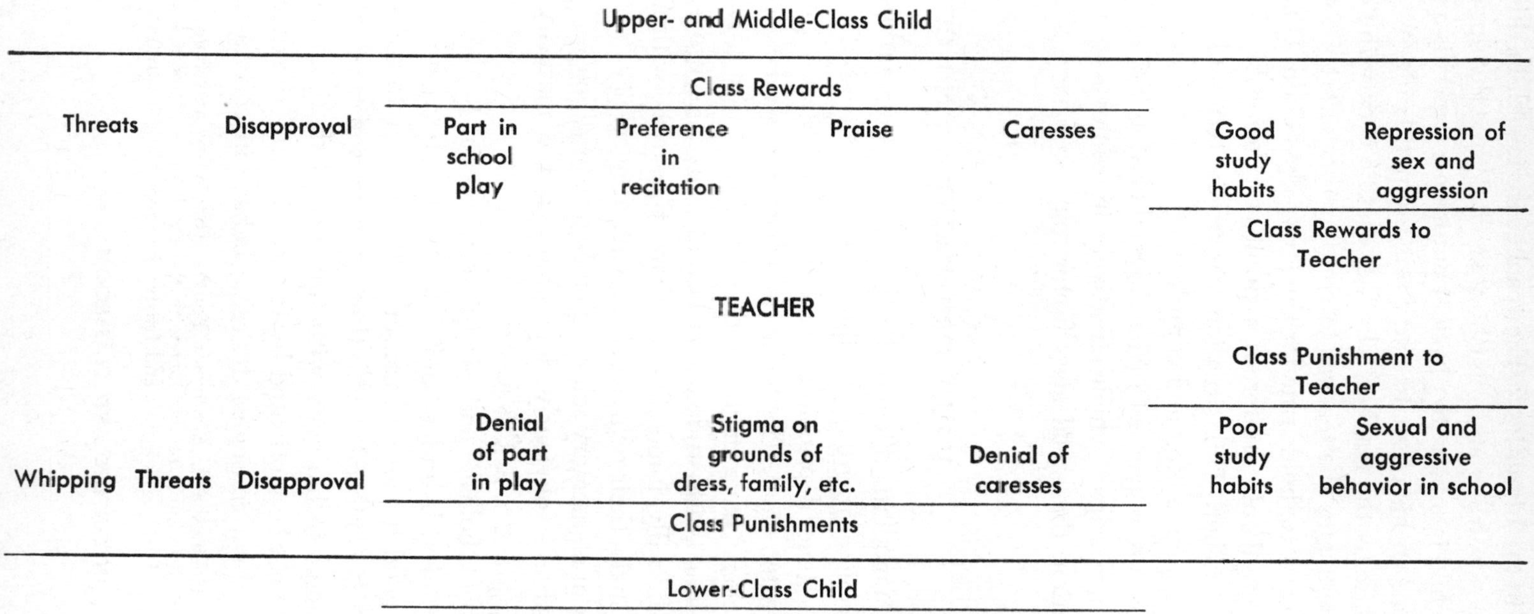

Upper- and Middle-Class Child

Class Rewards

Threats Disapproval Part in school play Preference in recitation Praise Caresses Good study habits Repression of sex and aggression

Class Rewards to Teacher

TEACHER

Class Punishment to Teacher

Whipping Threats Disapproval Denial of part in play Stigma on grounds of dress, family, etc. Praise Denial of caresses Poor study habits Sexual and aggressive behavior in school

Class Punishments

Lower-Class Child

FIGURE 19. Social Class, Controls, and Learning. (From Allison Davis and John Dollard, *Children of Bondage*, American Council on Education, 1940, p. 284.)

quently than in the big cities.[17] The teacher is viewed, in this interpretation, as a rewarding and punishing agent. While the upper- and middle-class child is subject to physical punishment and disapproval, he is reinforced in his effort to carry out the pupil role by the rewards given him by the teacher. The fact that he is carrying out the role in turn motivates the teacher to continue her efforts at encouragement. The reverse holds true for the lower-class child. His failure to fulfill the pupil role reinforces a punitive relationship between him and the teacher. This situation viewed in terms of principle shows how the augmenting and complementary sociative and dissociative relations are in part set by one's social class affiliation. On the other hand, in a school which effectively implements a humanist value orientation, the social class factor may be a very negligible one.

VALUE ORIENTATIONS AND CONTROL

The trend in modern education has been to equate good discipline with self-discipline or group discipline. These concepts have been announced as general principles, and their implications for action have not been too clear. The techniques have not always been successful. Teachers have floundered with futile discussions that achieved nothing, with student courts that sometimes proved to be arbitrary and finally impossible. Perhaps the areas within which children can make their own decisions will, of necessity, be small in the first years of elementary school. The degree to which self-government is feasible is obviously dependent on the maturity of the group and on practice in this area.

A recent book holds "good discipline to consist in the extent to which boys and girls understand what kind of behavior results in the greatest good for all and consciously endeavor to control their own behavior in conformity with these standards of conduct. In the school conducted in harmony with this idea of discipline, conduct control would not be motivated by fear of violating the dictation of authority, but by a conscious desire to behave in certain ways be-

[17] Cf. August Hollingshead, *Elmtown's Youth*, John Wiley and Sons, 1949, pp. 185–192, for a vivid example of this fact with the resultant resentment and hostility among students, and feelings of guilt and frustration among administrators.

cause this would most probably result in the greater satisfaction of basic needs and drives." [18] This statement needs careful thought. In the first place it is likely to involve a contradiction. It is quite possible that behavior which was supposed to result in that nebulous thing "the greatest good" would not coincide with behavior which would bring the greatest satisfaction of basic needs and drives. The whole conception is subjective and can be reduced only to a variety of mental states or feelings that are to guide a person, or it remains an empty abstract principle, pure verbalism. These announced theories of discipline are really superfluous, as the real answer given by the authors of this quotation lies in the way the work functions of the school are to be organized. They, like the teachers who compiled list of controls cited at the beginning of the chapter, have felt that it might be important to "organize a good work program." They have elaborated on this idea in the development of the core curriculum. [19] To spell out techniques that will facilitate fulfillment of the group project would be the logical development of their point of view on the subject of control—rather than turning back to the idea of discipline's depending on the individual's desires and efforts to act in certain ways. The work and play, the activity itself will dictate the necessary conditions and norms, and they will be accepted, if the activity is meaningful.

The systems of control that are used by teachers may not seem to be in harmony with their professed values. Control by domination of some sort, however subtle, is found in most teaching.

While Roman Catholic theory rejects "a pretended self-government and unrestrained freedom on the part of the child" which diminishes the teacher's authority, yet "if any of these terms are used less properly to denote the necessity of a gradually more active co-operation on the part of the pupil in his own education, if the intention is to banish from education despotism and violence, which, by the way, just punishment is not, this would be correct, but in no way new." [20]

This pronouncement, with emphasis on the teacher's authority

[18] Roland Faunce and Nelson Bossing, *Developing the Core Curriculum*, Prentice-Hall, Inc., 1951, p. 102.
[19] *Ibid.*, pp. 102–105.
[20] *Five Great Encyclicals*, The Paulist Press, 1939, pp. 54–55.

and the idea of punishment, seems to be not entirely consistent with the original spirit of religion as it springs out in the saintly or devotedly religious life. The teacher, to really express the religious model, would show the character virtues of humility, forbearance, love of God and man. His actions would exemplify the various sociative principles.

Controls handled in this way would be regarded as indulgence from a nativist and market point of view. Two-fisted men are not made by pampering. High group morale comes not from the awarding of opportunities but from curtailment and denial. Things must be made "tough." Spare the rod and spoil the child. There is power and authority in life, and people must learn to be obedient and carry out orders. Disobedience must be punished. Strictness, severity are felt and understood more easily than mildness and conciliation. The school is seen as an authoritarian organization, and controls express this authoritarian orientation.

The religious, the common man, and the humanist orientations all contain the point of view that the most profitable human experiences come out of sociative relations. The sociologist and modern educational theorists concur in pointing out that force and conflict are essentially repressive and destructive of creativity, and yet the better social principle of sociative relations is still not predominantly operative in most schoolroom situations. The maintenance of anything but a repressive and punitive order is dependent on a continuous sociative process. Until it is better understood how this is to be achieved, power and personal authority will hold sway.

Discipline and authority inhere in the nature and rationality of work. Self-discipline is found in response to a task or project. It is not some esoteric faculty or state inside the person. It is amazing what concentration, endurance, and work children can demonstrate when a project catches them. The discipline is in the job, not in the person, and in the job as articulated in a world. Thus we can go further and say that discipline and order are in the nature of the world. If the work lacks meaning, then discipline problems arise, be it in school, factory, office, or store. The humanist may be right in emphasizing the discipline of activity rather than rule by person.

The value orientations come to the fore in this area of discipline and the enforcement of the normative and functional order. We find that at this point much that is done is inconsistent with what is said, that often teachers cannot go beyond the logic of the moment, or of what is effective for achieving the immediate purpose. The significance of values comes out still more when we note how children interpret their work and rules.

Selected Readings

Curriculum in Intergroup Education, National Association of Secondary-School Principals, National Education Association, 1950.

Faunce, Roland, and Bossing, Nelson, *Developing the Core Curriculum,* Prentice-Hall, Inc., 1951.

Improving Human Relations, National Council for the Social Studies, 1941. See pp. 131–135 for programs instituted to rehabilitate two demoralized elementary schools.

Lowenfeld, Victor, *Creative and Mental Growth,* The Macmillan Company, rev. ed., 1952.

Piaget, Jean, *The Moral Judgment of the Child,* Harcourt, Brace and Company, 1932.

Read, Herbert, *Education Through Art,* Faber and Faber, 1943.

Redl, Fritz, "Group Psychological Elements in Discipline Problems," *American Journal for Orthopsychiatry,* January, 1943.

Robinson, John, "Students and Faculty Work to Improve School Life," *Journal of Educational Sociology,* May, 1948. Deals with the rehabilitation of a demoralized high school.

Rogers, Carl, *Client-Centered Therapy,* Houghton Mifflin Company, 1951, chaps. 8, 9.

"School Culture and Group Life," *Journal of Educational Sociology,* May, 1948, entire issue.

Sheviakov, George, and Redl, Fritz, *Discipline for Today's Children and Youth,* Department of Supervision and Curriculum Development, National Education Association, 1944.

The Student Council in the Secondary School, National Association of Secondary-School Principals, National Education Association, 1950.

Sullivan, Dorothea (ed.), *Readings in Group Work,* Association Press, 1952.

Wheeler, Raymond, and Perkins, Francis, *Principles of Mental Development,* Thomas Y. Crowell Company, 1932, chaps. 22, 23.

Yauch, Wilbur A. *How Good Is Your School?* Harper & Brothers, 1951, esp. pp. 139–148.

CHAPTER 12

The Meaning of the
Institutional Order of the School

OUR ANALYSIS so far has not taken into consideration what the persons who make up the school think about it. The work and play activities, the norms, and the system of enforcement are not just there. They have meaning for the boys and girls and for the teachers. They cannot participate in a neutral manner, for they are active agents. They sustain this institutional order in some phases and oppose it in others. All of them are evaluating the activities, the norms, the roles, and the personalities in the school. These evaluations may be shared with others, and they may not fit together. Situations may be interpreted in different ways. What an institutional order means to a participant depends upon the position he occupies, the experience he has had within this order, and what other attitudes and values he brings into it from outside.

We are interested in the positive and negative evaluations or assessments of the school's institutional order. Such an interpretation of the school from the point of view of the participants has not been extensively carried out. Children who have dropped out of school have given their reasons for leaving, and some of these reasons include an evaluation of the school. Teachers have been rated, but such ratings have little bearing upon the functional and normative orders. The data in this chapter are all taken from the study of West School in Mill City, the community described in Chapter 5.

To secure the necessary information from children is difficult. Some children are rather voluble; others cannot formulate any ideas, or they are inconsistent. To be reflective in this manner would be difficult even for adults. Responses were secured about the playground rules, work, the halls, classroom organization, and punishment. Generally a child was asked whether a rule was fair or not, reasonable or not. After the child had indicated his evaluation, he was asked to explain why he thought the rule was sensible or unreasonable. Teachers were interviewed on points stressed in the interview with the child. In this way one could check the degree to which pupils and teachers interpret events in similar or unlike fashion.

THE PUPIL'S INTERPRETATION OF THE SCHOOL

West School attempts to put the humanistic value orientation into effect. It has been noted, when this school was discussed in previous chapters, that practice is not always consistent with theory. The children interviewed were in the following grades: 4, 5, 6, 6–7, 8. In some instances children would refer to their experiences in earlier grades, and while there may be the danger of their projecting present interpretations into the past, these evaluations fit together. We will focus our analysis on the following areas: playground rules, work, classroom organization, and punishment.

WHAT STAYING ON THE PLAYGROUND MEANS

One of the more important rules, found also in most other schools, requires that pupils stay on the playground during recess and during the lunch hour unless they are going home for lunch. No child, unless he has written permission, should leave the grounds. The rule imposes a real restriction on freedom of movement.

All the children agreed that the rule was a fair and sensible one even though they might prefer to roam the streets, go "down street" to the business district, or buy a candy or ice cream in the little nearby stores. That they have done so was observed. Since children risk the imposition of sanctions by leaving the grounds, it is clear that their interests do not coincide with the norm. The norm, however, is public in meaning; that is, it promotes the safety and welfare of the child and also protects the teacher, i.e., from possible suit. Most children are aware of these points.

There were eight general reasons offered by the children as the rationale for the rule. (1) If one is off the playground during the recess or the lunch hour, one is likely to be late to class by not hearing the bells and not knowing the time. (2) One is apt to get into trouble with outside people. (3) One might get in an accident, get hurt or killed. (4) One might get "hollered" at by the teacher or be sent to the principal. (5) One is safe by staying on the playground. (6) It is a rule, and one is supposed to stay. Teachers and principal say so. (7) If one person went, all would leave the playground. (8) The school and the teachers are responsible for the pupils. The most frequent reasons given were a combination of the safety angle and teachers' responsibility. Such reasons are in accordance with the rationale of the institutional order.

The first five reasons represent an evaluation in terms of consequences to the child if he does not live up to the norm. Some of these assumed if not actual consequences link the playground norm to other norms that compose the institutional order. The "no tardiness" or "being on time" norms which support the functional order also support indirectly the "no off grounds" rule. Since it is bad to be late to class, the way to meet the "being on time" norms is by staying on the school grounds.

Of the other consequences, safety angle (being hurt or killed) may be the most serious. The emphasis on safety arises from the school's site, which is near some of the main traffic arteries. Pupils and teachers apparently assume that the probabilities of an accident are high. Being careful and staying on the grounds is drilled into the pupils by the teachers through safety campaigns and speeches by traffic policemen. Being late or scolded by the teacher may be the least serious of these consequences, though younger children seem more apprehensive than the older ones. These consequences involve a direct self-interest in terms of personal safety. In addition, the assessments by others may affect one's self-esteem and self-image; they may judge one as the person who is late, who violates norms, who is scolded by teachers, or who is sent to the principal.

The remaining reasons show other implications. One suggests a conforming attitude, the moral realism with which children regard rules established and maintained by adults. The norm is an objective fact. No deviation is possible. On the other hand, children conclude that without the norm completely atomistic behavior would result. If one person goes, all would go. Lastly, there is the realization that teachers are involved in a special way.

Children recognize that rights and duties are prescribed for teachers and pupils. They see those in the positional structure of the school with its division of authority, control, and duties, in the age and sex statuses of the community and society at large, and in the special positions within their families. They realize that responsibility, accountability, rights, and duties are graded. The child claims safety and well-being. The adult must meet this demand. The adult is fully accountable while the child is not. Such distinction in accountability is expressed in law. What the children state when they talk about the greater responsibility of the adult in the school is the *in loco parentis* rule. "Palmer is responsible for us." (What does that mean?) "He is supposed to take care of us and make sure that nothing happens to us," as a fifth-grader stated the rule. A fourth-grader put it this way: "If you go off the playground you may get hit by a car. The school is responsible. The school is responsible for whatever we do while in school. They get the blame for it. It's their fault. They get blamed for taking care of us. If we get hurt, that is their responsibility." Another said: "The school is responsible for you. If you run off and get hurt, the school is responsible. When mothers send children to school, they think their children are well taken care of." What responsibility means is not clear to many pupils. Most of them have learned that the school or the teacher is responsible and that, therefore, they should live up to the rule. The word takes on a crisis quality. Others interpret responsibility in terms of safety and welfare. One eighth-grader drew out the full implication. "If you run off and get hit by a car, it's the school's fault. They have to pay all the bills."

THE FUNCTIONAL ORDER AS STRESS AND STRAIN

The following points must be considered before we examine the interpretations of the pupils. In West School there is an almost absolute norm that children should be on their own in arithmetic and spelling. In these two areas there is little or no choice in the materials to be studied or the problems to work out. In the social studies and reading groups there is more emphasis on group activity. There is a certain amount of choice of topics to investigate and things to do. The result is a situation having two divergent emphases: one upon individual ability, initiative, and achievement, with a minimum freedom of choice; the other upon sharing, coöperating, common planning, sociability, and group responsibility with as much freedom of choice as is possible in the framework of the school. Pupils recognize these differences and accept them as part of the objective order in which they act. They seem to be most aware of the first emphasis.

Work load, the children thought, was all right, enough to keep one busy but not enough to cause strain. The leniency of teachers in accepting late work varied, but in general the children felt that they would give a person another chance. Furthermore, children knew that the teacher would help after school to improve their work or to complete it. The pupils understood that deadlines should be met and that a task assumed should be completed. Teachers tended to be less lenient when a pupil fell far behind in work or when the work was sloppily done.

When children were asked whether or not they could help one another, the overwhelming response was negative. It would, thus, seem that a school that wanted to encourage coöperation was doing the exact opposite. The children, as it finally became clear, had in mind arithmetic and spelling. The first typical response indicated acceptance of and conformity to the norm. One does not get help from others because asking others is bad, or one is not doing one's work if one secures help from others. Therefore, one should do it alone. The child conforms also through deference to the teacher as a person or to the authority of the teacher. One should not ask help from others because "the teacher does not like it." If the teacher gives permission, one may give or secure help, but this involves a restriction. When it was given, the child was not to secure answers but to gain an understanding of the process, the how of the task.

The second general response is in pragmatic terms. One might get the wrong answers. This involves other consequences. One might be caught and be exposed. One avoids then a painful situation, witnessed now and then by most children, by doing the work alone. If one were caught, there would be punishment, such as more checking and extra work in order to have the assignment accepted. If the answers one got were wrong, then one would learn improperly, i.e., learn how to make mistakes more readily. In sum, "You won't learn if someone helps. You should figure it out yourself." This idea is reinforced when pupils accept the definition that "copying is not learning; copying is cheating." Thus, some pupils will be labeled "copyers" or "cheater."

Pragmatic considerations are also extended into the future. If one does work alone, one can not only do it better but also handle hard problems and thus be prepared to meet the future. The future includes examinations. Getting help from others means a later inability to handle tests, and the test is a crisis situation. In order to surmount this crisis when one is on one's own, individual effort must be made. "We are not supposed to coöperate in arithmetic. The teacher says that's like copying. Plenty copy. If you copy, you don't learn anything. You can't do tests. We separate our chairs and you're on your own. If others do your work, you won't be able to be smart." The second reference to the future deals with the upper grades. "If you get in the higher grades, you won't know anything (i.e., if you get help from others)." Or: "You won't know what to do in the next grade." The expectation of promotion and future success supports an individualistic emphasis.

The report card also emphasizes individual striving and achievement. A pupil in the 6–7 combination class stated: "Report cards? I wish we had'm. You know where you stand. We're graded but don't get a report. We get graded on the work that is handed in, but no final report card. We get test marks. But at the end of the year we get a promotion card, name, and grade going in. That's all!" Another commented: "It's better to get report cards than just pass by the year. We get them every other month. You're worried until you get the first report card. Most people try for a five (the highest mark), to bring work up. Most kids working hard can't get their marks up. Lew had the same mark for three marking periods and he tried to make higher." Some pupils worry more and work harder because of report cards but better pupils, apparently, do not feel this anxiety. "With report cards you work hard to get marks. I feel I work harder." This statement also expresses the displacement of goals from the activity to the mark. Another pupil observed: "I worry more with report cards. Previously, we passed or not. Now we get it every two months."

Children resist the individualistic work pattern in word and in action with a resulting feeling of guilt and with a certain amount of moral ambivalence. A fourth-grader stated: "We're doing good if we help each other. Many just copy. Copying is not bad, but you shouldn't do it." A fifth-grader said: "We do help each other quite a bit. We feel wrong, but we do it anyway." An eighth-grader thought there was "no reason why you shouldn't get help from friends." The taboo on coöperation is not accepted. "Some kids can't wait too long, so they get the answers. They try, get stuck, get so mad, start swearing. So they go over and ask other people, and they give them the answers. Johnnie does this. Mac too. None of the girls do. [This is actually not true.] Most of them are smart." Most of them preferred the group situation, not only because there was this help and coöperation but also because it was a sociable situation.

DIFFICULTIES IN DEMOCRATIC ROOM ORGANIZATION AND IN THE TEACHER ROLE

Since West School's program is to develop democratic group experiences, teachers attempt to have some room organization which meets this intention. Such room organization began in the fourth grade in a rather minimal way. The interpretations of all this by the pupils bring out the difficulties in putting the program into effect. We will examine several grades.

Major offices in the fifth grade were those of president and vice-president. Office originally was held for four months, and tenure was then reduced to two so that more could have a chance at it. According to the pupils not many meetings were held during the year. At the time the class was observed, the class was planning a final school party with the sixth grade. Problems of class etiquette and conduct were usually discussed, "like walking out of seats and what to do about it." The teacher participated actively in the discussions. When pupils were asked whether they ever voted down the teacher, replies ranged from "never" to "once." To vote against the teacher seemed a breach of propriety, but the more typical response was: "We usually follow her suggestions because they are pretty good; nobody else usually has ideas, so we follow teacher's."

In the next grade the teacher made a more determined effort to foster group discussion and the formation of group decisions. The class has a set of officers—president, vice-president, and secretary. The children do not evaluate the president's office highly. There is little authority attached to it aside from bringing a meeting to order and closing it. The teacher usually takes over the direction during a discussion. Some of the pupils did not like the office because they did not want to be in front of the class. The secretary job was not liked because it involved too much writing. The secretary had to read the minutes of the previous meeting, a public performance that some abhorred. Furthermore, a policy of evaluative comments as well as the usual corrections had been instituted so that the experience tended to become embarrassing and uncomfortable.

A pupil summarized his experience as follows:

I like president and things like that. Other rooms do not have presidents, just other duties as in Dryer's and Krinsky's classes. If we had a problem we would go to Dryer and he would explain. The teacher handled the situation. I like the present arrangement better. The class has a right to think, to put in what they think. Miss Lewis isn't boss. She's just showing us how to work, wants us to know how to act and handle a group. In some cases we need her decision. Miss Lewis speaks out of turn. She makes decisions, like the seating arrangement. She suggested a committee to handle it. We don't follow her suggestions all the time. If we don't think she has a good suggestion, we vote her down. She doesn't tell you what to do all the time, like in third grade, but not in fourth and fifth. In other grades teachers are outside the group more. We have little to say about studies. Sometimes she gives us a choice.

Here we find a sense of freedom and self-direction, circumscribed, however, by the teacher's superior authority. Of fifteen children interviewed, all had a similar interpretation, though with some variations. Some evaluated this self-direction negatively, and others thought that the teacher really was boss.

The teacher isn't strict enough. Boys and girls can do what they want. I don't like that. I came from a stricter school. Miss Lewis isn't boss, but I'd like her to be though. In discussion she's part of the group. That's all right. Miss Lewis asks me why Gay, Peggy, and I fuss so much during discussion. Sometimes it's just boring to me. The more boring it gets the more temptation there is to talk to Gay. The class makes decisions unless Miss Lewis really disagrees. We can't go that far. The class turns down motions of Miss Lewis. Some of the class stick up for her. Others are against her. I really think Miss Lewis is boss. They made her teacher over us.

Interpretations are ambivalent. Thus, the class does make more decisions but only up to a certain limit. Meetings are interesting and a waste of time. The teacher is boss and is not boss. When this teacher, in carrying out the group idea, talks about the class as her family, pupils are not very sure what she means. As one girl commented, "Miss Lewis is the real leader of the class. Nobody feels that they're a real president. She is the teacher. Sometimes she's one of the group when she sits around as in discussion. One thing that's funny and it isn't done in other rooms, she calls us all her family. But in meetings, she doesn't always raise her hand. She doesn't have to because she's teacher. The class usually makes its own decisions except periods and studies. These are planned by her. When the class has something to decide, they do."

The sixth–seventh grade did not have a formal organization. A planning committee laid out topics to be studied a week in advance. Specific details would be worked out by the teacher. A class meeting was standard procedure in the morning as soon as the bell rang, and occasionally in the afternoon if there was a need for it. The teacher presided over the meeting. Any problem or concern that a pupil had could be brought forth at a meeting. If a pupil was too shy, he could put a note in the suggestion box. It was in this way, for example, that the teacher was made aware of the problem of a girl suffering from a collective crush on the part of the boys in the class. A note appeared in the box: "There are some boys in this room that made a nice girl cry they call her names. I hope you will tell them to stop. A friend of this girl."

The direction and content of thirty-four notes dropped in the box is given in Table 30. "Positive" means a suggestion for improvement, suggesting additional activities, or changing the program. Several notes suggested more joint activities with other rooms. Others criticized the planning committee for doing a poor job and indicated a need for a drastic shake-up. Most of the suggestions are considered in the class meeting if the teacher thinks it expedient. The class then decides what to do about the suggestion. In these meetings the teacher plays an active role, and the discussion comes out in line rather frequently with the teacher's ideas.

TABLE 30. Positive and Negative Comments by Major Activity Area in Suggestion Box, Grade 6–7, March 17-April 15

Direction of Comment		Major Areas				
	Total	Sports	Dancing	Studies	Class Organization and Management	Interpersonal
Positive	27	3	4	12	7	1
Negative	13	–	2	2	5	4
Total	40	3	6	14	12	5

Pupils regard this teacher as rather firm and strict, but this is approved. "She wants us to get as much out of school as you can get." Another thought that a teacher should be strict, "otherwise there would be too much foolishness."

In the eighth grade, events involving self-direction included two class parties, the selection of the class ribbon, and other activities associated with graduation. The teacher was regarded as the controlling influence in the class, handling all major decisions, disciplinary problems, and the planning of studies. In answer to a hypothetical case of infraction of rules children thought that the teacher would handle it herself without any group discussion. The teacher was regarded as both strict and not strict. Children stated both that she would and that she would not accept suggestions from pupils. The teacher was viewed, hence, in ambivalent terms, except on one point, namely, that she was the controlling factor in the class. The assessment of the class is in line with the teacher's conception of the class and its relation to the high school, namely, that the class should be a preparation for the high school and that activities should be organized to fit them into the high-school pattern.

The experience in all these classes shows the difficulty of putting into effect democratic group practices. The situation is difficult because of the very structure of the school, the division into teacher and pupil, a division supported by the legal order. It is also complicated by age status differences, which make for social distance between the children and the teacher as an adult. The range of group discussion seems limited to problems of class decorum and etiquette. The planning of the work and play activities is primarily in the hands of the teachers, for they have to coördinate their work to avoid duplication. The legal order also sets forth a certain amount of material that should be covered. Articulation with the local high school apparently affects how the activities of the two upper grades are carried out, the teachers putting into practice a traditional pattern, one that is found in the high school. There seems no consistency in what is done, so that the children will have democratic room organization in one grade and none in another. This may merely mean that the school has not fully realized its goal. In spite of the fact that the teachers in this school are interested in the humanistic orientation and have, in addition, the support of a local teachers college, the difficulties of putting this view into practice are great. It is not surprising that traditional practices are likely to prevail in schools lacking the facilities and support West School has.

SOME PUPIL REFLECTIONS ON PUNISHMENT

In the fourth grade the teacher did not believe in denying recess or having a pupil stay after school, a policy the children heartily approved. Most of them had experienced such penalties in earlier grades. One boy, referring to a denial of recess in the second grade, thought it was good punishment for running down the hall, " 'Cause we like to go out." Of all the types of controls listed by pupils in this class the worst was standing or sitting out in the hall. All had the same interpretation. "Everyones sees you there and know you wasn't good." "People come by and know how bad you are." "All people pass by and say, 'What are you doing there, you're bad.'" Being denied activities in class was regarded as next worst, for "you miss the fun." Sitting in the corner was regarded as easiest. One pupil did not care what the controls were.

In the fifth grade, staying after school was considered the worst punishment. The reason given by the pupils was the same—loss of playtime. On the matter of shaking up (i.e., teacher seizing child by shoulder and shaking him back and forth) and knuckling (hitting the knuckles with a ruler), all pupils agreed that such punishment would be just. Reasons varied, for the interpretations were colored by a special "problem" boy. "He got teacher really mad. Oh, yes! She was right. She was trying to help him all year." "The teacher was right. He was disturbing us, and we couldn't get work done." "My mother tells me that people who do not behave deserve to be punished. Children should behave themselves. The catechism book says always respect and obey teachers." "The teacher is fair. If you do something you must suffer consequences. Teacher won't hit for nothing." Knuckling was regarded as a test of discipline by the boys, not to flinch or show pain, and there is a trick of the trade. One boy said, "If you tighten your fist hard, it doesn't hurt anyway."

In the upper grades denial of recess and staying after school were considered the worst punishment. The reason, again, was the loss of playtime, and, for some boys, not being able to play on the class or school team. Being sent to the principal's office was regarded as a shameful experience, particularly by the girls. Some hardened boys did not care, for a penalty was a matter of form that you went through.

THE TEACHER'S ASSESSMENT OF THE FUNCTIONAL AND NORMATIVE ORDERS

A complete description of the assessments by the teachers is not attempted. We shall state their rationale for punctuality, work, quietness, and discipline.

BEING ON TIME

All teachers interviewed agreed that this rule is important. Children should be punctual, but the meaning of punctuality is rather broad. There are four reasons offered for this stress on time. One is that the school has to maintain a standard which is set by law. A child is to be in school a certain number of hours. There has to be some check on the child, and the most appropriate time, and for matters of attendance too, is at 9:00 A.M. and at 1:00 P.M. Insistence on punctuality is complying with the law. A second general reason relates to the operation of the functional order. This idea is well expressed by a teacher as follows: "One has to start some time, otherwise things would go on later and later. To get things done, there has to be a time when we get busy, and the easiest way and the one way is for all of us to be there. . . . There is something in knowing when to expect a definite thing. That does not mean to routinize the whole pattern, but you have to run a whole pattern and items have to fit in. Nine and one are the time pegs around which to organize the pattern." If the children arrive late, they may disrupt the class, and, in addition, they may fall behind in their work.

A third justification of the rule assumes that such punctuality is good character training. To state the point negatively, it is poor character training if a child comes into class at any old time and if consequently work is not done. Here punctuality is broadened to include promptness in completing tasks, but this links the idea once more with the functional order and the implied assumption that a certain amount of work must be accomplished. As we have seen, school standards include a certain amount of work that must be completed because prescribed in the statutes. To state the point positively, the teachers think that if appointments are met at the right time and work is handed in on time, there should be a sense of achievement and satisfaction.

A fourth point, closely related to the third, links being on time with adult training for the future. In actual life, they say, one has to be on time. If a person has a job, he is expected to be on time; therefore, children should learn to be punctual.

Since our culture is so completely time-centered, particularly in our urban society, this emphasis is not unrealistic. To be on time is necessary for efficient action. All groups have time schedules. The rationale for the norm becomes completely understandable as a condition necessary for a group as an ongoing system. The larger the group and the greater the variety of activities, the more important the time element and the scheduling of these functions. The teachers are aware of this necessity.

In conclusion, it should be noted that teachers are themselves subject to the norm of punctuality. Furthermore, there is or could be considerable flexibility in handling lateness. Unless a child is habitually late, a teacher in the lower grades pays little attention except for a casual inquiry. Some make the child go through the formal procedure of getting a late permit. In the grades up to the seventh this procedure is of little importance, a matter of routine, but in the last two grades, tardiness and absences are indicated on the report card. While the "being on time" rule as stated seems absolute, there is leniency in its enforcement which lessens as the child moves into the upper grades. This leniency is an expression of the humanistic orientation.

ON BEING "RELATIVELY" QUIET

How quiet children should be, according to the teachers, depends upon the activities taking place. In the library, for example, the rule tends to become somewhat absolute. There should be no talking, but if there is, the children should whisper. Talking is permitted in class as long as it is not disturbing to others, but this qualification is precisely the moot point: when is the talking disturbing? Miss Hendry interprets the rule as follows: "In the schoolroom, a good deal of the time, work has to be done. There has to be concentration. Nobody works very well in a noisy atmosphere. It is nerve racking. Children don't like it either. They say, 'It's so noisy you can think!'"

Quietness is thus linked with the working efficiency of the children. It is a condition that helps getting work done. Being quiet, however, also involves self-restraint; and the support of the norm, teachers think, makes for good character. It means they say, that one is considerate of others, realizing a responsibility to the group. Not to disturb others in the work is giving everybody a chance.

These teacher assessments show the impossibility of considering the meaning of a norm in isolation. Likewise, value implications cannot be avoided, for the norm may even become an end in itself. If it is assumed that quietness is an end value, it still will be interlinked in some way with other values on this level, e.g., good citizenship and fair play.

Another important implication of the quietness norm is a *sine qua non* for social interaction, i.e., it makes communication possible. When there is too much confusion and talking, directions cannot be heard. Requests for quiet, which sometimes are quite numerous, have generally been made so that adequate communication to all members of the class could be established. Communication breaks down, work breaks down when the norm is widely violated. When that occurs, a teacher is likely to impose "absolute" silence for a short time. In the rooms observed there is usually a low-pitched work hum when the class is proceeding in an interested and concentrated fashion. When this hum becomes louder and higher, deviation from the quietness norm occurs very rapidly. That means not only talking but walking around the room and visiting. The fact that there is this audible work murmur indicates a flexibility in supporting the norm. Quietness norms may be associated with certain kinds of activities that require concentration and contemplation. In the observed classes they have been most closely linked with arithmetic. In social studies, particularly if the class is split up in several small work groups, there is considerably more talking and visiting, but the teacher watches carefully to see that work is accomplished, that personal interests and gossip do not supplant the functional order.

INTERPRETATION OF WORK

We have already indicated that children must act individually as well as collectively, and they must act in these ways because of the direction of the teachers. The teachers direct them thus because of values they consider worth while.

The dual emphasis we have noted is expressed by a teacher in the following statement:

On my level [fourth grade] very few children work by themselves. They work by twos or threes in a group. I ask them not to transfer answers, not to get the answers but to ask each other for help on the process, how to secure the answer. [Yet] in case of talking, it is poor training for tests when they are absolutely on their own. I tell them "don't copy." Children tell on each other anyway, so I don't have to do detective work. I tell them to stand on their own feet, I emphasize that they will make mistakes but they will make mistakes less. So not to worry. To be independent. To take care of one's self. To listen, and not to ask too many questions. I believe in self-promotion.

I have three groups in reading. Children on their own initiative, spontaneously, ask to be given a chance for another group. Occasionally better readers sit in with those not so good, and I don't object if it's only for a period. Children want to advance on their own initiative, but this is stimulated by the progress of others. The result now is almost one large group.

Another teacher comments:

Even in group projects there is individual responsibility just the same. They are doubly of value. Arithmetic is largely individual, though not always. Each person should develop his own ability and his own thinking. One can't always work things with other people but by thinking things through one's self. That's part of our job to have them do that. To do our own thinking and not to depend on others.

Both of these statements involve a conception of the teacher's role and a social model of what is deemed good or excellent. It is the teacher's function to facilitate the progress of the pupil in the "tool" subjects but in such a way that there is self-initiative, individual responsibility, self-reliance. Group projects, as the teacher conceives them, act as a stimulus to this progress and individualism. That is to say, the pupil is accountable for the progress of the group. The teacher views his role as one that supports both individual and group orientation.

ON THE MATTER OF DISCIPLINE

"I can handle them with one hand tied behind my back," said the teacher in a lower grade. "The children will take care of me. I'm so old [said jokingly], they'll look out for me. There's nothing private on my desk. If the children want to look over the things on it that's all right." Here is a suggested attitude of teacher and pupil in a room which is greatly relaxed when the teacher is in charge. In this instance the teacher projects herself as a value into the action systems of the children. "The order or request has a validity for the social object [the children] because and insofar as the agent [the teacher] who expresses it is valuable in his eyes; its fulfillment would harmonize with the agent's accepted worth, its non-fulfillment would conflict with his worth." [1]

According to another, "The teacher has a responsibility in the classroom. It's all right to understand and look for causes but I have to act and do something in the immediate situation. For example, swearing is very vile in my room. What to do, I won't let them get away with it, not while I'm there." (She referred to some swearing involving such phrases as "god-damned son-of-a-bitch.") "Other children may not like it either." The assumption by the teacher of a common conventional morality is obviously not shared, but by the imputation of the morality to a majority, the teacher justifies her action. Prescription in the legal order would likewise sustain her. Considerations of her self-image are also involved. The teacher's concern with swearing is also related to the consequences that flow from the interaction. Swearing is contraventive, and if it is carried out with sufficient venom and spite, a fight is likely to result. Control of swearing means controlling a consequence that might be more serious. Such a course of action has been dubbed "preventive discipline" by one teacher. "See ahead of the child." "If they go out on the playground, see that they don't get too heated up and fight. See that they don't have emotional upsets. Likewise in class. Head off an outbreak. You save them and yourself." This appears to be a matter of manipulative technique which a teacher is forced to use. If she cannot solve underlying tensions and problems, she will at least smooth them over and present a smooth and even surface.

On defining a situation for children at the beginning of the year, a teacher pointed out that for two months during the summer children are relatively unsupervised, and then they go back to

[1] Florian Znaniecki, *Social Actions,* Farrar and Rinehart, Inc., 1936, p. 102.

school and routine. She discussed this situation in relation to the question of discipline. This teacher also observed that a child is not going to act wholly on his own accord, that a child in later life will be in situations where he must obey and where, furthermore, he may not even have too much to say. Children learn that also in school. This, as it will be noted, does not fit in with the ideas of self-expression, group direction, and democratic process.

Discipline involves the upholding of conventional morality and the prescriptions in the legal order. Maintaining these norms, however, insures the operation of the functional order, the safety of the child, the avoidance of possible suit and of negative reactions on the part of parents. Discipline is a means of maintaining appropriate conduct in the status structure, both the conduct appropriate for the positions of child and adult and that appropriate for the specialized institutional positions of teacher and pupil. In some instances, the control of the teacher is based on her attributes of personality highly assessed by pupils. The system of discipline is also future oriented, providing the kind of controls to which adults are subjected. The school, it is thought, furnishes in this way a real-life situation as children are prepared for adult functions.

IN CONCLUSION—THE SIGNIFICANCE OF THESE INTERPRETATIONS

People view an institutional order from the position they occupy in it. Some will see only a small part of it; others may see it as a whole. The narrow view is that of the pupils; the wider that of teachers and directors. The widest view, however, is that of the observer who tries to see the whole in its context, a sort of pupil-teacher-school-as-group vision.

A school is completely intelligible as a socio-cultural object without including the interpretations of the participants. What the pupils think may have no direct influence upon the overall structure and organization of the school, but the most effective education takes into account the biological potentialities and the social growth of the child and provides maximum conditions for the development of the child. Such a reference is to the nature of things and is objective. Science and philosophy attempt to provide this insight. The opinions of a child may be erroneous. A school built on error provides poor education. The response to such error lies in the action of the children. They reject and leave the school as soon as they are able, though in the meantime they are held there by compulsory school laws.

Yet we gain some insight into the school by studying these evaluations. They show how the child comes to terms with his pupil role. We see the complex interrelationship of norms. We see action in the school organized directly and indirectly through the legal order. It is an element in the thought of both pupils and teachers. We see a marked divergence in the work experience with pupils stressing coöperation and sharing in classroom work and then individualism supported by teachers. The outlook of the pupils is limited to the immediate situation and immediate future whereas teachers emphasize character training and the role of adults and citizens, a long-range point of view. We note the diverging and conflicting interpretations in room organization and the evaluation of the role of the teacher. Children bring into play conceptions of roles derived from other traditional schools and from their experience with parents and other adults in positions of authority. The teacher in a democratic role does not fit their ideas of proper adult behavior, and furthermore, it contradicts their conception of the allocation of authority in the school. Yet again, pupils like the permissive atmosphere of making decisions, of working in small groups, and of knowing somehow that the teacher is not the overpowering adult. Though they may feel mixed up about these inconsistent experiences, the pupils fulfill the jobs and tasks set out for them. It is the content that looms in their experience; the subtleties of room organization and teacher role are the dim background before which they perform their duties. We note how a pragmatic thread weaves through the interpretations. Rules and punishments are effective; they work, even though the child may dimly realize that the punishment works against him, against his growth, against his self-respect. Life in the institutional order of the schools is a complex, bewildering experience, approved, disapproved, decried, and justified. The multiplicity of views arrange themselves on the facets of the institutional order, reflecting like prisms the color of life within.

PART IV

INFORMAL SOCIAL STRUCTURE AND RELATIONS WITHIN THE SCHOOL

CHAPTER 13

Perspectives on the Nature of the Child

A CHILD does not come into the school as a neutral entity. All children by the time they enter school have had a history of love and hate, fear and joy, poverty or luxury. Form of speech, manners, appearance value in clothing, interests are embodied in each child in varying ways. As the child enters the school proper, he joins the formal organization. As he becomes involved with other children, he becomes part of an informal order, an order relatively independent of the formal structure which has been analyzed. This informal order deals with the interpersonal relations among the children, the evolving primary group structure, and the system of evaluation coupled with the resultant reputations. How this structure inhibits or facilitates the operation of the school is a problem to be investigated. Since the position of the child within the informal structure depends upon his past history, our initial analysis will take up certain aspects about the nature of children. What are children like?

If the nature of the child is to be known, the world in which he lives must be known. The following vignettes suggest both of these points. The range of such snapshots of child and world is very great. We limit ourselves to two, realizing that they have a problem slant.

I couldn't enter the *sobranie* (or church) dressed in American style; I must wear the Russian shawl over my head. However, I don't go; I just hate to go to that place. I used to go and sit on the bench and not take part. The old folks don't like it because I don't go to church. They feel awful about it.

The old folks have queer ways; that makes it hard on the children. It is impossible to change their ideas. Sometimes I feel sorry for the old folks, but after a person has been around Americans, he just can't stand the Russian way of living. What an awful hole I live in! I just can't bring my American friends here. . . . I always try to keep my friends away from my home and folks; they have that crazy old religion. . . . When some of the Russian girls go to American dances, their folks half kill them. The American boys are better than the Russian boys. If I can meet the right American man, one I think would make a good husband, I would marry him. I don't know what my folks would say; I know they raised an awful fuss when my older sister married a Russian Catholic. . . . As for me, I go out with a boy until he begins to think something of me; then he finds out about how queer my parents are and drops me like a hot cake. I can't blame him, however, for not wanting to get mixed up in a family like this. I know enough about American ways of living, enough to hate the Russian way.[1]

Here is the person growing up in two cultures, torn by tremendous cross pressures. In this case, the culture conflict is creating deep-seated personality disturbances.

Florida: "One of our public health nurses visited a nursery maintained on a private farm and found 48—and I did not say 4, I said 48—infants on two double beds. I might add that two of the babies in that location subsequently died."

Idaho: "When we dismiss our schools, we use children as soon as they can walk in the potato fields."

Oregon: "In bean picking the best group is a family group—mama, papa, and the kids picking beans."

Texas: "96 percent of the children in that camp had not consumed any milk whatsoever in the last six months."

Colorado: "I have never been so shocked as when I entered the one-room shacks with old iron bedsteads and thin pads, with one shaded bulb, in which as many as eight to ten people sleep, and with an old cook stove, dirt just as thick as you can find it, no toilet facilities, no water facilities."[2]

[1] Hannibal Duncan, *Immigration and Assimilation*, D. C. Heath and Company, 1933, pp. 763–764.
[2] *Migratory Labor in American Agriculture*. Report of the President's Commission on Migratory Labor, 1951, pp. 155, 162, 154.

Here is the child in the world of the migratory worker—diseased, uneducated, bowed with stoop labor, an outcast from any regular community, and, in the words of a county superintendent who used a warehouse for their classes, "sullen, resentful, and suspicious."

The maladjustments and personality problems which may disrupt the classroom and create countless conflicts and misunderstandings have their basis in the social world. In order to understand the child, or the child in the school, we must get as many perspectives as possible on the world in which he lives. In this way we widen our understanding of the nature of the child.

The school is one of the institutional groups in which the child develops his selfhood. Since he does not come to the school with a clean slate, he carries with him the marks and scars, the assets and liabilities of his life in the other institutional arrangements. This life history of the child in his family and of the family in the work-health-religion-recreation order which also organizes the life history facilitates or hinders his progress in school.

UNPOPULAR, A PROBLEM, MALADJUSTED

"One child out of 3 is regarded as a problem by teachers, 1 child out of 4 is an intellectual misfit in his grade, 1 child out of 4 has a serious reading deficiency, 1 child out of 6 is maladjusted according to personality tests, and 1 child out of 20 is repeating his grade." [3] From 18 to about 30 percent of the children in the three schools included in the cited study have adjustment problems of some sort. The degree of seriousness varies. Of the 1524 children studied in grades 1, 2, 4, 5, and 6, 12 percent were considered seriously maladjusted, i.e., having poor mental health and in need of expert guidance. Another 30 percent showed sufficient evidence of difficulty to be considered poorly adjusted, though not to a serious degree. [4] Table 31 shows that the number of children having problems increased with the grade level.

A series of studies on mental health was made among school children in Butler and Miami counties in Ohio, between 1946 and 1948.

[3] Carl R. Rogers, "Mental-Health Findings in Three Elementary Schools," *Educational Research Bulletin*, March 18, 1942, vol. XXI, p. 69.
[4] *Ibid.*, p. 70.

TABLE 31. Percentage Relationship of Maladjustment at Each Grade Level
in Three Schools, Columbus, Ohio

| Grade | Maladjustment | | Relatively |
Level	Serious	Moderate	Well Adjusted
1	11	18	71
2	13	19	70
4	9	24	67
5	15	44	41
6	12	39	49

Since slightly different criteria were used for grades 4–6 than were used for grades 1 and 2, comparison is safer within these groupings.
SOURCE: Carl R. Rogers, "Mental-Health Findings in Three Elementary Schools," *Educational Research Bulletin*, March, 1942, vol. XXI, p. 72.

These studies fit in with the trend of maladjustment just noted. In the first grade, 543 children living in rural farm and rural nonfarm homes including those in smaller towns of Butler County were given a physical examination and at the same time were scored on the presence or absence of eight nervous traits. Those who had four or more of these nervous traits were considered as having a low rating on mental health. Twenty percent of the children reported combinations of four or more, as nail biting, frequent colds, undue tiredness, bad dreams, insomnia, frequent eye pain, frequent illness, frequent crying.[5] The physical examination showed that 72 percent were free of gross physical defects. Of the remaining 28 percent, 42 percent were suffering from malnutrition, and 65 percent had other gross physical defects. Of the group with low mental health, 34 percent had gross physical defects not including malnutrition; 30 percent had gross physical defects including malnutrition; 24 percent had malnutrition as the only physical defect; 22 percent were without gross physical defects. What is significant in this group is the combination of low mental health with poor physical health, in which malnutrition is one of the more important components.[6]

In Miami County, Ohio, located in a predominantly rural and

[5] R. H. Woodward and A. R. Mangus, *Nervous Traits Among First Grade Children in Butler County Schools*, Division of Mental Health of the Ohio State Department of Public Welfare, 1949, p. 2; note that 20.6 percent were free of all the eight nervous traits.
[6] *Ibid.*, p. 4.

semirural region, a composite personality adjustment score was obtained for 1500 children in the third and sixth grades during 1946. A year later a follow-up study was made, and it included 340 of the children in the original studies. These children were now in the fourth and seventh grades. Table 32 compares the results of the two studies.

TABLE 32. Percentages of Children Showing Degrees of Adjustment in 1946 (N = 1500) and in 1947 (N = 340), Miami County

Type of Adjustment	1946	1947
Exceedingly well adjusted	13	12
Above average adjustment	22	22
Average adjustment	22	23
Below average adjustment	24	27
Poorly adjusted	19	15

SOURCE: A. R. Mangus, *Personality Adjustment of School Children*, F. J. Heer Printing Company, 1949, p. 14.

Roughly one out of every five children showed poor adjustment in 1946. Since adjustment is a matter of degree, it is conceivable that quite a few children would be on or near the margin between low average and poor adjustment. On the other hand, 35 percent of the children were well adjusted, about one out of every three children. Nevertheless, the weight is toward the lower end. The follow-up showed that the large majority of children did not change in their adjustment. Those who changed did so for the better, and the largest gains were made by those having the poorest adjustment. A study in Butler County of 1683 children in the fourth, fifth, and sixth grades fits in with the results discussed.[7]

In the same county a study of the mental health of 805 tenth-grade students in the high schools showed that nearly 28 percent had a rating of low mental health; 22 percent rated a high mental health status.[8]

[7] A. R. Mangus and R. H. Woodward, *An Analysis of Mental Health of Elementary School Children*, Division of Mental Health of the Ohio State Department of Public Welfare, 1949.

[8] A. R. Mangus and R. H. Woodward, *An Analysis of the Mental Health of High School Students*, Division of Mental Health of the Ohio State Department of Public Welfare, 1949, p. 20.

In West School, Mill City, of 161 tested pupils, 23 percent were rated as having a poor or very poor adjustment and 25 percent a good or superior adjustment. See Table 33. The scores of several

TABLE 33. Percentile Rank of 161 Pupils on the California Test of Personality for West School and by Grade, 1949

Percentile Rank	Total	Fourth	Fourth-Fifth	Fifth	Sixth	Sixth-Seventh	Eighth
					Grade		
80	21	1	1	9	4	2	4
70–75	19	4	2	5	2	2	4
35–65	84	18	8	8	17	21	12
25–30	21	3	8	2	3	2	3
1–20	16	2	7	1	3	2	1
Unclassified	3		2		1		
Total	164	28	28	25	30	29	24

SOURCE: Data from unpublished study by author.

In qualitative terms, starting at the top of the percentile column: superior adjustment, good adjustment, average adjustment, poor adjustment, very poor adjustment.

pupils lie close to the dividing points. If the percentile range of the middle group were reduced so that any pupil below the 40 percentile would be considered a poor or very poor adjustment and at the 65 percentile and above a good or superior adjustment, the percentages would be respectively 28 and 32. The first statement is the more conservative one. There was much variation in the classes. In the fourth grade those with good and superior adjustment and those with poor or very poor adjustment were each 18 percent of the class, and in the other grades, these percentages were respectively: in the fourth-fifth grade, 11 and 53; in the fifth, 56 and 12; in the sixth, 20 and 20; in the sixth-seventh, 14 and 14; and in the eighth, 33 and 17. The fourth-fifth grade was the only one with a large group of poorly adjusted pupils as defined by the California Test of Personality, Elementary Series, Form A. In the other classes the less well-adjusted children were surrounded by a large group of moderately or well-adjusted children. Chances of personality clash are thus reduced, and one might expect a more serene situation. This implication was confirmed by a sociometric test. The fourth-fifth grade was the only grade in which almost all children wrote down four rejection choices. In the other grades there was much reluctance to do so. One might assume that since most of the children felt well adjusted, they thought that they got along fairly well with everyone and hence there was no necessity to indicate negative choices. Most of the children had a pretty good conception or evaluation of themselves, but they felt that they lacked social skills.

Let us take a look at another country. An English study attempted to find out the extent of behavior and personality disorders in school children.[9] The study dealt with four boys' and four girls' schools including children between the ages 12 and 14. Schools differed in social class standing. The observed difficulties were classified under the following headings: *personality deviations* (timidity, sensitiveness, lack of sociability, daydreaming, emotional instability, etc.); *behavior disorders* (sex misdemeanors, truancy, wandering, lying, stealing, begging, cruelty); *habit disorders* (nail biting, thumb sucking, incontinence, habit spasm, masturbation, stammering); *scholastic difficulties* other than those due to mental defect. A questionnaire on the children was filled out by the teachers. What the study amounts to, then, is a problem evaluation by teachers. Keeping this qualification in mind, one notes that 46.2 percent of the children had one or more symptoms. The conclusion would be that the incidence of adjustment problems is roughly similar to that found in our country.

We have found so far that about 20 to 35 percent of children in schools have adjustment problems in moderately serious or serious form. This percentage is found even in the early grades. The proportion apparently does not change much from grade to grade, i.e., it applies to the elementary school as well as to the high school. The implication is obvious. A school should be a mental hygiene center and work as far as possible with children as soon as they enter school, for these children may well be the future psychotics in our mental hospitals. It also means that a teacher can expect in general to have from three to five emotionally disturbed children in her class. It is not implied that such children will exhibit only aggressive behavior, for shyness, awkwardness, and timidity are symptoms

[9] Bernice McFie, "Behavior and Personality Difficulties in School Children," *British Journal of Educational Psychology*, February, 1934, pp. 30–46.

usually overlooked in a "well-behaved" pupil. It is necessary to specify other findings of the cited studies in order to pin down this adjustment problem still further.

THE CHILD IN TERMS OF SEX AND AGE STATUS

The studies quoted show a marked sex difference in adjustment. Boys tend to have more adjustment problems than girls, and this tends to hold from the first grade through high school. The level of mental health is higher among girls than among boys, the Ohio studies found, whether the children lived on farm, in village, or in city. In West School, however, this association between personality adjustment and sex was not found. The lower ratings of boys may be due to the methods of composing the tests. The scoring of items may be in favor of girls and against boys so that the boys in general should score lower. As it has been pointed out, conduct required of children in the school fits in with the female sex status so that the school itself may favor better mental health in girls and contrariwise make for mental health problems in boys.

The growth of the child in its sex status is closely allied to the requirements of age status. From the point of view of the culture the movement of the child to the adult involves for the man the assumption of breadwinner, husband, and father positions and for the woman primarily the domestic, household manager, wife, and mother positions. The content of the sex status is designed to prepare the child for these adult sex statuses. This course of preparation is seen in more obvious form in preliterate and agricultural communities where many boy and girl activities are but the adult functions reduced and modified to fit the capacity of the child to deal with them. For example, take the drawing of water from a well in jugs as a female function. The young girl may be required to get water, but the size of the jug is small, adapted to her ability and strength. Her movements in handling the jug are the same as the adult's except again for their diminutive size. One might perhaps say that there is really no distinction between the adult and the child in the water drawing, for objective and method are the same, the only difference being the amount of water drawn. Children who milk cows, take care of chickens, drive tractors are performing such grownup functions. The extent to which the children are used as mere tools depends on the values of the culture. The tasks they perform here are linked with their family and community life, an organic relation that is not found in the usual forms of pure economic child labor.

In all cultures there is a provision made for play among children. Whether preliterate or twentieth century, many games are remarkably similar in content. Some may be open to both sexes, others particularized as to sex status, the obvious case being the doll and housekeeping games and play of girls in our culture. An eight-year-old boy playing with dolls would be considered an oddity. The play of boys is much more aggressive, whether it is the old-fashioned cowboys and Indians, cops and robbers, or the more current versions of playing at war and interplanetary hostilities. Thus, the activity is selected to fit in with the assumed temperament of male and female. In our activities the emphasis is derived from the ultimate domestic role the woman is to play and the breadwinner role of the husband. In the former there is to be gentleness, kindness, or meekness and in the latter, aggressiveness, domination, and a certain pontificality of the "superior" male. Thus, character training through activities is to lead the child to the adult sex role.

The sex role may also be viewed in terms of peer definition. The peer conception of the role constitutes an additional element to the adult's view of the sex role. Even though boys and girls maturate at different ages and even though other obvious biological differences exist, there may be social constants in the definition of the sex role, summed in the rather trite observation that a boy is to act like a boy and a girl like a girl. The question arises, however, as to what sort of boy and girl is envisioned.

The "ideal" as drawn by peers is found in Tryon's study of 12- and 15-year-old boys and girls. The children were studied at the age of 12 and restudied at the age of 15. Three-fourths of the 15-year-olds were of the original group.[10]

[10] Caroline Tryon, *Evaluation of Adolescent Personality by Adolescents*, Monographs of the Society for Research in Child Development, National Research Council, 1939.

The picture of the idealized boy at the age of 12 is one who is "skillful and a leader in games; his daring and fearlessness extend beyond his social group to defiance of adult demands and regulations. Any characteristic which can be construed as feminine by one's peers such as extreme tidiness or marked conformity to the class room is regarded as a weakness. However, some personableness and certain kindly and likeable qualities tend to be associated with the more highly prized masculine qualities." Prestige, for the 15-year-old boy, "is still in a large measure determined by physical skill, aggressiveness, and fearlessness. Defiance of adult standards has lost emphasis, though still acceptable and rather amusing to them tends to be associated with immaturity. . . . Much greater emphasis is placed upon personal respectability . . . unkempt-untidy related to this constellation is the only trait among the twenty on which the boys completely reversed their evaluation." [11]

The picture of the girl undergoes a marked shift between the ages of 12 and 15. The conception of the 12-year-old girl by her peers is one who is "quiet, sedate, nonaggressive, qualities associated with friendliness, likeableness, good-humor, and attractive appearance. Behavior which conforms to the demands and regulations of the adult world is admired. Tomboyishness is tolerated. At the 15 year old level admiration for the demure, docile rather prim lady-like prototype has ceased. Instead, many of the criteria for the idealized boy such as extroversion, activity, and good sportsmanship are highly acceptable for the girl. The ability to organize games for parties, involving both sexes, and the capacity to keep such activities lively and entertaining is admired. In addition the quality of being fascinating or glamorous to the other sex has become important but is looked upon as relatively specific or unrelated to other desirable qualities." [12] While there is a change, the change does not conflict with femininity, for it represents only a permissive variant in the role. Such variations are the "good sport," the "glamour girl," the "young lady," the "home girl." Only the "career girl" marks a major deviation toward the masculine role. [13]

[11] *Ibid.*, pp. 77–78.
[12] *Ibid.*, p. 77.
[13] Cf. Mirra Komarovsky, "Cultural Contradictions and Sex Roles," *American Journal of Sociology*, November, 1946, pp. 184–189.

Much is made of gang behavior, primarily a city phenomenon, among boys and to a certain extent among girls. The major significance of ganging is its reinforcement of the characteristics of sex status and its closure to others, especially adults. Most character-building organizations try to capitalize on this tendency.

SOCIAL CLASS AND THE CHILD

The content of the sex status of the child is also influenced by social class. What the social class factor means has been outlined in Chapter 5.

Evidence as to whether there is any association between socio-economic class and personality adjustment is inconsistent. The assumption is that children in the lower class will show greater maladjustment as compared to children of the upper. The English study concludes that the variations in the schools studied could not be explained by social class.[14] Of the Ohio studies only the Columbus study examined in rather gross fashion this relationship. "The more favored the neighborhood, the fewer the serious mental-health problems. In a favored school, one child out of twenty is seriously maladjusted, while in an underprivileged area, one child out of five presents serious problems."[15] On the other hand, a good average neighborhood area had about the same proportion of serious and moderately serious problems as the underprivileged. A study of sixth graders in St. Cloud, Minnesota,[16] showed a slight correlation ($r = .16 \pm .09$) between socio-economic status as measured by the American Home Scale and scores on a personality test, but this correlation is not significant (critical ratio, 1.77). In West School no relation was found between economic class and personality adjustment. Two other studies also substantiate this finding.[17] On the

[14] Bernice McFie, *op. cit.*, pp. 39–40.
[15] Carl R. Rogers, *op. cit.*, p. 73.
[16] Harris Gough, "Relationship of Socio-Economic Status to Personality Inventory and Achievement Test Scores," *Journal of Educational Psychology*, December, 1946, pp. 527–540.
[17] Helen Davidson, *Personality and Economic Background*, King's Crown Press, 1943, a study of highly intelligent children showing that most personality indices were independent of both intelligence and income of parents; B. J. Snyder and W. C. Snyder, "Some Relationships between Children's Symptoms of Maladjustment and Background Factors," *Journal of Clinical Psychology*, vol. 2, January, 1946, pp. 13–22.

other hand, two other studies show the opposite,[18] i.e., that there is a relationship between socio-economic status and personality traits and adjustment. The Coleman study was carried out on the junior-high level, using a national sample.

These personality tests, composed of questions about oneself and about certain activity areas such as school, home, and community, present certain difficulties and must be accepted rather cautiously. Just as the scored items may favor girls, so it is entirely feasible that they, like many of the intelligence tests, are unintentionally biased against the lower and favor the upper socio-economic classes. Also, the child may not be willing to answer the questions honestly, since they may represent a subtle attack on his self-estimate. Or the child may not understand a question and, hence, answer it incorrectly. Some of the questions may not apply to his life history and cannot be answered. Personality adjustment is also a difficult concept, for the crux of adjustment is in relation to others, in the sociative and dissociative relations, and not merely something inside the person. At any rate we do not reach any affirmative conclusions about the relationship between social class and personality adjustment.

What is a good home? A lower economic class child answered: "A place where there is enough to eat." Here is a life centered on the needs of the species, subsistence, shelter, protection—a matter of maintaining oneself. Species requirements are taken care of for the middle class, but the stress is upon moving ahead, striving and straining upward. The child in the upper class has to learn how to keep the strivers and strainers in their place. All these are the logical implications of the class principles.

There are several points one has to remember about this social class analysis. Most of the information deals with the middle and lower classes, as they have been studied most extensively. Furthermore, the great majority of children come from these two major groupings. The upper class in most studies comes to about 3 to 5

[18] H. A. Coleman, "The Relationship of Socio-economic Status to the Performance of Junior High Students," *Journal of Experimental Education*, vol. 9, September, 1940, pp. 61–63; N. R. Maddy, "Comparison of Children's Traits, Attitudes, and Intelligence with Parental Occupation," *Genetic Psychological Monographs*, vol. 27, 1943, pp. 3–65.

percent of a community's population. The school will thus deal primarily with middle-class and lower-class children, for many upper-class children are sent to private schools.

Differences between the middle-class and the lower-class child are as follows:

Lower Class	Middle Class
Work and Property	
Stress on getting job, and early.	Stress on saving, taking care of possessions, systematic hobbies.
Permissive versus Rigid Training	
More lenient and permissive.	More rigid and exacting.
More children breast fed and for long time, weaning late.	Fewer breast fed, more on bottle, shorter time, weaning early.
Bowel and bladder control later than MC.	Bowel and bladder control training early.
May stay out later at night.	Expected to be home early.
Go to movies alone early.	Go to movies alone at later age.
No special emphasis on etiquette, politeness, neatness.	Emphasis on neatness, taking care of things, training in etiquette and politeness.
Few sex taboos; early sex experience on group or single basis; masturbation and more overt homosexualism.	Strong sex taboos; emphasis on sex education; masturbation and light or heavy petting as coital substitutes.
Little or no taboo on overt aggression within and outside family.	Control of aggression except in self-defense, aggression as verbal.
Relation to Others and Authority	
Ganging in both social and unsocial manifestations.	Cliquing, selective association with proper children, snobbery.
Less concern for attitudes of others; impulse and wish into direct action.	Stress on good reputation, "other-directed"; conventionality.
Defiance and fear of authority—parents, police, teacher.	Respect and obedience to police, teacher, parents.
Achievement by being smart, hustling, able to get away with things.	Achievement supposedly on merit and according to the rules.
Parental control—harsh, violent, physical.	Parental control—shaming, withholding affection.

Lower Class	Middle Class
Education	
No long-time planning, immediate results wanted, skipping school not punished, homework not supervised, no supplementary opportunities.	Emphasis on school success; closer control and supervision, supplementary opportunities (music, dancing, camp, etc.)—child an educational striver and strainer.
Health	
Higher infant mortality rate; underweight, diseases longer and more frequent, less medical and dental care, malnutrition.	The converse of the lower-class child.

This comparison is made up of information drawn from a variety of sources.[19] Of course there are gradations within these economic classes and status groups. There are obviously families in the lower echelons who have higher aspirations and take on some of the patterns of the higher group. At the complete lower depths there are those who have repudiated the conventional patterns and given up hope.

THE CHILD IN NONWHITE GROUPS

The children in nonwhite groups are subjected to the advantages or disadvantages of economic class and status group as white children are. The similarities among upper-class people or lower-class people are very strong, despite color. The color bar, with all the associated spiteful and hateful evaluations, increases and com-

[19] Frank A. Shuttleworth, *The Adolescent Period: a Graphic Atlas*, Society for Research in Child Development, Vol. XIV, Serial No. 49, No. 1, 1949, Child Development Publications, 1951, Figures 53–56, 223, 248–252; Clyde Kluckhohn and Florence Kluckhohn, "American Culture: Generalized Orientations and Class Patterns," *Conflicts of Power in Modern Culture*, Lyman Bryson et al. (eds.), Harper & Brothers, 1947; Allison Davis and Robert Havighurst, *Father of the Man*, Houghton Mifflin Company, 1947; Allison Davis, "Socialization and Adolescent Personality," *Adolescence*, Part I, Forty-Third Yearbook, National Society for the Study of Education, 1944; Martha C. Ericson, "Child-Rearing and Social Status," *American Journal of Sociology*, November, 1946, pp. 190–192; A. C. Kinsey, W. B. Pomeroy, and C. E. Martin, *Sexual Behavior in the Human Male*, W. B. Saunders Company, 1948, chap. 10; Evelyn Duvall, "Conceptions of Parenthood," *American Journal of Sociology*, November, 1946, pp. 193–203; Allison Davis and John Dollard, *Children of Bondage*, American Council on Education, 1940; W. L. Warner and P. Lunt, *The Social Life of a Modern Community*, Yankee City Series, vol. 1, Yale University Press, 1945.

pounds the difficulties immensely. To be in a lower economic class and status group is bad enough, but to have in addition all the liabilities which color assessments bring about is much worse. Even middle- and upper-class families are subjected to much more strain and stress in getting ahead or maintaining their position, for they have to contend not only with the white world but with their own. What one would say about the Negro applies to a certain degree to other "nonwhite" groups, qualified to the extent that strong family systems prevail in such groups as the Mexicans and Japanese. We will focus our attention upon the Negro, since he composes the largest group.

A form which Negro society takes is shown in Figure 20. It shows the great gaps that separate Negroes from each other. The "axes of life" indicate the major orientations and problems—for the lower

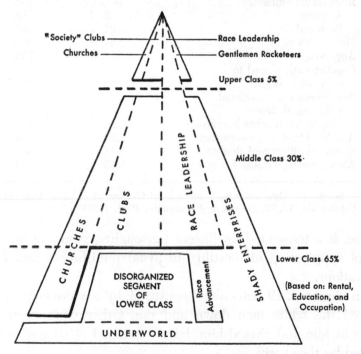

FIGURE 20.   Social Class Structure of Bronzeville, Chicago. Wide spaces indicate absence of social participation between individuals in adjacent segments. Broken lines indicate some social contacts between the segments. (From *Black Metropolis*, copyright, 1945, by St. Clair Drake and Horace R. Cayton. Reproduced by permission of Harcourt, Brace and Company, Inc.)

groups, subsistence; for the upper, getting ahead and gaining prestige. This is nothing new, though it seems that the lower economic and status group is more disorganized and the middle and upper more rigid in conduct than the corresponding white groupings. Each Negro group is hit deeply with the problem of deprivation in most of the areas of life.

What happens to the person is shown in Table 34. The result of this system of studied insult and contempt, of exploitation or dep-

TABLE 34. Rorschach Test Interpretations of 24 Negro Subjects

Interpretation	Subjects	Percent
Intelligence		
Average	14	58
Good average or better	10	42
Intellectual efficiency		
Average	2	8
Reduced	22	92
Deep anxiety	24	100
Aggression	24	100
Conflict with regard to		
aggressive urges	23	96
Suspiciousness, emotional		
isolation, deficient		
rapport with other humans	24	100
Apathy, passivity, compliance	24	100
Sexual conflicts and doubts	11	46
Above average desire for status	13	54

SOURCE: Abram Kardiner and Lionel Ovesey, et al., *The Mark of Oppression*, W. W. Norton and Company, 1951, p. 330.

rivation, is a tormented, inefficient personality, straining under the load of suppressing his hostility to avoid punishment and further deprivations.

John Simmons, 19 years old, "was struck by a white employer. He knocked the white man down and ran. Other white men threw bottles at him and chased him, but he escaped. That night he was arrested by the sheriff.

"Simmons' father told the white sheriff, 'Some white man hit my boy.'

"The sheriff answered, 'You mean, your boy hit a *white* man.'

"Simmons was fined by the court." [20]

A Negro school teacher, upper-middle class, had purchased an expensive suit in a small shop catering to middle-class whites and gave her name and address for the delivery of the suit. After writing down the information the white saleswoman said, "Margaret, what time do you want this purchased delivered?" Neither woman had ever seen the other before that time. The Negro woman later stated to her close friend, "I saw red. I was so mad. But I couldn't say a thing before all those white people. I made up my mind right then, though, that I'd never go there again to be insulted." [21]

And so the violent emotion is bottled up. It is in this situation of crass and subtle indignities that accumulate day after day, year after year that the Negro child suffers until he reaches his pariah adult status. The older the child becomes the less the chance of fighting back so that aggression is turned inward and he fights with other Negroes. The aggression may be relieved vicariously, as through the successful Negro boxer. Another way of getting along is through a pattern of servility—the "White Man's Nigger," jovial, clowning behavior, resignation.[22] These ways of acting will vary from social class to social class. The end result is the same; he is less of a person than he could be.

All these problems are right in the school. The school as a vehicle of social mobility has little meaning, for when the education is completed, there are few prospects of putting it to use. The world outside of school and the irrelevance of education state the conditions for truancy, delinquency, boredom in class, and discipline problems.

PROBLEMS THAT BOTHER CHILDREN

We want to indicate more concretely what it is that bothers children. To investigate this area many problem check lists have been constructed. The following are indicative—the SRA Junior and Youth Inventories, or the Mooney Problem Check List. In Table

[20] Allison Davis and John Dollard, *op. cit.*, p. 241.
[21] *Ibid.*, pp. 238–239.
[22] Robert L. Sutherland, *Color, Class, and Personality*, American Council on Education, 1942, chap. V. Cf. St. Clair Drake and Horace R. Cayton, *Black Metropolis*, Harcourt, Brace and Company, 1945, chaps. 19–23.

Table 35. Percent Checking Selected Items in the SRA Junior Inventory by Sex, Grade, and Socio-Economic Class

Item	Total	Sex		Grade					Socio-Economic Class	
		B	G	4	5	6	7	8	Upper	Lower
I wish I didn't have pimples on my face.	20	13	27	11	12	17	28	35	19	20
I get out of breath when I run or play.	44	41	47	56	48	43	36	36	35	46
Sometimes I get real dizzy.	22	21	24	29	26	20	19	16	17	24
I get tired of sitting.	37	38	36	40	38	38	34	34	32	39
I am hungry a lot.	26	29	23	29	26	24	23	22	26	26
I can't run as fast as the other kids.	21	23	18	26	24	19	16	16	15	22
I'd like to learn how to dance.	29	22	27	27	27	32	29	30	25	30
I don't like arithmetic.	22	22	22	24	21	21	23	23	18	23
I don't like geography.	21	19	24	18	23	29	19	15	17	22
I don't get good grades in school.	21	24	18	18	22	22	26	23	12	23
I'd like to find some good books to read.	30	30	30	33	33	28	27	28	30	30
I'd like to have more music in school.	20	14	26	22	23	21	18	15	20	20
Our school room gets too hot.	29	23	19	24	23	19	20	15	21	21
I can't read very well.	24	26	22	26	24	28	21	18	15	26
I can't write very well.	23	25	21	25	25	26	16	19	16	24
I can't do arithmetic very well.	28	25	31	27	25	27	29	30	21	29
I am not nice-looking.	23	19	28	21	23	25	23	23	18	25
I bite my finger nails too much.	35	32	38	32	30	37	37	35	32	35
I'd like a pet animal.	27	27	27	33	32	24	23	21	26	27
I'd like to get a job.	29	36	23	25	27	28	32	34	22	31
I'd like to know what I'm going to be when I grow up.	39	39	39	38	41	38	36	40	37	39
I wish we had more money.	24	26	22	29	29	20	20	20	15	26
I'd like to have my own room.	29	24	34	32	31	26	27	25	24	30
I don't like to rest when other kids are playing.	22	24	34	32	31	26	27	25	19	22
I wish I could go to more movies.	20	19	29	25	24	18	15	12	18	20

Source: H. H. Remmers and Robert Bauernfeind, *Examiner Manual for the SRA Junior Inventory Form A*, Social Research Associates, Inc., 1951, pp. 11–13. Reprinted with the permission of the copyright owners, The Purdue Research Foundation.

35 the problem items were checked by at least 20 percent of the 4517 children in the sample.[23] Here we see, in terms of the list, boys and girls who are active, concerned about their physical appearance, wanting social skills, disliking certain school subjects and wanting others, concerned about their school progress and better use of leisure time, better living. There are a few sex status and socio-economic class differences, and some interesting variations by grade, especially in the items dealing with health.

Table 36 is a sample of the Mooney Problem Check List, dealing with 603 students in a North Carolina high school.[24] Of the 330 problems, students checked on the average twenty-five problems. The lowest 25 percent marked thirteen and the third quartile thirty-

TABLE 36.   High-School Students' Problems as Determined
by a Problem Check List

Item	Number	Item	Number
Health and Physical Development		Not taking things seriously enough	174
Weak eyes	178	Losing my temper	143
Not as strong and healthy as I should be	120	Afraid of making mistakes	132
Frequent headaches	110	Taking things too seriously	131
Being underweight	106	Nervousness	104
Finance, Living Conditions, and Employment		Courtship, Sex, and Marriage	
Wanting to earn some money of my own	288	Wondering if I'll ever find a suitable mate	104
Learning how to spend money wisely	168	Social-Psychological Relations Wanting a more pleasing personality	113
Having to ask parent for money	164	Being disliked by a certain person	97
Learning how to save money	157	Morals and Religion	
Having no regular allowance (or regular income)	108	Can't forget some mistakes I've made	148
Having no family car	97	Adjustment to School Work	
Personal-Psychological Relations		Being a grade behind in school	139
Forgetting things	176		

[23] *Examiner Manual for the SRA Junior Inventory Form A*, Social Research Associates, Inc., 1951, pp. 11–13.

[24] Ross L. Mooney, "Surveying High-School Students' Problems by Means of a Problem Check List," *Educational Research Bulletin*, March, 1942, vol. XXI, pp. 57–69.

TABLE 36. High-School Students' Problems as Determined
by a Problem Check List (*Continued*)

Item	Number	Item	Number
Afraid of failing in school work	132	Taking care of clothes and other belongings	107
Worrying about grades	131	Wondering what becomes of people when they die	103
Trouble in mathematics	129	Being punished for something I didn't do	96
Not spending enough time in study	126	Home and Family	
Weak in writing	101		
Unable to express myself in words	94		
Curriculum and Teaching Methods			
Too much work required in some subjects	128		
So often feel restless in classes	124		
Lunch hour too short	105		
The Future: Vocational and Educational			
Wondering what I will be like ten years from now	312		
Wondering if I will be a success in life	192		
Deciding whether or not to go to college	140		
Wanting advice on what to do after high school	138		
Choosing best courses to prepare for college	114		
Not knowing what I really want	108		
Social and Recreational Activities			
So often not allowed to go out at night	139		

N = 603. Items concern only those checked by 16 percent or more of the students.
SOURCE: Ross L. Mooney, "Surveying High-School Students' Problems by Means of a Problem Check List," *Educational Research Bulletin*, March, 1942, vol. XXI, pp. 59–66.

three problems. Table 36 gives the major areas in which 16 percent of the students checked a problem.

Freshmen emphasized health problems above all others; sophomores put a greater emphasis on "social and recreational activities"; juniors led in problems of "adjustment to school work" and "curriculum and teaching methods"; seniors bunched problems in areas of "the future: vocational and educational," with some emphasis on "personal-psychological problems." Girls led boys with an emphasis in the area of "personal-psychological relations" and "social-psychological relations," and boys led girls in their interest in "the future: vocational and educational," and "adjustment to school work." These tendencies coincide with the demands of their respective sex statuses. Other schools may show a different emphasis on these problem areas, but the point is that the check list is a tool for securing some insight as to how the students look at the world. If there is any marked stress by age group or sex, the school can orient its curriculum to help the students up to its limits.

The technique also gives one insight into the constellation of problems that impinge upon a person, as in the following case of a high-school girl.[25] Out of thirty items in the list, nine, almost one-third, were in the area of health: poor teeth, poor hearing, nose or sinus trouble, not enough sleep, being underweight, not as strong and healthy as I should be, too tall, clumsy and awkward, not very attractive physically. The other problems were the following:

Employed late at night on a job
Not enough time for recreation
Too little chance to get into sports
Not spending enough time in study
Too little chance to go to shows
Wanting to learn how to dance
Unsure of my social etiquette
Lacking leadership ability
Too easily led by other people
Trying to break off a bad habit
Forgetting things
Cannot make up my mind about things
Unable to concentrate when I need to
Poor memory
Nervousness
Losing my temper
Worrying
Failure to go to church
Having no chance to go to church
Learning how to spend my money wisely
Too many personal problems

The girl's whole world is a problem, though the emphasis is upon health. It is a health-school-home-work-recreation problem, which is but saying that structure of the culture is so organized that there is lack of opportunity and integration, with the resultant personality

[25] *Ibid.*, pp. 58–59.

disturbances. The girl cannot function adequately anywhere. Since the school is only one of the institutions, its contribution to her dilemmas is limited. The worries come to a head as the child moves toward the adult status. A check list is not necessary to recognize the general problem of lack of cultural integration and lack of opportunity. We have already referred to this in our study of the community. The check list, however, concretizes problems in an immediate situation, but one has to be aware of the ramification of the problems into the community and into the culture.

For purposes of contrast, the incidence of disturbances as found in the English study is listed. Each grouping represents the percentage distribution among the whole group: [26]

Personality deviations:	sensitive, self-conscious, timid, nervous	13.7
	solitary, unpopular, very quiet	6.5
	sullen, resentful of authority	6.1
	day dreaming	3.8
	emotionally unstable, tempers	3.7
	lacking emotions, discouraged	.5
Behavior disorders:	lying, stealing, begging	3.4
	others	2.3
	bullying, quarreling	2.4
	shifty, unstable	2.4
	restless, fidgety	2.1
	clowning, limelight	2.0
	wandering, truancy	.5
Habit disorders:	nail biting, finger picking	22.2
	stammer	1.2
	masturbation	.4
	habit spasm	.4
	enuresis	.3
Scholastic difficulties:	lazy, erratic	4.4
	no interest	.4
	reading difficulty	.8
	arithmetic difficulty	.4
	very slow	.3

The information suggests a certain similarity to the adjustment problems as found in this country.

[26] Bernice McFie, *op. cit.,* pp. 36–37.

IN CONCLUSION: RECONSTRUCTING CHILDREN
BY RECONSTRUCTING WORLDS

In this analysis of the child we were always impelled to move from the child as such to the world in which he lives. The child of the agricultural worker is understood in terms of the excessive mobility of the family, the conditions of the camps and other habitation, the necessity to work, the hours worked and wages paid, community hostility, poor diets, inadequate medical care, and so on. The upper-class Negro child must be interpreted in terms of the over-conforming conduct, respectability, and "culture" which arise out of the interrelationships to his middle and lower class and the relations to the dominant white world. The immigrant child becomes understandable through his dual position in two cultures. There is a distinction in the content of the person because of his sex status, and this status is also modified by economic class and status group. The person is what he does and what he is prevented from doing. The limitations and expansion of action depend upon the total institutional pattern. To reduce the 25 to 30 percent of maladjusted children to a small proportion will involve more than giving check lists, personality tests, non-directive interviews, and all the variations of group therapy. Since no man is an isle unto himself, we are all affected by this distorted personal growth, either directly or indirectly by supporting all the palliative techniques and organizations. If the distortion is a matter of the institutional structure, then it can be rectified only by an effective reordering of our institutions.

Selected Readings

Davis, Allison, and Dollard, John, *Children of Bondage*, American Council on Education, 1940.

Dollard, John, et al., *Frustration and Aggression*, Yale University Press, 1939.

Frazier, E. Franklin, *Negro Youth at the Crossways*, American Council on Education, 1940.

Havighurst, Robert, and Taba, Hilda, *Adolescent Character and Personality*, John Wiley and Sons, 1949.

Kluckhohn, Clyde, and Murray, Henry, *Personality in Nature, Society, and Culture*, Alfred A. Knopf, 1948.

Langdon, Grace, and Stout, Irving, *These Well-Adjusted Children*, The John Day Company, 1951.

Lewis, Hylan, *Blackways of Kent*, University of North Carolina Press, 1955.

Mead, Margaret, and Wolfenstein, Martha, *Childhood in Contemporary Cultures*, University of Chicago Press, 1955.

Spinley, B. M., *The Deprived and the Privileged: Personality Development in English Society*, Routledge and Kegan Paul Ltd., 1953.

Warner, W. Lloyd, Junker, Buford H., and Adams, Walter, *Color and Human Nature*, American Council on Education, 1941.

West, James, *Plainville*, Columbia University Press, 1945.

Woods, Sister Frances Jerome, *Cultural Values of American Ethnic Groups*, Harper & Brothers, 1956.

CHAPTER 14

Informal Order Versus
Formal Order in the School

THE YEAR is 1925. The speaker is a very popular girl in the school. The question is: "What makes a girl eligible for a leading high school club?" The answer: "The chief thing is if the boys like you and you can get them for the dances. Then, if your mother belongs to a graduate chapter, that's pretty sure to get you in. Good looks and clothes don't necessarily get you in, and being good in your studies doesn't necessarily keep you out unless you're a 'grind.' Same way with the boys—the big thing is being on the basketball or football team. A fellow who's just a good student rates pretty low. Being good-looking, a good dancer, and your family owning a car all help." [1]

The year is 1952; the place, a high school in Texas. A boy is talking about a girl who is categorized negatively as a "mouse": "It seems as though there's an invisible barrier between us. If I dated her, it would be an exception to the rule because of the opinion of others. A lot of kids wouldn't think she was attractive. That's silly. If I really knew her, I don't know but what I'd think she's really pretty. She just hasn't entered into my thoughts, and I wouldn't know how to enter her in, if you know what I mean. There's too

[1] Robert S. Lynd and Helen M. Lynd, *Middletown*, Harcourt, Brace and Company, 1929, p. 216.

much attention paid to what others in your group have to say about that sort of thing. I wish I could be above such things. But if you try to, it appears as though you were peculiar." [2]

East, west, north, or south, today or yesterday invisible social barriers have risen within the school separating or grouping students, stigmatizing some and favoring others. What is noticed in the statements made by these "wheels" is the principle of inequality at work among adolescents, prestige group assumptions about the worth of persons. So one finds, upon the pinnacle of their social exclusiveness, a group of "peers" indulging in conspicuous consumption and social snobbery and viewing others with the same brutal contempt that is found among classes in the community. While some may view these social gymnastics with approval and with the wish that they could participate, others may respond with resentment and hatred. This informal order may be viewed as a system of preferential association based upon certain value assumptions. It is an order relatively independent of the formal order of the school, which has been examined. The problem is to find out the significance of the informal order.

The importance of the informal order varies with school level. While there are unfavorable comparisons made among children in the elementary school, the informal order in its more obviously invidious aspects is found in the high school and in the college. Running and howling with the pack in a series of self- and mutual-admiration circles is *par excellence* the activity of the teen-ager and his older prototypes Joe College and Betty Coed. Some of the studies such as the one made in Elmtown-Jonesville assume that the pattern found in high school also applies to the elementary school, even though their own evidence suggests the contrary. Many of the high-school studies, furthermore, have been made in communities having only one or at the most two high schools. In communities with eight or more high schools the informal pattern may be qualitatively different. Unfortunately, there are no studies which will shed light on this, so that most of our information will refer to the pattern as found in the community with one or two high schools.

[2] Carson McGuire and Rodney Clark, "Age-Mate Acceptance and Indices of Peer Status," *Child Development,* Summer, 1952, p. 152.

INFORMAL ORDER IN THE ELEMENTARY SCHOOL

Most of the information about preferential association on this educational level has been secured through sociometric techniques. Children are asked to choose or reject each other according to some specific criterion, such as the persons with whom one prefers or dislikes to sit, to work on a committee, to play. Choice and rejection patterns are worked out through sociograms, totals for each child are computed, and in this way some insight into the informal order is secured. Children may be interviewed as to why they made their selections. Family background information may be gathered to interpret the choices. As with all techniques the sociometric has to be used with caution and insight.[3]

WHO RATES HIGH AND WHO RATES LOW

John's father is a bookkeeper. The family lives in a nice residential area. John is considered one of the brighest pupils as measured by intelligence tests. He has a pretty good conception of himself as measured by a personality test. He is also one of the most hated children in his class. His social rating is about zero; nobody wants him around. This case states our problem. We will view such rating or prestige in terms of personality adjustment, economic class, sex status, and ethnic background.

We have already noted the amount of personality adjustment and maladjustment in the school. It would follow logically that the maladjusted have difficulty getting along, although this is perhaps merely saying that they are maladjusted. Do they also rate low? Are they rejected and does the converse hold true? In Butler County it was found that "among the popular children 36.1 percent of the girls and 26 percent of the boys received adjustment scores in the top quartile class. Among the unpopular or less popular group, only 25 percent of the girls and only 16 percent of the boys received the more favorable adjustment scores."[4] In Mill City it was found that

---

[3] Cf. H. Otto Dahlke and Thomas Monahan, "Problems in the Application of Sociometry to Schools," *The School Review*, April, 1949, pp. 223–234.

[4] A. R. Mangus and R. H. Woodward, *An Analysis of the Mental Health of Elementary School Children*, Division of Mental Health of Ohio State Department of Public Welfare, Ohio State University, Ohio Agricultural Experiment Station, Butler County Mental Health Association, July, 1949, p. 20.

personality adjustment was a significant but moderate factor in relation to prestige (x^2 significant at .01 and Q -.51). There was a moderate negative association between poor adjustment and high prestige on the one hand and between good adjustment and low prestige on the other. On the other hand, Bonney found little association between personality adjustment and friendship formation.[5]

We have to keep in mind that we are dealing with prestige as measured by a sociometric test, the cumulative choices for and against a child within a class, or a group of children within a school. The sociometric status of girls tends to be higher than that of boys, i.e., low prestige is associated with being male. This fact fits in with the better personality adjustment of girls as compared with boys.

On the elementary-school level it is not quite clear what the significance of socio-economic class is in rating. Studies vary from the contention that there is a "mirror-like reflection" between the family's social status and the friendship status of the child [6] to the finding that no such reflection is discoverable.[7] In the Elmtown-Jonesville (all referring to the same community) studies there is a tendency to understate the greater democratic relationships that are found in the elementary school, and this school system is organized on an 8–4 plan. A 6–3–3 plan might show different relations.

WHO CHOOSES WHOM

In a sociometric test it is difficult to separate actual, potential, and merely wished-for relations. Choices may include all three possibilities. We are now examining this question of being accepted or rejected from a slightly different angle. Our concern is not who rates high or low but the direction of the choices. This may be illustrated by the following constellation of choices, labeled a social atom in Figure 21. The figure involves two sisters in a sixth grade. Each sister has a unique social circle. Jane's pattern includes girls primarily from the lower economic class and status groups and with poor or average

[5] Merl Bonney, "A Sociometric Study of the Relationships of Some Factors to Friendships on Elementary, Secondary, and College Levels," *Sociometry*, February, 1946, pp. 21–47.
[6] Bernice Neugarten, "Social Class and Friendship Among School Children," *American Journal of Sociology*, January, 1946, pp. 305–313.
[7] Based upon two unpublished studies of West School in Mill City.

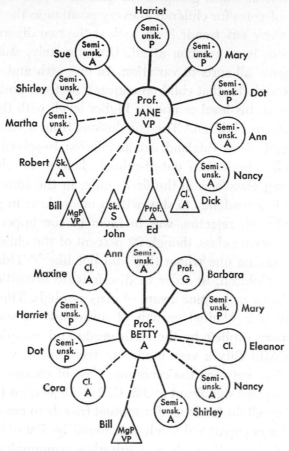

FIGURE 21. Social Atom of Two Siblings, West School, Mill City. Choices: mutual—heavy black line; positive—light black line; rejection—broken line. Occupation of father: MgP—managerial-proprietor; Cl.—clerical; Prof.—professional; Sk.—Skilled worker; Semi-unsk.—semi-unskilled worker. Personality adjustment. S—superior; G—good; A—average; P—poor; VP—very poor.

personality adjustments. Her rejections are centered upon boys. Her sister, Betty, is involved more with girls from the higher economic class and status groups, and her rejections include primarily girls. In these two cases we see something of this acceptance and rejection pattern of the direction of choices. What can be said in general about this direction of choices?

The first effort is to find out whether there is any relationship between the economic class or status group of the chooser and the economic class or status group of the chosen. Obviously, there will be a scatter of votes for children in every position in the social structure, but is there any trend? If we look at the two diagrams we will feel that there is no relation at all. Unfortunately, studies do not agree and show all sorts of variation. In one fifth and sixth grade, Neugarten concludes that children concentrate their positive choices on their own status level or upon a higher level, with the exception of the low-status children.[8] The conclusions from a study in Brasstown, located in New England, are as follows: In-school choices are less along class lines than out-of-school choices; in-school choices are least along class bias in the first grade; in the fourth and sixth grade there is a tendency to stay within one's class; in grade 8 this tendency falls off; rejection was in favor of the upper group and against the working class, though 20 percent of the children studied said "there was no one whom they did not like." [9] This study also showed that children, in order to discriminate according to social class, must know or become aware of class symbols. Throughout the grades there is a gradual growth of awareness of such symbols, becoming more explicit by the sixth grade and completed by the eighth.[10] In Mill City a very moderate relationship was found for positive choices between the economic class of chooser and that of chosen (chi square significant at .05. C. 21). Rejections tended to be similar. A very slight tendency for mutual friends to come from families of similar occupational levels was found by Potashin.[11] Finally, in a study of a seventh grade in a suburban community near Flint, Michigan, no relationship was found between parental occupation and friendship patterns.[12] Our conclusion is that on the elementary-school level economic class is a factor but not a decisive one. The

[8] Neugarten, op. cit., pp. 308–309.
[9] Celia Burns Stendler, Children of Brasstown, Bureau of Research and Service of the College of Education, University of Illinois, 1949, pp. 48–49. One trouble with this study is the lumping of many occupational groups into the three groupings with which the author works. To include under white-collar workers schoolteachers, small proprietors, clerks, and skilled craftsmen may obscure analysis. The study also does not test completely the class problem since upper-class children do not attend the public school.
[10] Ibid., pp. 92–93.
[11] Reva Potashin, "A Sociometric Study of Children's Friendships," Sociometry, February, 1946, pp. 48–70.
[12] Christopher Sower, "Social Stratification in Suburban Communities," Sociometry, August, 1948, pp. 235–249.

choice patterns in the school tended to be more democratic than those made outside.

Another way of looking at these choice patterns is to note the extent to which a group prefers itself as against any other group. For example, would children from professional families center their positive or rejecting choices among themselves or send them to a specific group, such as the clerical, managerial-proprietor? The details are shown in Tables 37 and 38. An index of 1.00 indicates indifference in choice; above 1.00, self-preference. The higher this index is above 1.00, the greater is the self-preference in relation to the particular group. Below 1.00 the preference is for the other group. It will be noted that most of the indexes center around 1.00. Self-preference is marked only in the clerical-semi-unskilled worker groups and skilled worker-clerical. Other group preference is directed to skilled worker and professional groups.

The rejection pattern, as the indexes show, is much stronger. Dislike is concentrated especially upon the children from semiskilled worker and clerical occupational groups. The managerial-proprietor group consistently rejects others, except those from professional families. Children from professional families seem self-depreciatory, tending to send their rejection choices among themselves. The position of children from skilled worker families is ambiguous. All groups tend to reject themselves more than they reject the managerial-proprietor group.

The first table would lead to the conclusion that the effort to make the humanistic orientation prevail in West School is successful. Choice is democratic. Rejection apparently is not. Yet there is a consistency, i.e., children from semi-unskilled worker and clerical families are disadvantaged, as contrasted with those from the skilled worker and professional families. The information does show that the economic class determination theory does not hold up entirely.

Another perspective involves boys and girls as respective in- and other-groups. Boys prefer to choose boys rather than girls (7.46), and girls choose other girls rather than boys (7.00). This tendency is very marked and strong, more so than the economic class and status group pattern. On the matter of rejections boys tend to be more self-rejecting (1.26), but girls direct their rejections in a

TABLE 37. Indexes of Self and Other Group Rejection by Economic Class, West School, Mill City

Group Rejecting	Group Rejected				
	Semi-Unskilled	Skilled	Clerical	Managerial-Proprietor	Professional
Professional	2.303	2.285	.788	2.424	
Managerial-proprietor	.013	.027	.650		a
Clerical	.762	1.015		2.308	.423
Skilled worker	.762		.406	1.247	1.100
Semi-unskilled worker		.750	.905	1.519	1.838

a No rejections sent to this group.
SOURCE: H. Otto Dahlke, "Determinants of Sociometric Relations Among Children in the Elementary School," *Sociometry* (ed.: J. L. Moreno), November, 1953, Table XI, p. 334.

TABLE 38. Indexes of Self and Other Group Preference by Economic Class, West School, Mill City

Subgroups Choosing	Subgroups Chosen				
	Semi-Unskilled	Skilled	Clerical	Managerial-Proprietor	Professional
Professional	1.296	.857	.591	1.364	
Managerial-proprietor	1.322	.677	1.040		.400
Clerical	3.759	.544		.461	.846
Skilled worker	1.362		3.309	1.273	.875
Semi-unskilled worker		.699	1.055	.974	.518

SOURCE: H. Otto Dahlke, "Determinants of Sociometric Relations Among Children in the Elementary School," *Sociometry* (ed.: J. L. Moreno), November, 1953, Table IX, p. 333.

marked manner to the boys (.51) rather than to their own sex. This fact explains the lower sociometric status of boys and the higher one of the girls. What seems to be coming to the fore in our analysis is not the importance of socio-economic class but the greater importance of the sex statuses.

Another strong cleavage is found among colored groups, a rather obvious point in view of the great cleavages that exist outside of the school. That children come to school with strong attitudes toward colored groups seems fairly well established.[13] The study of cleavage was first analyzed systematically by Moreno, who concluded that classroom cleavages along color line did not occur until the fourth grade.[14] The Criswell study is probably one of the most thorough.[15] It was carried out in three New York public schools, covering kindergarten through eighth grade in one school, kindergarten through 6B in another, and grades 4B, 5B, 6B, in a third. Negroes composed 74 percent, 47 percent, and 26 percent of the children studied in the three schools. The "white" group included Italians, Russian and Polish Jews, West Indian whites (primarily Puerto Ricans), and American whites. Negroes were rated on a six-point scale of skin color, and some of the Italians and West Indians rated low on this scale so that there was considerable color overlap. However, other physical characteristics were supposed to differentiate the children.

There are several findings of note. Sex cleavage was found to be greater than color cleavage from kindergarten to almost complete separation in grade 4 and a slight decrease of such cleavage in grades 7 and 8. This cleavage meant for example that a "white boy would almost invariably prefer (on the criterion of studying in proximity) a Negro boy to a white girl even if the girl in question was the only other white child in the class." [16] Self-preference of the white group was found from kindergarten on through the first and second grades. There was the least difference in these grades because of the cross-color friendliness of Negroes. Mutual withdrawal of color groups was consistent at the fifth grade. Prestige relations played a part, for in the younger children there was more interaction between popular members of the majority and the minority group. There was little of this in grades 4 and 5, and by grade 6 special

[13] Eugene L. Horowitz, "The Development of Attitude Towards the Negro," *Archives of Psychology*, 1936, No. 194. Cf. Joan Criswell, "A Sociometric Study of Race Cleavage in the Classroom," *Archives of Psychology*, 1938–1939, No. 235, pp. 5–11.
[14] J. L. Moreno, *Who Shall Survive?* Nervous and Mental Disease Publishing Company, 1934, p. 386.
[15] Joan Criswell, *op. cit.*
[16] *Ibid.*, p. 18.

prestige was accorded only their own members. Skin-color differences were important in the majority-colored classes. Moving up the grades, each color group tended more to prefer itself and to reject the darker group, and the converse held for the dark. There was the least amount of discrimination between white and light in the first three grades. The size of the minority group affected responses, girls adjusting more easily to small minorities than large, and boys to large minorities rather than small. There were some cross-sex choices among colored groups with Negro boys stopping at grade 2, Negro girls at grade 4 with a few white boys and girls choosing Negroes as late as grade 6 or 7. There were no cross-sex choices over color lines in the eighth grade.

Cleavage according to color is more complex than a first glance would seem to warrant. The cleavage is not simply white-nonwhite but is affected by sex cleavages. Distinctions in skin-color cleavages become most marked. Teachers must recognize these subtler differences in working with children in mixed color classes.

If we rank in order of importance factors affecting choice, sex status is first, type of personality adjustment second, color third, and economic class and status group fourth. The significance of these will vary from grade to grade, but the sex status and personality factor seem to be the more constant. In terms of these two factors, girls fare better than boys. The last two factors tend to become more significant in the later grades.

Many other variables have been tested to find out whether they affect friendship choices. Such analysis has included the factors of chronological age, mental age, intelligence quotient, height, weight, and scholastic achievement.[17] Result of these investigations are inconsistent. Correlations are usually so low as to have little or no

[17] Cf. John C. Almack, "Efficiency in Socialization," *American Journal of Sociology,* September, 1925, pp. 241–249; Merl E. Bonney, "The Relative Stability of Social, Intellectual, and Academic Status in Grades 2–4 and the Inter-relationships Between These Various Norms of Growth," *Journal of Educational Psychology,* February, 1943, pp. 88–102; Ernest Flotow, "Charting Social Relationships of School Children," *Elementary School Journal,* May, 1946, pp. 498–504; Reva Potashin, *op. cit.*; May Seagoe, "Factors Influencing the Selection of Associates," *Journal of Educational Research,* September, 1933, pp. 32–40; Mapheus Smith, "Some Factors in Friendship Selections of High School Students," *Sociometry,* August, 1944, pp. 303–310; Harold Soderquist, "Validity of the Measurement of Social Traits of High School Students by the Method of Rating Associates," *Journal of Educational Research,* September, 1937, pp. 29–44.

significance. Such trait analysis, moreover, cannot take into consideration the social-cultural context and the statuses that persons occupy.

THE HIGH SCHOOL—ORDERED BY THE STRUCTURAL PRINCIPLES

Friendships in the eighth grade suddenly cease when children transfer to high school. Obviously new alignments take place as there are many more contacts to make in a wider variety of situations. The new lines binding persons together in a system of preferential association are organized by many factors. For one thing the high school is a place where the process of assortive mate selection begins to take place. Dating and going steady in particular are patterns that bear upon a future marital partner. It is especially important for the girl to make the right choice in order to advance or maintain a general social position. Preferential association is both means and obstacle in this process. Career possibilities and domestic possibilities confront youth, and the informal order is a sorting device bearing upon these possibilities. In a relatively open class society such as ours a person's economic class and status group affiliation is a limiting condition. Elementary-school friends part. They are distributed into the various curricula, school clubs and organizations, and are separated in social functions by various invisible social barricades.

SOCIAL CLASS UNLIMITED

Almost all studies on the high-school level conclude that there is a significant relationship between the social behavior of students and the socio-economic status and education of parents.[18] For example, 500 students in a high school in a community of 7000 were classified by the researcher as successful leaders, attempted leaders, followers, voluntary nonparticipants, overlooked, and outcasts. Here something of this mirror-like relation between family status and

[18] Christopher Sower, *op. cit.*, p. 241, a dissenting study.

position of child in school was found.[19] The leader came from high levels. The Lynds had found the pattern as early as 1925.[20] It is very possible that the pattern took its rigid shape in that decade, for the high school earlier was highly restricted as to attendance. Mass education, i.e., in terms of large numbers of students on the high-school level, began after 1910.

Studies vary as to how significant this relation between social class and acceptance is. Most studies imply that social class is a major factor. A study in Texas, however, showed that the social class factor as affecting both boys and girls declined with age. The correlation between family status and peer status was at age 14 .457, at age 16 .325, and at age 18 .297.[21] We must, hence, look elsewhere in order to understand this informal order.

COLOR, NATIONALITY, RELIGIOUS GROUPS, AND PEER ACCEPTANCE

The focus now is upon the distinctions between white, nonwhite, Mexican, Japanese, Polish, Norwegian, Jewish, Protestant, etc. It is very likely that the social class factor as compared with the color, nationality, or religious affiliation may be less significant. Mexicans may be predominantly in the lower economic class and status group but what looms large is the fact that they are Mexicans. In Elmtown-Jonesville it was very apparent that Norwegian Lutheran, and Irish and Polish Catholic group affiliation united as well as separated students in the high school. The fact that the Lutheran minister opposed high-school activities as worldly and organized competing social affairs which the youth groups of the church were to attend indicated the significance of this religious and nationality group factor. The in- and out-group relation between the Norwegian Lutheran students and the others was recognized by all.

The complexity of the informal order and selective association is shown by Tables 39 and 40, based upon studies in Seattle high schools. The material was based upon several sociometric questions. Keeping in mind that the situations are hypothetical, we can, never-

[19] Katherine Miles, *Relationship between Certain Factors in the Home Background and Quality of Leadership as Shown by Children,* University of Minnesota Press.
[20] Robert and Helen Lynd, *op. cit.,* pp. 185–187.
[21] Carson McGuire and Rodney Clark, *op. cit.,* p. 146.

theless, see how the interrelationships change with each situation. An in- and out-group relationship is characteristic of all groups but the intensity varies. For example, Japanese have less of an in-group attitude in choosing leaders, work partners, and dates, but a stronger in-group attitude in choosing friends. Non-Jewish whites prefer leaders from their own group but are less in-group centered in choosing friends. The groups with the highest in-centric orientation are the Negro and Chinese. Table 39 spells out the details of inter-group selection.

There are several points worth noting. First is the highly advantaged position of the non-Jewish whites and the disadvantaged position of the Japanese and Negroes on all four of the criteria. Second, there is the mutual preference between non-Jewish whites and Jews on all questions. Third, we note a certain preference between Japanese and Chinese. Fourth, there is mutual dislike between Japanese and Jews. Fifth, Negroes prefer non-Jewish whites and Jews, who in turn find them more acceptable in the leader and work partner situation than in dating and friendship. Sixth, on the leadership, work, and dating criteria non-Jewish whites show more

TABLE 39. Groups Ranked from High to Low Self-Preference for Specified Sociometric Criteria of Choosing Leaders, Work Partners, Dates, and Friends in a High-School Population

Leadership	Work	Dating	Friendship
Non-Jewish white	Chinese	Chinese	Negro
Negro	Negro	Negro	Japanese
Chinese	Non-Jewish white	Non-Jewish white	Chinese
Japanese	Japanese	Japanese	Jewish
Jewish	Jewish	Jewish	Non-Jewish white

SOURCE: George Lundberg and Lenore Dickson, "Selective Association Among Ethnic Groups in a High School Population," *American Sociological Review*, February, 1952, p. 26.

prejudice to Jews, Japanese, and Negroes than these show to them. On the friendship criterion, the situation is reversed. Seventh, if we consider the four questions as a scale of impersonality, we note more scattering of choice in the impersonal situations of leadership and work and more narrowing of choice in friendship and dating. In the last, the most personal of the relations, the bars are up almost 100 percent against the Japanese and Negroes.

Some other group choices were made by various individuals. Non-Jewish whites frequently choosing outside their own group were likely to be (1) male, (2) under 16 years, (3) freshmen and sophomores, (4) not belonging to organizations, and (5) boys with low economic status. Out-group choices by the others were associated with (1) males, (2) juniors and seniors (on matters of leadership, work, and dating), (3) persons over 16 years of age, (4) those not participating in school organizations.[22]

Rejection choices or naming of "enemies" were made by (1) girls, (2) those less advanced in school, (3) those who planned to attend college, and (4) members of one or more organizations (Masonic, school, or the illegal fraternities and sororities). Members of nationality groups, of course, would reject students. The likelihood of naming of such students by a nationality group was as follows: Scandinavians, Jews, other whites, Chinese and Filipinos, Japanese, Italians, Negroes, and "not given." That Scandinavians are most likely to make rejection choices may be a matter of local circumstance. It must be noted that the students who appear most disadvantaged are less likely to make rejection choices. They have to forgo the luxury of hate. Members of religious groups rejected others. The likelihood of naming disliked students was highest among "other Gentiles" and least among non-churchgoers. Jews ranked second in this, then Protestants, and then Catholics. These data merely point out the ethnocentrism and in-out group relations that are possible and probable in our country. In other words, students will classify one another positively or negatively in terms of their group affiliations, both within and outside the school. Students not belonging to organizations were essentially nonentities; i.e., they were ignored, neither choosing nor rejected. They represent a sort of mass, unattached and floating from class to class until they leave.

Several other points are of note. There was a tendency for students to choose friends and "enemies" from within the groups to

[22] George Lundberg and Lenore Dickson, "Selective Association Among Ethnic Groups in a High School Population," *American Sociological Review*, February, 1952, pp. 29–32.

TABLE 40. Degrees of Friendliness Among Specified Groups in Choosing Leaders, Work Partners, Dates, and Friends in a High-School Population

Criteria and Group Choosing	Group Chosen			
	Most Liked	Second Liked	Third Liked	Least Liked
Leadership				
Non-Jewish white	Jewish 5.0	Negro 6.5	Chinese 18.7	Japanese 25.3
Chinese	Non-Jewish white 2.4	Negro 6.5	Jewish 9.6	Japanese 20.5
Japanese	Non-Jewish white 2.0	Chinese 4.4	Negro 4.5	Jewish 16.8
Jewish	Non-Jewish white .9	Negro 5.3	Chinese 8.9	Japanese 24.0
Negro	Non-Jewish white 5.3	Jewish 26.0	Chinese 27.3	Japanese 36.9
Work				
Non-Jewish white	Jewish 5.9	Chinese 9.5	Negro 113.4	Japanese 18.1
Chinese	Non-Jewish white 9.5	Japanese 12.3	Jewish 40.5	Negro 87.0
Japanese	Non-Jewish white 4.9	Chinese 5.3	Jewish 14.9	Negro 34.7
Jewish	Non-Jewish white 2.7	Negro 13.4	Chinese 16.9	Japanese 34.2
Negro	Non-Jewish white 7.7	Jewish 31.1	Chinese 65.3	Japanese 66.2
Dating				
Non-Jewish white	Jewish 6.9	Chinese 22.9	Negro 102.6	Japanese 116.2
Chinese	Japanese 25.3	Non-Jewish white 27.7	Jewish 62.4	Negro [a]
Japanese	Non-Jewish white 9.0	Chinese 9.3	Jewish 62.0	Negro [a]
Jewish	Non-Jewish white 2.6	Chinese 27.0	Japanese-Negro [a]	Japanese-Negro [a]
Negro	Non-Jewish white 15.4	Chinese 112.4	Japanese 136.9	Chinese [a]
Friendship				
Non-Jewish white	Jewish 4.3	Chinese 6.4	Japanese 11.6	Negro 12.6
Chinese	Japanese 33.9	Jewish 85.7	Non-Jewish white 57.2	Negro 179.5
Japanese	Chinese 22.8	Non-Jewish white 57.4	Jewish 76.1	Negro 81.8
Jewish	Non-Jewish white 13.5	Chinese 23.5	Japanese 57.2	Negro 126.3
Negro	Non-Jewish white 61.0	Jewish 72.8	Chinese 131.2	Japanese 132.9

[a] No choices given to that group by choosing group. Size of ratio after each group indicates the degree of self-preference of the choosing group in relation to the specified chosen group.

SOURCE: George Lundberg and Lenore Dickson, "Selective Association Among Ethnic Groups in a High School Population," *American Sociological Review*, February, 1952, p. 27.

which they belong. This fact tends to corroborate the point that the many unattached students are essentially in a stranger relation to the others. Since they do not belong, no one really knows them. As they are in the stranger relation, they are likely to be viewed negatively, though the terms of rejection may be rather mild. It was also found that the amount of in-group preference varied with the numbers in the various color, nationality, and religious groups. Non-Jewish whites were less ethnocentric when the other groups were a small portion of the total school population. They were more ethnocentric when the other groups were in large proportion. The larger the dominant out-group, the more ethnocentric are the minorities.

This discussion of the relation of these social categories of color, nationality, and religion to the informal order was to bring out the complexity of the pattern. In-group preference and out-group rejection are associated with all of the groups. There are no simple dichotomies such as Jew-Gentile or white-Negro. The Jew-Gentile dichotomy may, moreover, involve Jews who are orthodox, reformed, Zionist, etc., and the Gentiles may include Protestants (an omnibus category into which all forms of non-Roman Catholics are dumped), Roman Catholics, and the whole variety of nationality groups. This complexity is the same as the intricacies of the community pattern discussed in Chapter 5. The informal order is thus unified as well as broken up by these socio-cultural bonds of color, nationality, and religion.

To act effectively, the teacher must see these interrelations and gauge the amount of coöperation to be expected in these terms. We have noted that the least amount of ethnocentrism was shown in leadership and work situations. We can, therefore, expect that a well-designed activity program requiring coöperation among persons and groups may help to eradicate rejections and hostilities, whereas a program supposedly designed to bring out the "good" in each of these groups may serve to perpetuate divisions. If these groups are to be considered in any way, it should be as a by-product of the total program. Furthermore, the current emphasis on intergroup education is likely to deal with symptoms rather than basic factors. For example, the low position of the sharecropper is common to both many Negroes and many whites. To deal effectively with the disadvantaged position of these groups is to deal with the problems of the sharecropper rather than to emphasize a Negro-white relation. A resolution of the sharecropper problem means also a revision of the Negro-white relation.

ADDITIONAL FACTORS ORGANIZING THE INFORMAL ORDER

Just as sex status is a factor in the elementary school, so it is also in the high school. The informal order may be viewed as composed of two sections, one of males and the other of females. Minor variations occur which will be pointed out later. Attractions and rejections take place predominantly within one's sex status, and the in-group tendency is stronger among boys than among girls. On the group side this pattern is complemented by the unofficial or official fraternities and sororities, which also represent a status group principle.

In smaller communities and consolidated high schools a town-country difference is very likely to arise.[23] Since most of the country students come by school bus, they are labeled bus people. The distinction of town-country is more refined, for the social classification also involves the specific section, neighborhood, or township from which the student comes. An area's good or bad reputation automatically carries over to the boy and girl. This classification by rural area is similar to classification by ecological area in a city. In general, it appears that students coming in from the country rate lower than town students. They are not preferred as associates.

We might finally add that the very functions of the school may become factors in selective association. Here we have in mind the curricula, the various teams, and other organizations which build up a morale that carries over into the informal order. The same may be said of intellectual and artistic pursuits. Attention and achievement in such pursuits may not involve many students, since the norm of mediocrity is an effective barrier. Nevertheless, performance in the student status may carry over into the structure of the informal order, a preferential association of intellectuals.

[23] Harold Soderquist, *op. cit.*, p. 40.

Insight into the interrelations among school children is facilitated by use of the sociogram, a graphic device to show the pattern of acceptance or rejection choices based upon some criterion. Sociograms show a similar form, though different children may choose or reject each other depending upon the criterion used. Through the sociogram the teacher can secure an overall view of the attractions,

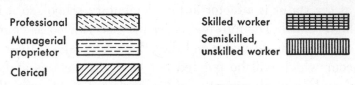

Professional

Managerial proprietor

Clerical

Skilled worker

Semiskilled, unskilled worker

Girl B has an average personality adjustment, lives in Baker Project; her father is a skilled worker.

Boy J' has a superior personality adjustment, lives in a disesteemed section in Area 6 where the family rents, and his father is a professional.

FIGURE 22.   Legend for Sociogram.

1. Identifying symbol: A, B, C., etc.—girls; A′, B′, C′, etc.—boys.
2. Personality adjustment: S—superior; G—good; A—average; P—poor; VP—very poor.
3. Father's occupation:
4. Ecological area: 1, 2, 3, 4, 5, etc.; O for home owner; T for tenant. P indicates residence at Baker Project, which is a disesteemed rental area. A negative sign indicates an especially disesteemed area.
    Example: 2^T = Area to, tenant; 4^P = Area, four, Baker Project
5. Choices (arrows indicate direction of choice): heavy black lines—mutual acceptance choices; heavy broken lines—mutual rejection choices; light line—unreciprocated choice; light broken line—unreciprocated rejection choice.

rejections, cliques, dyads, stars, and so-called isolates in a class (see Figures 23–28).

SOCIOGRAMS OF GRADE 8 IN WEST SCHOOL, MILL CITY

In this class the girls fall into two groups. There is a mutuality circle involving Ann, Carol, Gertrude, and Frances. Carol is the star among the girls. Doris is on the fringe of this group, but her choices are countered with rejections. Though Helen is a recent arrival in the class, she has been accepted by the girls. The other girls center on Kay, with the exception of Jane, who is completely rejected. Jane is a star in her own right, a rejected one. Such a person has usually been called an isolate, but Jane is in the midst of things. A true isolate would be one receiving no choices—in short, would be a nonentity. Inez, Jane, and Betty constitute a rejection triad. Jane, moreover, is rejected by both boys and girls. These dislikes apparently are very intense. Cross-sex choices are positive to King and Karl, negative to Ike, Garry, and Horace, who are all involved

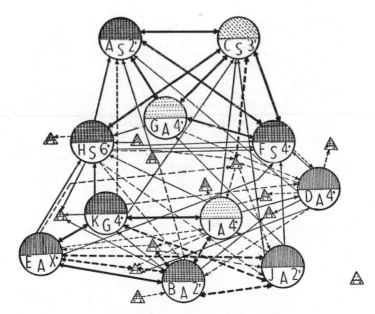

FIGURE 23.   Sociogram I, Grade 8.

INFORMAL ORDER VERSUS FORMAL ORDER IN THE SCHOOL   **343**

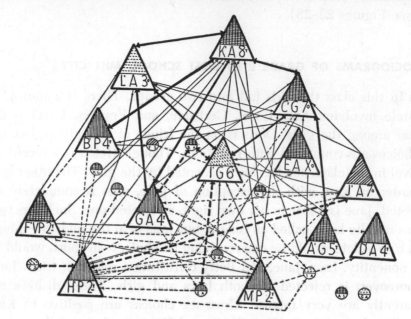

FIGURE 24. Sociogram II, Grade 8.

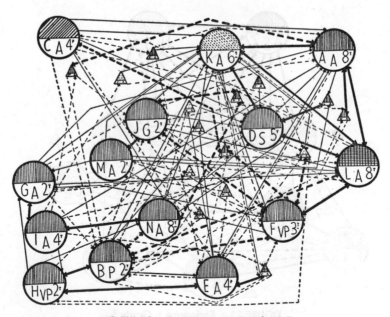

FIGURE 25. Sociogram III, Grade 6–7.

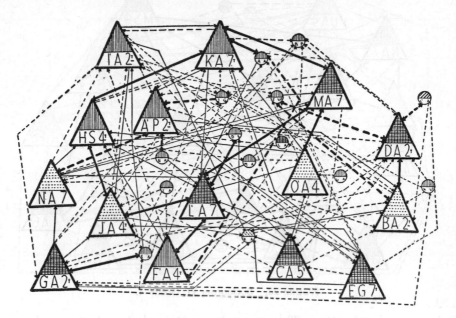

FIGURE 26. Sociogram IV, Grade 6–7.

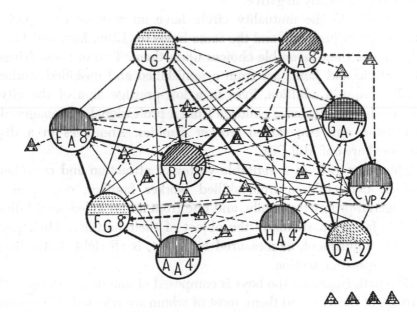

FIGURE 27. Sociogram V, Grade 4.

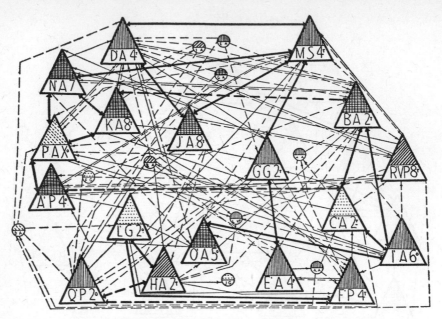

FIGURE 28. Sociogram VI, Grade 4.

in mutual rejections. The nonreciprocating choices between boys and girls are mostly negative.

The girls in the mutuality circle have an average or superior personality adjustment, and the same holds for Elsie, Kay, and Jane, who center their favorable choices upon them. Two of these fringe girls (Elsie and Jane) are from a semiskilled and unskilled worker family. Jane, in addition, lives in a low-prestige area of the city. The circle itself includes children from a professional, a managerial-proprietor, and two skilled worker families. Ann lives in a disesteemed area of Mill City.

The other girls, in a veritable vortex of attraction and rejection, include two children from skilled worker families, one from a managerial-proprietor family, and one from an unskilled-semiskilled family. Jane is particularly the object of their hostility. Their personality adjustment, as measured by a test, is all right. Betty lives in a low-prestige section.

The pattern among the boys is composed of one major group with a fringe of boys around them, most of whom are rejected. This group is made up of Lewis, Garry, Karl, Cole, and Ike. Arthur is linked to this group through Cole, and Bill through Lewis and Karl. Fred and Hank are the rejected ones, and also Miles, if one includes the girls' rejection choices. The outstanding popular star is Karl. Subsidiary stars are Lewis, Ike, and Cole. Hank is outstandingly rejected by both boys and girls. Ike, who is rejected by the girls, stands well with the boys. The situation of Ike is something that a sociogram will reveal, while an index of high or low standing could not bring out this configuration.

The boys in the mutual circle have average or good personality adjustments. They come from professional (Ike), skilled worker (Karl and Cole), managerial-proprietor (Lewis), and semi-unskilled worker (Garry) families. None live in a disesteemed section of the city.

Of the boys who compose the fringe, two have an average personality adjustment and three (Fred, Hank, and Miles) have poor or very poor adjustment. Three of them come from semi-unskilled

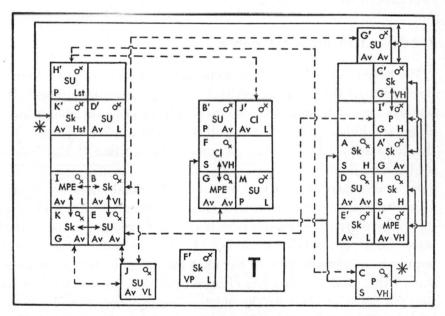

FIGURE 29. Seating Arrangement, Grade 8, Showing Mutual Choosing and Rejecting Choices. Upper left corner, initial of child. Upper right corner, sex. Center, father's occupation: SU—semiskilled, unskilled; Cl—clerical; Sk—skilled; P—professional; MPE—manager, proprietor, executive. Lower left corner, personality test score: P—poor; Av—average; G—good; S—superior. Lower right corner, prestige rating: LST—lowest; VL—very low; L—low; Av—average; H—high; VH—very high; HST—highest.

worker families, and two also live in the worst section of a low-prestige area. One of the fringe boys (Jack) comes from a clerical and another (Earl) from a skilled worker family.

Only two girls, Ann and Gertrude, are not involved within this choice pattern. The others are primarily involved in rejection relations.

Our detailed discussion brings out the complexity of the specific situation. It corroborates our previous analysis, which emphasized the significance of sex status and personality adjustment. The sociogram also brings out variations from the trend.

The seating arrangement in this class could also be viewed from the point of view of the sociogram. The seating arrangement tended to reinforce the groups in the class, though the order was part plan and part accident. Duke, Fred, and Harriet were deliberately separated from the rest of the class, as were also Hank and Donald. It is possible that the teacher placed Karl as a good influence by these two, though without results.

A GENERALIZED INFORMAL ORDER

We have examined a class in some detail in order to press home the point that this intricate network is a typical configuration that one can expect to find, that is very likely to occur in almost any class (see Figures 25–28). While this pattern applies primarily to the elementary school,[24] there is some evidence that it also holds for the high school.

In a class there is an actual or potential mutual circle or clique. Usually there are two, organized along sex lines. Within each sex status there are divisions in major and minor groupings. Stars may range from one to five in number. A star may shine in terms of popularity or unpopularity. At the most there may be two unpopular stars. Other students, in a less clear-cut position, receive both positive and negative choices. The outstanding rejections found within each sex group are among the pupils composing the fringe to the

[24] Based upon the Mill City study and upon data furnished by thirty-one elementary teachers ranging from grades 2 through 8. Cf. Mildred Peters, "A Study of Social Acceptance, Rejection, and Isolation from the Second Through the Tenth Grade," unpublished Ph.D. thesis, Ohio State University, 1946.

major group or those in the less acceptable second group. Frequently the children in the fringe are arranged in a series of mutual pairs. The members of the secondary group, i.e., a less inclusive mutual circle, are likely to send in negative relations to the rest of the class. On the high-school level the clique groups sometimes include boys and girls.

We have noted the great variety of structural principles of society that ramify into the school and organize this informal order. No primacy is assigned to the social class principle. Sex status, color, nationality, religious group, personality adjustment, and town-country distinctions bring about the cohesion and cleavages, the negative and positive social relations among the children. The task for a teacher is to have a total view, not only to see the general order of this informal configuration but simultaneously to understand it in terms of these intersecting principles. We have suggested that some pupils with very poor adjustment are highly accepted and some are rejected. Some well-adjusted pupils are ignored. These variations need examination. We need to define more explicitly the evaluations that focus upon or arise from actions and the various structural principles. To do this is to probe into the system of values in which children function and by which they assess one another. This will be our next task, but before we start it, we want to raise some problems about the meaning of the informal order.

THE INFORMAL ORDER AS IRRATIONALITY

If the informal order is organized in the manner analyzed, then as far as the operation of the school is concerned it is an irrational factor. It is a disturbing, tension-creating system that deflects the school from achieving its ends. It is dissociative, a war of striving, struggling cliques, triads, dyads, or isolates.

The cut, the slight, the contempt stemming from a pseudo-sophisticated snobbism reduces the holding power of the school. The informal order, riddled with cleavages, through which the "betters" saunter with their display of conspicuous consumption creates no respect for the person. A policy of studied insult sometimes supported by teachers and administrators becomes unbearable for those who feel the brunt of it. Pain and suffering or (more glibly) frustration is their lot, an experience for which there is no inherent rationale. It is not surprising that children strike back and leave school when the first opportunity presents itself. On the other hand, we must not overlook the unifying influence of the social triumphs upon the mutual admiration cliques, these tight little in-group islands, for the better they can practice their snobbism and run the show.

That this informal order is disturbing to the whole school is well recognized. In an Ohio high school it was claimed that the secret societies, which were eventually abolished, rigged elections, sabotaged school functions, and created competing factions.[25] It is an excellent demonstration of the point that a harmonious social order is not possible when based on an interest principle. A wider range of activities and organizations can eliminate not only these in-groups but also the disastrous consequences, provided, however, that the cost factor is negligible.[26]

The informal order is a mechanism that may distribute opportunity, preferential treatment (especially with regard to norm violations), and the receiving of awards in an inequitable manner. Social irrelevances are erected into major principles of discrimination. Education becomes in this manner privileged rather than truly public. School clubs and groups are twisted, perhaps unintentionally, to the furtherance of special interest. That participation in extra-curricular activities is associated with a higher socio-economic status has been amply documented.[27]

The informal order is a fact. Our analysis concludes that as now organized it is a divisive factor. Social facts are not immutable. They can be modified, reconstructed, or destroyed. Obviously, there are

[25] Martin Essex and Staff, "Club and Social Program as an Answer to Secret Societies," *The Nation's Schools,* October, 1951, p. 70.

[26] Cf. "Symposium on Secret Societies in High School," *NEA Journal,* March, 1952, pp. 141–142.

[27] Henry Smith, "A Study in the Selective Character of American Secondary Education: Participation in School Activities as Conditioned by Socio-Economic Status and Other Factors," *Journal of Educational Psychology,* April, 1945, pp. 229–246; David Wright, "Student Participation in Extra-Curricular Activities by Welfare Levels," unpublished master's thesis, Stanford University, 1939; Harold C. Hand, *Principal Finding of the Illinois Secondary School Curriculum Program,* Circular Series A, No. 51, Illinois Secondary School Curriculum Program, Bulletin No. 2, Office of the State Superintendent of Public Instruction, Springfield, May, 1949.

schools today in which the informal social order does not function as we have examined it, but the evidence supports the contrary tendency. The problem is first to recognize the informal order for what it is and then to change it, so that it will not conflict with the aims of the school. Market and nativist orientations may support it as we find it now. Religious, humanist, and common-man orientations may demand a real transformation, in so far as this is possible in the community context. A reformulation of an informal order does not mean that everybody has to accept everybody indiscriminately. The school is an agency of opportunity, and the aim must be to prevent deliberate discriminations on the part of student groups and in student affairs. Popular stars and hated stars there may be, cliques of various kinds, dyads, and even isolates, but color, creed, race, and status are irrelevant to capacity and achievement. They can become points for the awarding of privilege, but they need not. The choice in looking at this informal order is simple. The informal order can be integrated into the activity program of the school so that it supplements it. If it is not so integrated, then a school must take the consequences of maintaining a system of inequality with the resultant tensions, unrest, aggressiveness, derogatory nicknames, notes, and writing on the walls. To bewail such behavior and to control it with strong-arm methods on this or that student or clique is to no avail. The fault is in the order.

Selected Readings

Bonney, Merl, *Popular and Unpopular Children*, Sociometry Monographs No. 9, Beacon House.

Hollingshead, August, *Elmtown's Youth*, John Wiley and Sons, 1949, esp. chap. 9.

Lemann, Thomas, and Solomon, Richard, *Group Characteristics as Revealed in Sociometric Patterns and Personality Ratings*, Sociometry Monographs No. 27, Beacon House.

Moreno, J. L., *Who Shall Survive?* Beacon House, 1953. Basic work.

Segel, David, *Frustration in Adolescent Youth*, Bulletin 1951, No. 1, Office of Education, Federal Security Agency, 1951.

Taba, H., and Van Til, W. (eds.), *Democratic Human Relations*, Sixteenth Yearbook of the National Council for Social Studies, National Education Association, 1945.

Tryon, C. M., "The Adolescent Peer Culture," in Part I, *Forty-third Year-book*, National Society for the Study of Education, University of Chicago Press, 1944.

For studies of informal structure in other institutional groups:

Hughes, Everett C., "The Knitting of Racial Groups in Industry," *American Sociological Review*, October, 1946, pp. 512–519.

Miller, Delbert, and Form, William, *Industrial Sociology*, Harper & Brothers, 1951, pp. 272 ff.

Roethlisberger, F. J., and Dickson, W. J., *Management and the Worker*, Harvard University Press, 1939, chaps. 20–22.

CHAPTER 15

Reputational History

and Evalution in the School

OUR PREVIOUS analysis has shown some persistent uniformities in the interaction patterns of school children. We know some general factors related to these regularities. We also found some variations that need explanation. We can find out through a sociometric approach which children are preferred or rejected, but we do not know why these choices are made. Unless a teacher has some conception of the value basis of such choices, the sociometric approach will be rather sterile. The range of sociative and dissociative relations that organize the informal as well as the institutional order of the school takes place within this value context. Order and disorder are, then, relative to the evaluations made by the children. As this continuous process of evaluation takes place, a person develops his reputational history as a "good guy," a "smarty," and so on. While a single label may serve to characterize a person, the reputation is a flowing together of a great variety of points of evaluation.

The many facets of an evaluative system cohere around the various structural principles that we have been discussing: the pupil status, the sex statuses, ethnic affiliation, economic class, and prestige groups. We want to specify the content of these structural principles that constitute the source of evaluations. Such content may change as historical conditions change, but since the content is cultural, it is likely to change slowly. Here, then, are the specifics that will make the informal order intelligible.

In judging his peers, the child by direct experience, by observation, by hearsay and gossip notes how they play out the roles assigned to them. His rating of them expresses his estimate of how well they are carrying out the rights and obligations associated with their position in the social structure. It reflects his judgment as to whether they are exhibiting the personality attributes that inhere in a status. In the pupil status the evaluation may refer to the manner in which the pupil carries out his school activities, coöperates with or opposes others. Evaluations centered on age status would deal with activities appropriate to an age, the acquiring of maturity, leaving childish interests and developing adolescent and adult interests. Sex status involves maturation in matters of the masculine and feminine attributes associated with the status, and the assessment of certain physical qualities, as beauty, ugliness, strength and agility, and weakness. This status also includes heterosexual and/or homosexual relations, and erotic, affectional interests. Economic class involves not only the ecological area in which the child lives as a point of evaluation but also the kind of "front" value in terms of clothing, spending money, and personal appearance with which he is equipped.

Not all evaluations are linked with these structural principles. In the process of becoming an acceptable adult, the child acquires definitions of conduct from many groups and formulates, as he grows older, some general notions about appropriate conduct. Such a general system of valuation may coincide with the religious orientation, the humanistic, the common man, and so on. It will involve notions of right and justice in some form. Children may vary in their grasp of principle. Some will assess others directly in terms of their roles; others may evaluate in terms of general principle.

Piaget has attempted to show that a development takes place among children from a rigid application and respect for the rules of the game to a consideration of others on the principles of equity and justice.[1] According to his studies, 6- and 8-year-olds act on the

---

[1] Jean Piaget, *The Moral Judgment of the Child*, International Library of Psychology, Philosophy, and Scientific Method, 1932.

former principle and 9-year-olds on the latter. This change is correlated with a change in the child's major relationship, from one of submission to dominant adults and older children to one of cooperation and mutual respect among peers. In his English study Harrower found that the principle of equity appeared among middle-class children as young as 6 years old.[2]

There is an implication for educational theory and practice in this possibility of evaluating others beyond social categories and stereotypes in terms of equity, worth, and justice. The school can be so organized as to facilitate the realization of this possibility and, thus, avoid much destructive labeling that occurs among pupils and teachers. The possibility of a continuous development toward judgments based on equity needs investigation. Apparently in high schools peer evaluation by social categories and stereotypes is the major principle, and considerations of equity become minor.

Another implication that the principle of equity introduces is the idea of flexibility in judging conduct. In a seventh grade the class intellectual who was considered a "smarty" was mocking the failure of a boy with low emotional control to solve arithmetic problems. The boy had broken into tears, and the smarty was simulating his crying. A few seconds later he had pulled the smarty to the floor and was strangling him. It took the teacher and two assistants to separate the two. Not one child in the class blamed the attacker, and each thought that the smarty deserved what he had received. The breaking of the norm of not fighting was approved inasmuch as the smarty had violated a more basic norm by attacking the self-respect of the other boy. The children evaluated the situation in terms of fairness rather than applying a stereotyped rule.

THE PROCESS OF EVALUATION—TWO CASES

The actual record of evaluations made in a fourth and an eighth grade in the West School study will vivify the analytical statements with which this chapter was introduced. Our intention is not to present clear pictures of the children mentioned but to see how,

[2] M. R. Harrower, "Social Status and the Moral Development of the Child," *British Journal of Educational Psychology*, February, 1934, pp. 75–94.

on these two levels, the process of evaluation goes on—how it differs or, in some ways, is similar. The relative importance of the structural principles is implied, and the importance of the sex status, not usually recognized as so important on the elementary level, will lead to a further discussion of this point, with additional information from the study.

Our information is derived from the evaluative statements made by the pupils on their positive and negative choices on a sociometric question. These verbal statements do not mean that a child recognizes fully his motivations in choosing or rejecting others, but his response indicates the content of the standardized, conventional points of assessment. Children verbalize negative points with greater ease, but these negative features serve to indicate the areas where the greatest control is asserted by both teachers and pupils. Our source included children who were highly chosen or rejected and some who were both chosen and rejected.

VALUATION IN GRADE 4

The children considered in this class were: chosen—Jane, Irene, Betty, and Marvin; rejected—Ronald and Quentin; mixed assessment —Bob, Pug. These included the outstanding stars and clique leaders in this class. Positive assessments about the girls deal primarily with general sociability and the sharing of activities. No priority need be assigned to either point, for the general sociability of the child may induce the sharing of activities, and the fact that activities are shared promotes sociability and identification. This valuation is indicated by such phrases as "I just like to sit by Betty." "Betty is a good girl." "We have fun together. We sit by each other and talk to each other." With regard to Jane: "She likes to play with me. I ride up to the pines and play with her a lot, baseball. We go riding on bikes." "She knows how to do things, tells me words in the reader I don't know." In relation to Irene: "She does her work without talking." "She helps me with things. We draw pictures together. With Frances we go up in the woods for a hike." Some of these points deal with school work and classroom decorum and relate to favorable conduct in the pupil and sex status. The negative comments made about these girls referred to the writing of notes during class, a practice stopped by the teacher when a boy put one of the notes on her desk. Other negative comments were made by boys, of which the following is typical: "I don't like to sit by girls. Guess I'm bashful."

Marvin is valued as nice, friendly, not fighting, as a good ball player, as a good team captain. He is negatively assessed by Bob: "When we play baseball, and I get to first and then to second and make an out, he hollers at you all the time—almost every time I make an out." Since baseball competition is so important during spring, playing the game well is crucial. Bad playing merits censure which becomes extremely violent.

Negative assessments are revealing. We shall indicate all the comments dealing with Ronald and Quentin; a different significant aspect is shown in each.

Of Ronald:

Copying, he does a lot. Never got 100 this year, and that's why. One day, every minute, he was looking at my paper. He borrows pencils all the time. Chases you. Always tries to get you. In baseball always stretches bases and is out.

Hollers at you and hogs the field all the time.

Always trying to be everything. Games, trying every position, all over the field. Hollers out. If he doesn't have his way, he beats us up.

Always crabs, hollers. Tell'm to do something, he starts getting mad. Tries to stretch everything, three-bagger to home run and then usually gets out.

Ronald's evaluation involves his pupil and sex status. In the first he is violating the institutional norms that structure the pupil status, nor does he perform well. What is more important is his excessive aggressiveness and his effort to excel athletically. Strength, agility, and a certain amount of aggressiveness are components of the masculine role. Ronald goes beyond permissive limits and becomes, thus, the poor sport and something of a bully. The negative comments are so strong because Ronald's playing has resulted in several defeats for the class team.

Of Quentin:

Always hanging around girls. Sitting by girls. I don't like girls.

He's got a temper. Sticks out his tongue. Gets sent to the closet. Always playing with girls. Kinda sort of sissy. Told all the girls they could play baseball [apparently during a game], and all the girls came over and we had an argument.

He usually doesn't play.

Always bothers girls. Talks too much.

Always fooling around. Copies from my paper. Is mean. In social studies starts talking and gets you into trouble. Rips your paper. Punches and pokes.

He's an awful flirt. Kissed me before. I don't like it. Put his arms around me and I threw them off. Hit him in the arm today and hurt my hand. He made out as if he's crying [smiles]. In third grade he'd make out he'd have a secret and would tell a girl "I have a secret and I'll tell you." Then he kisses her [i.e., when her ear was close to his mouth].

The last three statements were made by girls. Sex status takes on a different significance from what it had in the case of Ronald. Aggressive heterosexual relations initiated by Quentin plus a cumulating reputation for such behavior resulted in his low rating. To a certain extent Quentin failed to fulfill the demands of the masculine role, since he fooled with girls and was a sissy. On the other hand, he did not participate in appropriate aggressive behavior and athletics, and this fact augmented the negative evaluation. He was also rated low because of violations of classroom decorum and failure to fulfill satisfactorily the requirements of the pupil status. Since he had evidently been punished repeatedly by being sent to the penal areas in the classroom, his reputation as an undesirable peer was sustained.

The following points relate to those assessed both positively and negatively. Bob is characterized by a member in his clique as "a good friend. He ain't stingy. If he's got sumpin, he shares it with me." Others, outside the intimate circle, say:

He always jokes and makes you laugh. [The implication is that the child reporting will be called down by the teacher for being noisy.] Or he hits you. You break out in a joke, he doesn't laugh. He only makes a face [demonstrates].

He is always fooling around a lot. Talking always. Talking and goes to the circle or cloakroom [i.e., penal areas in this class].

When I was reading in front of class, he made faces at me. He was showing off. That bothers me. He makes fun of me. Say something funny like [tells a joke], he goes "heh, heh, heh," and gives you a dull look.

Of Pug, children said:

He's a nice boy.

He's a big kid. He's interesting, knows lots about camping.

He doesn't talk too much.

Talks every minute. Can't do your work. Bothers you every minute.

He's crabby, hollers. Not a good sport. If I get an out in baseball, he says I missed them.

If you're nice to him, he's not nice to you.

He and me got mad at each other one day. [Refers to a dispute in a play the class was producing.] Today he used awful dirty words on the playground. I called him a pig. Then he stuck out his tongue at me. We practiced songs pretty good. He said after the play to me, "You're good but you should have sung louder." That felt good.

Pug also incensed the girls, who severely reprimanded him when he called the teacher "a crabapple ass."

In the two cases illustrated, both pupil status and sex status are involved. In addition certain reciprocities are violated—appreciation of humor and etiquette. Conventional morality becomes explicit with reference to "dirty words." Emphasis on sharing and knowledge are also points of evaluation. The badness of fighting also is a stated point, one that is current throughout the school. This would also include verbal aggressiveness: "hollering, arguing."

Aggression has to be interpreted carefully. There is the playful poke or punch that is acceptable, likewise retaliation in the same form. Standard games involving hitting—union, flinching, say "zero," gotcha in the goodies (a poke in the abdomen with a finger) and, under certain circumstances, tripping are regarded as legitimate by the children. From the point of view of the teachers these games are unacceptable. Efforts will be made to control them. There is also a permissive range of fighting. Boys as a rule will not strike back at a girl, but if the girl hits hard enough, the boy will retaliate. As one said: "Girls aren't afraid of boys. They'll hit right back." As a girl put it: "If he picks on me, hits me just to be mean, I hit'm back." The imputed meaning is all-important. Heterosexual teasing, including the snatching of hats or kerchiefs, mutual snowballing during winter, interfering with a game (hopscotch for example) insinuating an intimate girl-friend or boy-friend relation, name calling, and chasing a girl in a threatening manner, is also a modified form of aggression. "Girls get really mad, really fight when you call them names. I got kicked for fooling." Some of this teasing is regarded as legitimate, but any form of persistently carried out teasing meets with negative actions and evaluations.

VALUATION IN GRADE 8

In the process of assessment in this class the children compare the good with the good and the bad with the bad. Such comparisons suggest common standards of valuation. There is a continuity with the evaluative points in the fourth grade, but also certain differences stand out, particularly in the sex status. The children considered in this class include: chosen—Frances, Carol, and Annabelle, Lewis, Kurt, and Charles; rejected—Herbert, Josephine, and Beatrice. George is subject to a mixed evaluation. Annabelle is compared with Frances as a polite girl who helped us on a project. She has been evaluated as "one of the best in class, smart, a good drawer, a nice person, pleasant to talk with. She will talk with most everyone." Frances is "about the same as Annabelle. She works with people but at times just only with the friends she wants. Certain friends, that's all. She always speaks to you." "She's nice. She lives next to me. We play games together. She's full of fun, always funny. She doesn't like fights." A boy says of Frances that "she is nice, holds no grudges. If I have trouble with my work, she helps me if she knows about it. She isn't stuck up." Carol is considered as smart, good in sports, pleasant but somewhat erratic, "nice at times and the next day your dearest enemy." These assessments fit in with those of the other grades, the emphases upon the pupil and sex role well performed, favorable assessment of abilities, and recognition of sociability.

Kurt, Lewis, and Charles are also compared as being very similar. They are regarded as good in athletics, good students, and good workers. They are considered very sociable, polite, and helpful. A great emphasis is placed upon athletic ability and performance, but of itself that is insufficient for a high rating. Herbert, for example, has good athletic ability and plays well, but since he is considered a poor sport and since he does not fulfill satisfactorily other status requirements, his rating is very low.

Though there are these similar assessments of Kurt, Lewis, and Charles, there are differences which the children recognize. Kurt, the star of the class, is thought of as follows by girls:

He comes from a nice family. He is one of the decent boys in the room. Never heard him swear, not like the others. Nor call people names. He is well-mannered, well-dressed. He's on the basketball squad. He has many friends.

This statement, made by Beatrice, is revealing, for it shows that she also follows the conventional points of valuation. Beatrice herself is disesteemed on many of the points which she imputes to Kurt. The other girl says:

He's got a pretty good personality. He gets along well with everyone. He's also good in athletics.

The following statements by boys emphasize the same points which the girls mention.

Kurt is a nice guy. He's polite about the way he does things. I get along with him. I have no trouble with him, as breaking a rule. We go to a show once in a while.

He's like Lewis. He likes baseball. He's friendly and helps me with my studies.

He's a nice guy, friendly. He never gets in fights. He doesn't swear. You get sick of it if you hear it too much. He's good in sports and gets his work done.

Of Lewis the following assessments were made:

I was with him in every room except for one year, but we have been together since the fourth grade. He's a nice kid, big, tough. We get in fights but we don't like to fight hard. He has a powerful swing, loves baseball. He is on the basketball team. Almost every time there is a chance to work together on things, it's me and him. He doesn't swear often.

He's a nice guy. He's got lots of power behind his arms. He doesn't like to pick fights, keeps out of fights. We go fishing once in a while.

Lewis's favorable evaluations came only from boys. The emphasis was upon his athletic ability and love of sports. His athletic standing, it will be noted, is placed in a context of other points, such as not fighting, not swearing. The emphasis in the case of Charles, as compared to the sociability of Kurt and the athletic ability and performance of Lewis, is upon his intellectual ability and well-mannered conduct.

He's about the same as Kurt, but he's smarter than Kurt. Kurt is better in sports, but Charles is a square player and pretty good.

He's on our team. He's a pretty good guy. He seems to be smart in almost everything. He's kind and nice, Charles is. He doesn't swear, never heard him swear. He is good in athletics.

He is like Kurt, a respectable boy too. There is not a better family than Kurt's, but Charles is more of a gentleman than Kurt.

We might consider briefly at this point what being intellectual or smart means. One child can be considered smart, i.e., he knows a lot, and is rated highly on that account. Another child may also know a lot and be considered smart and is rated low on that account. "Smart" in this instance connotes smarty, intellectual show-off. This means that "smarty" creates a superiority-inferiority relation between himself and the others, a relation that is resented on implicit equalitarian assumptions. Being smart and sociable is probably the desired norm. The converse holds true. Being "dumb" and unsociable would tend to result in a low rating, but being dumb and sociable might result in a fair or even high rating. Children recognize and appreciate intellectual ability, the person who knows a lot, reads a great deal, can work problems easily, but it is relative to a social norm. When a child makes invidious comparisons between himself and others on these demonstrated abilities or becomes an intellectual exhibitionist, he will be rejected by others.

Herbert is the converse of the esteemed boys:

He's about the same as Frank. He's always looking for fights. He picks on small kids. He isn't too clean. He swears a lot and nobody seems to like him.

He swears and is always fooling around. Gus doesn't swear as much as Herbert. He uses all the four-letter words in front of boys and girls. Ollie does that sometimes.

He's always in trouble. He was blamed for the stolen watch. Everyone thought he stole. If he does many more things, he'll be in the reform school at Oldham.

I don't like his ways. He goes out all the time with girls. I don't like the way he plays sports. If he does, he wants to fight all the time.

He's the same as Beatrice, only a little worse. He's always telling dirty jokes.

This cross-sex comparison is probably one of the most invidious encountered in the study. From this comparison we already know how Beatrice is looked upon. We shall let the children speak.

She hangs around with bigger boys than she is, high school or graduates from high school. She's boy crazy. She tries to get boys to go after her. She swears but not at Miss Harrington, uses all swear words. She does not get along with people.

She's dirty, very rank. She has the wrong ideas of life. She's too interested in boys the wrong way. She tells dirty jokes. She uses language in school she shouldn't, dirty words.

If you make something, hers is always better than yours. All she does is best. I argue with her.

All the time I don't like her. She's jealous of the glee club where I and my sister sing duets. I'm afraid to go to the glee club. She's always wanting to pick fights with other girls. It was with Cay last year. She does her studies very well, though sometimes she lets them slide. She likes parties and is always trying to plan some, particularly in the earlier grades.

George, a Negro boy and the star pitcher on the school team, has an ambivalent position. He has many of the assessments of Herbert but he is accepted by the boys. Since he has a mutual choice with Kurt, his standing is helped. Kurt says of him:

He is always looking for a fight with Herbert. It used to be Herbert who picked the fights. He swears a lot. He's a nice guy to get along with if he didn't swear so much. If he would only do it quietly, it would be all right, but he hollers right out. During summer we go swimming. We used to go bicycle riding.

Girls are completely negative to George:

He's always in trouble. Never has a good word about anyone. He swears. He's a troublemaker. He likes to get in trouble. Sometimes he is pleasant, but he's got a grudge against the world. He's a rumor spreader.

THE EVALUATIVE PROCESS

A social situation is an intricate network of positive and negative assessments of activities, things, norms, and statuses. The assessment of a particular child is a complex social judgment which culminates in a reputation. The nature of this convergence of judgments we have noted in our two classes. The assessment involves many points: appearance values, capacities of individuals, conventional etiquette and morality, the institutional order of the school, aggressiveness or friendliness, intellectual achievement or intellectual snobbishness, ecological area of community, invidious reference to the poor, sexuality, swearing, and telling dirty jokes. These points cohere in the various structural principles, and in the various dyads and cliques that constitute the informal order. Most important, as the statements of the children show, is the sex and pupil status of the child. These and other less important points might be listed as follows:

Sex Status	Pupil Status	Economic Class and Prestige Group
Appearance values	Intellectual achievement	Ecological area
Capacities of person	or pupil performance	Invidious reference to
Aggressiveness	School norms	poor
Friendliness or socia-	Intellectual snobbishness	Conspicuous display
bility	Conventional etiquette	
Sexuality	Sharing of knowledge	
Swearing	and abilities	
Dirty jokes		
Teasing		

Ethnic or Color Group	Dyad and Cliques
Pride in one's affiliation	One of the gang
Teasing because of one's affiliation	An outsider
Negative references to one's group	Attempts at domination
Color references favorable or unfavorable	

The points of evaluation represent an unresolved amalgamation of the humanist, common-man, and nativist orientations. The first two center upon the pupil status and the sociable phases of the sex status. The last focuses upon the competitive and aggressive aspects of the statuses. In the economic class and prestige group we find a trace of the market orientation. These points mingle in many ways. Conspicuous display and pleasing appearance in the conduct of a girl may result in both favorable and unfavorable evaluations. Swearing, fighting, good athletic ability and performance may result in ambivalent evaluation, e.g., positive from the point of view of boys and negative from that of the girls, a peculiar intermixture of the humanist and nativist orientations.

Both boys and girls orient themselves to the plurality of these valuative points. They are the common base even though they apply differentially. Certain assessments of boys will be positive among themselves, negative if they apply them to girls, or vice versa. The significance of these points varies also with age. Younger children may evaluate primarily in terms of sex and pupil status. Older children will add the other structural points. Likewise the content will differ. The younger child does not evaluate the conduct in sex status the same as the older. Again we have to keep in mind the permissive limits that are implicit in all conduct. Teasing is all right up to a certain point. Fighting is acceptable given an appropriate situation. There is no way of defining what these permissive limits are. All one can say is that the principle of augmentation of negative relations is operative so that violent verbal or physical aggression is the culmination, but this outcome is based upon the evaluation of the situation. Content which is negatively assessed has a greater permissive range among boys than among girls.

From the point of view of social relations, the positive points promote sociative and the negative dissociative relations. Or we might say that in general associative acts will be highly assessed, and those that are dissociative will be condemned. This fact means that both the informal order and the institutional order of the school become disrupted when negative assessments are applied in a persistent fashion to a person, dyad, or clique. The disruption is more likely to occur when the assessed person resents and resists the negative evaluations. At this point a crisis breaks out which a teacher must resolve in some way in order to restore the disrupted normative and functional order. The positively assessed person insures the maintenance of order. The teacher has the obligation to promote the positive evaluations and to overcome the negative, and this problem includes herself as an active, evaluating agent in the schooling process. A positive orientation means a recognition of the social as the basic principle in life, i.e., that living is a coördinated, interdependent pattern of activities.

The significance of the pupil status has been worked out in our previous discussions and appears clear in the evaluative statements considered in this chapter. We want to explore further two other statuses, in order to determine their significance.

EVALUATION ON THE BASIS OF SOCIAL CLASS

Do all lower-class children in the elementary school have bad reputations? According to the Hometown-Jonesville-Elmtown study the answer is yes. "The lower-class child . . . has the reputation of being poorly dressed; not good looking; unpopular; aggressive; of not liking school; of being dirty and bad mannered; of never having a good time; and of not playing fair. The child of a family of upper status, on the other hand, enjoys a reputation almost exactly opposite." [3] None of these evaluative statements is a direct social class statement, so the assumption is made in the study that these factors are related to or associated with social class. The argument is clinched by assuming that children unconsciously use these criteria as class stereotypes even though they are not conscious of the class structure of the community. These data were secured by a guess-who test, a point we shall comment on later. Furthermore, the information shows that some of the higher status group children rate low and some of the lower rate high. These variations are not explained. On the basis of the assumptions they cannot be explained, unless it is assumed that the lower-class child acts like an upper-class child and vice versa, but then the analysis becomes inconsistent.

In the West School study and in Criswell's study, direct reference to social class as a point of evaluation was found infrequently, in fact almost negligibly. Criswell found little mention of good looks, physical traits, or prominence in class. [4] Positive points of evaluation found in this study included: *general approval* (he's nice; I like him; he's all right); *school ability* (he's smart; knows his work; reads

[3] Bernice Neugarten, "Social Class and Friendship Among School Children," *American Journal of Sociology,* January, 1946, p. 310.
[4] Joan Criswell, "A Sociometric Study of Race Cleavage in the Classroom," *Archives of Psychology,* January, 1939, pp. 48–51, 62–64.

good); *good conduct* (is quiet in class; doesn't copy; good, and I want to be good); *friends* (a pal; we like each other); *common activities* (we play together; work together; take walks on Sunday; have a club); *neighbor* (she lives next door; she lives across the street and we play together); *services performed by chosen for chooser* (lends me a pencil; gives me crackers); *length of acquaintance* (we've known each since kindergarten). Rejection points included: *bad conduct in class* (talks, bothers me; laughs too much; gets in trouble with teacher) and *truculent behavior* (fights, rowdy, tough, fresh, fussy, hot temper). The chief structural principles were sex and race in addition to pupil status. The points of evaluation were secured from the children through interview.

In *Children of Brasstown* social class evaluation was of no significance until the sixth grade was reached. While there was a tendency to assign the upper groups favorable evaluations as based upon a guess-who test, eighth-graders in effect denied "the existence of class differences when they report that nobody in their group fits the description in question."[5] The study also found about half the children in the eighth grade reversing the usual evaluation of social classes. The uppers, the children thought, "are selfish, snooty, don't care about others, do things behind people's backs. If they find money, they either hang onto it because no one would know they had it or they might even keep some and hand the rest in. The lowers are friendly, more generous, cooperative, hard working, tougher, unafraid, and honest. All they lack is 'a bringing up.'"[6] Stendler also found a tendency to evaluate upon individual differences rather than upon a basis of class, "commonly expressed by the statement about a particular kind of conduct, 'Anyone could do it.'"[7] This principle was voiced primarily by middle- and upper-middle-class children and was found from the first grade up. It represents the conception of equity and justice, and it likewise appeared in the many explanations and rationalizations about social class that children offered.

[5] Celia Burns Stendler, *Children of Brasstown*, Bureau of Research and Service of the College of Education, University of Illinois, 1949, p. 79.
[6] *Ibid.*, p. 86.
[7] *Ibid.*, p. 87.

Specific social class content is found infrequently in evaluative statements of children on the elementary-school level. There is also some evidence to suggest that this is true on the high-school level. The content of evaluative statements as derived from interview is quite different from that based upon guess-who tests. The Hometown and Brasstown studies were based upon these tests, the West School and Criswell studies upon interview. The results are different, so that the differences that appear are a question of technique. It is our opinion that the unstructured interviews are more revealing than the guess-who tests. Since these tests have been widely used and offered as diagnostic tools, we want to point out several limiting deficiencies. The test does not take into consideration the idea of permissive limits and forces a child to polarize his evaluations. If we exclude the question of reading difficulties in children, which may affect their response, there is, in addition, a question of meaning. A child may not interpret the items in terms of the meanings that the researcher has in mind. "Fighting," "clean," "dirty," for example, are complicated words. Also the range of items may not include the more important areas of evaluation of the children, so that a distorted picture results. The content of the sex status is touched upon but little by the test. Children may, furthermore, approve a child on one item and disapprove on another. The principle of the convergence of judgments is not met in this test. As the test is usually given, children are asked to consider *all* the children in the class. This request apparently assumes that children have knowledge about each other. That assumption is not valid. What happens in many negative responses is that children put down names of those whom they do not know or with whom they do not associate. Cliques tend to favor their own members and to devalue non-members. Finally, children will put down names merely to oblige the researcher. The form has to be filled out. The teacher wants them to do it, the researcher wants it, and so the children are considerate enough to comply. We have found this to be true even in sociometric questions. For these reasons we do not think that the guess-who test is an especially good diagnostic instrument. Unstructured interviews are preferable.

LOVE AND OBSCENITY AS POINTS OF EVALUATION

"Being dirty," "acting like a pig," "boy crazy" or "girl crazy," "dirty words," "dirty jokes"—all these labels refer to our culture patterns of love and obscenity. These terms cohere in the sex statuses, and like all evaluative terms have certain permissive limits. These limits will vary with the male and female status, so that the male may indulge in a certain amount of "dirtiness" as an expression of masculinity, behavior apparently tabooed to the female, even among children. From the official normative system attention to such things is frowned upon and proscribed.

The culture patterns of love and obscenity are pervasive. Attention is given to them from early childhood. The topic of sex and sexuality changes content as the child moves into the adult status. In this status the risqué, the titillations of the demimonde, and aphrodisiac commercialism flourish. The pattern has become extremely elaborate, a form of erotic teasing and erotic mystery. As we have already noted in our two classes, some of the most violent denunciations are made in terms of the patterns of love and obscenity, and even those who denounce others have been socialized into the patterns. We want to explore this topic a bit more to show how it affects the relations among children and so affects the functioning of the school.

EARLY SEXUALITY AND SEX HUMOR

The idea that children are not interested in sex *per se* and in the opposite sex is on a par with the notion that teachers are sexless and reproduce by fission. We have seen that Valentine's Day focuses on heterosexual relations with emphasis on love, and starts in the kindergarten. Teasing conduct between the sexes, usually in some form of a playful beating-up, is found on all levels. Some children will have had, by the time they are in high school, more sex experience than their teachers will ever have.

Ena, dena, dina, do
Put a baby on the po
When it's done, wipe its bum
[or When it's done, call its mum]
Ena, dena, dina, do [8]

This doggerel, an interesting transposition of "eeny, meeny, miny, mo," suggests the content of childish sex humor, a focus on the processes of elimination. This focus becomes a bit marginal on the adult level, where the emphasis is upon sexual intercourse as a content of humor. We can only suggest, in the absence of extensive systematic investigations, the nature of this early sexuality. A host of specific situations have been recorded by Susan Isaacs. The following gives something of the interaction among children through sex.

Christopher took a bowl from Benjie. Harold said: "I'll hit you in the face if you take mine." Benjie: "I'll wee-wee in your face." Benjie and Harold said to Timmy: "We'll put bim-bom-bee-wee water in your face. . . ." The children were getting water to drink in cups, and Harold told the others that he had given Frank some "wee-wee water" to drink. He often says "There is wee-wee water in the bowl" in which he washes his hands. Later he said that he had drunk "wee-wee" water and that the water in the cup was that. . . . Frank said: "Shall we make Benjie drink bee-wee water?" "Yes," Harold said, "and poison him." And another time, "and make spots come out all over him."

We note here that reference to sex is not only a form of humor but also a weapon of aggression. Threats to urinate upon another child are not untypical. It may also be a form of teasing behavior. To what extent the young child views this interest as tabooed is unclear, and that applies even to young middle-class children where rigid norms are thought to prevail. Even if the topics are tabooed, among themselves they are not, and apparently this talk about urine and feces becomes the epitome of humor. The following doggerels collected from first-graders illustrate our point:

Red, red, wet your bed
Wipe it up with ginger bread.

Brown, brown, go to town
Wear your britches upside down.

[8] Susan Isaacs, *Social Development in Young Children*, Routledge and Kegan Paul, Ltd., 1933, p. 140.

Ginny, guynee five by ten
Couldn't get through the bathroom door
So she got down upon the floor
And found the pee
And licked it up
And did some more.

These verses were quoted with a great deal of relish, and the amusement of the children was vast.

The young child has its ideas of what constitutes beauty in the female. It is not surprising that the class belle appears even in the prenursery school, and the phenomenon of the collective crush appears on the social scene, to the dismay frequently of the young girl showered with attention and the concern of the adult over this impetuous coltish conduct. The problem, of course, can become serious. A mother had brought her daughter to a prenursery school. The impact of the little girl upon the boys was immense. For some reason they thought she embodied all the attributes of feminine beauty. So compelling, so overpowering was her attraction that the boys showered her with friendly pats and big, wet, plashy kisses. For two days the girl bore the brunt of this mass affection until she finally became hysterical, immobile, and sobbing. The mother had to withdraw the girl. The boys settled back to normalcy. In one second grade the situation was somewhat reversed. This young class belle knew her power. The boys had to keep their distance. The belle, then, embarked on a sequence of bestowing her attention and favors upon each boy in the room individually, a few days with John, a week with Henry, and so on. Parents were suddenly confronted with an impossible situation when love-smitten youngsters, frantic from the tensions, implored them to find out when Sue was going to love them.

Such sexuality is but one of the phases in the younger child. In addition, one may expect exhibitionism, a showing of genitals, mutual inspection, sexual curiosity, and the whole complex of family play and ideas about babies and marriage. Much of this takes on a symbolic rather than a direct form at later ages. The direct approach to sex as seen in the younger child becomes veiled and verbal.

A CASE FOR SEX EDUCATION

Bee is too much like a pig. (You mean she's dirty?) Yes. She talks about boys all the time. Talks dirty about them. She hangs around boys in and out of school. She uses nasty words and tells dirty jokes, like "bugger faster," "boy in wagon, girl in wagon, boy on top . . ." Ann tells jokes but not like this. Bee told jokes to boys only once that I know of, to Kirby. Boys don't know what she's like.

Bee was considered by the teacher, on the other hand, as a well-behaved, quiet girl, neat and clean in dress, one who did her work, not brilliantly but steadily. Yet Bee was the center of a storm of inter-personal relations that raged among the girls in the class, opposition between the "dirty" and the "clean" and a struggle for the boy friend or girl friend. When a series of negative assessments takes place over a period of time, a fight or some emotional outbreak will occur, a major disruption of the schooling process, during which the system of evaluation comes to the fore. In the following we want to analyze the ramifications of such a crisis. We do not contend that in every school there will be an exact duplication of this event, but we do hold that from the nature of our statuses the likelihood that such a happening will take place is high. We might also note that the good, clean girls are a bit tarnished, for they precipitated the crises. Furthermore, their actions indicate that they were effectively socialized in "dirt."

Mary was having a crying spell in the girls' lavatory (a sanctuary during a great emotional strain, as we have pointed out) before the morning bell had rung. Eileen, from the fourth-fifth grade, informed Miss Lewis about it and also indicated that Lucy and Ann were involved. Eileen was considered by Miss Lewis one of the smuttiest children she knew: "I wouldn't want a daughter of mine to associate with her." Lucy was Mary's sister. Ann was one of the respected leaders in the class. Consoling Mary were Bee and Jane. Jane was regarded as one of the toughest fighters in the class and as a "pig." Harriet and Eve were also involved in this situation.

It was learned that as the children were returning from a bird walk Mary and Bee accidentally fell behind with Martin, Lee, and Carl, the most innocuous boys in the class. To the amusement and giggling of Ann, Cathy, and Harriet, Lucy shouted insinuatingly: "We know what you're getting. We know what you're after," a sex implication the "clean" girls enjoyed. Later on there was a lot of gossip among these girls about Mary and Bee, and as a result they decided to shun them. Later at home Lucy told Mary that she was not decent and implied that she was not fit to associate with nice girls such as Ann, Cathy, and Harriet. Mary broke down and cried. She resented the comments of her sister and the talk that had been spread. She thought that Ann was mainly responsible for spreading this unfavorable gossip. Upset about the whole matter, Mary wanted to talk to Ann but did not find opportunity. Still angry, Mary finally encountered Ann with her sister on the stairs going up to class. Lucy emphatically told Mary that she shouldn't or wouldn't lay hands on Ann or else. At this point Harriet appeared on the scene and took sides against Mary, making unpleasant comments and threatening her if she dared lay hands on Ann. Then, Mary was completely overwhelmed and broke down, fleeing to the lavatory. For over an hour Mary was completely incoherent, with uncontrollable weeping and huge sobs shaking her body, unable to speak, or blurting out broken phrases.

The teacher called the girls into a separate room. The discussion did not bring out clearly what was involved. It touched on class gossip, misinterpretation of events (such as the bird walk), dislikes, and cliques. When Harriet was brought in, the discussion became no clearer, except that Harriet indicated a perfunctory "it's too bad, I'm so sorry" attitude and defended her clique group. ("We had sworn an oath to defend each other.") Boy relations were touched upon. The whole matter of girl friendships was made much of—my friends versus your friends. The vocabulary throughout the discussion involved explosive words: jealous, mad, angry, fight, friends, best friends, only friend, all like, dislike, pig, and so on. Eventually the girls were sent out with the exception of Bee, Mary, and Lucy.

The discussion began on the boy angle and gradually gravitated to the sister relation. At this point Bee was sent back to class. The gist of the discussion with the two girls indicated a very strong sibling rivalry and jealousy which continued in the school. It indicated a home under a domineering, if not autocratic, father (whom the teacher up to this point had considered a very fine man) and a possibly neurotic, or at least highly sensitive, mother. The mother apparently was afflicted with crying spells over the dominance of the father. Household duties fell completely upon Mary, who regarded Lucy and her other sister Nancy (fourth-fifth grade) as the favorites.

From family relations the discussion veered back to boys, sex, and the dirty joke. Here the topic of Bee came up again. Lucy was in general very negative to Bee, referring to her constantly as "Bee, the pig." "Being piggish" meant having sexual interests, and perhaps the girls knew the vernacular meaning of "pig," i.e., prostitute. Mary said that Eileen was a purveyor of dirty jokes. She then indicated Bee's sources: (1) Bee's older sister in the eighth grade; (2) Eileen; (3) a friend of her sister who attended a parochial school; (4) a seven-year-old cousin who slept in a bed next to Bee when he visited. This boy would tell Bee about his activities. He was a member of a gang in a nearby town who indulged in sex exhibitionism, including a young girl who was regularly undressed. To associate with Bee, according to Lucy, was to become a pig. While Lucy's interest in sex was apparently strong too, she used negative terms which indicated her solidarity with the respectable girls forming the clique. Mary said that she was trying to stop Bee from telling dirty jokes if she was to remain her friend. The teacher's main efforts were directed to getting across the ideas of friendliness, distrust of gossip, family loyalty, greater participation of Mary and Bee in the group, and the wholesomeness of sex.

The teacher had little success discussing the situation with Bee. Bee admitted her relating of dirty jokes and confirmed the sources. Most of her answers were "I don't know" or vague and repressed. When the teacher tried to encourage her to use the books on sex education in the school's library, Bee's response was wholly negative. Bee had, nevertheless, once surreptitiously leafed through some of these books, apparently with a sense of guilt and shame. This feeling was increased, as she said: "When boys read the books in the library, and then look at us like *that*. That's why I don't want to look at them." Here knowledge was changed by an evaluation into a socially negative factor.

Bee's situation also dated back to an earlier grade and involved girls in the other half of the sixth grade. In this sixth-seventh combination there were some other girls considered "pigs," and one of them, Jo, was involved in the corruption of Bee, at least according to Belinda. Belinda characterized Jo: "I knew her last year. Bee and me got along fine till she came along. She came and now both are dirty. I fought her about this [to prevent the breakup of a friendship]. Jo isn't so dirty now, but last year she and some other girls went over to the church lawn, pulled up their dresses and whistled to the boys." Bee experienced a turnover of both boy and girl friends. Cindy was also involved in so far as she was able to entice Tom H. away from her. Tom was considered quite a prize, and Mary was also interested in him. Cindy was thoroughly disliked by both Bee and Mary.

The teacher also commented on the situation by stating that some of the mothers of the respectable girls had received complaints from their daughters that they had to indulge in such talk in order to get along and that the teacher should do something about the matter. The teacher, however, was limited by community disapproval of sex education, a disapproval which resulted, among other things, in the banishment of a male and female rabbit from the kindergarten. The teacher could only encourage the children to use the books in the school library and talk to them privately.

This particular case highlights the way in which sex, love, and obscenity are points of evaluation and so organize and disorganize relations among children in addition to contributing to a reputational history. The informal order becomes an arena of violent emotions, of hatreds and loves, of attacks and fighting, of shame and bravado as the children learn and live the male and female roles. The schooling process is carried out in this emotional vortex, at times completely upset when a crisis occurs or subtly sabotaged as children avoid or attract each other in terms of sex, love, and obscenity. By this we mean that some children may avoid others or be attracted to them because of these factors. The obscene may be alluring to some and they enjoy their obscenity. Others dislike it and are united by their purity. The girls in this class were separated as well as pulled together by these points of evaluation. As the event also showed, it ramified into other classes, schools, towns, and families. It included boys, though they tended to play a symbolic rather than an actual role. There was a history to the affair which emphasizes the continuity of attention, practice, and evaluation.

In contrast to the younger children, attention was no longer focused on the processes of elimination as an element of humor and on heterosexual teasing. The content among the older children included also specific reference to heterosexual relations and coitus, a content reflecting the growing maturation of the children. The pattern of obscenity included all the variations of swearing and the use of vernacular language when discussing sex and the body. A goodly part of activity and valuation were thus sex-directed, though not necessarily sex-motivated. There are many other ramifications, such as the tomboy, the stuffing and clogging of toilets, writing and drawing on lavatory walls, and so on.

Many of the points we have been discussing are recognized in English schools. Bibby lists the major problems in these schools as: the writing and passing of obscene or sexual notes, sexual conversation, sexual drawings, nude photographs, circulation of obscene magazines, nudity and exhibitionism, sexual experimentation, masturbation, homosexuality, crushes, and hero worship.[9] As a matter of fact, there is no difference in the nature of these problems in the English and our own schools.

Whether sex education and a value-neutral terminology can effectively substitute for the pattern of obscenity is a moot point. Educators think it will on the assumption that knowledge shared will dispel the mystery around sex. In this way sex and obscenity as points of evaluation would become less important. Education about sex in all its implications would then be a continuous process, starting in the prenursery school and continuing through high school, but to be effective it would also have to involve many modifications outside of the school, in families, in religion, in commerce, a revaluation of sex as positive, a reassessment in attitude and practice in relation to nudity. It may well be that, in cultures where nude communal bathing is customary, sex-directed attention and activity are more wholesome. As school life and our culture are now organized,

[9] Cyril Bibby, *Sex Education*, Emerson Books, Inc., 1946, pp. 107–131.

such revaluation is remote, and the patterns of love and obscenity will continue as they are.

THE COLLECTIVE CRUSH

Both boys and girls may be involved in a collective crush, though boys are likely to be more demonstrative. The collective crush already referred to is a more refined form of evaluation. It is still tinged with a modicum of sex, but other elements come to the fore. The collective crush is another variation on the organization of the informal order.

The case of Jenny will illustrate our point. Jenny was in a sixth-seventh class. She seemed to exemplify the good aspects of the female status. The way she carried out her role expectations fitted normative expectations. She was considered nice, pleasant, friendly. She did not interfere with school work, nor did she bother others. Jenny spoke nicely, i.e., did not swear, "holler," or argue. She was considered to be polite and have nice manners. She did not get mean or fresh or get into fights. She shared things, and was considered cute and pretty. Such assessments were made by both boys and girls. Discussing her, Belinda said: "She's hot and cute. She knows she's cute. Betsy is small but not cute. Jenny is so cute and better than Betsy that she gets everybody. She treats you to everything. If she buys ice cream, she'll almost force it down your throat. She has pretty eyes and teeth. One time she had long hair and curls and she wasn't so cute. She cut her hair, now she's cute. She is nice, decent, and kind. She talks to you, doesn't holler." "Petiteness," a favorable appearance value, and the ability to initiate sociative relations made Jenny a star. Furthermore, she did not exploit her standing, for if she had, evaluations such as snooty, snotty, or stuck-up would have appeared. She had to act out the role consistently. Finally during her history in the class she became the object of a collective crush.

Though it was recognized that Jenny had a special preference for Peter, who reciprocated, most of the boys paid Jenny the proper respect. One symptom of this was the tendency for boys to go out of their way to help her in some task. Another more expressive symptom was their milling around Jenny during recess, poking and pushing her gently, pulling her hair, and calling her endearing names such as "peanuts" and "honeybun." At times other girls would form a cordon around Jenny, an action which only contributed to the excitement. Eventually this awkward boyish attention became too much, and Jenny would cry. A note appeared in the class suggestion box: "There are some boys in this room that made a nice girl cry they call her nams. I hope you will tell them to Stop. a frined of this girl." The teacher, who was unaware of the situation, was able to identify the handwriting and called a class meeting. The boys admitted their unsubtle tactics but insisted: "But Jenny, we like you so *very* much." So Jenny cried again. After the proprieties of conduct were explored, the collective crush evaporated. Jenny's standing, however, remained unimpaired.

The collective crush is based upon the content of the male and female status. Our discussion has emphasized the crush as heterosexual, but the crush may also occur within one of the statuses. The points of evaluation remain the same.

SUMMARY

The ratings of the children and the significance of the structural principles are made meaningful by the content of valuation. Analysis of the children's assessments also makes understandable variations from the general trends in selecting one another as friends, work partners, and so on. In general the sociable child will have the better ratings and the sex-oriented child the lower, but this point is qualified by the principle of permissive limits. The teacher has the problem of determining which of the statuses is important in rating of the child, if she wants to organize the class intelligently. She has to find out what the convergence of judgments is that make a reputation if it is to be understandable to her.

Selected Readings

Bibby, Cyril, *Sex Education*, Emerson Books, Inc., 1946.
Freud, Sigmund, "The Origin and Development of Psychoanalysis," in J. S. VanTeslar (ed.), *An Outline of Psychoanalysis*, Modern Library, 1924, pp. 54–63.

Isaacs, Susan, *Social Development in Young Children,* George Routledge and Sons, Ltd., 1933.

Sears, Robert, *Survey of Objective Studies of Psychoanalytic Concepts,* Social Science Research Council, Bulletin 51, 1943, chaps. 1 and 2.

PART V

THE TEACHER IN
SCHOOL AND COMMUNITY

PART V

THE TEACHER IN
SCHOOL AND COMMUNITY

CHAPTER 16

Teaching as a Vocation

THE PROBLEM of getting teachers is readily solved by some who assert that teachers are born, not made. The proof of their contention is difficult to find, and perhaps the statement means no more than that there is a certain mystery, an ineffable quality, about good teachers. No scientific analysis can touch this x factor. An appeal to mystery produces awe and all sorts of other feelings which, titillating as they are, admit of no insight. On the other hand, to assert that teachers are made has an assembly-line, mass-production implication as if some standard mold stamped the human clay into a shape labeled teacher. This puppet concept of man is about as insightful as the appeal to mystery. To become a teacher means to make a choice, to acquire knowledge and skills, to obtain official certification of professional competence, as shown in Chapter 4. It is a creative act, a growth process. As there is no automatic process of getting either born or made teachers, people must be induced to take on the teacher status. Schools must have a qualified personnel, which necessitates recruitment and training.

THE SOCIAL RECRUITMENT OF TEACHERS

Teaching is part of the labor market, and it is subject to the variations of supply and demand in that market. As there is competition for personnel, a special effort has to be made to induce young people to enter teaching rather than some other profession or occupation. How are people persuaded and motivated to choose to be teachers? What is the social origin of this personnel? These are some of the topics to be considered.

THE SUPPLY OF AND DEMAND FOR TEACHERS

The demand for teachers is a function of the compulsory school laws and of the birth and mortality trends. The demand for certain types of teachers is a function of the curriculum and the value system of the school. Trends in school enrollment and school personnel have been presented in chapter 2. In Table 41 these trends are projected to 1960. For the first half of the decade a very large number of new pupils was expected to enter elementary school, but for the second half the number of new pupils was expected to diminish. The trend in high-school enrollment is the reverse, so that new additions in the first half of the decade are low as compared to estimates for the second half. The demand for teachers will vary with these trends.

The pupil-teacher ratio in these projections for the elementary school is around 38 to 1, and for the high school is 20 to 1. If the ratio for the elementary school were 30 to 1, the total teacher requirement for 1956–57 would be 941,600 teachers. There would not be the slightest possibility of securing the necessary number of qualified teachers for such a ratio. The student-teacher ratio for the high school can be achieved if past trends of teacher supply are maintained.

The problem of teacher supply and demand may become clearer when examined with reference to a specific year. In 1952 the total demand for qualified elementary teachers was 160,000.[1] It is broken down as follows: 10,000 to relieve overcrowding and eliminate dual and triple sessions per day; 20,000 to meet the demand of increased enrollment; 60,000 to replace annual loss; 70,000 to replace the worst of the undertrained, those who do not meet even half of the minimum requirements. If this minimum demand had been met for 1952, then the estimated annual need till 1957 would have been for

[1] Ray Maul, "How Many Teachers Do We Need?" *Journal of Teacher Education,* June, 1952, pp. 94–104.

TABLE 41. School Enrollment and School Personnel for Elementary
and High School, 1950–60

Year	Elementary School, Kindergarten Through Grade 8		High School, Grades 9–12		Professional [a] Other than Class Teachers
	Pupils (000)	Teachers	Students (000)	Teachers	
1950–51	22,793	608,131	6,493	325,143	71,790
1951–52	23,503	627,285	6,513	329,173	73,574
1952–53	25,044	646,111	6,619	334,983	75,469
1953–54	26,438	681,120	6,787	350,880	76,400
1954–55	27,565	709,500	7,075	365,500	76,800
1955–56	28,321	731,940	7,454	377,060	79,280
1956–57	28,777	755,040	8,152	388,960	81,700
1957–58	29,248	763,750	8,723	411,250	83,900
1958–59	29,385	773,500	9,091	416,500	85,000
1959–60	29,439	777,400	9,256	418,600	85,400

[a] Includes principals, supervisors, city and county superintendents and staffs.
SOURCE: Adapted from, "The Outlook for School Enrollments," Research Division, NEA, *Journal of Teacher Education*, March, 1953, pp. 45–52, and "Teacher Forecast for the Public Schools," Research Division, NEA, *Journal of Teacher Education*, March, 1953, pp. 53–58. The data after 1952–53 are estimates.

100,000 elementary teachers. The total supply in 1952 of qualified elementary teacher candidates was 32,433. This supply of new qualified elementary teachers was sufficient to cover only a little over half the annual teacher replacement.

The Bureau of Labor Statistics estimated that 560,000 elementary-school teachers would be required for the ten years following 1950 to replace those who died, retired, or left classrooms for other reasons.[2] The average annual replacement is estimated at 7 percent. Increased enrollment would create 240,000 new positions. The total demand would be 800,000 teachers, which would not include replacing those with emergency certificates. This estimate is similar to that of the Maul study, so that the annual average demand is for 100,000 elementary teachers. The conclusion is that the undersupply of elementary teachers is enormous. For the present there is little hope

[2] *Employment Outlook for Elementary and Secondary Teachers,* Bulletin No. 972, Occupational Outlook Series, Bureau of Labor Statistics, U.S. Department of Labor, 1949, p. 5.

that this fact will change very much, and the undersupply will continue.

The situation for the high school is quite different. The demand for September, 1952, was for 48,000 teachers in addition to the existing staffs. It is estimated that the demand will increase to 58,000 for 1958 and 63,000 for 1960.[3] The supply of qualified secondary-school teaching candidates was 62,692, an oversupply of teachers. However, the number of qualified teaching candidates has diminished. In 1950, 86,890 were prepared, as compared to the 62,692 for 1952, a decrease of 24,198. The oversupply of high-school teachers may be persistent. The Bureau of Labor Statistics estimates an annual replacement rate of 5 percent, or approximately 20,000 teachers per year by 1960. On a ratio of twenty-five pupils to a teacher, 85,000 new teachers would be needed in 1952–60.[4] This demand does not include the replacement of secondary-school teachers holding emergency or substandard certificates. In 1948–49, these came to 5.5 percent of the instructional staff or roughly 17,000 teachers. Oversupply of secondary teachers affects specific teaching fields. As a rule there is an oversupply in English and the social sciences and an undersupply in the natural sciences, mathematics, and some vocational subjects. It might be noted that the fit of the data and estimates of the two cited studies is not very close as compared to the material on the elementary school.

While the above discussion deals generally with teacher supply and demand, the labor market for teachers will vary by region and by state. It will vary by certification requirements and by certification reciprocity between states. It will vary by economic trend. In general there is an oversupply of teachers correlated with depression periods and an undersupply correlated with peak periods of prosperity.[5] Since 1900 the high points of oversupply were in 1901, 1903, 1915, 1928, 1933, 1940, 1949 (high school only) and the low points of undersupply were in 1907, 1912, 1918, 1921, 1942, 1945, 1950 (elementary only).[6] Since teacher salaries lag during inflation-

[3] Ray Maul, *op. cit.*, p. 95.
[4] *Op. cit.*, p. 8.
[5] J. Maske Roben, "Analysis of Trends and Teacher Supply and Demand, 1900–1950," *Journal of Teacher Education*, December, 1951, pp. 263–268.
[6] *Ibid.*, p. 265.

ary periods, this fact may contribute to a shift from teaching to more lucrative occupations.

THE SOCIAL ORIGINS OF TEACHERS

A widely held sociological generalization is to the effect that teachers originate in the lower income and occupational strata of the society and adopt the teaching profession as a means of moving socially into a higher status.[7] Since they are *arriviste* to the middle class, they tend to adhere to and promote strongly middle-class value and behavior patterns.

Table 42 compares two studies, one completed in 1910 and the other in 1948. The first was based upon 5215 schedules secured from teachers in twenty-two states.[8] The second was based upon 969 students attending Indiana University, of which 100 had decided to enter teaching, 174 were undecided, and 695 had decided against it.[9] As repeated mention will be made of this study, the group deciding to enter teaching will be referred to as group "T," and those deciding against it as group "O." These studies make it evident that a dramatic shift in the social origins of teachers has taken place. This change may merely exemplify the shift from a rural to an urban industrial culture so that teachers will be increasingly recruited from these new occupational strata—the professional, business, and public service groups. The notion that teachers stem predominantly from the lower occupational strata is historically dated, a view that also presumed that farming was a low-rating occupation, a somewhat disputable point. If farming is not regarded as a low-rating occupation, this particular interpretation was never correct. If business, profession, and public service may be regarded as composing the middle-class group, then it is evident that over half of the male and female teachers will now come from this class. The conclusion is

[7] William Lloyd Warner, Robert J. Havighurst, and Martin Loeb, *Who Shall Be Educated?* Harper & Brothers, 1944, chapter VIII; Robin M. Williams, Jr., *American Society,* Alfred A. Knopf, 1951, p. 286.

[8] Lotus Coffman, *The Social Composition of the Teaching Population,* Contributions to Education No. 41, Teachers College, Columbia University, 1911.

[9] Robert Richey and William Fox, *An Analysis of Various Factors Associated with the Selection of Teaching as a Vocation,* Bulletin of the School of Education, Indiana University, Division of Research and Field Services, May, 1948.

TABLE 42. Social Origin of Teachers and Future Teachers According to Occupation of Father and by Sex, 1910 and 1948

Type of Occupation	Percent in			
	1910		1948	
	Male	Female	Male	Female
Profession	7	7	15	16
Business	6	15	22	24
Farmer	66	42	4	20
Skilled worker	7	15 }	26	20
Unskilled worker	7	11 }		
Fine and practical arts	—	—	4	11
Public service	1	2	15	2
Retired	1	2	—	—
Not answered	5	6	13	6

SOURCE: Adapted from Lotus Coffman, *The Social Composition of the Teaching Population,* Contributions to Education No. 41, Teachers College, Columbia University, 1911, Tables XLVII and XLIX, p. 73, and Robert Richey and William Fox, *An Analysis of Various Factors Associated with the Selection of Teaching as a Vocation,* Bulletin of the School of Education, Indiana University, Division of Research and Field Services, 1948, Table VI, p. 18.

not surprising in light of the limited social mobility that takes place.[10] People tend to stay in the stratum in which they were born. However, the data also indicate that teachers tend to be recruited from those families at the lower end of the income range in these groups.[11] Teaching as a vocation may then be interpreted as a means of maintaining one's station in life.

The assumption of the key status of teaching, however, involves not only the social class position but also the sex status, and the latter may be of more significance. That most teachers are women is obvious, and one reason for this was seen in the cultural expectation that women supposedly deal more effectively with young children, a generalization of the mother role. There are other occupations which also involve this cultural expectation, such as nursing and social work. These are essentially "female" occupations, as the ratio of men to women shows.[12] Women will tend to choose such

[10] Cf., for a summary of data and discussion, Delbert Miller and William H. Form, *Industrial Sociology,* Harper & Brothers, 1951, chap. XIX.

[11] Lotus Coffman, *op. cit.,* pp. 76–77; Robert Richey and William Fox, *op. cit.,* p. 16.

[12] E. T. Hiller, *Social Relations and Structures,* Harper & Brothers, 1947, pp. 468–474.

occupations rather than those culturally "reserved" for males. Another way of looking at this choice is in terms of respectability or propriety associated with one's sex status. To put it as a question: What occupations are respectable for a woman, not only in terms of propriety but also in terms of income? Despite all the drawbacks to teaching, this profession has both of these elements. Of the eight most important reasons given for entering the profession by nearly 6000 women teachers, the second most important was "few other remunerative occupations for women in my county," the sixth, "greater prestige in teaching than in other occupations for women," and the seventh, "relative economic security." [13] This cultural view of occupation as linked with sex status explains the choice of teaching by women. If the earlier data are taken, Table 42, it is essentially a question of the occupational choice of farm children. Given our property and inheritance system, one of the children of the large farm families will receive the farm. All the rest must leave the farmstead. In choosing an occupation, teaching is the most natural choice for the unmarried female in terms of respectability and income. The latter data were interpreted to the effect that the choice of the profession is a means of maintaining a middle-class sex status. Other studies corroborate the view expressed here with the exception of the Kiely study, which showed that 36.7 percent of females attending several teachers colleges came from the skilled worker group.[14]

OTHER SOCIAL BACKGROUND FACTORS OF TEACHERS

Most teachers are native-born white. Coffman found this to be true of males (91 percent) and females (84 percent). Teachers foreign born with foreign-born parents came to 2 and 1 percent respectively. The in-between group in which the teacher is native-born but with one or both parents foreign-born came to 7 percent of the

[13] M. Margaret Stroh, Ida Lewett, and Vern Butler, *Better Selection of Better Teachers*, National Capital Press, Inc., 1943, p. 10.
[14] See Margaret Kiely, *Comparisons of the Students in Teachers Colleges and Students of Liberal Arts Colleges*, Contributions to Education No. 440, Teachers College, Columbia University, 1931, p. 32, but her data are inconsistent: cf. Table X, p. 32; M'Ledge Moffet, *Social Background and Activities of Teachers College Students*, Contributions to Education No. 375, Teachers College, Columbia University, 1929, pp. 16–17.

males, 15 percent of the females.[15] This last percentage is consistent with the sex status interpretation offered, namely, that these first-generation immigrant females could advance socially by choosing teaching as a profession. Kiely's study showed that of the students attending the teachers colleges 70 percent had native-born fathers and mothers and 30 percent foreign-born. In the liberal arts colleges studied the percentages were respectively 75 and 25.[16] These data indicate that the colleges are a vehicle for social mobility but that the teachers college presented a better opportunity than the liberal arts college. The nativity factor is of only historical significance today with possible exception in certain regions where Mexicans, French Canadians, and Puerto Ricans have settled.

In contrast to the earlier studies cited, Richey found that 70 percent of future teachers came from the small (40 percent) and large (30 percent) city.[17] The village and rural area are of less significance. Richey also found the following points: that younger women and older men students preferred teaching, that students from small high schools tended to favor teaching as a vocation, that education of mother and father had little bearing upon this occupational choice.[18]

THE RECRUITING PROCESS

Recruiting has three aspects. One involves the person's evaluation of occupations, opportunities, and experiences. A second may include the influence of immediate associates. The third phase consists of the recruiting efforts by the profession. The first two may be considered as factors propelling the person to the profession and the third as a factor attracting him.

THE PERSONAL EQUATION

As an individual's self is organized by his key role, essentially his vocation, his conception of it will be a factor in choosing it. The occupation not only may impart social recognition, such as a sense of

[15] Op. cit., pp. 56–57; data recomputed.
[16] Op. cit., p. 29.
[17] Op. cit., p. 16. This stress differs from that given by the author.
[18] Ibid., pp. 14–19.

worth and honor, but may serve as a means of self-fulfillment. In the Richey-Fox study over 90 percent of group T students rated teaching as comparable to or more desirable than other vocations requiring four years of college. This is quite in contrast to group O. Sixty-four percent of these found it less or much less desirable than other four-year-course vocations.[19] Both groups of students recognized desirable aspects of teaching. Five of these good features listed by both T and O groups were: security, pay advancement possibilities; working conditions, environment, hours; opportunity for social service; chance to work with young people; personal prestige and satisfaction. The evaluation of desirable features in both groups is quite similar. The same is true of the undesirable features. Some of these are: comparatively low pay, restricted private life, poor working conditions, monotonous routine work, low social standing or prestige, parental interference and uncoöperativeness. About 8 percent in each group listed no undesirable features.[20] Reasons for choosing teaching as a profession by group T included: good salary, desire for working with young people, social service opportunities or guidance possibilities, good vocational prestige and personal satisfaction, stimulating working conditions and environment, steady employment and retirement status. Reasons for not selecting teaching by group O were: low salaries as compared with other professions, little or no appeal, restricted personal life and limited social contacts, routine, dull and monotonous duties, preference for another vocation, little or no chance for advancement. Some other interesting differences in the two groups are shown in Tables 43 and 44. The attitudes of the students in group T show a leaning toward the humanist value orientation as compared with those selecting other occupations.

Comparing public school teachers (on twenty-four selected characteristics) with other persons students knew best in the community, "fewer than 20 percent of the students who planned to teach ranked teachers below average on any items, while 50 or more percent marked them above average on breadth of interest, culture, scholarship, leadership and dependability." In group O, "20 percent

[19] *Ibid.*, p. 26.
[20] *Ibid.*, pp. 40–43.

or more ranked teachers below average on happiness, magnetism, constructive community participation, open-mindedness, and originality, while on only one item, scholarship, did as many as 40 percent rank them above average."[21] The prospective teachers conceived of the teacher image along humanist lines, the nonteachers only approximately. Further, the teacher tended to be evaluated higher in these characteristics than other community members by the future teachers. This evaluation was not shared by the nonteachers.

Decision for teaching is conditioned by a high evaluation of the vocation despite the recognition of undesirable features. This evaluation is supported by a service concept of the vocation and by a favorable teacher image. It is possible that for some individuals this conception of the key role may root in the striving for social mobility.

TABLE 43. Percentage Distribution of Attitudes Toward Different Aspects of Teaching by Students Selecting and Not Selecting Teaching as a Profession

Agreement on Factors	Teacher Group	Nonteacher Group
Teaching offers greater cultural opportunities than do most other occupations.		
Agree	62	34
Uncertain	27	27
Disagree	11	38
Item not checked	0	1
Making a high salary is of first importance in considering a vocation.		
Agree	5	13
Uncertain	9	15
Disagree	86	70
Item not checked	0	2
Being of service to mankind is of first importance in considering a vocation.		
Agree	53	38
Uncertain	30	30
Disagree	17	30
Item not checked	0	2

SOURCE: Adapted from Robert Richey and William Fox, *An Analysis of Various Factors Associated with the Selection of Teaching as a Vocation*, Bulletin of the School of Education, Indiana University, Division of Research and Field Services, May, 1948, pp. 31–32.

[21] *Ibid.*, p. 26.

TABLE 44. Attitude Toward Different Aspects of Teaching by Students Selecting and Not Selecting Teaching as a Profession

Aspect of Teaching	Attitude in Percent			
	Agree	Uncertain	Disagree	Not Checked
A community has a right to expect a teacher to take part in a local church.				
Teacher students	45	23	32	0
Nonteacher students	33	22	45	0
A community has a right to expect a teacher to take part in in community activities.				
Teacher students	68	16	14	2
Nonteacher students	50	22	27	1
Demands, either school or community, should not be made upon the teacher's time after school has been dismissed in the afternoon.				
Teacher students	33	34	32	1
Nonteacher students	42	32	25	1
Teachers should discuss controversial social issues in the classroom.				
Teacher students	53	25	22	0
Nonteacher students	58	25	16	1
Teachers should be permitted to join unions.				
Teacher students	43	31	25	1
Nonteacher students	36	34	29	1
Teachers should be permitted to make political speeches.				
Teacher students	18	34	48	0
Nonteacher students	23	32	44	1
Community has a right to expect the teacher to buy such things as clothes and automobiles from merchants in the community where he teaches.				
Teacher students	11	11	78	0
Nonteacher students	10	11	78	1
The political views of a teacher should be examined when he is considered for a position.				
Teacher students	9	8	83	0
Nonteacher students	18	10	71	1

Aspect of Teaching	Attitude in Percent			
	Agree	Uncertain	Disagree	Not Checked
The religious views of a teacher should be examined when he is considered for a position.				
Teacher students	15	15	69	1
Nonteacher students	25	12	62	1
A teacher has an obligation to live in the community where he teaches.				
Teacher students	42	16	41	1
Nonteacher students	22	19	58	1
A teacher should not leave the community where he teaches more than 25 percent of week ends.				
Teacher students	20	18	62	0
Nonteacher students	5	20	73	2

SOURCE: Adapted from Robert Richey and William Fox, *An Analysis of Various Factors Associated with the Selection of Teaching as a Vocation,* Bulletin of the School of Education, Indiana University, May, 1948, pp. 31–32.

However, two other factors may condition this decision to teach. According to the Richey-Fox study both men and women students in group T (92 percent) had given considerable thought to this selection in contrast to group O, many of whom (64 percent) had never considered it.[22] This focus on teaching is related to the fact that those selecting teaching as a profession "had had more experience of a teaching nature than those who had decided not to be teachers."[23]

RECRUITMENT AND IMMEDIATE ASSOCIATES

Selection of a vocation is a social process. It not only involves the person's own assessment of vocations but also includes the advice and influence of others. Popular opinion believes that children follow the vocation of parents, especially in the professions. Doctors' sons become doctors, etc. Is this true for teaching? Table 45 con-

[22] *Ibid.*, p. 20.
[23] *Ibid.*, p. 25.

trasts group T and group O students whose parents or relatives were in the profession. The significance varies with sex. Mother, sibling, aunt, or uncle may direct the choice of the female to select teaching as a profession. One might surmise that the sibling is most likely to be a sister and the relative an aunt. The father with teaching background has a greater influence upon the male in the selection of teaching as a profession. Teacher families or kin may have only a moderate influence in recruiting future teachers. It would be interesting to study the extent to which such families and relatives may even advise against the selection of teaching as an occupation.

Friends in the vocation rank very high as helping an individual select a vocation. Friends outside the vocation have some influence. The paramount factor, however, is the influence of the parents.[24]

TABLE 45. Percentage Distribution of Students Selecting and Not Selecting Teaching as a Vocation Based upon the Numbers Who Had Relatives with a Teaching Background

| Relative | Teacher Group | | | Nonteacher Group | | |
	Male	Female	Total	Male	Female	Total
Father	19	13	16	8	10	10
Mother	14	26	21	15	16	15
Brother or sister	6	13	10	3	2	3
Aunt or uncle	35	58	47	36	39	37

SOURCE: Robert Richey and William Fox, *An Analysis of Various Factors Associated with the Selection of Teaching as a Vocation*, Bulletin of the School of Education, Indiana University, May, 1948, p. 20.

RECRUITMENT BY THE PROFESSION

While the influence of teachers is rated next to that of parents, most students in the Richey-Fox study had little or no direct personal assistance from teachers in selecting a vocation. The data suggests that students selecting teaching as a profession had more assistance than those who did not select it or who were undecided about it. On the whole more counseling and guidance of students needs to be done, and more students may be recruited for teaching.

Teachers colleges, colleges or schools of education have a vested

[24] *Ibid.*, p. 23.

interest in the recruitment of teachers. What approaches are used? To develop community awareness of teaching as a profession, thirty-four out of seventy-five colleges studied engaged in some public relations work. Of these thirty-four, 85 percent contributed newspaper articles, 44 percent gave talks to service clubs and other organizations, and 37 percent used radio spot announcements. A few had made movies on teaching.[25] Recruiting in secondary schools was done by the seventy-five colleges in the following ways: (1) visits by college public relations personnel to high school, 58 percent; (2) campus visiting day for high-school students, 48 percent; (3) promotional letters to follow visits by public relations personnel, 40 percent; (4) talks to high-school students by education majors, 20 percent. Other techniques included: sending bulletins on teaching to high schools, holding guidance conferences in high schools with college personnel officiating, having names of promising high-school students sent by college alumni to their college, sending kodachrome slides on teaching with wire recording to high school, colored movies of college activities on preparation for teaching, coöperation in recruitment with a community council or with professional organizations such as Delta Kappa Gamma or Phi Delta Kappa.[26]

Incentives stressed by sixty-six out of the seventy-five selected colleges in recruiting for teaching were, in order of frequency: (1) opportunity for service, 82 percent; (2) social significance, 63 percent; (3) joy of working with children, 58 percent. Reasonable security was stressed by colleges in states having good retirement systems, tenure laws, and relatively high minimum salaries.[27] The stress of these incentives fits in with the previously described evaluation of teaching by students.

Several techniques for recruitment among the lower-division students were used in the seventy-five colleges. Eighty-seven percent fostered observation in elementary-school classrooms. Meetings of staff advisers with students to give information on the profession

[25] Loretta Byers, "Organization and Procedures Employed by Colleges to Recruit Candidates for Elementary-School Teaching," *Journal of Teacher Education,* December, 1950, p. 296.

[26] *Ibid.,* p. 296.

[27] *Ibid.,* p. 295.

were held by 57 percent. Organization of groups such as Future Teachers of America was carried out by 53 percent. General courses giving information on opportunities in teaching were given by 52 percent of the colleges and education survey courses by 47 percent. Social service contacts with children of elementary-school age were sponsored by one-half of the studied colleges. Personnel interview and counseling were of minor significance.[28]

Responsibility for recruitment generally rested with the entire staff of the college rather than any particular staff member. However, in 34 percent of the colleges studied the president and the dean of education were most responsible for recruitment. Special recruiting committees were found in 23 percent of the colleges.[29]

Advertising of teaching as a profession is carried on by the NEA and affiliated groups. Much of this is of the general quality of advertising methods currently used, from glamour teacher to starry-eyed idealism. The outreach of this type of approach may be limited but will supplement somewhat the influence of parent, relative, teacher, or friend already in the vocation.

TEACHER TRAINING

Once the decision has been made, the prospective teacher must secure his training. The type of training received represents the modified heritage of the first normal school. In 1832 a New York regent's report cautioned against the establishment of public-supported teacher seminaries modeled after those in France and Germany as violating American traditions of individualism, self-government, and laissez faire. In Massachusetts, however, public and educational leaders who had attended European universities favored such teacher training institutions. The legislature was petitioned for a state normal school. When a wealthy Boston manufacturer put up $10,000 to be matched by the state, the first normal · school was opened in April, 1838, in Lexington. The normal school met much opposition. It was opposed by those favoring the New York regent report recommending distribution of state funds to the

[28] *Ibid.*, p. 296.
[29] *Ibid.*, p. 295.

private academies which had established departments of education. Religious antagonism was one of the most serious threats as the school became embroiled in sectarian warfare between Unitarians and orthodox Congregationalists who suspected the school of becoming a "real steam engine for Unitarianism." Because of a nonsectarian type of religious instruction the school was labeled "godless." There was opposition from older teachers, who felt that the school was a reflection on their teaching. The school was finally opposed by the liberal arts schools, by the faculty members and graduates of the private academies and liberal arts colleges, persons having contempt for the early normal school. To placate much of this opposition the decision was made to confine the curriculum to purely professional aims, i.e., the common school subjects, methods of teaching, and supervised teaching in a nearby school, sacrificing the general and cultural to the strictly professional and technical. The significance of the first normal school is fourfold.

1. It gave basic direction to the whole future of teacher training; 2. it helped open the breach between teacher education and liberal arts education which now, more than 100 years later, has not yet been closed; 3. it set precedent for secular, state control of teacher training and implicitly the power to establish and enforce definite standards of teacher preparation and competence; 4. it is a phase in the history of universal democratic education and thus for the cause of the ultimate elevation and enlightenment of common people.[30]

The controversy between teacher education and liberal arts education has not abated. Teacher training is viewed as preparing empty-headed technicians by subject-oriented departments, and in turn the purely liberal arts trained person interested in teaching is viewed as fact-cluttered and a bungler in methods. The either-or opposition needs amalgamation into a both-and view. This is the reason that a five-year program of teacher education has been advocated so that the person will be trained adequately both in subject and in method. The trend in this direction is seen in the decline of the normal school and the rise in teachers colleges. In 1900 there were 286 normal schools; in 1939 there were 61. In the

[30] Willis Rudy, "America's First Normal School: The Formative Years," *Journal of Teacher Education*, December, 1954, p. 270.

year 1925–26 teachers were prepared in high-school training classes, county normal schools, state normal schools, city normal schools, private normal schools, state and city teachers colleges, and land-grant colleges, liberal arts colleges, and universities. The first five institutions accounted for 37 percent of the teacher graduates. Table 46 gives the percentage distribution of teachers prepared by

TABLE 46. Percentage Distribution of Teachers Prepared by Type of Institution, 1949–50

Type of Institution	Percent of Teachers Prepared		
	Elementary	High	Total
Teachers colleges	33.6	16.9	21.9
Public colleges and universities	31.1	40.2	37.4
Private colleges and universities	28.3	38.9	35.8
Professional and technical schools	.2	3.9	2.8
Junior colleges	6.8	.1	2.1
Total	100.0	100.0	100.0
Numbers	37,171	86,047	123,218

SOURCE: T. M. Stinnette, "Accreditation and Professionalization of Teaching," *Journal of Teacher Education*, March, 1952, p. 34.

different types of institutions. As the data suggest, much of the teacher training is carried out by schools or colleges other than the teachers college. The continuity of the teachers college with the normal school is seen in the high proportion of teachers prepared for elementary education.

The process of assuming the teacher role has not been really studied. The future teacher participates in the general activities of a college. At the same time he is in a special group, by virtue of classes required, buildings, and libraries, and social activities sponsored by an education department or school or by its student organizations. This promotes in-group tendencies among such students. As a student progresses in his studies, he is preparing for a practical climax, namely, his practice teaching. This again has not been thoroughly explored. In general, one knows that pupils consider a practice teacher fair game, that often the student has difficulty relating theory to practice, that sometimes the experience is quite traumatic, especially in the higher grades. As a testing period it may have its rationale. Some students capitulate after the experience; others may feel encouraged. Until these facets are studied in detail, the socialization process from recruit to teacher remains obscure. At any rate, upon completion of his preparation a student takes a place in a school and in a community as well, unless he goes into some other field, as a surprisingly large number (35.6 percent) do.[31]

ON THE JOB

There are several aspects to be considered. The first is getting the job. The second is the teaching situation. The third involves the teacher in the community and teacher organizations.

GETTING THE JOB

The teacher, like most job holders, is not a free-wheeling particle of a labor force marching from school system to system according to the schedules of supply-demand and salary wage scales with a complete *sang-froid* and economic rationality. Channels of contact and information must be available, and these may be limited. Furthermore, the prospective teacher, without perhaps being aware of the fact, is confronted with many implicit prerequisites which must be met. Many have little or no bearing upon teacher competence. How these technical irrelevancies are viewed is shown in Table 47. Of the four groups rating the fifteen potential teacher-applicant types, the education students are the most liberal, school teachers next, lay persons third, and school board members the least liberal.[32] The type preferred by board members would be an individual who is Protestant, native-born white, conservative, without a foreign name, born and raised in the local community. This concept is at

[31] "1954 Teacher Supply and Demand, Report of the NEA," *Journal of Teacher Education*, March, 1954, p. 22. Military service, further formal study, other gainful occupations, and homemaking claim these individuals.
[32] Florence Greenhoe, *Community Contacts and Participation of Teachers*, American Council on Public Affairs, 1941, p. 33.

variance with the views of both the prospective teacher and the teachers themselves. Such differences may also be the seedbed for potential dissociative relations among these groups. FEPC legislation, wars and cold wars, and Supreme Court decisions may affect such rating today. A replication would be an interesting check on the persistence of these views. Local inbreeding, i.e., giving preference to local residents over outsiders if qualifications are equal, is especially characteristic of larger cities, and in some of these cities

TABLE 47. Employability Quotients of Potential Applicants for Teaching Positions in the Public Schools

Potential Applicant for Teaching Position	As Rated by			
	356 School Board Members	2095 Lay Persons	9122 Public School Teachers	3054 Education Students
1. A known Protestant	76.5	84.9	93.5	93.5
2. Native-born, foreign name	56.3	73.2	88.5	89.9
3. Nonlocal resident	48.3	46.0	78.4	89.1
4. City-reared person	45.8	66.6	85.4	90.8
5. Out-of-state applicant	15.4	27.5	69.4	64.9
6. A known Catholic	−21.3	9.5	53.1	68.0
7. A known pacifist	−22.8	5.3	29.7	40.4
8. A married woman	−32.1	−12.0	36.5	12.4
9. A known Jew	−41.3	2.3	44.8	41.5
10. A known militarist	−62.0	−50.1	−42.1	−25.0
11. A light Negro	−82.1	−54.2	−54.7	−33.6
12. A dark Negro	−85.7	−66.0	−63.4	−49.4
13. A known radical	−88.0	−72.5	−63.6	−48.2
14. Person in bad health	−93.3	−87.9	−54.7	−89.6
15. A known Communist	−94.1	−83.2	−77.5	−57.9

SOURCE: Florence Greenhoe, *Community Contacts and Participation of Teachers,* American Council on Public Affairs, 1941, p. 32.

this preference is stated in municipal ordinances. In 28 percent of 1684 city systems residence was not a factor in teacher selection, and in 13 percent no local residents were appointed as new teachers until they had one or more years of teaching experience elsewhere.[33]

Recruitment of applicants for teaching positions is done primarily

[33] NEA Research Bulletin, *Teacher Personnel Procedures: Selection and Appointment,* March, 1942, p. 63.

through the placement bureaus of teachers colleges, arts colleges, and universities and through use of applications sent in voluntarily by candidates. These two ways were found in over 80 percent of 1790 city school systems. Use of commercial teachers agencies and recruitment in other school systems were next in importance, then inquiries at conventions and similar gatherings, and lastly the securing of names from state departments of education or state employment services. Five percent of these city school systems published announcements of positions to be filled. The most productive practices were the first two. It also appears that the smaller the community the greater the reliance upon the academic placement bureaus. The larger the city the more frequently individual voluntary applications are used.[34]

Practices in selecting teachers as reported in 1795 city school systems in order of frequency are: (1) personal interviews with applicants; (2) filling out of formal applications; (3) checking references; (4) requiring submission of transcript of credits; (5) observing classroom work of applicant; (6) verifying experience records reported by applicants; (7) establishing eligibility list; (8) requiring applicants to submit to a physical examination; (9) requiring applicants to take a written examination. The interview is generally carried out by the superintendent of schools, and this varies with size of city. In the larger cities the principal or other supervisory officer to whom the teacher is responsible or an assistant superintendent or personnel officer will do the interviewing. In slightly over 25 percent of the cities over 100,000, a committee of the school staff was assigned the responsibility for interviewing applicants. In one-third of the communities between 2500–5000, school board members interviewed applicants. This proportion decreased with city size. The general purposes of the interview in order of frequency reported by 1779 city school systems were: (1) a general appraisal of the candidate's personality; (2) opportunity to gain some insight into the candidate's educational philosophy and professional outlook; (3) opportunity to evaluate candidate's voice; (4) opportunity to get information on the candidate's education and experience; (5) opportunity to learn of candidate's ambitions and plans for the

[34] *Ibid.*, pp. 64–65.

future. Of minor importance was an oral examination on the subject matter the candidate proposed to teach.[35]

Most schools issue written contracts to teachers. This procedure is set in most states by law, and no contract is binding unless it complies with the legal specifications. In some cities and states where there is permanent tenure a written contract is not required for tenure teachers. The status of oral contracts varies with the states and court decisions. Minimum essentials of a teacher's contract suggested by the Committee on Tenure of the NEA are:

1. Definite statement as to length of school term.
2. Definite statement as to amount of salary.
3. Phraseology which is legally enforceable.
4. Specific legal requirements, such as the kind of certificate and any special provisions of state law that apply.
5. Definite date of notification of reelection (at least 30 days before termination and preferably 60 or 90 days).
6. Provisions for equal protection to employer and employee.[36]

When the beginning teacher enters a school, he will undergo some adjustment and orientation. If friendly assistance and good supervision are forthcoming, the new teacher may make a good start. If nothing is done, the initial experience may become quite traumatic with resulting loss of efficiency and morale. The following procedures were used in order of frequency by 1756 city school systems. Help given the new teacher in locating living quarters was first, though this ranged from 40 percent in the largest cities to 89 percent in the smallest. In 71 percent, conferences with new teachers were held soon after school opened at which their special problems were discussed. The proportion following this procedure varied only slightly in all the cities reporting. Personal copies of rules and regulations governing the school system were given to the new teachers in 67 percent of the school systems without much variation in the proportion by size of city. In 47 percent, a reception, tea, or other social function was held early in the year to welcome new teachers. This ranged from 20 percent in the largest cities to 49 percent in the smallest. In 24 percent, new teachers reported several days

[35] *Ibid.*, pp. 66–67.
[36] *Ibid.*, p. 71.

earlier than the other teachers for special meetings and discussions—range 8 to 26 percent. Other procedures are used. For example, in some systems an older teacher is designated to act as counselor and friend to each new teacher.[37]

THE TEACHER AND HIS JOB

How the professional educator views the job, how the teacher looks at it, and what can be objectively determined are quite different things. The problems will only be suggested, for here again the analysis by researchers of the teaching role in context has hardly been begun. The reason for this has been the psychological orientation in examining the teacher, which approach has resulted in exhaustive lists of traits correlated and factorized. Some of these lists read more like a list of all possible virtues. This atomistic, out-of-context examination of traits is perhaps not too friutful. The most creative teacher the author has encountered was a woman with a speech defect, one who was firm, even strict at times. On the basis of trait analysis she might be rated as a mediocre if not poor teacher.

THE PROFESSIONAL VIEW

While there may be variations, the interpretations of the teacher role made by professional educators tend to be similar to that pictured in the following quotation: "The teacher is a participating member of the class group, a friendly counselor, an expediter of the group's plans and a technician in group process. . . . He has visited most of his students' homes and has met the parents on various occasions through his room parents club. He has seen his students react to all kinds of social situations as a result of his participation with them in picnics, games, theater and bowling parties, and other kinds of social affairs." [38] He plays a non-punitive role. This chummy concept of the teacher who is just "like one of the gang" fits in with the fun-leisure time emphasis in our culture and especially with adolescent culture. There are few occupations dealing with human relations containing these overtones of the overgrown big pal,

[37] *Ibid.*, p. 74.
[38] Roland Faunce and Nelson Bossing, *Developing the Core Curriculum*, Prentice-Hall, Inc., 1951, pp. 167, 163.

buddy-buddy, confessor, parental surrogate. This concept is unrelated to the actualities of the age statuses and the legal statuses structuring behavior. Doubtless, a teacher can be friendly without having to entice and jolly his students into trained minds and good citizenship. If the above description of the teacher's role were translated into a time schedule, how much of his life would be his own? Perhaps the statement implies that there shouldn't be any. Perhaps also the students would not want the teacher around too much either. The teacher then not merely is a teacher but becomes, or is expected to become, something of a mental hygienist, counselor, occupational adviser, tester, individual and group therapist, social worker, sociometrician, and community worker, all wrapped in one chummy package, an occupational megalomania *par excellence*.

A bit more modest, though stressing conforming behavior, are some general standards of professional conduct suggested by the NEA. While almost all teacher codes stress *wholesome personality* and *high moral character* as essentials in teaching service, these terms need clarification. They do suggest a narcissistic adulation as if wholesome personality and high moral character are not essential to other occupations. Everybody, no doubt, is for this kind of personality and character. The following axioms of professional conduct are offered. The teacher's conduct should be such as will:

Keep him physically and mentally fit.
Be a worthy example for pupils.
Bring no reproach upon himself.
Bring no reproach upon the profession.
Conform, in general, to accepted standards in the community.
Contribute to harmony and mutual advantage in all professional relationships.[39]

A teacher is obligated, according to the NEA, to maintain a higher standard of personal conduct than members of other occupational groups in the same community on the grounds that for building the character of impressionable children example is stronger than precept and that teachers hired by a community as public employees must reasonably conform to the moral and social standards of the

[39] *Ethics for Teachers,* Department of Classroom Teachers and Research Division, National Education Association, August, 1945, p. 9.

community.[40] These notions are all normative provisions. But keeping oneself physically and mentally fit is not a simple matter of personal decision. What is a worthy example in a community with a delinquent subculture? Everybody is for virtue in the abstract, or expressed in creedal statements unrelated to life situations. The concrete meaning on the job, however, will vary by age, sex, and experience and will be complicated by the history and traditions of the school and the community.

A CASE OF TEACHER DEFINITION

The following case is not necessarily typical.[41] It is used to clarify a point. The schools are typed by social class, ranging from the slum school to the school in the "better" residential sectors. Children in these schools were characterized by interviewed teachers as:

Slum: difficult to teach, uncontrollable and violent in the sphere of discipline, and morally unacceptable on all scores, from physical cleanliness to the spheres of sex and "ambition to get ahead."

Upper group: quick learners, somewhat "spoiled" and difficult to control and lacking in the important moral traits of politeness and respect for elders.

Middle group: hard working but slow to learn, extremely easy to control, and most acceptable on the moral level.[42]

The interviewed teachers considered parents of the high-status group as "interfering parents" and threatening to the teacher's authority. Some principals and long-established teachers were likewise so regarded. In this context, teaching, discipline, and accepting the child differed markedly.[43] The chummy teacher role concept may be quite unworkable by an individual teacher in the two extremes, nor are the general standards advocated too meaningful in these contexts.

In this situation two career patterns develop. In the one case the teacher endeavors to move from the slum school to a better school

[40] Ibid., pp. 9–10.
[41] Howard S. Becker, "The Career of the Chicago Public Schoolteacher," American Journal of Sociology, March, 1952, pp. 470–477.
[42] Ibid., p. 472.
[43] Howard S. Becker, "Social Class Variations in the Teacher-Pupil Relationship," Journal of Educational Sociology, April, 1952, pp. 451–465.

in a better neighborhood. As most beginning teachers start in the bottom group schools, they endeavor to move on as soon as possible. Given the evaluation, the beginning teacher starts his career with an unpleasant experience. If he stays there for a few years, he may develop methods of control and teaching standards that would unfit him for the other schools. Thus, a premium is placed upon moving out. A high teacher turnover is one result. The second career pattern is to remain in the bottom group school, and this tendency occurs when the teacher has adapted his working skills to fit the situation, is accepted by his colleagues, respected for firmness by children, and recognized by the parents in the area. Teaching in the upper-stratum school is also not viewed as the most desirable situation, for here disdain, if not veiled contempt, by students and by parents structure the job negatively,[44] hence, the preference for the middle group.

A job is not merely a prescription in a textbook or a well-sounding code published by a professional organization. Its meaning lies in a setting, and the life of a teacher is organized or disorganized by playing out his role in a particular setting. The setting, however, need not be taken as a given. The relations in a bottom- or upper-stratum group need not involve the implicit negative evaluations and dissociative relations. Teachers can help to restructure these situations. Gangdom need not prevail on the lower levels [45] or snobbery on the upper. However, such restructuring will demand the coöperation of many individuals and groups.

FURTHER CONSIDERATIONS OF THE TEACHER'S JOB—CONTROL

The question is a matter of directing one's job and life independently or on the basis of expectations and actual control of and by others. The teacher is one who is especially marked to cater to the community, to participate in organizations to contribute to all fund-raising drives, to lead a rather strait-laced life. This is a stereotype

[44] This is seen very clearly in *Elmtown's Youth*, pp. 185–192.
[45] Cf. Sophia Robison, Nathan Cohen, and Murray Sachs, "Autonomous Groups: an Unsolved Problem in Group Loyalties and Conflicts," *Journal of Educational Sociology*, November, 1946, pp. 154–162; I. A. Rodehaffer, "Gangdom—Fists to Reason," *Journal of Educational Sociology*, February, 1944, pp. 406–415.

perhaps of the teacher as a community beast of burden, an image to be deplored from the teacher's point of view, one taken for granted on the part of the community. One interpretation of this situation is the fact that the teacher is in the community but not of it—in short, a stranger. Furthermore, as a stranger he is in a very significant area of living, dealing with the lives of children. As the stranger is not of the in-group, an unknown X, a carrier of possible divergent modes of acting and thinking, the tendency is to treat him with mistrust, to deal with him through utilitarian rather than identifying relations. In addition, there is the public servant concept, and the servant is in a utilitarian subordinate position to the controlling master, viz., the community.

The first thesis is a sociological view of the teacher's standing in a community, and the second is part of the teacher-image promoted by professional educators. There may be a certain validity to this sociological view in smaller communities, provided the teacher really is an outsider, but in so far as there is selection from local candidates, the thesis is untenable. There is also a question of how long a teacher remains a stranger. Will this view of him continue after five, ten, twenty years of residence? In large cities where most people have segmental, utilitarian relations, where many of them are strangers to one another, this thesis may also be untenable. Perhaps the master-servant concept may be more fruitful in itself or in combination with the stranger thesis. Are there any data that may throw some light on this?

The stranger is a mobile person, shifting from community to community. Yet out of 9122 teachers asked about changing teacher location, i.e., from one school to another within the same community, or between different communities, almost 75 percent changed from zero to two times, and about 8 percent changed five or more times.[46] This fact does not suggest a high mobility. Teachers are not migratory persons. The amount of movement also varies with other factors. Fewer changes are found in the larger communities and in schools with higher salaries, but the longer the teaching the greater number of positions reported. The distance traveled by teachers tends to be rather restricted; i.e., they tend to stay within

[46] Florence Greenhoe, *op. cit.*, p. 20.

the local region.[47] A more recent study might show more mobility. At any rate this information does qualify the stranger thesis.

Perhaps the master-servant concept coupled with the social origins of teachers and sex status may be more useful in promoting understanding of the teacher-community relation. According to Richey and Fox, 38 percent of group T moderately or strongly approved of community control of teachers' out-of-school conduct as compared to 24 percent of group O. Woman future teachers were more conservative than the men. The proportions moderately or strongly disapproving of such control were 53 and 60 percent respectively.[48]

Table 48 shows an interesting ambivalence between these two student groups. Group T expect such controls over their activities and group O by implication do not. The future teachers suggest conforming, conservative conduct. The attitudes of group O also imply control on three points: (1) that a teacher's political and religious views should be examined when considering him for a position, (2) that teachers should not join a union, and (3) that teachers should not be politically active. Since students tend to originate in the lower occupational groups or at the lower end of a higher occupational group, acceptability and respectability are necessary phases for success in this mobility, hence, conforming, conservative conduct.

When specific items of control are examined, the generalized attitude noted is modified. This is seen in Tables 48 and 49. The two sets of data are not exactly comparable for in the one case approval and disapproval refers to control by a school board and in the second the behavior itself is evaluated. Despite this difference there is some similarity between the ratings of the students in the two cases. Group T again tends to be more conforming than group O. The latter are much more "liberal" in rejecting controls for the woman teacher. Control of personal behavior by a school board is firmly disapproved for both sexes by both student groups. However, these data suggest the assumption of greater liberality for men and stricter controls over women. Women raters are easier on men and

[47] *Ibid.*, p. 21.
[48] *Op. cit.*, p. 35.

TABLE 48. Approval and Disapproval of Control by the School Board of Specific Behavior Patterns of Men and Women Teachers by Students Selecting and Not Selecting Teaching as a Vocation

Behavior Patterns	Teacher Students			Nonteacher Students		
	Men	Women	Total	Men	Women	Total
Complete approval	100	100	100	100	100	100
Drinking in public						
Women	43	22	32	2	8	4
Men	38	20	28	−5	5	−2
Playing cards for money						
Women	14	3	4	−24	−24	−24
Men	10	−6	2	−27	−26	−26
Smoking in public						
Women	−20	−9	−14	−30	−41	−34
Men	−40	−51	−46	−33	−30	−32
Drinking in private						
Women	−28	−24	−26	−44	−50	−46
Men	−42	−28	−34	−44	−52	−46
Dating						
Women	−52	−50	−50	−53	−67	−57
Men	−55	−52	−54	−55	−68	−59
Playing cards for fun						
Women	−60	−50	−54	−54	−69	−58
Men	−63	−49	−56	−54	−68	−58
Dancing in public						
Women	−52	−54	−53	−54	−68	−58
Men	−53	−55	−54	−56	−70	−60
Smoking in private						
Women	−52	−46	−49	−57	−72	−62
Men	−61	−50	−55	−59	−70	−62
Index of median weight	−46	−48	−48	−49	−60	−52
Complete disapproval	−100	−100	−100	−100	−100	−100

SOURCE: Robert Richey and William Fox, *An Analysis of Various Factors Associated with the Selection of Teaching as a Vocation,* Bulletin of the School of Education, Indiana University, May, 1948, p. 39.

harder on their own sex. The reverse holds true for men. This fact indicates the significance of the sex status as a controlling factor. These various points are corroborated by Table 49. The degrees of liberality of the three groups of raters mentioned previously appear likewise in these specific ratings, with school board members the less liberal and the education students the most. The divergence of the student ratings from those of the school board members is

TABLE 49. Net Approval and Disapproval Reactions of Representative Groups to Teacher Behavior

| | As Rated By | | | | | |
| | School Board Members 356 | | Teachers 9122 | | Students 1363 | |
Teacher Behavior	Male [a]	Female	Male	Female	Male	Female
1. Owning an automobile	61.3	60.0	64.4	59.6	81.0	79.3
2. Dating a town person	31.7	28.9	49.7	46.5	65.8	64.2
3. Dating another teacher	19.6	19.5	35.2	40.5	67.3	66.7
4. Leaving area over week ends [b]	0.8	0.9	9.9	5.5	5.8	−6.7
5. Pay for coaching, speaking, etc.	2.8	−3.1	30.4	29.0	23.3	21.8
6. Single teachers living in apartment	−6.2	11.2	24.6	24.5	36.4	29.7
7. Buying clothes, etc., outside area	−8.5	19.4	−4.3	−4.0	−1.6	−1.5
8. Smoking in private	−9.8	−46.2	11.5	11.2	35.0	1.4
9. Not attending church	−9.9	−69.0	−54.8	−54.5	−61.6	−62.2
10. Playing cards for money	−18.2	−56.6	−69.2	−70.0	−72.3	−77.6
11. Joining teachers union	−22.5	−23.1	9.1	8.5	22.2	22.4
12. Dancing at public dance	−23.9	−26.4	5.7	4.2	25.7	19.0
13. Playing pool or billiards	−25.0	−28.2	−8.0	−17.8	−3.6	−47.2
14. Living outside community	−27.2	−29.7	−11.7	−10.8	−37.4	−39.1
15. Teaching controversial issues [c]	−34.9	−36.7	−1.2	−1.4	34.2	32.9
16. Smoking in public	−48.1	−80.7	−25.2	−61.0	−16.1	−66.7
17. Playing cards for fun	−48.1	16.9	54.3	54.5	66.8	76.1
18. Making a political speech	−55.7	−55.9	−34.9	−40.5	−53.7	−60.3
19. Running for political office	−56.1	−56.4	−33.4	−34.2	−58.4	−57.7
20. Drinking alcoholic liquors	−80.1	−81.3	−71.8	−73.2	−76.5	−76.7
21. Dating a student	−86.0	−65.7	−84.4	−86.4	−68.8	−76.7
22. Use of rouge, etc., by a woman		0.4		45.5		65.3
23. Woman teaching after marriage [d]		−43.2		4.7		25.5

[a] Male (teacher); female (teacher).
[b] Item reads in questionnaire: "Leaving community often over week-ends."
[c] Item reads: "Teaching controversial social issues in the classroom."
[d] Item reads: "A woman who continues to teach after marriage."
SOURCE: Florence Greenhoe, *Community Contacts and Participation of Teachers*, American Council on Public Affairs, 1941, p. 51.

quite marked. The school board members apparently conceive of teachers as emotional, social, political, and intellectual eunuchs. Doubtless, few board members would like to have such restrictions placed upon their lives. Given the erotic, leisure-time, political patterns of the culture, where exhortation to get out and participate in all these areas is blared at everyone through the mass media of communication, where most people, with some social class variation, indulge in these activities anyway, the notion of the aseptic, astringent, asexual teacher is unrealistic if not schizoid. In their evaluation the students reject this idea, preferring to be like anyone else. This jejune view is diplomatically modified by the teachers in a somewhat compromise set of ratings, but this fact signifies acquiescence to control over their personal lives by board and community. In these data the woman teacher is again most subject to control, in contrast to men, and the sex status determination of ratings also appears.[49] In addition, there is an inverse relation between size of community and disapproval of the types of teacher behavior studied. There are two exceptions—drinking in public and dating a student.[50] On teachers' reaction to community control of their conduct about 45 percent reported acceptance, 10 percent rebellion, 1 percent protest, 5 percent evasion, around 18 percent education of community to greater tolerance, 5 percent miscellaneous, with 15 percent not reporting.[51]

If teachers are strangers, practice a master-servant relation in a community, or are socially mobile individuals, this should reflect itself in their participation in organizations. On the basis of the first point, they would be less likely to be in or support community organizations. Teachers are outsiders and not too acceptable. On the basis of the second point, they might be required indirectly to participate in and support various organizations. And on the basis of the last, teachers would join for matters of furthering their mobility. The data show that in general teachers do not participate in or support community organizations or social groups, with the exception of their professional and school related organizations and

[49] *Ibid.*, pp. 52–53; John Huer, "A Public View of the Teacher," *Journal of Teacher Education*, September, 1954, pp. 202–204.
[50] Florence Greenhoe, *op. cit.*, p. 51; John Huer, *op. cit.*, p. 204; Phillipps Breman, "Community Control of Teacher Behavior," *Journal of Teacher Education*, December, 1951, p. 299.
[51] Florence Greenhoe, *op. cit.*, p. 56.

the church. A few participate in relief-welfare groups and fraternal organizations.[52] The first point appears validated until the question is raised as to how typical or untypical the behavior of the teacher is as compared with that of other groups.[53] The Komarovsky study of urbanites concludes that the majority of the citizens are non-participants in special social groups. Except for members of the upper strata who belong for matters of influence and control, most persons either do not belong to special groups or follow the teacher pattern, i.e., belonging to groups linked with the occupation, church, welfare, and fraternal groups. This is the American pattern. The teacher moves within this pattern as set by his profession, by his sex, and by expense and time considerations. Many groups are monosexual rather than bisexual in composition, and many service and economic organizations are for men only. Given the number of females in the teacher field, this fact may account for the small proportion of teachers in some of these organizations. Further, many companies, for matters of public relations and influence, encourage their personnel to join special groups, frequently paying membership fees, dues, and other assessments.

As to the problem of control, the following may be concluded. By virtue of the master-servant concept of the teaching job, teachers may implicitly invite such control even though they are against it, an interesting ambivalence between the job concept and the personal, private life concept. The master-servant idea may have a linkage with sex status in terms of a spinster-drudge view of teachers,[54] i.e., the odd, single female who does all the dirty work in the house, the member of the family who is the servant—and in this context, servant to the community. Much of the control is likely to represent the heritage of the protection of the female, who not so

[52] *Ibid.*, pp. 62–74; Leo Alilunus, "The Community Life of Teachers," *Journal of Teacher Education*, September, 1955, pp. 193–195; Martin Quanbeck, "A Study of the Alumni of Ten Minnesota Colleges," *Journal of Teacher Education*, December, 1953, pp. 295–299.

[53] Mirra Komarovsky, "The Voluntary Associations of Urban Dwellers," *American Sociological Review*, December, 1946, pp. 686–698. Cf. W. Lloyd Warner, Marchia Meeker, and Kenneth Eells, *Social Class in America*, Science Research Associates, 1949, p. 95.

[54] Cf. William Dean Howells' comment on teachers and education in *A Traveler from Altruria*, quoted in Howard Jones and Ernest Leisy (eds.), *Major American Writers*, Harcourt, Brace and Company, 1939, pp. 1305–1339.

long ago was considered a minor in law. The Puritan heritage may also animate this control, and this heritage may be stronger in small communities. If the teacher hired is nonlocal and if the community is under 10,000 or rural, more control is likely to take place, diminishing as the community increases in size. This control presents a source of friction and conflict which cannot be rationalized away, and it is a factor in teacher turnover. One way out of the dilemma is to strengthen teaching as a profession. Professionalization is a slow process; only in the past forty years has much progress been made. Professionalization is a collective process, carried out by groups rather than individuals. This leads to our next topic.

TEACHER ORGANIZATION

The improvement of the prospects of an occupational group is linked up with organization, collective action on the part of the members. The obvious case is the trade union movement. The objective is to control the job for its members. To attain this objective the group attempts a high degree of closure, setting forth admission requirements to limit membership, and it also attempts a job imperialism by controlling as many job opportunities as possible. Once the workers are organized, efforts can be directed to controlling or influencing wages and conditions of work. This approach to improving one's vocational status is traditionally associated only with the unions. It seems quite clear that professional organization does not differ one bit from union organization, except perhaps in the narcissistic illusions of superiority of the white collar over the sweaty collar. The close-knit, monopolistic, monolithic organizations of the American Medical Association and the American Bar Association would draw sighs of envy from any trade union leader. There is an extraordinary degree of closure, of control of members, and of working conditions by these organizations. In fact, without membership in these groups it is extraordinarily difficult or almost impossible to practice the profession; in short, a real closed shop is in existence. Professionalization means, then, the developing of closure and the controlling of conditions of work. The closure is set by high training requirements, licenses, and certification. Ideally, it would also include limiting access to training, either by high entrance requirements or by limiting the number of training institutions. An artificial scarcity of trained personnel could thus be maintained, and in this way the group can become powerful, especially when in strategic positions such as in medicine and law. This tendency appears in all the professions, including teaching. The difference with teachers is that there is no one great encompassing organization but a split between those who would ally themselves with the trade union movement and those who would follow professional pretensions. The one sector feels that a teacher is a worker, like any other worker, and thus should follow aggressive collective bargaining tactics. The other thinks that such conduct is not becoming to a profession and thus would prefer a more genteel, dignified approach. The first sector is organized as the American Federation of Teachers, affiliated with the American Federation of Labor, now AFL-CIO. The second sector comprises the National Education Association of the United States, usually referred to as the NEA.

THE AMERICAN FEDERATION OF TEACHERS, AFL-CIO

The first labor union oriented teacher organization was organized in 1897 as the Chicago Teachers Federation, which has continued, since then, to be a strong and vigorous group. The group first to affiliate with the American Federation of Labor was the San Antonio, Texas, Public School Teachers Association, 1902. Growth of such locals has not been spectacular In 1916 there were twenty locals with the American Federation of Labor, and in that year the American Federation of Teachers was organized. In 1951 there were 50,000 members in locals of the American Federation of Teachers, concentrated primarily in large industrial centers. In 1952 the AFT claimed locals in all of the twenty-five largest cities in the nation except for three in Texas. It had locals in 75 percent of the cities of 100,000 and over and in 50 percent of the cities 25,000 and over. One might surmise that the AFT is conspicuously absent in smaller communities. Given the type of teacher control previously described, and given also the animus against teacher unions by school board members, lay persons, and even teachers themselves, it is not surprising that the growth of the AFT has been slow and concentrated in the large urban centers. Locals of the AFT are found in all states with the exception of Mississippi, New Mexico, Oklahoma, South Carolina, Utah, and Wyoming.

This group attempts to follow collective bargaining procedures or at any rate a more aggressive approach than the NEA. Twenty-nine percent of the strikes shown in Table 50 were carried out by

TABLE 50.   Work Stoppages Involving Teachers, 1940–52

Year	Stoppages Beginning in Year		Average Duration Calendar Days	Number of Work Stoppages by Issue		
	Number	Workers Involved		Wage and Hours	Organiza-tional [a]	Other [b]
1940	2	100	9.5	—	—	2
1941	1	120	2.0	1	—	—
1942	2	170	28.5	—	—	2
1943	2	100	3.5	2	—	—
1944	4	1,710	11.3	3	—	1
1945	1	15	17.0	—	1	—
1946	16	3,060	13.3	—	4	1
1947	20	4,720	7.3	16	—	4
1948	12	4,210	8.3	4	3	5
1949	9	440	3.7	3	2	4
1950	4	90	8.3	2	2	—
1951	10	4,510	12.1	4	1	5
1952	7	1,570	4.4	4	—	3
Totals	90	20,815	9.1	50	13	27
Percent				56	14	30

[a] Organizational: strike to gain recognition of a union or professional association, strengthening bargaining position, and to protest discrimination. Wages and hours are an important element also.
[b] Job security, physical and administrative school conditions and policies, and re-lated problems.
SOURCE: Bernard Yabroff and Lily David, "Collective Bargaining and Work Stop-pages Involving Teachers," *Monthly Labor Review,* May, 1953, p. 478.

locals of the AFT. This group also attempts to influence public opinion through publication and other propaganda methods. It has lobbied before state legislatures and Congress. In general it has a no-strike policy, first stated in 1947 and reaffirmed in 1951. Some states prohibit strikes by government employees, so that teachers could not strike anyway. However, the AFT has supported two strikes, the first in St. Paul, Minnesota, in 1946. In this particular strike the entire personnel of the school system stopped work, supported by almost every community group. The second case was in Pawtucket, Rhode Island, in 1951.

THE NATIONAL EDUCATION ASSOCIATION
OF THE UNITED STATES

The NEA in its own words makes no small claims: "The National Education Association is the only organization that represents or has the possibility of representing the great body of teachers in the United States. . . . The NEA is related to the teacher profession of this country somewhat as the American Medical Association is to the medical profession and the American Bar Association is to the legal profession." [55] It further characterizes itself as an independent, voluntary, nongovernmental organization of educators living and working in the United States.

The growth of the NEA has been quite slow. It began in 1857 with forty-eight members. Between 1887 and 1918 it fluctuated between nine and ten thousand members, a minute proportion of teachers. In 1906 it received a charter from Congress "to elevate the character and advance the interests of the profession of teaching, and to promote the cause of education in the United States." In 1920 the membership was 52,850. The progress of the organization dates from this period. In 1955 the NEA claimed 613,000 individual members and 1,083,000 affiliated members in sixty-six state and 5542 affiliated associations.[56] Pressure to participate in the NEA or affiliates is strong and may account in part for the large membership.

The structure of the NEA is quite complex with 30 departments, 13 headquarters divisions, and 24 commissions and committees. The NEA believes in a decentralized system of schools and in local and state control of public education, though supporting federal aid to schools by vote of its Representative Assembly. The NEA does not

[55] *National Education Association of the United States,* pamphlet, n.d., pp. 6–7, 1.
[56] *Ibid.,* p. 6.

control selection of textbooks, curriculum content, or teaching methods and materials, as some critics maintain. It has no authority to do that. It carries on international activities through membership in the World Confederation of Organizations of the Teaching Profession and through its membership in UNESCO. It supports teachers who claim that they have been unjustly treated. It conducts research and carries on an extensive program of publication. It has represented teachers before legislatures and Congress. For this activity it has been accused of being a school lobby by other lobbying organizations, e.g., state chambers of commerce.

Prior to World War II the NEA was characterized as an administrator-dominated organization with a very conservative attitude toward social action.[57] Officials were reluctant to stand up for local teachers and fend off attacks upon the schools until teachers forced a constitutional reform in 1934. The NEA during this period did publish fair salary schedules and lists of fair personnel practices. It did advocate some local NEA representation, but on the whole the organization as controlled was timid and very conservative. In 1947 it was realized that the teachers' situation on the matter of salaries was not to be improved by individual bargaining, and a resolution was passed to use group action to obtain salary increases. This policy correlated with the increase in teacher strikes (Table 49). The NEA also has a no-strike policy, and striking is considered an utterly unprofessional type of behavior or, in the words of one commentator, a "professional disgrace."[58] Instead of plebeian worker tactics, professional decorum and "democratic persuasion" are to be used. However, some rank and file disagree with this view. Of the strikes given in the table, 25 percent were carried out by local NEA affiliates. The one case in which the NEA supported a teacher work stoppage was in Norwalk, Connecticut, in 1946, but it was argued that there was no strike since the teachers had not signed any contract; no contract, no work—thus, no existing agreement was violated by the strike.

[57] Howard K. Beale, *Are American Teachers Free?* Charles Scribner's Sons, 1936, pp. 52–53, 692–702.
[58] S. Mackenzie, "Teacher Strikes, a Professional Disgrace," *Nation's Schools*, July, 1947, pp. 54–55.

IMPROVING CONDITIONS—STRIKE OR PERSUASION

Teacher strikes are not peculiar to the United States. They have occurred in recent years in France, Norway, and Italy.[59] The trend in the United States correlated with the rapid inflation which occurred after removal of price controls. As the table shows, the majority of the cases involved the problem of wages and hours. It might be assumed that the decision to strike must have occurred in a most intolerable situation, given professional scruples against such behavior. Even in labor relations the strike is a last resort to the breakdown of collective bargaining, and again it may be assumed that boards of education may have turned deaf ears to requests for better salaries. It is difficult for a teacher to enforce a request for an increase in salary since each contract is an individual contract. Furthermore, if a strike takes place, a teacher may be discharged for conduct unbecoming to the profession or for insubordination, violating an order of the board to desist from such behavior. The teacher finds himself in a social trap. Unless teacher bargaining includes all school districts in an area, equivalent to industry-wide bargaining, the results are of little value. A strike may dramatize the teacher's plight, and for that reason may be of propaganda value. If there is public support, crucial in all work stoppages, then progress may be made, as happened in St. Paul, in Norwalk, and in the state of Utah.

While a school district is an independent corporation, it still is regarded as an agency of the state, its special creation to further its purposes. For this reason and also because of legal restrictions, the strike is not an effective approach. Democratic persuasion with a local board may be equally ineffective, especially if a board views its relation to teachers in master-servant terms. In order to advance the welfare of the profession as a whole, action of teachers must be political, i.e., to lobby for favorable legislation, for the legal order sets the basic framework for schools. While there is an animus against political activities by teachers, political action appears to be

[59] *Time Education Supplement,* March 23, 1951, p. 230; November 13, 1953, p. 963; April 16, 1954, p. 375; December 9, 1955, p. 1269.

the main route not only to professionalization but also to better salaries, pensions, and other conditions of work.

Lobbying is a form of democratic persuasion involving the right to petition. As groups attempt to persuade legislators to follow a course of action, they do not look upon one another with favor or respect. Each lobby hopes to appear righteous and concerned with public welfare, implying that any other lobby is greedy and selfish. In contrast to their own conduct, lobbies based on economic interest try to portray the lobbying of teachers as untruthful, selfish, and power-mad, raiding the public treasury for higher salaries and demanding other privileges, such as tenure (the shield for the incompetent), pensions (at taxpayers' expense), etc. Since part of the lobbying which teachers indulge in does involve a quest for money, it is easy to charge crass materialism to a group supposedly devoted to service. Implicit in such attack is the assumption that teachers should not have the right to petition or at any rate that they should not use it. A servant should not act as the master does. Such unfriendly attacks are a natural phase of lobbying. Representatives of teacher organizations have forthrightly denounced such unethical imputations to their actions. Since details of the teacher's status are legally determined in most cases, change must be through law. The lobby approach is the only alternative to acquiescing to an unchanging *status quo*.

SUMMARY

As an occupation teaching involves both economic and noneconomic factors. The supply of and demand for teachers vary with economic conditions so that in good times people are more likely to enter more remunerative fields. Chronic shortage in the elementary field has not brought about higher salaries to attract personnel. Taking salary schedules as they are found in different systems, one can see that entrance to the field is motivated by more than monetary considerations. It appears that persons entering the teaching field have a service ideal. Recruitment techniques stress this point. Teaching also represents for some an avenue of advancement from lower occupational strata. For others it is a means to maintaining status.

The social position of the teacher and the associated sex status (a job usually for females) imparts a great stress on conformity and respectability. When a person formally enters a teaching position, he is frequently subjected to strong community controls, stemming out of a community evaluation of the teacher which is tacitly supported by a master-servant concept entertained by the profession. If the teacher is regarded as a stranger in the community, controls are likely to be firm. These controls fall unequally upon men and women teachers, with greater restrictions placed upon the latter. To better his position, the teacher, like the worker, has organized, though he prefers to use methods that he thinks befit his profession. One of the major means to advance the profession is favorable legislation. Teachers become lobbyists. Consequently they are involved in the rough and tumble of politics and propaganda, pressure and counterpressure. In Part VI we want to examine the pressures and attacks that have been made upon the profession and the schools.

Selected Readings

EDUCATION

Elsbree, Willard, *The American Teacher*, American Book Company, 1939.

Huggett, Albert, and Stinnett, T. M., *Professional Problems of Teachers*, The Macmillan Company, 1956.

Kirkpatrick, William (ed.), *The Teacher and Society*, First Yearbook of the John Dewey Society, D. Appleton-Century Company, 1937.

Opinions of the Committee on Professional Ethics, National Education Association, June, 1955.

Richey, Robert, Dunfee, Maxine, and Hoppe, Arthur, *Planning for Teaching*, McGraw-Hill Book Company, 1952.

Rugg, Harold, and Brooks, Marian, *The Teacher in School and Society*, World Book Company, 1950, chap. 9.

Teachers' Opinions on Ethics in the Teaching Profession,

SOCIOLOGY

Hiller, E. T., *Social Relations and Structures*, Harper & Brothers, 1947, chaps. 33 and 34.

Parsons, Talcott, *Essays in Sociological Theory Pure and Applied*, The Free Press, 1949, chap. 8.

Waller, Willard, *The Sociology of Teaching*, John Wiley and Sons, 1932, chap. 5.

CHAPTER 17

Teaching and Bureaucracy

As A teacher is certified and employed, he immediately and simultaneously is involved in many social dimensions. These will consist of the legal order, especially as crystallized in a state department of education, the local school system (the county, city, or township board and schools under its jurisdiction), the particular school, and the local community. The first three dimensions may be viewed as a unit. Each may be analyzed independently of the other. Nevertheless, these various phases work together, are connected in many ways, and thus may be considered as one pattern. This type of structure is labeled a bureaucracy. Unfortunately, the word "bureaucracy" has a negative quality in popular thinking, standing for inefficiency, red tape, official buck passing, regimentation, and similar emotional evaluations. The word "bureaucrat" calls forth an image of a narrow-minded, regulation-conscious, inflexible, petty, and autocratic individual. The terms "bureaucracy" and "bureaucrat" are simply epithets. Where emotional responses prevail, insight is likely to be lacking. To rail against bureaucracy is something like Don Quixote's attacking windmills. Bureaucratic structures are a stubborn fact of modern life. They represent the dominant form in which modern life has shaped itself. Hence, the cultural landscape is dotted with religious bureaucracies, business and industrial bureaucracies, trade union bureaucracies, political bureaucracies, and educational bureaucracies. The form of all of these types tends to be similar, and the problems arising in each likewise tend to be the same.

The objective in this section is to examine the operation of this type of structure as a whole. The position of the teacher is one among many within a bureaucratic structure. Our focus is upon the nature of these positions and upon the problems which arise in this type of organization. Our use of the word "bureaucracy" is wholly objective, in the sense that the term refers to a phase of living that needs understanding. Praise or blame is irrelevant. Bureaucracy will not be downed by individual attitude or fiat.

THE NATURE OF BUREAUCRATIC ORGANIZATION

Wherever large-scale organization takes place, it will be in the form of bureaucracy. In fact, there is as yet no device to take its place. The coördination of large numbers of persons is not the crux of bureaucratic organization. It may be provisionally defined as a technical and/or administrative organization designed to carry out the purposes of a group. This is to suggest the cultural and social quality of the organization. The words "technical" and "administrative" imply both a planned or rational organization and a complex division of labor. The definition may be extended by stating that bureaucracy is an organization operated by experts according to rationally determined principles or that it is an organization operating according to calculable rules and calculable results without regard to persons. The last phrase stresses the impersonal character of this type of organization, the irrelevance of personal bonds and loyalties, an idea similar to that of a government by law rather than by men.

There are three important phases of bureaucratic organization: spheres of jurisdiction, hierarchy, and professionalization. The first refers to functions, the second to control, and the third to the expert.[1]

[1] Max Weber, *Grundriss der Sozialökonomik*, J. C. B. Mohr, 2nd ed., 1925, pp. 650–678.

SPHERES OF JURISDICTION

A bureaucracy may be viewed as an organization composed of departments, bureaus, divisions, offices. Each of these represents an area of official duties. The functions and authority of each are fixed and defined: what is to be done, what cannot be done, and what the proper relations to other areas are. Such a bundle of tasks and authority is a sphere of jurisdiction. It may be narrow or large depending upon its position in the overall structure. Thus, some spheres may be dominantly decision making, as a board of education, or they may be executive and administrative, as in the superintendency, or they may be task performing, as in teaching. The areas of jurisdiction are fixed by rules or administrative regulations. In the school these are defined basically in the legal code. A board of education, moveover, has the power to prescribe additional duties and delegate authority to the various divisions and offices under its jurisdiction, provided these do not conflict with the state code. It is this type of job specification that involves the calculable rules. In this way precision and efficiency of action are to be maximized. An individual, thus, knows what he can and cannot do, and he can act in a determinate way by orienting himself to the fixed and defined functions and authority prescribed for his position.

Two other characteristics of bureaucratic organization are linked with the spheres of jurisdiction. One is the development of office or bureau management. This is an area of official duties itself, and the major task here is to facilitate the operation of the total structure. The personnel consists of administrators, administrative assistants, supervisors, minor executives, divisional superintendents, and others. Office and bureau management represents specialization in dealing with rules and regulations. These functionaries have the task of telling the technicians, professionals, and "bosses" what they can do and cannot do. They have a rule- and duty-clarifying function. Personnel management is one form of this type of jurisdiction. Its job is to see that the organization runs smoothly, that grievances and disputes are appropriately handled, that conflict is held down to a minimum, that the division of labor is geared together effectively. The second characteristic involves methodical provisions for the regular and continuous fulfillment of the prescribed duties by a qualified personnel. This is a problem of recruiting trained persons and the rule of competence is the determining one. This is another way of saying that position in bureaucratic structure is not for amateurs. To check on competence of performance, job ratings usually are made, upon which decisions about dismissal, promotion, demotion, or transfer to another position will be made. The criterion, it must be emphasized, is that of competence, so that evaluations based on race, creed, color, or national origin are irrational from the standpoint of bureaucratic organization.

HIERARCHICAL STRUCTURE

The various spheres of jurisdiction are organized on a scale of authority, i.e., a system of graded authority. Authority in this case has reference to the right and duty to issue directives in accordance with the rules to achieve the purposes of the organizations. This type of authority, as in the case of Plato's pilot, is based on the rule of competence. It is not power as an end in itself. The concept of graded authority means that the lower offices will be supervised and directed by the higher. In general, task functions prevail in the lower and policy making in the upper positions. The bottom offices, then, have no authority.

The hierarchical structure involves two additional characteristics. Since it is a graded structure of authority, proper lines or channels of communication are worked out. Authority is, thus, not capricious or arbitrary. The transmission of directives is clearly demarcated as they are sent from one area of jurisdiction to the other. As a rule, appeals, requests for information or interpretation, or progress reports move from the lower offices to the higher, and this type of information also moves in a set pattern. The violation of this procedure is referred to as "going over somebody's head," ignoring intermediary authorities and contacting the higher. The concepts of appropriate channels of communication has reference to facilitating the operation of the organization. The second feature in this structure is the reliance upon the written document. Bureaucracy may be viewed as management and performance based upon the written document, summed in the concept of "the files." Correspondence, reports, circulars, originals or copies, top-secret, secret, confidential, for administrative use only—all this constitutes the paper work that is thought to be the major characteristic of bureaucratic organization. Without such material circulating through the proper channels of communication, bureaucracy could not function. The permanence of bureaucracy rests in its files; access to the files becomes of crucial importance. Access will be differentiated according to the authority of a sphere of jurisdiction. Unauthorized access is a major problem, whether in terms of personnel within the structure or in terms of outsiders attempting to secure confidential information.

PROFESSIONALIZATION

The relation of an incumbent to his job is that of the trained expert. It is the acceptance of the obligation to fulfill faithfully his official duties in return for income. The loyalty of the incumbent is not to persons but to the office, to impersonal purposes. Duty to office in a relatively closed system is one feature, and this relation is also spelled out in the legal code.

Professionalization means that the office is viewed as a vocation or career. Prerequisites of training are set forth, thus excluding the unqualified from incumbency. Certification, licensing, or examinations qualify the individual as a trained expert. The professional vocation is a career, a lifetime preoccupation of the person. In terms of bureaucratic organization, this means that personal position involves appointment by a superior, tenure, and a fixed salary according to kind of function or rank, and length of service. It means that career opportunities are within the organization, and a successful career represents advancement to the policy-making or top administrative spheres of jurisdiction.

POSSIBILITY OF CHANGE

In recent years, modifications have been taking place in bureaucratic organization. Instead of monolithic units of specialized functions and graded authority, there is a tendency to "decentralization." In business this trend is toward the operating independence of the producing unit. In religion, some form of congregationalism has always limited central control. In education, there is a slow trend toward the relative autonomy of the local school unit. This trend may modify greatly the notions of higher and lower levels in school organization and foster the concept of the equality of colleagues.

SCHOOL SYSTEMS AS BUREAUCRATIC STRUCTURES

"School system" will refer to the administrative area over which a board of education has jurisdiction, be this on a township, district, county, or municipal basis. Each of these will involve variations in bureaucratic organization. Since all of them cannot be considered, only certain types will be examined.[2]

SPHERES OF JURISDICTION IN THE SCHOOL

When a teacher enters a school system, his view of the whole will be limited by his particular spot. The significance of his spot will vary with the size of the school and the position of the school in the total structure. The concept of the school may thus range from a primary group quality to a very impersonal quality, since bureaucratic structure is in some cases rather rudimentary and in others quite complex, depending on size and location.

The smaller the school and school system, the less bureaucratic it is. We find this illustrated in the following data, taking the high school as our example. Most high schools tend to be rather small (Table 51). Seventy-five percent had an enrollment of less than 300 students. The giant high school is rather rare. Of 24,314 high schools in 1946, 3 percent had enrollments of 1500 and over, and one-tenth of one percent (nineteen schools) of 5000 and over.[3] The size of professional staff in 1946 for four-year high schools ranged from one to over a hundred. In 82.5 percent of these schools the professional staff had twelve or less individuals. Ninety-five schools (.8 percent)

[2] Cf. Arthur Moehlman, *School Administration*, Houghton Mifflin Company, 1940, for a summary of variations.
[3] *How Large Are Our High Schools*, Circular No. 304, Office of Education, Federal Security Agency, Government Printing Office, 1949, p. 19.

TABLE 51. Size of High School by Enrollment, 1930, 1938, 1946

Enrollments	1930		1938		1946	
	Number	Percent	Number	Percent	Number	Percent
10– 24	2,077	9.4	1,372	5.6	975	4.1
25– 49	3,866	17.4	2,643	10.7	2,686	11.2
50– 74	3,521	15.8	3,051	12.4	3,117	13.0
75– 99	2,543	11.4	2,661	10.8	2,548	10.6
100– 199	4,603	20.7	6,407	26.1	5,920	24.7
200– 299	1,633	7.3	2,561	10.4	2,643	11.0
300– 499	1,478	6.7	2,271	9.2	2,376	10.0
500– 999	1,421	6.4	1,940	7.9	2,212	9.3
1,000–2,499	934	4.2	1,444	5.9	1,328	5.5
2,500 and over	161	.7	240	1.0	142	.6
Total	22,237	100.0	24,590	100.0	23,947	100.0

SOURCE: *How Large Are Our High Schools,* Circular No. 304, Office of Education, Federal Security Agency, 1949, p. 19. Includes all public high schools except those enrolling fewer than ten pupils and the ungraded or evening high schools.

had over one hundred.[4] In 1951–52 in high schools from 500 to 5000 enrollment there were 26,347 custodians, of which 19,525 were male and 6822 female. There was an average of six custodians per school. The average number of professional staff per custodian was 7.7.[5] For the same year and type of schools there were 10,668 full-time clerical workers, of which 10,096 were female and 572 male. Average number of clerks per school was 2.4. The average number of professional staff per clerk was 18.9.[6] The structure of the school in terms of professional staff, custodians, and clerical workers, thus, varies enormously, creating a real qualitative and organizational difference. In 1949, for example, Seward Consolidated High School, Illinois, had twelve students and one teacher, while Austin High School, Chicago, had 5671 students and 204 teachers. However, the bureaucratic structure becomes most evident in those systems where enrollment is in the thousands and teachers and other professional staff number in the hundreds.

[4] *Ibid.,* p. 20.
[5] Ellsworth Tompkins and Mabel Rice, *Clerical and Custodial Staff in Public Secondary Schools,* Circular No. 445, Office of Education, U.S. Department of Health, Education, and Welfare, Government Printing Office, 1955, pp. 8–9.
[6] *Ibid.*

The Board of Education. As we have previously seen, the state establishes a corporation, the school district, as the instrument to further educational objectives. The legal agent responsible for the carrying out of these general goals is the board of education. The powers of the board are set by statute and include the right to acquire and dispose of property, to determine educational policies, to hire and discharge personnel, to construct buildings, to make contracts for supplies, equipment, and services, to levy taxes upon the school district for the support of the program, to make its own rules and procedures, and many other powers. All these are subject to the legal phrasing in the statutes and the interpretations given by the appellate courts. A board may thus perform legislative, "judicial," and executive functions.

The responsibility of the board is in two directions. As an agent of the state it is responsible to the state. Board members are in the legal status of public officials with all the rights and immunities of such officials when the board is in legal session. Board members may be removed from office for demonstrated malfeasance or misfeasance. They are subject to procedure in civil and criminal courts for such action as board members. The second direction of responsibility is to the community or, more specifically, to the electorate. The board is responsible to the people of the school district for an effective educational program. In theory at least, the accountability of the board is through the election. If the operation of the board is not efficient, the people may have the opportunity to remove them. This possibility does not apply to appointed boards or to boards elected by other agencies than the electorate. Two-thirds of the members of county school boards are elected. Of city boards of education about 85 percent are elected. In the other instances, the members are appointed or selected by agencies other than the voters.

The manner by which persons become members of a board may have a bearing upon its operation. In a sense, that sphere of jurisdiction which is at the apex of the educational bureaucracy is peculiarly dependent on the state, the voter, or the appointing agency. This not only bears upon the powers that may be exercised but also is relevant as to who will be the incumbents. This fact is a deviation from the pure type of bureaucratic structure, so that considerations other than technical competence bear upon the incumbency of school boards—for example, political party policies.

There are no special qualifications for membership on a school board with the exception of citizenship or residence. In general, this means that an educational policy is in the hands of amateurs or dilettantes, as a board of laymen may be characterized. They are amateur in the sense that they have, usually, no special training or experience in educational matters, although on occasion former school personnel become members of a board. However, a typical board tends to have members whose socio-economic status is middle or upper class, i.e., merchants, manufacturers, bankers, brokers, real-estate men, doctors, lawyers, housewives, and in rural areas farmers as well. Few board members originate in worker occupations. Because of this social background it is frequently alleged that boards are conservative toward most educational, social, and economic issues and that consequently school programs are likely to become inflexible. This allegation and result have not been definitely shown. In view of the diversity in American schools, the contention may seem questionable. Doubtless some boards are very rigid and conservative as others are flexible and progressive. At any rate, a good school man can also educate the board. Superintendents, in rating board members, prefer housewives and professionals (except ministers) to businessmen, prefer members having children to those who have none, prefer neither too young nor too old (best age, 40 to 50), and a moderate tenure. The longer the service, the more conservative and less useful the members seem to become.[7] The typical composition of a school board deviates from the bureaucratic concept of the trained expert.

The operation of a board is conditioned by its financial powers and sources. This area constitutes an important phase in the definition of its sphere of jurisdiction. There are two types of board: the financially dependent and the financially independent. In the first, the financing of the schools is controlled either by city or by county fiscal authorities. In some cities the mayor may exercise a veto over

[7] G. G. Struble, "A Study of School Board Personnel," *American School Board Journal*, October, 1922, pp. 137–138.

school budgets and expenditures through the budget bureau. In some New England states budget and taxes are approved in the town meeting. In these cases there is a division of authority so that financing of the school is carried out by one agency and the school program by another. Financially independent school districts in general have authority to prepare the budget and vote necessary taxes, subject to statutory limitations.

Lastly, the operation of the board is a phase of its sphere of jurisdiction. A board may organize in a variety of ways. It may attempt executive functions in addition to its planning and appraising functions, or it may delegate the executive function to professional personnel, retaining planning and appraising functions. When a board attempts executive activity, it operates through a series of standing committees to which members are assigned. These typically will be a finance committee, an instruction committee, and a plant committee. A board may delegate executive functions to professional personnel, e.g., a business manager, superintendent, and superintendent of building and grounds. A board, then, acts as a coördinating agency, usually through standing committees with overlapping membership. Another form of organization is the delegation of executive authority as a unit to the superintendent of schools with the board acting as a planning and appraising body. With such a structure a board can act as a committee of the whole, relieved of executive activities, devoting its time to developing educational policy.[8]

Variations in Line-Staff Organization. It has been suggested that bureaucratic structure will vary with size of school district and school population: the smaller the size, the less complex the structure and the more likely it will be that primary-group type of relations prevail. Except for the provision in the legal code, spheres of jurisdiction may be less well defined. Two different types of organization will be examined, the small-scale and the large-scale. In both types some form of line-staff organization occurs. Line organization refers especially to the division of graded authority—child to teacher, teacher to principal, principal to division superintendent, division superintendent to superintendent. Each of these, of course,

---

[8] Cf. Arthur Moehlman, *op. cit.,* pp. 218–225, chaps. 10 and 11.

involves functions as well as certain amounts of authority. Staff organization refers primarily to a division of function without much of an intervening line of authority, e.g., a legal department, an accounting department, a school plant department directly responsible to the superintendent.

A simple form of organization is shown in Figure 30. In the small district there is a supervising principal or superintendent. If there

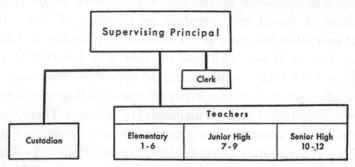

FIGURE 30. Organization with Independent Principal. (Reprinted from *School Administration* by Arthur B. Moehlman, by permission of Houghton Mifflin Company. Copyright 1940 by Arthur B. Moehlman. P. 297.)

is a titular high-school principal under the superintendent, he is usually a full-time teacher with added record and disciplinary duties. The executive activities of the supervising principal include: "preparation of detailed rules governing procedure; supervision of instruction; purchase of educational and non-educational supplies; enforcement of the compulsory attendance laws; selection of textbooks; recommendation of teachers for appointment or dismissal, and sometimes preparation of the budget." [9] He may also do some teaching. The supervising principal is a kind of educational jack-of-all-trades. A clerk, full or part time, prepares the reports required by county and state agencies, handles correspondence, keeps books, and makes out requisition forms. Student help may be used to assist in this management of the files, the justification being direct educational experience. Custodial problems are simplified in such small districts, as one school building does the complete housing job. Line-staff organization is very simple—teacher to principal to board, custodial and clerical.

[9] *Ibid.*, p. 297.

Large-scale organization is shown in Figure 31. It represents both a quantitative and a qualitative expansion: an increased number of personnel and the addition of new functions. Every position above the teacher is administrative. At the top is the specialized staff, centering in the superintendent if there is unit organization. This type of organization is represented in the diagram. The superintendent's relation to the teacher, as can be seen, is most likely to be

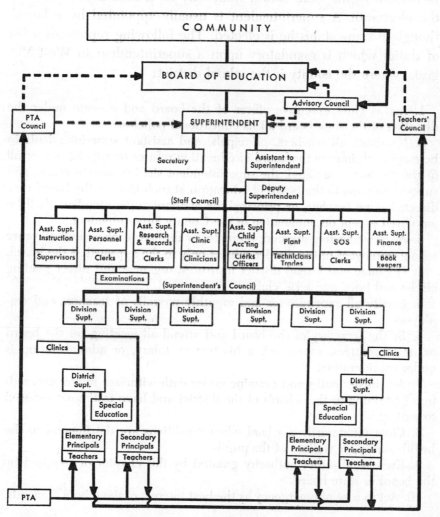

FIGURE 31. Large Organization with Specialized Staff. (Adapted and reprinted from *School Administration* by Arthur B. Moehlman, by permission of Houghton Mifflin Company. Copyright 1940 by Arthur B. Moehlman. Pp. 304, 308.)

distant and remote. This may be true also of the lower echelons of the administrative staff. The functions of the superintendent are primarily planning and coördinating. The other staff positions represent a delegation of his duties.

The duties of the superintendent are manifold. They are specified in the legal code. A superintendent is a state as well as local official. He is a de facto public official. He is responsible both to the local board and to the state board. Indirectly he is held accountable by the electorate. A superintendent is usually appointed by a board, though in some states he is elected. The following represents a list of duties which is mandatory upon a superintendent in West Virginia, where the county is the school district:

1. Act as chief executive officer of the board and execute under the direction of the state board all its educational policies.
2. Nominate all teachers, principals, and assistant superintendents to be employed; in case the board of education refuses to appoint any or all of the persons nominated, the superintendent shall nominate others and submit the same to the board of education at such time as the board may direct; but no teacher, or principal, or assistant superintendent shall be employed except on nomination of the County Superintendent.
3. Assign, transfer, suspend, promote, or dismiss teachers and all other school employees of the district subject only to the approval of the board.
4. Organize and attend district institutes; organize and direct reading circles and boys' and girls' clubs.
5. Certify all expenditures and monthly payrolls of teachers and employees.
6. Be the secretary of the board and attend all meetings of the board or its committees, except when his tenure, salary, or administration is under consideration.
7. Administer oaths and examine under oath witnesses in any proceedings pertaining to the schools of the district and have testimony reduced to writing.
8. Close temporarily a school when conditions are detrimental to the health, safety, or welfare of the pupils.
9. Exercise all other authority granted by this chapter or required by the board or state board.
10. Act in case of emergency as the best interest of the school demands.

These represent the duties in one section of the code, and in another the following are added:

11. Visit the schools as often as practical; observe and make suggestions concerning the instruction and classroom management of the schools and their sanitary conditions.

12. Report to the board cases of incompetence, neglect of duty, immorality, or misconduct in office of any teacher or employee.

13. Recommend for condemnation buildings unfit for school use.

14. Direct the taking of the school census.

15. Call, at his discretion, conferences of principals and teachers to discuss the work of the schools of the district.

16. Report to the board the progress and general conditions of the schools.

17. Make such reports as are required by the state superintendent. In case the superintendent fails to report as required, the state superintendent may direct that the superintendent's salary be withheld until an acceptable report is received.

18. Perform all other duties prescribed in this chapter or required by the board or the state board.[10]

We thus see personnel and supervisory functions, financial duties, instructional and curricular duties, school plant and equipment duties, special board obligations, and public relations duties. The list represents official duties, and many informal obligations may accrete. In a large system it becomes obvious why a superintendent needs special assistants to carry out educational policies.

The second officer of importance is the principal, who differs little from the superintendent in terms of function. The difference is in scope of authority. The principal is responsible for a particular administrative area or school plant. The various functions stated above are carried out by the principal, delegated to him by board and superintendent. In a very large school the principal may have several assistants. He will then exercise for this school the planning, supervising, and coördinating functions that the superintendent exercises for the system as a whole.

The duties of the other administrative personnel are in part indicated on the chart. As one proceeds down the line, the duties of the personnel are roughly as follows:

Deputy superintendent—technical manager, and co-ordinator of detail.
Division superintendent—responsible for the management of total educa-

[10] *West Virginia Code*, The Michie Company, 1955, pp. 902–903.

tional activity within a section of the district or division, such as, elementary education within total district.

District superintendent or district principal—responsible for the administration of a section of a total district, either on a territorial basis including all aspects of education or by divisions such as elementary or secondary; may include specialized schools for atypical children.

Building principal—responsible for part or all of the educational program within the building.

Specialized subject principal or administrative supervisor in charge of a subject division, such as, languages or social studies, or an administrative division, such as, kindergarten, primary, special education, etc.[11]

The various councils suggested in the chart are possibilities. They may be formally established or simply function in advisory capacity. There are few cases of PTA or teachers' councils, and in a strict sense they are outside of the real structure. However, they may serve as additional channels of information whereby any processing of data through regular channels is avoided.

Professionalization. This term refers not only to a support of an occupation in the mores and value orientation of the supporting culture but also to a specific recognition and approval in law. Professionalization is associated with occupational associations whose purpose it is to foster the type of recognition stated. The objective is to insure a qualified personnel in the occupation, the elimination of the incompetent and the quack, and some measure of control over conditions of work, such as salary, tenure, and retirement. A professional group is generally recognized by high requirements for training coupled with certification of competence. This certifying is considered a function of the state, and some certifying agency or board of examiners will provide the accreditation. A few professional organizations, medicine and law especially, also issue certificates, conferring membership in the professional group, which are practically necessary in order to work in the occupation. In teaching, this level of professional development has not been reached.

The process of accreditation begins with the high school, but for our purposes it starts with professional education. To make sure

[11] Arthur Moehlman, *op. cit.*, pp. 286, 306–307.

that the instructional institutions are qualified, accreditation is provided by both private and public agencies. "Of 1,200 colleges preparing teachers in 1952, 300 had no accreditation except that which comes with approval of their respective state departments to prepare teachers." [12] The remainder are accredited by six regional accrediting bodies and by the American Association of Colleges for Teacher Education. A new group, the Council for Accreditation of Teacher Education, has been organized. The composition of its members gives a concept of the various groups involved in this process. There are twenty-one members, distributed as follows: six from colleges and universities appointed by the American Association of Colleges for Teacher Education; six from state departments of education, three appointed by state directors of teacher education and certification and three by state commissioners of education; six teachers and administrators from schools appointed by the National Commission of Teacher Education and Professional Standards of the National Education Association; three school board members appointed by the National Association of School Board Members.[13] However, despite the attention given to teacher certification, it is "still in a chaotic state. . . . On such problems as the major element that should constitute a program of teacher education, the kinds of responsibility that will be placed upon institutions in the total certification procedure, and the bases on which reciprocities (so that a teacher can readily practice in any state) can be practiced among the states, there is still no general agreement." [14] The problem of professionalization among administrators tends to be similar.

Of the various aspects of professionalization two more will be briefly considered: income and tenure. Since bureaucratic organization operates according to calculable rules, both income and tenure should be so structured. In other words, there should be an objective reference in terms of salary scales and retirement plans and benefits on the one hand and specified rules concerning the con-

[12] W. Earl Armstrong, "Teacher Education," in *Education for Professions*, Office of Education, U.S. Department of Health, Education, and Welfare, Government Printing Office, 1955, p. 226.
[13] *Ibid.*
[14] *Ibid.*, p. 228.

tinuous fulfillment of the job on the other. In both instances capriciousness, arbitrariness, favoritism on the part of administrators and board members are to be controlled if not completely suppressed, for the avoidance of such acts fits in with the rational nature of bureaucratic organization. Caprice is not calculable.

For every position in a bureaucratic structure there ought to be a corresponding salary. "Ought" is used to mean consistent with bureaucratic organization. A salary schedule is a rationally devised plan for the payment of teachers. It determines the beginning salary, the amount and number of increments, and the maximum salary. Rationally it should be based on training, experience, and teaching efficiency as opposed to salary differences based on grade taught, sex, race, color, belief, residence, or economic or marital status.[15] Since education is regarded as a function of the state, a salary schedule can be set up through legislation. For the school term 1950–51, thirty-one states, Alaska, and Hawaii had minimum-salary laws for teachers.[16] The range of the salary schedule in the law at this time was from $522 (South Carolina) for the lowest certificate recognized to $5100 minimum salary for teacher with maximum credit for experience (Alaska, MA degree or five years).[17] However, many of these salary schedules have been revised. Furthermore, a board may have a salary schedule on which the beginning minimum may be considered above the legislative minimum-salary provision. In those states where there are no minimum-salary laws, where no provisions are made for increments, the salary schedule, if there is one, is set by the local board of education.

[15] NEA Research Bulletin, *Teacher Personnel Procedures: Employment Conditions in Service,* May, 1942, p. 87.

[16] "In 17 states there is a minimum *schedule* which includes certain required increments for experience. In nine states the minimum salaries are classified, usually according to the teacher's level of preparation, resulting in two or more *flat-rate salaries,* but increments for experience are not required. In seven states a *single flat-rate salary* is stated as the minimum. Of the 17 states that have no minimum-salary law, three grant state aid to local districts on the basis of salary apportionments that vary with the qualifications of the individual teacher employed, but do not require local districts to observe the apportionment rates as a minimum in paying individual teachers." NEA Research Bulletin, *State Minimum-Salary Laws for Teachers, 1950–51,* November, 1950, p. 3.

[17] *Ibid.*

Any person holding a job has a tenure, but conditions of tenure vary. Bureaucratically to insure efficiency on the job, to avoid arbitrary dismissal, permanent tenure is a necessary condition. Terms of employment vary considerably. The most general practice is annual election. Teachers are appointed for only one year at a time and are released or reappointed at the end of the year. A second practice is the continuing contract between school board and teachers. In this type of contract teachers are employed for an indefinite period. Annual reappointment is not necessary. If a teacher is not notified at a set date that his services are not desired, the contract continues automatically for another year. However, the plan permits a teacher to be discharged at the end of any year, irrespective of the reason, provided he has been properly notified. The third type is permanent tenure. Teachers have a job security after completing successfully a probationary period. Dismissal cannot take place except upon proved charges of specified causes. A teacher is entitled upon dismissal to a hearing and may appeal to higher authority such as the courts or chief state school official. Tenure protection is accorded to city teachers in thirty-nine states and to rural teachers in thirty-four states. In some tenure is statewide or it may apply only to cities and not to the rural areas. City schools may have their own tenure regulations. In city school systems the type of employment condition varies with size: the smaller the city, the larger the proportion having annual election or appointment and the smaller the proportion with permanent tenure. In cities of 100,000 or more 26 percent had annual election as compared with 52 percent in cities 2500 to 5000. Sixty-seven percent of these large cities had a policy of permanent tenure as compared to 31 percent in the small ones. The continuing contract type was 6 and 17 percent respectively.[18]

Under a tenure system not only must there be a careful screening of teachers during the probationary period but there must also be provision for rating for advancement, promotion, etc. Efficiency

[18] NEA Research Bulletin, *Teacher Personnel Procedures: Selection and Appointment*, March, 1942, p. 73.

rating appears to be declining rather than growing. In city school systems studied in 1922–23, 57 percent reported teacher rating as compared to 40 percent in 1940–41.[19] In two-thirds of the city schools reporting for 1940–41 a teacher is not given a copy of his rating, though the ratings are used for several purposes: (1) as a supervisory aid; (2) in deciding on reappointment of teachers not on tenure; (3) in recommending probationary teachers for permanent appointment; (4) in selecting teachers for promotion; (5) in paying regular increments on the salary schedule; (6) in selecting teachers to receive supermaximum salaries.[20] Teachers do not object to ratings provided the rating system is a valid one. A discussion of this topic concludes: "While the theory and ideal behind it are acceptable to all, the unscientific nature of existing systems, the faults of the methods of administration, and the frailties of rating officials inevitably provoke opposition. Undoubtedly even a cumulative personnel record which is rather a collection of evidence than a judgment would arouse disapproval because of the nature of items included or excluded. Nevertheless, teachers and administrators should work together to find a system of evaluating teachers' work that is acceptable to a substantial majority of the teaching staff." [21] The whole topic is, thus, a moot one.

The assumption that tenure is a sinecure for teachers is unwarranted. In the first place, teachers under permanent tenure are sometimes dismissed, though in not as large a proportion as in the other types of tenure. Cities reporting dismissal of experienced teachers compare as follows: with annual election, 35 percent; with continuing contract, 37 percent; and with permanent tenure, 22 percent.[22] Secondly, by law, by explicit or implicit policy, or by rating, a teacher is expected, if not required, to advance in professional growth.

[19] NEA Research Bulletin, *Teacher Personnel Procedures: Employment Conditions in Service*, May, 1942, p. 95.
[20] *Ibid.*, p. 96.
[21] *Teacher Rating*, Department of Classroom Teachers and Research Division, National Education Association, December, 1946, pp. 21–22. Cf. NEA Research Bulletin, *The Teacher Looks at Personnel Administration*, December, 1945, pp. 124–127.
[22] NEA Research Bulletin, *Teacher Personnel Procedures: Employment Conditions in Service*, May, 1942, p. 106.

One way to understand bureaucratic organization is to view it in terms of the problems that arise within it. A problem is an impairment of function, something that violates the rational technical requirements of bureaucratic structure. By looking at the problems, one may also derive a concept of the bureaucracy in its "pure" form. We shall do this by referring to sixteen cases in which the NEA was asked to make an investigation. This amounts to a definition of what is desirable and undesirable in school administration and organization from the viewpoint of the educators. However, it must be kept in mind that the principle of rationality and competence underlies this educational approach, and furthermore, the type of problem that educators have encountered is similar to those found in other institutional organizations, business and industrial establishments, government, trade unions, and other large-scale associations. Lastly, the conditions in the cases cited may have changed. They are used to make a point. How prevalent these situations are nobody knows, though optimistically one may hope that they are few in number. That these strains and stresses may disorganize a school may seem self-evident, but they also reach disorganizingly into the community, as happened, for example, in the North College Hill case. "The refusal of the board to re-engage the superintendent led to repercussions all but unprecedented. There followed prolonged student strikes, mass community protests, a series of disorderly board meetings attended by hundreds of citizens culminating in a riot and arrests, mass resignations of teachers, and finally, resignation of the entire school board at a meeting from which certain board members left under the protection of police."[23]

FACTIONALISM AS A FORM OF BUREAUCRATIC STASIS

Some sort of factionalism occurs in almost all of the sixteen cases. This may occur in a dispute between spheres of jurisdiction, but it more frequently involves some type of primary group development within the structure, the clique, the administrative "machine," and

[23] *North College Hill, Ohio*, National Commission for the Defense of Democracy Through Education, National Education Association, November, 1947, p. 7.

other types of stabilized and personalized relations. The factions may occur in a board of education, among administrators, or among teachers. The factionalism may take place within and among these three sectors. As a form of stasis the coöperative structure breaks down. Frequently these diverse factions are pursuing ends other than educational, such as power, prestige, and money. The factionalism may extend outside the structure to include other organizations. In this case, the faction within represents an outside interest.

Conflicts Among Spheres of Jurisdiction. This problem involves two aspects. One is concerned with the appropriate delegation of authority and function. The second is a matter of maximizing a sphere of jurisdiction.

Since a bureaucratic structure is organized by clearly defined areas of official duties, a failure to specify such areas results in dissociative relations. Since a person orients himself to the calculable rules in the theoretical model of bureaucracy, he cannot act effectively when these are not properly worked out. The failure to specify these areas may arise in conflicts within the board. Such difference may arise between "conservative" and "liberal" members (Houston), Roman Catholic and Protestant (North Hill), pro-administrative machine and non-machine (Chicago, New York, Kelso, McCook), old and new board members (Kansas City). Many board members have little or no conception of what they are supposed to do except they know that they have power, and this they use with insolence of office, stamping roughshod over superintendent, principals, teachers, and community protest, as almost all the cases show. The public servants act as public masters, defying the community to change their arbitrary decisions. Board members attempt to combine both policy-making and administrative functions. Frequently the board chairman arrogates both areas, and when he is through, the result has commonly been a demoralized school system and a community in conflict. When this takes place, open board meetings become tremendously charged with emotion, verging on the expression of violence. Ignorance plus power equals chaos (e.g., Kelso, North Hill, McCook, Grand Prairie, Chandler, Kansas City).

Maximizing a sphere of jurisdiction is a kind of imperialism within the structure, an encroachment on and a subtle absorption of duties and functions belonging to other areas. This problem has occurred most frequently on the policy-making and top administrative levels. Thus, the board secretary, a deputy or assistant superintendent, or a business manager may gradually usurp duties and functions of the superintendent. Where a dual control system has been in effect, this problem has always arisen. This system allocates financial matters to a business manager and educational matters to the superintendent, in the hope of greater efficiency. The result has been the contrary, and the dual control system has been rejected by the NEA on the following grounds:

The first is that all matters relating to the school, whether they concern building construction, the arrangement and number of rooms, lighting, roofing, sanitation, maintenance, janitorial service, cafeterias, personnel, instruction, etc., all have educational implication, and thus should be under the supervision of the superintendent. Secondly, when the business manager is responsible to the board of education and not to the superintendent, the board of education may be forced to choose between recommendations made by the business manager and those made by the superintendent.

Moreover, a business manager who is not responsible to the superintendent can, to the detriment of education, gain an ascendancy over the clerical staff, instructional staff, and the superintendent. He can build a political machine within the school system that may cause factionalism and a multitude of attendant evils. By the threat of withholding funds for school improvements, he can block the appointment of personnel or force the appointment and promotion of personnel of his choice.[24]

This dual control issue was found in Kansas City, Houston, New York City. It is found in those states where financial matters are entrusted to one board and educational affairs to another.

Primary Groups in Relation to Stasis. That friendships and cliques develop in a school staff is axiomatic. They are informal structures similar to the informal structure that develops among pupils. These cliques may be organized according to age, sex, teaching field, support of athletics and sports, marital status, and, frequently, smoking, drinking, and card playing.[25] Some cliques may be

[24] *Report of an Investigation, Los Angeles Heights, Texas,* Committee on Tenure and Academic Freedom, National Education Association, November, 1948, pp. 10–11.
[25] Wilbur Brookover, *A Sociology of Education,* American Book Company, 1955, pp. 192–201.

primarily sociability groups, but others may be concerned to influence policy. Opposition among such groups may contribute to stasis, as they struggle against or support one another through the grapevine, in faculty meetings, etc.

A phase of this behavior which has not been studied very much refers to erotically tinged (teasing, for example) and voyeuristic behavior. This may take place especially in relation to single teachers of requisite eligibility and attributes, though married teachers may likewise be so involved. Sexual evaluations and attractions take place, and it is quite plausible to hypothesize that this is an element uniting both mono- and bi-sex cliques. It may be an important element in homosexual and heterosexual pair relations. How this reverberates back into the formal structure is difficult to say, but the matter would be an interesting study.

The clique or coterie may also develop between teacher and pupil and involve the favoritism referred to in a previous chapter. The basis of such a following may be manifold, from an appreciation of competence and friendliness to relations erotically tinged. Unabashed voyeurism may be directed toward their teacher by students, beginning with the physical maturation of the boys and girls. The young female teacher may thus be confronted with sixty or eighty ogling and appraising eyes. There may be a crush on the young male teacher. There may be also reciprocation, so that sex is used as a subtle method of control.[26] In passing, it should be observed that the behavior referred to is not peculiar to the school, for it also takes place in other large-scale organizations. The stereotype in business is the "office wife."

THE FILES AS A PROBLEM

This issue is not as likely to arise on the elementary level as on the high-school level. Reference here is to the "office gang" or "office clique," a group of elite students (upper-middle or upper class) favored by teachers and principals, who give them semi-official roles. In such roles they will have access to the files and information, which makes them a powerful group. In Elmtown such a

[26] Fritz Redl, "Group Emotion and Leadership," *Psychiatry*, November, 1942, pp. 573–584.

group was a factor in precepitating a breakdown in some of the school's rules.[27] This group manipulated admission slips to classes until a faculty meeting had to be called to deal with the issue. The extent to which such office cliques use and manipulate information is not known.

The second aspect of this issue is the failure of principals, superintendents, and boards to keep accurate records. This is a part of their official duties and is generally prescribed in the statutes. However, as several of the NEA cases show, the greatest lack has been in keeping adequate personnel records of teachers. In the instances involving dismissal of teachers, the actions appeared completely arbitrary because of the lack of information and the refusal of boards to produce any. In all likelihood none was available. In addition, it was found that some boards manipulated their minutes and records according to their interests, changing or expunging them to conceal information as well as to save face.

Sometimes record keeping becomes an end in itself. This aspect of the problem of the files was expressed to the author by one teacher: "If they would only let us teach instead of keeping all those records." This overstress on records, as she sees it, is fostered by the administrators. Here again the bearing on state aid should be noted, for the great stress on the attendance records is linked with this financial aspect of the school. On the elementary level some trial efforts have been made with the "teacher's aides," similar in idea to nurse's aides. The teacher is to be supplied with an individual to do all the record keeping. This individual will be paid at a much lower rate than the teacher and meanwhile the pupil load per teacher is to be increased as theoretically she is now free to devote her time exclusively to instruction. The NEA has contended that schools instead of hiring a roster of teacher's aides should take the funds and hire more teachers and thus also make classes smaller so that instruction can be individualized. The question of the burdensome aspect of file keeping remains at present an unsolved problem.[28]

[27] August Hollingshead, *Elmtown's Youth,* John Wiley and Sons, 1949, pp. 185–187; cf. Wilbur Brookover, *op. cit.,* pp. 221–222.
[28] The Fund for the Advancement of Education, *Teachers for Tomorrow,* Bulletin No. 2, November, 1955, pp. 40–46; Alexander Stoddard, *Schools for Tomorrow,* The Fund for the Advancement of Education, January, 1957.

EXPLOITATION OF OFFICE

Using an office for personal gain and advantage constitutes exploitation of office. As an aspect of bureaucracy it is found in almost all types, though the one most publicized is the political. This type of perversion [29] of bureaucratic structure expresses the working maxim "to the victor belongs the spoils" and in the absence of a civil service represents the dilettante and special interest traditions. Exploitation of office is usually for gaining money and property or as a means of consolidating and maintaining power. This type of practice involves the substitution of private goals (which might be culturally acceptable in other situations) for the group goals. The incumbent of office may fulfill his duties and at the same time exploit the possibilities. The higher the position in the structure, the greater are the opportunities for such exploitation, for the higher positions are the policy-making ones and the incumbents have complete access to the files.

That exploitation of office is regarded as harmful and undesirable is recognized in law as the "conflict of interest" principle. This principle implies that private interest is not identical with public welfare, safety, and morality. When a person enters a public office, he is to divest himself of private interest in accordance with this principle. For example, if he is in a position involving the awarding of contracts, he may be required to divest himself of his stockholding in corporations. A judge may disqualify himself from hearing a case because of previous involvement. In all the legal codes of the states there are provisions dealing with conduct in public office, and a part of these statutes deal with exploitation of office. Such provisions are found in the statutes dealing with education, and they apply to the board of education, the superintendent and staff, the teachers, and other employees connected with the school. A review of such statutes will give some idea of the extent to which exploitation of office has taken place. Violations of such acts are a criminal offense. Exploitation of office may, thus, be viewed as a form of white-collar criminality,[30] crime committed in the pursuit of one's

[29] Cf. the discussion of destructive processes in Leopold von Wiese and Howard Becker, *Systematic Sociology*, John Wiley and Sons, 1932, pp. 368–398.

[30] Edwin Sutherland and Donald Cressey, *Principles of Criminology*, J. B. Lippincott Company, 5th ed., 1955, pp. 38–47, 197–201.

occupation. While the term has been applied to persons in the upper socio-economic strata—managerial, proprietor and professional occupations, and corporations—"blue-collar" criminality, pilfering of goods by employees, for example, is also of this type. The statutes cover malfeasance and misfeasance in office, especially with reference to the awarding of contracts in building, equipment and supplies, and textbooks. The law also covers bribery and corruption in securing such contracts.

The amount of exploitation of office is unknown. Six of the sixteen NEA cases showed evidence of such exploitation. Some of the practices skirt the boundary lines of legality, as, for example, nepotism and favoritism. There is the bestowal of privilege, advantage, or patronage in the first instance by reason of kin relationship and in the second because of personal preference unrelated to the principle of competence. In three schools this type of practice took place. Boards of education hired relatives or close friends for administrative and clerical positions. In one case a board, dominated by a particular religious group, attempted to reinstate a demoted school principal to the former position because of their common religious affiliation and against the recommendation of the superintendent. In another case school board members were alleged to have participated in school work contracts in violation of state laws. In the remainder of the cases teachers had to kick back part of the salary first to secure a position, second to hold it, and third to get promotion. Failure to pay involved dismissal.

The magnitude of exploitation of office may be illustrated in one case. It represented an interaction between superintendent, president of the board, the mayor, the "pro-administration" machine within the school, and the political machine outside of the school. Nepotism and favoritism occurred in appointments, promotions, and demotions. It was characterized by irregularities in a principals' examination. It involved the adoption of twenty-three textbooks written or co-authored by the superintendent, many of them in fields in which the superintendent had no training or experience. However, no court case was instituted to test whether or not the superintendent had violated the state constitution and statutes on this point. There were financial irregularities which, according to the NEA report,[31] "may be taken for granted in school systems having 'one-man boards' and which are closely connected with political machines in the making of appointments and the awarding of contracts." A state's attorney investigation revealed in 1939 (the report being later suppressed) "evidence of payments of bribes to public school officials, the contribution of money to political campaign funds by firms that received school board contracts, the rejection of low bids in certain cases, the substitution of low-grade material for first-class material specified in contracts, and the awarding of contracts to firms owned by a well-known racketeer." At the time of its investigation in 1944, the Defense Committee felt that the coal, heating, and plumbing contracts needed a thorough checking. In addition the Committee claimed reliable information of which the following practices were regarded as typical:

1. Payment of $2,500 to a certain ward committeeman by a prominent high-school principal for the purpose of securing passing grades in the 1937 principals' examination.
2. Obtaining the endorsement of ward committeeman, sometimes by payment of money in order to secure appointments as substitute teachers for long assignments, as truant officers and other school officers.
3. Payment of money to politicians to secure night school, summer school, and other school board appointments.
4. Making of contributions to political funds on the basis of goods or services sold to the schools by certain firms.
5. Rejection of low bids for school milk and other supplies.[32]

It is not implied that these conditions still obtain in this city. The data were introduced to clarify the meaning and ramifications of exploitation of office.

Exploitation of office may also be destructive of teacher morale, encourage factionalism, weaken confidence in public officials, increase the costs of schooling, and seriously affect the health and welfare of children, especially when such corruption takes place in relation to buildings, equipment, and supplies. To cite a case: In one large city school system it was found that the board collusively had awarded catering contracts to firms in which they had an inter-

[31] *Certain Personnel Practices in the Chicago Public Schools*, National Commission for the Defense of Democracy Through Education, National Education Association, May, 1945, p. 61.
[32] *Ibid.*, p. 62.

est and these firms sent inferior if not dangerous food products to the schools, resulting in the sickness of many children. When this situation was exposed by a courageous principal, several of the board members were indicted and convicted. The principal, ironically enough, was dismissed from her position by this very board for "insubordination," a decision upheld later by a court. Exploitation of office must be seen as more than a perversion of bureaucratic structure. It becomes destructive of moral order, in the community and in society at large.

REPRISAL AND CONTROL TECHNIQUE

A bureaucratic structure is a coöperative system based upon well-defined areas of function and responsibility. Bureaucratic management is to facilitate the operation of the system. This management has to orient itself to the defined rules and policies. Proper and adequate procedures must be established so that difficulties may be worked out—for example, adequate grievance machinery. In the absence of such policies and rules, and in the lack or inadequacies of personnel practices, administration becomes an *ad hoc* matter, dealing with this and that case, according to the predilections, animus, and humor of supervisors, principals, superintendent, and board. Action becomes attached to personalities rather than being oriented to the calculable rules and so becomes an element in factionalism. When administration is personalized, reprisal and dissociative control techniques are likely to come into play. When this type of management takes place, the bureaucratic order is not capable of functioning and in the extreme case completely breaks down. Such a breakdown will be evident in student strikes and mass resignation of teachers.

Personalized administration is contrary to the nature of bureaucratic organization. In many of the NEA investigations such school management has been labeled "dictatorial, fascist, undemocratic, unethical or professionally unsound." In twelve out of the sixteen cases the problem arose out of arbitrary administrative actions, usually involving the dismissal of teachers. Dismissal of incompetent teachers is a justifiable act, but dismissal as a method of control, a technique of intimidation, is not. The former conforms to the requirements of bureaucratic organization; the latter does not. A technique of intimidation, bureaucratically viewed, is irrational. Personalized administration is most likely to involve two sociological principles: the augmentation of negative relations and dissociative complementary relations. One may therefore expect fear, worry, uncertainty, hate, spite, and resentment, the destroying emotions and relations, to arise within the system.

All these anxieties are well reflected in the Houston investigation, to cite a case. Despite the fact that from 75 to 94 percent of respondents to a questionnaire felt that the salary schedule was good, that support by the PTA was regarded as good, that supervisors and principals understood teachers' problems, that job security was reasonably high, that school buildings and maintenance were good, and that there was fair support from nonschool groups, 55 percent did not think the school situation satisfactory. Furthermore, in seeming contradiction, 44 percent of the teachers felt that there was a likelihood of losing their positions regardless of their skill and ability as teachers. Though few teachers had been dismissed, this belief was held. Other types of reprisals that teachers feared were: transfer to a less desirable job—48 percent; withholding earned promotion—42 percent; loss of reputation by false charges by school authorities—42 percent; attack from nonschool groups—42 percent; withholding of annual contract after others have received theirs—31 percent. These fears were linked with pressures brought upon teachers by principals, members of the board of education, the business manager, and school administrators, by the absence of grievance machinery, and by community controversy.

What is important for our analysis is the matter of expected reprisals. The ones listed apparently are fairly common and found in the other cases. In the Miami case, similar fears and complaints were voiced: withholding contracts until after close of school; unjust transfers of teachers; dismissal of teachers without proper notice; threats of loss of positions if teachers failed to agree with the opinion of the director of vocation education; political intimidation; unprofessional remarks made by the director of vocational education;

reprisals for failure to give support and rewards for service in connection with state and local political campaigns. These techniques are not new; they have been used in large and small school systems. Every technique discovered by the NEA investigations in these cases, which begin in the middle forties, was found in a report published in 1936. This report concludes by stating: "If, then, teachers are to be free, they must be protected, not only against pressure from groups outside the schools but also against the powerful restrictive forces inside the school: various methods of control short of dismissal, the play of favoritism, student opinion, interfering parents, donors of school funds, other teachers, supervisors, principals, school boards, and superintendents. Until these elements are deprived of control over teachers or are won to freedom, and until a tradition of free expression that affects them all is established, no effective freedom for teachers can be established." [33]

Espionage as a Method of Control. The culmination of a non-bureaucratic system of control is the organization of a spy or spotter system. This method is a form of psychological terrorism. No one knows who the informer is—student, fellow teacher, custodian, supervisor. To prove the existence of a spy system may be difficult. In six of the sixteen cases it was alleged that administrators had encouraged such spying. A spy system is designed to ferret out the "troublemakers," those indicating lack of submission to an incumbent school administration. It separates the loyal from the disloyal—loyalty defined in terms of allegiance and uncritical subordination to administrators and school board. A spy system isolates person from person, indicates a lack of respect for the rights and opinions of others, and stifles freedom of thought and discussion.[34] In one state, New York, this method of control has been legitimatized by the Feinberg law, a law upheld by the courts. When the state education commissioner ruled that teachers were not compelled to inform, a member of the New York City Corporation Council announced that an appeal

[33] Howard K. Beale, *Are American Teachers Free?* Part XII: Report of the Commission on the Social Studies, American Historical Association, Charles Scribner's Sons, 1936, chap. XIX, and pp. 620–621.
[34] Cf. the articles published in *The Mirror*, Los Angeles, California, March 22–25, 1954.

would be taken.[35] In this case spying not only is to be legal but also is to be made compulsory—the epitome of an irrational perversion of a bureaucratic organization.

VALUE ORIENTATIONS AND BUREAUCRATIC STRUCTURE

The topic can be introduced by the following evaluation of bureaucratic organization:

Observation of the largest school districts leads to the conclusion that as the district increases in size there is loss in flexibility, a growth in bureaucratic rigidity and greater emphasis upon form, less continuing provision for growth, and too often an attempt to provide for high centralization in operation without permitting sufficient freedom and variation on part of individual schools to adjust the specific needs of their attendance areas. There is almost complete loss of the partnership concept of community participation, an increasing remoteness from the people, and a diminishing participation of teacher expression. . . . From the simple first colleague relationship of the small district, the superintendent develops in the largest cities into an officer who is remote from the classroom. To the average city teacher the superintendent is a shadowy but potent *force* instead of an understanding colleague. . . . The teachers believe that changes may be effected in the selection of this chief administrative officer so that he will be of them rather than superimposed upon them. . . . Instruction is the supreme purpose of the schools and the most important aspect of the executive activity. . . . The teacher is the most important agent in the instructional process, and all other specialized personnel must be considered purely as facilitating agents to make the work of the teacher proceed more efficiently. From this point of view the currently accepted division of personnel into "executive" and "worker" is an artificial one and, even worse, tends to be misleading in the establishment of relations and attitudes within organization. . . . The transference to educational practice of the concepts of corporate management, stimulated unfortunately by teachers of school administration during the early decades of the twentieth century, has placed altogether too much emphasis on mere mechanical concepts of efficiency and hierarchical organization. This tendency, coupled with the still strong aristocratic academic tradition, has produced an autocracy in the practice of executive activity that has had unfortunate results in the schools themselves. This autocracy is not confined to the superintendency, but is also strongly evident in the principalship and particu-

[35] *Civil Liberties*, American Civil Liberties Union, October, 1956, p. 4.

larly in teacher-pupil relations. While it may have expedited the mechanics of organization, it has undoubtedly retarded the possibility of growth and improvement in the educational process itself. This executive autocracy that grew out of a combination of professional incompetency, blind worship of business efficiency concept, and the aristocracy of the academic tradition is one of the most serious problems confronting the administration of the education process today.[36]

The evaluations in this statement are corroborated by a study of teacher attitudes toward personnel administration. Hindrances and helps to good teaching were listed by urban teachers as follows. Helps: (1) understanding, coöperative principal; (2) congenial fellow teachers; (3) interested and appreciative pupils; (4) helpful, sympathetic supervisors; (5) good equipment and building facilities; (6) freedom to use initiative; and (7) coöperative parents. Hindrances: (1) overload in number of pupils; (2) indifferent, unresponsive pupils; (3) inadequate equipment and building facilities; (4) low or unfair salaries; (5) interruptions in classroom work; (6) extracurricular and extra duties; (7) lack of teaching materials.[37] It was found that helps emphasized in high-morale cities were "professional leadership and the degree of recognition and respect shown to the teacher," and hindrances emphasized in low-morale cities were "lack of administrative and supervisory leadership and lack of recognition of the teacher's work and professional problems."[38] It appears, then, that one of the crucial phases of the structure is the type of social relations that exist, i.e., the extent to which sociative or dissociative relations prevail. At the minimum the relation may be exclusively utilitarian, symbiotic, where "some working relations are kept up solely by the dependence of each party upon the other, without any sense of responsibility or sympathy, and with a minimum respect for norms . . . an equilibrium maintained by force or fear of force."[39]

Social relations manifest or embody the value orientations. If we translate the above data into the different value orientations, we find that the basic concern of the educators is implementing the humanist

[36] Arthur Moehlman, op. cit., pp. 307–309, 232, 249.
[37] NEA Research Bulletin, The Teacher Looks at Personnel Administration, December, 1945, p. 133.
[38] Ibid., p. 136.
[39] E. T. Hiller, Social Relations and Structures, Harper & Brothers, 1947, p. 168.

value orientation and minimizing if not excluding especially the nativist and market orientations. Bureaucratic structures embodying nativist or market orientations, or both, may approximate symbiotic structures. The problem in humanistic terms is how, in a structure of differential function and authority, an equalitarian colleague concept may prevail. Differences in function and authority do not necessarily involve invidious comparisons and deferential behavior. If attention is focused on the purpose of schooling, the top-heavy superstructure may not be necessary. It seems an oddity that a professionally trained personnel require such an enormous supervisory staff, a staff that can misconstrue its function because of traditional ideas. Humanistically, the administrative staff should be subsidiary to the instructional, to the ultimate end of education. This would mean that the order of Figure 31 would be reversed. At the top would be the children, then the teachers, and the remainder of the administrative staff essentially a series of service departments, supporting and assisting teachers and children. The idea of turning a hierarchical structure upside down may be difficult to grasp. If this idea can be seen in connection with decentralized schools, schools with greater autonomy to build curricula as fits their situation, then the restructuring is possible. According to Moehlman, "a logical extension of the idea of the responsible principal would be the responsible school in which the entire instructional staff is recognized as the true executive unit. . . . The professional personnel within a building can be held to group responsibility, and under these conditions will select its own leaders, and administration becomes in fact as it is in theory a facilitating device rather than a dominating activity." [40] This has led to the concept of multiple principalship based upon a series of committees, staffed by elected teachers who will devote a certain amount of their teaching time to administrative duties.[41] The concept of task-performing lower echelons and policy-making higher echelons is done away with; instead of a bifurcation there is a unity. The reason for this inheres in the nature of teaching. A competent teacher does not need supervision and is capable of fulfilling his duties as an autonomous agent. As

[40] Arthur Moehlman, *op. cit.*, pp. 542, 538.
[41] See *ibid.*, p. 539, for further details.

long as finances, building, equipment, and maintenance are provided, the control of the schooling process can be carried out by the teachers of the local school. The concept suggested here is similar to that of administrative agencies in government. A board will establish policy, as Congress does, but the execution and the details are left to the agency—in this case the local school.

While the decentralized type of school administration is only in embryonic state, there are other ways of democratizing the structure, or bringing it more into line with the humanist orientation. The first of these is tenure legislation. "To some boards of education the degree of independence which tenure accords teachers is abhorrent. . . . Teacher tenure is equally repellent to certain administrators . . . because it necessitates the alteration of their methods of dealing with teaching personnel. To work successfully with teachers, freed from the constant threat of losing their positions, requires the substitution of administrative leadership for authority." [42] Stable tenure is an essential aspect of bureaucratic structure, and such tenure insures freedom of action and limits arbitrary dismissal of teachers of demonstrated competence. Sound tenure legislation does make provision for the dismissal of incompetent teachers. The question of incompetent principals and superintendents is another matter. It is not surprising that teachers are almost unanimous in their attitudes toward tenure, though this consensus is higher among urban teachers (94 percent) than rural (81 percent), higher among secondary teachers than elementary, and higher among male teachers than female.[43] Almost two-thirds of the teachers responding felt that school authorities should be more aggressive in dismissing incompetent teachers, but dismissal should be rational. The following procedures are regarded as reasonable before a decision to dismiss is made:

1. Warning that services are not satisfactory.
2. Opportunity to improve service.
3. A written statement of deficiencies, of specific reasons why services are unsatisfactory.

[42] Willard Elsbree, *The American Teacher*, American Book Company, 1939, pp. 482–483.
[43] NEA Research Bulletin, *The Teacher Looks at Personnel Administration*, December, 1945, p. 123.

4. An opportunity, if the person desires, to appear before the employing board to answer to the reasons stated, before the board makes its decision to dismiss.[44]

These procedures also imply that all decisions, and especially the hearing, are conducted on the basis of norms of fairness, open-mindedness, and equity. This may be insured through counsel for the teacher considered for dismissal or through investigation by the local professional organization. Ninety-four percent of urban teachers and 89 percent of rural teachers responding thought that the local professional educational orgagnization should act when questions arise over the dismissal of teachers; i.e., on the request of the teacher concerned, it should investigate the facts and make recommendations to the school authorities.[45] A necessary adjunct is adequate grievance machinery, a serious lack in many school systems.

Democratizing the school system means that it will operate essentially along humanist lines, that norms of competence and justice prevail, that communication is unrestricted, that there is willingness to listen and to change. Other ways of implementing this are suggested in Figure 31. The sharing of decision making through principals' and/or staff councils is a possibility. Greater participation by teachers is necessary. A sizable proportion of urban (41 percent) and rural (43 percent) teachers feel that participation in policy-forming groups should be increased. A much greater proportion (84 percent urban, 69 percent rural) expressed the opinion that the local inclusive professional educational organization should be recognized by school authorities as spokesman for professional employees, an idea with trade union overtones. A still larger proportion (94 percent urban, 84 percent rural) of teachers endorsed the statement that an administrative council, representing teachers and other groups, should consider educational policies and make recommendations to school authorities.[46] A PTA council and/or lay advisory

[44] *Dismissals in Fort Myers, Florida,* Committee on Tenure and Academic Freedom, National Education Association, December, 1951, p. 20.

[45] NEA Research Bulletin, *The Teacher Looks at Personnel Administration,* December, 1945, p. 123.

[46] *Ibid.;* cf. NEA Research Bulletin, *Teacher Personnel Procedures: Employment Conditions in Service,* May, 1942, pp. 110–112.

council are also possibilities in making the school a common venture in democratic living.

The following cases were investigated by the National Education Association of the United States through its Committee on Tenure and Academic Freedom, the Professional Investigation Committee on Teacher Dismissals, and, especially, the National Commission for the Defense of Democracy Through Education. These cases show what is desirable and undesirable in school organization and administration as viewed by this organization and its committees.

Interferences with the Independence of the New York City Board of Education, National Commission for the Defense of Democracy Through Education, NEA, February, 1944.

Certain Personnel Practices in the Chicago Public Schools, National Commission for the Defense of Democracy Through Education, NEA, May, 1945.

McCook, Nebraska, An Example of Some Effects of Undemocratic School Administration in a Small Community, National Commission for the Defense of Democracy Through Education, NEA, March, 1947.

North College Hill, Ohio, An Example of Some Effects of Board of Education Interference with Sound Administration of Public Education, National Commission for the Defense of Democracy Through Education, NEA, November, 1947.

Chandler, Arizona, An Example of the Need for Fair Dismissal Procedures, National Commission for the Defense of Democracy Through Education, NEA, October, 1948.

Grand Prairie, Texas, A Case Involving the Civil Rights of Teachers and the Ethical Responsibilities of Boards of Education, National Commission for the Defense of Democracy Through Education, NEA, September, 1949.

Report of the NEA-WEA Investigation Committee on Kelso, Washington, National Education Association of the United States and the Washington Education Association, June, 1950.

Newport, New Hampshire, National Education Association of the United States and the New Hampshire State Teachers' Association, August, 1950.

Twin Falls, Idaho, An Example of Unfair Dismissal Practices When Supervisory Responsibilties Are Indefinite, Idaho Education Association and National Commission for the Defense of Democracy Through Education, NEA, September, 1950.

Oglesby, Illinois, A Case Involving Unfair Dismissal Practices and Unethical Conduct on the Part of Teachers, National Commission for the Defense of Democracy Through Education, NEA, May, 1951.

Mars Hill, North Carolina, A Case Involving the Coercion of Teachers Through Political Pressures, National Commission for the Defense of Democracy Through Education, NEA, October, 1951.

Dismissals in Fort Myers, Florida, An Investigation of Employment Procedures Which Caused Community Disturbances, Committee on Tenure and Academic Freedom, NEA, December, 1951.

Miami, Florida, An Example of the Effects of the Injection of Partisan Politics into School Administration, National Commission for the Defense of Democracy Through Education, October, 1952.

Houston, Texas, A Study of Factors Related to Educational Unrest in a Large School System, National Commission for the Defense of Democracy Through Education, NEA, December, 1954.

Kansas City, Missouri, A Study of Some Problems Arising Out of the Failure to Clarify the Respective Responsibilities of a Board of Education and Its Administrative Staff, National Commission for the Defense of Democracy Through Education, NEA, October, 1955.

Dismissals in Cherokee County, South Carolina, A Study of Faulty Human Relations, Committee on Tenure and Academic Freedom, NEA, March, 1956.

Bridgewater Township, New Jersey, A Study of Difficulties Growing Out of Misunderstandings Between a Board of Education and Its Chief Executive Officer, National Commission for the Defense of Democracy Through Education, NEA, May, 1956.

Selected Readings

EDUCATION

American Association of School Administrators and National School Boards Association, *Written Policies for School Boards*, the Association, September, 1955.

American Association of School Administrators, NEA: *School Boards in Action*, Twenty-fourth Yearbook, 1946.

Lay Advisory Committees, Twenty-ninth Yearbook, 1951.

Staff Relations in School Administration, Thirty-third Yearbook, 1955.

Dreiman, David, *How to Get Better Schools*, Harper & Brothers, 1956.

Hagman, Harlan, *The Administration of American Public Schools*, McGraw-Hill Book Company, 1951.

Moehlman, Arthur, *School Administration*, Houghton Mifflin Company, 1940.

SOCIOLOGY

Blau, Peter M., *Bureaucracy in Modern Society*, Studies in Sociology, Random House, 1956.

Broom, Leonard, and Selznick, Philip, *Sociology,* Row, Peterson, and Company, 1955, chap. VI.

Dubin, Robert (ed.), *Human Relations in Administration,* Prentice-Hall, Inc., 1951.

From Max Weber: Essays in Sociology, translated by H. H. Gerth and C. Wright Mills, Oxford University Press, 1946.

Gouldner, Alvin (ed.), *Studies in Leadership,* Harper & Brothers, 1950.

Gouldner, Alvin (ed.), *Patterns of Industrial Bureaucracy,* The Free Press, 1954.

Merton, Robert, Gray, Ailsa, Hockey, Barbara, and Selvin, Hana (eds.), *Reader in Bureaucracy,* The Free Press, 1952.

von Mises, Ludwig, *Bureaucracy,* Yale University Press, 1946.

Simon, Herbert, *Administrative Behavior,* The Macmillan Company, 1945.

Weber, Max, *The Theory of Social and Economic Organization,* translated by A. M. Henderson and Talcott Parsons, Oxford University Press, 1947.

PART VI

THE SCHOOL IN THE CENTER OF CONTROVERSY

CHAPTER 18

Special Interests and Education

OUR ANALYSIS now shifts back to a consideration of the school in its socio-cultural context. The inner structure and operation of the school has been examined in its formal and informal dimensions. We want to find out now how the school maintains its identity as an autonomous institution as against other institutions and groups. The problem is one of cultural and social integration, the extent to which there is harmony and consistency in values and policy, and the extent to which relations are sociative rather than dissociative. We will deal with the relation of various special interest groups to the school, their criticisms, proposals, strategies, and tactics, with the counter-tactics of the school, and finally with the role of the courts in these issues.

Let us assume that you have been approached by the local chamber of commerce to develop a program of business-industry-school coöperation. You have decided that the idea seems good. Schools ought to coöperate with the community, and here is also an opportunity for contact with reality outside the cloistered school halls. The program involves among other points a series of field trips to businesses and plants. In some cases students will be permitted to take over the concern and operate it for a day. That sounds like a fine idea, and the publicity that will be in the paper will be good public relations. As the program is being formulated, you are visited by a delegation from the local unions. They object to the whole idea on the grounds that the program is management and business oriented to the exclusion or at least minimization of the significance of the unions. The program, they contend, is biased, if not antilabor. The delegation argues that the program should be dropped or that a corresponding amount of time and effort should be spent on union activities and programs. School-community coöperation no longer seems simple. While you are trying to resolve this dilemma, another small delegation marches in with a lot of questions about the textbooks. The books need a voluntary weeding out on the part of the school or else. You already know from what happened in communities in California, New Jersey, Colorado, and Ohio what this "or else" means. Your school is suddenly in the midst of sound and fury. Though your intentions were good and well meaning, you discover that each group is interested primarily in its point of view to the exclusion of the others. It seems as if each group wanted an orthodoxy in the school—its own. There are various ways by which groups try to get their orthodoxy, their value orientation, institutionalized in the school.

In a culturally integrated society such pressures would not face school administrators. But we have seen, in Chapter 3, how our culture is diversified into major alternative patterns out of which conflict may arise. In modern thought this situation has been characterized as a pluralistic society, a society of special interest groups. The word "pluralistic" is implicitly used as good or praiseworthy, in contrast to a "monolithic" totalitarian type of society, but the basic principle in both types actually is the same, namely, the interest principle. What this interest principle means has been readily recognized by earlier writers such as Hobbes and Hegel. It has been cogently stated by Madison in the tenth essay of *The Federalist*: the tendency to factionalism or stasis, the inability of functional groups in a society to get along with one another. On the interest principle —and by interest is meant self-advantage—a society is characterized by conflicts, truces, temporary liaisons, balance of power, a splintering into innumerable interests jockeying for positions of power. For Hobbes the answer to the situation was the state as Leviathan, the supreme power. For Madison the state was the umpire between the contending interests. Since the state itself is thought of as an interest group, it also has to fend for itself as against the others, and in this process is likely to become a totalitarian type, as Plato centuries ago rightly cognized. The concept of society as well as of the world is, then, of groups supposedly having harmony within and enmity without, a view found in *The Federalist* (essay VI),[1] the social Darwinism of the nineteenth century, and its attenuated form in much of contemporary sociological thinking.

The characteristic social relations on the basis of this traditional view would be dissociative, i.e., relations of hate, of enmity, and of power. If cultures are modeled in this fashion, such results are to be expected. One finds this in preliterate cultures with highly individualistic trends, such as the Mundugumor and Dobu,[2] also in classic culture, Periclean Athens, and Caesarian Rome.[3] Our modern world, as has been already suggested, is likewise modeled on the interest principle. However, no society is capable of maintaining itself exclusively on the interest principle and its corollaries of expediency and utility, for these are not principles of organization. The reference is subjective, particularistic. The proposition that the pursuit of self-interest automatically sums itself into the welfare of the whole is not necessarily true, as evidenced, for example, in racketeering and white-collar criminality. Interest means conflict and enmity. By enmity is meant "overt opposition to or aggression against a specific person or group; it may or may not be accompanied by hatred. In either event, it is open and recognized hostility, arising from conflicting interests, ideas, ways of life, or other separative tendencies. It is the opposite of coöperation and is expressed by acts

---

[1] Alexander Hamilton, John Jay, and James Madison, *The Federalist,* Everyman's Library, pp. 20–25. The theory of human nature correlates with the theory of society, viz., "That men are ambitious, vindictive, and rapacious" (p. 20), that momentary passions, and immediate interests, have a more active and imperious control over human conduct than general and remote considerations of policy, utility, and justice (p. 22). Cf. Gerard DeGré, "Freedom and Social Structure," *American Sociological Review,* October, 1946, pp. 530–536. The concept of freedom employed here is the traditional "freedom from external restraint."

[2] Margaret Mead, *Sex and Temperament in Three Primitive Societies,* New American Library, 1950, pp. 119 ff.; R. F. Fortune, *Sorcerers of Dobu,* E. P. Dutton and Company, 1932.

[3] Stanley Casson, *Progress and Catastrophe,* Harper & Brothers, 1937; Harry E. Barnes and Howard Becker, *Social Thought from Lore to Science,* D. C. Heath and Company, 1938, pp. 135–164; Ludwig Friedlaender, *Sittengeschichte Roms,* Phaidon Verlag, 1934; Carl C. Zimmerman, *Family and Civilization,* Harper & Brothers, 1947, on the "atomistic family system."

of injury, ill will, and refusal to communicate."[4] It is unlikely that in this situation truth and standards of integrity are elements in the dissociative relation; in other words, this opposition is not likely to be a conflict of impersonal ideals,[5] though that may vary with the value orientation supported. Appeals to truth, the facts, and standards of integrity are more likely to be associated with the humanist and common-man value orientations whereas appeals to traditional authority or prestige are more likely to be associated with the other value orientations. In the extreme form there is the hate organization and the "professional hate monger," sellers of hate and enmity for those who will pay the fee. The problem, then, is to view the school in this particular socio-cultural matrix. Given this condition, what happens?

CONTROVERSY AND CONSENSUS AND THE SCHOOL

The consensus of a society is expressed in a commonly shared and accepted system of beliefs, values, or agreeements on conduct and valuations of the major spheres of living. Even dissenting individuals and groups must recognize and deal with them. A continuous problem in every society is the transmission of this consensus from generation to generation. If there is no or little disagreement with regard to the areas of consensus, cultural transmission is easier. In highly differentiated societies such as ours this problem becomes more complicated, especially when there is controversy. The existence of controversy is an indication of lack of consensus. It means that consensus becomes highly relative, less common and shared. This relativized consensus is exemplified in the divergent value orientations.

In its formal program the school transmits culture in two broad areas: (1) the so-called tool subjects, writing, reading, arithmetic, science, vocational training, etc.; (2) attitudes and values, art, literature, and social studies. The former were thought to be neutral in nature until the publication of the *Nazi Primer*, for example, demonstrated explicitly how these "neutral" tool subjects can become

[4] E. T. Hiller, *Social Relations and Structures*, Harper & Brothers, 1947, p. 163. The entire analysis of dissociative relations by Hiller merits careful consideration.
[5] *Ibid.*, p. 174.

vehicles for the inculcation of attitudes and values. Perhaps the assumed neutrality of tool subjects in our country is not without value implication. It is in the area of the social studies that controversy and the assertion of control by diverse groups have been most manifest.[6] There has been distrust and suspicion of teachers precisely in the question of dealing with controversial issues.[7] The imposition of loyalty oaths upon teachers in many states and the activities of the Un-American Activities Committee during the past sixteen years highlight this situation.

THE SIGNIFICANCE OF THE SPECIAL INTEREST GROUP

Controversy is associated with the rise of special interest groups. These may rise spontaneously or may be created as a delegate or satellite group by a parent organization. The function of the special interest group is to further the acceptance of its value orientation. The special interest group identifies its particular subculture with the culture as a whole and usually advocates its value orientation, using such terms as "public welfare" or "for the good of the country," and similar broad appeals. Most groups are, doubtless, sincere in their convictions and actions, and so they try to induce the school to transmit their subculture rather than that of other groups. Transmission by the schools would represent an institutionalization of their values. Other groups naturally would oppose such efforts. Those groups which emphasize strongly the transmission of traditional values with which they identify themselves will be most active in this surveillance of the schools. Thus, the schools become a battleground of contending value emphases, and the schools become surrounded by a ring of militant special interest groups which are watching, censorious, and praising depending on the kind of event or crisis that may develop.

Many years ago De Tocqueville recognized the great role that special interest groups played in furthering a cause in the United

---

[6] Cf. Howard Beale, *A History of Freedom of Teaching in American Schools*, Charles Scribner's Sons, 1941; Bruce Raup, *Education and Organized Interests in America*, G. P. Putnam's Sons, 1936.

[7] *What People Think About Youth and Education*, Research Division, National Education Association, November, 1940, pp. 197–198.

States. While this tendency has continued, it has become much more complex and also professionalized. Its epitome is seen in the lobbying process, whether on the national or local level.[8] The special interest group in this instance is a pressure group striving for control over others. It is an attempt to influence or direct the policies and programs of other individuals and groups. These groups function on the national, state, and local level. Inasmuch as some of these groups are federated organizations, they represent a relatively unified organization of influence and pressure on all three levels. This fact is important as it makes possible one of the more effective techniques—pseudo grass-roots democracy. The national organization or the advertising public relations agency handling the contract supplies the general directives, formats, etc., to the local groups, who handle these as if they themselves had thought of them spontaneously.

It is difficult to know how many groups are involved in this process. Most business and industrial corporations have organized a variety of commodity or producer associations, trade associations, institutes, and chambers of commerce. There are numerous trade unions which also attempt control on the three levels mentioned. There are the farm organizations, coöperative groups, and consumer groups. To these one may add the patriotic, professional, and fraternal groups, all of which at some time may attempt to influence or control others. A rough estimate as to the proportion of such groups may be gleaned from the number of organizations which registered under the Lobby Act for the years 1946–49 (Table 52). The total number of groups came to 1295.

The funds spent in control efforts have been estimated as over a billion dollars,[9] and this only in connection with federal lobbying. The total amount spent in pressure and influence must be considerably over a billion dollars. This amount does not include a large hidden subsidy. One device of these groups is to have their material

[8] *Economic Power and Political Pressures*, Monograph No. 26, Temporary National Economic Committee, Investigation of Concentration of Economic Power, 76th Congress, 3rd Session, Senate Committee Print, Government Printing Office, 1941. Cf. Reports of the House Select Committee on Lobbying Activities, House of Representatives, 81st Congress, 2nd Session, 1950–51; Karl Schriftgiesser, *The Lobbyists*, Little, Brown and Company, 1951.

[9] Karl Schriftgiesser, *op. cit.*, pp. 146–168.

entered into the *Congressional Record,* print enormous numbers of copies by using the very low-cost government printing press, and distribute them free through the franking privilege of friendly congressmen. This amounts to a several million dollar subsidy.[10]

TABLE 52. Number and Percent of Groups Registered Under the Lobby Act, by Value Orientation, 1946–49

Value Orientation	Number	Percent
Market	873	67
Humanist	133	10
Common-man [a]	108	8
Nativist	69	5
Religious	19	1
Combinations [b]	59	4
Unclassified [c]	34	3

[a] Mostly trade unions.
[b] Mostly Indian tribes.
[c] Mostly individuals.
SOURCE: *Lobby Index,* 1946–49, A Report of the House Select Committee on Lobbying Activities, House of Representatives, 81st Congress, 2nd Session, Washington, 1950.

The amount of material poured forth by these various groups must be stupendous. One very active and high-powered group has claimed in one of its pamphlets that within a seven-year period, 1937–44, it had sent out:

82,000,000 pieces of literature—booklets, pamphlets, reprints of editorials and articles, specially addressed letters.
760,000 books.
More than 10,000 transcriptions, carrying 15-minute radio talks on national issues, besides frequent national hook-up for representatives of the committee.
350,000 telegrams to citizens to arouse them to actions on great issues.
Many thousands of releases to daily and weekly newspapers—full-page advertisements in 536 newspapers with a combined circulation of nearly 20,000,000.[11]

[10] *Ibid.,* pp. 205–207. For a specific case, see *Hearings* before the House Select Committee on Lobbying Activities, Part 5, 81st Congress, 2nd Session, Government Printing Office, 1950, pp. 97–107.
[11] *Hearings* before the House Select Committee on Lobbying Activities, Part 5, 81st Congress, 2nd Session, Government Printing Office, 1950, p. 6.

Another active group sent out around 4,000,000 pamphlets and booklets 1946–50, and its articles were used in 389 newspapers and magazines.[12] In contrast to these groups a third, for example, distributed, June, 1948–August, 1949, only 17,492 copies of its studies, but these studies were sent usually to opinion leaders and to persons professionally concerned with the subject matter of each study.[13] The three cases suggest the amount of activity typical of these groups. If we again consider the large number of groups that are involved, the struggle for control and influence is tremendous.

It is not our task to evaluate these groups but to note their bearing on education. There are two general ways by which the special interest and pressure groups attempt influence and control. The first is simply a matter of coöperation; the second is direct attack.

CONTROL THROUGH COÖPERATION

The action of special interest groups in this method is twofold: first, the services rendered are genuine, a "free will" offering to help the school; second, the services rendered include special pleading. The special pleading of its value orientation may assume either a minor or a major portion of the service. In either case the relation between donor and school is that of the exchange of a gift. A gift involves a mutual relation. There is the side of the donor and his bestowal of the gift. The giver may be on either an equal, a superior, or an inferior level. In the last case the action represents a token of lowly status and the object is ingratiation. In the second case the action represents high status and the object is condescension and the bestowal of a favor. In the first the objective involves mutual and willing admiration among equals. Since the gift is a social relation involving status and norms of conduct, the recipient of the gift is thus constrained to respond. He is obligated to respond in some affirmative fashion. The minimum is mere acknowledgment. The maximum is approval and support of the donor, i.e., the donor is to be preferred and favored as against non-donors. The more that gifts are accepted the more obligated does the recipient become.

[12] *Ibid.*, Part 8, p. 1.
[13] *House Report* No. 3233, House Select Committee on Lobbying Activities, 81st Congress, 2nd Session, Government Printing Office, 1950, p. 11.

The gift may promote a genuine or a spurious relation; genuine in conformance with norms of charity, sympathy, and admiration; spurious when the action is to minipulate the recipient to one's interest.[14] This manipulative aspect is more likely to occur when the paired relation is between unequals; however, it may be concealed in a relation of presumed equals. When the gift is not manipulative, there is implicit a respect for the other person, as demonstarted most vividly in gift sharing among family members and between lovers. This value of respect and concern for the other is a constant element in the gift relation even if the giving is manipulative, for the donor must at least pretend adherence to these values. No donor would dare give a gift openly stating and claiming a manipulative intent. Not only would such an offer be refused but the response might also involve resentment and hostility because of the norm and value violation. Unfortunately, in our Western society the gift has been used as a sales tool so that the bestowal of gifts becomes suspect outside of a primary group context and in social relations of a utilitarian type. The aphorism "don't look a gift horse in the mouth" no longer applies.

It is difficult to disentangle genuine and spurious gift relations as such appraisal involves the imputation of motives unless some objective data make this unnecessary. The clue for our analysis lies in the nature of the groups and their value orientations as discussed in Chapter 3. In addition, an examination of the gift may reveal the presence or absence of special pleading. Our premise also is that society is structured on the interest principle. On this principle we would deduce that the gift, especially between groups, will take on a manipulative quality, as the gift is for the advancement of one's interest.

The school is involved in the gift pattern, primarily as a recipient. As recipient it is thus constrained to be under obligation to the donor. This means that the policy of the school to the donors should be friendly, coöperative rather than skeptical and evaluative. It also means that the school is constrained to accept gifts. In this

[14] See Robert K. Merton et al., *Mass Persuasion*, Harper & Brothers, 1946, pp. 142–146, for a discussion of the pseudo-*Gemeinschaft*, the pretense of common values in order to promote private interests.

sense the school is an object of charity, and a refusal of a gift publicly may seem unreasonable and antagonistic. The gift, thus, places administrators in a social trap, for their response permits no in-between relation; the response is either sociative or dissociative. The odds are that the sociative response will be forthcoming, and the special interest will have reached its goal.

THE GIFT AND THE CURRICULUM

The amount of free materials prepared by special interest groups is fabulous. This material is not always designed for school use, but it can be used by almost any type of group. However, some of the material is especially designed for the school. The special interest groups may have educational bureaus of their own to prepare the material. In some cases the preparation is contracted out to advertising and public relations agencies or to educators who may be induced to prepare the material.

The type of free classroom material is also vast. It includes: films, film strips, pamphlets, books, posters, comic books, work sheets, maps, charts, tape and record transcriptions. To direct the use of the material, study outlines, tests, teacher guides, and scripts are furnished free. What is seen here is a subtle usurpation of the teacher's functions. The free material provides for everything. The use of the material thus directs the educational process.

The special interest group advertises and urges its free wares upon the schools. Any issue of the *NEA Journal* is replete with this type of free offer. A review of sixty-seven advertisements in this journal shows a variety of reasons for the offers. Some of the free material is offered as an inducement for the school to buy a particular product—example: the Ditto Company, which has prepared sixty-five workbooks with mats which can be used only on its machines. Compton's Encyclopedia includes an offer of free problem-solving units. Childcraft has similar offers. Periodicals such as *Time* and *Newsweek* offer free teaching aids. Some of the material is used to plug a product. The Cereal Institute has provided booklets on breakfasts, bar charts for nutritional education. Wrigley's gum advertises all sorts of free educational gimmicks in the promotion of their product. The Wheat Flour Institute has furnished materials for a nutritional program on all educational levels, including food charts, bulletins, and booklets. Some of the material contains special pleading. This has been so of the advertising posters offered by the Association of American Railroads and the American Meat Institute, and the comic booklets of the B. F. Goodrich Company. A trade union offered a film plus descriptive booklet on its activities. Lastly, there are materials simply portraying facts, like some of the booklets of General Motors on research.

Groups that have nothing to sell will either indulge in special pleading or attempt to be objective. However, most groups will feel that their material is objective and that of other groups likely to be biased, full of special pleading, especially when the groups are involved in controversy. This would be true of the way trade unions are likely to evaluate materials put out, for example, by the National Association of Manufacturers, the National Economic Council, Inc., the Committee for Constitutional Government, or the Conference of American Small Business Organizations. In turn, these groups are suspicious of trade union material, of which there is also a considerable amount. Patriotic groups will view with alarm both trade union and "liberal" publications and other material, e.g., that of the Americans for Democratic Action. The listing of such groups would become interminable. The point, however, is that in an era of relativized consensus the concept of truth tends to become relativized too, so that truth becomes the property and virtue of the in-group and error or falsity the vice of the out-group. This situation does not preclude the possibility of objective analysis. It does mean that any published material has to be very carefully scrutinzed, and a teacher in the rush and pressure of duties is unlikely to do this. Since the donor appears legitimate and respectable, an impression many groups give by adding educators to its trustees and educational committees, the teacher proceeds on faith that the donation is also legitimate.

The free offer directed to schools in general may or may not be taken up. A direct way of getting materials into the schools is simply by an unsolicited donation. The group sending the material adds a letter of transmittal. Such material is sent directly to school administrators and teachers. Some organizations design their material only for such officials. Another tactic is to send the material to the school library. These gifts are anonymously endowed by individual business concerns and other groups. Since many school libraries are rather inadequate, such unsolicited gifts may be quite welcome. Since this type of gift giving is impersonal, the obligations to donor are more tenuous. If some sort of follow-up, involving a personal contact by some local person, could be made, the gift would fall more completely into the pattern. The donation of materials to schools in this manner is a function of the financial resources of the group. The larger the resources, the more the group is capable of putting its materials into the schools to the disadvantage of those who lack such economic power and backing. The chances of the school's transmitting the value orientation of these groups is thereby increased.

Another tactic involving the gift and the captive audience is through lectures, speeches, and demonstrations furnished either free or at a most nominal cost by various organizations. These speakers may be supplied by organizations outside the community, or they may be supplied by local units. Here again, there may be several possibilities: an objective account of a topic, an objective account coupled with special pleading, or outright special pleading. The chances are that the last two possibilities will prevail, though this varies with the subject matter. The special pleading is most likely to occur in the social studies and to be more indirect in other areas of study. The advantage of this approach is the personal contact, with administrators, with teachers, and with students.

PRIZE CONTESTS AS A MEANS OF CONTROL

This approach is more limited as far as outreach and participation are concerned. Working on the contest by students and teachers is a control of the educational process. If study materials are furnished with the contest, the control is increased. Even though prizes are limited, the objective of controlling the curriculum is achieved. An added fillip would be the presentation of an award, which thus focuses on the donating group, good publicity for school and donor, notices in the school and local newspaper, announcement on the local radio, etc.

Attempts to influence the school through contests of various types became so notorious that the schools have reacted against them. There is considerable disagreement among educators as to the value of such contests, a controversy so far unresolved. To weed out the desirable from the undesirable contests, a national contest committee of the National Association of Secondary School Principals announces each year a list of national school contests by firms, organizations, and institutions outside the organized educational agencies. The list prepared by this committee is not binding on any school. In 1948–49 the committee approved thirty-four contests. Nine were art contests, ten essay contests, four forensic contests, six scholarships, and five miscellaneous. Twelve of these were sponsored by business groups or trade associations, four by nativist groups, four by groups interested in health and safety, three by teacher groups, two by fraternal organizations, two by periodicals, the remainder by groups with a humanistic orientation. This list is simply a suggestion of the types of contests that are involved. Some of them recur every year; others are temporary.

The listing does not tell anything about the content of these contests, though one can infer from the sponsor what sort of result is expected. The following may serve as an illustration. Beginning in 1947 and for several succeeding years the Association of American Physicians and Surgeons sponsored a national essay contest: "Why the Private Practice of Medicine Furnishes This Country with the Finest Medical Care," with prizes of $1000, $500, $100, and $25.[15] Materials for the contest were supplied to participants and libraries. The contest was supported by a ten-dollar levy upon the members of the organization. In order to win, the student had no choice but to be for this program and against any other program. It would be difficult to conceive how an awarding committee could judge any other way.[16] The effectiveness of such a tactic is hard to assess. However, the Purdue University public opinion polls of high-school

[15] Jean Begeman, "The Doctors' 'Freedom Program,'" *New Republic*, April, 1953, p. 10.

[16] For other examples of this technique, see Wilbur Brookover, *A Sociology of Education*, American Book Company, 1955, p. 69.

students showed that, in 1944, 77 percent of students favored "government providing medical service for all." In 1948, on the same question, 80 percent of the student response was favorable. After three years of the essay contest, a poll taken in 1950 showed that 53 percent favored such a program.[17] Whether this sizable percentage difference was due to the essay contest cannot be determined with any accuracy, though the propagandist would maintain that the method was successful. Every group sponsoring a contest hopes to achieve such success.

The idea of the field trip is an old one, but its use as a method of control is rather new. The original assumption is that the field trip is a learning experience if carefully prepared and directed by the teacher. It can become a method of propaganda when the control is in hands outside of the school. Plant tours in the form of Business-Industry-Education days are widespread. On such days school is dismissed. Teachers and students in small groups are guided through industrial plants and business firms. Just what is learned is difficult to ascertain, but evidence suggests that the participants are thoroughly impressed.[18] The tendency for a pro-management slant to develop is very high, even if no manipulation is intended. It is to this tendency that unions object.[19] The problem centers not in viewing and examining the technical phases of production but in the social implications and discussions, which may constitute a preferential treatment. A field trip is not necessarily neutral in the conflict of value orientations, and this aspect needs to be recognized.

An extended version of the field trip is in the form of scholarships or fellowships to teachers who participate in some firm or institute as an educational experience. Subsidization of teachers for such a purpose has been carried out by almost all groups, regardless of value orientation. It is simply another phase of the attempt to control the transmission of value orientations in the school. The subsidy, of course, is a gift, and thus, the norms and obligations of the gift pattern are instituted in another form.

[17] Jean Begeman, *op. cit.*, p. 10.
[18] Cf. testimonials offered in *Trends in Education-Industry Cooperation* and in the new format *Trends in Church, Education, Industry Cooperation*, National Association of Manufacturers, any issue.
[19] J. Austin Burkhardt, "Big Business and the Schools," *The Nation*, November 10, 1951, p. 402.

DIRECT ATTACK ON THE SCHOOLS

Direct action to control the school may dovetail with the coöperative approach. The same groups may be involved, or they may operate through a "front" organization. A front organization is one whose real purposes, clientele, methods of operation, or sources of financial support are different from those stated by it. There are also those groups which wholly or in part derive their income from propaganda or so-called public relations work. The function of such groups is to arouse, manipulate, and engineer public opinion, to put a concentrated pressure upon the school and upon that point which seems most vulnerable, the board of education. As the board is the decision-making body, the pressure eventually has to be placed upon it to force decision in conformance with the desires of the agitating groups. The right to petition for redress of grievance, of course, is a basic one in a democratic society, though the right to petition through pressure group methods may be a perversion of the original intention. The right of petition is premised on the natural law conception of the person, i.e., the rational, reasonable, self-directing individual. This concept involves a willingness to communicate, to listen, to weigh, to arrive at a judicious judgment by the participants. Those involved in a direct attack upon the schools do not adhere to this view. In so far as they seem to be attacking some shadowy internal enemy personified eventually in school teachers and administrators, the ensuing dissociative relation involves unwillingness to communicate.

Doubtlessly, the motives of many who are going to save the schools are sincere. They are convinced of the absolute rightness of their value orientation, and their actions flow naturally from their value premises. What they do, however, may be skillfully manipulated by those having a vested interest in agitation. How such individuals view the situation may be glimpsed in the following sardonic statement written in the middle thirties by a former liberal:

At the present moment the best system for men and women who want to be writers and also want to be rich is to trade upon the fears of the rich. The world is full of alarums. The Red Menace sparkles on every

SPECIAL INTERESTS AND EDUCATION   *477*

side. Raids upon his money bags are threatened from every quarter. This is the natural atmosphere for the rich man's terrors. Therefore, the first thing to do is to play upon these terrors. Scare him some more. Then invent some racket for protecting him from those perils.

One good field—which is the occasion for this outburst to the acquisitive writer—is the schools. There the Bolsheviki are ceaseless. They are stealing the souls of our children and poisoning the minds of our teachers. They are being taught the wickedness of wealth and undermining the constitutional props. Therefore, what better racket than to save the schools from this monster. Therefore, organize an agency like, for instance, the National Republic Lettergram Service of Washington D.C. Send out letters, bulletins, circulars, and pamphlets keeping loyal teachers advised of the march of the Reds upon the school. Then you can call upon patriotic rich men to subscribe $100, $150, or maybe $1,000 to carry on this great work.[20]

Much of the ammunition for the local groups is supplied by the professional agitators, for a fee. This fact means, among other things, that considerable financial backing has to be furnished. The locus of such backing is either corporate or in the middle and upper classes.

Direct attacks on education are not new.[21] The attacks have generally coincided with some sort of critical period: the revolutionary period, ending in the Alien and Sedition Acts, the Civil War period, the turbulent nineties, the post-World War I 1920's with their "red scare" and fracas about teaching evolution, the depressed thirties, and the cold war aftermath of World War II. In the current situation both state and national government through special committees, which presumably were collecting facts for legislative proposals, took on the role of Star Chamber court proceedings and attempted directly to influence the use of textbooks and the employment of teachers. While these committees have dealt with the public school, their primary target was the universities, colleges, and foundations.

THE ISSUES

From a humanist point of view the issue is educational freedom. What this means may be summarized under the following six points:

[20] John T. Flynn, "To Get Rich, Scare the Rich," *New Republic,* September 9, 1936.

[21] Howard Beale, *A History of Freedom in American Schools,* Charles Scribner's Sons, 1941; Howard Beale, "Teacher as Rebel, His War for Freedom," *The Nation,* May 16, 1953, pp. 412–412.

1. That no religious, political, social, racial, or other noneducational factor shall influence the appointment of teachers.
2. That teachers shall be protected against dismissal for religious, political, racial, or social views or for membership in any religious, political, racial, or national-origin group, while remaining liable to dismissal for incompetence, neglect of duty, moral turpitude, violation of the freedom of others, or conviction of crime under the laws of the land.
3. That teachers have the right to a fair hearing when accused.
4. That their freedom of conduct, both public and private, shall be no more restricted than that of other citizens.
5. That students shall be allowed to hear all points of view on controversial subjects fairly presented, and to formulate their own opinions.
6. That there should be access to all materials necessary for study.[22]

The humanist takes the Jeffersonian view that in the free interplay of ideas, in free discussion, truth will prevail, or as expressed by Chief Justice Hughes in the De Jonge case (299 U.S. 353), "The greater the importance of safeguarding the community from incitements to the overthrow of our institutions by force and violence, the more imperative is the need to preserve inviolate the constitutional rights of free speech, free press, and free assembly in order to maintain the opportunity for free political discussion."

It is the humanist and common-man point of view that generally is under attack, and in so far as the schools may incorporate these value systems, they must perforce come under attack.

The programs of three organizations will be examined to determine the issues. Of these the overall broad stand will be examined to show that the school is but one issue. Detailed charges will be taken from one organization.

The legislative positions taken by the National Economic Council, Inc., are shown in the following, as filed under the Federal Regulation of Lobbying Act and in the correspondence from its files. For the period 1949–50:

Favors:
Additional restrictions on labor unions.
Removal of present Supreme Court and barring of its Justices from holding judicial office.
Limiting of Government's taxing power through constitutional amendment.

[22] Howard Beale, "Teacher as Rebel," p. 412.

A ceiling on income-tax levies.
Aid to Spain.
Withdrawal of Federal claims to tidelands in favor of States.
Taxation of cooperatives.
Opposes:
Federal aid to education.
Displaced-persons legislation.
Further immigration.
Public housing.
Middle-income housing bill.
United States participating in United Nations.
United States participating in International Trade Organization.
United States participating in International Labor Organization.
United States ratification of Genocide Convention.
FEPC, anti-lynching bill, and other civil-rights measures.
Rent control.
Marshall plan.
United States support for an independent Israel.
Social security.
Farm-price support.
Point 4 program.
Reciprocal Trade Agreement Act.
TVA.
Atomic Energy Act.
World Federation resolution.

Other positions reflected in the same material:
For:
Private enterprise.
Private property.
Individual initiative.
American independence.
Against:
Communism.
World Government.
United Nations.
Bipartisan foreign policy.
Militant Zionism.
Antitrust suits against A. & P., Du Pont.[23]

While some of the issues are dead, the general view is that of the nativist and market orientations, and this combination also accounts

[23] *Hearings,* House Select Committee on Lobbying Activities, House of Representatives, 81st Congress, 2nd Session, Part 4, Government Printing Office, 1950, pp. 60–61.

for the attack on government. There may also be a trace of anti-Semitism in this program, though this attitude is but a variant of nativism.

Content analysis of materials published by the Foundation for Economic Education and the Committee for Constitutional Government is similar. A study of themes in 200 paragraphs published by the first group shows that 71 percent deals with the advent of socialism, 19 percent with free enterprise, and 10 percent with taxes. Socialism is equated with all the welfare legislation supported by the Democratic party in 1932–52. Attempts are made to show that this legislation is anti-Christian. The second theme is to demonstrate the worth of free enterprise. The third theme deals with high taxes. The thesis defended is that taxation is governmental stealing and anti-Christian. The Committee for Constitutional Government follows a similar line except it does not undertake a religious justification for its view. The implied criticism of the schools would be that they support welfare legislation, thus also support socialism, therefore are against free enterprise and individualism—and the secularism of the public school is against Christianity.

This type of criticism becomes vehemently articulate in the attacks of the professional hucksters of suspicion, doubt, and hatred. A good example is a pamphlet entitled "Progressive Education Causes Juvenile Delinquency." A cartoon on the title page pictures a scrawny, spinsterish, elderly female chopping spitefully if not gleefully with a broad-headed ax at the tree of the American Way of Life, attempting to bring down the fruits of fair play, honesty, justice, etc.

In a detailed content analysis of eight pamphlets and ten papers issued by one of these organizations each paragraph was analyzed for theme, and the themes were grouped into major topics. Topics and themes are discussed in order of their importance as judged by the amount of space allotted to them.

1. *Communism and Socialism.* This topic appeared in various forms in 84 out of 320 paragraphs. Americanism is presented as the antithesis of communism and socialism. Related themes charge that

Academic freedom is used to dispense communism and socialism.
Academic freedom is academic license.

"They" (Communists or Socialists)
    advocate concentration of power.
    conceal the origin of Communist ideas.
    use good but misguided people.
    want world conquest.
    want to control the schools.
    use distortion, but have found that outright lying does not work.
Socialism is moving in, is a threat.

The New Deal is an example of how socialism enters the campus and then moves out into the world.

Socialism is linked with strikes, with attacks on private property, with pacifism.

Communism breeds hate, destroys its promoters, hopes to control American education in order to destroy it.

International communism is a threat.

A secret number of teachers are Communists.

2. *Progressive Education.* The interpretation here is that progressive education teaches that truth is not absolute or everlasting. The theme is broadened into an attack on pragmatic philosophy and specifically against the statements of John Dewey, who becomes the intellectual scapegoat. Clifford Kilpatrick is a close second. The charges are:

Pragmatism, which underlies progressive education, is atheism and selfishness, is antisocial, an ivory tower philosophy; teaches that a moral order does not exist, teaches that decisions should be made on own immediate experience, that the immediate desire of the pupil is all that matters, that truth is mere utility.

Progressive education is a problem, wrecks individualism, is against indoctrination (although progressive educators are inconsistent about indoctrination), is all method and no goal.

The public-school system is dedicated to progressive education and the educators, rather than the parents, determine the methods and aims of education. Modern methods of education are ignored by progressive education.

Progressive education is on the way out since it
    increases social delinquency, juvenile delinquency.
    has no substance.
    is an outmoded grotesquerie.
    is noneducational.
    rejects knowledge.

rejects morality.

teaches social, not individual values.

3. *What Should and Should Not Be Taught in the Schools.* The main theme is that education should make children loyal Americans. This should be the major function of the schools and colleges in the country. The development of this topic is inconsistent and self-contradictory. It contains some of the following themes:

Education is not for opinion but for facts.

Opinions have no place in the classroom.

Only Americanism should be taught.

There should be freedom with control.

There should be a balance between facts and thinking.

Education should be adaptable to individual differences and interests.

In education there is a need for freedom of choice of values.

Educated man is moral man, informed and thinking man.

There is disagreement among educators over transmitting knowledge.

There has been a change from scientific studies to "dynamism."

Federal control would mean a transformation of the curriculum.

4. *Teachers.* The main theme is a criticism of academic freedom.

Teachers should be pro-American.

Their loyalty is needed.

They go beyond their responsibility and teach opinion.

They want a special freedom.

It is pointed out that professors are the same as everybody else, that only a few are unstable, but that the present faculty must be screened.

5. *Money.* The main point here is that federal aid to education would bring federal control of education. Other points made:

Federal aid would mean that the individual state would take a loss.

Tax money should be refunded if not used in public school.

Our schools are not free because they are tax supported.

Education costs; our schools do not have sufficient funds to operate.

Tuition for private schools should be deductible from income tax.

It would be a moral thing to remove this double taxation for Catholics.

World government would bring the problem of money.

World government would precipitate world-wide inflation.

America is now supporting the rest of the world.
Americans would have to pay more taxes.

6. *Public and Private Schools.* In general the argument is a plea for the private school and the superiority of the private school over the public. There is a plea for bigger and better private schools.

Public school has an inherent political character.
Parents should be responsible for education.
There are not enough private schools now but soon will be.

7. *Freedom and Religion.* The main theme is "we get our American ideals from the Christian religion."

Public schools destroy American ideals of freedom.
American freedom is connected to the Christian religion.
United States is famous because of its freedom.
Americans would have to share wealth under world government.
Americans are decent people.
Freedom is more important than possessions.
Our forefathers believed in this ideal; we should do the same.
Americans would lose their national sovereignty for world government.
World government would bring chains and slavery.

8. *Peace.* The major theme is that world government would not make for peace.

Advocates of world government expect everyone to cease antagonism.
Americans do not want peace at any price.

9. *American Superiority.* This stresses the dangers of world government.

There is a conspiracy to undermine the American way of life.
World government would have to be organized and run either by the United States or by Russia.
Americans are superior.
Oriental tradesmen are not up to standards.
World government would have to be democratic for us.
World majority is not favorable to Americans.
Tariffs and immigration barriers would have to come down.
World government would
 ruin American industry and labor.
 harm small businessmen.
 bring problem of enforcement.
 mean foreign armies here.

take over police power.

have power of life and death.

America would resist world government forces.

10. *Discrimination.*   This is approved.

There should be and are inequalities in the United States.
Competition is the law of life.
Majority rule should not apply to education.
Material things for the masses are not necessary.

11. *Individualism.*   The major theme is individualism versus statism. Statism is equated with the welfare state, bureaucrats, regimentation, and centralization. The second theme is that individualism is now rare.

12. *Either-Or.*   There are two themes: Either the self or society, and "either we or a world majority must be masters in our house."

13. *Miscellaneous.*

Today there is a battleground of ideas.
We must use propaganda.
Capitalism has been lax.
We have stated the case of progressive education fairly and sympathetically.
These are serious times.
The situation in the colleges is terrible.
Your generation must carry on the American tradition.
There is subversive work carried out by students.

In Table 53 the proportionate distribution of the themes is summarized. Over one-half of the examined paragraphs are devoted to interlinking education, communism, and socialism. The overall picture of this type of propaganda is one based on nativist and market principles with oligarchic overtones.[24] Whether the allegations in these materials are true or not is irrelevant to the analysis. However, it must be pointed out that there is almost no documentation, an uncritical use of the files of the federal and California Un-American Activities Committees, files which have a tendency to quote one another, a reliance upon alleged authorities, use of glittering generalities, name calling, and appeals to patriotism, prejudice, and

[24] Cf. Morris Mitchell, "Fever Spots in American Education," *The Nation*, October 27, 1951, pp. 344–347; for a periodical which consistently follows the attack pattern outlined, see *The National Republic*.

TABLE 53. Distribution of Themes in Pamphlet Material
of the National Council for American Education

Theme	Number	Percent
Linkage of education, socialism, and communism	84	26
Criticism of "progressive education	75	23
What should and should not be taught in the schools	37	12
Criticism of teachers	23	7
Money, federal aid to education	23	7
Freedom, freedom and Christianity	19	6
American superiority	18	6
Anti-public and pro-private school	9	3
Pro-discrimination and inequality	8	3
Anti-world government, pro-national sovereignty	5	1
Individualism, anti-state	4	1
Either-or	3	1
Miscellaneous	12	4
Total paragraphs	320	100

especially fear—fear of Russia, fear of loss of job and security, fear of others, and even fear of our own government. Very few constructive statements are made.

PATTERN OF ATTACK

There are few new twists in the pattern of attack on schools. The techniques were hatched and refined during the turbulence of the late thirties, when the organization of workers in the mass industries was opposed, by methods of control that finally became systematized in the Mohawk Valley formula.[25] Today both sophistication and crudity mark the methods and techniques that are designed to motivate and move special publics to action.[26] How, then, to attack the schools in the most effective way? The arsenal of ideas has been

[25] Wilbert Moore, *Industrial Relations and the Social Order*, The Macmillan Company, 1946, pp. 399–449; Alfred McClung Lee, *How to Understand Propaganda*, Rinehart and Company, 1952, pp. 145–176.

[26] Alfred McClung Lee, *op. cit.*; Carey McWilliams, "Government by Whitaker and Baxter, III," *The Nation*, May 5, 1951, pp. 418–421.

examined; the inventory now has to deal with choice of weapon, strategy, and tactic.[27]

When is a good time to commence an attack on the schools? There are several occasions that are auspicious: (1) a school bond issue campaign; (2) a school tax levy issue; (3) a school board election; (4) factionalism in the school, especially in the type where there is a dual control as between superintendent and business manager; (5) any type of new program or reorganization; (6) the use of school facilities by outside groups. Some of these situations may occur together so that the chances for a broad attack are increased. The first two occasions are rather obvious because of the issue of money; the financing of the schools can readily lead into a criticism of the use of the moneys. Thus, the issue may shift from school financing to school program. In the third case, there may be division among board members as between "conservatives" and "liberals" and also on the basis of religious differences, usually a Roman Catholic-Protestant division. Each division may have its followers, and thus, the struggle is on. Factionalism within the school is somewhat similar in nature to case three. As we have seen in Chapter 14, there is a great tendency to friction when there is a dual system of control in the school. This problem may also arise when an official attempts to maximize his sphere of jurisdiction, e.g., a business manager attempts to control curriculum by his approval or disapproval of expenditures. The fifth occasion is a clash between those who

[27] The pattern of attack is based upon: David Dreiman, *How to Get Better Schools*, Harper & Brothers, 1956, pp. 16–22, 40–51; the *Denver Post, Faceless Informers and Our Schools*, 1954; The *Houston Post*, October 11–October 28, 1953; Frank Buchanan, "Lobbying and Its Influence on the Public Schools," *The Nation's Schools*, July, 1951, pp. 23–27; David Hulburd, *This Happened in Pasadena*, The Macmillan Company, 1951; Dick Brunner, "Priests vs. Parishioners," *The Nation*, July 28, 1951, pp. 68–70; Carey McWilliams, "Our Town in Turmoil," *The Nation*, June 16, 1951, pp. 558–560; Ernest Melby, *American Education Under Fire*, Freedom Pamphlet, Anti-Defamation League of B'nai B'rith, 1951; Kenneth M. Gould, "The Scarsdale Story," *The Humanist*, No. 4, 1952, pp. 145–159; National Commission for the Defense of Democracy Through Education, Proceedings of the Commission's Open Meeting at the 93rd Annual Meeting of the National Education Association of the United States, July 5, 1955; *Report of an Investigation, Houston, Texas*, National Commission for the Defense of Democracy Through Education, NEA, December, 1954; *Censorship Bulletin*, American Book Publishers Council, March, May, 1956; *Defense Bulletin*, National Commission for the Defense of Democracy Through Education, NEA, January, 1954–September, 1956; Edward Darling, *How We Fought for Our Schools*, W. W. Norton and Company, 1954; Max Lowenthal, *The Federal Bureau of Investigation*, William Sloane Associates, 1950; James Rorty, "The Attack on Our Libraries," *Commentary*, June, 1955.

become upset by a change within the school and those who presumably benefit by the change. If the change is not clearly understood by the community, then an unenlightened public may become involved, especially when skillfully led by some particular faction. The sixth occasion represents a clash between the programs and views of different community groups so that one attempts to prevent another from using the school building for meetings. The attack may also be directed against speakers which a group may invite to discuss some issue or problem. All these situations can introduce a network of angry dissociative actions.

The attacking units must be organized. This works out in about three ways. An existing organization may marshal its own forces to attack. This organization may attempt to induce other organizations to join or coöperate with it, forming a united front against the school as well as against organizations defending the school. If there is no established group to spearhead the attack, a local group will be specially formed. The group will usually adopt a name suggesting that it is operating for the welfare of the school and the welfare of the community. Membership is highly selected and meetings are usually closed. Control frequently is autocratic. Such a special established group may then attempt liaisons with other groups. If the community is large enough, more than one such group will be organized. Lastly, contact may be made with groups outside the community for propaganda materials. Agents of such propaganda groups may be invited in, for a fee, to assist in the agitation. Ex-FBI agents operating private detective or investigating agencies are frequently brought into the fray as "impartial" consultants.

It is not possible to indicate all of the tactics used in attacking the schools. That guidance is given to local groups from the outside is very clear. This can be seen in the uniformities of the attacking pattern and the materials used. The standardized pattern has the following characteristics. As in all propaganda, heavy use is made of the media of communication. A calculated letter campaign to newspapers criticizing schools is an opening gambit. This criticism may refer to any of the six occasions mentioned above. If a newspaper is friendly to the criticism, it will tend to print more of these critical letters and limit or ignore defending letters. The tactic is to send in the letter as an individual though the sponsorship and content of the letter are organizational. Thus, it is the irate taxpaper, the worried mother, the proud patriot who sends in the complaining letter. As the groups always seem well financed, they are able to do quite a bit of printing on their own of fliers, leaflets, newsletters, etc. The material may be either homespun, standard organizational diatribe, or purchased from the hate hucksters. Radio commentators may be solicited to join the cause. If a friendly newspaper also owns a local radio station, the channels are clear. As most commentators are conservative and an attack is spectacular, the odds of his jumping on the band wagon are good. Lastly there is the telephone. On the one extreme is wire tapping. The other extreme is the anonymous call late at night to make threats. A planned telephone campaign directed to persons of influence in school or otherwise may be used. Again persons will speak as individuals, not as members of an organization. To insure fast organizational action the phone chain system is used. This technique roots in an autocratic system, i.e., commands from the top, obedience in the lower levels. Leader X contacts his subordinates. Each of these contacts five members. Each of these five members contacts five other members, and so on. Furthermore, which member is to be called is specifically assigned.

Personal contact with persons of influence or officials is an important tactic. It has been already stressed, i.e., to make the contact as an individual and to suppress the organizational affiliation which prompted the attack. When a leader or official is attacked on an issue by individuals over a period of time, it may seem to him that a grass-roots uprising is taking place. This is the impression it is hoped will be conveyed even though the grass roots are all in the upper-middle and lower-upper classes. It is actually a pseudo-democratic movement. It was thus possible for a small group of women plus a few men to upset the Houston school system. The united front of these doughty females came to .0007 percent of the population 21 years and over, or .0005 percent if the population of the Houston metropolitan area is used as the base. This extremely tiny fraction of the total voting population presumed to dictate and to control school policy and the intellectual life of the community. The tactic works, and an official harassed by a few, articulate, middle-aged women may think that they represent large numbers. A well-planned public opinion survey would show up the pretensions of such individuals to speak for the community as a whole. However, such a survey would be denounced as biased by such groups and individuals, who would also claim that the masses do not have the inside information. They have, and thus their voice is *vox populi* and therefore also *vox dei*. Part of the tactic is to deny organizational affiliation when the linkage is indicated. This procedure is to make certain of creating the impression that the persons speak as individuals. The reason for the whole tactic is that officials will pay more attention to individuals than to organizations. An organization can speak only once, but through its members, posing as concerned individuals, it can speak as many times as members will speak up. Such hammering away at leaders and officials in a tactic of planned, pseudo-spontaneous, pseudo-grass-roots "public opinion" is effective.

The content of accusations directed against school board members, superintendents, teachers, and textbooks has been indicated. The technique primarily is the "big lie" technique, a repeated statement of distortions which increase as time goes on. Character assassination, ample use of anonymous but "reliable" sources, access to confidential files, use of official and unofficial black lists, censored book lists, all contribute to an aggressive offense which presumes that the victim is guilty and must be so judged until he clears himself. This presumption of guilt is a repudiation of a hard-won cultural achievement, a reversal of all judicial procedures, a Star Chamber atavism. If a charge is successfully challenged, one simply shifts ground to another issue or charge. The affirmative statement is better than a denial. The victim is always placed in a protesting role, and in a conflict situation that is a weak one. If any sort of counterattack takes place, the cry of "smear" or "undemocratic" is raised.

The next tactic is applied to the wrecking or controlling of a meeting, such as a school board meeting, PTA meetings, or forums and public discussions of school matters. To set the tone some sort of demonstration, involving patriotic symbols, is threatened. As soon as the meeting comes to order, if not before, the discussion must be monopolized. If the chairman attempts control, he must be accused of dictatorial tactics, branded an enemy of freedom of speech. Several members of the group must be planted in various parts of the hall. The function of these individuals is to form a heckling panel. As one member leaves off, another takes up. Other speakers should be interrupted with trivial insinuating questions. If this is successful, the meeting will fall apart and break up. If heckling and other disturbance-creating tactics fail and if there is an opportunity to become an official part of the meeting, this should be attempted. In official position one can more readily throw a meeting. Prolonging a meeting into late hours is a way of killing future interest. Raising questions about it as an audience member, before, during, and after a meeting, is essential. If a meeting is concluded, it should be denounced the next day through the various media of communication. Action in a meeting is premised on the assumption that the attacking side is absolutely right and everyone else is the enemy, and there is no reason why any attention should be paid to the enemy.

Another procedure is a boring from within technique. This works in two ways. The first is to develop a spy system in the attacked organization. Students, teachers, supervisory and administrative personnel are all possible informers. This is the technique of the faceless informer. It weakens opposition as it destroys trust. The second way is to place one's own members in strategic positions so that they will have access to the files and other information essential for the attack. Also, when members are in official strategic positions, they can effectively weaken a counterattack.

The pattern of attack described is not inherently associated with the school. It can be directed to any institutional group. This generality of the attack pattern is the important point. Variations of it have taken place in business organizations, trade unions, and many other social action groups. This type of destroying pattern should not be identified with political groups, and our analysis has made that clear. The incidence of attacks on schools is fortunately not high in light of the many communities where such turmoil has not occurred. That these attacks are successful in the short run is clear. Superintendents and teachers have been discharged. Textbooks, library books, and periodicals have been removed. Special activities have been cut out. Bond and tax levies have been defeated. Teachers refuse to discuss controversial issues. Though the incidence may be relatively small, the general aftermath may be great. One does not need a controversial attack on one's own school when the lesson of such attack appears within the walls of other schools. The handwriting on the wall spells out "conformity, play it safe, don't think—too much." Such a situation is not only anti-education but also anti-man, inhibiting his growth potentialities, favoring the robot mind.

What can be done to check the destructive tactics and attempts at control by militant groups? The partiality and narrowness of special interest must be overcome. The best protection is to know the facts, and these facts must be shared. Objectivity and the common acquisition of insight, a creative growth process, both intellectual and social in nature, are the components in furthering the good. In this process opposition may be overcome. In terms of sociological principles previously discussed, this is a case of transforming a dissociative tendency into a sociative one. The analysis of this problem will be our next topic.

Selected Readings

Dreiman, David, *How to Get Better Schools*, Harper & Brothers, 1956, Part I.

Hulburd, David, *This Happened in Pasadena*, The Macmillan Company, 1951.

Katz, Daniel, et al. (eds.), *Public Opinion and Propaganda*, The Dryden Press, 1954, chaps. 3, 5, 8.

Lee, Alfred M., *How to Understand Propaganda*, Rinehart and Company, 1952.

Schriftgiesser, Karl, *The Lobbyists*, Little, Brown and Company, 1951.

CHAPTER 19

The Development of Mutuality

DENUNCIATION OF the schools has brought forth few if any positive results, aside from contributing to the income of the professional agitator or heightening the sense of self-importance of the self-appointed guardian of the society. The clamor of the special interest group is to have education organized solely on its terms regardless of the facts of child nature and of the world. That the school has deficiencies has been noted in previous chapters. There is much concern about improving education in many quarters where criticism has attempted to be fair in terms of available facts. The bull-in-the-china-shop approach is replaced by tough reasonableness based upon investigation and study. Criticism is a legitimate function provided it is carried out according to norms of fairness and objectivity.

The aim of the analysis in this chapter is not to provide a public relations handbook.[1] The problem is educational planning. This planning should be objective, carried out with due regard for the facts of child growth and the changes taking place within the culture. It should minimize opposition and facilitate coöperation. Much opposition to planning is like a witch's caldron fuming special interest, ignorance, and hostility. Our job is to see how persons and

[1] David Dreiman, *How to Get Better Schools,* Harper & Brothers, 1956, is as good a handbook as can be found; also Wilbur Yauch, *How Good Is Your School?* Harper & Brothers, 1951, chap. XIV.

groups can design their patterns of action on the basis of knowledge —specific knowledge of the school system in question, a background of knowledge derived from the natural and social sciences. In the context of controversy the answer lies in a creative process of self-education of all concerned with changing or improving schools. The process is creative in so far as ignorance is dispelled and enlightenment is gained. It is self-education to the extent that this enlightenment is secured by effort rather than absorbed as a handout from authority. The process is social in so far as the development of insight is a mutual, coöperative project.

What this means will be clarified by examining the approach of the National Education Association, by reviewing five cases involving opposition, and lastly by summarizing the implications of these materials.

THE NEA AND CRITICISM OF THE SCHOOLS

Since the NEA is the professional organization for school personnel, an examination of its approach to school planning and to school criticism may cast light upon the problem under analysis. This organization has also come under attack by the type of group discussed in the previous chapter. The attacks, in part, have arisen because the NEA through one of its commissions has been active in attempting to solve many of the community controversies centering on the school. How, then, does the NEA function in this situation?

EDUCATOR'S VIEW OF THE ATTACKS

The following account is based upon a content analysis of two pamphlets and five articles. Of 264 paragraphs, 167 were devoted to an examination of the attacks and the attackers. The remainder dealt with a statement of the educator's stand. There are seven areas into which the themes of these paragraphs can be classified. As the last is a "miscellaneous" category, it will not be considered.

The first topic deals with "the attacks and their composition." Only the major themes will be considered, and these are as follows:

1. Criticism is not wrong, but the grounds of attack are bad.
2. The attacks are an attempt to undermine the schools under the guise of patriotism.

3. The attacks express an authoritarian philosophy of life.

4. The attacks are based either on ignorance of education or on intentional distortion of facts.

5. The attacks threaten democracy.

What educators perceive in the attack is the idea that free public schools are wrong in principle. One of the premises in the attack is a laissez-faire individualism, and on this premise there is the judgment that the free public school is socialistic. There is also the implication that an unthinking majority continuously subdues and dominates a thinking minority. In so far as the attack advocates rigid discipline, indoctrination, curtailing access to information and expression of opinion, educators regard it as expressing an anti-democratic and, hence, an authoritarian view. However, educators are not averse to using the bad label, classifying the attackers as fascist, Nazi, or, last but not least, communist-minded. In general, the educators think that the attacks reveal a lack of understanding of what education means in a predominantly urban-industrial-technological world.

The second topic deals with an exposé of the enemies, especially the "professional enemy" of public schools. The themes are similar to those discussed except that they are linked up with specific organizations, such as the National Council for American Education, the American Education Association (Keep Our American Schools American), the Church League of America, the Conference of American Small Business Organizations Committee on Education, the Employers Association of Chicago (How Red Is the Little Red School House?), and others. An attempt is made to show what tactics these groups use and what type of literature they publish so that people can be on guard against their propaganda.

The third topic deals with the role of education. The themes tend to be an affirmation of the humanistic value orientation. The major themes are: (1) that education in America is rooted in democratic philosophy; (2) that the goal of education is the development of an intelligent and active citizenry; (3) that education is a changing, dynamic process. Minor themes support these. For example, public schools are not for the teaching of religion. The three "R's" are still important, but education should equip the child to meet the problems of the day. Man is more important than the state. Inquiring minds are needed. The past was simple.

The fourth topic deals with solutions. The major theme is that school-community coöperation will solve educational problems. A second major theme is that the citizens themselves must take the initiative. Minor themes stress the importance of knowledge, an informed lay public, and the responsibility of educators to inform the public.

The fifth topic represents an attempted explanation of the attacks on the school. The theme is that the schools are used as a scapegoat. In a tense situation people are looking for something upon which to release their fears, anxieties, and hatreds. The schools have become the target for such persons. Whether or not this explanation is valid is another question.

The sixth topic deals with the public. The themes are that educators have been lax in their public information relations and that the public is not aware of the problem.

BASIC PREMISES ON CRITICISM OF SCHOOLS

The following statement summarizes the position of the NEA. Criticism is accepted as a part of living, as vital to the democratic process. Constructive criticism made by laymen may keep the school responsive to the needs of the community. "Criticism has its greatest value when citizens and educators use it in working cooperatively to solve school problems."[2] There are several specific premises involved, as follows:[3]

1. Public schools belong to the people. They exercise their prerogatives through lay representatives on boards of education.
2. The need for public education is accepted and supported by the people. Conflict about educational procedures arises because of (a) lack of information about them, and (b) differences of opinion about objectives, methods, and techniques.
3. Teachers are employees of the public. This does not mean, however, that they should sacrifice sound principles for the sake of placating unwarranted criticism. The teaching profession is obligated to protect the

[2] Local Association Activities Leaflet, No. 22, National Education Association, n.d., p. 1.
[3] Ibid.

good reputation of an institution which society has created for its own welfare.

4. Experience shows that if in those communities where two-way channels have been established and utilized citizens have confidence in teachers and education because they are acquainted with what schools are doing.

5. When coöperation between schools and community is at a high level, sudden outbursts of unwarranted criticism do little harm. Leaders among citizens will rise to the occasion and give full support to the schools in coöperation with school officials.

6. When unwarranted criticisms are made, teacher leaders should exercise restraint. It should be assumed at the start that those who criticize, no matter how loudly, are sincere, honest, well-intentioned people, even though they may be lacking in information about the schools and their problems.

These working principles represent the humanist value orientation. It shows that the problem is interpreted to be one of understanding (knowledge) and communication. The statement assumes that the social model of the humanist value orientation is generally accepted. The thematic analysis above suggests that this concept of the attacker is not adhered to. The concept of the "professional enemy" does not assume that the critics are sincere, honest, and well-intentioned, merely lacking adequate information about the schools. The "enemy" view is expressed in phrases such as "wild charges from the destructive-minded group."[4] The image of the critics is thus twofold—the good but uninformed person who is reasonable and willing to communicate and the bigoted person. Strategy would be based on these two concepts.

ACTION AGAINST CRITICISM

The NEA proposes that certain steps be taken. The first is to find out whether or not the criticism is justifiable. Are the alleged weaknesses found in the school program? If they are found, then corrective measures can be taken. If not, then the criticism is judged unwarranted, and countermeasures should be taken.

Unfortunately, what is right or wrong frequently is relative to a value orientation. For example, let us assume the educator thinks

[4] *Ibid.*, p. 4.

that a letter type of report card should be abolished and a written report substituted, and that there are good grounds for so doing. Criticism is made of this change and it is asserted that the former type of report card should be maintained as it supports and spurs competition, and competition is asserted to be a law of life which the educator is repealing. The nativist thinks he is right, that his criticism is just. In a relativistic view each contention is right and just, i.e., as viewed from the standpoint of each value orientation. How could this be handled? The NEA suggests two approaches. The first is simply a power play, of lining up sufficient supporters to out-weigh the opposition. As a temporary tactical maneuver this proce-dure may be useful. The second is education of the opposition, and this is a long-run proposition. The assumption is that truth will out— that a resolution of differing views on life can be had by reference to life itself, that the close study and observation upon which knowl-edge rests will produce invincible evidence of the best way in which to order acts so that harmony and meaning result. The process of coöperative investigation involves greater coöperation between teacher organizations, administrators, PTA, and other community organizations. It will ultimately result in the unmasking of pressure groups, if they exist.

CASES ON PUBLIC RELATIONS

To focus our analysis, we shall examine five communities in which controversy about the schools had arisen. What can be learned from these communities? Is there any discernible pattern of events? Are there any uniformities? How was the criticism handled?

THE SCARSDALE CONTROVERSY

This residential suburban community of 14,000 is composed pri-marily of business executive and professional families. They may be described as ranging from upper-middle to upper-upper class. The community is politically conservative. The majority of the citizens are college or university graduates. The community has a non-partisan type of government in which citizens regardless of party are enlisted to serve. The mechanism for this enlistment is through two civic organizations, the Town Club, composed of 900 leading men forming a cross section of the community, and the Woman's Club. They nominate a slate of governmental officials, a nomination that amounts to election. The board of education is also nominated in this manner, by a nonpartisan committee. The school budget for the community is around two million dollars a year. The average per pupil expenditure of $585 a year is very high. The school program is a mean between traditionalism and so-called progressivism.

The attack on the schools began in 1948 when a Wall Street broker organized a Committee of Ten, later calling itself the Scarsdale Citizens Committee. This individual, on the basis of some grand jury experience and readings about communism, assumed that communists were attempting to take over Scarsdale schools. The first phase of the attack was on books used in the high-school library or on those approved as textbooks. The books were alleged to be discreetly subversive, anti-American or pro-Russian in spots. The group also complained that the library contained no books or material critical of Russia or communism.

Beginning in the fall of 1949, members of the committee began to attend board of education meetings and to heckle the board with their charges, doing this for ten out of the twelve meetings.

How to handle these charges became a problem as tension mounted. There were those who hoped that a policy of cautious silence would be successful as the opposition might gradually die out for lack of a public response. This policy was not regarded as successful, for the committee would not give up. Another group was not so certain that the principle of ignoring the controversy was a reasonable idea. In October of 1949 this informal group drafted a manifesto expressing its faith in the democratic process, its faith in the school board, and its opposition to the charges voiced by the committee. The document was signed by eighty-one prominent members of the community and published in the *Scarsdale Weekly* and in the metropolitan press.

In June, 1950, the board of education held a special open meeting at which the committee could present its evidence. In the meanwhile the board had directed its committee on educational policy to review the controversy and the methods of selecting the books. The committee did not find subversive influences at work and upheld the existing method of selecting books. The superintendent of schools presented a report defending the loyalty of the 133 members of the teaching staff. On the basis of these reports and the lack of adequate facts on the part of the Committee of Ten, the president of the school board ruled that no more time would be given to the committee's charges in open meetings and that complaints to the board should henceforth be in writing. This ruling was denounced by the committee as a gag rule.

During this controversy the *Scarsdale Inquiry*, a local paper owned and operated by the Woman's Club, covered the charges and opened up its pages to the indefatigable letter writers supporting the committee as well as balancing it with letters from other citizens.

When the attack on the books failed, the committee turned its attention to exposing alleged "leftish" speakers in the Scarsdale schools and community organizations. Charges against speakers were mailed to every household in the community, a campaign continuing to June, 1952.

In the meanwhile, school board elections were being held, and it was feared that the committee would propose its slate of candidates from the floor to oppose the official nonpartisan nominees. However, the committee, while voicing accusations against incumbent members, did not enter candidates of its own. Turnout for school elections was unusually high because of the controversy, and the nonpartisan slate was elected, in 1950, 1951, and 1952, in increasing numbers.

Because of the attacks on persons, a group of sixty, meeting in private homes, began, in February, 1952, to discuss ways and means of protecting the schools and individuals. The original plan to organize a citizens' council on public education, as advocated by the National Citizens Commission for the Public Schools, was shelved on the grounds that the community was over-organized. However, a steering committee of sixteen members was formed, selected from the leading town organizations and composed of prominent individuals.

In March, 1952, the Committee of Ten was granted permission by the board of education to hold a public meeting in one of the schools. In a somewhat autocratically controlled meeting, the committee rehearsed again its charges, and thus indicted the board of education for permitting questionable books and speakers to enter the school.

The community reaction was as follows. First, the superintendent and principals of the schools issued a statement to the community challenging it to decide what kind of education it wanted for the children. Second, the four PTA's the Woman's Club, and the League of Women Voters passed resolutions endorsing the board of education and condemning the Committee of Ten. The Town Club also endorsed the board and instructed its education committee to report on the controversy and the Committee of Ten. Third, radio broadcasts (tape recorded) presented the views of community leaders on the controversy, the Committee of Ten declining to participate. Fourth, the newly organized steering committee was circulating an open letter to the board of education and the teaching staff, expressing its confidence in them and condemning the Committee of Ten. Fifth, in April the board of education issued a report reviewing the controversy and summarizing its educational philosophy and administrative principles. Lastly, in May at the time of the school election, the nonpartisan members of the board were reëlected, and the open letter, signed by 3100 citizens of Scarsdale and several hundred from neighboring communities, was presented to the board president. A resolution to establish permanent machinery to oppose further attacks was passed. The presidents of the four major civic organizations were to constitute themselves an informal nucleus to develop further support needed for the schools.[5]

CONTROVERSY IN MINNEAPOLIS

The genteel history of Scarsdale is quite in contrast to the turbulence that has characterized Minneapolis. Aside from the depression of the 1930's which threatened to wreck the school system, the city as a community was ripped apart in a series of industrial disputes

[5] Kenneth Gould, "The Scarsdale Story," *The Humanist*, No. 4, 1952, pp. 145–159.

culminating in bloody street fighting in 1937 and a trial of the union leaders for alleged subversion in 1941. The controversies arising in and about the schools centered in three areas: (1) financing, (2) the curriculum, and (3) personnel policies. The first was a continuous problem inasmuch as the tax levy on real estate for school purposes was set by the 1921 city charter, and this provision had not been revised. Problems of personnel policy likewise were continuous. The controversy about the curriculum arose when a common learnings curriculum was introduced, which consisted of double class periods in English and social studies.[6]

An off-and-on citizens' committee, activated only in crisis, had been organized in the city since 1934. The original impetus to organize the group was a question of school relief, the quest for funds to keep the schools operating in light of decreased property values, increased tax delinquencies, increased enrollments, and cuts in teachers' salaries. The group was organized with representatives from the Parent-Teachers Council, the League of Women Voters, the American Association of University Women, the National Council of Jewish Women, the Junior Chamber of Commerce, and from the schools. Later, representatives from other groups participated. This committee saw that the problem was more than school relief. It was an overall problem of school financing which also involved the system of state aid. The committee prepared facts on the economic situation of the schools and acted as a pressure group on the legislature. In this way it was able to double the allotment of state aid in a four-year period. Then, the committee became dormant.

In 1941 another crisis arose when school janitors and engineers threatened to strike. The committee became reactivated. It reorganized, broadening its activities beyond the financial phase, and took on the name Citizens Committee on Public Education. It was soon realized that the problem involved the operation of the whole school system, especially the way the board of education and the superintendent functioned. The committee urged the state to finance a complete survey of the Minneapolis schools. When the situation became worse, the survey was authorized and carried out by the

[6] David Dreiman, *op. cit.*, pp. 16–27; Miles E. Cary, "The Fight over Common Learnings in Minneapolis," *Progressive Education*, May, 1951, pp. 205–211.

University of Chicago's public administration department. The report recommended a better school board and better school administration. Voters elected a coalition slate of reform candidates to the school board, an election in which the Citizens Committee was quite active. A new superintendent was employed in 1944. The committee again became dormant.

The next problem was again financial as the city was unable to increase the tax levy in a period of mounting enrollment and inflation. Here the barrier was the tax levy on real estate set in the 1921 city charter. In 1946 the committee was activated again. Its chairman, a vice-president of one of the city's leading flour milling companies, decided that the committee had to broaden its representation and that it should become permanent, for school problems seemed persistent. As a result of broadening representation, more citizens at large and more organizations participated. Eventually 100 organizations were represented on the committee and an equal number of citizens at large. Almost one-third of the representatives were from labor unions, and this representation was a new fact.

The problem was how to raise more money. Sponsoring a series of studies, the committee advocated a special 1 percent across-the-board earned-income tax levy to help the schools. This was defeated in 1947. The financial problem, however, became still more acute so that the board voted to cut off four weeks from the school year, an equivalent of a 10 percent cut in teachers' salaries. In the winter of 1948 this action led to a twenty-seven-day teachers' strike, carried out by the teachers' union. The board restored the cut, granted a small increase, and requested the city council to secure a two-million-dollar loan to finance the settlement. In 1948 the Citizens Committee proposed an amendment to the city charter to increase the tax levy by eleven mills. This proposal was defeated, receiving 47 percent of the votes out of a required 60 percent. The defeat took place in the "labor" wards of the city. There was also an antischool Property Owner's Association which advocated lower taxes for schools and especially lower salaries for teachers. The Citizens Committee set up a research panel under the direction of experts from the University of Minnesota and of an advertising agency with which members of the committee were affiliated. On the basis of the report the committee saw that it had to broaden still more its representation, and it also saw how it should educate the public. This meant closer and more work with and by labor's representatives.

To assist the school board in its financial problem, the state legislature, on the grounds that public education is a responsibility of the state, gave it special permission to levy an extra tax of 8.5 mills for three years, the first year outright and the following two years upon approval of a simple majority of the voters. To make certain that this approval would be forthcoming, the Citizens Committee engaged in a series of activities. It sponsored a city-wide Public Education Institute held in one of the schools in a "labor" ward. It sponsored a "modern school day" in which around 50,000 persons visited both Minneapolis schools and the better schools in the suburbs. The committee set up a special *ad hoc* organization called the Vote Yes School Committee. This was also a nonpartisan committee working on a ward-precinct-block organization, with special efforts by the labor unions, and other informational and dramatic devices. In the 1950 election set by the legislature the vote carried 2-1.

In the year 1945-46 a new curriculum was tried out provisionally in some schools. The new approach consisted of double class periods in English and social studies. If the experimental effort was deemed satisfactory, the curriculum was to be introduced generally in the senior and junior high schools. A series of workshops studied the curriculum during the years 1945-50. Meetings were held with parents and their attitudes checked by a questionnaire. In the meanwhile a new superintendent was employed in 1948 who continued the program.

In February of 1950 an opposition group came into existence, labeling itself a Parents' Council, which began to attack the program, using techniques discussed in the previous chapter. About two months after the attack was rolling along, the superintendent issued a statement refuting the charges of the group. Then, two instructors of the College of Education made talks to PTA's, school luncheons, and other groups, presenting findings from school studies. The principal in a junior high school where the program had been in effect for four years gave talks in the city, at the university, and to outside communities, presenting evidence that the program was successful. Two newspapers gave good coverage to the controversy, one of them advocating a conciliatory, experimental attitude toward the program. At the request of the Citizens Committee the Minneapolis Branch of the American Association of University Women made a report on the program, giving it a qualified, tentative approval. In this controversy apparently community groups were reluctant to speak out, and the PTA took no stand. Since the first vote on the tax levy was to take place in September, the attack on the curriculum which started in February may not have been wholly coincidental. During this controversy the superintendent resigned, and a new one came into the community.

In 1951 the state legislature on the basis of the 1950 vote approved a permanent nine-mill increase over the charter limit. In the same year the janitors in the school went on strike for more pay during the coldest days, forcing the schools to close. The Citizens Committee appointed, after some argument among the members, a fact-finding committee to meet with janitors and union and nonunion teachers. With the coöperation of the governor, a settlement was effected. The Citizens Committee set up a subcommittee of management and labor representatives as an advisory group to the school board's personnel director.

In 1954 voters again were asked to raise the tax levy six mills. The vote fell short of the 60 percent required to change the city's charter. However, the state legislature authorized an increase of three mills.

In order to minimize public apathy, the Citizens Committee has sponsored special programs, e.g., a Citizens School Week in 1952, a twentieth anniversay of the committee's founding in 1954. The Minneapolis story shows a continuity of problems and demonstrates the necessity for continuous scrutiny and solutions proposed on an informed, organized, lay basis.

FUROR IN HOUSTON, TEXAS

School difficulties in Houston were of long standing but came to a head in the latter part of the forties and early fifties. The problems were rooted in the school system itself as well as in the community. Within the school factionalism had become quite strong. It was found in the school board, among administrators, among teachers. It took place between the teachers' professional organization and that of the administrators. The community was divided between "conservatives" and "liberals." Attacks were made on outside speakers, even if they were not sponsored by educators, as "Communist-fronters." Teaching materials were attacked as subversive. United Nations and UNESCO were especially denounced as un-American and subversive, and the annual nation-wide U.N. essay contest was dropped. The attacks were made by members of the board and by outside groups, especially by a super-patriotic group of middle-aged women. Events crowded on from 1949 to 1953, culminating in the discharge of a deputy superintendent who had become "controversial."

How was this situation handled? The initiative came from a group of thirty young women disturbed by the lack of participation in school elections and board meetings and worried about the school situation. In 1949 they organized the Houston Forum on Public Education. The first year was spent on fact finding, establishing contact with the National Citizens Commission for the Public Schools, and finally publishing a booklet on the schools in 1951. Since the forum was nonpartisan, a political action group was needed. This was organized, and labeled the Parents Council for Improved Schools. In the school election of that year, the candidates supported by this group were defeated, with only 20,000 voters participating.

Leaders from the forum, the council, and other civic organizations saw that certain legal changes had to be instituted before the board could be made more responsive to the people and before a larger vote could be registered. The state legislature was persuaded to introduce two changes. The first was to tie in the school board election with the other general elections, and the second was to reduce the term of the board members from six to four years. Then the groups were able to pressure the board to hold its meetings at a place and time to accommodate interested citizens.

In 1952 forum leaders requested forty other civic groups to send representatives to discuss the Houston school situation. A representative from the National Citizens Commission was present as a resource person. Out of this meeting came the suggestion for a town meeting on the schools. With a dozen other organizations as co-sponsors, the forum organized the meeting. Three hundred persons attended, including an unofficial delegation of patriotic middle-aged women who attempted to wreck the meeting by heckling and by attempting to dominate the various buzz groups. However, this effort failed as a questionnaire on the meeting revealed that from 75 to 80 percent of the participants felt that discussion was free and the meeting useful. Town meetings were continued for the next three years, and during this period the forum began a series of neighborhood sessions. In the November, 1954, election the efforts of the groups were realized. The voters elected four liberal or moderate candidates and three conservative.

A month later a report prepared by the Defense Commission of the National Education Association on the Houston schools shook the community. The investigation, made by southern members of the NEA, took place at the request of the Houston Teachers Association after the old board had refused to renew the contract of Dr. Ebey, a deputy superintendent, who was a newcomer to the community. Dr. Ebey was accused of communist leanings, none of which were substantiated. Nevertheless, the board voted not to renew his contract. The report by the Defense Commission spelled out the troubles of the Houston school system, condemned the old board for acting hastily on Dr. Ebey's case, and suggested on several pages recommendations to improve the school system.[7]

SPRINGFIELD, MASSACHUSETTS, STRENGTH IN UNITY

Springfield came into the limelight for the first time when the community inaugurated a program to promote intergroup understanding. One impetus to this plan was the very heterogeneous population of this manufacturing town. However, despite this at-

[7] *Houston, Texas,* a Study of Factors Related to Educational Unrest in a Large School System, National Commission for the Defense of Democracy Through Education, National Education Association, December, 1954; David Dreiman, *op. cit.,* pp. 40–51.

tempt, attacks were made by patrons in some elementary schools. The content of the attack is standard, and so also are the methods, with protest meetings and publicity on radio and by newspapers. In this case, however, the attack did not go very far. When the publicity became a bit heavy, the board of education authorized a study of the entire school system, including also the allegations made in the attack. The study, carried out by a research team from the University of Illinois, showed that the schools as a whole were doing a good job, though pointing out some deficiencies in the training of the children. Although the critics were not satisfied, pointing out that educators would naturally support one another, the report was accepted by the community. The question arises as to why the controversy was so brief and easily handled in this community.

The following factors are of relevance to the question. This community of 162,000 had small elementary schools, only two of them having as many as fifteen classrooms. This fact apparently facilitated a close working relationship between parents and teachers. It was felt that there were no strong moneyed interests to take the time and effort to fight for a reduction in school costs. The superintendent had been in the community for twenty-five years. Past and present school board members, around forty citizens, had faith in his competence. However, what was more important was the policy of the superintendent in making changes. He worked for gradual, planned change, concentrating on specific items. Each departure from tradition was given a trial for concentrated study and for interpretation to parents and to community. In this way many new procedures and methods were adopted. Finally, and quite important, there was solidarity and unity among school personnel. The teachers were vigorous in their defense of the schools, evidently feeling a strong proprietary interest. Various procedures brought this about. Workshops were sponsored to study new methods and materials. Teachers were sent to summer schools with expenses paid to work on curriculum changes. No teacher was compelled to adopt a change until he saw the significance of it. Teacher administration was strong. Major decisions were made only after wide discussion and teacher participation. The Community Teachers Association shared in the selection of teachers, the formulation of salary schedules, the planning of workshops, and other in-service activities.[8]

PASADENA—THE AFTERMATH

In 1950 troubles centering in and around the schools came to a head, resulting in the dismissal of the superintendent. Aside from a certain amount of factionalism in the schools, the usual series of charges were levied against the schools—not enough Americanism was taught, textbooks were subversive, the schools were socialistic, etc. School redistricting was opposed by property and class interests, and a proposed tax levy increase was defeated. During the heat of the controversy over the superintendent, demands were made for a school survey. The board consented and organized a twelve-man citizens' survey committee composed of the different elements involved in the struggle. Two educators were selected to direct the study.

The directors realized that a traditional type of survey would not accomplish much. True, a report would be published, and placed before the board, which then could accept as much as it wanted. Given the divisions in the community, they realized that a report made by educators would not carry weight. The various charges could be refuted by the objective report of a research team, but the community might not accept the verdict. The directors then conceived of the report as a project in community education. The citizens themselves had to make the report, and the educational experts would serve as resource persons. If a group of citizens considered the charge of subversive books, read the books, discussed controversial points, and rendered a judgment, their consensus might be more acceptable.

The two directors and the Citizens' Survey Committee agreed on fourteen areas of study. Each area was assigned to a committee composed equally of citizens and school employees. The area topics were further divided among subcommittees. There were a total of 117 committees with a membership of 1019 citizens. There was

[8] Alice Pittman and H. P. Study, "Newer Practices Survive at Springfield," *Progressive Education*, May, 1951, pp. 211–213.

additional community participation in the hearings and polls conducted by the committees. The work began in April of 1951, and the work was completed in March of 1952. The report comprised a 1012-page volume.

Some results of the survey are interesting. No textbook used in the schools contained a single line of subversion. The appointment of an assistant superintendent in charge of personnel was recommended as the school system was weak in its personnel relations. The organization of the school system was not good, with too much responsibility and detail concentrated at the top. It was recommended that two types of advisory committee be established, one to be named by the board and to consist of nine lay citizens to consult with it on community wishes, the other to be an elected committee drawn from the school to consult with the superintendent. It was found that around three-fourths of the citizens were willing to pay more taxes for the schools. A majority believed that junior-high-school students should discuss all sides of controversial questions. On the 6–4–4 educational plan of the schools the survey reached no definite conclusion. It was felt that this citizens' survey helped to integrate the community as well as dispel charges as unfounded.[9]

THE QUEST FOR OBJECTIVITY

The five cases eventually end on a successful note, though considerable dissension had lacerated the communities. The extent to which the controversy is overcome may vary with the presence of militant special interest groups or a setting of social unrest. The task at present is to examine these cases as a whole and then to proceed to some systematic considerations.

COMMON ELEMENTS AND UNIFORMITIES

Perhaps the first element common to these cases is the delay in responding to a critical attack. The initial advantage belongs to the opposition when the surprise attack is launched. The longer the

[9] Joseph A. Brandt, "This, Too, Happened in Pasadena," *Harper's Magazine*, November, 1951, pp. 76–79.

delay in responding, the more the attacking group can consolidate its position and thus the more difficult it is to dislodge it. This hesitation may be partly due to a lie-low attitude, a hope that the attack may wear itself out if no attention is given to it. This attitude is an absolutely forlorn hope if a militant group is involved. Nevertheless, hesitation does occur and serves to disunite those who may want to counter. The failure to act quickly and forcefully may also involve disunity within a school system, i.e., within the teaching staff, the administrators, and the board of education, so that no effective leadership can be given by educators. Lastly, teachers and administrators are not sure of their standing in the community and may be reluctant to speak out for fear some retaliation will take place. To cope with criticism expressed during a long period of hostility is difficult, for an affirmative, constructive view is harder to state and to maintain against a barrage of emotionalized accusations.

A second element is the ambivalent role of press and radio. This may include an unintentional or intentional distortion of news to outright support of the attack. In Houston, for example, a monitored radio commentator not merely supported the attack but even encouraged espionage in the school. In Pasadena the press was unfavorable. As long as headlines play up the charges, the attack receives support. The public receives a biased account. In the context of sensational crimes, this tendency has been described as "trial by newspaper" or "trial by mass media," [10] and the handling of attacks on the schools is similar. On the other hand, there is the attempt to be objective and neutral in the controversy, as exemplified in the *Scarsdale Weekly* and the Minneapolis press. In Houston, one of the papers delegated a reporter to uncover the behind-the-scenes manipulations in the school controversy and as a result published an exposé—a series of articles on the activities and organization

[10] Joseph T. Klapper and Charles Y. Glock, "Trial by Newspaper," *Scientific American*, February, 1949, pp. 16–21; Martin Millspaugh, "Trial by Mass Media," *Public Opinion Quarterly*, Fall, 1949, pp. 328–329; Alfred M. Lee, *How to Understand Propaganda*, Rinehart and Company, 1952, chap. 5; Dorothy Bromley, "Free Press vs. Fair Trial," *Harper's Magazine*, March, 1951, pp. 90–96. Cf. Mitchell Charnley, "A Study of Newspaper Accuracy," *Journalism Quarterly*, December, 1936, pp. 394–401; Carl O. Smith and Stephen Sarasohn, "Hate Propaganda in Detroit," *Public Opinion Quarterly*, Spring, 1946, pp. 24–52; Milton and Hortense Gabel, "Texan Newspaper Opinion," *Public Opinion Quarterly*, Spring, 1946, pp. 55–70; Gunnar Myrdal, *An American Dilemma*, Harper & Brothers, 1944, pp. 1372–1373.

of the Minute Women of America. The fact that the press and radio are thought to be significant in affecting public opinion has led the NEA to formulate two action principles: "Utilize informed laymen and teachers to explain the work of the schools on radio, television. . . . Arrange face-to-face conferences with local editors and radio and television broadcasters in order to be sure that they will have the facts about the local school situation." [11] These suggestions are a move in the direction of objectivity. Their significance will be discussed later.

The third aspect, already alluded to, refers to the position of administrators and teaching staff. Where unsatisfactory personnel relations occur (Houston, Pasadena, Minneapolis), headway against criticism is difficult to achieve. In fact, factions within the school system may more or less openly support the attack. On the other hand, where there is a good working relation within the school system and in addition between school and community (Scarsdale and Springfield), there will be a unified, forthright, and forceful counterattack. The situation in these two communities tends to corroborate the fourth and fifth working principle mentioned on page 497. This last case may be viewed as an instance of the augmentation of sociative relations.

The fourth element that is outstanding is the fact that the controversy is begun and carried out by an extraordinarily small group of people. Since these very few individuals feel that they are supporting a cause, they may bring a fanatical, vociferous zeal to their quest. In short, they are successful intimidators. They are also individuals who must have time (leisured middle-aged if not superannuated women) and money (professional and managerial occupational status). Males who may be involved stem from similar groups and statuses. One of the axes around which they structure their actions is the nativist value orientation. The fact that there are these militant, agitating individuals frequently leads to a faulty appraisal of the situation, and in this one may be misled also by the publicity given to them. A newspaper poll in Minneapolis on the common learnings controversy shows clearly, on two questions, this tendency to misinterpret and exaggerate the nature of a con-

[11] Local Association Activities Leaflet, No. 22, National Education Association, p. 4.

troversy. On the question "Have you heard or read anything about the common schools program in some Minneapolis schools?" Minneapolis respondents answered: yes 55 percent, no 44 percent, no opinion 1 percent; and informants in neighboring communities: yes 17 percent, no 78 percent, no opinion 5 percent. The second question was: "What is your opinion of the common schools program: do you approve of it, disapprove, or are you indifferent?" This question was directed to those answering yes, and the answers were: Minneapolis interviewees—approve 18 percent, disapprove 11 percent, indifferent 9 percent, no opinion 17 percent; neighboring communities informants—approve 6½ percent, disapprove 3 percent, indifferent 3 percent, no opinion 4½ percent.[12] Too often a blatant, vociferous minority may be taken to represent the voice of the people. A well-conducted public opinion poll may put things in proper perspective.

The cases show, fifthly, that these upper groups are not of identical stripe. The sociological generalizations that members of the upper-middle and upper groups are *eo ipso* conservative if not "reactionary" is not upheld, at least with reference to the school (Scarsdale, Minneapolis, Pasadena). In Scarsdale, the upholding of the humanist value orientation is quite clear. What the data show is that these top groups are not unified social strata, especially when viewed in the local community context. Most sociological studies do show conservatism in these strata in relation to economic issues, especially labor relations, but it does not follow that the same must hold true in noneconomic areas.[13] In smaller communities, this unity of thought and action may be found. In larger communities it may be less the case, and the influence on policy may be not merely a matter of access to channels and face-to-face contact but also a matter of group organizations, so that an upper-middle- or upper-class person may, inconsistently perhaps, uphold diverse value orientations. Thus, members of these strata may be on both sides of school controversies.

[12] Miles E. Cary, *op. cit.*, p. 211.
[13] Arthur Kornhauser, "Analysis of 'Class Structure' in Contemporary American Society—Psychological Bases of Class Divisions," in George W. Hartmann and Theodore Newcomb (eds.), *Industrial Conflict*, The Cordon Company, 1939. Richard Centers, *The Psychology of Social Classes*, Princeton University Press, 1949.

Sixthly, we see the ambivalence of community groups in these controversies. Many apparently lack the initiative or fortitude to take a stand. The ineptness of the Parent-Teacher Association is evident in most of the cases. This is the group that should be in the front of the controversy instead of being an anemic bystander. However, this inaction of the PTA is understandable inasmuch as in many communities it is relegated to the position of a money-raising organization without much insight into the operation of the school. Also the PTA tends to be found only on the elementary level whereas the area of controversy involves the junior and senior high school. Perhaps this may account for the creation of special pro-school organizations which have arisen in these conflicts. We also see that such a group attempts to secure as wide a community par-ticipation as possible (Scarsdale, Minneapolis, Houston). The mem-bership also tends to involve persons having children in the schools, apparently a younger generation than those attacking. These groups are nonpartisan, nonpolitical organizations. Their major functions appear to be fact finding, education, and conciliation. For matters of political action another organization, which may be temporary, is set up. What happens at the polls counts, whether the issue is a board election or a bond or tax levy. The political action group is necessary at this point of the controversy. By setting it up, the other citizens' group may maintain its character as a fact-finding, educating organization, again a movement toward objectivity.

Lastly, there is a determinate effort to find out what the facts are, i.e., the organization and functioning of the school system, whether it be a matter of books, of methods, of finance, or of special services. It is an analysis of what is, of trends, of results, and this is the quest for objectivity. The cases show two tendencies. First, there is a recital of facts, directed in part to the attackers and to an amorphously conceived public. Such facts as given by educators or teachers are not likely to convince. This result is seen clearly in the wrangling taking place during open board meetings. Yet despite the inconclusiveness of the meetings, such open discussion is a very rudimentary move toward objectivity. The second approach is the survey. Surveys fall into four types: (1) a survey conducted by teachers and administrators of the school system (important, but not very satisfactory); (2) a survey made by an outside research team, usually from the School of Education of a well-known university (fairly satisfactory if the conflicts are not too deep and intense); (3) a survey by an investigating team sent into the controversy by the NEA only at the request of the local and state teachers' association (important); (4) some form of community self-survey (the better of the methods). All of these are a form of problem solving and tend to be objective, as any rational approach is. The first three, however, cannot effect what is quite important, namely, reconciliation within the community. The fourth approach does, and why it does is the topic of our systematic consideration.

THE RATIONALE OF SOCIAL ACTION RESEARCH

This type of research is not concerned with the advancement of knowledge but with the changing or improvement of a problem situation. Indeed, some of the facts discovered by such a study are ones that are to be changed or destroyed. For example, the fact of bad housing in a community is to be replaced by the fact of good housing. This type of research is a tool to facilitate the reconstruction of the social world. The completion of a project does not automatically mean success. The implementation of recommendations may have to be through political action, and the fact that the report is the result of lay-citizen action not under political control may lead to its circumvention by incumbent political officials and bureaus.[14] Nevertheless, even such opposition can be realistically dealt with in so far as the nature of the problem and its resolution are clearly perceived.

Social action research has been used extensively in minority group problems and community health problems,[15] and some of the techniques have been developed in the survey of such problems. Much of the theoretical underpinning is expressed in the current label

[14] Cf. the case of Bellevue, Washington. Dreiman, *op. cit.*, pp. 52–59.
[15] Ronald Lippitt, *Training in Community Relations*, Harper & Brothers, 1949; Clare Seltiz and Margot Haas (eds.), "Community Self Survey," *Journal of Social Issues*, Spring, 1949 (entire issue).

"group dynamics,"[16] discussed in Chapter 9. In the present discussion we shall attempt to see the interrelations between the quest for objectivity and reconciliation as a phase of social action research. This quest is a way of controlling opposition by asking it to participate in working out a problem. The word "control" is not precise. What is meant is that opposition is resolved in a new unity through the process of working out a problem. This unity is found through overcoming conflicting ideas in new insights, and it is found socially in the replacement of dissociative relations by sociative ones.

THE MEANING OF "OBJECTIVE"

By this word we do not refer to a traditional distinction between the inner life of the individual and the world outside. Reference to the individual, his feelings and states of mind, is usually termed "subjective." The world outside of his skin, especially the world of nature, is referred to as "objective." This distinction is not very useful, and we shall use these words in a different way.

The word "objective" will denote systematic relationship, summed in the concept of whole. The objective in terms of ideas is the whole of knowledge, designating logical relations and possibilities in reality. The objective in terms of culture is best seen in work and art, examples of concrete wholes. As creative acts, both work and art are means-ends rational, i.e., an embodiment of craftsmanship. Craftsmanship is an appropriate interrelating of materials through design. It involves an appropriate use of tools. It is this systematic appropriate interrelationship of materials, tools, and intelligence that constitutes the action pattern of work. The agent is one element in the pattern, shaping and shaped by the design that integrates tools and materials to their proper end. The painter must know the quality of his pigments, must know color, brush technique, and so forth. The mechanic's action is organized in relation to the demands of the motor, its physics, its construction, the type of repair needed,

[16] Cf. Kurt Lewin, *Resolving Social Conflicts*, Harper & Brothers, 1948; J. L. Moreno, *Who Shall Survive? Foundations of Sociometry, Group Psychotherapy, and Sociodrama*, Beacon House, 1953; Dorwin Cartwright and Alvin Zander (eds.), *Group Dynamics*, Row, Peterson, and Company, 1953; Murray G. Ross, *Community Organization*, Harper & Brothers, 1955.

the materials and tools to do the job well. The surgical act is an integration of the knowledge of physiology, anatomy, operating technique—a coördination of effort by specialists to the end of a healthy person. This objectivity to the facts of the world as seen in work and crafts activities is found in even the most "primitive" group, though this means-ends rational phase of their life may be overlayered with the subjectivity of magical beliefs.

The subjective will be viewed as the fragmented, the unrelated, the disconnected, the irrelevant. The subjective in terms of ideas is error, superstition, false belief, and in terms of culture it is interest, expressed as honor, prestige, notoriety, power. In the person, the ultimate expression of the subjective is psychosis; in society it is tyranny and totalitarianism. Morally, subjectivity is expressed as utility and expediency. It perverts the means-ends rationality of work and art. Wherever the subjective principle becomes significant, the life process is to that extent distorted. In the social world this means a tendency to stasis, uneasy and uncertain truces, corruption, compromises, and renewed conflicts, a fact recognized by many American thinkers and writers, such as Emerson, Whitman, Mark Twain, William Dean Howells, and Lincoln Steffens. Sociologically, the operation of the interest principle as analyzed by Ratzenhofer and Gumplowicz meant a society at war within itself and without, a sort of Hobbesian war of all against all. We see the principle in schools where the granting of awards and prizes is biased by the social class status of the student. We see it in the mass entertainment function of schools. We find it in the booster groups, pushing their interest unrelated to the school program as a whole. We find it in administrators maximizing authority and control for the sake of prestige and power. We discover it in board members who exploit their office for gain. But the principle is not merely located in schools. Fee splitting and ghost surgery, fraudulent advertising, adulterated drugs and foods, the various forms of the "fix," cartels and monopoly prices, faith healing and associated quackery are manifestations of subjectivity and interest. We can see the problem in the United Nations. In the Security Council and in the General Assembly where the subjective principle prevails little of consequence is achieved, in contrast to many of the programs and projects carried out by the problem-centered organizations such as FOA, WHO, and other specialized agencies. The subjective principle is an invitation to sterility and death. Fortunately the logic of human life so far has been such that the subjective has not prevailed.

Objectively, the quest for the good school is also the quest for the good life. The good school is one which embodies the most adequate organization of materials, methods, personnel, and social relations promoting growth in knowledge, work, and art—not life destroying but life sustaining and fulfilling. The quest for objectivity in education is then a matter of understanding the growth of children, understanding methods, understanding books, understanding finance—in sum, all that understanding which issues into a harmonious, dynamic social cultural complex called a school. Social action research is one instrument in this quest.

The Objective as Moral. What this means is that the craftsman must understand and properly work with his material. This is the morality of work, of the vocation. One phase of the objective as systematic interrelation is normative—not merely norms of competence but norms of rightness, a proper respect for the materials and a proper respect for others contained within the relation. It is the absence of fraud, of adulteration, of perverted use of materials. It is honesty and fairness with others. It does not matter whether these concepts involve "things" or persons. Even nature cannot be violated without consequences.

As social action research is a modified application of the scientific point of view, we may understand the objective as moral by examining science as a system of action. Science as work or as vocation has a normative order little different from that of any other type of work: honesty in dealing both with materials and with others, openmindedness to ideas and suggestions, suspended or tentative judgment, understanding rather than condemnation, tolerance, impartiality, control of bias and emotion (self-discipline in short), patience, application of energy, coöperation, and, if necessary, demonstrated in the lives of scientific heroes, self-sacrifice. A rejection of this normative aspect results in the perversion of scientific endeavor, fraud (Piltdown man), or sterility (Lysenkoism).

The scientific attitude is a correlate of scientific ethos, the latter referring to certain social conditions which are necessary for science as work to exist. The basic condition here is freedom of communication, the circulation of ideas, access to materials, freedom to study, to investigate, and to transmit to others the results. It means freedom to coöperate with others regardless of race, creed, color, or social status. In this sense the scientific ethos is equalitarian, for the norm recognizes only the competence of the man's work. The theatrical façades of life, such as prestige and distinctions of creed, color, and status, are properly discarded as irrelevant. This is true of the ethics of work. Achievement is the criterion, not the "sacred" arrogance resting upon inherited social position.

We can now see the significance of social action research from this perspective. In so far as persons and groups participate in problem solving, the ethic requires the relinquishing of special interest and subjectivity—utility and expediency. The mere fact that something works is no criterion of goodness, and opportunism involves no point of view at all; it is a twin sister of nihilism. Honesty, fairness, and tolerance to the facts and to those with whom one is looking for and examining the facts—this is the way. It is not surprising that critics of education are frequently reluctant to participate in such projects. They might have to practice the virtues that they deny as well as change their ideas, to which they cling rather rigidly. The method of social action research implies reconciliation as the work progresses and persons express in conduct the requisite virtues of the science method. The reconciliation will be in ideas, in morality, and in social relations. This last aspect must be considered.

The Social Dimension of Action Research. The significance here is the conversion of dissociative relations into sociative. This change comes about not by propagandizing or attempting to convert persons or groups. Such a procedure may have the opposite effect. Action is not directed against a person or group but against an issue. Nor is the issue a matter of propaganda, for such marshaling of "facts" on various sides reaches a dead end with the participants convinced of the rightness of their facts as against those of the others. The start of the action research is an issue and/or disagreement. The objective of the research is to resolve the issue and, thus, also the disagreement. The process is one of mutual education, as well as self-education. The question is not one of who is right or wrong, who will gain prestige, who will control—all these are the subjective in reference. The question is objective, i.e., how can the problem be best resolved. The social dimension is a coöperative venture in problem solving, joint planning, fact collecting, analysis, and reporting.

The various phases of problem solving just enumerated imply a division of labor, and this in itself demands coöperative, sociative relations. That differences of opinion will arise can be taken for granted, involving a certain amount of momentary dissociation. The function of the research is not to augment the differences, to "resolve" them by domination and authority. Quite the contrary, effort will be made to change negative responses to positive ones intentionally, again not by preaching or moralizing but by working with others on the problem. The differences may be resolved in the coöperative venture of developing greater and more accurate insights.

This coöperative venture takes place among individuals and representatives of organizations in the community. The greater the base of such involvement of persons and groups, the greater the chances for reconciliation through commonly gained understanding. The greater also the odds of the community's accepting recommendations. This outreach into the community's organizations cannot be overemphasized. Without it, effective community action is not possible. This has been seen in moderately successful community chest drives when representation was primarily from upper-middle- and upper-class strata and organizations. By including labor representatives much greater success was obtained.[17] The necessity for this was found by the Minneapolis group. An attempt by members representing business to torpedo the Northtown Survey on human relations failed when it was pointed out that the questions on the survey had been worked out and agreed to by all the participants including the business representatives. It was, therefore, not right or proper (appeal to norms) for these representatives to jeopardize the project or undo the work achieved by the whole group. The

[17] James B. McKee, "Status and Power in the Industrial Community, a Comment on Drucker's Thesis," *American Journal of Sociology*, January, 1953, pp. 368–369.

business representatives, then, withdrew their objections and supported the project. This result could only have been achieved on the basis of wide community representation on the one hand and the fact that the questions were the joint accomplishment of all the participants.[18]

A Final Caveat. Social action research is not a panacea. To plunge willy-nilly into some community self-survey may be a certain invitation to disaster and failure. The issue must be widespread enough to warrant the establishment of a survey, and participation must be genuine. It has been indicated that the very process itself is sociative. However, where participants come in with the intent of deliberately obstructing, the survey may have rough going, though the fact of broad participation may minimize the occurrence of this approach. But social action research as method is concerned with the operation of the survey group itself, and effort will be made to clarify how the program is progressing, how members are participating, how improvement can be made.

There are some who may hold to their actions in an absolute sense, i.e., adhere to them regardless of consequences. Individuals from such groups may be most difficult to work with. Persons holding to actions and beliefs because of tradition may be more amenable to change. Some may be opportunistic and consequently may go along with the program. There are those willing to coöperation, to investigate, to experiment, and these naturally present no problem. In spite of these various action schemata, a person is a member of different groups upholding different value systems. How he responds in the social action research situation depends upon which group he is consciously or unintentionally representing. However, it is difficult to conceive of other methods in which there will be a more objective, mutual, self-correcting, insightful, progressive interplay among a group of participants than there is in social action research.

Selected Readings

Corey, Stephen, *Action Research to Improve School Practices,* Columbia University Press, 1953.

[18] Cf. A. J. Marrow, *Living Without Hate,* Harper & Brothers, 1951, one popular summary of much work in this area.

Dreiman, David, *How to Get Better Schools,* Harper & Brothers, 1956, Part III.

Hunter, Floyd, Schaffer, Ruth, and Sheps, Cecil, *Community Organization: Action and Inaction,* University of North Carolina Press, 1956. Reaches a very skeptical conclusion as to the value of community self-study, though on the basis of a somewhat contrived problem.

Lewin, Kurt, *Resolving Social Conflicts,* Harper & Brothers, 1948, chaps. 2, 4, 7, 13.

Lippitt, Ronald, *Training in Community Relations,* Harper & Brothers, 1949.

Menge, J. Wilmer, and Faunce, Roland, *Working Together for Better Schools,* American Book Company, 1953.

CHAPTER 20

Educational Controversy and Law

THE HUE and cry of demagogues about education may give rise to concern and anxiety; yet, unless some kind of specific action takes place affecting the school, the shouting of the propagandists remains the hot air that it is. Pressure groups exist, as we have noted, but since the public school is a creation of the state, changes in education must be made through law—either legislation or the decisions of the courts or both. Our attention will center on the courts, for the court in its review of a case is reviewing principles.

Law is not merely a technique of social control. It is a principle of ordering life, the good life or the just life. Public education as set forth in law is considered a good, and the courts have corroborated this in decisions determining whether or not the principle is sound. Courts do not function in a cultural vacuum. Value orientations and theories about the state influence the interpretations and decisions made by the courts. The possibility of the courts' assisting in a disordering of life is real, as courts will function in ambivalent ways. This dual prospect of order and disorder as mediated through the courts is applicable to education. As we proceed in our analysis, we will note how the courts are concerned with the problem of the organization of American culture and society, and specifically with education.

There are three major areas of controversy. One deals with the relation of religion and education. A second takes up the problem of segregation and education. A third centers upon the control of dissent. The first two are general problems of socio-cultural organization. The third deals with the values of free speech and communication. The greater part of our analysis will deal with decisions made by the United States Supreme Court.

SECULARISM, RELIGION, AND THE COURTS

It would be too simple to phrase the problem as a public school-parochial school issue. The fundamental problem is a question of the significance of religion in American life. Once this problem has been worked through, then another immediately arises as to the relation of religion and education. The question may be rather bluntly expressed, as in a statement by the president of Texas Christian University: "Any school in America which does not teach belief in God is actually teaching atheism. Our schools cannot prepare the kind of citizens we need unless they return pure religion to its rightful place in education." We are thus confronted with the problem of an interpretation of religion. We will also investigate the specific educational problems of religious education on released time, and the situation of church-supported schools.

RELIGION AS THE BASIS OF ORDER?

That religion has a profound impact on the activities of the public school is very clear, as we have seen. The notion that there is no religion in the public schools is a figment of the imagination. For a dyed-in-the-wool secularist, however, there is still too much of it; for the religionist, of course, too little. The former would prefer a scientific-secular education, the latter a Christian education. To resolve the dilemma, the courts have to decide on the significance of religion as *a* or *the* component in life. There is no important judicial decision in this matter that does not contain an assessment of religion. The specific point of departure, however, is the First Amendment of the Constitution: "Congress shall make no law respecting an establishment of religion, or prohibiting the free exercise thereof."

The interpretation of this amendment has been through the writings of James Madison and Thomas Jefferson, especially Madison's *Memorial and Remonstrance against Religious Assessment* and Jefferson's *Bill for Establishing Religious Freedom,* adopted by the Virginia legislature in 1799. The former was a protest against a prospective law compelling the state or a person to make an annual contribution to Christian religion or some specific denomination. Madison thought that such a law would make for sectarian conflict, "the denial of liberty and imposition of clerical control upon the state." Jefferson's Bill stated "that to compel a man to furnish contributions of money for the propagation of opinions which he disbelieves and abhors is sinful and tyrannical," that no citizen "should be compelled to support this or that teacher of his own religious persuasion," that "no man shall be compelled to frequent or support any religious worship, place, or ministry whatsoever." It must be emphasized that Madison and Jefferson were not against religion—both were probably deists—but that they opposed a church or religion as the official church or religion of the state, supported by public funds. This principle was to apply to every form of public aid to church and/or religion, and the principle, in a phrase, is "the separation of state and church."

The courts, and for our purpose of analysis the United States Supreme Court, have interpreted the amendment, basing their declaration in part on Madison and Jefferson, in part on other court decisions, thus summarizing a point of view. Two court decisions (Everson v. Board of Education, 330 U.S. 1; McCollum v. Board of Education, 333 U.S. 203) embody the opinion of the United States Supreme Court today, the former a 5–4 decision and the latter an 8–1. The position of the court is as follows:

"The establishment of religion" clause of the First Amendment means at least this: Neither a state nor the Federal Government can set up a church. Neither can pass laws which aid one religion, aid all religions, or prefer one religion over another. Neither can force nor influence a person to go or to remain away from church against his will or force him to profess a belief or disbelief in any religion. No person can be punished for entertaining or professing religious beliefs or disbeliefs, for church attendance or non-attendance. No tax in any amount, large or small, can be levied to support any religious activities or institutions, whatever they may be called, or whatever form they may adopt to teach or practice religion. Neither a state nor the Federal Government can, openly or secretly, participate in the affairs of any religious organizations or *vice versa*.[1]

It was emphasized that the public schools were "more consistent with Protestant than with Catholic culture and scheme of things." [2] It was stressed that the separation of church and state was "to keep advantage from getting control of public policy or the public purse." [3] The court also stressed the point that religion was an individual or private matter. Thus, the court stated an anticlerical principle and a point of view that fitted in with the deistic ideas of the Enlightenment and Protestant traditions. Religion, politics, and law are distinct areas and achieve "their ends if left free each in its own sphere." [4]

Religion and civic life are, however, not two distinct spheres. Justice Reed, dissenting in the McCollum decision, elaborated in great detail the interlocking between religion, civic life, and governmental activities: public prayers and invocations, chaplains, tax-exempted church properties, etc.[5] Madison and Jefferson are interpreted by some as favoring religion in civic life and governmental activities. The Court has stressed the point that ours is a religious, if not Christian, nation. The crux of the problem is not whether religion integrates with political and civic life but whether a church or sectarian group should receive public funds or other legislative preferment in propagating its particular belief and sacramental system. The issue, for the time, seems resolved on an abstract level but in the application of the separation of state and church principle there is uncertainty and ambiguity. Hence, continued litigation can be expected as the courts are called to judge particular cases.

THE SPECIFIC ISSUE OF RELIGION AND EDUCATION

The linkage between religion and education is shown in Table 54. These various practices are carried out by the forty-eight states,

[1] Everson, pp. 15–16.
[2] *Ibid.*, p. 23.
[3] *Ibid.*
[4] McCollum, p. 211.
[5] Cf. "Religion and the State," *Law and Contemporary Problems*, vol. 14, 1949, pp. 23–44, 73–99; note also the article "Preferment of Religious Institutions in Tax and Labor Legislation," pp. 144–159.

District of Columbia, Alaska, and Hawaii. Practices differ among the various political divisions, and even within a particular state some practices will be approved and others prohibited. A great deal is left to the decisions of the local school boards. What practice takes place depends upon the state constitution, permissive legislation, and judicial decision. There is no special consistency in state court decisions. For example, eight state supreme courts upheld statutes granting free transportation to parochial-school pupils on the theory that the aid was a benefit to the child rather than to the school, and seven held such statutes to be unconstitutional. Four courts decided that such a practice aided both child and sect. A few courts handed down conflicting decisions. Much of the litigation has centered on the practices listed in the table. An underlying issue is the question of public support of private schools.

The right of parents to send children to schools of their own choice was upheld by the United States Supreme Court, *Pierce v.*

TABLE 54. Practices and Usage in Aid to Sectarian Schools and Sectarianism in Public Schools as Reported by State Superintendents of Education

Practice Reported	Number of Political Divisions Reporting				
	Yes	No	?	Required	Permitted
Bible reading in public school		8	4	12	27
Free textbooks for parochial-school pupils	5	44	2		
Transportation of parochial-school pupils at public expense	19	21	2		
Excusing pupils for attendance at "weekday" church schools [a]	35	14	2		
Religious instruction by church teachers inside public school during school hours	10	38	3		
Employment of school teachers wearing religious garb	16	22	13		
Use of public schools by religious groups after school hours	34	13	4		
Rental of church-owned buildings for public school purposes	30	5	17		

[a] This information was secured before the McCollum decision.
SOURCE: NEA Research Bulletin, *The State and Sectarian Education*, February, 1946, Table 1, p. 36, adapted. ? includes: law silent; no comment by superintendent; no answer.

Society of Sisters, 268 U.S. 510 (1925). The decision declared unconstitutional, under the Fourteenth Amendment, an Oregon law compelling all children to attend public schools. The private school, however, had to meet the educational requirements established by the state. Private schools are of two types, the religious oriented and the secular, the latter approximating in many cases the nonsectarian orientation of the public schools. The religious-oriented private school is the parochial school. Commonly the notion of the parochial school is associated with the Roman Catholic Church, but there are numerous religious groups—Lutherans, Quakers, and Seventh-Day Adventists, for example—that support schools of their own. The *St. Louis Lutheran* describes the "parochial school" as follows:

For what is a parochial school? It is an instrument by which a religious body establishes, confirms, and propagates its religious beliefs. It is not the primary purpose of a church school to serve the public good, but to serve its own purposes, i.e., the perpetuation of its own beliefs—religious, social, scientific, economic, for it is no longer a religious education principle that geography or mathematics may be divorced from religious teaching.[6]

This blunt but candid interpretation disposes of a casuistical distinction between subjects that are merely secular and those that are religious in the church-supported schools. Education is one, namely, religious, and this view fits in with those formulated by other church groups.

Since parents have the right to choose either public or private school, should private schools be supported by public funds derived from taxes? Presumably no "secular" private school would entertain the notion that it should be state supported. The issue has arisen in connection with the religious-oriented private school. Yet even here there is much disagreement. In general most Protestant groups are against such support while the Roman Catholic Church in principle is for such support. In the briefs *amicus curiae,* six Protestant church groups, one Jewish organization, and three nonreligious groups filed in favor of the view of Everson and McCollum. The opposing briefs

[6] Conrad Moehlman, *The Wall of Separation Between Church and State,* The Beacon Press, 1951, p. 140.

were filed primarily by the attorney generals of states having a stake in the case, one Roman Catholic lay organization, and one Protestant organization. They illustrate very well the division that centers upon religion, education, and the state.

The two cases referred to throughout our analysis are regarded as crucial decisions. In the Everson case the Court upheld a New Jersey statute providing for payment of transportation of pupils to public and Roman Catholic schools. The case was judged on the basis of the child benefit principle, and at the same time the principle of separation of church and state was affirmed. Since the decision was a 5–4 decision, the issue is by no means resolved. In the McCollum case the Court decided against an Illinois school board that had undertaken in collaboration with a local religious council a program of religious instruction on released time on school premises. The decision here was 8–1. This issue also is not settled and might be examined a bit more closely.

RELIGIOUS EDUCATION ON RELEASED OR DISMISSED TIME

This practice usually involves a one-hour-a-week program of religious instruction by a religious group for its members. Children are released or dismissed for the one hour from their classes to attend the special class in religious and/or denominational instruction. Programs of this sort date back at least as far as 1936. A study of 3790 communities in 1940 showed that 3063 never had such a program; 133 gave it up; 488 had it in some form. In 357 communities an enrollment of 164,013 pupils was reported, primarily from the fourth, fifth, and sixth grades.[7] A 1948 poll of 5100 school superintendents, with 2639 replies returned, showed that 1621 communities never had a released time program; 301 abandoned theirs; 708 (26.8 percent) had some sort of program, 8 of them on an after-school basis. The enrollment in the released time schools was some 5 percent of the total enrollment in these schools. In New York City the percentages of children on released time were 81.43 Roman Catholic, 13.36 Protestant, 5.18 Jewish. The enrollment centered in 1949 in the first through fourth grades. Older children apparently

[7] *Ibid.*, p. 157.

do not participate.[8] From about 23 to 32 percent of the pupils in the school studied were on released time.[9]

A variety of problems arise out of the released time program. To what extent is this religious education only sectarian, e.g., Methodist, Roman Catholic, Presbyterian, etc.? To what extent can non-Christians and dissident sects participate in such a program? How adequate is the instruction? How far is the school involved in supporting the program? Schools have been involved to the extent of announcing the program, recruiting pupils, dismissing students, keeping records on them, readjusting the studies for those not participating, and canceling the religious classes when necessary. When the children are released, does the safety responsibility fall on the school or the particular church group? Should the school provide the escorts and monitors? If any of the released children are truant, how is this to be handled and who should handle it? There seems to be no clarity on these points. Truancy, according to three studies published by the Public Education Program, is one of the more serious persistent problems.[10] Aside from many of these practical problems there is the question of principle. For the time the McCollum decision is a setback for proponents of religious education on released time. The response to the decision has been varied. In 162 communities the program has been dropped. In other communities school officials have contended that the decision does not apply to them, and the New York Supreme Court held that the decision does not apply to the New York law. The controversy of the content and organization of education through law and courts continues.

WHAT IS DONE IN THIS CONTROVERSY?

There are several approaches contending groups are using and will use to further their ideas and policies about religion and education. The first of these is publicity, a propaganda battle of attack and counterattack. This is primarily a function of the intellectuals and

[8] *Released Time for Religious Education in New York City Schools,* Public Education Association, 1949. The research study was carried out by the Center for Field Services, New York University.

[9] *Ibid.,* p. 8.

[10] *Ibid.,* pp. 18–21.

persons speaking in authority as officials for their group. Books are written, lawyers prepare briefs, all to show that their side is right and the other completely wrong. A certain amount of vituperation and name calling provides additional color to the ideological battle. Thus the Supreme Court justices can be denounced as being part of a conspiracy formed by Communists, materialists, agnostics, and secularists to wreck freedom of education.[11]

Another approach is to secure legislation enacted to favor one's cause. With ample funds, it is possible to fight the case through all necessary courts with the hope that one's side will be upheld. This procedure involves the hazard that an unfavorable decision may establish precedent against one's side. Split decisions may be encouraging, for they indicate ambiguity in the case and, hence, possibilities of a later reversal. If judges in the court are steeped in your point of view, they may unconsciously steer their decision your way.

A final step is to secure a constitutional amendment, either to a state constitution or to the Federal Constitution. For example, the New York State constitution was amended to provide free transportation for parochial-school pupils. The technique is a workable one. The referendum as a way of securing the necessary legislative sanction has also been used. The resulting wild, if not unethical, campaigning aggravates existing group differences.

THE COURTS AND SEGREGATION IN EDUCATION

Segregation by color and nationality in education is widespread. It is found in the North as well as in the South, East, and West. It involves Negroes, Indians, Mexicans, and low-income whites. The segregation is explicitly stated in the law of a state or more covertly embodied in an administrative policy of a school board. If the law states that there should be separate schools on the basis of color, a dual school system results. By administrative policy a school board can so district the schools that the result amounts to a segregation by color or by social class.

The problem arises as to the adequacy of segregation as a principle of social organization. In resolving this question, the courts are

[11] *New York Times*, April 3, 1948, p. 16, col. 3.

not concerned to know only whether segregation "works." A social scientist could point out that it works after a fashion but has dysfunctional long-range effects on the society. The courts may consider what implications segregation has for the status of the individual or group segregated, and may also view the practical consequences. The facts of the case may show whether or not the law involves a violation of constitutional rights, especially as regards the Fourteenth Amendment. Indirectly such an approach is also an evaluation of segregation as a principle of social organization.

"SEPARATE BUT EQUAL" DOCTRINE

The United States Supreme Court first announced what has come to be known as the "separate but equal" doctrine in Plessy v. Ferguson in 1896. The decision upheld a Louisiana law providing for separate facilities on railway cars for whites and nonwhites. This case established a major precedent, and many subsequent decisions were made in accordance with this principle. A school case was decided in 1929, Gong Lum v. Rice. A Chinese citizen was required to attend an elementary school for Negroes in Mississippi. He claimed he was entitled to admission to the school for whites. The Supreme Court concluded that he was "colored," and that facilities available to Negroes and thus available to the Chinese citizen were equal to the white. The cumulation of such decisions makes change extraordinarily difficult.

The challenge to segregation in education received its impetus from cases centering upon professional, graduate-school training. At this level inequalities in opportunities and facilities would seem more patent. In a series of decisions segregation as a principle of ordering professional graduate training was gradually rejected. In the Gaines case (1938) the Court ruled that Gaines was denied equal protection in the law, that he had a right to the same legal education as whites, that the University of Missouri had to either admit him to its regular law school or establish a separate Negro law school. A similar decision was handed down against the University of Oklahoma in the Sipuel case, 1948. In the Sweatt case, 1950, the

Court upheld a petition that the Negro plaintiff had the right to attend the University of Texas Law School rather than the Negro law school, the decision resting on the inequalities of opportunity and facilities and the equal protection clause of the Fourteenth Amendment. In the McLaurin case, 1950, the Court ruled against a law to establish a policy of segregation *within* the University of Oklahoma Graduate School. The plaintiff was a Negro seeking his doctor's degree in education. He was compelled to sit in a special "colored" row in the classroom, was assigned a special table in the library and a special table in the cafeteria. The Court ruled that the differences in treatment not only were a handicap in his education but also deprived him of his equal protection in the law. It thus seems that on the level of graduate professional training segregation as a principle is on its way out.

Once a trend is in evidence, it broadens its scope. With the precedents established on the graduate-school level, more legal moves were made on the elementary. Cases from Oklahoma, Maryland, Virginia, Delaware, and South Carolina were argued through the lower courts, and finally all five were considered at one time by the United States Supreme Court in 1953. The decision as announced was a reversal of the Plessy-Ferguson decision and with it the invalidation of all the laws that the decision had upheld. The Court was deciding not only a question of constitutional rights but also a principle of order in education, and by implication a principle of order in American society.

The summary of the unanimous United States Supreme Court decision given in Brown et al. *v.* Board of Education of Topeka et al. is as follows:

Segregation of White and Negro Children pursuant in the public schools of a State solely on the basis of race, pursuant to state laws permitting or requiring such segregation, denies to Negro children the equal protection of the laws guaranteed by the 14th Amendment—even though the physical and other "tangible" factors of white and Negro schools may be equal.

a. The history of the 14th Amendment is inconclusive as to its intended effect on public education.

b. The question presented in these cases must be determined, not on the basis of conditions existing when the 14th Amendment was adopted but in the light of the full development of public education and its present plan in American life throughout the Nation.

c. Where a State has undertaken to provide an opportunity for an education in its public schools, such an opportunity is a right which must be made available to all on equal terms.

d. Segregation of children in public schools solely on the basis of race deprives children of the minority group of equal educational opportunities even though the physical facilities and other "tangible" factors may be equal.

e. The "separate but equal" doctrine adopted in Plessy v. Ferguson has no place in the field of public education.[12]

This decision was followed one year later by a decision describing how desegregation was to be implemented.[13] The Court reaffirmed its original decision by declaring that all provisions in federal, state, and local law requiring or permitting racial segregation in education had to yield to the principle of admittance to public schools on a nondiscriminatory basis. The court decided that the lower courts were best qualified to provide the judicial supervision necessary to determine whether local school authorities were attempting in good faith to comply with the desegregation decision and at the earliest practicable date. The lower courts were directed to evaluate the adequacy of any plans submitted by public-school authorities to effect a smooth transition to a nondiscriminatory school system. The burden of establishing the need for additional time was placed upon the school authorities. In this way the Court hoped to achieve a systematic and orderly transition.

One has to keep in mind that the Court decisions are also in fields other than education. The Mitchell and Henderson cases dealt with equality of facilities on the railways. The constitutionality of FEPC laws on state and municipal levels is also part of this trend. These decisions affirm the value orientation given in many of our constitutions, as in that of Ohio: that men have certain inalienable rights; that they are all by nature free and independent; that the rights include enjoying and defending life and liberty, acquiring, possessing, and protecting property, and seeking and obtaining happiness and safety.

[12] 347 U.S., 483.
[13] Brown v. Board of Education of Topeka, 349 U.S. 294.

THE RESPONSE TO THE TREND

On the upper levels of education including both undergraduate and especially graduate training, the segregation principle has been either abolished or greatly weakened. About eleven states which had segregation laws applying to university training changed these laws to comply with the Court decision. In some states white students began to attend Negro colleges; in West Virginia, for example, in one such college white students have become a majority—an integration in reverse.

Following the Sipuel decision governors of fourteen southern and border states made an arrangement, subject to ratification by their state legislatures, for interstate regional education. The purpose of the compact was to coöperate toward the establishment and maintenance of jointly owned and operated regional educational institutions in the southern states in the professional, technological, scientific, literary, and other fields so as to provide greater educational advantages and facilities for the citizens of the several states who reside within such region.[14]

Regional education on the advanced levels is perhaps a sound educational plan, especially for states not having the finances to provide a first-grade graduate training for all its citizens. In fact eleven western states have made arrangements for such regional education. Since the plan came into being immediately after the Sipuel decision, some have interpreted the move as a last-ditch stand for segregation in higher education.[15] Whether this interpretation is correct may be seen if the plan is continued after the Sweatt and McLaurin decisions.

The response to the desegregation decision was extraordinary. It was hailed practically as a Magna Charta in civil rights and as indication of the democratic values of the nation. This shower of praise arose especially in that area best described as the Civil War North. Contrariwise, abuse, vituperation, spite, hate, and fury rolled like an avalanche from the Civil War South. At the minimum the

[14] Pauli Murray, *State Laws on Race and Color,* Women's Division of Christian Service, 1951, p. 666.
[15] *Ibid.,* p. 665.

Supreme Court was accused of using a political and social approach rather than a legal approach to the issue. At the other extreme, the Supreme Court was slandered as composed of New Deal, left-wing-dominated, communist-inspired, and brain-washed, Negro-loving carpetbag Yankees. The regional mores of the South were struck a mortal blow by this decision, but the diehards were ready once more to march to the strains of "Dixie," fighting a final rear-guard action for white supremacy. The immediate issue was how to avoid obeying the law. The rationale for action rested on a states' right position, and Calhoun's concepts of interposition and concurrent majority were exhumed to support the legal skirmishing that was to take place. Apparently the Civil War had not settled the issue of sovereignty and power. The house was still divided against itself, indeed so badly that rumor snaked its way across the sunny South and smoky North to the effect that federal troops would be used to enforce the decision . . . John Brown marching again . . . grapes of wrath . . . no stillness at Appomattox.

The response in seven of the old South states was a ringing affirmation of the segregation principle and racialist dogma. These states passed either constitutional amendments or statutory requirements permitting the abolition of the public-school system or assignment of pupils. Such action is meaningful in terms of a nativist-racialist value orientation tucked in a democratic framework. If there is a choice between a public-school system and a wider system of integration, then it is proposed that the public school must be abandoned, a shocking idea in terms of the religious, humanist, and common-man orientations.

That the South is not a monolithic bloc is seen in steps toward integration in Maryland, Kentucky, Tennessee, Texas, Missouri, West Virginia, Oklahoma, and New Mexico. In these states constitutional and statutory changes have been introduced to facilitate desegregation. In various cities and counties desegregation has been introduced though the transition is slow. In one year's time about 500 school districts in the South desegregated, and given the regional mores and tradition, this is considerable progress. Unfortunately, the press and other media have centered upon the more sensational activities and events of obstructionists, ignoring compliance and integration. In general, it appears that children and adolescents are quite capable of making a sensible adjustment if they are not hindered by interfering adults. It should be noted that northern states are also not monolithically united in liberalism, as is evidenced in school gerrymandering, segregated housing and hospitals, and employment discrimination.

The response to the decision also included the revival of vigilantism, violence, a resurgence of the KKK, but, more cleverly, the development of Citizens' Councils. The Citizens' Council attempts to put into effect economic boycotts against Negroes and whites supporting the Supreme Court decision. The councils are most active in Mississippi, Alabama, Texas, Georgia, and Arkansas. This is a move centering in the middle and lower-upper classes of the South. The boycott is used with the hope that violence can be restrained as the segregation lines are held. Violence is poor publicity. A boycott is less dramatic. The boycott tends to be total, involving all the commercial, industrial, and financial establishments of a community. It is likely that this is to be found most effective in smaller communities.

Lastly, the attack has centered upon the National Association for the Advancement of Colored People, which has fought the legal battles. Legislation has been introduced in some states practically outlawing the organization. In others, restrictions and controls have been imposed on its activities. Membership in the organization has led to loss of civil rights and job opportunities.

The type of response shown is consistent with the value orientation embodied in these actions. The initial response to the decision is to close ranks, the white in-group versus all the rest. The impact of the decision will be to accentuate the faith and actions of those who may be described as prejudiced and discriminating. They will come into positions of control or will be active in the organization of new groups to preserve the *status quo*. In so far as the NAACP is regarded as a subversive, internal enemy, this fact will also consolidate the views and actions of the extremists. The non-prejudiced and non-discriminating person or group in the South may mark time for the moment. Others may vacillate, depending upon the pressures in the community. At any rate a certain amount of unrest and violence is to be expected for the time, but this will diminish as the decisive factor is the larger society and not the regional. The old idea that the South is homogeneous and unchanging is disproved by the actions of some of the churches against segregation and by the action of the Negro. It follows from a sociological principle that "submission continues as long as the domination by force or economic coercion persists, but self-assertion returns if the power of the dominant agent diminishes relatively," [16] and the Supreme Court decision has diminished it.

THE STATUS OF DISSENT

Dissent in ideas produces controversy; dissent in action, conflict. Difference in views and opinions has no bearing upon validity, or soundness, or upon the rightness of ethical implications. Dissent is not an end in itself. Humanistically, it is but a phase of progressive clarification of ideas and insight. In the other value orientations dissent is more likely to mean heresy, and difference cannot be tolerated; hence religious and political inquisitions. Dissenting forefathers may be regarded as cultural heroes; dissenting contemporaries are subversives or an internal enemy. The dissent of the South from the Supreme Court decision makes for controversy, and if there is a willingness to discuss, the controversy may resolve itself. Forcing the acceptance of or compliance with the dissent on others is another matter, for this attempts to structure the society on an unsound principle. Perhaps there is a lurking, haunting realization of the unsoundness of the idea, a realization that segregation, universalized as a principle, could just as well be turned against the dominant white. The social Darwinism implicit in the segregation idea stands for the non-human, the non-moral—in short, the non-social. To support such an idea is to uphold error, and to act upon the idea is to be unethical or immoral. The Supreme Court decision attempts to uphold a moral order by proscribing the segregation principle, and in this case it does not proscribe the right to think differently or incorrectly.

Thinking and action are not totally distinct realms. If it is assumed

[16]E. T. Hiller, *Social Relations and Structures*, Harper & Brothers, 1947, p. 180.

that man is a social creature, neither beast nor god, then thinking is directed to good action. The extent to which this is not so makes thinking a perversion and action unsocial. The type of dissent that can be considered sound is best exemplified in the self-corrective action and progress of the scientific method, and in the often protested innovations which are always challenging orthodoxy in the arts. How, then, have the courts viewed dissent as a factor in culture, and how does this view involve education? There are three pertinent areas: censorship, group libel, and security. All three are interlinked, and all three eventually are concerned with the control of thought. The issues center especially on Amendment I of the Constitution: "Congress shall make no law . . . abridging the freedom of speech or of the press; or the right of the people peaceably to assemble and to petition the Government for a redress of grievances," and on the Fourteenth Amendment: ". . . No State shall make or enforce any law which shall abridge the privileges or immunities of citizens of the United States, nor shall any State deprive any person of life, liberty, or property without due process of law. . . ." Judicial decisions and *stare decisis* may be considered intervening factors.

EXCISING THOUGHT THROUGH CENSORSHIP

In Chapter 285 of the Session Laws of Minnesota for the year 1925 Section I provides:

Any person who, as an individual, or as a member or employee or a firm, or association or organization, or as an officer, director, member or employee of a corporation, shall be engaged in the business of regularly or customarily producing, publishing or circulating, having in possession, selling or giving away

(a) an obscene, lewd, and lascivious newspaper, magazine, or other periodical, or

(b) a malicious, scandalous, and defamatory newspaper, magazine, or other periodical,

is guilty of a nuisance, and all persons guilty of such nuisance may be enjoined, as hereinafter provided.

This particular statute covers the general content of censorship laws. Most censorship laws take the form of obscenity statutes designed to prevent the corruption of the morals of youth in specific and the public in general. They cover not only newspaper, magazine, and periodical but also book, pamphlet, ballad, printed paper, phonographic record, print, picture, figure, image, and "other thing." In recent years, on the ground of controlling the trend of juvenile delinquency, laws have been passed banning comic books containing "fictional deeds of crime, bloodshed, lust, or heinous acts, which tend to incite minors to violent or depraved or immoral acts." There is a tendency for the objection to the obscene and the indecent to be broadened and to gradually include other areas and forms of communication, as seen in section b of the cited statute.

Censorship is exercised on all levels of government, the federal, the state, and the municipal. Federally, the customs office and the post office are the two agencies which have been involved in censorship lawsuits testing the validity of some individual's negative classification of material. In some cases they have been upheld, in others overruled. Most active control is on the municipal level, on the basis of either a state law or a municipal censorship ordinance. A censorship board, a chief of police, or an assigned member of a police department will perform the censorship functions. Local support may be given by so-called watchdog societies, well-intentioned citizens frequently condemning books and other materials without having read or investigated them, on the basis of censorship lists prepared by private organizations, such as the National Organization for Decent Literature. Such check lists are circulated throughout the country. Pressure will be put upon local authorities to use the lists if they have not already used them voluntarily.[17] The heat is then turned on publishers, distributors, and librarians, and to dramatize the situation public burning of books is advocated.[18]

The state has the power to protect its citizens and especially its youth against obscenity in its various forms. This type of control is based upon the police power of the state, and has been upheld by the courts either directly or indirectly in many decisions.[19] These decisions are mutually reinforcing and tend to reappear as cases

[17] *Censorship Bulletin,* American Book Publishers Council, March, 1956.
[18] *Ibid.,* p. 4.
[19] Commonwealth *v.* Holmes, 17 Mass. 336; State *v.* McKee, 73 Conn. 18; Gitlow *v.* New York, 268 U.S. 652, 667; Fox *v.* Washington, 236 U.S. 273; Chaplinsky *v.* New Hampshire, 315 U.S. 568; Commonwealth *v.* Isenstadt, 318 Mass. 543.

come under the purview of the courts. Impure thought and action which is to be controlled is traditionally characterized as sexual impurity, the pornographic, the scatological. The problem is where to draw the line between art or science and obscenity. Is an art book containing pictures of undraped human figures obscene? Is the nude the same as the naked? Are the *Canterbury Tales* or Shakespeare's plays and sonnets obscene? Are Kinsey's studies in sexual behavior pornography? Many of the great works of literature have at one time or another been denounced as unacceptable, as have also scientific works investigating tabooed conduct. On the community level the issue seems fairly clear. An all-or-none position is taken. If the material is thought to be bad for children, it is also assumed to be bad for adults. The courts have been reluctant to accept such a simple standard, and they also have been reluctant to expand the concept of obscene to include such phrasing as the improper, the suggestive, or the violent. The courts have rejected such extension (Winters *v.* New York, 333 U.S. 507). They have been chary of ruling against freedom of speech and of the press even in alleged obscenity cases. In this way freedom of communication is maintained.

The extension of censorship has been resisted by the Supreme Court. Though a conviction was upheld by the state courts in a case involving section b of the statute cited above, the United States Supreme Court declared the statute unconstitutional (Near *v.* Minnesota, 283 U.S. 697). In this case a permanent injunction had been issued preventing the publication of a newspaper. Articles in this newspaper had made serious charges against public officials and others in connection with prevalence of crimes and the failure to punish them. The chief of police, for example, was accused of gross neglect of duty, illicit relations with gangsters, and participation in graft. The county attorney, also accused by the publishers, secured an injunction on the ground that the publication was a nuisance as defined in section b. The Court ruled that section b of the law constituted an infringement of the liberty of the press as guaranteed by the Fourteenth Amendment. "The conception of the liberty of the press in this country had broadened with the exigencies of the colonial period and with efforts to secure freedom from oppressive administration. That liberty was especially cherished for the immunity it afforded from previous restraint of publication of censure of public officers and charges of official misconduct. . . . The fact that the liberty of the press may be abused by miscreant purveyors of scandal does not make any the less necessary the immunity of the press from previous restraint in dealing with official misconduct." The Court recognized certain exceptional cases as limiting—war, obscenity, insurrection, but also indicated remedies open to plaintiffs, namely, the criminal libel law and interference with the proper discharge of judicial functions. The decision was 5–4, suggesting the differences in the Court.

Freedom of communication is one of the necessary conditions for human growth. Untruthful and harmful communication can be changed only by progressive clarification of ideas and values and the practice of tolerance. Censorship imposes an embargo on the exchange of experience through all the avenues of communication. It is very apt to become the tool for special interest. A society in which rigorous censorship is applied is not likely to be one conducive to education and free inquiry. Untruth and harmful communication may also involve the reputation or privacy of groups and individuals. An individual has protection in common law against libel and slander. To extend the law of libel and slander to include groups is something recent, and such a tendency involves an extension of censorship.

GROUP LIBEL AS A MEANS OF LIMITING THOUGHT

The professed aim of group libel laws, now found in some form in five states, is to insure harmonious relations among persons and groups. It is supposed to make for frank and free discussion without malice, hatred, or falsehoods and misrepresentation. Of two cases of alleged violations of such laws, one of the laws was declared unconstitutional by the state court (Klapprott v. New Jersey, 127 N.J. 395), but the other was declared constitutional with very vigorous dissent in the United States Supreme Court (Beauharnais v. Illinois, 343 U.S. 250). The nature of the Illinois law is as follows:

It shall be unlawful for any person, firm or corporation to manufacture, sell, or offer for sale, advertise or publish, present or exhibit in any public place in this state any lithograph, moving picture, play, drama, or sketch which publication or exhibition portrays depravity, criminality, unchastity, or lack of virtue of a class of citizens, of any race, color, creed or religion which said publication or exhibition exposes the citizens of any race, color, creed or religion to contempt, derision, or obloquy or which is productive of breach of the peace or riots. . . .

This law is based on analogy of the law of libel involving individuals. Criminal libel generally outlaws statements attacking the "virtue" of another or prohibits statements tending to bring another into "public ridicule." Many states require that a defendant in libel suit show that the utterance state the facts and that the publication be made with good motives for justifiable ends. The defendant challenged the law, claiming that it violated freedom of speech and of press guaranteed as against the states by the due process clause of the Fourteenth Amendment, and that the provisions of the law were vague and too broad.

The decision of the Supreme Court (5–4) upheld the conviction.

But if an utterance directed at an individual may be the object of criminal sanctions, we cannot deny to a State power to punish the same utterance directed at a defined group, unless we can say that this is a wilful and purposeless restriction unrelated to the peace and well-being of the State. . . . It would, however, be arrant dogmatism, quite outside the scope of our authority in passing on the powers of a State, for us to deny that the Illinois legislature may warrantly believe that a man's job and his educational opportunities and the dignity accorded him may depend as much on the reputation of the racial and religious group to which he willynilly belongs, as it does on his own merits. This being so, we are precluded from saying that speech concededly punishable when immediately directed at individuals cannot be outlawed if directed at groups with whose position and esteem in society the afflicted individual may be inextricably involved. [The Court refused to accept the possibility of an abuse of such a law as valid ground to deny the Illinois legislature the power to adopt such a measure, continuing] "While this Court sits" it retains and exercises authority to nullify action which encroaches on freedom of utterance under the guise of punishing libel. Of course, discussion cannot be denied and the right, as well as the duty, of criticism must not be stifled.

The majority also dismissed the contention that the terms of the statute were too vague and broad. They also took cognizance of racial and religious intergroup problems with special emphasis on the professional agitator or the willful perpetrator of falsehoods to promote hatred, strife, violence, and breaches of the peace. The statute upheld by refusal to reverse the conviction was an attempt to suppress the manipulation of a fluctuating public opinion by use of calculated falsehood and vilification.

The dissenting judges took issue with the majority decision on every reason proffered to sustain the conviction. The sum view of the minority was that the majority decision sanctioned the spread of censorship. "The Court's opinion 'is notice to the legislatures that they have the power to control unpopular blocs' and 'a warning to every minority that when the Constitution guarantees free speech it does not mean what it says.' . . . State experimentation in curbing freedom of expression is startling and frightening doctrine in a country dedicated to self-government by its people. I reject the holding that either state or nation can punish people for having their say in matters of public concern." Some of the dissenting judges thought that the majority decision abridged not only freedom of speech and press but also freedom of petition and assembly. "I think the First Amendment with the Fourteenth, 'absolutely' forbids such laws without any 'ifs' or 'buts' or 'whereases.' Whatever the dangers if any, in such public discussions, it is a danger the Founders deemed outweighed by the danger incident to the stifling of thought and speech. The Court does not act on this view of the Founders. It calculates what it deems to be the danger of public discussion, holds the scales are tipped on the side of state suppression and upholds state censorship."

Alternate proposals to control hate propaganda have been offered, such as (1) compulsory retraction in which the judgment requires the defendant to print a revised version of the facts; (2) compulsory reply in which publishers are required to print a rebuttal; (3) disclosure measures forbidding anonymously published defamation.

The significance of the group libel laws is seen in the views of the dissenting judges, a possibility which the majority also recognized, namely, the suppression of discussion dealing with public issues for fear of libel. An aggressive group might effectively stifle any criticism on the grounds of group libel. In the absence of a standard with respect to group libel, it becomes difficult to determine defamatory acts. For example, one segment of a community may think an utterance defamatory and another segment may not. The problem in education becomes clear. The teacher may be confronted with a group libel charge directly by a group or through administrative channels upon complaint. Dealing with controversial issues may become an occupational hazard. The split decision indicates the uncertainties within the Supreme Court, and these become more marked in the problem of security and loyalty, especially since World War II.

SECURITY AND CONFORMING BEHAVIOR

The first action taken on the part of a political party in power to stifle criticism and opposition occurred in the Alien and Sedition Act of 1789. The bill was passed during a crisis period—possible war with France, fear of and hostility to the ideas of the French Revolution, rumors of French plots and French espionage, and antagonism to French and Irish immigrants. The Enemy Alien act provided for "protective custody of non-naturalized aliens subject of a hostile nation in case war or invasion were attempted or threatened." This idea, in modern terms, is the concentration camp. A second aspect of the law gave the President the power to order the deportation of any alien judged dangerous to the peace and safety of the United States or suspected on reasonable grounds of being concerned with treasonable or secret plotting against the government. In addition aliens were required to take out a license to reside in the country. The prohibitions of the Sedition Act are worth citing in full:

That if any person shall write, print, utter or publish, or shall cause or procure to be written, printed, uttered, or published, or shall knowingly and willingly assist or aid in writing, printing, uttering or publishing any false, scandalous and malicious writing or writings against the government of the United States, or either house of the Congress of the United States, with intent to defame the said government, or either house of Congress, or the said President, or to bring them or either of them into contempt or disrepute; or to excite against them, or either or any of them, the hatred of the good people of the United States, or to stir sedition within the United States, or to excite any unlawful combinations therein, for opposing or resisting any laws of the United States, or any act of the President of the United States, done in pursuance of any such law, or of the power in him vested by the constitution of the United States, or to resist, oppose, or defeat any such law or act, or to aid, encourage or abet any hostile designs of any foreign nation against the United States, their people or government, then such person, being thereof convicted before any court of the United States having jurisdiction thereof, shall be punished by a fine not exceeding two thousand dollars and by imprisonment not exceeding two years.

The Federalists enforced this act vigorously against their political opposition headed by Jefferson and Madison. Many editors and publishers of newspapers were brought to trial, frequently before hostile Federalist judges. The Federalists lost the election of 1800. The act expired in 1801. Jefferson pardoned all those convicted under the law, and Congress repaid most of the fines.

This early situation and law show the type pattern: crisis, fear of an external enemy, fear of an internal enemy (aliens and social critics), fear of ideas and discussion; control, alien registration, deportation, protective custody, concentration camps, fine and imprisonment, suppression of freedom of speech, of press, of assembly, of petition, by declaring such seditious. The First Amendment was a victim of the cold war between the United States and France. To generalize: whenever the described crisis takes place, the indicated controls will be put into effect. In contemporary times the Smith Act, the McCarran Act, the Japanese-American "Relocation," security hearings, and loyalty oaths are phases of this issue. These laws and methods of control have arisen out of the recent war crises.

Our examination of the judicial response to such legislation will begin with the cases arising under the Espionage Act of World War I. The anti-sedition cases in this type of act, on both federal and state levels, dealt with charges of interfering with the operation of the war. The first set of cases involving seditious utterance alleged to interfere with the conduct of the war were those of Schenck, Debs, Sugarman, and Frohwerk. Of these the Schenck case is basic because of the handling of the First Amendment and because of the later fact that this decision became the basic precedent to follow.

The question of free speech was handled by Justice Holmes as follows in a unanimous decision:

We admit that in many places and in ordinary times the defendants in saying all that was said in the circular would have been within their constitutional rights. But the character of every act depends upon the circumstances in which it is done. *Aikens v. Wisconsin*, 195 U.S. 194, 205, 206. The most stringent protection of free speech would not protect a man in falsely shouting fire in a theatre and causing panic. It does not even protect a man from an injunction against uttering words that may have all the effect of force. *Gompers v. Bucks Stove and Range Co.*, 221 U.S. 418, 439. The question in every case is whether the words used are used in such circumstances and are of such a nature as to create a clear and present danger that they will bring about the substantive evils that Congress has a right to prevent. It is a question of proximity and degree. When a nation is at war many things that might be said in time of peace are such a hindrance to its effort that their utterance will not be endured so long as men fight and that no Court could regard them as protected by any constitutional right. . . . The statute of 1917 #4 punishes conspiracies to obstruct as well as actual obstruction. If the act, (speaking, or circulating a paper,) its tendency and the intent with which it is done are the same, we perceive no ground for saying that success alone warrants making the act a crime. . . .

Succeeding decisions based upon the Schenck case fortify the principle of clear and present danger. Other decisions upholding restriction on freedom of speech and press in peacetime included the Gitlow (1925), Whitney (1927), Burns (1927) cases. These cases dealt with state criminal syndicalism statutes.

From 1931 to the middle forties the Supreme Court built up a body of principle and precedent strongly limiting government authority and power in the area of political expression, as especially embodied in the First Amendment. The first decision involved was the Near case, previously discussed. Major decisions include the De Jonge (1937), Stromberg (1931), Herndon (1937), Taylor (1943), Barnette (1943), and Schneiderman (1943) cases.

The De Jonge case involved a violation of an Oregon criminal syndicalism statute. This law defined criminal syndicalism as a doctrine "which advocates crime, physical violence, sabotage or any unlawful acts or methods as a means of accomplishing or effecting industrial or political change or revolution." The act defined specific offenses such as the teaching of criminal syndicalism, printing or distribution of materials advocating the doctrine, organization of a society or meeting to advocate it, and presiding over or assisting in conducting of such a society or meeting. De Jonge was charged and convicted for participating in and conducting such a meeting. Since previous decisions (Gitlow and Fiske) include the free speech guarantees of the First Amendment under the scope of the Fourth Amendment and as thus applicable to the states, the Court reversed the conviction on the grounds that the statute as interpreted by the state court violated the due process clause. Chief Justice Hughes writing the majority decision commented:

The greater the importance of safeguarding the community from incitements to the overthrow of our institutions by force and violence, the more imperative is the need to preserve inviolate the constitutional rights of free speech, free press and free assembly in order to maintain the opportunity for free political discussion, to the end that government may be responsive to the will of the people and that changes, if desired, may be obtained by peaceful means. Therein lies the security of the Republic, the very foundation of constitutional government. . . . If the persons assembling have committed crimes elsewhere, if they have formed or are engaged in a conspiracy against the public peace and order, they may be prosecuted for their conspiracy or other violation of valid laws. But it is a different matter when the State, instead of prosecuting them for such offenses, seizes upon mere participation in a peaceable assembly and a lawful public discussion as the basis for a criminal charge.

In West Virginia State Board of Education v. Barnette, 319 U.S. 624, the issue involved a compulsory flag salute in the schools. Failure to comply was insubordination dealt with by expulsion and readmission to the school upon compliance. An expelled child was considered "unlawfully absent" and thus proceded against as a delinquent; the parents were liable to prosecution and if convicted subject to a fine not to exceed $50 and a jail term not to exceed thirty days. Members of Jehovah's Witnesses, a religious group teaching that the laws imposed by God are superior to those imposed by temporal government, sought an injunction to restrain enforcement of the regulation against their children and parents. The flag salute was regarded as idolatry. Children of Jehovah's Witnesses were expelled.

Threats were made to send them to reformatories and threats were made to the parents that they would be prosecuted for contributing to the delinquency of minors. The sole issue was the flag salute. A lower court granted the injunction. The board of education then took the case to the United States Supreme Court, denying that the law and regulation was an unconstitutional denial of religious freedom, of freedom of speech, and invalid under the due process and equal protection clauses of the Fourteenth Amendment.

The decision of the Court affirmed the judgment of the lower court granting the injunction against the West Virginia Board of Education:

The sole conflict is between authority and rights of the individual. The State asserts power to condition access to public education by making a prescribed sign and profession and at the same time to coerce attendance by punishing both parent and child. The latter stand on a right of self-determination in matters that touch individual opinion and attitude. . . . Here the power of compulsion is invoked without any allegation that remaining passive during a flag salute creates a clear and present danger that would justify an effort even to muffle expression. To sustain the compulsory flag salute we are required to say that a Bill of Rights which guards the individual's right to speak his mind, left it open to public authorities to compel him to utter what is not in his mind. . . . Struggles to coerce uniformity of sentiment in support of some end thought essential to their time and country have been waged by many good as well as evil men. . . . As governmental pressure toward unity becomes greater, so strife becomes more bitter as to whose unity it shall be. . . . Those who begin coercive elimination of dissent soon find themselves exterminating dissenters. Compulsory unification of opinion achieves only the unanimity of the graveyard. . . . If there is any fixed star in our constitutional constellation, it is that no official, high or petty, can prescribe what shall be orthodox in politics, nationalism, religion, or other matters of opinion or force citizens to confess by word or act their faith therein. If there are any circumstances which permit an exception, they do not now occur to us. . . .

Since World War II more legislation, administrative regulations, and intensified pressure by private groups have greatly restricted many provisions of the constitutional amendments, particularly the First, Fourth, Fifth, Sixth, Eighth, and Fourteenth. The trend has been similar on both federal and state level. These limitations involve (1) the activity of legislative committees, (2) the enforcement of anti-sedition legislation, (3) the denial of privileges or positions of influence to alleged subversives, (4) loyalty qualifications for employment, (5) internal security and similar legislation, (6) the increasing tendencies to use licensing as a method of control. By 1951 thirty-one states and territories had anti-sedition laws similar to the Smith Act, twenty had criminal syndicalism laws, sixteen had criminal anarchy laws, thirty-four had red flag laws.

The number of court cases involved in all these areas is enormous, and for our purposes only two will be briefly considered: Dennis et al. *v.* United States, 341 U.S. 494, and Adler *v.* Board of Education, 342 U.S. 485. The first was a test of the Smith Act, the second of the Feinberg law and the rules promulgated under it by the State Board of Regents.

In the Dennis case four judges joined the decision written by Chief Justice Vinson and two judges wrote concurring opinions. Two judges, Mr. Black and Mr. Douglas, dissented. The charge was that the indicted individuals had willfully and knowingly organized as the Communist party a society and group of persons teaching and advocating the duty and necessity of doing this, and all this in violation of the Smith Act. The Court argued that Congress had the power to protect the government of the United States from change by violence, revolution, and terrorism, but that the means to do this might conflict with the First and Fifth amendments. The Court relying upon Schenck, Gitlow, and Whitney and dismissing Fiske, De Jonge, and Barnette as insubstantial, agreed with the trial judge that the requisite danger existed by referring to the world situation and the disciplined nature of members of the Communist party. "And this analysis disposes of the contention that conspiracy to advocate, as distinguished from the advocacy itself, cannot be constitutionally restrained, because it comprises only the preparation. It is the existence of conspiracy which creates the danger." The clear and present danger rule, it may be recalled, held that speech could be restrained only when it is likely to lead immediately to acts that are legally punishable. If the connection between speech and act is only remote, restraint is not legitimate. Only acts, and speech which has an immediate connection with acts, can be controlled by law. This view is set aside by the Court as indicated and also by its rejection of "the contention that success or probability of success is the criterion" of danger. The Court also rejected the argument that the statute was vague. Justice Jackson concurring did not think that the statute, while constitutional, was an effective way of dealing with the problem:

Communism will not go to jail with these Communists. No decision by this Court can forestall revolution whenever the existing government fails to command the respect and loyalty of the people and sufficient distress and discontent is allowed to grow up among the masses. Many failures by alien governments attest that no government can long prevent revolution by outlawry. Corruption, ineptitude, inflation, oppressive taxation, militarization, injustice, and loss of leadership capable of intellectual initiative in domestic or foreign affairs are allies on which the Communists count to bring opportunity knocking to their door.

The two dissenting judges agreed that the Smith Act flatly violated the First Amendment and was therefore unconstitutional, that the clear and present danger rule was repudiated, that the determination of the crucial issue of fact by judge rather than jury took on a Star Chamber quality, that the extension of the law of conspiracy to include speech was unwarranted, and finally that maintaining free speech as the rule rather than the exception was worth the risk. "The restraint to be constitutional must be based on more than fear, on more than passionate opposition against the speech, on more than a revolted dislike for its contents. There must be some immediate injury to society that is likely if the speech is allowed. . . . Seditious conduct can always be punished. But the command of the First Amendment is so clear that we should not allow Congress to call a halt to free speech except in the extreme case of peril of the speech itself. The First Amendment makes confidence in the common sense of our people and in their maturity of judgment the great postulate of our democracy."

The Feinberg law assumes that there has been a large-scale infiltration into the public schools of New York of persons advocating the overthrow of the government by force or violence or by any other unlawful means, that persons propagandize such views in the classes, and that to protect the children these persons must be removed. Specific reference is made to the Communist party and other organizations having a similar purpose. Each year a report has to be filed on personnel by the designated supervisor or administrative head.

The majority held that the law did not abridge freedom of speech and assembly of persons employed or seeking employment in the public schools of New York. A person seeking such employment could not do it on his terms but upon reasonable terms laid down by the proper school authorities, and this law was held a reasonable condition. The Court also ruled that membership in an organization listed as allegedly subversive by the Board of Regents as a presumption of guilt did not violate due process. The Court finally dismissed the charge that the word "subversive" was vague and indefinite. The decision was a 6–3 judgment.

Justice Black, dissenting, thought that the Court should not sustain a law which "effectively penalizes school teachers for their thoughts and their associates" and Justice Douglas:

I have not been able to accept the recent doctrine that a citizen who enters the public service can be forced to sacrifice his civil rights. . . . The present law proceeds on a principle repugnant to our society—guilt by association. . . . The law inevitably turns the school system into a spying project. . . . This is not the usual type of supervision which checks a teacher's competency; it is a system which searches for hidden meanings in a teacher's utterances. . . . What happens under this law is typical of what happens in a police state. Teachers are under constant surveillance; their pasts are combed for signs of disloyalty; their utterances are watched for clues to dangerous thoughts. A pall is cast over the classrooms. There can be no real academic freedom in that environment. . . . Of course the school systems of the country need not become cells for Communist activities; and the classrooms need not become forums for propagandizing the Marxist creed. But the guilt of the teacher should turn on overt acts. So long as she is a law-abiding citizen, so long as her performance within the public school system meets professional standards, her private life, her political philosophy, her social creed should not be the cause of reprisals against her.

The continuity of point of view of the dissenting judges should appear clear. What these variations in court decisions show is (1) the preponderance favoring curtailment of the constitutional amendments and (2) a basic clash of value orientations.

VALUE ORIENTATIONS—THE BASIC ISSUE

This examination of court decision and law shows the tremendous significance of the legal order as a fact in life. What happens to the school occurs within the setting of a legal framework. The bearing of court decision and law has been examined in three areas: the relation of religion and education, discrimination and education, and significance of dissent. In all of these areas there is a clash of points of view, and this difference is also manifested in the court decisions. The variations in the legal reasoning involve two opposite value orientations, the nativist and the humanist, or to put it into more traditional terms, the principle of sovereignty as opposed to natural rights.

Sovereignty is the power principle *par excellence*, and legal finesse in locating sovereignty in this person or in that group is immaterial to its nature, which is "supreme power over citizens and subjects, unrestrained by law," as Jean Bodin defined it. Supreme power unrestrained by law—what better concept of the tyrant could be found? What exists is at the will if not the whim of the sovereign. In this situation there are no rights, only privileges and duties bestowed by the sovereign, who is also free to take them away, as he is unrestrained by law. As sovereignty is identified with the state, the state is this absolute power center, a group among other groups concerned with maintaining itself as against any other group. As it is the supreme power, the issue is resolved which no special pleading for the goodness of a pluralistic society can overcome. A sovereign deals only with subjects, issuing directives and commands which must be obeyed under penalty of incurring all the force of an absolute power. Education may be given or withheld, voting may be universal or limited, discrimination may be upheld or withdrawn, speech, assembly, petition all may be controlled as the sovereign wills, and so it has been with the absolute monarchs and the alleged enlightened despots of the past. It is the continuation of the Hobbesian Leviathan which structures the judicial views abridging or limiting the Bill of Rights and subsequent pertinent amendments. A fundamental distrust of the person, of inquiry, of free communication is evidenced in the actions of a sovereign. Under these conditions the life of the person is always uncertain and insecure as he attempts to order his actions in a situation which is basically irrational and nonmoral as the unanimity of the graveyard is reached. In so far as the principle of sovereignty is a working principle in our institutional life, one should not be surprised at the results. The fact that things are not worse is due not to the magnanimity and graciousness of the sovereign but to the counterprinciple of natural rights.

On the assumption that man is a social as well as a rational being, the natural rights view asks what conditions are necessary for man to realize himself. The concept of the right to life, liberty, and the pursuit of happiness or property roots in the natural rights tradition. Such rights are universal to the category man, and every individual partakes of them. To deny them is to deny man. The question is, then, not a matter of power at all but a matter of structuring life to realize these rights. The Declaration of Independence and the Bill of Rights express the essential conditions. It is not surprising that these are attacked and whittled away, when a sovereign point of view is maintained. The right to revolution is a natural rights concept, the right to abolish, change, and institute new forms of government, a venture which Jefferson pointed out is not to be undertaken lightly. Free speech, free press, religious toleration, free education—all are necessary conditions to realize man's nature. The concept of man under sovereignty is that of subject; the corresponding natural rights concept is that of citizen. It involves respect for the person as the other involves deference and servility. It views man as an accountable agent, "conscious of his intentions, capable of choice and self-direction, and able to take the consequences of his choices and actions," [20] not as a loyal, indoctrinated robot. The enlightened citizen, the social, rational, educated man, is the model, in the natural rights view. It is this concept of man that manifests itself in legal reasoning of those upholding freedom of speech, etc., and limiting authority and power.

We see now the dilemma of our culture in terms of incompatible principles. Each structures the institutional life differently; hence the strains and stresses in our institutional order. Under conditions

[20] E. T. Hiller, *op. cit.*, p. 195.

of crisis the sovereignty view is likely to prevail and the natural rights view to be devalued. Under conditions of relative peace the natural rights view is likely to prevail. It is never completely downed because its fit to the facts of life is closer than that of sovereignty. What is necessary is to implement the natural rights view in our modern corporate society—a venture, based on the restatement of a social philosophy, which would make full use of the findings of the psychological and social sciences. With such reinterpretation of natural rights in our schools and our society, the conditions could be established to allow for full growth of personality, to bring about a kaleidoscopic richness and diversity of life in an era of genuine fulfillment of human potentialities.

Selected Readings

American Civil Liberties Union, *America's Need: a New Birth of Freedom*, 34th Annual Report, July 1, 1953–June 30, 1954.

American Civil Liberties Union, *Clearing the Main Channels*, 35th Annual Report, July 1, 1954–June 30, 1955.

American Civil Liberties Union, *Liberty Is Always Unfinished Business*, 36th Annual Report, July 1, 1955–June 30, 1956.

Barth, Alan, *The Loyalty of Free Men*, The Viking Press, 1951.

Biddle, Francis, *The Fear of Freedom*, Doubleday and Company, 1951.

Chaffee, Zechariah, *Free Speech in the United States*, Harvard University Press, 1946.

Fraenkel, Osmond, *The Supreme Court and Civil Liberties*, American Civil Liberties Union, 1955.

Gellhorn, Walter, *The State and Subversion*, Cornell University Press, 1950.

Konvitz, Milton, *Bill of Rights Reader*, Cornell University Press, 1954.

Newman, Edwin S. (ed.), *The Law on Civil Rights and Civil Liberties*, Oceana Publication, 1955.

Pfeffer, Leo, *Church, State, and Freedom*, The Beacon Press, 1953.

Reutter, Edmund, *The School Administrator and Subversive Activities*, Columbia University Press, 1951.

Selekman, Sylvia, and Selekman, Benjamin, *Power and Morality in a Business Society*, McGraw-Hill Book Company, 1957.

Valien, Bonita, *The St. Louis Story: A Study in Desegregation*, Anti-Defamation League, n.d.

Williams, Robin, and Ryan, Margaret, *Schools in Transition*, University of North Carolina Press, 1954.

Appendix: Sample of a Descriptive Report Card

[This report is a summary of a boy's work in the third grade.]

Paul Jones   Date *June 4, 1956*

Paul has made quite a spurt in reading. The June achievement test shows that he has grown more than two years. His arithmetic shows a growth of better than a year. His spelling and language growth is the least, but it is approximately a year. The tests indicate that Paul can read some fifth grade materials.

Paul's coördination and physical and emotional control show improvement in a number of ways but still require considerable guidance. He tries harder to watch where he is going and to keep from falling down. His posture when sitting or standing is somewhat improved. He is more conscious of the need for controlling himself on his chair. His work with carpenter tools and art materials shows improvement in coördination. He is more responsible for himself and listens better to directions and suggestions. He is improving in temper control but needs to keep trying.

Paul has good ideas and is improving in learning to express them better through art and other activities. His ability to communicate with others has been given special attention through his lip reading and speech work. He coöperates very well, but has a short attention span.

His work as circulation manager of the newspaper was good for him. It gave him more prestige and more experience in group work. In play activities he usually starts with the group but is soon day dreaming or off playing by himself. He is one of the strongest in the group and can perform isolated basic skills well. He doesn't play in the seasonal games unless closely supervised to see that he does so. His hearing difficulty is a real handicap to some of his group activities.

Paul is using his singing voice more frequently. He is very sensitive to phrases. He reads his songs rather well.

Paul shows a good understanding of science.

Paul is to go to the fourth grade in the fall.

Jean Trumbull
Teacher
Third Grade

INDEXES

Index of Names

Abrams, Frank, 56
Adams, Walter, 324
Alexander, William M., 39
Alilunus, Leo, 413
Almack, John, 334
Anderson, Elin, 110, 204
Anderson, Harold, 211, 212
Armstrong, W. Earl, 437

Barnes, Harry E., 465
Barrows, Alice, 133
Barth, Alan, 555
Bauernfeind, Robert, 318
Baxter, Bernice, 62, 138, 181
Beale, Howard K., 418, 451, 467, 478, 479
Beatty, Thomas, 205
Becker, Howard, 446, 465
Becker, Howard S., 406
Begeman, Jean, 475, 476
Bell, Earl, 119
Benne, Kenneth, 220, 225, 279, 404
Bergler, Egon, 118
Bernard, Jessie, 119
Bibby, Cyril, 376, 378
Biddle, Francis, 555
Biesanz, John, 12
Biesanz, Mavis, 12
Blanshard, Paul, 67
Blau, Joseph, 19, 39
Blau, Peter, 458
Bonney, Merl, 328, 334, 351
Bossing, Nelson, 22, 277, 279, 404
Brady, Robert, 66
Brandt, Joseph, 510
Bredemeier, H., 16

Bremeans, Phillipps, 412
Brewer, Helen, 211, 212
Brewer, Joseph, 211
Brodinsky, B. P., 60
Bromley, Dorothy, 511
Brookhover, Wilbur, 212, 443, 445, 475
Brooks, Marian, 182, 421
Broom, Leonard, 459
Brunner, Dick, 487
Brunner, Edmund, 119
Buchanan, Frank, 487
Burkhardt, J. Martin, 476
Butler, Vern, 389
Butts, R. Freeman, 21, 39, 86
Byers, Loretta, 396, 397

Caplow, Theodore, 119
Carr, Lowell, 119
Cartwright, Davis, 225, 516
Cary, Miles, 502, 513
Caudill, William, 129, 133, 144
Cayton, Horace R., 100, 120, 315, 317
Casson, Stanley, 465
Centers, Richard, 513
Chaffee, Zechariah, 555
Charnley, Mitchell, 511
Chatto, C. I., 262
Clark, Robert, 326, 336
Cocking, Walter, 144
Coffman, Lotus, 387, 388
Cohen, Nathan, 407
Coleman, H. A., 312
Commager, Henry, 19, 66
Cook, Lloyd, 127
Corey, Stephen, 231
Cressey, Paul, 272, 446

Criswell, Joan, 333, 366
Cross, Gertrude, 181
Cubberly, Ellwood, 21, 22, 86
Cuber, John, 12
Cummings, Howard H., 262
Cunningham, Ruth, 225

Dahir, James, 119
Dahlke, H. Otto, 62, 327, 332
Danford, H. C., 205
Darling, Edward, 487
David, Lilly, 416
Davidson, Helen, 311
Davis, Allison, 119, 275, 314, 317, 323
Davis, Kingsley, 66
DeGré, Gerard, 465
Dewey, Richard, 119
Dickson, Lenore, 337, 338, 339
Dickson, W. J., 352
Dollard, John, 120, 275, 314, 317, 323
Drake, St. Clair, 120, 315, 317
Dreiman, David, 458, 487, 492, 493, 502, 515, 522
Dubin, Robert, 459
Duncan, Hannibal, 302
Dunfee, Maxine, 421
Dunne, George, H., 67
Duvall, Evelyn, 314

Edwards, Alba, 98
Edwards, Newton, 72, 86
Eells, Kenneth, 413
Elsbree, Willard, 421, 455
Engelhardt, N. L., 144
Ericson, Martha C., 314
Essex, Martin, 350

Faunce, Roland, 222, 277, 279, 404, 522
Fenimore, Watson, 202, 205
Fleming, W. S., 50, 68
Flotow, Ernest, 334
Flynn, John T., 478
Foner, Philip, 18, 19
Folger, O. Hershel, 205
Form, William, 100, 352, 388
Fortune, R. F., 465
Fox, William, 387, 388, 390, 391, 392, 393, 394, 395, 410, 412
Fraenkel, Osmond, 555
Frank, Lawrence, 12
Frazier, Franklin, 323
Freud, Sigmund, 378
Friedlaender, Ludwig, 465
Froehlich, Gustav, 231, 232, 233, 234
Frohlich, Philip, 197

Gabel, Hortense, 511

Gabel, Milton, 511
Gallion, Austin, 119
Gardner, Burleigh B., 119
Gardner, Mary, 119
Gellerman, William, 52
Gellhorn, Walter, 555
Gerth, Hans, 12, 101, 459
Ginsberg, M., 73
Gist, Noel, 119
Glock, Charles Y., 511
Goodlad, John, 181
Gough, Harris, 311
Gould, Kenneth, 487, 501
Gouldner, Alvin, 459
Gray, Ailsa, 459
Greenhoe, Florence, 400, 401, 408, 409, 411, 412, 413
Gregg, Russell, 167, 168, 170
Group, Don, 205
Gruber, Frederick, 205

Haas, Margot, 515
Haas, Robert, 221, 225
Hagman, Harlan, 458
Halbert, L. A., 119
Hall, Clifton, 16, 17, 21, 39
Hallegan, Alice, 262
Hallenback, Wilbur, 119
Hamburger, Ernest, 98
Hamilton, Alexander, 465
Hammond, Barbara, 156, 157
Hammond, J. I.., 156, 157
Hand, Harold C., 167, 171, 350
Harlow, Alvin, 127
Harrower, M. R., 355
Hatt, Paul, 119
Havighurst, Robert, 314, 323, 387
Hayes, Margaret, 250
Herrick, Theral, 231, 273
Hess, Walter, 205
Hiller, E. T., 6, 12, 213, 226, 252, 254, 388, 421, 453, 466, 538
Hillman, Arthur, 119
Hockey, Barbara, 459
Hollingshead, August, 32, 103, 107, 163, 179, 201, 276, 351, 407, 445
Hoppe, Arthur, 421
Horowitz, Eugene L., 333
Howard, Ebenezer, 119
Howe, Irving, 66
Howells, William Dean, 413 n.
Huer, John, 412
Huggett, Albert, 421
Hughes, Everett C., 352

Isaacs, Susan, 370, 379

Jacobson, Paul B., 167, 168
Jay, John, 465
Jefferson, Thomas, 18, 19, 325
Johnson, Alvin, 86, 228
Junker, Buford, 324

Kahler, Alfred, 98
Kallen, Horace, 67
Kardiner, Abram, 316
Katoona, Arthur, 212
Katz, Daniel, 492
Kelley, Earl C., 271
Kelley, Florence, 181
Kiely, Margaret, 389, 390
Kingery, Gordon, 191
Kinsey, A. C., 314
Kirkpatrick, William, 421
Klapper, Joseph T., 511
Kluckhohn, Clyde, 67, 324, 334
Kluckhohn, Florence, 67, 334
Knight, Edgar, 16, 17, 21, 39, 73
Kolb, J. H., 119
Kolb, William L., 12
Kollmorgen, Walter, 120
Komarovsky, Mirra, 310, 413
Konvitz, Milton, 555
Kornhauser, Arthur, 513
Krug, Edward, A., 222

Lafferty, H. M., 182
Langdon, Grace, 324
Laycock, S. R., 248, 249
Lee, Alfred Mclung, 486, 497, 511
Leggett, 144
Lemann, Thomas, 351
Leonard, Olson, 120
Levine, Michael, 160
Levy, Marion, 66
Lewett, Ida, 387
Lewin, Kurt, 207, 210, 515, 522
Lewis, Gertrude, 181
Lewis, Hylan, 324
Lindeman, Eduard C., 67
Lindman, Erick L., 40
Lippitt, Ronald, 207, 515, 522
Loeb, Martin, 387
Loomis, Charles, 120
Lowenfeld, Victor, 279
Lowenthal, Leo, 194
Lowenthal, Max, 487
Lundberg, George, 337, 338, 339
Lunt, P., 314
Lynd, Helen, 120, 163, 169, 198, 325, 336
Lynd, Robert, 120, 163, 169, 198, 325, 336

McFie, Bernice, 307, 311, 322
McGuire, Carson, 326, 335
McDonald, Lois, 120
McKay, Claude, 120
McKee, James B., 520
McKelvey, F. H., 131
McKibben, Frank, 49, 68
McLeish, Kenneth, 120
McWilliams, Carey, 486, 487
MacKenzie, S., 418
Maddy, N. R., 312
Madison, James, 465, 525
Mangus, A. R., 304, 305, 327
Marrow, A. J., 521
Martin, C. E., 314
Martin, Walter, 12
Maul, Ray, 384, 386
Mead, Margaret, 324, 465
Meeker, Marcia, 413
Melby, Ernest, 487
Menge, J. Wilmer, 522
Merton, Robert K., 459, 471
Miels, Alice, 226
Miles, Katherine, 336
Miller, Delbert, 100, 352, 388
Miller, Herbert, 108
Mills, C. Wright, 12, 98, 101, 459
Millspaugh, Martin, 511
Mitchell, Elmer, 200
Mitchell, G. S., 100
Mitchell, J. C., 250
Mitchell, Morris, 485
Moe, Edward, 120
Moehlman, Arthur, 427, 431, 432, 433, 436, 453, 454, 458
Moehlman, Conrad, 68, 528
Moffett, M'Ledge, 389
Monahan, Thomas, 327
Mooney, Ross L., 319, 321
Moore, Wilbert E., 100, 486
Moreno, J. L., 221, 333, 351, 516
Morgan, Arthur E., 120
Morison, Samuel, 19
Morphet, Edgar L., 40
Mulhern, James, 40
Mumford, Lewis, 89, 119
Muntyan, Bozidar, 220, 225
Murray, Henry, 324
Murray, Pauli, 535
Myrdal, Gunnar, 67, 511

Neugarten, Bernice, 328, 330, 366
Nevard, Norm, 200
Newman, Edwin S., 555
Nightingale, R. T., 73
Northrop, F. S. C., 67

O'Brien, Robert, 12
Olson, Willard, 226
Ovesey, Lionel, 316

Park, Robert, 108
Parsons, Talcott, 421
Perkins, Francis, 279
Perkins, Laurence B., 144
Peters, Mildred, 348
Pfeffer, Leo, 555
Piaget, Jean, 254, 279, 354
Pittman, Alice, 509
Pomeroy, W. B., 314
Pope, Liston, 120
Pope Pius XI, 44
Potashin, Reva, 330, 334

Quanbeck, Martin, 413
Quoist, Michel, 114

Raup, Bruce, 86
Read, Herbert, 279
Redl, Fritz, 267, 279, **444**
Reed, Mary, 211
Reid, Kenneth, 154
Reiss, Albert, 119
Reisner, Edward, 86
Remmers, H. H., 318
Reutter, Edmund, 555
Rice, Mabel, 428
Richey, Robert, 387, 388, 390, 391, 392, 393, 394, 395, 410, 412
Reisman, David, 267
Roben, J. Maske, 386
Robinson, John, 279
Robison, Sophia, 407
Rhodehaffer, I. A., 407
Roethlisberger, F. J., 352
Rogers, Carl, R., 279, 303, 311
Rorty, James, 487
Ross, Murray, 516
Roth, Alfred, 133, 154
Rudy, Willis, 398
Rugg, Harold, 182, 421
Ryan, Margaret, 555

Sachs, Murray, 407
Sarasohn, Stephen, 511
Savage, 202
Saylor, Galen, 39
Schaffer, Ruth, 522
Schriftgiesser, Karl, 468, 497
Schultz, Raymond E., 167, 168, 169, 170
Seago, Mary, 334
Sears, Robert, 379
Segel, David, 351

Selekman, Benjamin, 555
Selekman, Sylvia, 555
Selitz, Clare, 515
Selvin, Hana, 459
Selznick, Philip, 459
Sheats, Paul, 220
Sheps, Cecil, 522
Sheviakov, George V., 267, 279
Shrag, Clarence, 12
Shuttleworth, Frank, 314
Simon, Herbert, 459
Sinclair, Robert, 114
Smith, Carl O., 511
Smith, Gerald, 43, 68
Smith, Henry, 350
Smith, Mapheus, 334
Snyder, B. J., 311
Snyder, W. C., 311
Soderquist, Harold, 334, 341
Solomon, Richard, 351
Sorokin, Pitirim, 254
Sower, Christopher, 330, 335
Spinley, B. M., 324
Srole, Leo, 109
Steffen, Lincoln, 155
Stein, Clarence, 119
Stendler, Celia Burns, 330, 367
Stermer, James, 119
Stiles, Dan, 182
Stinnette, T. M., 399, 421
Stoddard, Alexander, 445
Stouffer, Samuel S., 67
Stout, Irving, 324
Strang, Ruth, 182
Stroh, M. Margaret, 389
Strubble, G. G., 430
Stuber, G. M., 205
Study, A. P., 509
Sullivan, Dorothy, 279
Sutherland, Edwin, 272, 446
Sutherland, Robert L., 317

Taba, Hilda, 323, 351
Tangent, Pierre, 101
Tawney, H., 114
Taylor, James, 154
Taylor, Carl C., 120
Thayer, V. T., 68
Tompkins, Ellsworth, 428
Tryon, Caroline M., 309, 310, 352
Tuck, Ruth, 120

Upson, L. D., 114
Useem, John 104
Useem, Ruth, 104
Usher, Roland, 70 n.

Valien, Bonita, 555
Van Pool, Gerald, 271
Van Til, W., 351

Walker, Mabel, 110
Walker, Charles, 120
Waller, Willard, 9, 182, 205, 421
Warner, William Lloyd, 109, 163, 165, 314, 324, 386, 413
Weber, Max, 101, 423, 459
Weems, Saucier, 61
Weigle, Luther, 68
West, James, 121, 159, 324
Wheeler, Raymond, 279
White, Ralph K., 207
Whyte, William, 121
Wickman, E. K., 248, 249
Widick, B. J., 66
Wiese, Leopold von, 446
Williams, Robin, 12, 555

Wilson, Logan, 12
Wineman, David, 267
Winslow, Jones, 121
Wolfenstein, Martha, 324
Woods, Sister Frances Jerome, 324
Woodward, R. H., 304, 305, 327
Woywood, Stanislaus, 67
Wright, David, 350
Wrinkle, James, 182
Wynne, Walter, 121

Yabroff, Bernard, 416
Yauch, Wilbur, 279, 493
Yeager, William, 182
Young, Kimball, 120

Zander, Alvin, 225, 516
Zimmerman, Carle C., 121, 465
Znaniecki, Florian, 296
Zollman, Carl, 67

Index of Subjects

Accreditation, 436, 437
Action, possibility of as limited by law, 68
Activities: as integrative or individualizing, 224; as source of good discipline, 277
Adjustment, and sex status, 308
    See also Personality adjustment
AFL-CIO, 415
Age status, and occupation, 308
Aggression, degrees of, 359, 365
American Federation of Labor, and educational policy, 57
American Federation of Teachers: 415; policies of, 416
American Legion, 52
American public school system, *see* Public education
Americanism, 42
Anti-intellectualism, 199, 201
Architecture, and humanist values, 129
Athletic association, 195
Athletics: malpractices in, 202; financing of, 204
Attacks on education: historical examples of, 478; present day, 478–492; content analysis of propaganda used in, 481–485; strategies in, 487–491; checking of, 492
Authority, and the bureaucratic hierarchy, 425

Band association, 195
Behavior, integrative and dominative, 211, 212
Behavior problems, studies of, 250
Binding-out system, 16

Board of Education: as employer, 75; accountability of, 429; responsibilities of, 429; functions of, 429, 431; and politics, 429, 430, 448; financial powers and sources of, 430; membership of, 430; delegation of functions, 431; misuse of authority by, 442; as object of pressure, 477
Booster clubs, 196
Building and equipment, as reflecting values, 129
Bureaucracy: and modern life, 422; defined, 423; spheres of jurisdiction in, 424; and hierarchical structure of, 425; importance of files in, 426; and professionalization, 426
Bureaucratic career, and duty to office, 426
Bureaucratic organization, phases of, 423–426

Catholic education: claims of, 45; and symbolism, 46; environment in, 46
Censorship: Minnesota law, 539; police power, 540; governmental and private, 540; problems of judging, 541; Winters decision, 541; Near decision, 541–542; implications for education, 542
Ceremonial occasions: and state laws, 84; order of importance, 184
Certification of teachers: 75, 437; and professionalization, 426
Cheating: 177; controls to prevent, 177
Chicago Teachers Federation, 415
Child, legal status of, 77, 78

Christmas, as affecting school, 185–186
Chromo-therapy, 139
Church and state, in Catholic theory, 45
    See also Separation of church and state
Citizen, in democratic theory, 61
City: 88; growth of, 90, 91; size, 93; zoning, 94
City design: 90; and market orientation, 91; and private interest groups, 94
Class, size of as affecting methods, 222, 223
Collective action, and labor, 57
Color, as factor in sociometric choice, 333–334
Commercialization, in school athletics, 203
Committee for Constitutional Government, 481
Committee system, a democratic technique, 222
Company town, 99
Competence, as job criterion in bureaucracy, 425
Community: size, 87; forms of settlement, 89; ends and purposes, 93; facilities, 94; reform, 117; as municipality, 118; solidarity through mass entertainment, 198; coöperative action, 520
Community-school relation, loss of, 452
Community cleavage: 117; and mass entertainment, 203
Community living, and subordination of the market orientation, 116
Competition: 54; through examination, 175; as a spur, 176; and poor sportsmanship, 200; and hostility, 201
Consolidated schools, and neighborhood spirit, 142, 143; and town-country split, 341
Contests, as means of control, 474–476
Control: based on rationality, 257; as subjective or objective, 264; techniques of, 265; through segregation, 266; through humiliation, 266; through exhortation, 267; student courts as, 270–273; of teachers, 450; over education by special interest groups, 470–492
    See also Corporal punishment
Contracts, written and oral, 403
Controversy: in Scarsdale, 498–501; in Minneapolis, 501–505; in Houston, 505–507; in Springfield, 507–509; in Pasadena, 509–510; role of press and radio in, 511; delay in response to, 511; and school personnel, 512; and public opinion, 512–513; and conserva-
tism, 513; and the quest for objectivity, 514; and role of PTA, 514; and pro-school nonpolitical organizations, 514; and political action groups, 514; and reconciliation, 515.
Coöperation, as limited by activities, 285
Conventionalism, 51
Copying, 285
Core curriculum: 222; as objective approach to control, 277
Corporal punishment: and law, 82; as control, 266
Corporate interest groups, 100
Corruption: in municipal life, 115; in sports, 203; in public office, 447; and the subjective, 517
Counseling, 265
County, as source of revenue, 32, 33
Courts: and principles of order, 523; decisions based on sovereignty, 553–554
Criticism of schools: objective, 493; NEA proposals, 497–498
Courses of study: 162–163; and social class, 165
Culture: aspects of, 5; as value reality, 5; defined, 5
Culture conflict, 302
Cultural drag, due to inadequate school buildings, 144
Curriculum, expansion, 158

Democracy: in the classroom, 61, 62; in community life, 118; pseudo grassroots, 468
Democratic group practices, difficulty of, 290
Democratic theory, as stated by NEA, 60–61
Decentralization: in bureaucratic organization, 427; of schools, 454; of school administration, 455
Discipline: arising from nature of activity, 256; sources of problems, 257–264; preventive, 296; and law, 297; as preparation for adult life, 297; see also Control
Discrimination: as deliberate, in the school, 351; by teachers, 260
Dismissals: as intimidation, 449; of incompetent teachers under tenure, 455; teacher attitudes on, 455–456; fair procedures of, 455–456
Dissent: and constitutional law, 539; and scientific method, 539
Dissociative, defined, 213
Dissociative relations, increased by negative assessments, 365, 372

Domination-submission control techniques, 265
Drop-out problem, 258
Dual school system: in England, 73; in Germany, 73
Dualism, sacred-secular, 49

Economic class: and status group, 101; as factor in sociometric choice, 329–332
　　See also Socio-economic class
Education: colonial period in, 15–17; amount attained, 28–30; differences in access to, 30; as economic fact, 30, 31; financing of, 32–33; and business groups, 37; as controversial issue, 39; as Christian, 43–44; official Catholic policy on, 44; law and Christian, 50; as function of government, 71; defined by law as privilege, 80; studies of costs of, 166–171
　　See also Attacks on education; Catholic education; Private schools; Public education; School; Secondary education
Education associations, 39
Educational problems and world outside, 317
Enrollment: in elementary education, 25, 26; in secondary education, 25, 26; in schools, 29
Environment, cultural, 126
Equality of opportunity, and status factors, 171
Equity, 354–355
Equipment, and opportunities, 142
Espionage, in school systems, 451
Ethnocentrism, 340
Evaluation of peers: in grade 4, 356–359; in grade 8, 360–363; point of, 364; on basis of individual differences, 369
Examinations: and anxiety, 174; and schedules, 174–175; as self-evaluation, 176; and cross pressures, 178
Expenditures of public funds: 34–37; by state, 36
Exploitation of office: 446; a criminal offense, 446–447; effect of, 448

Federal aid to education, 18, 20, 34, 36
Federal government as source of revenue, 33
Feudal structure, and status, 104
Field trip, as means of control, 476
Foundation for Economic Education, 481
Fraternities and sororities, in high school, 341

"Front" organizations, 477
Functional order: 7; reconstruction of, 225, 260

Gangs, 311
Gerrymandering, 160
Gifts: in elementary school, 186; as social relation, 470; as means of control, 471–474; and curriculum, 472–474
Grades: as ends, 179; as invidious comparison, 179
Grading: based on reputation, 176; as preferential, 179
Gridiron street plan, 91, 92
Grievance machinery, 450, 456
Group discipline, 276
Group discussion: case of, 216–217; functions in, 219; as control, 270, 287, 290
Group dynamics: 206; in social action research, 516
Group dynamics techniques: 222; group observer, 220; group recorder, 220; group resource person, 220; consistent use of, 225
Group leadership, democratic, authoritarian, laissez faire, 207–211, 212
Group libel: Illinois statute, 542–543; intent of law, 542; Beauharnais decision, 542–544; methods of controlling hate propaganda, 544; deterrent to discussion and education, 544–545
Group process, democratic, authoritarian, laissez faire, 207–211
Groups: economic, 39; and value orientation, 41; policies of, 42; religious, 43; nativist, 51; business, 54, 99, 100; labor, 57; educational, 60; nationality or color, 105; private, volunteer, 116

Heroes, 194
Heroics, in mass entertainment pattern, 197
Holidays, public, 183
Human welfare, as highest value, 60
Humanist value orientation: supported in legal order and school norms, 229; and choice of teaching as vocation, 391; and equalitarian colleague concept, 454; and democratizing of school structure, 456

"Idols of consumption," 194, 199
"Idols of production," 194
Inconsistency: in conception of state in U.S., 85; in legal order, 85
Individual, and state, 71
Individualized instruction, 181

Inequality: in community life, 103; principle of, among adolescents, 326; informal order a system of, 351
Informal order: importance for sociological analysis, 9; defined, 326; complexity of, 336, 340
Informal order generalized: 342–349; star, 348; clique, 348, 349; mutual pairs, 349; triads, 349; isolates, 349
Institutional groups, common characteristics of, 9
Interest principle, 464, 465
Intergroup education, 109, 262, 340
Intergroup selection, in high school, 336–340
Interview: unstructured, 368; of job applicant, 402
"Isms," opposed, 53, 56

Jacksonianism: and equality, 19; and vocational training, 20
Jefferson, Thomas: theory of natural right, 18; as advocate of intellectual elite, 19; interpretation of the 1st amendment, 525
Job information, 400
Justice, in children's relations and judgments, 354, 355

Labor market for teachers, factors influencing, 386
Lancasterian and Madras systems of education, 155, 156
Law: as a means to order, 69; as safeguard of rights, 72
Laws: "Old Deluder Satan" act of 1624, 16; Order of king of Prussia (1854) on education, 70; on school attendance, 20, 80; in loco parentis, 283; minimum salary, 438; Feinberg, 451
    See also Released time for religious education, Segregation, Security, Group libel
Light, in classroom, 139
Living space, 90
Lobbying: by AFT, 416; by NEA, 418; as democratic right, 420; funds spent in control of, 468
Local school unit, autonomy of, 427
Lower-class child, 313
Loyalty oaths, 467

Maladjustments of children, solution of, 323
    See also Personality adjustment
Mass audience, crowd characteristics, 192

Mass entertainment: background of, 192–194; opposed by educators, 199, 200, 202; as big business, 203
Mental health, See Personality adjustment
Middle-class child: 313; and principle of equity and justice, 367
Migratory worker, world of, 302–303
Monastic life, as social model, 44
Monitorial system, 156
Municipal government, as set by communal ends, 114

Nazi primer, 466
National Economic Council, legislative positions, 479–481
Nationality groups: and stereotyped interpretations, 107; adjustment phases, 108
Natural rights view, 71, 554, 555
Naturalism, Catholic rejection of, 47
NEA: under attack, 54; claims, 417; growth, 417; structure, 417; policies, 417–418; international activities, 418; investigation of dual control system, 443; investigation of exploitation of office, 447; investigations of problems in school administration listed, 457
Negro society, 315–316
Neighborhoods, rural, 143
New Haven grammar school, norms of conduct for scholars in, 227
Norm of mediocrity, 180, 341
Normal schools, 397
Normative order, 6, 7
Norms: reflecting values, 6; of punishment, 228; permissive range of, 228, 251, 252; proscriptive, 228; as traditional ends, 228, 251; as role defining, 228, 252; and law, 229, 252; transmission of, 238, 300; formulated by students in two High Schools, 231; rated by faculty and pupils of the University of Chicago high school, 231–235; of work and decorum, 240; listed for sixth grade, 242–244; as found in functional areas, 237–247; their violation, two studies of, 248–249; of sex, 250; code of, 250; evaluated by mental hygienists, 250; enforcement of, 252, 265; as favoring female status, 252; reflecting inconsistent goals, 253; related to school order, 253; and middle-class values, 253; evaluated by pupils, 281

Objective: meaning of, 516–517; as moral, 518
Occupation: trends, 98; and status, 100

Opening exercises, 173
Opportunity, and power, 99
Organization, of teachers, 414, 415

Parochial schools, 49, 528
Personality adjustment: 303–307; and social class, 311–312; and prestige, 328
Personalized administration, 449, 450
Play, as socializing, 309
Plenary power, of legislatures over education, 71
Politics: and the financing of education, 32; and school contracts, 39
Population: school, 25; problems, 94
Practice teaching, 399
Pressure groups, see Special interest groups
Private schools, public support for, 528
Problem children, 261
Problem solving, through sociodrama, 221
Problems of children, 317–322
Professional agitators, 478, 481, 493
Professionalization: of teaching, 414; of an occupation, 436
Property tax, 100
Protestant education, 48
Psychodrama, 224, 225
Public education: as cultural achievement, 15, 22; in New England, 17; Constitutional provisions for, 18; as controversial, 20–21; arguments for, 21; development of, 23; as democratic, 74; and hidden costs, 166
Public office, and conflict of interest principle, 446, 447
Punctuality, 292–293
Punishment: and status, 274; as rated by pupils, 291
Pupil-teacher ratio, 384

Quietness, 293–294

Race and color, as tests of admission, 81
Reconciliation, techniques of, 520
Record keeping, 445
Recruitment of teachers: through counseling, 395; by colleges, 395–396; through NEA, 397; by placement bureaus, 402
Relations: of domination and submission, 241; interpersonal, as affecting discipline, 260
Religion, as promoting education, 15, 16
Religion and education: Protestant view, 48; a basic issue, 524
Religious events, 184
Religious groups, opposition between, 51

Released time for religious education, 50, 529 531
Report cards: substitutes for, 180; pupil interpretation of, 285; descriptive, 557
Reprisals, feared by teachers, 450
Reputation: as result of examinations, 176; and punishment, 274; due to place of residence, 341; structural principles as source of, 353–354
Revenue, sources of, 32, 33
Rituals, as socializing, 4
Role-playing: in sociodrama, 221; and reputation, 354
Rote drill, 157

Safety, in school environment, 140
Salary scales, 437
Scientific attitude and ethos, 518, 519
School: scientific study of, 3; as related to culture, 5; as institutional group, 9; attendance problems, 28; types of, 22–24; equipment, 38; as agency of state, 72, 85; as reflecting quality of community life, 89; and vocational adjustment, 98; as community center, 127; choice of, 160, 161; pupil evaluation of, 280–291; conformity in, 492
School administration: 452, 453; as facilitating device, 454; NEA investigations of problems in, 457; surveys, types of, 515
School buildings: extent of need for, 25; underuse of, 25, 27; guides to evaluation of, 130; as influencing educational practices, 130; surveys, 131, 132, 135, 136; in cities, 132; codes, 134; overcrowding in, 135; color in, 139; size of, 427, 431
School bus, and children's opportunities, 142
School district: organization of small, 432; organization of large, 433; dual control system of administration of, 443
School personnel: and school enrollment, 385; duties of, 435, 436; and cliques, 444; and sexual evaluations, 444
School principal, 435, 453
School superintendent, duties of, 434
Secondary education: enrollment in, 25–26; holding power of, 28; extent of, 28
Sectarianism and education, 527
Security: Alien & Sedition Act, 545–546; factors favoring sedition acts, 546; Schenck decision and freedom of speech, 546, 547; rights of individual

safeguarded, 547; De Jonge decision, 547–548; Barnette decision, 548–549; post World War II, 549–550; communism and Dennis decision, 550–551; education and Feinberg decision, 551–552

Segregation: as fact, as principle, 531–532; "Separate but equal" doctrine, 532; Supreme court decisions, Plessy v. Ferguson, (1896), 532, Brown et al. v. Board of Ed. of Topeka et al. (1953), 533; court decisions in non-educational areas, 534; implementation of supreme court decision of 1953, 534; interstate regional education compact, 535; response to U.S. supreme court decision, 535–536; integration of schools, 536–537; legislation to abolish public education, 536; states rights, 536; southern attack on NAACP, 537; white citizens councils, 537

Self-discipline, 276

Self-made man, 55

Separation of church and state: 17, 49, 525; U.S. supreme court on, 525; uncertainty about, 526

Sex: as aggression, 370, information as negatively evaluated, 374; problems in school, 376; and reputation, 375; as method of control, 444; crush on teachers, 444; voyeurism, 444

Sex education: 375; and social change, 376

Sex humor, content of, 370, 371, 376

Sex roles: and special activities, 165; in mass entertainment pattern, 197, 198; peer definition of, 309–310; adolescent changes in, 310

Sex status: as structuring functional order, 165; and Valentine's Day, 187; and punishment, 274; and social class, 311; as factor in sociometric choice, 331–332; and collective crush, 377; and teacher role, 414

Sexuality: and age and sex status, 369; in the younger child, 371; indirect, 371

Slum, 110–114; schools in, 116

Social, defined, 213

Social action research: 515–516; and mutual education, 519; and objectivity, 519, 520; difficulties in, 521

Social atom, 328, 329

Social class: and punishment, 274; See also Socio-economic class

Social Darwinism, 465

Social discipline, 59

Social disorder, 117

Social distance, 101

Social relations: principles of, 213–215; intergroup, 215; interpersonal, 215; in school systems, 453

Social model: defined by norms and values, 6; of a group, 42; varying with grade, 252

Socialization: defined, 5; as inconsistent, 253

Sociative, defined, 213

Sociative relations, encouraged by positive evaluations, 365

Socio-economic class: as factor in child's prestige, 328; and sociometric choice in high school, 335–336

Sociodrama: 221; danger possible in, 225

Sociogram, use of, 342

Sociometric choices: in the elementary school, 327–334; in the high school, 335–351

Sociometric techniques, uses and limitations, 327

Sound, in classroom, 140

Sovereignty: 85; doctrine of absolute, 71

Special interest group: as influencing schools, 10; dealing with education, 39; and graduation ceremonies, 188; and school awards, 188–190; and the school, 463; claims of, 467; attempts to control or influence others, 468; and hidden subsidies, 468–469; relation to education, 470–478

Spontaneity: 143; and integrative behavior, 212

Sports: commercialized, 192; spectator, and loyalty, 194

State: as source of revenue, 33; conceptions of in U.S., 70; nature of, as influencing education, 70; as ultimate parent, 78, 79; its nature reflected in law, 84–85; and the interest principle, 464, 465

Status: and values, 8; as structuring society, school, 8, 9; as rights and duties, 8; and education in Prussia, 73; and duality in education, 104; and educational discrimination, 116, 117

Statutory laws: as embodying concept of state, 71; on socialization, 79, 80; on the delinquent child, 79; and curriculum, 81; and authority, 82; and conduct, 82; on ceremonial occasions, 83; on the flag, 84; on censorship, obscenity, 539; and conduct in public office, 446

Strikes, by teachers, 416, 417, 419

Student courts, as control, 270–273

Student government, 274, 286–287
Students, preferential treatment of, 444, 445
Subjective, meaning of, 517
Success: 55; as end in sports, 199, 202
Supreme court decisions: on equal opportunity in education, 74; on released time for religious education, 528–531; on segregation, 532–534; on censorship, 541–542; on group libel, 543; on security, 546–552
Suspension, 82, 267

Taxes, as source of revenue, 32
Tax rates, 94, 115
Teacher-community relation, 409, 412, 421
Teacher behavior, control of, 409, 410, 413
Teacher education, controversy over, 398
Teacher employment, outlook for, 385
Teacher loads, study on, 223
Teacher morale: and exploitation of office, 448; and personalized administration, 449, 450
Teacher role: pupil interpretation of, 288, 289, 298; within bureaucracy, 452; viewed by educators, 404; and NEA standards, 405; as influenced by type school, 406
Teacher selection: factors influencing, 400, 401; practices in, 402
Teachers: and sex role, 28; legal status of, 74–76; administrative task of, 174; as value objects for children, 296–297; demand for, 384; obligations regarding peer evaluation, 365; as interpreters of reputations, 378; undersupply of, 385, 386; oversupply of, in high school, 386; social origins of, 387; and social mobility, 388, 390; national origin of, 389, 390; "public servant" concept of, 408, 421; "stranger" concept of, 408, 421; as participators in organizations, 412, 413; conformity of, 421; service ideal of, 420; freedom for, 451, 453; as autonomous, 454
Teacher's aides: 445; NEA policy on, 445
Teachers college, rise of, 398

Teachers' organizations, as pressure groups, 75
Teaching: as female occupation, 27; as part of the labor market, 383; and sex status, 389; as rated by students, 391; as self fulfillment, 391
Tenure: 439; opposition to details of system, 440; legislation, 455
Tests: personality, limitations of, 312; guess-who, 366, 367, 368
Theoretical conceptions, necessity of for sociological analysis, 11
Time schedules, in school, 143
Trade unions, and teachers, 415
Tradition, and the nativist, 51, 52, 53
Truancy, 229

Ungraded schools, 181
United States: inconsistency in conception of state in, 85; supreme court, see Supreme court decisions

Vacation patterns, as having no rationale, 27
Value orientations: religious, 43–51, 63; nativist, 51–54, 63; market, 54–56, 64; common man, 57–59, 65, 66; humanist, 60–62, 66; and commencement ceremony, 190; and control, 277–279; and evaluation of peers, 364, 365; and bureaucratic structure, 453, 454; and controversy, 466; and the meaning of dissent, 538
    See also Humanist value orientation
Value reality, of the school, 171
Values: as determining norms, 6; expressed in school buildings, 143, 144; conflicting in diversified culture, 41, 464; as contending for transmission by the schools, 467
Vocabulary of social sciences, 213
Vocational training, implications of, 159
Vocational policies, and education, 100
Vocational opportunities, and communities, 95

War, 52
White House Conference on Education, 34
Work, individual or group, 284–285, 295
Work groups, 222

Set in Linotype Caledonia
Format by James T. Parker
Manufactured by Kingsport Press, Inc.
Published by HARPER & BROTHERS, *New York*